A Hackett Test Prep Manual
for Use with AP® Latin

A Hackett Test Prep Manual for Use with AP® Latin

Ed DeHoratius

Hackett Publishing Company, Inc.
Indianapolis/Cambridge

For further information, please address
    Hackett Publishing Company, Inc.
    P.O. Box 44937
    Indianapolis, Indiana 46244-0937

    www.hackettpublishing.com

Cover design by Brian Rak
Composition by Integrated Composition Systems

ISBN-13: 978-1-62466-852-4 (pbk.)

AP® is a trademark registered by the College Board, which was not involved in the production of, and does not endorse, this product.

CONTENTS

For Lee Krasnoo, my friend and Wayland High School colleague since 1999, in gratitude for his unending patience and the constancy of his integrity.

ACKNOWLEDGMENTS

I want to offer my heartfelt thanks to the following people for their support, encouragement, and assistance in the completion of this project.

First and foremost, my colleagues and students. The students in my 2017–2018 Latin 3/4 class assisted with some of the research for the book; it was a learning experience for all of us. And Lee Krasnoo's 2017–2018 and 2018–2019 AP® Latin classes piloted some of the materials in their preparation for the AP® Exam.

I can't thank enough my colleagues in the language department at Wayland High School for their understanding and patience in the face of the multitude of projects beyond my teaching load. I want to especially thank Melissa Bryant, then Language Department Chair, for her support of my work both at Wayland and beyond.

I also want to thank the following: William Broadhead of the Massachusetts Institute of Technology for his assistance with the character glossary and other Caesar details; Mary English of Montclair State University and Chief Reader of the AP® Latin Exam for fielding questions about the AP® Exam; and the College of the Holy Cross for the use of their library.

To the two anonymous readers: thank you. Your detailed and deliberate reading of and insightful comments on an admittedly bloated initial manuscript streamlined and clarified its content. The manuscript is stronger for your work, corrections, and suggestions. I appreciate the time you took and the work you did to make this a better book. I did not accept all of your recommendations but know that they were all carefully considered.

Finally, I want to thank Hackett Publishing. This ever-expanding project would not have happened without their patience and support. Brian Rak has shepherded this project from beginning to end, and Jennifer McBride and Ellen Douglas found mistakes in the original manuscript that I wouldn't even have thought to look for.

In the end, though, many have read this manuscript, but only one has written it. While I thank everyone for their help, I take full responsibility for any errors that remain.

I cannot close here without thanking my family, Liz, Will, Matthew, Andrew, the Kennedys, and my parents, whose patience before the constant presence of my laptop, especially stretching into the summer of 2018, when the manuscript was overdue, has been Herculean. I love you all and I thank you for all that you do for me.

INTRODUCTION

You have read hundreds of lines of Latin. You have read pages and pages of English. You have studied vocabulary, grammar, and rhetorical figures; analyzed passages; parsed forms; and scanned lines. You likely learned history, maybe art history, all culminating in the AP® Latin Literature Exam that you are thinking about taking or planning to take.

This book is not intended to replace your teacher or your textbook; it is not a teaching text. You are familiar with the Latin; you've read the syllabus. What you need to prepare for the exam is something to organize all of that information for you:

- Which vocab words are most important to know?

- Which grammatical forms and constructions are used most commonly?

- Who are the most important characters in each text?

- Where are all of the places mentioned in each text?

- How can I easily review important grammatical structures?

Additionally, you need to supplement the test-specific information your teacher provides you and to be able to practice what you'll be asked to do on the exam.

The goal of this book is to answer those questions and more so that you have quick references for the varied information that you need to master, and to provide that information and practice, all of which will help you to be successful on the AP® Exam.

It is likely that you will not need every chapter in this book; you might already know and understand certain information in a given chapter. The book assumes nothing about your knowledge, understanding, or preparation. It is intended to allow you to focus on your weaknesses and to provide you the necessary information to address those weaknesses. Toward that end, some information that might be considered basic or fundamental is included, should that be the information you happen to need to prepare for the exam.

There is too some redundancy built into the book; for example, there is a proper names glossary that includes both frequency-of-appearance and basic vocabulary information for those names. Those names also appear in the general vocabulary frequency list. Because the book is intended to be used discretely rather than sequentially, information is included wherever it is deemed necessary, even if it appears elsewhere, to ensure your exposure to it.

The most important Latin skill for successful completion of the AP® Exam is being able to use the Latin to support directly what you are saying. Thus, to whatever extent possible, Latin references from the syllabus are included; for example, in the character glossary, a quote or quotes from the Latin syllabus about each character are included to give you extra reinforcement interacting with and understanding the Latin.

The book does not include an entire practice exam. Rather it approaches preparing for the test more through analysis and discrete practice; that is, all sections of the exam are represented, discussed, and analyzed, but they are not included together in a single test.

In the end, the AP® Exam is a measure of both your preparation over the course of the syllabus and your preceding Latin instruction, and your ability to articulate that preparation on the day of the exam. Your teacher is faced with any number of drains on her class time, both Latin- and non-Latin-related; few teachers ever send their students off to the AP® Exam congratulating themselves for having covered not only the syllabus but also all of the necessary supporting content as well as adequately reviewing it all in the days leading up to the exam. This book is intended to fill those gaps, to provide you that new information or extra review that your school and non-school schedule might not have allowed. Congratulations on taking the AP® Latin Exam and good luck.

If you have any suggestions or corrections, I welcome them. You can reach me at dehlatinteach@gmail.com or @dehlatinteach on Twitter.

RESOURCES

- The resources here will be largely confined to web resources; I will also include the print resources that I used in the preparation of this book.

- It is essential when using web resources that you are discerning in your choices; too many resources, especially in Google's early results, are at best of questionable quality and at worst downright wrong.

- Your best bet is to use the resources in your textbooks or readers. These glossaries are specifically tailored to the text that you are reading, while online dictionaries will provide more general, and often longer, definitions, which make it more difficult to determine the meaning of a word in context.

- The grammar guides in your book(s) might include exceptions particular to an author or might emphasize certain constructions that an author uses more commonly. If, however, you are looking for resources to supplement your print resources, the resources below are good places to start.

- I include QR codes for longer links to make accessing the sites more streamlined, albeit via a smartphone or tablet.

GLOSSARY

- latinlexicon.org

  - Not the most polished visually of interfaces, but gives access to both the Elementary and the full Lewis and Short Latin Dictionaries.

  - Click on "Search" in the upper left and type the Latin word at the upper left.

  - Suggestions will autopopulate below if you pause in your typing.

- [print] Glare, P. G. W. *The Oxford Latin Dictionary*. 2nd ed. Oxford: Oxford University Press, 2012.

TRANSLATIONS

Bellum Gallicum
- [print] Wiseman, Anne, and Peter Wiseman. *The Battle for Gaul*. Boston: David R. Godine, 1980.

- The Perseus Project [see QR code below for link]

  - Navigate chapters and sections in the box to the upper right of the translation.

Aeneid

- [print] Virgil. *Aeneid*. Translated by Stanley Lombardo. Indianapolis, IN: Hackett, 2005.

- [print] Virgil. *The Aeneid*. Translated by David West. London: Penguin, 2003.

- https://www.poetryintranslation.com/PITBR/Latin/Virgilhome.php

  - an excellent translation that combines readability and literalness

  - And if you are studying, or interested in studying, ancient literature further, the parent site has translations of other important classical texts.

C. Julius Caesar, Gallic War.
The Perseus Project.

Virgil, The Major Works.
Poetry in Translation.

COMMENTARIES

Both *Bellum Gallicum* and *Aeneid*

- Caesar. *Selections from His "Commentarii de bello gallico."* By Hans-Friedrich Mueller. Mundelein, IL: Bolchazy-Carducci, 2013.

- Virgil. *The Aeneid*. Edited with introduction and commentary by J. W. Mackail. Oxford: Clarendon Press, 1930.

- Virgil. *The Aeneid of Virgil, Books 1–6 and 7–12*. Edited by R. D. Williams. New York: Macmillan, 1972.

- Dickinson College Commentary

  - Latin text in segments with commentary at right

  - Tabs at the top of the commentary window provide vocabulary and media (the latter of which is empty for some segments).

Caesar, Selections from the Gallic War.
Dickinson College Commentaries.

Vergil, Aeneid Selections.
Dickinson College Commentaries.

- The Perseus Project

  - A Latin text with each word hyperlinked to vocabulary and morphological information, but in a more general sense; Perseus provides all possibilities because it does not know the original context of the word.

- There is commentary and a translation in the menus at right; the translations will tend to be of an archaic English.

C. Julius Caesar, De Bello Gallico.
T. Rice Holmes, ed., *The Perseus Project*.

P. Vergilius Maro, Aeneid.
J. B. Greenough, ed., *The Perseus Project*.

AP® EXAM RESOURCES

- The College Board website provides a wealth of material:

  - AP® Latin Home Page [see QR code below for link]

  - At the bottom of the AP® Latin Home Page, under the "Exam Preparation" heading, are the most recent exam's released Free Response Questions as well as the Free Response Question and Scoring Information Archive.

    - The archive includes Free Response Questions dating back to 2013.

    - The archive also includes links to sample student responses.

AP® Latin. Home page,
The College Board

Chapter 1

INTRODUCTION TO THE AP® EXAM AND COURSE

1.1   OVERVIEW OF THE EXAM

- Two sections:
    - o   Multiple choice: 50 questions, 1 hour, 50 percent of grade
    - o   Free Response: 5 questions, 15 minute reading period + 1 hour, 45 minutes = 2 hours, 50 percent of grade

1.2   SPECIFIC EXAM GRADING BREAKDOWN

- 50 percent: multiple choice section
- 50 percent: free response section
    - o   7.5 percent: Vergil translation
    - o   7.5 percent: Caesar translation
    - o   20 percent: analytical essay
    - o   7.5 percent: Vergil short answer question
    - o   7.5 percent: Caesar short answer question

1.3   THE AP® LATIN SYLLABUS

The AP® Latin Exam includes the following requirements:
- *Readings in Latin* (the first number refers to book numbers and the second to Vergil's line numbers or Caesar's chapter numbers):
    - o   *Aeneid* 1.1–209; 1.418–40; 1.494–578
    - o   *Aeneid* 2.40–56; 2.201–49; 2.268–97; 2.559–620
    - o   *Aeneid* 4.160–218; 4.259–361; 4.659–705
    - o   *Aeneid* 6.295–332; 6.384–425; 6.450–76; 6.847–99
    - o   *Gallic War* 1.1–7
    - o   *Gallic War* 4.24–35 + sentence 1 of 36: *Eodem die legati … venerunt*

- o *Gallic War* 5.24–48

- o *Gallic War* 6.13–20

- • *Readings in English*:

- o *Aeneid* 1, 2, 4, 6, 8, 12

- o *Gallic War* 1, 6, 7

1.4   SPECIFIC INFORMATION YOU NEED TO KNOW

1.4.1   TERMINOLOGY

This is the list of terminology included on p.129 of the Fall 2019 Course and Exam Description. Each term (as well as others) will be defined and expanded upon in the grammar chapter.

modifies	indirect command	dative of reference
complements	conditionals	dative with special verb
is dependent on	mood	accusative of duration of time
antecedent	imperative	accusative of respect
gerundive	hortatory or jussive subjunctive	ablative absolute
gerund	passive periphrastic	ablative of separation
supine	deponent	ablative of comparison
fearing clause	partitive genitive	ablative of specification
result clause	genitive with impersonal verb	ablative of cause
purpose clause	genitive with adjective	ablative of description
relative clause	genitive with verb of remembering (forgetting)	ablative of degree of difference
relative clause of characteristic	objective genitive	ablative with special verb
relative clause of purpose	dative of possession	ablative of time when
cum clauses	dative of purpose	ablative of time within which
indirect statement	dative with compound verb	vocative
indirect question	dative of agent	

1.4.2   LITERARY STYLE

Each term (as well as others) will be defined and expanded upon in the rhetorical figures chapter.

alliteration	hyperbole	rhetorical question
anaphora	litotes	simile
apostrophe	metaphor	synchesis
asyndeton	metonymy	synecdoche
chiasmus	onomatopoeia	tmesis
enjambment	personification	transferred epithet
hyperbaton	polysyndeton	

1.5   THE MULTIPLE CHOICE SECTION

1.5.1   OVERVIEW

- 50 questions

- 1 hour to complete

- counts for 50 percent of the exam grade

- one Vergil passage

- one Caesar passage

- one sight poetry passage

- one sight prose passage

- topics covered:

  o   vocabulary

  o   syntax

  o   grammatical terminology

  o   political, historical, and cultural contexts

  o   scansion (for poetry)

  o   stylistic features

  o   general comprehension

1.6   THE FREE RESPONSE SECTION

1.6.1   OVERVIEW

- 5 questions
- 2 hours total to complete
  - 15-minute reading period
  - 1 hour, 45 minutes to answer questions
- counts for 50 percent of the exam grade
- one Vergil translation (suggested time: 15 minutes)
- one Caesar translation (suggested time: 15 minutes)
- one analytical (long) essay (suggested time: 45 minutes)
  - focuses on linguistic and literary aspects of the texts through a comparison
- one Vergil and one Caesar short answer question (suggested time: 15 minutes each)
  - five to seven discrete (i.e., not necessarily related) questions on each passage
- questions may be answered in any order

Chapter 2

TAKING THE TEST

- This chapter provides strategies, samples, and practice questions.

- Every aspect of the AP® Exam will involve translating and understanding Latin.

- Toward that end, some general tips on reading and translating are provided here.

READING TIPS

- Reading Latin is a combination of knowledge and understanding.

  o Knowledge refers to whether you know what you need to know:

    ▪ Do you know vocabulary information so that you can tell the difference between *regis* (3rd declension genitive singular) and *puellis* (1st declension dative or ablative plural)?

      • Many texts will make this distinction with macrons (*regis* vs. *puellīs*) but the AP® Exam will not use macrons.

    ▪ Do you know your endings and forms?

  o Understanding refers to when you combine your knowledge with the specific context of a text.

    ▪ You might know that a word is ablative by knowing its vocabulary information but can you use the context of a sentence to correctly translate that ablative?

HOW TO READ A LATIN SENTENCE

- **Read through the entire sentence** in Latin. If the sentence is long, read it clause-by-clause.

- As you read through the sentence, **make mental (or physical) notes** about what you know and don't know.

  o Horum omnium fortissimi sunt Belgae (*Bellum Gallicum* 1.1)

    ▪ You might note that *horum omnium* are genitive plural and agree.

    ▪ *Fortissimi* can be genitive singular or nominative plural.

    ▪ *Sunt* is plural, which suggests that *fortissimi* will be nominative plural.

    ▪ *Belgae* is plural, which confirms that *fortissimi* is plural and agrees with *Belgae*.

- On the other hand …

- You might think that *horum omnium*, because of the *-um* ending and because it is the first word, is nominative singular (neuter).

- *Horum*, especially, might be tricky to identify as a genitive plural; often one letter stems (in this case, *h-*) are harder to identify. (*Rerum*, the genitive plural of *res, rei*, is commonly misidentified.)

- If you make a mistake like this, recognize it as early as you can; the moment the sentence stops making sense, stop and start over.

- If you don't start over, often you will make a second mistake to try to correct the first mistake you made; starting over allows you to try to correct the initial mistake.

- If you translate *horum omnium* as the subject, the other words in the sentence can't be correct.

  - You might translate the sentence "all of them are the bravest Belgians."

  - That translation makes some sense in isolation, but doesn't fit the broader context and mistranslates *horum omnium* as nominative plural.

  - Recognize that it doesn't sound quite right and start over, rather than try to make them fit incorrectly: if *horum omnium* can't be the subject, what else can it be?

- **Make sure to translate each Latin word.**

- It is a good idea to cross out Latin words in the translation to ensure that you have accounted for each in your English translation.

- **Don't expect Latin to work like English** does. It doesn't, and, when you assume that it does, you make mistakes.

  o It is common in English that the first noun in a sentence is the subject.

  o You will want Latin to operate similarly, that the first noun in the sentence be the subject.

  o Latin, however, uses endings rather than word order to convey this. Focus on the Latin, the endings, to identify the subject and other parts of the sentence.

  o *Horum omnium* in the above example is the first noun of the sentence but, because of its ending, can't be nominative.

- **Triage forms**; that is, understand which forms are easier to identify and which forms are more difficult to identify.

  o A form that ends in a *-t* is most likely a verb (exceptions being relatively obvious non-verbs like *et*).

- A form that ends in a -*us* is most likely a nominative, although be careful of 4th declension nouns, which use the -*us* ending for genitive and accusative as well.

- A form that ends in -*i*, however, can be any number of forms: nominative plural or genitive singular, dative singular, 1st person singular perfect active, present passive infinitive.

- It is important to know which endings are more straightforward and which endings are more ambiguous.

- As you are reviewing the Latin of the syllabus, focus on those words that are ambiguous in context and make sure that you know them.

- **Know the misleading forms:** there are certain endings that are commonly one form but less commonly another form; it is difficult to identify those less commonly used forms.

  - **the -e ending**

    - It is most commonly the **3rd declension noun ablative singular** ending.

    - It is also the **3rd declension adjective neuter nominative and accusative singular** ending.

      - sed esse Galliae **commune consilium** (*Bellum Gallicum* 5.27)

      - saxa vocant Itali mediis quae in fluctibus Aras, / **dorsum immane** mari summo (*Aeneid* 1.109–10)

      - Other instances of this form occur at *Bellum Gallicum* 1.2, 1.3, 1.5, 1.6, 5.27, 5.47, and *Aeneid* 1.149, 2.583, 2.184, 6.408.

    - A further complication is that 3rd declension adjectives do not use the -*e* ending for the ablative singular but rather the -*i* ending.

  - **the -i ending**

    - 2nd declension, genitive singular or nominative plural

    - 3rd declension nouns, dative singular

    - 3rd declension adjectives, dative and ablative singular

    - perfect active indicative, 1st person singular

    - present passive infinitive

- Understand how the **Venn Diagram of Endings** can help identify nouns joined by a conjunction or noun-adjective agreement; that is, when you have two linked forms with different endings, the forms of those endings will overlap:

  - cum ad fines regni sui **Sabino Cottaeque** praesto fuissent frumentumque in hiberna comportavissent (*Bellum Gallicum* 5.26)

    - The -*que* joins *Sabino* and *Cottae*.

- The -o ending of *Sabino* can be either dative or ablative singular.

- The -ae ending of *Cottae* can be genitive or dative singular or nominative plural.

- The only form that the endings share is dative singular, and so they must both be dative singular; that is, the overlap of the Venn Diagram of their endings is dative singular.

- **Latin word order** is designed to help you, if you know how to read it.

  o **Chunking.** Break the Latin sentence into more easily digestible chunks.

  o Translate those and put them together to make the sentence.

    - et regno occupato per tres potentissimos ac firmissimos populos totius Galliae sese potiri posse sperant (*Bellum Gallicum* 1.3)

      - *Regno occupato* agree; that's a chunk.

      - *Per* is a preposition that takes the accusative. The conjunction *ac* links the two adjectives *potentissimos* and *firmissimos*, both of which agree with *populos*, all of which, plus *tres* are the complete object of *per*. That's a big chunk.

      - *Totius Galliae* agree; another chunk.

      - *Sese* to *sperant* isn't as straightforward because of the two infinitives *potiri* and *posse*, but the key word is *sperant*.

      - As a head verb, *sperant* can take an infinitive in indirect statement.

      - Of the two infinitives, only one, *posse*, can also take an infinitive, so *posse* is dependent on *sperant* and *potiri* is dependent on *posse*.

      - *Sese* is the subject accusative of *posse*.

    - et **regno occupato** <u>per tres potentissimos ac firmissimos populos</u> *totius Galliae* sese potiri posse sperant (*Bellum Gallicum* 1.3)

    - And, with the kingdom occupied by the three most powerful and established peoples, they hope that they can control all of Gaul.

  o **The Verb at the end** functions as a punctuation mark that marks the end of a clause.

  o **A verb followed by a conjunction or a comma** very likely marks the end of a clause.

    - quae tamen, ancoris iactis, **cum fluctibus complerentur,** necessario adversa nocte in altum provectae, continentem petierunt. (*Bellum Gallicum* 4.28)

      - *Cum* marks the beginning of the clause.

      - *Complerentur*, followed by a comma, marks the end of the clause.

  o **Conjunctions.** Conjunctions link like elements, from clauses to individual words, and help to organize a sentence by marking chunks of words.

- et regno occupato per tres *potentissimos* **ac** *firmissimos* populos totius Galliae sese potiri posse sperant (*Bellum Gallicum* 1.3)

  - The conjunction *ac* links the adjectives *potentissimos* and *firmissimos*.

- **Framing.** Latin will sometimes separate a word and its modifier to identify grammatically connected words or phrases.

  - **Omnibus rebus** ad profectionem **comparatis**, diem dicunt (*Bellum Gallicum* 1.6)

  - Si adire non possit, monet ut tragulam **cum epistola** ad amentum **deligata** intra munitionem castrorum abiciat (*Bellum Gallicum* 5.48)

    - *Comparatis* agrees with *rebus* and *deligata* with *epistola* but are separated from them to show that *ad profectionem* and *ad amentum* are translated with them, rather than with another part of the sentence.

- **Annotating the Text.** You might already do this but marking chunks, frames, vocabulary, and so on is a useful approach to navigating a Latin sentence or text.

  - Have your own system: for example, full brackets for clauses and lower half brackets for phrases or chunks.

  - Write definitions above words on your first read-through, so you don't have to recall them when translating, which could interrupt your momentum.

  - Arrows and other connectors are useful for connecting modifiers and nouns or subjects and verbs, especially in the more convoluted word order of poetry.

2.1 THE MULTIPLE CHOICE SECTION

2.1.1 OVERVIEW

- 50 questions
- 1 hour to complete
- counts for 50 percent of the exam grade
- one Vergil passage from the syllabus: 10–12 questions
- one Caesar passage from the syllabus: 10–12 questions
- one sight poetry passage: 13–15 questions
- one sight prose passage: 13–15 questions
- topics covered:
  - vocabulary, including the definition of words or phrases in context
  - syntax

- o   grammatical terminology

- o   political, historical, and cultural contexts

- o   the scansion of dactylic hexameter or elegiac couplet (for poetry)

- o   stylistic features

- o   understanding of references to Roman culture, including history and mythology

- o   general comprehension of Latin texts

- • Note that literal translation is not tested in the multiple choice section.

2.1.2   STRATEGIZING THE MULTIPLE CHOICE SECTION

- • Four passages in an hour means 15 minutes per passage.

- • 50 questions over four passages means on average 12 questions per passage.

- • At a minute per question, that leaves 3 minutes remaining per passage.

- • Use that 3 minutes to scan the passage:

   - o   What context can the title give you?

      - ▪ The sample sight poetry passage on the College Board website is entitled "A request from an admirer."

         - • This title suggests that the poem is about a relationship, likely an amorous one, and possibly an unrequited one.

         - • Expect then related vocabulary: friend words, love words, and so on

   - o   Assess vocabulary.

      - ▪ Are there vocabulary words you definitely don't know? These will require context to figure out.

      - ▪ Are there vocabulary words you definitely know?

      - ▪ Do any specific vocabulary words give you a sense of context or meaning?

      - ▪ Are there proper names, gods' names, heroes' names, place names, that might suggest what the passage is about?

   - o   Can you identify any words as potentially a specific construction?

      - ▪ Are there clearly identifiable subjunctive verbs?

      - ▪ Are there infinitives that might be in an indirect statement?

      - ▪ Are there gerunds or gerundives?

   - o   Try to get a broad sense of what the passage is about, for example, war, love, relationships, and so on.

   - o   Note structural elements that might be helpful:

- Is there dialogue? That will mean more 1st and 2nd person verbs.

- Are the sentences long and periodic or short and concise? If the former, you'll need to spend some time analyzing the structure.

2.1.3   CHOICE OF PASSAGES

- Passages included in the multiple choice section are chosen in general with the following criteria in mind:

  o Caesar and sight prose: selections of between 75 and 100 words or around 7 to 10 lines

  o Vergil and sight poetry: selections of between 10 and 15 lines

  o sight prose: a selection from a recommended author (this list is suggested but not complete): Nepos, Cicero (not including letters), Livy, Pliny the Younger, Seneca, or the non-syllabus Latin of Caesar

  o sight prose: macrons are used only for necessary clarity, for example, to distinguish the 1st declension ablative singular from nominative singular

  o sight poetry: a selection written in dactylic hexameter or elegiac couplet

  o sight poetry: a selection from a recommended author (this list is suggested but not complete): Ovid, Martial, Tibullus, Catullus, or the non-syllabus Latin of Vergil

  o both sight prose and poetry: passages uncommonly taught in school or from textbooks will be favored, for example, Ovid's Apollo and Daphne or Catullus 64 will likely not be included

  o self-contained episodes; that is, one that begins and ends in those 10 to 15 lines, or a single poem (for the sight poetry)

  o little to no obscure vocabulary: 1–2 words at most need their definitions provided for you

  o relatively easy to identify the episode

2.1.4   THE TYPES OF MULTIPLE CHOICE QUESTIONS AND ANSWERS

- Questions will cover a range of difficulty.

  o Most will fall in the medium range with a few easier and a few more difficult.

- Questions will be distributed throughout the selection and will cover most if not all of the selection; that is, there will be not be large chunks of the selection left unasked.

- Grammar questions ask for the following types of information:

  o part of speech

- noun, pronoun, verb, adjective, adverb, preposition, conjunction, interjection
  - the subject or object of a verb
  - the case and number of a noun
  - the grammatical context of a noun—that is, what word dictates what case that noun will be in
  - the tense and mood of a verb
  - the translation of words or phrases
  - the understanding of the meaning of a line or phrase
    - This differs from translation in that translation will be more literal while understanding will be more of a summary.
  - scansion: the scanning of the first four feet of a line
    - The answers will be given in either verbal or symbol form.
      - dactyl, dactyl, spondee, spondee
        ‾◡◡   ‾◡◡   ‾‾   ‾‾
    - the number of elisions in a line
  - which figure of speech appears in a line or lines
- Negative questions in general will not be asked.
  - For example, which of the following is NOT true?
- "None of the above" will not be used as an answer choice.
- Questions that ask whether one, two, or three choices are correct will not be asked.
  - For example, What case is the word _____ (line #)?
  - I. nominative / II. accusative / III. ablative
  - a = I only / b = I and II / c = I and III / d = I, II, and III
- Nonexistent or impossible Latin forms will not be included as incorrect choices.
  - For example, *amiant* will not be included as an incorrect choice for a question about subjunctive verbs because the form *amiant* does not exist.
- Translation answer choices will always make sense; that is, they will test your comprehension of the Latin rather than your ability to identify nonsensical English.

2.1.5   THE FORMAT OF MULTIPLE CHOICE QUESTIONS

- The line numbers included with the texts in the multiple choice section do not correspond to the line numbers of the original text.

- Each question includes a text with self-contained line numbers used only for that question; for example, line numbering for each passage will begin at line 1 and continue to the end rather than the line numbering from the original text.

  o For example, *Aeneid* 1.65–75 would appear in a multiple choice question as below, formatted lines 1 to 11 rather than 65 to 75 (only the first few lines are included).

    1. "Aeole (namque tibi divum pater atque hominum rex
    2. et mulcere dedit fluctus et tollere vento),
    3. gens inimica mihi Tyrrhenum navigat aequor
    4. Ilium in Italiam portans victosque penates:

- Questions will appear in the order in which they appear in the text.

  o For example, a question on line 3 will precede a question on line 4.

2.1.6 SAMPLE MULTIPLE CHOICE PASSAGES

- Included here are four sight prose passages, four sight poetry passages, two Caesar passages, and two Vergil passages.

- Following the final Vergil passage is an answer key for all passages that includes a question rating of easy, easy/medium, medium, medium/difficult, or difficult, and an explanation of why the answer is correct and how the correct answer can be deduced.

- I have attempted as best I can to model both potential passages and questions, in content and language, that might appear on the AP® Exam.

- If you are interested in pursuing the passages further, passage citations are included with the Latin of the answer key only; passage citations are not included on the AP® Exam and so are not included in the questions.

2.1.7   SAMPLE MULTIPLE CHOICE PASSAGES—SIGHT PROSE

The Death of Remus

1   Priori Remo augurium[1] venisse fertur,[2] sex vultures; iamque nuntiato augurio cum duplex

2   numerus Romulo se ostendisset, utrumque regem sua multitudo consalutaverat:[3]

3   tempore illi[4] praecepto, at hi[4] numero avium regnum trahebant. Inde cum altercatione

4   congressi certamine irarum ad caedem vertuntur; ibi in turba ictus Remus cecidit.

5   Vulgatior fama est ludibrio[5] fratris Remum novos transiluisse muros; inde ab irato

6   Romulo, cum verbis quoque increpitans[6] adiecisset, "Sic deinde, quicumque alius

7   transiliet moenia mea," interfectum. Ita solus potitus imperio Romulus; condita urbs

8   conditoris nomine appellata.

[1.] augurium, -i: auspices, prophecy

[2.] fertur: "is said"

[3.] consaluto, -are: to greet

[4.] illi, hi: the supporters of Remus, the supporters of Romulus

[5.] ludibrium, -i: mockery, contempt

[6.] increpito, -are: to scold repeatedly

1. The case and number of <u>Remo</u> (line 1) are

    a. nominative singular

    b. dative singular

    c. ablative singular

    d. genitive plural

2. From the words <u>priori</u> … <u>ostendisset</u> (lines 1–2), we learn that

    a. Romulus saw more birds than Remus

    b. Romulus saw fewer birds than Remus

    c. Romulus and Remus saw the same number of birds

    d. Romulus saw his birds first

3. In line 2, <u>se</u> refers to

    a. himself

    b. herself

    c. itself

    d. themselves

4. The case and number of <u>avium</u> (line 3) are

    a. nominative singular

    b. accusative singular

    c. genitive plural

    d. ablative singular

5. The subject of <u>vertuntur</u> (line 4) is

    a. the birds

    b. Romulus and Remus

    c. the followers of Romulus

    d. the followers of Remus

6. From the words <u>ibi</u> ... <u>cecidit</u> (line 4), we learn that

    a. Romulus died

    b. Remus died

    c. the crowd revolted

    d. Remus slaughtered the crowd

7. The subject of <u>transiluisse</u> (line 5) is

    a. fama (line 5)

    b. ludibrio (line 5)

    c. Remum (line 5)

    d. muros (line 5)

8. In lines 5–6, <u>ab irato Romulo</u> is an ablative of

    a. place from which

    b. degree of difference

    c. comparison

    d. agent

9. In line 6, <u>verbis</u> is an ablative of

    a. time when

    b. means

    c. accompaniment

    d. separation

10. From the words <u>sic deinde</u> … <u>moenia mea</u> (lines 6–7), we learn that

    a. Romulus hopes to expand the size of the kingdom

    b. the walls of Rome will now grow quickly

    c. anyone is welcome to settle in Rome

    d. what happened to Remus will happen to anyone that mocks the walls

11. In line 7, <u>ita solus potitus imperio Romulus</u> is translated

    a. thus, the ruler alone gave Romulus power

    b. thus, the sun set on Romulus' reign

    c. thus, Romulus alone enjoyed power

    d. thus, Romulus enjoyed the powerful sun on his empire

12. On what word is the translation of <u>conditoris</u> (line 8) dependent?

    a. condita

    b. urbs

    c. nomine

    d. appellata

Introducing a Virtuous Matron

1   Matrona quaedam Ephesi[1] tam notae erat pudicitiae, ut vicinarum quoque gentium

2   feminas ad spectaculum sui evocaret. Haec ergo cum virum extulisset,[2] non contenta

3   vulgari more funus passis prosequi crinibus aut nudatum pectus in conspectu

4   frequentiae plangere,[3] in conditorium[4] etiam prosecuta est defunctum, positumque in

5   hypogaeo[5] Graeco more corpus custodire ac flere totis noctibus diebusque coepit. Sic

6   adflictantem se ac mortem inedia[6] persequentem non parentes potuerunt abducere, non

7   propinqui; magistratus ultimo repulsi abierunt, conplorataque[7] singularis exempli

8   femina ab omnibus quintum iam diem sine alimento[8] trahebat. Adsidebat aegrae

9   fidissima ancilla, simulque et lacrimas commodabat lugenti,[9] et quotienscumque

10   defecerat positum in monumento lumen renovabat.

[1] Ephesus, -i: Ephesus, a town on the western coast of modern-day Turkey

[2] effero, -ferre: to bury (as in a body after a funeral)

[3] plango, -ere: to beat (in mourning), to mourn

[4] conditorium, -i: tomb

[5] hypogaeum, -i: tomb

[6] inedia, -ae: starvation

[7] conploro, -are: to mourn

[8] alimentum, -i: nourishment, food

[9] lugeo, -ere: to mourn

1. The case and number of pudicitiae (line 1) are

    a. nominative plural

    b. dative singular

    c. ablative plural

    d. genitive singular

2. In lines 1–2, the subjunctive of evocaret is

    a. cum clause

    b. result clause

    c. purpose clause

    d. noun clause of result

3. In line 2, haec refers to

    a. matrona (line 1)

    b. pudicitiae (line 1)

    c. feminas (line 2)

    d. spectaculum (line 2)

4. In line 3, <u>aut</u> connects

    a. funus (line 3) and pectus (line 3)

    b. vulgari (line 3) and conspectu (line 3)

    c. prosequi (line 3) and plangere (line 4)

    d. crinibus (line 3) and frequentiae (line 4)

5. In line 4, <u>defunctum</u> refers to

    a. Ephesi (line 1)

    b. virum (line 2)

    c. funus (line 3)

    d. conditorium (line 4)

6. The words <u>positumque</u> … <u>coepit</u> (lines 4–5) tell us that the matron

    a. returned home to Greece and stayed up all night missing her husband

    b. killed herself because of her grief for her dead husband in the tomb

    c. carried her husband's body into the tomb and departed quickly

    d. kept watch over her husband's body and wept continuously

7. In line 6, the words <u>adflictantem se ac mortem inedia persequentem</u> are translated

    a. herself, causing pain through starvation and pursuing death

    b. causing herself pain and pursuing death by starvation

    c. causing him pain and starving herself

    d. pursuing her own starvation and causing herself pain through death

8. The case and number of <u>magistratus</u> (line 7) are

    a. nominative singular

    b. genitive singular

    c. nominative plural

    d. accusative plural

9. In line 8, the words <u>quintum</u> … <u>trahebat</u> tell us that

    a. she has five days' worth of food with her

    b. she hasn't eaten for five days

    c. in five days food will be delivered to her

    d. she left the tomb for five days to eat

10. In lines 8–9, the words <u>adsidebat aegrae fidissima ancilla</u> are translated

    a. the most faithful maid was sitting by the weary woman

    b. the weary maid was sitting by the most faithful woman

    c. the most faithful maid was weary from sitting by the woman

    d. the weary woman was sitting by the most faithful maid

CHAPTER 2

11. The case and number of <u>lugenti</u> (line 9) are

      a. genitive singular

      b. dative singular

      c. ablative singular

      d. nominative plural

12. In lines 9–10, the words <u>quotienscumque</u> … <u>renovabat</u> tell us that

      a. the morning light illuminated the inside of the tomb

      b. the light in the tomb kept going out and the maid kept relighting it

      c. the tomb is too dark for the matron to see anything

      d. the matron brought a light with her into the tomb so she could see

CHAPTER 2

A Successful Hunt

1   Ridebis, et licet rideas. Ego, ille quem nosti, apros[1] tres et quidem pulcherrimos cepi.

2   "Ipse?" inquis. Ipse; non tamen ut omnino ab inertia mea et quiete discederem. Ad retia

3   sedebam; erat in proximo non venabulum[2] aut lancea, sed stilus et pugillares;[3] meditabar

4   aliquid enotabamque, ut si manus vacuas, plenas tamen ceras reportarem. Non est

5   quod contemnas hoc studendi genus; mirum est ut animus agitatione motuque corporis

6   excitetur; iam undique silvae et solitudo ipsumque illud silentium quod venationi[4] datur,

7   magna cogitationis incitamenta sunt. Proinde cum venabere, licebit auctore me ut

8   panarium[5] et lagunculam[6] sic etiam pugillares feras: experieris non Dianam magis

9   montibus quam Minervam inerrare. Vale.

[1] aper, -pri: wild boar

[2] venabulum, -i: a hunting spear

[3] pugillar, -aris: a writing tablet

[4] venatio, -onis: hunting, a hunt

[5] panarium, -i: breadbasket

[6] laguncula, -ae: small bottle

1. From line 1 (<u>ridebis</u> … <u>cepi</u>), we can infer that Pliny

    a. enjoys hunting

    b. has never hunted before

    c. is normally a bad hunter

    d. was gored by three boars

2. In line 1, <u>licet rideas</u> is translated

    a. you should laugh

    b. you will laugh

    c. you are laughing

    d. you must laugh

3. The second <u>ipse</u> in line 2 is translated

    a. him, himself

    b. it, itself

    c. I, myself

    d. we, ourselves

4. From line 2 (<u>non</u> … <u>discederem</u>), we learn that Pliny

    a. was able to hunt without exerting much energy

    b. hunted all of his meals

    c. was not motivated to hunt

    d. was forced by his friend to hunt

5. In line 2, <u>ad</u> is translated

    a. to
    b. toward
    c. by
    d. from

6. We learn from line 3 (<u>erat</u> … <u>pugillares</u>) that Pliny was preparing to

    a. write
    b. hunt
    c. sleep
    d. eat

7. The subjunctive of <u>reportarem</u> (line 4) is

    a. purpose clause
    b. conditional
    c. indirect command
    d. indirect question

8. The form of <u>studendi</u> (line 5) is

    a. subjunctive
    b. participle
    c. imperative
    d. gerund

9. The function of the ut clause in lines 5–6 (<u>ut</u> … <u>excitetur</u>) is

    a. subject
    b. object
    c. purpose
    d. result

10. The case and number of <u>incitamenta</u> (line 7) are

    a. nominative singular
    b. ablative singular
    c. nominative plural
    d. accusative plural

11. The translation of <u>cum</u> (line 7) is

    a. with
    b. when
    c. although
    d. by

12. The case and number of <u>me</u> (line 7) are

    a. genitive singular

    b. dative singular

    c. accusative singular

    d. ablative singular

13. The allusions <u>Dianam</u> and <u>Minervam</u> (lines 8–9) are used to

    a. recall myths in which each loved a mortal man

    b. suggest hunting and artistic pursuits

    c. imply that only men should be hunting

    d. encourage the reader to go hunting

14. The translation of <u>quam</u> (line 9) is

    a. which

    b. whom

    c. than

    d. how

A Guard Introduces Himself to a Mourning Woman

1   Proxima ergo nocte, cum miles, qui cruces asservabat, ne quis ad sepulturam corpus

2   detraheret, notasset sibi lumen inter monumenta clarius fulgens et gemitum lugentis

3   audisset, vitio[1] gentis humanae concupiit scire quis aut quid faceret. Descendit igitur in

4   conditorium,[2] visaque pulcherrima muliere, primo quasi quodam monstro infernisque

5   imaginibus turbatus substitit; deinde ut et corpus iacentis conspexit et lacrimas

6   consideravit faciemque unguibus[3] sectam, ratus (scilicet id quod erat) desiderium extincti

7   non posse feminam pati, attulit in monumentum cenulam suam, coepitque hortari

8   lugentem ne perseveraret in dolore supervacuo,[4] ac nihil profuturo[5] gemitu pectus

9   diduceret: "omnium eundem esse exitum et idem domicilium" et cetera quibus

10 exulceratae[6] mentes ad sanitatem revocantur.

[1] vitium, -i: flaw, fault
[2] conditorium, -i: tomb
[3] unguis, -is: fingernail, claw

[4] supervacuus, -a, -um: unnecessary
[5] nihil profuturus, -a, -um: useless
[6] exulceratus, -a, -um: shredded, destroyed

1. In line 1, <u>proxima nocte</u> is an ablative of

    a. time
    b. place where
    c. means
    d. agent

2. In line 1, <u>quis</u> is translated

    a. who
    b. whoever
    c. by which
    d. anyone

3. From the words <u>qui ... detraheret</u> (lines 1–2) we learn that the soldier is there

    a. to protect the matron from her husband's family
    b. to prevent crucified bodies from being taken down
    c. to prevent the matron from killing herself
    d. to oversee the killing by crucifixion of criminals

4. In line 3, the subjunctive of <u>faceret</u> is

    a. relative clause of characteristic
    b. fearing clause
    c. indirect question
    d. indirect command

CHAPTER 2

5. Which of the following is associated with <u>quodam monstro infernisque imaginibus</u> (lines 4–5)?

    a. religious sacrifice

    b. the underworld

    c. gladiatorial games

    d. imperial succession

6. The word <u>ut</u> (line 5) is translated

    a. so that

    b. that

    c. as

    d. to

7. The use of the infinitive of <u>pati</u> (line 7) is

    a. indirect statement

    b. subjective

    c. exclamation

    d. complementary

8. The word <u>suam</u> (line 7) refers to

    a. the soldier

    b. the dead husband

    c. the matron

    d. the tomb

9. In line 8, the subjunctive of <u>perseveraret</u> is

    a. indirect command

    b. purpose clause

    c. result clause

    d. indirect question

10. The words <u>omnium eumdem esse exitum et idem domicilium</u> (line 9) refer to which of the following ideas?

    a. everyone deserves appropriate housing

    b. everyone will eventually die

    c. a tomb is no place for a woman to live

    d. there is a limit for how long a woman should mourn her dead husband

11. The words <u>et cetera quibus</u> (line 9) are translated

    a. and other things by which

    b. and certain things with which

    c. and those things for which

    d. and the rest to which

2.1.8   SAMPLE MULTIPLE CHOICE PASSAGES—SIGHT POETRY

The Death of Turnus

1	Stetit acer in armis
2	Aeneas volvens oculos dextramque repressit;
3	et iam iamque magis cunctantem flectere sermo
4	coeperat, infelix umero cum apparuit alto
5	balteus[1] et notis fulserunt cingula[2] bullis[3]
6	Pallantis pueri, victum quem vulnere Turnus
7	straverat atque umeris inimicum insigne gerebat.
8	Ille, oculis postquam saevi monimenta doloris
9	exuviasque hausit, furiis accensus et ira
10	terribilis: "Tune hinc spoliis indute[4] meorum
11	eripiare mihi? Pallas te hoc vulnere, Pallas
12	immolat et poenam scelerato ex sanguine sumit."
13	Hoc dicens ferrum adverso sub pectore condit
14	fervidus; ast illi solvuntur frigore membra
15	vitaque cum gemitu fugit indignata sub umbras.

[1] balteus, -i: baldric (a belt worn over the shoulder typically to hold a weapon)
[2] cingula, -orum: swordbelt
[3] bulla, -ae: stud (decorative protrusion)
[4] induo, -ere, indui, indutus: to clothe

1. In line 3, <u>cunctantem</u> describes
   a. Aeneas
   b. Turnus
   c. Pallas
   d. Juno

2. <u>Flectere</u> (line 3) is dependent for its translation on
   a. magis (line 3)
   b. cunctantem (line 3)
   c. sermo (line 3)
   d. coeperat (line 4)

3. Which of the following figures of speech occurs in lines 4–5 (<u>infelix</u> … <u>balteus</u>)?

    a. synchesis

    b. personification

    c. transferred epithet

    d. asyndeton

4. The ablative of <u>umero alto</u> (line 4) is

    a. manner

    b. accompaniment

    c. comparison

    d. place where

5. From the words <u>victum</u> … <u>gerebat</u> (lines 6–7) we learn that

    a. Pallas escaped Turnus' attack

    b. Turnus killed Pallas and is wearing his belt

    c. the gods will intervene to save Turnus' life

    d. Aeneas has finally conquered Turnus upon seeing Pallas' belt

6. The case and number of <u>insigne</u> (line 7) are

    a. nominative singular

    b. accusative singular

    c. ablative singular

    d. vocative singular

7. <u>Ille</u> (line 8) refers to

    a. Aeneas

    b. Turnus

    c. Pallas

    d. Jupiter

8. The metrical pattern of the first four feet of line 9 is

    a. dactyl-spondee-dactyl-spondee

    b. spondee-spondee-dactyl-spondee

    c. dactyl-spondee-spondee-dactyl

    d. spondee-dactyl-spondee-spondee

9. In line 10, <u>indute</u> modifies

    a. tu (line 10)

    b. spoliis (line 10)

    c. meorum (line 10)

    d. mihi (line 11)

10. The form of <u>eripiare</u> (line 11) is

    a. indicative

    b. imperative

    c. infinitive

    d. subjunctive

11. In line 11, <u>mihi</u> is translated

    a. from me

    b. to me

    c. for me

    d. with me

12. Which of the following figures of speech occurs in lines 11–12 (<u>Pallas</u> … <u>immolat</u>)?

    a. anaphora

    b. asyndeton

    c. alliteration

    d. apostrophe

13. From the words <u>Pallas</u> [1st one] … <u>sumit</u> (lines 11–12) we learn that

    a. Pallas is about to kill Turnus

    b. Turnus' death will avenge the death of Pallas

    c. the blood from Turnus' wound stains the earth

    d. Aeneas cares about Pallas more than Turnus

14. The case and number of <u>illi</u> (line 14) are

    a. nominative singular

    b. genitive singular

    c. dative singular

    d. nominative plural

The Unexpected Arrival of a Husband

1   "Mittenda est[1] domino (nunc, nunc properate, puellae)
2   quamprimum[2] nostra facta lacerna[3] manu.
3   Quid tamen auditis (nam plura audire potestis)?
4   Quantum de bello dicitur esse super?
5   Postmodo victa cades: melioribus, Ardea,[4] restas,
6   improba, quae nostros cogis abesse viros.
7   Sint tantum reduces.[5] Sed enim temerarius[6] ille
8   est meus, et stricto qualibet[7] ense ruit.
9   Mens abit et morior, quotiens pugnantis imago
10   me subit, et gelidum pectora frigus habet."
11   Desinit in lacrimas inceptaque fila[8] remisit,
12   in gremio[9] vultum deposuitque suum.
13   Hoc ipsum decuit: lacrimae decuere pudicam,
14   et facies animo dignaque parque fuit.
15   "Pone metum. Veni," coniunx ait; illa revixit,
16   deque viri collo dulce pependit onus.

[1] The speaker is Lucretia, a Roman woman whose husband is away fighting.
[2] quamprimum: as soon as possible
[3] lacerna, -ae: cloak
[4] Ardea, -ae: the name of a town near Rome against which Rome was fighting
[5] redux, -cis (adj): returning
[6] temerarius, -a, -um: rash, thoughtless
[7] qualibet: in any direction, all over the place
[8] filum, -i: thread
[9] gremius, -i: lap

1. The metrical pattern of the first four feet of line 1 is
    a. dactyl-spondee-spondee-dactyl
    b. dactyl-dactyl-spondee-dactyl
    c. spondee-dactyl-spondee-dactyl
    d. spondee-spondee-spondee-spondee

2. In line 1, <u>mittenda est</u> is translated
    a. had to be sent
    b. must send
    c. has to send
    d. must be sent

3. In line 2, <u>nostra</u> modifies

      a. quamprimum (line 2)

      b. facta (line 2)

      c. lacerna (line 2)

      d. manu (line 2)

4. The subject of <u>auditis</u> (line 3) is

      a. puellae (line 1)

      b. lacerna (line 2)

      c. manu (line 2)

      d. plura (line 4)

5. Which of the following figures of speech occurs in lines 5–6 (<u>melioribus</u> … <u>viros</u>)

      a. anaphora

      b. aposiopesis

      c. apostrophe

      d. asyndeton

6. The case and number of <u>quae</u> (line 6) are

      a. nominative singular

      b. nominative plural

      c. accusative plural

      d. vocative singular

7. From lines 7–8 (<u>sed enim</u> … <u>ense ruit</u>) we learn that

      a. Lucretia's husband has died in battle because of his impulsivity

      b. Lucretia's husband fights recklessly

      c. Lucretia's husband won the battle for the Romans

      d. Lucretia's husband uses the sword that she made for him

8. In line 9, <u>pugnantis</u> is translated

      a. of fighting

      b. having been fought

      c. of the man fighting

      d. fighting

9. From the words <u>desinit in lacrimas</u> (line 11), we can infer that

      a. Lucretia is distraught

      b. Lucretia is overjoyed

      c. Lucretia's husband is distraught

      d. Lucretia's husband is overjoyed

10. In line 12, <u>suum</u> refers to

    a. Lucretia

    b. Lucretia's husband

    c. the puellae of line 1

    d. soldiers

11. The form of <u>decuere</u> (line 13) is

    a. indicative

    b. infinitive

    c. imperative

    d. subjunctive

12. The words <u>et facies</u> … <u>parque fuit</u> (line 14) tell us that Lucretia

    a. made herself more attractive for the return of her husband

    b. is angry at her husband for still being away

    c. is genuine in both her feelings and her appearance

    d. considers herself equal to her husband in courage

13. In line 15, <u>veni</u> is translated

    a. I have come

    b. come!

    c. I am coming

    d. coming

14. From line 16 we learn that Lucretia

    a. fainted in shock at the sight of her husband

    b. gave her husband the cloak that she and her assistants had been weaving

    c. fled the room because of the weight of her emotions

    d. hugged her husband

The Helmsman Disappoints

1   Iamque propinquabant scopulo metamque tenebant,

2   cum princeps medioque Gyas[1] in gurgite victor

3   rectorem navis compellat voce Menoeten:[2]

4   "Quo tantum mihi dexter abis? Huc derige cursum;

5   litus ama et laeva stringat sine palmula[3] cautes;[4]

6   altum alii teneant." Dixit; sed caeca Menoetes

7   saxa timens proram pelagi detorquet ad undas.

8   "Quo diversus abis?" Iterum, "Pete saxa, Menoete!"

9   Cum clamore Gyas revocabat, et ecce Cloanthum[5]

10   respicit instantem[6] tergo et propiora tenentem.

11   Ille inter navemque Gyae scopulosque sonantes

12   radit iter laevum interior subitoque priorem

13   praeterit[7] et metis tenet aequora tuta relictis.

[1] Gyas, -ae: the name of the captain of one of Aeneas' ships

[2] Menoetes, -is (acc = -en): a companion of Aeneas and the helmsman of Gyas' ship

[3] palmula, -ae: oar

[4] cautes, -is, f.: a rock, crag

[5] Cloanthus, -i: the name of the captain of one of Aeneas' ships

[6] insto, -are (+ dat): to approach

[7] praetereo, -ire: to overtake

1. In line 3, the subjunctive of <u>compellat</u> is

   a. purpose clause
   b. result clause
   c. jussive
   d. cum clause

2. The case and number of <u>navis</u> (line 3) are

   a. nominative singular
   b. genitive singular
   c. dative plural
   d. ablative plural

3. The form of <u>derige</u> and <u>ama</u> (lines 4 and 5) is

   a. indicative
   b. infinitive
   c. imperative
   d. subjunctive

4. In line 6, <u>altum</u> refers to

    a. the rock

    b. the mast of the ship

    c. Menoetes

    d. the sea

5. In line 6, <u>caeca</u> modifies

    a. Menoetes (line 6)

    b. saxa (line 7)

    c. proram (line 7)

    d. pelagi (line 7)

6. From the words <u>sed caeca</u> … <u>ad undas</u> (lines 6–7), we learn that

    a. Menoetes fears the other ships and follows Gyas' orders

    b. Menoetes smashes the ship on the rock and it sinks

    c. Menoetes loses control of the ship

    d. Menoetes steers the ship away from the rock

7. The speaker of the direct speech in line 8 is

    a. Menoetes

    b. Gyas

    c. Cloanthus

    d. Aeneas

8. In line 9, <u>cum</u> is translated

    a. with

    b. when

    c. since

    d. although

9. In line 11, to whom does <u>ille</u> refer

    a. Menoetes

    b. Gyas

    c. Cloanthus

    d. Aeneas

10. How many elisions are in line 12?

    a. 0

    b. 1

    c. 2

    d. 3

11. In line 12, <u>iter</u> is translated

    a. route

    b. journey

    c. trip

    d. direction

12. From the words <u>metis</u> … <u>relictis</u> (line 13) we learn that

    a. Gyas' ship has retaken the lead

    b. Cloanthus has turned around the meta in the lead

    c. Cloanthus' ship has struck the meta and is sinking

    d. Gyas' ship is safe at sea but out of the race

Dido's Lament to Aeneas

1   Certus es ire tamen miseramque relinquere Didon[1]

2   atque idem venti vela fidemque ferent.

3   Certus es, Aenea,[2] cum foedere solvere naves

4   quaeque ubi sint nescis, Itala regna sequi.

5   Nec nova Karthago, nec te crescentia tangunt

6   moenia nec sceptro tradita summa tuo.

7   Facta fugis, facienda petis; quaerenda per orbem

8   altera, quaesita est altera terra tibi.

9   Ut terram invenias, quis eam tibi tradet habendam?

10   Quis sua non notis arva tenenda dabit?

11   Alter habendus amor tibi restat et altera Dido

12   quamque iterum fallas, altera danda fides.

13   Quando erit, ut condas instar[3] Karthaginis urbem

14   et videas populos altus ab arce tuos?

15   Omnia ut eveniant, nec di tua vota morentur,

16   unde tibi, quae te sic amet, uxor erit?

[1] an irregular accusative form of Dido, -onis, f.   [3] instar (indecl.), n.: image

[2] Aeneas, -ae, m.: Aeneas, Trojan hero

1. Which of the following grammatical constructions occurs in line 1 (certus … Didon)?
    a. indirect statement
    b. indirect command
    c. indirect question
    d. passive periphrastic

2. Which of the following figures of speech occurs in line 2 (atque … ferent)?
    a. hendiadys
    b. chiasmus
    c. asyndeton
    d. zeugma

3. The case and number of Aenea (line 3) are
    a. nominative singular
    b. ablative singular
    c. vocative singular
    d. accusative plural

4. The antecedent of <u>quae</u> (line 4) is

    a. Aenea (line 3)
    b. foedere (line 3)
    c. naves (line 3)
    d. regna (line 4)

5. In line 4, the subjunctive of <u>sint</u> is

    a. cum clause
    b. indirect question
    c. indirect command
    d. purpose clause

6. The metrical pattern of the first four feet of line 5 (<u>nec</u> … <u>tangunt</u>) is

    a. dactyl-spondee-spondee-spondee
    b. dactyl-dactyl-spondee-spondee
    c. spondee-dactyl-spondee-spondee
    d. dactyl-spondee-spondee-dactyl

7. Which of the following figures of speech occurs in lines 5–6 (<u>nec nova</u> … <u>summa tuo</u>)?

    a. apostrophe
    b. anaphora
    c. aposiopesis
    d. onomatopoeia

8. In line 7, <u>facta fugis, facienda petis</u> is translated

    a. you flee and seek walls that must be built
    b. you seek to flee walls that must be built
    c. you must build the walls that you flee
    d. you flee already built walls, you seek walls not yet built

9. In line 8, <u>altera</u> … <u>altera</u> is translated

    a. one … the other
    b. both … and
    c. not only … but also
    d. this one … that one

10. The form of <u>tradet</u> (line 9) is

    a. indicative
    b. subjunctive
    c. participle
    d. infinitive

11. The antecedent of <u>sua</u> (line 10) is

    a. quis (line 10)
    b. notis (line 10)
    c. arva (line 10)
    d. tenenda (line 10)

12. From <u>quamque iterum fallas</u> (line 12), we can infer that Aeneas

    a. has deceived Dido
    b. will not succeed in establishing his new land
    c. will deceive another woman
    d. will suffer without Dido in his life

13. The case of <u>instar</u> (line 13) is

    a. nominative
    b. genitive
    c. accusative
    d. ablative

14. In line 14, <u>altus</u> is translated

    a. from above
    b. tall
    c. deep
    d. all around

15. The case and number of <u>vota</u> (line 15) are

    a. nominative singular
    b. ablative singular
    c. nominative plural
    d. accusative plural

16. The dative of <u>tibi</u> (line 16) is

    a. agent
    b. purpose
    c. possession
    d. direction

2.1.9 SAMPLE MULTIPLE CHOICE PASSAGES—CAESAR

Tasgetius, the Carnutian

1   Erat in Carnutibus summo loco natus Tasgetius, cuius maiores in sua civitate regnum

2   obtinuerant. Huic Caesar pro eius virtute atque in se benevolentia, quod in omnibus

3   bellis singulari eius opera fuerat usus, maiorum locum restituerat. Tertium iam hunc

4   annum regnantem inimici multis palam ex civitate auctoribus interfecerunt. Defertur ea

5   res ad Caesarem. Ille veritus, quod ad plures pertinebat, ne civitas eorum impulsu

6   deficeret, L. Plancum cum legione ex Belgio celeriter in Carnutes proficisci iubet ibique

7   hiemare quorumque opera cognoverat Tasgetium interfectum, hos comprehensos ad se

8   mittere. Interim ab omnibus legatis quaestoribusque, quibus legiones tradiderat, certior

9   factus est in hiberna perventum locumque hibernis esse munitum.

1. In line 1, the first <u>in</u> (<u>in Carnutibus</u>) is translated
    a. on
    b. at
    c. to
    d. among

2. In lines 1–2 (<u>cuius … obtinuerant</u>), we learn that Tasgetius
    a. led a revolt to assume power
    b. had ancestors who established rule
    c. fled the kingdom for a neighboring state
    d. had more land than anyone else in the kingdom

3. Lines 2–3 (<u>huic</u> … <u>restituerat</u>) reflect Caesar's tendency to
    a. punish those who cross him
    b. reward those loyal to him
    c. use locals to gain allies for the Romans
    d. infiltrate local peoples to put down rebellions

4. In line 2, <u>eius</u> refers to
    a. Tasgetius
    b. Caesar
    c. the Carnutians
    d. the ancestors of Tasgetius

5. In line 3, <u>singulari</u> modifies

    a. bellis (line 3)

    b. eius (line 3)

    c. opera (line 3)

    d. usus (line 3)

6. From lines 3–4 (<u>tertium … interfecerunt</u>), we learn that

    a. Tasgetius invited fellow citizens to rule with him

    b. Tasgetius was killed by his fellow citizens

    c. Tasgetius stepped down from power after the third year

    d. Tasgetius allied with Caesar to conquer neighboring peoples

7. The antecedent of <u>eorum</u> (line 5) is

    a. Tasgetius

    b. Caesar

    c. Tasgetius' ancestors

    d. Tasgetius' killers

8. In line 6, the subjunctive of <u>deficeret</u> is

    a. purpose clause

    b. indirect command

    c. indirect question

    d. fearing clause

9. The translation of <u>proficisci</u> (line 6) is

    a. to depart

    b. I departed

    c. depart!

    d. having departed

10. In line 7, <u>se</u> refers to

    a. Tasgetius

    b. Caesar

    c. Lucius Plancus

    d. the killers of Tasgetius

11. The ablative of <u>ab omnibus legatis quaestoribus</u> (line 8) is

    a. agent

    b. means

    c. absolute

    d. place from which

CHAPTER 2

The Romans Under Siege

1   Quibus rebus perturbatis nostris novitate pugnae tempore opportunissimo Caesar

2   auxilium tulit: namque eius adventu hostes constiterunt, nostri se ex timore receperunt.

3   Quo facto, ad lacessendum et ad committendum proelium alienum esse tempus

4   arbitratus suo se loco continuit et, brevi tempore intermisso, in castra legiones reduxit.

5   Dum haec geruntur, nostris omnibus occupatis, qui erant in agris reliqui discesserunt.

6   Secutae sunt continuos complures dies tempestates quae et nostros in castris

7   continerent et hostem a pugna prohiberent. Interim barbari nuntios in omnes partes

8   dimiserunt paucitatemque nostrorum militum suis praedicaverunt et quanta praedae

9   faciendae atque in perpetuum sui liberandi facultas daretur, si Romanos castris

10   expulissent, demonstraverunt. His rebus celeriter magna multitudine peditatus

11   equitatusque coacta ad castra venerunt.

1. The case of pugnae (line 1) is dependent on

    a. rebus (line 1)

    b. novitate (line 1)

    c. tempore (line 1)

    d. Caesar (line 1)

2. Caesar's use of the noun Caesar (line 1) indicates that

    a. Caesar the writer is referring to Caesar as a character in his own narrative

    b. a writer other than Caesar has written this passage

    c. Caesar the writer is emphasizing Caesar the character's role in this passage

    d. Caesar only refers to himself in the 3rd person in the *Gallic Wars*

3. From the words se ex timore receperunt (line 2) we can infer that Caesar's soldiers

    a. fought valiantly

    b. were terrified by the enemy

    c. were no longer terrified by the enemy

    d. retreated

4. The form of lacessendum (line 3) is

    a. infinitive

    b. imperative

    c. subjunctive

    d. gerundive

5. The case and number of <u>tempus</u> (line 3) are

    a. nominative singular

    b. genitive singular

    c. accusative singular

    d. nominative plural

6. Which part of speech is <u>reliqui</u> (line 5)?

    a. noun

    b. adjective

    c. verb

    d. adverb

7. What is the grammatical function of <u>continuos complures dies</u> (line 6)?

    a. accusative direct object

    b. accusative extent of time

    c. subject accusative

    d. accusative place to which

8. The subjunctive of <u>prohiberent</u> (line 7) is

    a. relative clause of result

    b. relative clause of purpose

    c. indirect question

    d. indirect command

9. In line 8, <u>suis</u> is translated

    a. themselves

    b. them

    c. they

    d. their people

10. In line 8, <u>et</u> connects

    a. barbari (line 7) and praedae (line 8)

    b. partes (line 7) and perpetuum (line 9)

    c. dimiserunt (line 8) and daretur (line 9)

    d. praedicaverunt (line 8) and demonstraverunt (line 10)

11. From lines 8–9 (<u>quanta</u> ... <u>daretur</u>), we learn that

    a. the enemy has plundered much of the Roman booty

    b. the Romans are ready to fight

    c. the Romans are vulnerable

    d. the Gauls have won their freedom forever

12. The subjunctive of <u>daretur</u> (line 9) is

    a. indirect question

    b. indirect command

    c. conditional

    d. relative clause of characteristic

13. The case and number of <u>peditatus</u> (line 10) and <u>equitatus</u> (line 11) are

    a. nominative singular

    b. genitive singular

    c. nominative plural

    d. accusative plural

14. The participle <u>coacta</u> (line 11) modifies

    a. rebus (line 10)

    b. multitudine (line 10)

    c. peditatus equitatusque (lines 10–11)

    d. castra (line 11)

2.1.10 SAMPLE MULTIPLE CHOICE PASSAGES—VERGIL

The Arrival of the Trojans

1   "O regina, novam cui condere Iuppiter urbem

2   iustitiaque dedit gentes frenare superbas,

3   Troes te miseri, ventis maria omnia vecti,

4   oramus: prohibe infandos a navibus ignes,

5   parce pio generi et propius res aspice nostras.

6   Non nos aut ferro Libycos populare penates

7   venimus, aut raptas ad litora vertere praedas;

8   non ea vis animo nec tanta superbia victis.

9   Est locus, Hesperiam Grai cognomine dicunt,

10   terra antiqua, potens armis atque ubere glaebae;

11   Oenotri coluere viri; nunc fama minores

12   Italiam dixisse ducis de nomine gentem.

13   Hic cursus fuit,

14   cum subito adsurgens fluctu nimbosus Orion

15   in vada caeca tulit penitusque procacibus Austris

16   perque undas superante salo perque invia saxa

17   dispulit; huc pauci vestris adnavimus oris.

1. The case and number of <u>regina</u> (line 1) are
    - a. nominative singular
    - b. ablative singular
    - c. vocative singular
    - d. nominative plural

2. The grammatical function of <u>cui</u> (line 1) is
    - a. nominative subject
    - b. genitive possession
    - c. dative indirect object
    - d. subject accusative

3. The conjunction -<u>que</u> (line 2) connects
    - a. regina (line 1) and iustitia (line 2)
    - b. condere (line 1) and frenare (line 2)
    - c. Iuppiter (line 1) and iustitia (line 2)
    - d. urbem (line 1) and gentes (line 2)

4. The number of elisions in line 3 is

    a. 0

    b. 1

    c. 2

    d. 3

5. In line 3, <u>vecti</u> modifies

    a. Troes (line 3)

    b. miseri (line 3)

    c. ventis (line 3)

    d. maria (line 3)

6. The form of <u>prohibe</u> (line 4), <u>parce</u> (line 5), and <u>aspice</u> (line 5) is

    a. imperative

    b. infinitive

    c. subjunctive

    d. gerund

7. The infinitive <u>populare</u> (line 6) expresses

    a. purpose

    b. result

    c. cause

    d. characteristic

8. The grammatical function of <u>animo</u> (line 8) and <u>victis</u> (line 8) is

    a. dative indirect object

    b. dative of possession

    c. ablative of means

    d. ablative absolute

9. The metrical pattern of the first four feet of line 10 (<u>terra</u> ... <u>atque</u>) is

    a. spondee-spondee-spondee-spondee

    b. spondee-dactyl-spondee-spondee

    c. dactyl-dactyl-spondee-dactyl

    d. dactyl-spondee-dactyl-spondee

10. In line 11, <u>coluere</u> is translated

    a. (they) have cultivated

    b. to have cultivated

    c. to cultivate

    d. (they) cultivate

CHAPTER 2

11. Which of the following characteristics of the *Aeneid* is illustrated in the shortness of line 13?

    a. Vergil's use of artistic language

    b. Vergil's indebtedness to Homer's epics

    c. the incomplete nature of the *Aeneid* at Vergil's death

    d. the lasting influence of the *Aeneid* on later writers

12. Which of the following figures of speech occurs in lines 14–16 (cum … saxa)?

    a. hendiadys

    b. asyndeton

    c. alliteration

    d. hysteron proteron

13. Which of the following is associated with Orion (line 14)?

    a. storms

    b. war

    c. refugees

    d. peace

14. Which part of speech is penitus (line 15)?

    a. noun

    b. adjective

    c. adverb

    d. verb

15. The grammatical function of vestris oris (line 17) is

    a. dative of direction

    b. ablative of means

    c. genitive of possession

    d. nominative subject

Aeneas Addresses Dido

1   "Infelix Dido, verus mihi nuntius ergo

2   venerat exstinctam ferroque extrema secutam?

3   Funeris heu tibi causa fui? Per sidera iuro,

4   per superos et si qua fides tellure sub ima est,

5   invitus, regina, tuo de litore cessi.

6   Sed me iussa deum, quae nunc has ire per umbras,

7   per loca senta situ cogunt noctemque profundam,

8   imperiis egere suis; nec credere quivi

9   hunc tantum tibi me discessu ferre dolorem.

10   Siste gradum teque aspectu ne subtrahe nostro.

11   Quem fugis? Extremum fato quod te adloquor hoc est."

12   Talibus Aeneas ardentem et torva tuentem

13   lenibat dictis animum lacrimasque ciebat.

14   Illa solo fixos oculos aversa tenebat

15   nec magis incepto vultum sermone movetur

16   quam si dura silex aut stet Marpesia cautes.

1. The metrical pattern of the first four feet of line 2 (<u>venerat</u> … *the first syllable of extrema*) is

    a. spondee-spondee-spondee-dactyl

    b. spondee-spondee-dactyl-spondee

    c. dactyl-spondee-dactyl-spondee

    d. dactyl-spondee-spondee-spondee

2. The grammatical function of <u>exstinctam</u> (line 2) and <u>secutam</u> (line 2) is

    a. gerundive expressing purpose

    b. indirect statement

    c. circumstantial cum clause

    d. result clause

3. From the word <u>ferro</u> (line 2), we learn that Aeneas knows that Dido killed herself

    a. by burning herself

    b. by poisoning herself

    c. by stabbing herself

    d. by throwing herself off of a cliff

4. The case of <u>funeris</u> (line 3) depends on

    a. heu (line 3)

    b. tibi (line 3)

    c. causa (line 3)

    d. fui (line 3)

5. The translation of <u>per</u> (line 3) is

    a. through

    b. near

    c. in

    d. by

6. The translation of <u>qua</u> (line 4) is

    a. which

    b. by which

    c. any

    d. this

7. From line 5, we learn that Aeneas

    a. was cursed by the gods for leaving Dido

    b. lost a ship when leaving Carthage

    c. fought a fierce battle at sea

    d. didn't want to leave Dido

8. The case and number of <u>deum</u> (line 6) are

    a. nominative singular

    b. accusative singular

    c. nominative plural

    d. genitive plural

9. The antecedent of <u>quae</u> (line 6) is

    a. me (line 6)

    b. iussa (line 6)

    c. deum (line 6)

    d. umbras (line 6)

10. The ablative of <u>imperiis</u> (line 8) is

    a. accompaniment

    b. means

    c. degree of difference

    d. respect

11. The grammatical function of <u>me</u> (line 9) is

      a. subject accusative

      b. ablative of comparison

      c. ablative of place where

      d. accusative place to which

12. In line 9, the form of <u>ferre</u> depends on

      a. credere (line 8)

      b. quivi (line 8)

      c. me (line 9)

      d. discessu (line 9)

13. In line 10 (<u>siste</u> … <u>nostro</u>), Aeneas asks Dido to stop

      a. walking away

      b. crying

      c. talking

      d. attacking him

14. In line 11, <u>quem</u> is translated

      a. which

      b. whom

      c. who

      d. what

15. In line 12, <u>talibus</u> modifies an understood Latin word translated as

      a. steps

      b. tears

      c. fear

      d. words

16. In line 14, the ablative of <u>solo</u> is

      a. place where

      b. means

      c. cause

      d. comparison

2.1.11 SAMPLE MULTIPLE CHOICE QUESTIONS ANSWER KEY AND EXPLANATIONS

The Death of Remus

1   Priori Remo augurium[1] venisse fertur,[2] sex vultures; iamque nuntiato augurio cum duplex

2   numerus Romulo se ostendisset, utrumque regem sua multitudo consalutaverat:[3]

3   tempore illi[4] praecepto, at hi[4] numero avium regnum trahebant. Inde cum altercatione

4   congressi certamine irarum ad caedem vertuntur; ibi in turba ictus Remus cecidit.

5   Vulgatior fama est ludibrio[5] fratris Remum novos transiluisse muros; inde ab irato

6   Romulo, cum verbis quoque increpitans[6] adiecisset, "Sic deinde, quicumque alius

7   transiliet moenia mea," interfectum. Ita solus potitus imperio Romulus; condita urbs

8   conditoris nomine appellata. [Livy, *Ab urbe condita* 1.7]

[1.] augurium, -i: auspices, prophecy
[2.] fertur: "is said"
[3.] consaluto, -are: to greet

[4.] illi, hi: the supporters of Remus, the supporters of Romulus
[5.] ludibrium, -i: mockery, contempt
[6.] increpito, -are: to scold repeatedly

1. The case and number of <u>Remo</u> (line 1) are

    a. nominative singular

    b. dative singular

    c. ablative singular

    d. genitive plural

Question Rating: Easy / Medium. Priori *comes from* prior, prioris, *a 3rd declension adjective, which makes* priori *either dative or ablative (remember that 3rd declension adjectives use the -i ending for both dative and ablative).* Remo *too can be either dative or ablative by ending. There is no ablative that makes immediate sense with a proper name and no preposition (accompaniment, e.g., would require* cum*).* Augurium venisse fertur *means "Auspices are said to have come" with* Remo *following logically as "to Remus." Normally, such direction would be* ad *plus the accusative but here is a dative of direction.*

2. From the words <u>priori</u> … <u>ostendisset</u> (lines 1–2), we learn that

    a. Romulus saw more birds than Remus

    b. Romulus saw fewer birds than Remus

    c. Romulus and Remus saw the same number of birds

    d. Romulus saw his birds first

Question Rating: Easy. The key word here is duplex, *meaning "twice as many": "when twice as many birds (as Remus saw) showed themselves to Romulus."*

3. In line 2, <u>se</u> refers to

    a. the number of birds
    b. Romulus
    c. Remus
    d. the auspices

Question Rating: Easy. As the reflexive pronoun, se reflects on the subject of the verb. Duplex numerus is the subject and so se refers to it, the number of birds.

4. The case and number of <u>avium</u> (line 3) are

    a. nominative singular
    b. accusative singular
    c. genitive plural
    d. ablative singular

Question Rating: Easy. Avis, avis is a 3rd declension noun and so the -ium ending is genitive plural. Genitives are often linked with nouns and the two choices for avium are numero and regnum. "Number of birds" makes more sense than "a kingdom of birds."

5. The subject of <u>vertuntur</u> (line 4) is

    a. the birds
    b. Romulus and Remus
    c. the followers of Romulus
    d. the followers of Remus

Question Rating: Easy. Romulus and Remus not only are nominative but also make the most sense as the subject: "Romulus and Remus are turned to slaughter."

6. From the words <u>ibi</u> … <u>cecidit</u> (line 4), we learn that

    a. Romulus died
    b. Remus died
    c. the crowd revolted
    d. Remus slaughtered the crowd

Question Rating: Easy / Medium. Cado, -ere means "to fall" with the specific connotation of falling down dead. Icio, -ere means "to strike" and agrees with Remus. Turba could be distracting with the -a ending a potential nominative but, after the preposition in, that -a ending will be ablative.

CHAPTER 2

7. The subject of <u>transiluisse</u> (line 5) is

    a. fama (line 5)
    b. ludibrio (line 5)
    c. Remum (line 5)
    d. muros (line 5)

Question Rating: Medium. Transiluisse is an infinitive which takes its subject in the accusative. Of the choices, both Remum and muros are accusatives but Remum makes the most sense as the subject. As an active verb, transiluisse can also take a direct object and so muros is that direct object.

8. In lines 5–6, <u>ab irato Romulo</u> is an ablative of

    a. place from which
    b. degree of difference
    c. comparison
    d. agent

Question Rating: Easy. The preposition ab narrows the choices of ablative to place from which, separation, or agent; neither ablative of comparison nor ablative of degree of difference uses a preposition. Romulo is a person, which suggests agent but agent also requires a passive verb. That passive verb is the perfect passive participle interfectum: "killed by the angry Romulus."

9. In line 6, <u>verbis</u> is an ablative of

    a. time when
    b. means
    c. accompaniment
    d. separation

Question Rating: Medium. Cum is the distracting word here in that the preposition cum takes an ablative object and the ablative verbis follows it. Cum here, however, is the conjunction, which the subjunctive verb adiecisset suggests; because cum is a conjunction rather than a preposition, verbis cannot be an ablative of accompaniment, which requires the preposition cum. Ablative of manner can, but does not have to, use the preposition cum, but verbis would be a stretch as an ablative of manner. Verbis also is not a time word and so cannot be an ablative of time. Verbis explains how Romulus "scolded repeatedly" (increpitans) and so is an ablative of means.

10. From the words <u>sic deinde</u> … <u>moenia mea</u> (lines 6–7), we learn that

    a. Romulus hopes to expand the size of the kingdom
    b. the walls of Rome will now grow quickly
    c. anyone is welcome to settle in Rome
    d. what happened to Remus will happen to anyone that mocks the walls

Question Rating: Medium. Quicumque *is the indefinite pronoun "whoever" and* transiliet *is future (with that -e-), which suggests that Romulus is extending what happened to Remus to anyone else who acts similarly.*

11. In line 7, <u>ita solus potitus imperio Romulus</u> is translated

    a. thus, the ruler alone gave Romulus power
    b. thus, the sun set on Romulus' reign
    c. thus, Romulus alone enjoyed power
    d. thus, Romulus enjoyed the powerful sun on his empire

Question Rating: Medium. Potitus *comes from* potior, -iri, *one of the five deponent verbs that take an ablative object, which makes* imperio *the object of* potitus. Solus *is from* solus, -a, -um, *the adjective meaning "alone" (as opposed to* sol, solis, *the 3rd declension noun "sun"), and agrees with* Romulus.

12. On what word is the translation of <u>conditoris</u> (line 8) dependent?

    a. condita (line 7)
    b. urbs (line 7)
    c. nomine (line 8)
    d. appellata (line 8)

Question Rating: Medium. Conditoris *comes from the 3rd declension noun* conditor, -oris, *which makes it genitive singular. Genitives are often associated with nouns, which eliminates* condita *and* appellata *as probable choices.* Appellata *refers to calling or naming something and so it makes sense that the city (*urbs*) would be called after the name (*nomine*) of its founder (*conditoris*).*

Introducing a Virtuous Matron

1   Matrona quaedam Ephesi[1] tam notae erat pudicitiae, ut vicinarum quoque gentium

2   feminas ad spectaculum sui evocaret. Haec ergo cum virum extulisset,[2] non contenta

3   vulgari more funus passis prosequi crinibus aut nudatum pectus in conspectu

4   frequentiae plangere,[3] in conditorium[4] etiam prosecuta est defunctum, positumque in

5   hypogaeo[5] Graeco more corpus custodire ac flere totis noctibus diebusque coepit. Sic

6   adflictantem se ac mortem inedia[6] persequentem non parentes potuerunt abducere, non

7   propinqui; magistratus ultimo repulsi abierunt, conplorataque[7] singularis exempli

8   femina ab omnibus quintum iam diem sine alimento[8] trahebat. Adsidebat aegrae

9   fidissima ancilla, simulque et lacrimas commodabat lugenti,[9] et quotienscumque

10   defecerat positum in monumento lumen renovabat. [Petronius, *Satyricon* 111]

[1] Ephesus, -i: Ephesus, a town on the western coast of modern-day Turkey
[2] effero, ferre: to bury (as in a body after a funeral)
[3] plango, -ere: to beat (in mourning), to mourn
[4] conditorium, -i: tomb
[5] hypogaeum, -i: tomb
[6] inedia, -ae: starvation
[7] conploro, -are: to mourn
[8] alimentum, -i: nourishment, food
[9] lugeo, -ere: to mourn

1. The case and number of <u>pudicitiae</u> (line 1) are

    a. nominative plural

    b. dative singular

    c. ablative plural

    d. genitive singular

Question Rating: Medium. By ending, pudicitiae *cannot be ablative plural, which eliminates choice c. With the singular verb* erat, pudicitiae *can't be nominative plural, which eliminates choice a. The key word is* notae: *because it agrees with* pudicitiae, *rather than with* matrona, *the genitive of description makes the most sense, "a matron of noted virtue."*

2. In lines 1–2, the subjunctive of <u>evocaret</u> is

    a. cum clause

    b. result clause

    c. purpose clause

    d. noun clause of result

Question Rating: Medium. The key word is tam, *which is one of the "so" words that signal a result clause: "was of such noted virtue that she …"*

3. In line 2, <u>haec</u> refers to

    a. matrona (line 1)
    b. pudicitiae (line 1)
    c. feminas (line 2)
    d. spectaculum (line 2)

Question Rating: Easy / Medium. By agreement, haec *cannot refer to* spectaculum, *which is a neuter singular, while* haec, *if neuter, has to be plural, which eliminates choice d. The singular verb* extulisset *suggests that* haec *is singular, which means it cannot agree with the plural* feminas *or* pudicitiae, *which eliminates choices b and c. If* haec *is the subject, which the accusative* virum *suggests, then it makes more sense that the* matrona *is burying her husband.*

4. In line 3, <u>aut</u> connects

    a. funus (line 3) and pectus (line 3)
    b. vulgari (line 3) and conspectu (line 3)
    c. prosequi (line 3) and plangere (line 4)
    d. crinibus (line 3) and frequentiae (line 4)

Question Rating: Medium. The key word here is contenta *because of how it governs everything up to* plangere *(line 4). The two infinitives,* prosequi *(line 3) and* plangere *(line 4), are directly dependent on* contenta *and each infinitive governs the other constructions. The* aut *then connects the two infinitives.*

5. In line 4, <u>defunctum</u> refers to

    a. Ephesi (line 1)
    b. virum (line 2)
    c. funus (line 3)
    d. conditorium (line 4)

Question Rating: Difficult. Defunctum, *from which the English word "defunct" comes, means "dead." With this meaning, it only makes sense that it refers to* virum.

6. The words <u>positumque</u> … <u>coepit</u> (lines 4–5) tell us that the matron

    a. returned home to Greece and stayed up all night missing her husband
    b. killed herself because of her grief for her dead husband in the tomb
    c. carried her husband's body into the tomb and departed quickly
    d. kept watch over her husband's body and wept continuously

Question Rating: Easy / Medium. The descriptive verbs are custodire, *"to guard," and* flere, *"to weep," both of which are infinitives dependent on* coepit. *The conjunction* ac *joins these infinitives, which govern the rest of the constructions.*

7. In line 6, the words <u>adflictantem se ac mortem inedia persequentem</u> are translated

    a. herself, causing pain through starvation and pursuing death

    b. causing herself pain and pursuing death by starvation

    c. causing him pain and starving herself

    d. pursuing her own starvation and causing herself pain through death

Question Rating: Easy / Medium. The key word is se, *the reflexive pronoun, but a word that is often misunderstood or mistranslated. Se here is the object of* adflictantem: *"causing herself pain." The conjunction* ac *connects* adflictantem *with the other participle* persequentem, *which governs both the direct object* mortem *and the ablative* inedia: *"pursuing death by starvation."*

8. The case and number of <u>magistratus</u> (line 7) are

    a. nominative singular

    b. genitive singular

    c. nominative plural

    d. accusative plural

Question Rating: Easy. Magistratus *is a fourth declension noun, so all four choices can be correct because of the* -us *ending. The nominative plural* repulsi, *however, combined with the plural verb* abierunt *and the short clause suggest that* magistratus *is nominative plural.*

9. In line 8, the words <u>quintum</u> … <u>trahebat</u> tell us that

    a. she has five days' worth of food with her

    b. she hasn't eaten for five days

    c. in five days food will be delivered to her

    d. she left the tomb for five days to eat

Question Rating: Easy. The key to this question is the idiom trahebat quintum diem, *that* traho *with* diem *means "to spend time": "she was spending her fifth day." Even if that idiom isn't known, though, the meaning of* sine alimento *is relatively clear and should yield the correct answer.*

10. In lines 8–9, the words <u>adsidebat aegrae fidissima ancilla</u> are translated

    a. the most faithful maid was sitting by the weary woman

    b. the weary maid was sitting by the most faithful woman

    c. the most faithful maid was weary from sitting by the woman

    d. the weary woman was sitting by the most faithful maid

Question Rating: Easy / Medium. The key to understanding this fragment is that fidissima ancilla *agree and that they are the subject of* adsidebat; *this combination eliminates choices b and d. It is helpful to understand as well that* aegrae *is a substantive adjective that is dative with the compound* adsidebat. *Even without realizing how* aegrae *works, however, the Latin yields choice a more easily than choice c, which would require a separate word for "woman."*

11. The case and number of <u>lugenti</u> (line 9) are

    a. genitive singular
    b. dative singular
    c. ablative singular
    d. nominative plural

Question Rating: Medium. Lugenti *is a present active participle, which means that it takes 3rd declension endings, which eliminates choices a and d. But the difficulty to this question is the meaning of* commodabat, *to lend or to add, which suggests the possibility of a dative indirect object. Even without knowing the meaning of* commodabat, *however, the accusative* lacrimas *as the direct object suggests, albeit not as definitively, that* lugenti *is dative.*

12. In lines 9–10, the words <u>quotienscumque</u> … <u>renovabat</u> tell us that

    a. the morning light illuminated the inside of the tomb
    b. the light in the tomb kept going out and the maid kept relighting it
    c. the tomb is too dark for the matron to see anything
    d. the matron brought a light with her into the tomb so she could see

Question Rating: Medium / Difficult. The difficulty to this question is the vocabulary, specifically quotienscumque, *"as often as," and* defecerat, *"had failed" or "had gone out." Beyond the meaning of* quotienscumque *and* defecerat, lumen positum in monumento *potentially removes choices a and c and some understanding of* renovabat *as "renew" suggests choice b.*

A Successful Hunt

1   Ridebis, et licet rideas. Ego, ille quem nosti, apros[1] tres et quidem pulcherrimos cepi.

2   "Ipse?" inquis. Ipse; non tamen ut omnino ab inertia mea et quiete discederem. Ad retia

3   sedebam; erat in proximo non venabulum[2] aut lancea, sed stilus et pugillares;[3] meditabar

4   aliquid enotabamque, ut si manus vacuas, plenas tamen ceras reportarem. Non est

5   quod contemnas hoc studendi genus; mirum est ut animus agitatione motuque corporis

6   excitetur; iam undique silvae et solitudo ipsumque illud silentium quod venationi[4] datur,

7   magna cogitationis incitamenta sunt. Proinde cum venabere, licebit auctore me ut

8   panarium[5] et lagunculam[6] sic etiam pugillares feras: experieris non Dianam magis

9   montibus quam Minervam inerrare. Vale. [Pliny, *Epistulae* 1.6]

[1] aper, -pri: wild boar
[2] venabulum, -i: a hunting spear
[3] pugillar, -aris: a writing tablet

[4] venatio, -onis: hunting, a hunt
[5] panarium, -i: bread-basket
[6] laguncula, -ae: small bottle

1. From line 1 (<u>ridebis</u> … <u>cepi</u>), we can infer that Pliny

    a. enjoys hunting

    b. has never hunted before

    c. is normally a bad hunter

    d. was gored by three boars

Question Rating: Medium. The Latin of this opening line is relatively straightforward. The difficulty to the question comes from the ability to understand Pliny's tone in the Latin: he pokes fun at himself for actually being able to kill not only three boars but also really nice ones (quidem pulcherrimos).

2. In line 1, <u>licet rideas</u> is translated

    a. you should laugh

    b. you will laugh

    c. you are laughing

    d. you must laugh

Question Rating: Easy. The subjunctive rideas eliminates the indicative choices b and c. And both context and licet suggest choice a as the correct answer. The literal translation "it is permitted that you laugh" becomes "you should laugh."

3. The second <u>ipse</u> in line 2 is translated

    a. him, himself
    b. it, itself
    c. I, myself
    d. we, ourselves

Question Rating: Medium. Pliny is imagining a conversation with his recipient in which Pliny has to convince his recipient that he actually killed three nice boars. The repetition of ipse *conveys that convincing: "'you yourself?' I myself." The force of both* ipses *is similar to the emphasis of italics in English.*

4. From line 2 (<u>non</u> … <u>discederem</u>), we learn that Pliny

    a. was able to hunt without exerting much energy
    b. hunted all of his meals
    c. was not motivated to hunt
    d. was forced by his friend to hunt

Question Rating: Medium. The correct answer lies in the second half of the clause, ab inertia … discederem, *"and I didn't even have to leave my peace and quiet." The first half of the clause,* non … omnino, *plus the subjunctive* discederem, *can prove distracting, of course, but is not as necessary for understanding the clause as a whole.*

5. In line 2, <u>ad</u> is translated

    a. to
    b. toward
    c. by
    d. from

Question Rating: Easy. Translating sedebam *correctly yields the correct translation of* ad: *"I was sitting by my nets." Choices a and b are correct possible translations for* ad *but not for this particular context.*

6. We learn from line 3 (<u>erat</u> … <u>pugillares</u>) that Pliny was preparing to

    a. write
    b. hunt
    c. sleep
    d. eat

Question Rating: Easy / Medium. The correct answer relies on recognizing the meaning of stilus, *which is associated with the glossed* pugillares *and* lancea, *associated with* venabulum, *both of which establish the contrast between what he might be expected to be doing (hunting) and what he is doing (writing).*

7. The subjunctive of <u>reportarem</u> (line 4) is

    a. purpose clause
    b. conditional
    c. indirect command
    d. indirect question

Question Rating: Medium. The ut *of line 4 governs* reportarem *but the* si, *also of line 4, might suggest that* reportarem *is a conditional. Why was Pliny writing things down (*enotabam*)? So that he might bring back full tablets, if empty hands.*

8. The form of <u>studendi</u> (line 5) is

    a. subjunctive
    b. participle
    c. imperative
    d. gerund

Question Rating: Easy. The -nd- *of* studendi *eliminates choices a and c; it can be by form either the future passive participle or the gerund. The participle, as a verbal adjective, must agree with a noun (though participles can be used substantively, it is very rare for the future passive participle to be used substantively); the gerund, as a verbal noun, will function in isolation. Because nothing agrees with* studendi *and it makes sense that it is a genitive after* genus, *the correct answer is d.*

9. The function of the ut clause in lines 5–6 (<u>ut</u> … <u>excitetur</u>) is

    a. subject
    b. object
    c. purpose
    d. result

Question Rating: Difficult. Mirum est *is an impersonal construction: "it is amazing." In such a construction, the clause that follows, more often an infinitive, functions as the subject of the verb; the pronoun "it" stands for the clause that follows: "it is amazing that the mind is moved," which is equivalent to "that the mind is moved is amazing."*

10. The case and number of <u>incitamenta</u> (line 7) are

        a. nominative singular
        b. ablative singular
        c. nominative plural
        d. accusative plural

Question Rating: Difficult. The correct answer hinges on recognizing incitamentum *as a neuter noun, which eliminates choices a and b, and recognizing the role of* sunt. *There are three subjects:* silvae et solitudo ipsumque illud silentium *with* sunt *as the verb and* incitamenta *as the predicate, which makes it nominative.*

11. The translation of <u>cum</u> (line 7) is

        a. with
        b. when
        c. although
        d. by

Question Rating: Difficult. The identification of cum *as a conjunction in general is relatively straightforward but two details make this a more difficult identification: the* cum *clause is short, only two words, and* venabere *is a tricky verb form. Even though* venabere *has been glossed, the* -bere *ending is an uncommon form, the alternate 2nd person passive:* venabere = venaberis. *The identification of* venabere *as a verb eliminates choices a and d and choice c does not make sense given the context.*

12. The case and number of <u>me</u> (line 7) are

        a. genitive singular
        b. dative singular
        c. accusative singular
        d. ablative singular

Question Rating: Medium / Difficult. Knowing the forms of ego *eliminates choices a and b. Distinguishing between the accusative and ablative, however, relies on understanding that* auctore me *is an ablative absolute: "with me as author" ("idea-originator") for the* ut *clause that follows.*

13. The allusions <u>Dianam</u> and <u>Minervam</u> (lines 8–9) are used to

        a. recall myths in which each loved a mortal man
        b. suggest hunting and artistic pursuits
        c. imply that only men should be hunting
        d. encourage the reader to go hunting

Question Rating: Medium / Difficult. The correct interpretation of the allusion relies on understanding throughout the passage the contrast established between hunting and artistic pursuits, that Pliny has consistently been drawing this distinction, and that he closes that distinction by using the goddesses in charge of these pursuits as reference points: "you will find that Diana does not wander in the mountains more than Minerva does"; that is, there is as much art to be found in the woods as there is prey.

14. The translation of <u>quam</u> (line 9) is
     a. which
     b. whom
     c. than
     d. how

Question Rating: Easy. The use of the comparative magis *triggers the meaning of* quam *as "than," choice c. The relative pronoun, choices a and b, would require another clause / verb.*

A Guard Introduces Himself to a Mourning Woman

1   Proxima ergo nocte, cum miles, qui cruces asservabat, ne quis ad sepulturam corpus

2   detraheret, notasset sibi lumen inter monumenta clarius fulgens et gemitum lugentis

3   audisset, vitio[1] gentis humanae concupiit scire quis aut quid faceret. Descendit igitur in

4   conditorium,[2] visaque pulcherrima muliere, primo quasi quodam monstro infernisque

5   imaginibus turbatus substitit; deinde ut et corpus iacentis conspexit et lacrimas

6   consideravit faciemque unguibus[3] sectam, ratus (scilicet id quod erat) desiderium extincti

7   non posse feminam pati, attulit in monumentum cenulam suam, coepitque hortari

8   lugentem ne perseveraret in dolore supervacuo,[4] ac nihil profuturo[5] gemitu pectus

9   diduceret: "omnium eundem esse exitum et idem domicilium" et cetera quibus

10   exulceratae[6] mentes ad sanitatem revocantur. [Petronius, *Satyricon* 111]

[1] vitium, -i: flaw, fault
[2] conditorium, -i: tomb
[3] unguis, -is: fingernail, claw
[4] supervacuus, -a, -um: unnecessary
[5] nihil profuturus, -a, -um: useless
[6] exulceratus, -a, -um: shredded, destroyed

1. In line 1, <u>proxima nocte</u> is an ablative of

   a. time
   b. place where
   c. means
   d. agent

   Question Rating: Easy. The ablative of agent requires a preposition and the ablative of place where usually uses a preposition, and nocte *is neither a person nor a place word, which eliminates choices b and d. As a time word,* nocte *works as an ablative of time: when did this happen? "On the next night."*

2. In line 1, <u>quis</u> is translated

   a. who
   b. whoever
   c. by which
   d. anyone

   Question Rating: Easy. After si, nisi, num, *or* ne, *words that would begin with* ali- *drop the* ali-, *so* ne quis *is really* ne aliquis *and* aliquis *means "anyone."*

3. From the words <u>qui</u> … <u>detraheret</u> (lines 1–2) we learn that the soldier is there

   a. to protect the matron from her husband's family
   b. to prevent crucified bodies from being taken down
   c. to prevent the matron from killing herself
   d. to oversee the killing by crucifixion of criminals

   Question Rating: Difficult. The interpretation of these clauses depends on recognizing quis *as "anyone,"* detraheret *as "to take down," and* ad sepulturam *as "for burial."*

4. In line 3, the subjunctive of <u>faceret</u> is

   a. relative clause of characteristic
   b. fearing clause
   c. indirect question
   d. indirect command

   Question Rating: Medium. The identification of quis *and* quid *as interrogative words is key to identify* faceret *as an indirect question. A relative clause of characteristic would require a relative pronoun, rather than an interrogative pronoun, and both a fearing clause and an indirect command would require a clause word (*ut *or* ne*).*

5. Which of the following is associated with <u>quodam monstro infernisque imaginibus</u> (lines 4–5)?

   a. religious sacrifice
   b. the underworld
   c. gladiatorial games
   d. imperial succession

   Question Rating: Medium. An understanding of the meaning of monstro, *"monster," and* infernis, *"having to do with the underworld," is necessary to associate this phrase with the underworld.*

6. The word <u>ut</u> (line 5) is translated

   a. so that
   b. that
   c. as
   d. to

   Question Rating: Easy. Ut with the subjunctive can be translated as choices a, b, or d, but ut *with the indicative is translated "as." Because* conspexit *is indicative, choice c is correct.*

7. The use of the infinitive of <u>pati</u> (line 7) is

> a. indirect statement
> b. subjective
> c. exclamation
> **d. complementary**

Question Rating: Easy / Medium. Pati is an infinitive that depends on posse, *thus it is a complementary infinitive.* Posse *is also an infinitive, dependent on* ratus *(line 6), in indirect statement.*

8. The word <u>suam</u> (line 7) refers to

> **a. the soldier**
> b. the dead husband
> c. the matron
> d. the tomb

Question Rating: Medium. A common misconception of the possessive adjectives is that their ending determines the gender of their translation or their reference. But the ending of these adjectives is determined by the gender of the noun that they are modifying, in this instance cenulam. *Because* cenulam *is feminine,* suam *must be feminine as well to agree with it, but that in no way means that* suam *refers to a feminine (no different from "his sister" where "his" is feminine to agree with "sister" but refers to a masculine). Context must determine to whom* suam *refers: the soldier is bringing "his dinner."*

9. In line 8, the subjunctive of <u>perseveraret</u> is

> **a. indirect command**
> b. purpose clause
> c. result clause
> d. indirect question

Question Rating: Difficult. The use of ne *eliminates choices c and d, as a result clause would use* ut non *in the negative and an indirect question would require an interrogative introductory word, which* ne *can be but uncommonly. The meaning of* hortari, *to encourage, confirms that* perseveraret *is an indirect command: "began to encourage the mourning woman not to persist."*

10. The words <u>omnium eumdem esse exitum et idem domicilium</u> (line 9) refer to which of the following ideas?

    a. everyone deserves appropriate housing

    b. everyone will eventually die

    c. a tomb is no place for a woman to live

    d. there is a limit for how long a woman should mourn her dead husband

Question Rating: Difficult. The translation of the words is "that there is the same end and the same destination for everyone," which suggests choice b. It is helpful to understand the previous clause as well, that the soldier was encouraging the matron to stop uselessly grieving; that is, that she should live in the moment and stop mourning her dead husband.

11. The words <u>et cetera quibus</u> (line 9) are translated

    a. and other things by which

    b. and certain things with which

    c. and those things for which

    d. and the rest to which

Question Rating: Medium / Difficult. The recognition that the soldier has finished speaking and the association of quibus *with* revocantur *are the most helpful for understanding what* cetera quibus *means: "and other things by which destroyed minds are brought back to sanity."* Cetera *can mean "the rest" but does not mean "certain" or "those," which eliminates choices b and c. Choice d works for* cetera *but not for* quibus, *which is ablative of means with the passive* revocantur.

The Death of Turnus

1	Stetit acer in armis
2	Aeneas volvens oculos dextramque repressit;
3	et iam iamque magis cunctantem flectere sermo
4	coeperat, infelix umero cum apparuit alto
5	balteus[1] et notis fulserunt cingula[2] bullis[3]
6	Pallantis pueri, victum quem vulnere Turnus
7	straverat atque umeris inimicum insigne gerebat.
8	Ille, oculis postquam saevi monimenta doloris
9	exuviasque hausit, furiis accensus et ira
10	terribilis: "Tune hinc spoliis indute[4] meorum
11	eripiare mihi? Pallas te hoc vulnere, Pallas
12	immolat et poenam scelerato ex sanguine sumit."
13	Hoc dicens ferrum adverso sub pectore condit
14	fervidus; ast illi solvuntur frigore membra
15	vitaque cum gemitu fugit indignata sub umbras. [*Aeneid* 12.938–52]

[1] balteus, -i: baldric (a belt worn over the shoulder typically to hold a weapon)
[2] cingula, -orum: swordbelt
[3] bulla, -ae: stud (decorative protrusion)
[4] induo, -ere, indui, indutus: to clothe

1. In line 3, <u>cunctantem</u> describes

   a. Aeneas
   b. Turnus
   c. Pallas
   d. Juno

Question Rating: Medium. Because the -em ending can be masculine or feminine, any of the four answers can be correct grammatically. The keys to the question are (1) recognizing sermo *as the subject; (2) understanding the context of Turnus' pleas beginning to affect Aeneas; and (3) knowing that* cunctantem *means "hesitating" and refers to Aeneas.*

2. <u>Flectere</u> (line 3) is dependent for its translation on

   a. magis (line 3)
   b. cunctantem (line 3)
   c. sermo (line 3)
   d. coeperat (line 4)

Question Rating: Easy. The only distractor that might prove possible is cunctan-tem *(b) but* flectere, *as an infinitive, follows logically after* coeperat, *"he had begun (to …)."*

3. Which of the following figures of speech occurs in lines 4–5 (<u>infelix</u> … <u>balteus</u>)?

    a. synchesis

    b. personification

    c. transferred epithet

    d. asyndeton

Question Rating: Easy. Recognizing the meaning of infelix *as "unhappy" and how that would not apply to a baldric but rather to the owner of the baldric yields the correct answer.*

4. The ablative of <u>umero alto</u> (line 4) is

    a. manner

    b. accompaniment

    c. comparison

    d. place where

Question Rating: Easy / Medium. The difficulty to this question lies in the not uncommon poetic practice of omitting the preposition in *from an ablative of place where. The distractors, however, can be eliminated relatively easily:* umero, *"shoulder," could not work as an ablative of manner; accompaniment should have the preposition* cum; *and comparison requires a comparative word.*

5. From the words <u>victum</u> … <u>gerebat</u> (lines 6–7) we learn that

    a. Pallas escaped Turnus' attack

    b. Turnus killed Pallas and is wearing his belt

    c. the gods will intervene to save Turnus' life

    d. Aeneas has finally conquered Turnus upon seeing Pallas' belt

*Question Rating: Medium. The syntax of this relative clause is a bit muddled in that the second half (*umeris … gerebat*) is dependent on a genitive relative pronoun that is not stated.*

6. The case and number of <u>insigne</u> (line 7) is

    a. nominative singular

    b. accusative singular

    c. ablative singular

    d. vocative singular

Question Rating: Difficult. Insigne *is a 2-form 3ʳᵈ declension adjective and so uses that -e ending for its neuter nominative and accusative singular. In this instance, Turnus is the subject of* gerebat, *so* insigne, *as a neuter, cannot be nominative and so is accusative. The overlap in ending with the more commonly used -e ending of the ablative singular of 3ʳᵈ declension nouns (not 3ʳᵈ declension adjectives, which use -i for the ablative singular) makes identifying this form particularly difficult.*

7. <u>Ille</u> (line 8) refers to

    a. Aeneas
    b. Turnus
    c. Pallas
    d. Jupiter

Question Rating: Easy / Medium. Ille *is masculine, so any of the four distractors can be correct, but the only one that makes any sense in context is Aeneas. Both the quote in lines 10–12 and the* accensus *and* terribilis *fit better with Aeneas than any of the other choices.*

8. The metrical pattern of the first four feet of line 9 is

    a. dactyl-spondee-dactyl-spondee
    b. spondee-spondee-dactyl-spondee
    c. dactyl-spondee-spondee-dactyl
    d. spondee-dactyl-spondee-spondee

Question Rating: Easy / Medium. The key to scanning these four feet correctly is the elision of -que and hausit. *An additional potential difficulty is* exuvias: *sometimes students can misread single-vowel syllables as diphthongs;* exuvias *is four syllables, the first three the initial dactyl and the final the first long syllable of the next foot.*

9. In line 10, <u>indute</u> modifies

    a. tu (line 10)
    b. spoliis (line 10)
    c. meorum (line 10)
    d. mihi (line 11)

Question Rating: Difficult. By ending, indute *can only be vocative; that is, as the perfect passive participle using 2ⁿᵈ and 1ˢᵗ declension endings the only case for the -e ending is vocative. That it then modifies* tu *further complicates the question: the modification of a 2ⁿᵈ person subject by a vocative adjective is not uncommon in poetry.*

10. The form of <u>eripiare</u> (line 11) is

    a. indicative

    b. imperative

    c. infinitive

    d. subjunctive

Question Rating: Difficult. The trap distractor is c, infinitive, because of the -re ending. The -re here, however, is the alternate 2ⁿᵈ person singular passive ending (-re for -ris), which also eliminates choice b. The distinction between indicative and subjunctive then comes down to vocabulary: that eripio *is a 3ʳᵈ -io verb means that -are (-aris) is subjunctive. And, although you might not know* eripio, *you might recognize it as a compound of* rapio, -ere.

11. In line 11, <u>mihi</u> is translated

    a. from me

    b. to me

    c. for me

    d. with me

Question Rating: Medium. That mihi *is a dative suggests that "to me" (b) or "for me" (c) is the correct answer. But, with* eripiare, mihi *here is a dative of separation (used with verbs of taking away): "snatched from me." Though this is a less common use of the dative, it is the one too that makes the most sense in context and with the verb* eripiare.

12. Which of the following figures of speech occurs in lines 11–12 (<u>Pallas</u> … <u>immolat</u>)?

    a. anaphora

    b. asyndeton

    c. alliteration

    d. apostrophe

Question Rating: Easy. The repetition of Pallas *is a relatively clear anaphora, especially since the other choices do not apply.*

13. From the words <u>Pallas</u> [1ˢᵗ one] … <u>sumit</u> (lines 11–12) we learn that

    a. Pallas is about to kill Turnus

    b. Turnus' death will avenge the death of Pallas

    c. the blood from Turnus' wound stains the earth

    d. Aeneas cares about Pallas more than Turnus

Question Rating: Easy / Medium. Much of the interpretation of this section hinges on the recognition of immolat *as "to destroy" and an understanding of* poenam sumit *as "to undergo punishment." From those expressions, the rest of the lines suggest b as the correct answer.*

14. The case and number of <u>illi</u> (line 14) are
    a. nominative singular
    b. genitive singular
    c. dative singular
    d. nominative plural

Question Rating: Easy / Medium. The proximity of illi solvuntur *might suggest that* illi *is a nominative plural but the (neuter) plural* membra *is the subject of* solvuntur. Illi *is rather the dative singular of* ille, illa, illud, *and here a dative of reference.*

The Unexpected Arrival of a Husband

1   "Mittenda est[1] domino (nunc, nunc properate, puellae)

2   quamprimum[2] nostra facta lacerna[3] manu.

3   Quid tamen auditis (nam plura audire potestis)?

4   Quantum de bello dicitur esse super?

5   Postmodo victa cades: melioribus, Ardea,[4] restas,

6   improba, quae nostros cogis abesse viros.

7   Sint tantum reduces.[5] Sed enim temerarius[6] ille

8   est meus, et stricto qualibet[7] ense ruit.

9   Mens abit et morior, quotiens pugnantis imago

10   me subit, et gelidum pectora frigus habet."

11   Desinit in lacrimas inceptaque fila[8] remisit,

12   in gremio[9] vultum deposuitque suum.

13   Hoc ipsum decuit: lacrimae decuere pudicam,

14   et facies animo dignaque parque fuit.

15   "Pone metum. Veni," coniunx ait; illa revixit,

16   deque viri collo dulce pependit onus. [Ovid, *Fasti* 2.743–60]

---

[1] The speaker is Lucretia, a Roman woman whose husband is away fighting.

[2] quamprimum: as soon as possible

[3] lacerna, -ae: cloak

[4] Ardea, -ae: the name of a town near Rome against which Rome was fighting

[5] redux, -cis (adj): returning

[6] temerarius, -a, -um: rash, thoughtless

[7] qualibet: in any direction, all over the place

[8] filum, -i: thread

[9] gremius, -i: lap

1. The metrical pattern of the first four feet of line 1 is

    a. dactyl-spondee-spondee-dactyl

    b. dactyl-dactyl-spondee-dactyl

    c. spondee-dactyl-spondee-dactyl

    d. spondee-spondee-spondee-spondee

Question Rating: Medium. *The difficulty to scanning this line is the elision of* mittenda est / mittendast. Nunc, nunc *are both long because of the double consonant and the* -a- *of* properate *is a naturally long syllable but identifiable as the first syllable of the standard dactyl-spondee with which lines of dactylic hexameter end.*

2. In line 1, <u>mittenda est</u> is translated

> a. had to be sent
> b. must send
> c. has to send
> **d. must be sent**

Question Rating: Medium. The -nd- of mittenda *signals the gerundive which, in general, signifies obligation or necessity (translated by "must" or "have to"). The gerundive combined with a form of* sum, esse *produces the passive periphrastic, which is passive and conveys obligation or necessity. All choices convey obligation or necessity; choice a is past tense and choices b and c are active. Choice d is the only one that is passive and present.*

3. In line 2, <u>nostra</u> modifies

> a. quamprimum (line 2)
> b. facta (line 2)
> c. lacerna (line 2)
> **d. manu (line 2)**

*Question Rating: Medium / Difficult. The two other -a endings (*facta *and* lacerna*) make this answer tricky but scansion confirms that* nostra *is ablative and so agrees with* manu. *The -a of* facta *and* lacerna *scans short, which makes them nominative. The -a of* nostra *scans long and the -u of* manu *has to be ablative, which means that* nostra *has to agree with* manu.

4. The subject of <u>auditis</u> (line 3) is

> **a. puellae (line 1)**
> b. lacerna (line 2)
> c. manu (line 2)
> d. plura (line 4)

Question Rating: Difficult. The key to this question is recognizing that properate *in line 1 is an imperative and that* puellae *is a vocative and that they are both plural. The plural 2nd person is carried down to* auditis *with the* puellae *remaining the subject.*

5. Which of the following figures of speech occurs in lines 5–6 (<u>melioribus</u> … <u>viros</u>)

    a. anaphora

    b. aposiopesis

    c. apostrophe

    d. asyndeton

Question Rating: Medium / Difficult. Apostrophe is the direct address of someone or something not present. Ardea, as a vocative and the town where Lucretia's husband is fighting, is not present and being addressed directly by Lucretia.

6. The case and number of <u>quae</u> (line 6) are

    a. nominative singular

    b. nominative plural

    c. accusative plural

    d. vocative singular

Question Rating: Difficult. Quae by form can be choices a, b, or c, but only b if its antecedent is feminine or neuter plural or c if its antecedent is neuter plural. Viros is plural but masculine; melioribus, *while plural and potentially all three genders with the -ibus ending, remains ambiguous.* Ardea, *however, is feminine singular,* cogis *is singular, and* viros *is likely the direct object of* cogis, *which suggests that* quae *is singular. The one difficulty here is that the relative pronoun (*qui, quae, quod*) does not have to be 3rd person; that is, it is here nominative but nominative as the subject of a 2nd person verb (*cogis*) because* Ardea *is still being addressed directly.*

7. From lines 7–8 (<u>sed enim</u> … <u>ense ruit</u>) we learn that

    a. Lucretia's husband has died in battle because of his impulsivity

    b. Lucretia's husband fights recklessly

    c. Lucretia's husband won the battle for the Romans

    d. Lucretia's husband uses the sword that she made for him

Question Rating: Medium / Difficult. The key Latin words or phrases necessary to answer this question are temerarius, meus, stricto ense, *and* ruit. Temerarius *and* meus *both describe Lucretia's husband,* meus *confirming that she's talking about her husband and* temerarius *establishing his recklessness.* Stricto ense ruit *confirms that he is fighting: "he rushes around with his sword drawn" (rather than dying, winning, or using, as the other choices suggest).*

8. In line 9, <u>pugnantis</u> is translated

    a. of fighting
    b. having been fought
    c. of the man fighting
    d. fighting

Question Rating: Difficult. Pugnantis is the present active participle, signified by the -nt-, in the genitive, which eliminates choice b. Choice a is the translation of the gerund, which pugnantis is not either, but the gerund and the present active participle are both translated with the English -ing, which often causes confusion. Choice d assumes that pugnantis agrees with another genitive noun, which it does not. Pugnantis is the participle used substantively; that is, there is not a stated noun for it to agree with and one must be supplied when translating it. The "man" in choice c is that supplied noun.

9. From the words <u>desinit in lacrimas</u> (line 11), we can infer that

    a. Lucretia is distraught
    b. Lucretia is overjoyed
    c. Lucretia's husband is distraught
    d. Lucretia's husband is overjoyed

Question Rating: Medium. In lacrimas suggests sadness rather than joy and Lucretia, having just finished speaking, is still the subject with no nominative to introduce a new subject.

10. In line 12, <u>suum</u> refers to

    a. Lucretia
    b. Lucretia's husband
    c. the puellae of line 1
    d. soldiers

Question Rating: Medium. A common misconception of the possessive adjectives is that their ending determines the gender of their translation or their reference. But the ending of these adjectives is determined by the gender of the noun that they are modifying, in this instance vultum. *Because* vultum *is masculine,* suum *must be masculine as well to agree with it, but that in no way means that* suum *refers to a masculine (no different from "his sister" where "his" is feminine to agree with "sister" but refers to a masculine). Context must determine to whom* suum *refers: "Lucretia puts her face in her lap."*

11. The form of <u>decuere</u> (line 13) is

> **a. indicative**
> b. infinitive
> c. imperative
> d. subjunctive

Question Rating: Medium. The perfect active, 3ʳᵈ person plural ending -erunt can be syncopated (contracted) to the ending -ere, more often in poetry than in prose. There are three ways to distinguish a syncopated perfect from a present active infinitive. First, recognizing that the -ere ending is on a 3ʳᵈ, rather than a 2ⁿᵈ, principal part. While you might not recognize this verb or know its principal parts, you can work backward to reconstruct its first two principal parts: if the infinitive is decuere, *its first principal part must be* decuo *(if 3ʳᵈ conjugation) or* decueo *(if 2ⁿᵈ conjugation); the latter especially seems a far-fetched form. Second, the first -e- of the -ere ending will scan long. So too will the first -e- of a 2ⁿᵈ conjugation present infinitive, but 2ⁿᵈ conjugation verbs are less common than 3ʳᵈ conjugation verbs; if that -e- is long, consider the possibility that it is a syncopated form. Third, grammatical context: does it make sense to have an indicative verb here or an infinitive? Especially in a relatively short clause, it will be more difficult for an infinitive to make sense than an indicative.*

12. The words <u>et facies</u> … <u>parque fuit</u> (line 14) tell us that Lucretia

> a. made herself more attractive for the return of her husband
> b. is angry at her husband for still being away
> **c. is genuine in both her feelings and her appearance**
> d. considers herself equal to her husband in courage

Question Rating: Difficult. Facies *and* animo *establish the connection between what she is feeling on the inside (*animo*) and how she appears on the outside (*facies*). Digna and* par *agree with* facies *and govern* animo *(strictly speaking,* digna *takes the ablative and* par *the dative but, since* animo *is closer to* digna*, it is ablative): "Her face / appearance was worthy of and equal to her feelings."*

13. In line 15, <u>veni</u> is translated

> **a. I have come**
> b. come!
> c. I am coming
> d. coming

Question Rating: Medium. Veni *looks like, and can be, an imperative form and, since* pone *is also imperative, it is tempting to think that* veni *is imperative. Rather, because of context,* veni *is the 1ˢᵗ person singular, perfect active: "I have come."*

Taken with Pone metum: *"Put aside your worry. I have come." A further clue is* coniunx *which identifies the husband, rather than Lucretia, as the speaker. Finally, the -e- in* veni *scans long, which makes it the 3rd rather than the 2nd principal part, whose -e- is short.*

14. From line 16, we learn that Lucretia

    a. fainted in shock at the sight of her husband

    b. gave her husband the cloak that she and her assistants had been weaving

    c. fled the room because of the weight of her emotions

    d. hugged her husband

Question Rating: Medium. *This line is a periphrasis (a long way of saying something) for hugging: "And she hung, as a sweet burden, from the neck of her husband." (Because* onus *is neuter,* onus dulce *can be read as the direct object of* pependit *but this seems the weaker reading.)*

The Helmsman Disappoints

1   Iamque propinquabant scopulo metamque tenebant,

2   cum princeps medioque Gyas[1] in gurgite victor

3   rectorem navis compellat voce Menoeten:[2]

4   "Quo tantum mihi dexter abis? Huc derige cursum;

5   litus ama et laeva stringat sine palmula[3] cautes;[4]

6   altum alii teneant." Dixit; sed caeca Menoetes

7   saxa timens proram pelagi detorquet ad undas.

8   "Quo diversus abis?" Iterum, "Pete saxa, Menoete!"

9   Cum clamore Gyas revocabat, et ecce Cloanthum[5]

10   respicit instantem[6] tergo et propiora tenentem.

11   Ille inter navemque Gyae scopulosque sonantes

12   radit iter laevum interior subitoque priorem

13   praeterit[7] et metis tenet aequora tuta relictis. [Vergil, *Aeneid* 5.159–71]

[1] Gyas, -ae: the name of the captain of one of Aeneas' ships

[2] Menoetes, -is (acc = -en): a companion of Aeneas and the helmsman of Gyas' ship

[3] palmula, -ae: oar

[4] cautes, -is, f.: a rock, crag

[5] Cloanthus, -i: the name of the captain of one of Aeneas' ships

[6] insto, -are (+ dat): to approach

[7] praetereo, -ire: to overtake

1. In line 3, the subjunctive of <u>compellat</u> is

    a. purpose clause
    b. result clause
    c. jussive
    d. cum clause

Question Rating: Easy / Medium. Cum *here is followed by* princeps, *a nominative, which confirms that* cum *is not a preposition but rather is a conjunction. The difficulty to this question is how delayed the verb of that* cum *clause is. But there is no personal verb between* cum *and* compellat, *which suggests that* compellat *is the subjunctive verb in that* cum *clause.*

2. The case and number of <u>navis</u> (line 3) are

    a. nominative singular
    b. genitive singular
    c. dative plural
    d. ablative plural

Question Rating: Medium. Navis, -is *is a 3rd declension noun, which eliminates choices c and d. The vocabulary information for the passage identifies* Gyas *as a nominative singular and* victor *is also a nominative singular, both of which suggest that* navis *is not a nominative singular. The only choice left is genitive singular, which makes sense when* navis *is read with* rectorem: *"when he exhorted the helmsman of the ship."*

3. The form of <u>derige</u> and <u>ama</u> (lines 4 and 5) is

    a. indicative

    b. infinitive

    c. imperative

    d. subjunctive

Question Rating: Medium. The imperative is formed by removing the -re from the present infinitive, so the imperative of derigere *becomes* derige *and* amare *becomes* ama. *Direct speech is more likely to have 1st and 2nd person verbs and the imperative, of course, is a 2nd person form.*

4. In line 6, <u>altum</u> refers to

    a. the rock

    b. the mast of the ship

    c. Menoetes

    d. the sea

Question Rating: Medium. Altus, -a, -um *can mean either high / tall or deep. In this case, because of both the boat race in general and, more specifically, Gyas' exhortations to Menoetes to take the inside lane while rounding the* meta, altum *refers to the deep water; that is, the water farther away from the* meta. *He concludes his speech by saying "Let the others have the deep (water)."*

5. In line 6, <u>caeca</u> modifies

    a. Menoetes (line 6)

    b. saxa (line 7)

    c. proram (line 7)

    d. pelagi (line 7)

Question Rating: Medium. Caeca *is neuter, plural, accusative to agree with the neuter, plural, accusative* saxa, *which is the direct object of the participle* timens. *The grammatical trap is that it is placed next to* Menoetes *and the two words are isolated at the end of the line, further suggesting their association (to English speakers). Menoetes, however, is masculine, nominative, singular and so* saxa *cannot be read with it (in addition to which,* saxa *is a noun). Vergil, however, ingeniously intentionally isolates these two words to associate them visually, if not grammatically:* caeca *is a transferred epithet; that is, it agrees with* saxa *but describes* Menoetes. *By placing them next to each other, Vergil further emphasizes the transferred epithet.*

6. From the words <u>sed caeca</u> … <u>ad undas</u> (lines 6–7), we learn that

    a. Menoetes fears the other ships and follows Gyas' orders

    b. Menoetes smashes the ship on the rock and it sinks

    c. Menoetes loses control of the ship

    d. Menoetes steers the ship away from the rock

Question Rating: Medium. Menoetes *is the subject of* detorquet *with* timens *a participle agreeing with him, so* Menoetes *is fearing the blind rocks and twisting the ship (*proram*) to the sea (*ad undas pelagi*).*

7. The speaker of the direct speech in line 8 is

    a. Menoetes

    b. Gyas

    c. Cloanthus

    d. Aeneas

Question Rating: Medium. Gyas *is the captain of the ship (*princeps, *line 2) and* Menoetes *is the helmsman (*rectorem, *line 3).* Gyas *orders* Menoetes *to take the inside lane on the meta (lines 4–6) but* Menoetes *doesn't out of fear of the rocks (lines 6–7).* Gyas *reiterates his order in line 8.* Menoete *is a vocative form and* Cloanthum *is the direct object of* respicit *(line 10).*

8. In line 9, <u>cum</u> is translated

    a. with

    b. when

    c. since

    d. although

Question Rating: Medium. This answer hinges on whether cum *is a conjunction or a preposition; choice a is the only non-conjunction choice, so, if* cum *is a preposition, the answer must be a. Two clues suggest that* cum *is a preposition rather than a conjunction. First, that it is followed by the ablative* clamore; cum *the conjunction can be followed by a non-preposition ablative but the ablative* clamore *means that* cum *is more likely a preposition than if it were followed by a nominative. Second, the* et *after* revocabat *would seem to connect two independent clauses, whose verbs are* revocabat *and* respicit. *If* cum … revocabat *is an independent clause, then* cum *cannot be a conjunction.*

9. In line 11, to whom does <u>ille</u> refer

    a. Menoetes

    b. Gyas

    c. Cloanthus

    d. Aeneas

Question Rating: Medium. Ille *here indicates a shift in perspective. While Gyas and Menoetes had been the focus, the focus now shifts to the swiftly approaching Cloanthus: "That guy now …"*

10. How many elisions are in line 12?

    a. 0

    b. 1

    c. 2

    d. 3

Question Rating: Medium. Laevum interior *elides because* laevum *ends in* -m *and* interior *begins with a vowel.*

11. In line 12, <u>iter</u> is translated

    a. route

    b. journey

    c. trip

    d. direction

Question Rating: Medium / Difficult. Iter *here refers to the path that Cloanthus' boat takes, tight to the meta, and so means "route." Choice d is a possible, but worse, answer because of the verb* radit. *Direction is difficult to make work as a direct object; it would work better as a prepositional phrase (to go in a direction) while route works better as the direct object of* radit.

12. From the words <u>metis</u> … <u>relictis</u> (line 13) we learn that

    a. Gyas' ship has retaken the lead

    b. Cloanthus has turned around the meta in the lead

    c. Cloanthus' ship has struck the meta and is sinking

    d. Gyas' ship is safe at sea but out of the race

Question Rating: Medium. Metis relictis *is an ablative absolute explaining that the meta has been left behind; that is, Cloanthus' ship has successfully navigated the inside route, rounded the meta, and is now in the lead.* Tenet aequora tuta *refers to the safe seas that Cloanthus' ship has ahead of it now that it is in the lead.*

Dido's Lament to Aeneas

1   Certus es ire tamen miseramque relinquere Didon[1]

2   atque idem venti vela fidemque ferent.

3   Certus es, Aenea,[2] cum foedere solvere naves

4   quaeque ubi sint nescis, Itala regna sequi.

5   nec nova Karthago, nec te crescentia tangunt

6   moenia nec sceptro tradita summa tuo.

7   Facta fugis, facienda petis; quaerenda per orbem

8   altera, quaesita est altera terra tibi.

9   Ut terram invenias, quis eam tibi tradet habendam?

10   Quis sua non notis arva tenenda dabit?

11   Alter habendus amor tibi restat et altera Dido

12   quamque iterum fallas, altera danda fides.

13   Quando erit, ut condas instar[3] Karthaginis urbem

14   et videas populos altus ab arce tuos?

15   Omnia ut eveniant, nec di tua vota morentur,

16   unde tibi, quae te sic amet, uxor erit? [Ovid, *Heroides* 7.7–22]

---

[1] an irregular accusative form of Dido, -onis, f.   [3] instar (indecl.), n.: image

[2] Aeneas, -ae, m.: Aeneas, Trojan hero

1. Which of the following grammatical constructions occurs in line 1 (<u>certus</u> … <u>Didon</u>)?

    a. indirect statement
    b. indirect command
    c. indirect question
    d. passive periphrastic

Question Rating: Easy. Indirect statement is the only choice that uses the infinitive (ire and relinquere), choice a. While the two infinitives can also be interpreted as different uses of the infinitive (e.g., complementary), the question focuses on distinguishing the different verb forms that each construction uses: choices b and c require the subjunctive and choice d the gerundive.

2. Which of the following figures of speech occurs in line 2 (<u>atque</u> … <u>ferent</u>)?

    a. hendiadys

    b. chiasmus

    c. asyndeton

    d. zeugma

Question Rating: Difficult. The identification of venti vela fidemque ferent *as a zeugma relies on both an understanding of these words and the context of the couplet and the poem as a whole: "the winds will take your sails and your faithfulness."*

3. The case and number of <u>Aenea</u> (line 3) are

    a. nominative singular

    b. ablative singular

    c. vocative singular

    d. accusative plural

Question Rating: Easy. The vocative is often set off by commas; especially a single word surrounded by commas will most likely be a vocative (ablatives absolute are also sometimes, though less often, set off by commas but cannot be a single word). The glossed vocabulary information eliminates choice a and both an ablative, especially without a preposition, and a plural proper name would make little sense.

4. The antecedent of <u>quae</u> (line 4) is

    a. Aenea (line 3)

    b. foedere (line 3)

    c. naves (line 3)

    d. regna (line 4)

*Question Rating: Medium / Difficult. By agreement, choices c and d can be correct (*Aenea *is of course masculine and* foedere *is neuter singular). The difficulty to this question, however, lies in the postponement of* regna, *that the antecedent of* quae *is placed after, rather than before, its antecedent.*

5. In line 4, the subjunctive of <u>sint</u> is

    a. cum clause

    b. indirect question

    c. indirect command

    d. purpose clause

Question Rating: Easy / Medium. Choices a, c, and d require cum *or* ut, *which are not present. The difficulty of this question, however, lies in the brevity of the clause (ubi sint) and that it is embedded in another short clause (quae nescis). Nonetheless, the combination of an interrogative word,* ubi, *and a subjunctive,* sint, *necessitates that it be read as indirect question.*

6. The metrical pattern of the first four feet of line 5 (<u>nec</u> ... <u>tangunt</u>) is

    a. dactyl-spondee-spondee-spondee
    b. dactyl-dactyl-spondee-spondee
    c. spondee-dactyl-spondee-spondee
    d. dactyl-spondee-spondee-dactyl

Question Rating: Medium / Difficult. The scansion of the first three words determines the answer. The key is recognizing that nova *agrees with the nominative Karthago, which makes* nova *nominative singular and so makes the "a" in* nova *short.*

7. Which of the following figures of speech occurs in lines 5–6 (<u>nec nova</u> ... <u>summa tuo</u>)?

    a. apostrophe
    b. anaphora
    c. aposiopesis
    d. onomatopoeia

Question Rating: Easy. The repetition of nec *throughout the couplet should be relatively easy to identify as an anaphora.*

8. In line 7, <u>facta fugis, facienda petis</u> is translated

    a. you flee and seek walls that must be built
    b. you seek to flee walls that must be built
    c. you must build the walls that you flee
    d. you flee already built walls, you seek walls not yet built

Question Rating: Medium / Difficult. The translation remains relatively straightforward if each clause is treated separately and the distinction in tense between facta *and* facienda *is understood:* facta *is a perfect passive participle, while* facienda *is a future passive participle. Both participles modify* moenia *from the previous line.*

9. In line 8, <u>altera</u> ... <u>altera</u> is translated

    a. one ... the other
    b. both ... and
    c. not only ... but also
    d. this one ... that one

Question Rating: Easy. Alter ... alter *means "one ... the other."*

10. The form of <u>tradet</u> (line 9) is

    a. indicative
    b. subjunctive
    c. participle
    d. infinitive

Question Rating: Easy. Tradet is a 3rd conjugation verb, so the -e- makes it future indicative.

11. The antecedent of <u>sua</u> (line 10) is

    a. quis (line 10)
    b. notis (line 10)
    c. arva (line 10)
    d. tenenda (line 10)

Question Rating: Medium / Difficult. Choices b and d are not nouns; notis is an adjective and tenenda *is a participle. Sua agrees with* arva *but* arva *is not its antecedent—that to which it refers. The possessive adjectives* (meus, noster, tuus, vester, suus) *agree with one noun but refer to a different noun, for example, in "his sister" /* sua soror *the translation of* sua *depends on to whom it refers rather than with what it agrees; a common mistake is to assume that* sua, *in this example, means "her" because it is feminine, when it is only feminine because it agrees with* soror. *Since* quis *is the subject,* sua, *as the reflexive possessive, will reflect on it: "Who will give their (his/her) land to be kept by unknown people?"*

12. From <u>quamque iterum fallas</u> (line 12), we can infer that Aeneas

    a. has deceived Dido
    b. will not succeed in establishing his new land
    c. will deceive another woman
    d. will suffer without Dido in his life

Question Rating: Medium. The subjunctive fallas *is in a relative clause of purpose or characteristic: "another Dido whom you intend to deceive again" (purpose) or "another Dido of the sort that you will deceive again" (characteristic).*

13. The case of <u>instar</u> (line 13) is

    a. nominative
    b. genitive
    c. accusative
    d. ablative

Question Rating: Easy / Medium. The "you" subject of condas *eliminates choice a and the general meaning of the clause suggests accusative. That* instar *is indeclinable requires you, however, to use context entirely to determine its case rather than using its form or ending to help you.*

14. In line 14, <u>altus</u> is translated

    a. from above
    b. tall
    c. deep
    d. all around

Question Rating: Easy / Medium. When the nominative adjective is used with a pronominal subject, it is often best translated adverbially: "you see your people from above from the citadel."

15. The case and number of <u>vota</u> (line 15) are

    a. nominative singular
    b. ablative singular
    c. nominative plural
    d. accusative plural

Question Rating: Medium. Votum *is a neuter noun, which eliminates choices a and b. The nominative* di *eliminates choice c. That* morentur *is a deponent proves important, however, because if it is read as a passive, it might be easier to think that* vota *is ablative.*

16. The dative of <u>tibi</u> (line 16) is

    a. agent
    b. purpose
    c. possession
    d. direction

Question Rating: Medium. Choice a requires a passive verb and choice d requires a verb of motion, neither of which is present. The dative of possession is frequently used with sum, esse (erit) *and makes sense: "from where will you have a wife who loves you in this way" or "from where will a wife be for you who loves you in this way."*

Tasgetius, the Carnutian

1 Erat in Carnutibus summo loco natus Tasgetius, cuius maiores in sua civitate regnum
2 obtinuerant. Huic Caesar pro eius virtute atque in se benevolentia, quod in omnibus
3 bellis singulari eius opera fuerat usus, maiorum locum restituerat. Tertium iam hunc
4 annum regnantem inimici multis palam ex civitate auctoribus interfecerunt. Defertur ea
5 res ad Caesarem. Ille veritus, quod ad plures pertinebat, ne civitas eorum impulsu
6 deficeret, L. Plancum cum legione ex Belgio celeriter in Carnutes proficisci iubet ibique
7 hiemare quorumque opera cognoverat Tasgetium interfectum, hos comprehensos ad se
8 mittere. Interim ab omnibus legatis quaestoribusque, quibus legiones tradiderat, certior
9 factus est in hiberna perventum locumque hibernis esse munitum. [*Bellum Gallicum* 5.25]

1. In line 1, the first <u>in</u> (in Carnutibus) is translated

    a. on

    b. at

    c. to

    d. among

Question Rating: Easy. As long as Carnutibus *is read as the people rather than a place, choice d is the only choice that makes sense in the translation: "There was among the Carnutians …"*   .

2. In lines 1–2 (<u>cuius</u> … <u>obtinuerant</u>), we learn that Tasgetius

    a. led a revolt to assume power

    b. had ancestors who established rule

    c. fled the kingdom for a neighboring state

    d. had more land than anyone else in the kingdom

Question Rating: Easy / Medium. The correct answer hinges on an understanding that maiores *refers to the ancestors of Tasgetius. The rest of the translation is relatively straightforward: "whose ancestors had obtained power in their state."*

3. Lines 2–3 (<u>huic</u> … <u>restituerat</u>) reflect Caesar's tendency to

    a. punish those who cross him

    b. reward those loyal to him

    c. use locals to gain allies for the Romans

    d. infiltrate local peoples to put down rebellions

Question Rating: Easy / Medium. The correct answer lies in understanding the meaning of pro, *"in return for," and the referent of* huic, *Tasgetius.*

4. In line 2, <u>eius</u> refers to

    a. Tasgetius

    b. Caesar

    c. the Carnutians

    d. the ancestors of Tasgetius

Question Rating: Easy / Medium. The potential difficulty to this question is delineating the three pronouns: huic, eius, *and* se. *Both* huic *and* eius *refer to Tasgetius, while* se *refers to Caesar: "To this man [Tasgetius], Caesar, in return for his [this man's / Tasgetius'] courage and kindness to him [Caesar]."*

5. In line 3, <u>singulari</u> modifies

    a. bellis (line 3)

    b. eius (line 3)

    c. opera (line 3)

    d. usus (line 3)

Question Rating: Easy / Medium. The -i ending can be difficult here because not only is singularis *a 3ʳᵈ declension adjective but, unlike 3ʳᵈ declension nouns, 3ʳᵈ declension adjectives take their ablative in -i rather than the -e of nouns. In addition,* opera, *as a 1ˢᵗ declension noun, is not as obvious an ablative.*

6. From lines 3–4 (<u>tertium</u> … <u>interfecerunt</u>), we learn that

    a. Tasgetius invited fellow citizens to rule with him

    b. Tasgetius was killed by his fellow citizens

    c. Tasgetius stepped down from power after the third year

    d. Tasgetius allied with Caesar to conquer neighboring peoples

Question Rating: Easy / Medium. The meaning of interfecerunt, *the identification of* inimici *as its subject, and the understanding that Tasgetius is the object all yield the right answer: "His enemies killed him."*

7. The antecedent of <u>eorum</u> (line 5) is

    a. Tasgetius

    b. Caesar

    c. Tasgetius' ancestors

    d. Tasgetius' killers

Question Rating: Medium. Pronouns must agree with their antecedent in gender and number; because eorum *is plural, choices a and b can be eliminated. Context suggests that the state would not revolt at the encouragement of Tasgetius' ancestors but rather his killers.*

8. In line 6, the subjunctive of <u>deficeret</u> is

    a. purpose clause

    b. indirect command

    c. indirect question

    d. fearing clause

Question Rating: Medium. The correct answer hinges on knowing that veritus *means "fearing." The* ne *introduces a positive fearing clause, a reversal from the conventional use of* ne *as a negative conjunction: "That man [Caesar], fearing … that the state would revolt because of their encouragement."*

9. The translation of <u>proficisci</u> (line 6) is

    a. to depart

    b. I departed

    c. depart!

    d. having departed

Question Rating: Easy / Medium. The -i ending is difficult because it can be so many different forms. Knowing that proficiscor *is a deponent suggests that choice a is correct as a present passive infinitive form but recognizing that* iubet *is the main verb should eliminate choices b and c, which would be impossible to have next to a 3rd person verb. The meaning of* iubet, *"he orders," also suggests that* proficisci *is an infinitive.*

10. In line 7, <u>se</u> refers to

    a. Tasgetius

    b. Caesar

    c. Lucius Plancus

    d. the killers of Tasgetius

Question Rating: Medium. In a sentence of such complexity, keeping track of pronouns becomes as much a question of translation and understanding as it is of grammar. The reflexive se *should reflect on the subject but does it reflect on the subject of the main verb? The infinitive? Latin will reflect on the subject of the main verb,* iubet, *and, since Caesar is doing the ordering,* se *refers to Caesar: "Caesar orders him to send to him(self)." (Note that English would not use the reflexive.)*

11. The ablative of <u>ab omnibus legatis quaestoribus</u> (line 8) is

    a. agent
    b. means
    c. absolute
    d. place from which

Question Rating: Easy / Medium. *The ablative of agent requires the preposition a/ab and a passive verb. The difficulty with this passage is that the passive verb,* factus est, *is separated from its ablative of agent and can have an active meaning: without the ablative agent,* certior factus est *can be translated "became more certain" but with the ablative of agent must be translated "was made more certain by."*

The Romans Under Siege

1   Quibus rebus perturbatis nostris novitate pugnae tempore opportunissimo Caesar

2   auxilium tulit: namque eius adventu hostes constiterunt, nostri se ex timore receperunt.

3   Quo facto, ad lacessendum et ad committendum proelium alienum esse tempus

4   arbitratus suo se loco continuit et, brevi tempore intermisso, in castra legiones reduxit.

5   Dum haec geruntur, nostris omnibus occupatis, qui erant in agris reliqui discesserunt.

6   Secutae sunt continuos complures dies tempestates quae et nostros in castris

7   continerent et hostem a pugna prohiberent. Interim barbari nuntios in omnes partes

8   dimiserunt paucitatemque nostrorum militum suis praedicaverunt et quanta praedae

9   faciendae atque in perpetuum sui liberandi facultas daretur, si Romanos castris

10   expulissent, demonstraverunt. His rebus celeriter magna multitudine peditatus

11   equitatusque coacta ad castra venerunt. [*Bellum Gallicum* 4.34]

1. The case of <u>pugnae</u> (line 1) is dependent on

    a. rebus (line 1)
    b. novitate (line 1)
    c. tempore (line 1)
    d. Caesar (line 1)

Question Rating: Easy / Medium. *The placement of the genitive* pugnae *between* novitate *and* tempore *might prove confusing but* pugnae *makes more sense with* novitate: *"the novelty of this fighting."*

2. Caesar's use of the noun <u>Caesar</u> (line 1) indicates that

    a. Caesar the writer is referring to Caesar as a character in his own narrative
    b. a writer other than Caesar has written this passage
    c. Caesar the writer is emphasizing Caesar the character's role in this passage
    d. Caesar only refers to himself in the 3rd person in the *Gallic Wars*

Question Rating: Easy / Medium. *Caesar refers to himself in the 3rd person when he is functioning as a character in his own narrative and uses the 1st person when he is commenting as a writer on what he is writing.*

3. From the words <u>se ex timore receperunt</u> (line 2) we can infer that Caesar's soldiers
   a. fought valiantly
   b. were terrified by the enemy
   c. were no longer terrified by the enemy
   d. retreated

Question Rating: Easy. The correct answer hinges on the understanding of the meaning of receperunt, "to take back."

4. The form of <u>lacessendum</u> (line 3) is
   a. infinitive
   b. imperative
   c. subjunctive
   d. gerundive

Question Rating: Easy / Medium. The -nd- signifies that lacessendum *has to be a gerund or gerundive; although it is separated from the noun that it modifies,* proelium, *its role as a modifier (participle) makes choice d the correct choice. (It should be noted too that gerund is not a choice, so choice d is the only choice that fits the* -nd- *form.)*

5. The case and number of <u>tempus</u> (line 3) are
   a. nominative singular
   b. genitive singular
   c. accusative singular
   d. nominative plural

Question Rating: Medium. Tempus, -oris is a neuter, 3rd declension noun, which eliminates choices b and d. Arbitratus introduces the indirect statement of which esse *is the infinitive and* tempus *is the subject and the subject of an infinitive is accusative.*

6. Which part of speech is <u>reliqui</u> (line 5)?
   a. noun
   b. adjective
   c. verb
   d. adverb

Question Rating: Medium / Difficult. Reliqui looks like a form of the verb relinquo, -ere *but, if it is, it has to be the 1st person perfect active indicative, which would not make sense with the 3rd person verb* discesserunt *next to it. Reliqui also looks like it's a noun, with the -i ending and placed next to the verb. It is, however, a substantive adjective: "those left behind (departed)."*

7. What is the grammatical function of <u>continuos complures dies</u> (line 6)?

    a. accusative direct object

    b. accusative extent of time

    c. subject accusative

    d. accusative place to which

Question Rating: Easy. The presence of the time word dies *identifies this construction as accusative extent of time.*

8. The subjunctive of <u>prohiberent</u> (line 7) is

    a. relative clause of result

    b. relative clause of purpose

    c. indirect question

    d. indirect command

Question Rating: Difficult. This question relies on an understanding of the nuance of the subjunctives continerent *and* prohiberent. *The result of the continuous storms was that the Romans stayed in camp and the enemy couldn't fight. Those subjunctives could also be read as relative clauses of characteristic: "storms of the type that kept our men in camp and prohibited the enemy from fighting."*

9. In line 8, <u>suis</u> is translated

    a. themselves

    b. them

    c. they

    d. their people

Question Rating: Medium. The distinction between the reflexive pronoun se *and the reflexive possessive adjective* suus *determines the correct answer. The pronoun* se *would mean "themselves" (and would not make as much sense), while the possessive adjective* suis *is used substantively and means "their people": "they sent messengers and told their people."*

10. In line 8, <u>et</u> connects

    a. barbari (line 7) and praedae (line 8)

    b. partes (line 7) and perpetuum (line 9)

    c. dimiserunt (line 8) and daretur (line 9)

    d. praedicaverunt (line 8) and demonstraverunt (line 10)

Question Rating: Difficult. The difficulty in this answer lies in the separation of the two verbs, especially with two subordinate clauses in the demonstraverunt *half. Nonetheless, a conjunction following a verb, as in* praedicaverunt et, *will most likely join verbs. Both* daretur *and* expulissent *are in subordinate clauses, which leaves* demonstraverunt *as the main verb that* et *connects.*

11. From lines 8–9 (quanta … daretur), we learn that
    a. the enemy has plundered much of the Roman booty
    b. the Romans are ready to fight
    c. the Romans are vulnerable
    d. the Gauls have won their freedom forever

Question Rating: Medium / Difficult. This clause separates the subject, facultas, *and its modifier,* quanta: *"how much ease." The genitive gerundives go with that subject with* daretur *as the passive verb: "how much ease of taking plunder and freeing themselves forever is given (to them)."*

12. The subjunctive of daretur (line 9) is
    a. indirect question
    b. indirect command
    c. conditional
    d. relative clause of characteristic

Question Rating: Medium / Difficult. The interrogative word quanta *is the signal that* daretur *is in an indirect question. But* quanta *is a less traditional interrogative word and the noun it modifies,* facultas, *is separated from it.*

13. The case and number of peditatus (line 10) and equitatus (line 11) are
    a. nominative singular
    b. genitive singular
    c. nominative plural
    d. accusative plural

Question Rating: Medium / Difficult. Both equitatus *and* peditatus *are 4th declension nouns, which allows all four choices to be correct. Of those choices, the genitive singular is the least frequently used and the most difficult to identify. Nonetheless,* coacta *agrees with* multitudine, *which frames* peditatus *and* equitatus *and suggests that they are associated with the phrase. The only way they can be connected is as a genitive with the noun* multitudine; *the ablative and passive* coacta *cannot take a nominative or accusative.*

14. The participle <u>coacta</u> (line 11) modifies

>   a. rebus (line 10)
>   **b. multitudine (line 10)**
>   c. peditatus equitatusque (lines 10–11)
>   d. castra (line 11)

Question Rating: Medium / Difficult. *The primary distractor is* castra, *which has the same ending as* coacta, *but "a forced camp" does not make a lot of sense. Rather,* coacta *agreeing with* multitudine *not only makes sense but also confirms the association of* peditatus equitatusque, *two genitives, with* multitudine coacta: *"a multitude of infantry and cavalry brought together."*

The Arrival of the Trojans

1   "O regina, novam cui condere Iuppiter urbem

2   iustitiaque dedit gentes frenare superbas,

3   Troes te miseri, ventis maria omnia vecti,

4   oramus: prohibe infandos a navibus ignes,

5   parce pio generi et propius res aspice nostras.

6   Non nos aut ferro Libycos populare penates

7   venimus, aut raptas ad litora vertere praedas;

8   non ea vis animo nec tanta superbia victis.

9   Est locus, Hesperiam Grai cognomine dicunt,

10   terra antiqua, potens armis atque ubere glaebae;

11   Oenotri coluere viri; nunc fama minores

12   Italiam dixisse ducis de nomine gentem.

13   Hic cursus fuit,

14   cum subito adsurgens fluctu nimbosus Orion

15   in vada caeca tulit penitusque procacibus Austris

16   perque undas superante salo perque invia saxa

17   dispulit; huc pauci vestris adnavimus oris. [*Aeneid* 1.522–38]

1. The case and number of <u>regina</u> (line 1) are

    a. nominative singular
    b. ablative singular
    c. vocative singular
    d. nominative plural

Question Rating: Easy / Medium. The "o" plus the comma after regina *signals the vocative case. The potential difficulty is that this vocative looks like the nominative, which is by far the more commonly used case.*

2. The grammatical function of <u>cui</u> (line 1) is

    a. nominative subject
    b. genitive possession
    c. dative indirect object
    d. subject accusative

Question Rating: Easy. The form cui *can only be a dative and the indirect object is confirmed by the verb* dedit, *which takes an indirect object.*

3. The conjunction <u>-que</u> (line 2) connects

    a. regina (line 1) and iustitia (line 2)
    b. condere (line 1) and frenare (line 2)
    c. Iuppiter (line 1) and iustitia (line 2)
    d. urbem (line 1) and gentes (line 2)

Question Rating: Medium. The primary distractor is choice c because iustitia, *although ablative, appears nominative. Nonetheless, the only two parallel elements among the choices are* condere *and* frenare.

4. The number of elisions in line 3 is

    a. 0
    b. 1
    c. 2
    d. 3

Question Rating: Easy. Maria *and* omnia *elide.*

5. In line 3, <u>vecti</u> modifies

    a. Troes (line 3)
    b. miseri (line 3)
    c. ventis (line 3)
    d. maria (line 3)

Question Rating: Medium. The commas around ventis … vecti *might suggest that* vecti *modifies* ventis *but, by ending, they can only agree if* ventis *is a 3rd declension nouns (which it is not) in the genitive singular.* Troes *is the only noun among the choices with which* vecti *agrees in gender, number, and case: masculine, plural, nominative.*

6. The form of <u>prohibe</u> (line 4), <u>parce</u> (line 5), and <u>aspice</u> (line 5) is

    a. imperative
    b. infinitive
    c. subjunctive
    d. gerund

Question Rating: Easy. The imperative is not a commonly used form but makes sense in the context (it is used more often in direct speech than in narration) and translation, and by its form: the present active infinitive with the -re *removed.*

7. The infinitive <u>populare</u> (line 6) expresses

> **a. purpose**
> b. result
> c. cause
> d. characteristic

> *Question Rating: Easy / Medium. The infinitive of purpose is rare but appears here: why did we come? Not to conquer Libyan peoples.*

8. The grammatical function of <u>animo</u> (line 8) and <u>victis</u> (line 8) is

> a. dative indirect object
> **b. dative of possession**
> c. ablative of means
> d. ablative absolute

> *Question Rating: Medium / Difficult. Choice a can be eliminated because there is no verb of giving, showing, telling that would take an indirect object. Choice d can be eliminated because* animo *and* victis *would have to agree to be an ablative absolute. The difficulty to the question is that the form of* sum, esse *that confirms the dative of possession is understood: "This force is not for our mind and such arrogance is not for conquered peoples" or "Our mind does not possess this force and conquered peoples do not have such arrogance."*

9. The metrical pattern of the first four feet of line 10 (<u>terra</u> … <u>atque</u>) is

> a. spondee-spondee-spondee-spondee
> **b. spondee-dactyl-spondee-spondee**
> c. dactyl-dactyl-spondee-dactyl
> d. dactyl-spondee-dactyl-spondee

> *Question Rating: Medium. There are two elisions,* terra antiqua *and* atque ubere, *which affect the scansion. Otherwise, the number of double consonants makes this a relatively straightforward line to scan and yields all spondees except for the second foot.*

10. In line 11, <u>coluere</u> is translated

    a. (they) have cultivated
    b. to have cultivated
    c. to cultivate
    d. (they) cultivate

Question Rating: Medium. This is the syncopated perfect 3rd person indicative, which uses -ere as an alternate ending for -erunt. The -u- in coluere indicates the 3rd principal part, from which the present infinitive cannot be formed.

11. Which of the following characteristics of the *Aeneid* is illustrated in the shortness of line 13?

    a. Vergil's use of artistic language
    b. Vergil's indebtedness to Homer's epics
    c. the incomplete nature of the *Aeneid* at Vergil's death
    d. the lasting influence of the *Aeneid* on later writers

Question Rating: Easy / Medium. Upon Vergil's death, he ordered, legend has it, the manuscript of the Aeneid *to be burned because he had not yet completed it; his wish was not honored. Evidence of this incompletion is seen in half lines such as this, of which there are 57 throughout the twelve books of the* Aeneid.

12. Which of the following figures of speech occurs in lines 14–16 (<u>cum</u> … <u>saxa</u>)?

    a. hendiadys
    b. asyndeton
    c. alliteration
    d. hysteron proteron

Question Rating: Medium. The very length of text within which the figure appears makes this question somewhat difficult. Nonetheless, the consistent repetition of the "p" and "s" sound create alliteration.

13. Which of the following is associated with <u>Orion</u> (line 14)?

    a. storms
    b. war
    c. refugees
    d. peace

Question Rating: Medium / Difficult. The constellation Orion sets in November and rises in midsummer and is then associated with the storms that occur during these times.

14. Which part of speech is <u>penitus</u> (line 15)?

    a. noun

    b. adjective

    c. adverb

    d. verb

Question Rating: Medium. *The -us on* penitus *can make it look like a noun or adjective but it is an adverb that means "completely."*

15. The grammatical function of <u>vestris oris</u> (line 17) is

    a. dative of direction

    b. ablative of means

    c. genitive of possession

    d. nominative subject

Question Rating: Medium. *The dative of direction is the only choice that makes sense, "we swam to your shores," but it is a rarer use of the dative. There is a 3rd declension noun,* os, oris, *which might make* oris *here look genitive, but this is the 1st declension noun* ora, -ae.

Aeneas Addresses Dido

1   "Infelix Dido, verus mihi nuntius ergo

2   venerat exstinctam ferroque extrema secutam?

3   Funeris heu tibi causa fui? Per sidera iuro,

4   per superos et si qua fides tellure sub ima est,

5   invitus, regina, tuo de litore cessi.

6   Sed me iussa deum, quae nunc has ire per umbras,

7   per loca senta situ cogunt noctemque profundam,

8   imperiis egere suis; nec credere quivi

9   hunc tantum tibi me discessu ferre dolorem.

10   Siste gradum teque aspectu ne subtrahe nostro.

11   Quem fugis? Extremum fato quod te adloquor hoc est."

12   Talibus Aeneas ardentem et torva tuentem

13   lenibat dictis animum lacrimasque ciebat.

14   Illa solo fixos oculos aversa tenebat

15   nec magis incepto vultum sermone movetur

16   quam si dura silex aut stet Marpesia cautes.

17   Tandem corripuit sese atque inimica refugit

18   in nemus umbriferum, coniunx ubi pristinus illi

19   respondet curis aequatque Sychaeus amorem. [*Aeneid* 6.456–74]

1. The metrical pattern of the first four feet of line 2 (<u>venerat</u> … *the first syllable of* <u>extrema</u>) is

    a. spondee-spondee-spondee-dactyl

    b. spondee-spondee-dactyl-spondee

    c. dactyl-spondee-dactyl-spondee

    d. dactyl-spondee-spondee-spondee

Question Rating: Easy / Medium. A relatively easy bit of scansion but the elision of ferroque *and* extrema *is necessary for the correct answer. Otherwise, as long as the double consonants throughout the opening syllables are identified, all syllables will be long except for the -erat of* venerat.

CHAPTER 2

2. The grammatical function of <u>extremam</u> (line 2) and <u>secutam</u> (line 2) is

     a. gerundive expressing purpose

     b. indirect statement

     c. circumstantial cum clause

     d. result clause

Question Rating: Medium. The absence of the infinitive esse *makes this indirect statement more difficult to identify, but the only other choice that might have some possibility is choice a, although, of course, neither* exstinctam *nor* secutam *is a gerundive.*

3. From the word <u>ferro</u> (line 2), we learn that Aeneas knows that Dido killed herself

     a. by burning herself

     b. by poisoning herself

     c. by stabbing herself

     d. by throwing herself off of a cliff

Question Rating: Easy. Ferro *is a not uncommon synecdoche for sword and here is an ablative of means.*

4. The case of <u>funeris</u> (line 3) depends on

     a. heu (line 3)

     b. tibi (line 3)

     c. causa (line 3)

     d. fui (line 3)

Question Rating: Easy / Medium. Funeris *is a fairly straightforward genitive dependent on* causa. *The potential difficulty lies in their separation and that* causa, *because of its use with the gerund and gerundive, can sometimes be a less obvious noun to govern a genitive.*

5. The translation of <u>per</u> (line 3) is

     a. through

     b. near

     c. in

     d. by

Question Rating: Easy / Medium. The translation of per *is intuitive as long as* iuro *is translated correctly: "I swear by the stars." ("On," of course, can also work.)*

6. The translation of <u>qua</u> (line 4) is

    a. which
    b. by which
    c. any
    d. this

Question Rating: Medium. Any ali- *word that occurs after* si, nisi, num, *or* ne *will lose its* ali- *prefix, so* qua *here is really* aliqua, *which, because it modifies* fides, *means "any."*

7. From line 5, we learn that Aeneas

    a. was cursed by the gods for leaving Dido
    b. lost a ship when leaving Carthage
    c. fought a fierce battle at sea
    d. didn't want to leave Dido

Question Rating: Easy / Medium. The correct understanding of invitus, *"unwilling," and* cessi, *"I left," are necessary to yield the correct answer.*

8. The case and number of <u>deum</u> (line 6) are

    a. nominative singular
    b. accusative singular
    c. nominative plural
    d. genitive plural

Question Rating: Medium. The syncopation of the genitive plural -orum *to* -um *is not uncommon, especially in poetry, but the affinity of its ending with the accusative singular ending can still cause confusion.*

9. The antecedent of <u>quae</u> (line 6) is

    a. me (line 6)
    b. iussa (line 6)
    c. deum (line 6)
    d. umbras (line 6)

Question Rating: Medium. The confusion lies in the different possibilities for quae: *feminine nominative singular or plural; neuter plural nominative or accusative. Because* quae *is a pronoun, only gender and number matter, which eliminates choices a and c. Placing an antecedent after the relative pronoun, as* umbras *is placed, is rare but not unheard of but if there is an antecedent that works grammatically and falls before the pronoun, that is the better choice, as* iussa *is.*

CHAPTER 2

10. The ablative of <u>imperiis</u> (line 8) is

    a. accompaniment

    b. means

    c. degree of difference

    d. respect

Question Rating: Medium. The form egere *is the syncopated perfect of* ago, -ere, egi, actus. *The ablative* imperiis *explains how Aeneas was driven ("by their power[s]"). The difficulty in this question lies in recognizing the meaning of* egere.

11. The grammatical function of <u>me</u> (line 9) is

    a. subject accusative

    b. ablative of comparison

    c. ablative of place where

    d. accusative place to which

Question Rating: Medium / Difficult. The indirect statement begins with hunc tantum, *whose placement and length suggest that it, rather than* me, *is the subject accusative. Nonetheless, the indirect statement only makes sense with* me *as the subject and* hunc tantum dolorem *as the object: "that I brought so much of this grief to you."*

12. In line 9, the form of <u>ferre</u> depends on

    a. credere (line 8)

    b. quivi (line 8)

    c. me (line 9)

    d. discessu (line 9)

Question Rating: Medium. The verb quivi *governs the complementary infinitive* credere *which itself is a head verb that introduces an indirect statement whose infinitive is* ferre.

13. In line 10 (<u>siste</u> … <u>nostro</u>), Aeneas asks Dido to stop

    a. walking away

    b. crying

    c. talking

    d. attacking him

Question Rating: Medium. The line's meaning depends on an understanding of the two periphrases (a longer way of saying something simple): siste gradum *means "stop your step" and* te … nostro *means "and don't pull yourself away from my presence."*

14. In line 11, <u>quem</u> is translated

    a. which

    b. whom

    c. who

    d. what

Question Rating: Easy / Medium. This sentence contains a basic use of quem *but* quem *traditionally is a difficult form to translate. Generally, a nominative relative or interrogative pronoun will be followed directly by a verb, while a non-nominative relative or interrogative pronoun (the interrogative here) will be followed by a noun (with a helping verb in between for the interrogative): "Whom do you flee?"*

15. In line 12, <u>talibus</u> modifies an understood Latin word translated as

    a. steps

    b. tears

    c. fear

    d. words

Question Rating: Easy / Medium. The conclusion of direct speech in Latin is generally signified by some expression that includes something about speaking and/or words. In this instance, Aeneas' speech is closed with talibus (verbis): *"with such words."*

16. In line 14, the ablative of <u>solo</u> is

    a. place where

    b. means

    c. cause

    d. comparison

Question Rating: Medium / Difficult. The identification of this ablative is dependent on the meaning of solo, *the neuter 2ⁿᵈ declension noun, "ground." As "ground," a place word, ablative of place where is correct.*

2.2   FREE RESPONSE QUESTIONS—TRANSLATION

2.2.1   TRANSLATION OVERVIEW

- one translation from the Caesar syllabus

- one translation from the Vergil syllabus

- 15 minutes for each translation

- Each translation counts for 7.5 percent of the overall grade.

- The College Board's Fall 2019 AP® Latin Course and Exam Description breaks translation down into four component parts (p.14):

  1. knowledge of vocabulary
  2. knowledge of morphology [forms]
  3. knowledge of grammar and syntax [grammar refers to specific grammatical constructions, while syntax refers to how those constructions are assembled]
  4. knowledge of the differences between Latin and English usage that require adjustments so that the translation is in fact correct English

- Translations for the AP® Exam should be as literal as possible while still maintaining conventional English usage:

  o *The goal is not to produce the artistically best translation but rather the most literal one that is consistent with English usage. (Course Description 144)*

- The two questions you should ask yourself when translating are as follows

  o Does my translation reflect the Latin grammar?

  o Does my translation sound like English?

- The AP® Exam allows for a departure from precise aligning of Latin and English when Latin structures are not reflected in English:

  o English indirect statement does not, and, in most cases, cannot, use an infinitive, as Latin does.

  o The connective relative—the relative that begins a new sentence—is difficult, if not impossible, to preserve in English.

- **The College Board's Learning Objectives and Evidence Statements for Translation**

- All of the below bullets are quoted directly from the 2012 Course Description, p.11:

- *[The Fall 2019 Course and Exam Description organizes this information differently, spreading it out as Learning Objectives for each Unit Guide. There is further expansion of translation achievement in the 2019 Achievement Level Descriptions found on pp.116–18.]*

  o Primary Objective: The student translates previously prepared Latin texts into English as literally as possible.

- The student demonstrates knowledge of Latin vocabulary when translating Latin texts into English.

    - rendering in English that reflects an appropriate meaning of the Latin words

    - rendering in English that reflects the parts of speech of the Latin words

- The student demonstrates knowledge of Latin morphology when translating Latin texts into English.

    - rendering in English that reflects the grammatical forms of the Latin words (e.g., gender, case and number of nouns, adjectives, and pronouns; person, number, tense, voice, and mood of verbs; degree of adjectives and adverbs)

- The student demonstrates knowledge of Latin grammar and syntax when translating Latin texts into English.

    - rendering in English that reflects the Latin grammatical constructions (e.g., subject-verb agreement, pronouns and their antecedents, subordinate clauses)

    - rendering in English that reflects the relationships between clauses

- The student demonstrates an understanding of differences between Latin and English usage when translating Latin texts into English.

    - rendering in English of Latin constructions that demonstrates an understanding of differences between Latin and English usage (e.g., indirect discourse, conditions, impersonal constructions, double datives)

2.2.2   THE GRADING OF THE TRANSLATIONS

- Each passage is divided into 15 word groups, also referred to as segments or sense units.

- Each translation is graded based on a successful translation of each of these word groups.

- For each word group translated correctly, a student receives credit; for each word group translated incorrectly, a student receives no credit.

- The entire word group must be translated correctly for a student to receive credit.

    o   For example, if the word group is a nominative and genitive and the student translates the genitive correctly but renders the nominative a direct object (rather than a subject), no credit is received for that word group.

2.2.2.1 Word Groups

- The 2017 AP® Exam included the following Vergil passage for translation:

  Rex erat Aeneas nobis, quo iustior alter
  nec pietate fuit, nec bello maior et armis.   545
  Quem si fata virum servant, si vescitur aura
  aetheria neque adhuc crudelibus occubat umbris,
  non metus.

- For grading, the passage was broken up into these word groups:[1]

  o   Rex Aeneas

  o   erat nobis

  o   quo

  o   alter nec fuit nec

  o   iustior pietate

  o   maior

  o   bello et armis

  o   si fata si

  o   servant

  o   quem virum

  o   vescitur aura aetheria

  o   neque adhuc

  o   occubat

  o   crudelibus umbris

  o   non metus

- The first two word groups illustrate both the literal and idiomatic possibilities for translations.

  o   Rex Aeneas

  ▪   King Aeneas, with synonyms for "king" also accepted

  o   erat nobis

  ▪   to/for us; of us

  •   *Nobis* is a dative of possession which can be translated literally (Aeneas was a king **for us**) but which produces somewhat awkward English.

---

1. As delineated in Mary C. English, "Report on the 2017 Advanced Placement Latin Examination," *Classical Outlook* 92, no. 3 (2017): 82.

CHAPTER 2

- The published grading of this question includes this note: "Segments 1 and 2 [*Rex Aeneas erat nobis*] can be translated idiomatically: "we had a king," "our king was Aeneas."[2]

2.2.2.2 Translation Analysis

- Two analyses are included.

  o First, a more general analysis that looks at sample translations and compares them to trends identified across all submitted translations.

  o Second, a more specific analysis that uses sample translations and word groups to illustrate the grading process and to identify correct and incorrect translations.

- Both passages include Latin that is no longer on the syllabus.

- This approach provides students with practice sight translating, rather than relying on a passage with which they might already be familiar, which in turn forces them to focus more carefully on the Latin and their analysis of it.

- The published analysis of the 2012 exam does not include the traditional word-group analysis because of the change in the AP® Latin syllabus in 2013, but rather provides a more general summary of common mistakes among all translations, which will be used here.

2.2.2.3 General Analysis of Translation Trends

- Below is the *Aeneid* translation passage from the 2012 AP® Exam.

- Below the passage are four translations from student AP® Exams, followed by a correct translation.

- *[The use of* sic *within a translation indicates that what precedes it indeed belongs; that is, that what precedes it is not a typo or mistake.]*

> Sopor fessos complectitur artus.
> Et iam Argiva phalanx instructis navibus ibat
> a Tenedo tacitae per amica silentia lunae   255
> litora nota petens, flammas cum regia puppis
> extulerat, fatisque deum defensus iniquis
> inclusos utero Danaos et pinea furtim
> laxat claustra Sinon. [*Aeneid* 2.253–59]

Sample Translation 1

And now a Greek fleet with ships having been instructed was going from Tenedos through the friendly silence of the quiet moon, seeking familiar shores, when the royal ship had thrown off flames and having defended the inclosed [*sic*] Greeks in the belly by *iniquis* [*sic*] fates and Sinon loosed the pine barrier secretly.

---

2. Ibid.

Sample Translation 2

The *sopor* [*sic*] completes the final skill. And now the Greek fleet was going in instructed ships from Tenedos through the friendly silence of the silent moon, seeking noted shores, when the kingdom had dragged the ships from the flames, and having been defended by the fate of the god the enclosed Greeks hid in the stomach and Sinon secretly opened the pines.

Sample Translation 3

Sleep overcame the tired limbs. And now the Greek troop went by means of ships having been guided from Tenedos through friendly silences of the quiet moon seeking known shores, the kingdom having been led out with flaming ships, and Sinon having been protected by unequal fates and the gods stealthily let out the Greeks having been enclosed in the belly and the wooden enclosure.

Sample Translation 4

The limbs are taken over by a still tiredness. And now the phalanx at Argos sails on ships having been instructed from Tenedos quietly through the silent friendly moon. Seeking the natural shores, when the flames from the royal tombs was [*sic*] brought out, and the team feel [*sic*] defense by the fate of the gods and stealthily Sinon lets the Greeks having been inclosed [*sic*] in the crowded pine out of the stomach.

Analysis of Sample Translations

Acceptable Full Credit Translation. Sluggishness embraces his tired limbs. And now the Greek fleet, with their ships lined up, was going from Tenedos through the friendly silence of the quiet moon, seeking familiar shores, when the royal fleet had raised flames, and Sinon, having been protected by the hated fates of the gods, releases the closed pine boards and the enclosed Greeks from the belly.

- Common grammar mistakes made in submitted translations:[3]

  - line 253: not identifying *complectitur* as a deponent verb

    - Sample 1 omits this half line.

    - Sample 2 translates *complectitur* actively but with an incorrect meaning.

    - Sample 3 translates *complectitur* correctly.

    - Sample 4 translates *complectitur* passively as "are taken over."

---

3. These grammar mistakes and the vocabulary mistakes below are taken from Robert W. Cape Jr., "An Overview of the 2012 Advanced Placement Latin: Vergil Examination," *Classical Outlook* 89, no. 4 (2012): 97.

- o   line 254: not identifying *Argiva* as an adjective
    - ▪ Samples 1, 2, and 3 translate *Argiva* correctly.
    - ▪ Sample 4 translates it as the noun Argos: "the phalanx at Argos."
- o   line 255: not recognizing that *tacitae* agrees with *lunae*
    - ▪ All four samples translate *tacitae* correctly.
- o   line 255: not identifying *amica* as an adjective
    - ▪ Samples 1, 2, and 3 translate *amica* correctly.
    - ▪ Sample 4 translates *amica* as agreeing with *lunae*: "through the silent friendly moon."
- o   line 256: translating *cum* as the preposition "with" rather than the conjunction
    - ▪ Samples 1, 2, and 4 translate *cum* correctly.
    - ▪ Sample 3 does not translate *cum* as the preposition but rather translates the *cum* clause as an ablative absolute rather than as a *cum* clause: "the kingdom having been led out with flaming ships."
- o   line 256: not identifying *regia* as an adjective
    - ▪ Sample 1 translates *regia* correctly.
    - ▪ Samples 2 and 3 translate *regia* as the noun "kingdom."
    - ▪ Sample 4 translates *regia* as an adjective but modifying "tombs," which is not in the Latin.
- o   line 257: not identifying *extulerat* as a pluperfect
    - ▪ Samples 1 and 2 translate *extulerat* correctly as a pluperfect.
    - ▪ Sample 3 translates *extulerat* as a perfect passive participle: "having been led out."
    - ▪ Sample 4 translates *extulerat* as a perfect passive indicative: "was brought out."
- o   line 257: not identifying *defensus* as a perfect passive participle
    - ▪ Sample 1 translates *defensus* as a perfect active participle: "having defended."
    - ▪ Samples 2 and 3 translate *defensus* correctly.
    - ▪ Sample 4 translates *defensus* incorrectly as a noun: "defense."
- o   line 257: not recognizing that *iniquis* agrees with *fatis*
    - ▪ Samples 1 and 3 translate *iniquis* correctly as an adjective but both get the meaning wrong:
        - • Sample 1 leaves the Latin word in its translation without translating it.
        - • Sample 3 translates it as "unequal," mixing it up with the adjective *inaequalis*.
    - ▪ Samples 2 and 4 omit *iniquis* from their translations.

- Common vocabulary mistakes made in submitted translations:

  o line 253: reading *complectitur* incorrectly as *completur*

    ▪ Sample 1 omits this half line.

    ▪ None of the other samples read it as *completur* (though, as above, two others translated it incorrectly in different ways).

  o line 253: reading *artus* incorrectly as *ars*

    ▪ Sample 1 omits this half line.

    ▪ Sample 2 translates *artus* as *ars*: "the final skill."

    ▪ Samples 3 and 4 translate the meaning of *artus* correctly, though Sample 4 translates it as a nominative subject rather than the correct accusative direct object.

  o line 255: reading *a* incorrectly as *ad* or *apud*

    ▪ All four samples translate *a* correctly.

  o line 257: reading *iniquis* incorrectly as *inquis*, "you say."

    ▪ None of the samples read *iniquis* incorrectly as *inquis*, though other mistakes in the translation of *iniquis* were made (see above).

2.2.2.4 Word Group Analysis and Grading

- Below is the *Aeneid* translation passage from the 2011 AP® Exam; these lines are no longer included in the syllabus.

- Below the passage are two translations from student AP® Exams.

- You can use these sample translations to assess them in general and to practice seeing how word groups are used to grade translations.

- I suggest trying to analyze the translations yourself, especially in terms of word groups, before reading the included analysis.

- Below the sample translations are the word groups that the AP® Readers used and an analysis of the translations.

- The transcription of each translation reflects the original: the presence of brackets or parentheses indicates that the translator used them rather than any insertion by me.

> Ipsa sed in somnis inhumati venit imago
> coniugis, ora modis attollens pallida miris,
> crudeles aras traiectaque pectora ferro   355
> nudavit, caecumque domus scelus omne retexit.
> Tum celerare fugam patriaque excedere suadet,
> auxiliumque viae veteres tellure recludit
> thesauros, ignotum argenti pondus et auri.
> 　　[*Aeneid* 1.353–59]

Sample Translation 1: 14 of 18 points

But the image itself of [her] husband having been buried came [to her] in sleep, raising its shining head in wondrous ways; it revealed the cruel altars and the chest having been pierced with a sword and it uncovered the dark evil of the whole house. Then it urges [her] to quicken her flight and to leave behind her country, and as help, it discloses the locations of old treasures in the earth, an unknown weight of silver and of gold.

Sample Translation 2: 16 of 18 points

But the image itself of her unburied husband comes (to her) in sleep, lifting its pale mouth(s) with miraculous measures; it (he) revealed the bloody altars and the chest(s) having been pierced by iron, and it uncovered the whole dark sin of the house. Then it urges (her) to hasten (her) flight and to leave (her) country, and it discloses the help of roads and ancient treasures on the land, an unknown weight of silver and gold.

Analysis of Sample Translations

Acceptable Full Credit Translation. But in her dreams the image itself of her unburied husband came, lifting its pale face in amazing ways; it bared the cruel altars and its chest pierced with a sword and revealed the whole hidden crime of the house. Then it urges her to hasten her flight and leave her fatherland and reveals, as an aid for her journey, ancient treasures in the ground, an unknown weight of silver and of gold. [4]

- When reviewing the individual word groups below, remember that an "incorrect" means no credit for that word group.

- There is no partial credit given for word groups; the entire word group must be translated correctly to receive credit for it.

Word Group 1, *sed in somnis*: but in her dreams
- correct for both samples

- Both samples translate *in somnis* as "in sleep," which is acceptable, and, although "in sleep" is postponed in both samples to the end of the clause, it is translated with the verb, which makes it acceptable.

Word Group 2, *ipsa imago venit*: the image itself came
- correct for both samples

Word Group 3, *inhumati coniugis*: of her unburied husband
- incorrect for Sample 1; correct for sample 2

- Sample 1 forgets the negative meaning of *inhumati*, translating it as "having been buried" rather than "not having been buried" or "having been unburied."

---

4. Mary Pendergraft, "The Grading of the 2011 Advanced Placement Exam in Latin: Vergil," *Classical Outlook* 88, no. 4 (2011): 105.

- Sample 1 translates *inhumati* more participially, "having been buried," while Sample 2 translates it more adjectivally, "unburied," both of which are acceptable translations, if Sample 1 had negated the participle.

Word Group 4, *attollens ora pallida*: lifting its pale face
- correct for both samples

- The Sample 1 translation of *ora* as "head" is acceptable and *ora* can acceptably be translated as a singular or a plural.

Word Group 5, *modis miris*: in amazing ways
- correct for Sample 1; incorrect for sample 2

- Sample 2 seems to understand *modis* as a metrical term, translating it as "measures."

- Sample 2 also seems to read *modis miris* as an ablative of means, translating it "with miraculous measures," suggesting that the face is raised by means of these ways, rather than the more descriptive, albeit general, rendering of it as "in amazing ways."

Word Group 6, *nudavit*: it bared
- correct for both samples

- Both samples read "it" as the subject, with Sample 2 including "(he)" in parentheses. Both subjects are acceptable.

Word Group 7, *crudeles aras*: the cruel altars (as object of *nudavit*)
- correct for both samples

Word Group 8, *traiectaque pectora ferro*: and its chest pierced with a sword (as object of *nudavit*)
- correct for both samples

Word Group 9, *-que retexit*: and revealed
- correct for both samples

Word Group 10, *caecum domus scelus omne*: the whole hidden crime of the house
- incorrect for Sample 1; correct for Sample 2

- Sample 1 translates the neuter, singular, accusative *omne* with *domus* rather than with the correct *scelus*.

Word Group 11, *tum suadet*: then it urges
- correct for both samples

- *Suadet* and *recludit* below are present tense verbs, often referred to as the historical present—that is, a present tense verb used to tell a story in the past or to refer to a past event. These verbs may be translated in the present or the past but they must be translated consistently: if *suadet* is translated in the present, then *recludit* must be as well, and likewise for the past.

Word Group 12, *celerare fugam*: to hasten her flight
- correct for both samples

Word Group 13, *patriaque excedere*: and leave her fatherland
- correct for both samples

Word Group 14, *-que recludit tellure*: and reveals in the ground

- correct for Sample 1; incorrect for Sample 2

- Sample 2 translates *recludit* correctly but misunderstands where the treasures lie, translating *tellure* as "on the land" rather than "in the land."

Word Group 15, *auxilium viae*: as an aid for her journey
- incorrect for Sample 1; correct for Sample 2

- Sample 1 translates *auxilium* correctly but forgets to include the genitive *viae*.

- Sample 1 translates *auxilium* as an appositive, signified by "as," to the object of *recludit*, while Sample 2 translates it as a direct object of *recludit*. Both translations are acceptable; if Sample 1 had included *viae*, it would have received credit for this word group.

Word Group 16, *veteres thesauros*: ancient treasures
- incorrect for Sample 1; correct for sample 2

- Sample 1 includes the word "locations" as the object of *recludit* which forces *veteres thesauros* to be translated as a genitive, "of old treasures."

- In the published student responses (in the article in footnote 4), a student scored 17 out of 18 for the passage, losing a point because of the translation of *thesauros* as singular rather than plural.

Word Group 17, *ignotum pondus*: an unknown weight
- correct for both samples

Word Group 18, *argenti et auri*: of silver and gold
- correct for both samples

2.2.3   LIST OF TRANSLATIONS FROM PREVIOUS CAESAR-VERGIL AP® EXAMS (2013 TO 2019)

- The 2017 to 2019 translations include a one sentence English summary of the Latin.

- The 2013 to 2016 translations include no such summary.

Caesar

Vergil

2019

The failure of Orgetorix's conspiracy

Aeneas laments a disastrous decision.

Hac oratione adducti inter se fidem et ius iurandum dant et, regno occupato, per tres potentissimos ac firmissimos populos totius Galliae sese potiri posse sperant. Ea res est Helvetiis per indicium enuntiata. Moribus suis Orgetorigem ex vinculis causam dicere coegerunt. (1.3–4)

"O patria, o divum domus Ilium et incluta bello moenia Dardanidum! Quater ipso in limine portae substitit atque utero sonitum quater arma dedere; instamus tamen immemores caecique furore et monstrum infelix sacrata sistimus arce." (2.241–45)

2018

Pullo attacks and is attacked.

Mediocri spatio relicto, Pullo pilum in hostes immittit, atque unum ex multitudine procurrentem traicit; quo percusso et exanimato, hunc scutis protegunt, in hostem tela universi coiciunt neque dant regrediendi facultatem. Transfigitur scutum Pulloni et verutum in balteo defigitur. (5.44)

Iris approaches the dying Dido.

Ergo Iris croceis per caelum roscida pennis mille trahens varios adverso sole colores devolat et supra caput astitit. "Hunc ego Diti sacrum iussa fero teque isto corpore solvo." Sic ait et dextra crinem secat. (4.700–704)

2017

Caesar, although shorthanded, comes to the rescue.

Caesar, consilio eius probato, etsi opinione trium legionum deiectus ad duas redierat, tamen unum communis salutis auxilium in celeritate ponebat. Venit magnis itineribus in Nerviorum fines. Ibi ex captivis cognoscit quae apud Ciceronem gerantur quantoque in periculo res sit. (5.48)

Ilioneus praises the missing Aeneas.

Rex erat Aeneas nobis, quo iustior alter
nec pietate fuit, nec bello maior et armis.
Quem si fata virum servant, si vescitur aura
aetheria neque adhuc crudelibus occubat umbris,
non metus. (1.544–48)

2016

Nostri, simul in arido constiterunt, suis omnibus consecutis, in hostes impetum fecerunt atque eos in fugam dederunt; neque longius prosequi potuerunt, quod equites cursum tenere atque insulam capere non potuerant. Hoc unum ad pristinam fortunam Caesari defuit. (4.26)

"Troius Aeneas, pietate insignis et armis,
ad genitorem imas Erebi descendit ad umbras.
Si te nulla movet tantae pietatis imago,
at ramum hunc" (aperit ramum qui veste latebat)
"agnoscas." Tumida ex ira tum corda residunt.
(6.403–7)

2015

Natio est omnis Gallorum admodum dedita religionibus, atque ob eam causam qui sunt adfecti gravioribus morbis quique in proeliis periculisque versantur aut pro victimis homines immolant aut se immolaturos vovent, administrisque ad ea sacrificia Druidibus utuntur. (6.16)

Nunc etiam interpres divum Iove, missus ab ipso (testor utrumque caput), celeres mandata per auras detulit: ipse deum manifesto in lumine vidi intrantem muros vocemque his auribus hausi. Desine meque tuis incendere teque querelis; Italiam non sponte sequor. (4.356–61)

2014

Galli se omnes ab Dite patre prognatos praedicant, idque ab Druidibus proditum dicunt. Ob eam causam spatia omnis temporis non numero dierum sed noctium finiunt; dies natales et mensum et annorum initia sic observant ut noctem dies subsequatur. (6.18)

Aeole (namque tibi divum pater atque hominum rex et mulcere dedit fluctus et tollere vento), gens inimica mihi Tyrrhenum navigat aequor, Ilium in Italiam portans victosque penates: incute vim ventis submersasque obrue puppes. (1.65–69)

2013

Pronuntiatur prima luce ituros. Consumitur vigiliis reliqua pars noctis, cum sua quisque miles circumspiceret, quid secum portare posset, quid ex instrumento hibernorum relinquere cogeretur. Omnia excogitantur, quare nec sine periculo maneatur et languore militum et vigiliis periculum augeatur. (5.31)

Hic, ubi disiectas moles avulsaque saxis saxa vides, mixtoque undantem pulvere fumum, Neptunus muros magnoque emota tridenti fundamenta quatit totamque a sedibus urbem eruit. Hic Iuno Scaeas saevissima portas prima tenet … (2.608–13)

2.3   FREE RESPONSE QUESTIONS—ANALYTICAL ESSAY

2.3.1   ANALYTICAL ESSAY OVERVIEW

- one question, worth 20 percent of the total score

- recommended time: 45 minutes

- two passages to be compared

- Passages can be two from Vergil, two from Caesar, or one from each.

- If one passage from each, they will be thematically related.

2.3.2   ANALYTICAL ESSAY ACHIEVEMENT LEVELS

- The College Board uses five achievement levels, 1–5, 1 being the worst, to measure "the degree to which student performance meets learning objectives in each skill category." (Fall 2019 Course and Exam Description, p.115)

- Achievement levels do not necessarily correspond to final AP® Exam scores.

- Included here are summaries of the Achievement Levels for Textual Analysis and Argumentation (Fall 2019 Course and Exam Description, pp.120–24).

- Each Achievement Level is divided into five subcategories:

   o   Development of an Argument

   o   Use of Latin Textual Examples

   o   Inferences and Conclusions

   o   Analysis of Language Usage and Stylistic Features

   o   Use of Contextual Knowledge

- Development of an Argument
    - Level 5
        - coherent, logical structure
        - Analysis demonstrates a balanced, nuanced understanding of the Latin.
        - main ideas stated clearly
        - full supporting details
        - provides evidence from throughout the passage as support
        - Analysis addresses all aspects of the question.
    - Level 4
        - lacks the nuanced understanding of the passage of level 5
        - goes beyond summary to analyze
    - Level 3
        - an excessive reliance on summary
        - an underdeveloped argument
        - Some supporting details are provided but more in isolation than as part of a cohesive analysis.
    - Level 2
        - attempts to summarize but without organization or focus
        - Content may be vague or irrelevant.
    - Level 1
        - less ability than level 2
- Use of Latin Textual Examples
    - Level 5
        - accurately paraphrases or translates from the entire passage
        - supports the analysis with specific and relevant Latin
    - Level 4
        - lacks some accuracy in translation or paraphrase
        - Passages might not be wholly relevant to the analysis.
    - Level 3
        - lacks balance in the response, either analyzing without citing Latin or citing Latin without applying it to the analysis

- Level 2
  - cites individual words or short phrases to support analysis
  - some incorrect assumptions or conclusions
  - misinterprets author's point of view, tone, or opinions
- Level 1
  - less ability than level 2

- Inferences and Conclusions
  - Level 5
    - supports the analysis with implied rather than directly stated information
    - refers to the author's implied point of view, tone, or opinions
  - Level 4
    - uses some implied information but uses more directly stated information
    - Minor errors may exist in references to the author's point of view, tone, or opinion but these errors do not undermine the analysis as a whole.
  - Level 3
    - lacks a complete understanding of implied information in the passage
    - demonstrates only a limited understanding of point of view, tone, or opinions
  - Level 2
    - focuses more on what is stated than what is implied
    - includes incorrect interpretations of point of view, tone, or opinions
  - Level 1
    - less ability than level 2
- Analysis of Language Usage and Stylistic Features
  - Level 5
    - use of rhetorical or stylistic feature or word choice, word order, or ambiguity to support analysis
    - able to explain how such features are relevant to analysis
  - Level 4
    - includes an underdeveloped incorporation of rhetorical or stylistic features, word choice, word order, or ambiguity

- o Level 3
  - ▪ includes rhetorical or stylistic features, word choice, word order, or ambiguity with limited or ineffective connection to the Latin
- o Level 2
  - ▪ includes rhetorical or stylistic features with little or no connection to the Latin
- o Level 1
  - ▪ less ability than level 2
- Use of Contextual Knowledge
  - o Level 5
    - ▪ specific references to relevant cultural or historical information or information about the author, genre, or traditions of classical literature, to whatever extent relevant
  - o Level 4
    - ▪ includes an underdeveloped incorporation of relevant cultural or historical information or information about the author, genre, or traditions of classical literature, to whatever extent relevant
  - o Level 3
    - ▪ includes relevant cultural or historical information or information about the author, genre, or traditions of classical literature with limited or ineffective connection to the Latin
  - o Level 2
    - ▪ includes cultural or historical information or information about the author, genre, or traditions of classical literature that is incorrect or irrelevant to the Latin
  - o Level 1
    - ▪ less ability than level 2

2.3.3   SAMPLE RESPONSE ANALYSIS

- Below is included an analytical essay from the 2014 AP® Exam.
  - o Depending on your time, at least outline your response to the question, including the Latin you would use to support your answer; if time permits, write out your response in full.
  - o Then use the analysis of student responses to gauge the success of your own essay.
  - o Remember, the recommended time for completion of this question is 45 minutes.

- Every analytical question includes the following instruction after the question itself (emphasis theirs):

BE SURE TO REFER SPECIFICALLY TO THE LATIN THROUGH THE PASSAGES TO SUPPORT THE POINTS YOU MAKE IN YOUR ESSAY. DO NOT SIMPLY SUMMARIZE WHAT THE PASSAGES SAY.

(When you are asked to refer specifically to the Latin, you must write out the Latin and/or cite line numbers AND you must translate, accurately paraphrase, or make clear in your discussion that you understand the Latin.)

2014

- The 2014 exam included two Caesar passages and asked students to analyze Caesar's opinions of his soldiers' actions in battle:[5]

Iusserunt pronuntiare ut impedimenta relinquerent atque in orbem consisterent. Quod consilium etsi in eiusmodi casu reprehendendum non est, tamen incommode accidit: nam et nostris militibus spem minuit et hostes ad pugnam alacriores effecit, quod non sine summo timore et desperatione id factum videbatur. Praeterea accidit, quod fieri necesse erat, ut vulgo milites ab signis discederent, quae quisque eorum carissima haberet ab impedimentis petere atque arripere properaret. (5.33)

At tanta militum virtus atque ea praesentia animi fuit ut, cum ubique flamma torrerentur maximaque telorum multitudine premerentur suaque omnia impedimenta atque omnes fortunas conflagrare intellegerent, non modo demigrandi causa de vallo decederet nemo sed paene ne respiceret quidem quisquam, ac tum omnes acerrime fortissimeque pugnarent. Hic dies nostris longe gravissimus fuit, sed tamen hunc habuit eventum ut eo die maximus numerus hostium vulneraretur atque interficeretur. (5.43)

In the passages above, Caesar describes Roman soldiers, under different leaders, facing enemy attacks. In a well-developed essay, analyze how Caesar's accounts of the battles reveal his judgment about the soldiers' actions.

BE SURE TO REFER SPECIFICALLY TO THE LATIN THROUGH THE PASSAGES TO SUPPORT THE POINTS YOU MAKE IN YOUR ESSAY. DO NOT SIMPLY SUMMARIZE WHAT THE PASSAGES SAY.

(When you are asked to refer specifically to the Latin, you must write out the Latin and/or cite line numbers AND you must translate, accurately paraphrase, or make clear in your discussion that you understand the Latin.)

---

5. Texts and question taken from Robert W. Cape Jr., "Report on the 2014 Advanced Placement Latin Examination," *Classical Outlook* 90, no. 3 (2015): 77–81.

- Possible overarching ideas:
  - Caesar's use of positive or negative connotations conveys his satisfaction or lack thereof with his troops' behavior.
  - Caesar attributes the inevitability of his troops' reactions to the decisions made by the commanders; a well-conceived plan will produce positive results, while an ill-conceived plan will produce negative results.
- Latin from 5.33 that you could use to support an answer, with translation or paraphrase and analysis:
  - Quod consilium etsi in eiusmodi casu reprehendendum non est, tamen incommode accidit:
    - The order to abandon the supplies and form into a circle (from the previous sentence) was sound advice given the situation (*consilium ... est*) but still did not work out well (*tamen incommode accidit*).
      - The use of *eiusmodi (casu)* emphasizes that this particular situation influenced the decision, rather than the decision being one that is universally applicable.
      - Caesar uses litotes (*reprehendum non est*) to undercut his praise of the decision; that is, he allows that it was a sound decision but ultimately criticizes its outcome.
      - The adversative *tamen* introduces and emphasizes the corrective judgment of *incommode accidit*.
      - The use of the negated adverb *incommode*, a litotes, albeit a weak one, emphasizes Caesar's negativity similar to how *reprehendum non est* does.
  - nam et nostris militibus spem minuit et hostes ad pugnam alacriores effecit, quod non sine summo timore et desperatione id factum videbatur:
    - The strategy decreased Caesar's soldiers' hope and increased the enthusiasm of the enemy for fighting because the decision of Caesar's soldiers seemed done out of fear and desperation.
      - The use of *et ... et* and the implicit comparisons in *minuit*, which, while not a comparative word itself, implies the comparative *minor*, plus *alacriores* establish the opposite nature of the reaction of the two armies to the result of the strategy, the Romans' hope decreasing, while the enemy's enthusiasm increases.
      - The framing of *ad pugnam* by the noun-adjective pair *hostes alacriores* emphasizes the focus of the enthusiasm: the fight.
      - The postponement of the subject and indirect statement (*id factum*) allows the emotion that the enemy attributed to the Romans to be emphasized by appearing first in the clause (*non sine ... desperatione*).

- The litotes of *non sine* and the superlative *summo* further highlight the fear and desperation the enemy attributed to the Romans.

o Praeterea accidit, quod fieri necesse erat, ut vulgo milites ab signis discederent, quae quisque eorum carissima haberet ab impedimentis petere atque arripere properaret.

- It's no surprise that the soldiers abandoned their posts and tried to save whatever they thought important.

  - Both the adverb *praeterea* and *quod fieri necesse erat* reveal the inevitability of the soldiers' reactions.

  - The adverb *vulgo*, "commonly" or "universally," has its origin in the noun *vulgus, -i*, "crowd," which creates a greater sense of the collective behavior of the soldiers.

  - The simplicity of the statement *ab signis discederent* and the use of *signis*, to which Caesar attributes such importance, reveals both the inevitability of the action and the emotional state of the army to abandon their most important possession.

  - The asyndeton of *discederent* and *properaret*, both of which are dependent on *accidit*, reveals the swiftness and chaos with which the soldiers were acting.

  - The framing of *quisque eorum* by *quae carissima* illustrates the attachment of the soldiers to their possessions: the soldiers are literally surrounded and enveloped by their dearest possessions.

- Latin from 5.43 that you could use to support an answer, with translation or paraphrase and analysis:

o At tanta militum virtus atque ea praesentia animi fuit ut …

- The courage and presence of mind of the soldiers was so great that …

  - The primary position of *tanta* expresses how impressed Caesar was with their behavior: the first idea in the sentence is "so great."

  - The separation of *tanta* and *virtus* with the visual association of *tanta* and *militum* by placing them next to each other transfers the meaning of *tanta* to *militum*; that is, the soldiers are so great, in addition to their *virtus* being so great.

o cum ubique flamma torrerentur maximaque telorum multitudine premerentur suaque omnia impedimenta atque omnes fortunas conflagrare intellegerent

- although the soldiers were being attacked by flame on all sides and enduring a huge number of weapons and thought that their supplies and valuables were being burned

- The concessive meaning of *cum*, "although," allows Caesar to establish all of the adverse conditions under which his soldiers were fighting but, at the same time, to increase their valor through mention of those adverse conditions.

- The tricolon crescens of the subjunctive verbs in the *cum* clause, the third of which, *intellegerent*, includes an indirect statement, illustrates the escalation of the adverse conditions under which the soldiers were fighting and further emphasizes Caesar's positivity toward the soldiers because of those adverse conditions.

o ut … non modo demigrandi causa de vallo decederet nemo sed paene ne respiceret quidem quisquam, ac tum omnes acerrime fortissimeque pugnarent.

  ▪ The soldiers were so courageous that not only did they not flee but they didn't even look back and all of them fought most bravely and fiercely.

    - The structure of *non modo … sed* establishes both parallelism between the act of not leaving and not looking back and hierarchy: it was commendable that they didn't flee but even more so that they didn't even look behind them out of fear.

    - The double superlative *acerrime fortissimeque* illustrates Caesar's admiration for his men's bravery.

o Hic dies nostris longe gravissimus fuit, sed tamen hunc habuit eventum ut eo die maximus numerus hostium vulneraretur atque interficeretur.

  ▪ This day was the worst for our men but still they managed to wound and kill the greatest number of the enemy.

    - The use of a superlative intensified by an adverb (*longe gravissimus*) reflects how bad Caesar wants to portray this day.

    - The superlative *gravissimus* is echoed in the superlative *maximus*, providing a juxtaposition between how bad the day was and how successful his soldiers were.

SAMPLE STUDENT PARAGRAPHS[6]

- Sample paragraphs from three essays are included with their scores and a brief description for that score from the rubric used to grade the essays.

- Paragraphs that cover similar material and represent a range of scores are included in full and then again with comments and observations.[7]

- Use the uninterrupted responses to form your own conclusions about what was done well and poorly.

6. Scores and transcribed paragraphs taken from Robert W. Cape Jr., "Report on the 2014 Advanced Placement Latin Examination," *Classical Outlook* 90, no. 3 (2015): 78–80.
7. Observations about the essays are mine unless otherwise noted.

Response 1 without commentary; Score: 5/5

- A 5/5[8]

    - … analyzes how Caesar judges his soldiers' actions by consistently incorporating Latin evidence

    - … uses Latin that is copious, accurate, specific, and relevant, as well as properly cited and distributed throughout each passage

    - … draws inferences and conclusions

First off, Caesar describes the approach each group of soldiers took as they fought. In the first passage, the soldiers were given orders to leave their baggage and come together in a circle ("*ut impedimenta relinquerent atque in orbem consisterent*") and they were able to follow—at first. Then they began to fall out of place and especially they began to lose hope ("*nostris militibus spem minuit*") and compared to the enemy, who were fighting even more fiercely ("*hostes ad pugnam alacriores effecit*"), this was not good. Caesar places these descriptions of opposite sides to highlight the differences in fighting, and the fact that the enemy was doing better is not something that Caesar praises, the soldiers are filled with greatest fear and desperation ("*summo timore et desperatione*"). On the other hand, the soldiers in the second passage display great strength and presence of mind since the beginning ("*tanta militum virtus atque ea praesentia animi*"). No one backed away from the wall for the reason of deserting ("*non modo demigrandi causa de vallo decederet nemo*") and instead almost no one took a rest from their duty ("*sed paene ne respiceret quidem quisquam*"). These men kept fighting on most fiercely and most strongly ("*tum omnes acerrime fortissime pugnarent*") although the day was most grave ("*hic dies … gravissimus fuit*"). This is the kind of attitude Caesar approves of and even exalts in his writing. The soldiers were not put down by anything, and Caesar wanted it this way.

Next, Caesar also described the attitude that the soldiers in each passage manifested with respect to their material goods, in order that he may show what their priorities are and what they should be. In the first passage, the soldiers at first obeyed orders to leave the baggage (line 1) but when the fighting became very fierce and the soldiers became more frightened and desperate, they withdrew from the battle ("*ut vulgo milites ab signis discederent*"). Once this happened, they went to search and to seize ("*petere atque arripere*") from the baggage whatever was most dear to them ("*quae quisque eorum carissima haberet ab impedimentis*"). Caesar clearly showed with this passage that the soldiers did not have their priorities straight. They should have forgotten their bags and kept fighting on with bravery, like a Roman should. Caesar then tells how a Roman ought to do this (set their priorities) with the second passage. He tells that although on all sides they were burned by flames ("*cum ubique flamma*

---

8. This and the 4/5 and 2/5 scoring guide below taken from Robert W. Cape Jr., "Report on the 2014 Advanced Placement Latin Examination," *Classical Outlook* 90, no. 3 (2015): 77–78.

terrerentur") and a great number of weapons oppressed them ("*maxima telorum …
premerentur*") and they knew all their baggage an [*sic*] all their property to be burning
("*suaque omnia impedimenta atque omnes fortunas conflagrare intellegerent*"), they still
kept fighting on (lines 4–5: "*ac tum … pugnarent*"). These are the priorities that Roman
soldiers should have, points out Caesar. Even if they know everything they hold dear
is being destroyed (material-wise), their main focus should be the battle and to uphold
the Roman spirit if [*sic*] *virtus* and *Romanitas*.

Response 1 with bulleted commentary (emphasis mine); Score: 5/5

First off, Caesar describes the approach each group of soldiers took as they fought.

- *An opening sentence that, if somewhat general, nonetheless describes what the paragraph is about.*

In the first passage, the soldiers were given orders to leave their baggage and come
together in a circle ("*ut impedimenta relinquerent atque in orbem consisterent*") and
they were able to follow—at first. Then they began to fall out of place and especially
they began to lose hope ("*nostris militibus spem minuit*") and compared to the enemy,
who were fighting even more fiercely ("*hostes ad pugnam alacriores effecit*"), this was
not good.

- *This next sentence shows understanding of the Latin by both summarizing what the Latin says and by using the Latin to draw conclusions.*

Caesar **places these descriptions of opposite sides to highlight the differences in
fighting**, and the fact **that the enemy was doing better is not something that Caesar
praises**. The soldiers are filled with greatest fear and desperation ("*summo timore et
desperatione*").

- *This sentence illustrates good use of the Latin to analyze.*

On the other hand, **the soldiers in the second passage** display great strength and presence of mind since the beginning ("*tanta militum virtus atque ea praesentia animi*").

- *The paragraph includes citations from both passages.*

No one backed away from the wall for the reason of deserting ("*non modo demigrandi
causa de vallo decederet nemo*") and instead **almost no one** took a rest from their duty
("*sed paene ne respiceret quidem quisquam*").

- *The inclusion of "almost" (paene) in the paraphrase shows a detailed understanding of the Latin.*

These men kept fighting on most fiercely and most strongly ("*tum omnes acerrime fortissime pugnarent*") although the day was most grave ("*hic dies … gravissimus fuit*"). **This is the kind of attitude Caesar approves of and even exalts in his writing. The soldiers were not put down by anything, and Caesar wanted it this way.**

- *The paragraph is concluded decisively and definitively in a way that addresses the question.*

Next, Caesar also **described the attitude** that the soldiers in each passage manifested with respect to their material goods, **in order that he may show what their priorities are and what they should be.**

- *A good opening sentence that both establishes the focus of the paragraph and makes an assertion about the passages.*

In the first passage, the soldiers at first obeyed orders to leave the baggage (line 1) but when the fighting became very fierce and the soldiers became more frightened and desperate, they withdrew from the battle ("*ut vulgo milites ab signis discederent*"). Once this happened, they went to search and to seize ("*petere atque arripere*") from the baggage whatever was most dear to them ("*quae quisque eorum carissima haberet ab impedimentis*").

- *Good summary that uses Latin consistently, accurately, and throughout and that sets up the analysis that follows.*

Caesar clearly showed with this passage that the soldiers did not have their priorities straight. **They should have forgotten their bags and kept fighting on with bravery, like a Roman should.** Caesar then tells how a Roman ought to do this (set their priorities) with the second passage. He tells that although on all sides they were burned by flames ("*cum ubique flamma terrerentur*") and a great number of weapons oppressed them ("*maxima telorum … premerentur*") and they knew all their baggage an [*sic*] all their property to be burning ("*suaque omnia impedimenta atque omnes fortunas conflagrare intellegerent*"), they still kept fighting on (lines 4–5: "*ac tum … pugnarent*").

- *Good analysis that draws a conclusion and transitions into the counterpoint of the following passage that uses Latin again consistently, accurately, and throughout.*

These are the priorities that Roman soldiers should have, points out Caesar. Even if they know everything they hold dear is being destroyed (material-wise), **their main focus should be the battle and to uphold the Roman spirit if [*sic*] *virtus* and *Romanitas*.**

- *An excellent closing sentence that not only concludes the analysis but also introduces a relevant contextual idea beyond the scope of the passages:* Romanitas.

- *Other than the opening sentence, there is little wasted space in the essay: it stays focused on the topic and consistently uses Latin throughout to support its answer.*

- *The Latin used is from both passages and distributed throughout each passage.*

- *The essay shows a precise understanding of the Latin and is able to connect that Latin to the analysis.*

- *The essay organizes its paragraphs around ideas, each paragraph introducing a different analysis of the question and each including Latin from both passages to support that analysis.*

- *The second paragraph has more awkward phrasing than the first paragraph but none of these detract from the overall argument.*

- *From the AP® Report:*[9]

  - *"With 17 different citations and additional use made of some, the amount of Latin used qualifies as copious."*

  - *"The student demonstrates a solid understanding of Roman culture and military practice. For example, 'Even if they know everything they hold dear is being destroyed (material-wise), their main focus should be on the battle and to uphold the Roman spirit of* virtus *and* Romanitas.'"*

Response 2 without commentary; Score: 4/5

- A 4/5

  - … may lack nuance in its analysis but still shows a sound understanding of the Latin

  - … uses Latin that might not be copious enough but is distributed throughout each passage

  - … includes inference but also summary when there should be inference

First Caesar reveals a model soldier with the account of an enemy attack on their fort. In Lines 2–3, Caesar sets the dismal scene with three observations. (*cum ubique flamma*, line 2) reveals that "flames are raging on all sides" ad [*sic*] ("*maximaque telorum multitudine premeretur*" line 2) shows that "they are being pressed by the very greatest multitude of spears." Even with their backs against the walls, these soldiers refuse to back down. Even with all of this going on, the soldiers in Line 4 (*de vallo decederet nemo*) remain in the fight as "no one jumps down from the fortification wall." After this Caesar highlights the fighting style in Line [*sic*] 4 and 5 with the words

---

9. Robert W. Cape Jr., "Report on the 2014 Advanced Placement Latin Examination," *Classical Outlook* 90, no. 3 (2015): 79.

CHAPTER 2

accerrime and *fortissime*. Caesar lauds the soldiers with very fierce and very brave fighting, that followed when they did not abandon their fort. Caesar includes many sentences with the conjunction of *sed* and *tamen* in order to highlight the courage of the soldiers at this instance. This is utilized in the final sentence of the passage from Line [*sic*] 5 to 6 (*Hic dies ... interficeretur*). Caesar begins the sentence by saying that the day was long and very serious. He then adds in *sed* to reveal they wounded and killed the very greatest number of enemies (*maximus interficeretur* Line 6). Caesar writes this section as a guide for being a model soldier. Even though the soldiers were pressed by the enemy, they managed to not give in and then fight very bravely for Rome. Even in Line 1, Caesar opens the selection by telling how this was such great courage of soldiers, with Caesar's favorite words such as *virtus* and compound sentences that show the severity of the situation, Caesar writes a favorable piece on how Roman soldiers should fight. The account of soldiers fighting fiercely with their backs against the walls, reveals Caesar's positive judgement [*sic*] of the soldiers.

However in section 33 of Book five, Caesar is not as praiseworthy of the soldiers' actions. Caesar first begins the selection with a description of a plan the soldiers are following. In Line 1 (*iusserunt ... consisterent*), they ordered by an announcement to leave behind and stand firm on the Earth. The plan is carried out to loosen the load of unneeded items and form a protective post. In Line 3, Caesar explains the results of this plan, as he describes how the soldiers fights [*sic*]. In line 4, Caesar uses such language as "*non sine summo timore*" or not without the greatest fear. Caesar also highlights in the same sentence "*desperatione id factum videbatur*," or "It was seemed to have been done out of desperation." This act leads to their downfall as shown in Line 5 "*ut vulgo milites ab signis discederent*." This phrase, which loosely translates to the "soldiers departed from their signs," this is a cardinal sin in the book of Caesar, as the Standard Bearer is integral for organizing soldiers into the correct formation. Due to the plan and the fear they felt, the soldiers became disorganized, which ultimately led to their downfall. Caesar begins the passage with the plan given to the soldiers at hand and shows the effects. The word placement such as "*timore*" and "*desperatione*" show little grace under pressure. The repetition of the word *accidit*, which means to happen as a slight negative connotation, as he explains the ultimate failures of the soldiers. Due to the discombulation [*sic*] and panic of the soldiers, Caesar chastizes [*sic*] the actions of the soldiers in Section 33.

Response 2 with bulleted commentary (emphasis mine); Score: 4/5

First Caesar reveals a model soldier with the account of an **enemy attack on their fort**.

- *The opening sentence establishes the focus of the paragraph but references only the second passage (the first focuses on a battle away from the fort).*

In Lines 2–3, Caesar sets the dismal scene with three observations. (*cum ubique flamma*, line 2) reveals that "flames are raging on all sides" ad [*sic*] ("*maximaque telorum multitudine premeretur*" line 2) shows that "they are being pressed by the very greatest multitude of spears." Even with their backs against the walls, these soldiers refuse to back down. Even with all of this going on, the soldiers in Line 4 (*de vallo decederet nemo*) remain in the fight as "no one jumps down from the fortification wall."

- *The essay uses Latin well, translating it well and applying it to the focus of the essay.*

After this Caesar highlights the fighting style in Line 4 and 5 **with the words *accerrime* and *fortissime*.** Caesar lauds the soldiers **with very fierce and very brave fighting,** that followed when they did not abandon their fort.

- *The use of* accerrime *and* fortissime *could be more precise: they are relatively easy forms to understand and little is done with them beyond their meaning.*

Caesar **includes many sentences with the conjunction of *sed* and *tamen* in order to highlight the courage of the soldiers** at this instance. This is utilized in the final sentence of the passage from Line 5 to 6 (*Hic dies … interficeretur*). Caesar begins the sentence by saying that the day was long and very serious. **He then adds in *sed* to reveal** they wounded and killed the very greatest number of enemies (*maximus interficeretur* Line 6).

- *The focus on the adversatives (conjunctions that signal a shift in focus)* sed *and* tamen *is an attempt to analyze but one that lacks precision. In the end, there is no real conclusion drawn; the essay summarizes rather than analyzes.*

Caesar writes this section **as a guide for being a model soldier.** Even though the soldiers were pressed by the enemy, they managed to not give in and then fight very bravely for Rome. Even in Line 1, Caesar opens the selection by **telling how this was such great courage of soldiers, with Caesar's favorite words such as *virtus* and compound sentences that show the severity of the situation,** Caesar writes a favorable piece on how Roman soldiers should fight.

- *This section is attempting to analyze (as a guide … soldier) but the writing is less precise. There are no clear ideas or analysis from "telling how … severity of the situation."*

The account of soldiers fighting fiercely with their backs against the walls, **reveals Caesar's positive judgement** [*sic*] of the soldiers.

- *This concluding sentence lacks specificity or punch: "fighting with their backs against the walls" is too cliché and "reveals Caesar's positive judgement" is too imprecise.*

However in section 33 of Book five, Caesar is not as praiseworthy of the soldiers' actions. Caesar first begins the selection with a description of a plan the soldiers are following. In Line 1 (*iusserunt ... consisterent*, they ordered by an announcement to leave behind and **stand firm on the Earth**.

- *This next paragraph opens well enough but a misreading in the translation undermines its effectiveness: "Earth" seems the translation of* orbem, *which should be "circle."*

The plan is carried out to loosen the load of unneeded items and form a protective post. In Line 3, Caesar explains the results of this plan, as he describes how the soldiers fights [*sic*]. In line 4, Caesar uses such language as "*non sine summo timore*" or not without the greatest fear. Caesar also highlights in the same sentence "*desperatione id factum videbatur*," or "It was seemed to have been done out of desperation."

- *Latin here is mentioned and translated correctly but not connected to any analysis.*

This act leads to their downfall as shown in Line 5 "*ut vulgo milites ab signis discederent*." This phrase, which loosely translates to the "soldiers departed **from their signs**," this is a cardinal sin in the book of Caesar, as **the Standard Bearer is integral for organizing soldiers into the correct formation**.

- *The citation of* ab signis *is a good one but its translation and analysis lack precision. Although in the analysis it is referenced as "standard (bearer)," it is translated as "signs." Also, the standards were the representative of a Roman army and to lose them was the most significant disgrace of a Roman army. To focus on military organization and formation is to miss the point of the* signis.

Due to the plan and the fear they felt, the soldiers became disorganized, which ultimately led to their downfall. Caesar begins the passage with the plan given to the soldiers at hand and **shows the effects. The word placement such as "*timore*" and "*desperatione*" show little grace under pressure. The repetition of the word** *accidit*, which means to happen as a **slight negative connotation, as he explains the ultimate failures of the soldiers**.

- *The opening sentence is a good one and hints at potential analysis, but the analysis itself is too vague: word placement is a good way to analyze but nothing specific is said about the word placement. The analysis of* accidit *is similar in that a "negative connotation" is mentioned without any explanation of how it is negative.*

Due to the discombulation [*sic*] and panic of the soldiers, Caesar chastizes [*sic*] the actions of the soldiers in Section 33.

- *A plain, if not ineffective, concluding sentence to the paragraph but without enough specific analysis within the paragraph to make the point convincingly.*

- *Overall, the paragraphs incorporate the Latin well with a few misreadings but a good sense of its meaning and a wide range of it from the passages.*

- *The analysis, however, lacks the focus, consistency, and nuance of the first essay, the 5/5.*

- *From the AP® Report:*[10]

  - *"The student presents a good—though unpolished—analysis of both passages and comments about performance and courage of the soldiers. Draws inferences and conclusions from the Latin about Caesar's judgments."*

  - *"Use of Latin is generally accurate, though not elegant or plentiful."*

  - *"Shows understanding of the overall context of both passages and establishes the terms of analysis at the beginning and at the end, demonstrating critical thinking about the passages before writing."*

  - *"The English style sometimes distracts from the analysis of the Latin. Demonstration of how specific Latin words and phrases support the argument is sometimes imprecise."*

Response 3, without commentary; Score: 2/5
  - A 2/5
    - … uses minimal analysis that may be confusing or relies on summary as well as avoiding parts of the passages or only focusing on one
    - … uses little to no Latin support that may be misunderstood
    - … draws few inferences or makes incorrect assumptions

In the first passage, Caesar details an attack on the Roman army in which the Romans created an "*orbem*" (an orb) (line 1). This made it very easy for the enemy to attack. On the surface it seems that Caesar is praising his army for their bravery. But he says that the "*milites ab signis discederent*" (line 5, they left their signs) and their "*spem minuit*" (line 3, their hope diminished). Clearly, Caesar is unhappy with the performance of his army. Not only do they make a tragic formation mistake, but they do not exhibit the bravery and courage, for which Roman soldiers were known. Caesar tries to cover up the mistake of his men with phrases like "*quod fieri necesse erat*" (lines 4–5, because it was necessary to do) and "*Praetera accidit*" (line 4, after which it happened).

---

10. Robert W. Cape Jr., "Report on the 2014 Advanced Placement Latin Examination," *Classical Outlook* 90, no. 3 (2015): 80.

By using phrases like this Caesar subtly makes what happened not the responsibility of the soldiers or of him, but of the gods and other uncontrollable forces in order to make his army seem better.

Unlike the first passage, Caesar seems to be very happy with the performance of his soldiers in the second passage. He attributes their accomplishments to them rather than an unknown being. Rather than using impersonal verbs Caesar uses 3rd person plural endings throughout the entire passage. Some examples include "*torrerentur,*" "*premerentur,*" "*intellegerent,*" and "*pugnarent.*" In fact in the very first sentence, Caesar makes a direct reference to the soldiers' bravery and spirits ("*tanta militium* [sic] *virtus atque praesentia anima*" line 1). Caesar details how the soldiers were willing to jump straight into the action by "*discederet vallo*" (climbing the rampart into the enemy camp). He shows that Roman soldiers are willing to risk their lives for the cause. Caesar's reaction and commentary to this is a start [sic] contrast to that of the first passage.

Response 3, with commentary; Score: 2/5

In the first passage, Caesar details an attack on the Roman army in which the Romans created an **"*orbem*" (an orb)** (line 1).

- *Only one Latin word is used and it is translated at best awkwardly and at worst incorrectly.*

This made it very easy for the enemy to attack. On the surface it seems that **Caesar is praising his army for their bravery**.

- *There is no evidence provided for this statement.*

But he says that the **"*milites ab signis discederent*" (line 5, they left their signs) and** their "***spem minuit***" **(line 3, their hope diminished)**. Clearly, Caesar is unhappy with the performance of his army. Not only do they make a tragic formation mistake, but they do not exhibit the bravery and courage, for which Roman soldiers were known.

- *There is an attempt at analysis with "not only … were known" but little Latin is used as support and what is used includes the awkward "signs" for* signis *rather than "standards."*

Caesar tries to cover up the mistake of his men with phrases like "*quod fieri necesse erat*" (lines 4–5, because it was necessary to do) and "*Praetera accidit*" (line 4, after which it happened). By using phrases like this **Caesar subtly makes what happened not the responsibility of the soldiers or of him, but of the gods and other uncontrollable forces** in order to make his army seem better.

- *Another attempt at analysis with little Latin to support it. Additionally, the introduction of the gods and "other uncontrollable forces" is not supported by the text and seems a naive attempt to create a conclusion where there is no evidence to support it.*

Unlike the first passage, Caesar seems to be **very happy with the performance of his soldiers in the second passage**.

- *A good, if plainly written, opening sentence.*

He attributes their accomplishments **to them rather than an unknown being**. Rather than using impersonal verbs **Caesar uses 3rd person plural endings throughout the entire passage. Some examples include** "*torrerentur*," "*premerentur*," "*intellegerent*," and "*pugnarent*."

- *The assertion here isn't entirely clear. A reference to the previous paragraph's introduction of the gods is included and the role of 3rd person plural endings isn't explained, with examples included without any analysis.*

In fact in the very first sentence, **Caesar makes a direct reference to the soldiers' bravery and spirits** ("*tanta militium* [sic] *virtus atque praesentia anima*" line 1). Caesar details how the **soldiers were willing to jump straight into the action by "*discederet vallo*" (climbing the rampart into the enemy camp)**. He shows that Roman soldiers are willing to risk their lives for the cause.

- *The opening sentence of this section seems promising: it is specific and seems intended to introduce analysis. The Latin, however, is not used effectively. The first quote does not include a verb and indicates only a keyword understanding: "bravery" and "spirits" are uncontextualized translations of* virtus atque praesentia anima. *And the second quote is misused. The preposition* de *is omitted and it is translated the opposite of what it means.*

Caesar's reaction and commentary to this is a start [*sic*] contrast to that of the first passage.

- *Identifying something as a contrast alone, without any qualification or explanation, is not a sufficient conclusion.*

- *From the AP® Report:*[11]

  - "Weak, somewhat faulty argument about Caesar's judgment of the events/ soldiers' actions. This seems to stem from a general understanding of the contexts of the passages, not from being firmly grounded in the Latin."

---

11. Robert W. Cape Jr., "Report on the 2014 Advanced Placement Latin Examination," *Classical Outlook* 90, no. 3 (2015): 80–81.

- "Some accurate Latin, but many individual words used, some of negligible value to the argument."

2.3.4   LIST OF PREVIOUS ANALYTICAL QUESTIONS

- Only included here are questions from the Caesar-Vergil syllabus, whose first year was 2013.

- 2014 is not included here because it was included in the previous section.

- The questions themselves are bolded and italicized here but will not be on the exam itself.

- Remember that all analytical questions include the following reminder, which will not be repeated for each question:

> BE SURE TO REFER SPECIFICALLY TO THE LATIN THROUGH THE PASSAGES TO SUPPORT THE POINTS YOU MAKE IN YOUR ESSAY. DO NOT SIMPLY SUMMARIZE WHAT THE PASSAGES SAY.
> *(When you are asked to refer specifically to the Latin, you must write out the Latin and/or cite line numbers AND you must translate, accurately paraphrase, or make clear in your discussion that you understand the Latin.)*

2019

A. Caesar, id quod erat suspicatus, aliquid novi a barbaris initum consilii, cohortes quae in stationibus erant secum in eam partem proficisci, ex reliquis duas in stationem cohortes succedere, reliquas armari et confestim sese subsequi iussit. Cum paulo longius a castris processisset, suos ab hostibus premi atque aegre sustinere et conferta legione ex omnibus partibus tela coici animadvertit. Nam quod omni ex reliquis partibus demesso frumento pars una erat reliqua, suspicati hostes huc nostros esse venturos noctu in silvis deliuerant; tum dispersos depositis armis in metendo occupatos subito adorti, paucis interfectis reliquos incertis ordinibus perturbaverant, simul equitatu atque essedis circumdederant. [*Bellum Gallicum* 4.32]

B. Ambiorix pronuntiari iubet ut procul tela coiciant neu propius accedant et, quam in partem Romani impetum fecerint, cedant: levitate armorum et cotidiana exercitatione nihil his noceri posse; rursus se ad signa recipientes insequantur. Quo praecepto ab eis diligentissime observato, cum quaepiam cohors ex orbe excesserat atque impetum fecerat, hostes velocissime refugiebant. Interim eam partem nudari necesse erat et ab latere aperto tela recipi. Rursus cum in eum locum unde erant egressi reverti coeperant, et ab eis qui cesserant et ab eis qui proximi steterant circumveniebantur. Sin autem locum tenere vellent, nec virtuti locus relinquebatur, neque ab tanta multitudine coiecta tela conferti vitare poterant. [*Bellum Gallicum* 5.34–35]

In Passage A, the Britons attack some of Caesar's men, and in Passage B, Ambiorix advances against Cotta's army. In a well-developed essay, analyze the enemy's strategy in each situation.

2018

Quod ubi Caesar animadvertit, naves longas, quarum et species erat barbaris inusitatior et motus ad usum expeditior, paulum removeri ab onerariis navibus et remis incitari et ad latus apertum hostium constitui atque inde fundis, sagittis, tormentis hostes propelli ac submoveri iussit; quae res magno usui nostris fuit. Nam et navium figura et remorum motu et inusitato genere tormentorum permoti barbari constiterunt ac paulum modo pedem rettulerunt. Atque nostris militibus cunctantibus, maxime propter altitudinem maris, qui decimae legionis aquilam ferebat, contestatus deos, ut ea res legioni feliciter eveniret, "Desilite," inquit, "milites, nisi vultis aquilam hostibus prodere; ego certe meum rei publicae atque imperatori officium praestitero." Hoc cum voce magna dixisset, se ex navi proiecit atque in hostes aquilam ferre coepit. [*Bellum Gallicum* 4.25]

> Maximus Ilioneus placido sic pectore coepit:
> "O regina, novam cui condere Iuppiter urbem
> iustitiaque dedit gentes frenare superbas,
> Troes te miseri, ventis maria omnia vecti,
> oramus: prohibe infandos a navibus ignes,
> parce pio generi, et propius res aspice nostras.
> Non nos aut ferro Libycos populare penates
> venimus, aut raptas ad litora vertere praedas;
> non ea vis animo, nec tanta superbia victis.
> …
> Quod genus hoc hominum? Quaeve hunc tam barbara morem
> permittit patria? Hospitio prohibemur harenae;
> bella cient primaque vetant consistere terra.
> Si genus humanum et mortalia temnitis arma,
> at sperate deos memores fandi atque nefandi."
>   [*Aeneid* 1.521–29, 539–43]

In the passages above, Romans and Trojans face difficulties in coming to shore safely. In a well-developed essay, analyze how they each attempt to overcome these difficulties.

2017

Exarsere ignes animo; subit ira cadentem
ulcisci patriam et sceleratas sumere poenas.
"Scilicet haec Spartam incolumis patriasque Mycenas
aspiciet, partoque ibit regina triumpho?
Coniugiumque domumque patres natosque videbit
Iliadum turba et Phrygiis comitata ministris?
Occiderit ferro Priamus? Troia arserit igni?
Dardanium totiens sudarit sanguine litus?
Non ita. Namque etsi nullum memorabile nomen
feminea in poena est, habet haec victoria laudem;
exstinxisse nefas tamen et sumpsisse merentes
laudabor poenas."   [*Aeneid* 2.575–86]

"Infelix Dido, verus mihi nuntius ergo
venerat exstinctam ferroque extrema secutam?
Funeris heu tibi causa fui? Per sidera iuro,
per superos et si qua fides tellure sub ima est,
invitus, regina, tuo de litore cessi.
Sed me iussa deum, quae nunc has ire per umbras,
per loca senta situ cogunt noctemque profundam,
imperiis egere suis; nec credere quivi
hunc tantum tibi me discessu ferre dolorem.
Siste gradum teque aspectu ne subtrahe nostro.
Quem fugis? Extremum fato quod te adloquor hoc est."
          [*Aeneid* 6.456–66]

Aeneas sees Helen in passage (A) and Dido in passage (B). In a well-developed essay, analyze Aeneas' reactions to these encounters.

2016

"Tantane vos generis tenuit fiducia vestri?
Iam caelum terramque meo sine numine, venti,
miscere et tantas audetis tollere moles?
Quos ego—sed motos praestat componere fluctus.
Post mihi non simili poena commissa luetis.
Maturate fugam regique haec dicite vestro:
non illi imperium pelagi saevumque tridentem,
sed mihi sorte datum. Tenet ille immania saxa,
vestras, Eure, domos; illa se iactet in aula
Aeolus et clauso ventorum carcere regnet." [*Aeneid* 1.132–41]

"Iuppiter omnipotens, cui nunc Maurusia pictis
gens epulata toris Lenaeum libat honorem,
aspicis haec? An te, genitor, cum fulmina torques
nequiquam horremus, caecique in nubibus ignes
terrificant animos et inania murmura miscent?
Femina, quae, nostris errans in finibus, urbem
exiguam pretio posuit, cui litus arandum
cuique loci leges dedimus, conubia nostra
reppulit ac dominum Aenean in regna recepit.
Et nunc ille Paris cum semiviro comitatu,
Maeonia mentum mitra crinemque madentem
subnexus, rapto potitur: nos munera templis
quippe tuis ferimus famamque fovemus inanem." [*Aeneid* 4.206–18]

In the passages above, Neptune and Iarbas express indignation at the actions of others who hold different levels of power than they themselves do. In a well-developed essay, analyze how each speaker justifies his feelings to the one(s) he is addressing.

2015

Contra ea Titurius sero facturos clamitabat, cum maiores manus hostium adiunctis Germanis convenissent aut cum aliquid calamitatis in proximis hibernis esset acceptum. Brevem consulendi esse occasionem … Magno esse Germanis dolori Ariovisti mortem et superiores nostras victorias; ardere Galliam tot contumeliis[1] acceptis sub populi Romani imperium redactam,[2] superiore gloria rei militaris exstincta. Postremo quis hoc sibi persuaderet, sine certa re Ambiorigem ad eiusmodi consilium descendisse? Suam sententiam in utramque partem esse tutam: si nihil esset durius, nullo cum periculo ad proximam legionem perventuros: si Gallia omnis cum Germanis consentiret, unam esse in celeritate positam salutem … Si praesens periculum non, at certe longinqua obsidione fames esset timenda? [*Bellum Gallicum* 5.29]

[1] contumelia, -ae, f.: insult   [2] redactam: "brought under"

"O socii (neque enim ignari sumus ante malorum),
o passi graviora, dabit deus his quoque finem.
Vos et Scyllaeam rabiem penitusque sonantes
accestis[1] scopulos, vos et Cyclopia saxa
experti: revocate animos maestumque timorem
mittite; forsan et haec olim meminisse iuvabit.
Per varios casus, per tot discrimina rerum

[1] accestis: "you approached"

tendimus in Latium, sedes ubi fata quietas
ostendunt; illic fas regna resurgere Troiae.
Durate, et vosmet rebus servate secundis."

In the passages above, both Quintus Titurius Sabinus and Aeneas address their men in different situations. In a well-developed essay, analyze the ways in which each speaker tries to persuade his men to take a certain course of action.

_____

2014   [see essay analysis above]

_____

2013

(A)

Caesari cum id nuntiatum esset, eos per provinciam nostram iter facere conari, maturat ab urbe proficisci et quam maximis potest itineribus in Galliam ulteriorem contendit et ad Genavam pervenit. Provinciae toti quam maximum potest militum numeram imperat (erat omnino in Gallia ulteriore legio una), pontem qui erat ad Genavam iubet rescindi … Caesar, quod memoria tenebat L. Cassium consulem occisum exercitumque eius ab Helvetiis pulsum et sub iugum missum, concedendum non putabat; neque homines inimico animo, data facultate per provinciam itineris faciendi, temperaturos ab iniuria et maleficio existimabat. Tamen, ut spatium intercedere posset dum milites quos imperaverat convenirent, legatis respondit diem se ad deliberandum sumpturum. [*Bellum Gallicum* 1.7]

(B)

"Solvite corde metum, Teucri, secludite curas.
Res dura et regni novitas me talia cogunt
moliri et late fines custode tueri.
Quis genus Aeneadum, quis Troiae nesciat urbem,
virtutesque virosque aut tanti incendia belli?
Non obtunsa[1] adeo gestamus pectora Poeni,
nec tam aversus equos Tyria Sol iungit ab urbe.
Seu vos Hesperiam magnam Saturniaque arva,
sive Erycis[2] fines regemque optatis Acesten,
auxilio tutos dimittam opibusque iuvabo.
Vultis et his mecum pariter considere regnis?

[1]tundo, -ere, -tudi. -tunsum: insensible, without feeling   [2]Eryx, -icis. m.: Sicilian king Eryx, brother of Aeneas

Urbem quam statuo vestra est; subducite naves;
Tros Tyriusque mihi nullo discrimine agetur.
Atque utinam rex ipse Noto[3] compulsus eodem
adforet Aeneas! Equidem per litora certos
dimittam et Libyae lustrare extrema iubebo,
si quibus eiectus silvis aut urbibus errat." [*Aeneid* 1.562–78]

[3]Notus, -i, m.: the south wind

In the passages above, Caesar and Dido respond to requests from foreigners to pass through their territories. In a well-developed essay, analyze how both Caesar and Dido reveal their leadership styles in their responses.

2.4　FREE RESPONSE QUESTIONS—SHORT ANSWER

2.4.1　SHORT ANSWER OVERVIEW

- one passage from the Caesar syllabus

- one passage from the Vergil syllabus

- 5–7 questions, called subquestions, per passage that cover (Course Description 155):
  - literal translations
  - scansion (for Vergil)
  - grammatical constructions
  - context
  - connections to the English readings

- The subquestions of the short answer are similar, though not identical, in content to the questions of the multiple choice section.

- 15 minutes for each passage

- Each passage counts for 7.5 percent of the overall grade for 15 percent total.

- Included here are the Short Answer questions from the previous Caesar-Vergil exams.

- Below the questions is a separate section that includes the answers.

- Because these questions are largely objective in nature, the best practice is to become accustomed to the types of questions asked and the preparation necessary to answer them.

- The Short Answer questions will include the following text:
  - Answer the following questions **in English** unless the question specifically asks you to write out Latin words. Number your answer to each question.

- Typically, 1 of the 5–7 subquestions will ask you to write out Latin words to support your answer.

- Typically, the line of scansion from Vergil will contain an elision.

- The line numbers in each question refer to the line numbers from the AP® Exam text; they will not necessarily correspond to the line numbers of the text reproduced here (but will be close, if not correct).

2.4.2   SHORT ANSWER PASSAGES AND QUESTIONS FROM PREVIOUS EXAMS

2019—Question 4

> Qualis apes aestate nova per florea rura
> exercet sub sole labor, cum gentis adultos
> educunt fetus, aut cum liquentia mella
> stipant et dulci distendunt nectare cellas,
> aut onera accipiunt venientum, aut agmine facto
> ignavum fucos pecus a praesepibus arcent:
> fervet opus, redolentque thymo fragrantia mella.
> "O fortunati, quorum iam moenia surgunt!" [*Aeneid* 1.430–37]

1. Name the stylistic device introduced by <u>Qualis</u> (line 1).

2. **(A)** Name **one and only one** of the bees' tasks described in lines 2–5 (<u>cum gentis</u> … <u>venientum</u>). **(B)** Write out the Latin for that task.

3. **(A)** Translate in context <u>agmine facto</u> (line 5) and **(B)** identify the construction.

4. Write out **all** of line 6 (<u>ignavum</u> … <u>arcent</u>) and mark the scansion.

5. In what historical war were the city walls (<u>moenia</u>) mentioned in line 8 destroyed?

6. In Book 12, what Rutulian leader is compared to a lion?

2019—Question 5

Viri, quantas pecunias ab uxoribus dotis nomine acceperunt, tantas ex suis bonis aestimatione facta cum dotibus communicant. Huius omnis pecuniae coniunctim ratio habetur fructusque servantur: uter eorum vita superarit, ad eum pars utriusque cum fructibus superiorum temporum pervenit. Viri in uxores, sicuti in liberos, vitae necisque habent potestatem; et cum pater familiae illustriore loco natus decessit, eius propinqui conveniunt et, de morte si res in suspicionem venit, de uxoribus in servilem modum quaestionem habent. [*Bellum Gallicum* 6.19]

1. Identify the case and number of <u>dotis</u> (line 1).

2. To what custom do lines 1–2 (<u>Viri</u> … <u>communicant</u>) refer?

3. According to lines 3–4 (<u>uter</u> … <u>pervenit</u>), how much of the family's money does the surviving spouse receive?

4. Translate in context <u>vitae necisque habent potestatem</u> (lines 4–5).

5. **(A)** Translate in context <u>illustriore loco natus</u> (line 5) and **(B)** identify the case of <u>loco</u>.

6. According to lines 6–7 (<u>de morte</u> … <u>habent</u>), under what circumstance are Gallic wives treated like Roman slaves?

2018—Question 4

> Cerberus haec ingens latratu regna trifauci
> personat adverso recubans immanis in antro.
> Cui vates horrere videns iam colla colubris
> melle soporatam et medicatis frugibus offam
> obicit. Ille fame rabida tria guttura pandens
> corripit obiectam, atque immania terga resolvit
> fusus humi totoque ingens extenditur antro. [*Aeneid* 6.417–23]

1. Name one and only one characteristic of Cerberus mentioned in lines 1–2 (<u>Cerberus</u> … <u>antro</u>). Write out the specific Latin word or words for that characteristic.

2. Earlier in Book 6, which deity speaks through the Sibyl (<u>vates</u>, line 3)?

3. Translate in context the word <u>videns</u> (line 3) **AND** identify its tense.

4. Write out **all** of line 4 (<u>melle</u> … <u>offam</u>) and mark the scansion.

5. Name **one and only one** thing that Cerberus does in lines 5–7 (<u>Ille</u> … <u>antro</u>).

6. What mythical hero was sent to retrieve Cerberus from the Underworld?

2018—Question 5

In omni Gallia eorum hominum qui aliquo sunt numero atque honore genera sunt duo. Nam plebes paene servorum habetur loco, quae nihil audet per se, nullo adhibetur consilio. Plerique, cum aut aere alieno aut magnitudine tributorum aut iniuria potentiorum premuntur, sese in servitutem dicant nobilibus: in hos eadem omnia sunt iura quae dominis in servos. [*Bellum Gallicum* 6.13]

1. Translate in context the words <u>aliquo numero atque honore</u> (line 1).

2. What Latin word is the antecedent of <u>quae</u> (line 2) ?

3. Name **one and only one** of the circumstances that, according to lines 3–4 (<u>Plerique</u> … <u>nobilibus</u>), force the common people of Gaul to become slaves.

4. Translate in context the word <u>sese</u> (line 3) **AND** identify its case.

5. Identify the case of <u>dominis</u> (line 5).

6. In Roman society, what was a slave called after manumission?

2017—Question 4

> "Heu pietas, heu prisca fides invictaque bello
> dextera! Non illi se quisquam impune tulisset
> obvius armato, seu cum pedes iret in hostem
> seu spumantis equi foderet calcaribus armos.
> Heu, miserande puer, si qua fata aspera rumpas,
> tu Marcellus eris. Manibus date lilia plenis
> purpureos spargam flores animamque nepotis
> his saltem accumulem donis, et fungar inani
> munere." [*Aeneid* 6.878–86]

1. Who is the speaker of the lines above?

2. In lines 1–2 (<u>Heu</u> … <u>dextera</u>), the speaker lists characteristics of Marcellus. Name **one and only one** of these characteristics. Write out the specific Latin word or words for that characteristic.

3. What are the tense and mood of the verb <u>tulisset</u> (line 2)?

4. Write out and scan **all** of line 3 (<u>obvius</u> … <u>hostem</u>).

5. Translate in context the words <u>miserande puer</u> (line 5) **AND** identify the case.

6. In which Roman ritual would the actions described in lines 6–9 (<u>Manibus</u> … <u>munere</u>) be appropriate?

2017—Question 5

> Caesar, quod memoria tenebat L. Cassium consulem occisum exercitumque eius ab Helvetiis pulsum et sub iugum missum, concedendum non putabat; neque homines inimico animo, data facultate per provinciam itineris faciendi, temperaturos ab iniuria et maleficio existimabat. Tamen, ut spatium intercedere posset dum milites quos imperaverat convenirent, legatis respondit diem se ad deliberandum sumpturum: si quid vellent, ad Id. April. reverterentur. [*Bellum Gallicum* 1.7]

1. Translate in context the phrase <u>memoria tenebat</u> (line 1).

2. Under what circumstances in war does the ritual indicated by the phrase <u>sub iugum missum</u> (line 2) occur?

3. Translate <u>data facultate</u> (line 3) **AND** identify the grammatical construction.

4. According to lines 2–4 (<u>neque homines</u> … <u>existimabat</u>), why did Caesar not want to grant the Helvetii's request?

5. According to lines 4–5 (<u>Tamen</u> … <u>convenirent</u>), why does Caesar want a delay?

6. Later in Book 1, where does Caesar send the Helvetii after he defeats them?

2016—Question 4

> Primus ibi ante omnes magna comitante caterva
> Laocoon ardens summa decurrit ab arce,
> et procul "O miseri, quae tanta insania, cives?
> Creditis avectos hostes? Aut ulla putatis
> dona carere dolis Danaum? Sic notus Ulixes?
> Aut hoc inclusi ligno occultantur Achivi,
> aut haec in nostros fabricata est machina muros." [*Aeneid* 2.40–46]

1. Translate <u>magna comitante caterva</u> (line 1) in context **AND** name the grammatical construction.

2. According to line 2 (<u>Laocoon</u> … <u>arce</u>), what is Laocoon's state of mind?

3. To what proposed action of the Trojans does <u>insania</u> (line 3) refer?

4. Write out and scan **all** of line 4 (<u>Creditis</u> … <u>putatis</u>).

5. Identify the case of <u>dolis</u> (line 5).

6. Name a stylistic device that occurs in line 6 (<u>Aut</u> … <u>Achivi</u>). **Write out** the specific Latin word or words that illustrate that figure.

2016—Question 5

Deum maxime Mercurium colunt. Huius sunt plurima simulacra, hunc omnium inventorem artium ferunt, hunc viarum atque itinerum ducem, hunc ad quaestus pecuniae mercaturasque habere vim maximam arbitrantur. Post hunc Apollinem et Martem et Iovem et Minervam. De his eandem fere quam reliquae gentes habent opinionem: Apollinem morbos depellere, Minervam operum atque artificiorum initia tradere, Iovem imperium caelestium tenere, Martem bella regere. Huic, cum proelio dimicare constituerunt, ea quae bello ceperint plerumque devovent. [*Bellum Gallicum* 6.17]

1. Identify **one and only one** of Mercury's roles described in lines 1–3 (hunc omnium … arbitrantur). **Write out** the specific Latin word or words for that role.

2. Translate ferunt (line 2) in context.

3. According to lines 4–5 (De his … opinionem), how do the Gauls' beliefs about the gods compare with those of other peoples?

4. According to Roman belief, Apollo is a god of many things other than healing. Name **one and only one** of these things.

5. Translate the words cum constituerunt (lines 6–7) **AND** identify the mood of constituerunt.

6. Later in Book 6, Caesar describes the religious beliefs of another people. Name that people.

CHAPTER 2

2015—Question 4

"Tempus erat quo prima quies mortalibus aegris
incipit et dono divum gratissima serpit.
In somnis, ecce, ante oculos maestissimus Hector
visus adesse mihi largosque effundere fletus,
raptatus bigis ut quondam, aterque cruento
pulvere perque pedes traiectus lora tumentes." [*Aeneid* 2.268–73]

1. Name the speaker of these words.

2. Identify the case of divum (line 2).

3. Accurately write out and scan **all** of line 3 (In somnis … Hector).

4. Translate in context the word fletus (line 4) **AND** identify its case.

5. Name **one and only one** aspect of Hector's physical appearance described in lines 5–6 (aterque … tumentes).

6. What decisive event prompted Hector's visit?

7. According to what is described in Book 1, who dragged Hector's body around the walls of Troy three times?

2015—Question 5

Apud Helvetios longe nobilissimus fuit et ditissimus Orgetorix. Is, M. Messala et M. Pupio Pisone consulibus, regni cupiditate inductus coniurationem nobilitatis fecit et civitati persuasit ut de finibus suis cum omnibus copiis exirent: perfacile esse, cum virtute omnibus praestarent, totius Galliae imperio potiri. [*Bellum Gallicum* 1.2]

1. Translate in context the word <u>ditissimus</u> (line 1).

2. Based on your knowledge of Roman history, what was the usual length of time in office for a consul serving in Rome in the Roman Republic?

3. Translate <u>ut de finibus suis exirent</u> (line 3) **AND** identify the type of subjunctive clause.

4. Identify the case of <u>omnibus in cum virtute omnibus praestarent</u> (lines 3–4).

5. According to lines 3–4 (<u>perfacile</u> … <u>potiri</u>), what was Orgetorix's goal?

6. Later in Book 1, which Gallic chieftain intercedes on behalf of the Helvetii in support of their migration?

2014—Question 4

> Instamus tamen immemores caecique furore
> et monstrum infelix sacrata sistimus arce.
> Tunc etiam fatis aperit Cassandra futuris
> ora dei iussu non umquam credita Teucris.
> Nos delubra deum miseri, quibus ultimus esset
> ille dies, festa velamus fronde per urbem. [*Aeneid* 2.244–49]

1. Translate <u>immemores caecique furore</u> (line 1) **AND** identify the use of the ablative in <u>furore</u>.

2. To what specifically does <u>monstrum infelix</u> (line 2) refer?

3. Accurately write out and **scan** all of line 2 (<u>et monstrum</u> … <u>arce</u>).

4. To whom specifically does <u>quibus</u> (line 5) refer?

5. What activity is described in lines 5–6 (<u>Nos</u> … <u>urbem</u>)?

6. In Book 1, Cupid is sent in disguise into the city of Carthage. What is his mission there?

2014—Question 5

Moribus suis Orgetorigem ex vinclis causam dicere coegerunt. Damnatum poenam sequi oportebat ut igni cremaretur. Die constituta causae dictionis Orgetorix ad iudicium omnem suam familiam ad hominum milia decem undique coegit, et omnes clientes obaeratosque suos, quorum magnum numerum habebat, eodem conduxit: per eos, ne causam diceret, se eripuit. Cum civitas ob eam rem incitata armis ius suum exsequi conaretur, multitudinemque hominum ex agris magistratus cogerent, Orgetorix mortuus est; neque abest suspicio, ut Helvetii arbitrantur, quin ipse sibi mortem consciverit. [*Bellum Gallicum* 1.4]

1. According to line 1 (<u>Moribus</u> … <u>coegerunt</u>), why was Orgetorix forced to plead his case in chains?

2. According to lines 1–2 (<u>Damnatum</u> … <u>cremaretur</u>), what was the specific punishment if Orgetorix lost the case?

3. Name **one and only one** group mentioned in lines 2–4 (<u>Orgetorix</u> … <u>conduxit</u>) that helped Orgetorix to escape.

4. Translate <u>ne causam diceret</u> (line 5) as literally as possible **AND** identify the type of ne-clause.

5. According to lines 7–8 (<u>neque abest</u> … <u>consciverit</u>), what was suspected about Orgetorix's death? Write out the Latin that supports your answer.

6. Later in Book 1, what is **one and only one** strategy that Caesar uses to prevent the migration of the Helvetii?

CHAPTER 2

2013—Question 4

> At vero Aeneas aspectu obmutuit amens,
> arrectaeque horrore comae et vox faucibus haesit.
> Ardet abire fuga dulcesque relinquere terras,
> attonitus tanto monitu imperioque deorum.
> Heu quid agat? Quo nunc reginam ambire furentem
> audeat adfatu? Quae prima exordia sumat? [*Aeneid* 4.279–84]

1. To what or whom is Aeneas reacting?

2. According to lines 1–2 (<u>At</u> … <u>haesit</u>), what is one physical effect of Aeneas' reaction? Write out the Latin to support your answer.

3. Translate <u>fuga</u> (line 3) and identify the case.

4. Accurately write out the Latin of line 4 (<u>attonitus</u> … <u>deorum</u>) and scan the line.

5. In lines 5–6 (<u>Heu</u> … <u>sumat</u>), Aeneas asks himself three questions. What is one of these questions?

6. Later in the *Aeneid*, what is one way by which Dido tries to prevent Aeneas from <u>dulcesque relinquere terras</u> (line 3)?

2013—Question 5

> His rebus adducti et auctoritate Orgetorigis permoti constituerunt ea quae ad proficiscendum pertinerent comparare, iumentorum et carrorum quam maximum numerum coemere, sementes quam maximas facere ut in itinere copia frumenti suppeteret, cum proximis civitatibus pacem et amicitiam confirmare. Ad eas res conficiendas biennium sibi satis esse duxerunt: in tertium annum profectionem lege confirmant. Ad eas res conficiendas Orgetorix deligitur. Is sibi legationem ad civitates suscepit. [*Bellum Gallicum* 1.3]

1. In lines 1–2 (<u>constituerunt</u> … <u>comparare</u>), what do the Helvetii decide to do?

2. Identify the grammatical construction of <u>ut</u> … <u>suppeteret</u> (line 3).

3. According to lines 4–5 (<u>Ad</u> … <u>duxerunt</u>), how much time did the Helvetii estimate it would take them to get ready?

4. Translate the phrase <u>Ad eas res conficiendas</u> (line 4) and identify the verb form of <u>conficiendas</u>.

5. To whom does <u>sibi</u> (line 6) refer?

6. What is one reason Caesar gives later in the *Bellum Gallicum* for attacking the Helvetii?

2.4.3   ANSWERS TO SHORT ANSWER PASSAGES AND QUESTIONS FROM PREVIOUS EXAMS

2019—Question 4

> Qualis apes aestate nova per florea rura
> exercet sub sole labor, cum gentis adultos
> educunt fetus, aut cum liquentia mella
> stipant et dulci distendunt nectare cellas,
> aut onera accipiunt venientum, aut agmine facto
> ignavum fucos pecus a praesepibus arcent:
> fervet opus, redolentque thymo fragrantia mella.
> "O fortunati, quorum iam moenia surgunt!" [*Aeneid* 1.430–37]

1. Name the stylistic device introduced by <u>Qualis</u> (line 1).

   - **simile**

2. **(A)** Name **one and only one** of the bees' tasks described in lines 2–5 (<u>cum gentis</u> … <u>venientum</u>). **(B)** Write out the Latin for that task.

   - **bring out the mature young bees (*adultos educunt fetus*); press / stamp down liquid / flowing honey (*liquentia mella stipant*); stretch the cells (of the hive) with sweet nectar (*distendunt nectare cellas*); receive the loads of the arriving bees (*onera accipiunt venientum*)**

3. **(A)** Translate in context <u>agmine facto</u> (line 5) and **(B)** identify the construction.

    - with their battle line formed: ablative absolute

4. Write out **all** of line 6 (<u>ignavum</u> … <u>arcent</u>) and mark the scansion.

    - ignavum fucos pecus a praesepibus arcent:

       - ‐ | ‐ ‐ | ‐ ˘ ˘ | ‐ ‐ | ‐ ˘ ˘ | ‐ ‐

5. In what historical war were the city walls (<u>moenia</u>) mentioned in line 8 destroyed?

    - Punic Wars

6. In Book 12, what Rutulian leader is compared to a lion?

    - Turnus

2019—Question 5

Viri, quantas pecunias ab uxoribus dotis nomine acceperunt, tantas ex suis bonis aestimatione facta cum dotibus communicant. Huius omnis pecuniae coniunctim ratio habetur fructusque servantur: uter eorum vita superarit, ad eum pars utriusque cum fructibus superiorum temporum pervenit. Viri in uxores, sicuti in liberos, vitae necisque habent potestatem; et cum pater familiae illustriore loco natus decessit, eius propinqui conveniunt et, de morte si res in suspicionem venit, de uxoribus in servilem modum quaestionem habent. [*Bellum Gallicum* 6.19]

1. Identify the case and number of <u>dotis</u> (line 1).

    - genitive singular *[this question caused difficulty among students]*

2. To what custom do lines 1–2 (<u>Viri</u> … <u>communicant</u>) refer?

    - The husband and wife contribute to a shared account: the wife contributes her dowry and the husband the same amount from his own property. *[accepted responses did not require technical knowledge of dowries but rather an awareness of the combination of husband and wife's finances]*

3. According to lines 3–4 (<u>uter</u> … <u>pervenit</u>), how much of the family's money does the surviving spouse receive?

    - the accumulated wealth of the joint account (the wife's original dowry and the husband's original matching amount), plus any interest that has accrued *[similar to question #2, descriptive responses that showed an understanding of the Latin, without technical knowledge of the precise terminology, were accepted]*

4. Translate in context <u>vitae necisque habent potestatem</u> (lines 4–5).

    - husbands have power of life and death (over their wives and children)

5. **(A)** Translate in context <u>illustriore loco natus</u> (line 5) and **(B)** identify the case of <u>loco</u>.

    - A. born in a more distinguished station / class
    - B. ablative

6. According to lines 5–6 (de morte … habent), under what circumstance are Gallic wives treated like Roman slaves?

    - If there is a suspicion about how their husbands died, the wives are questioned under torture in the same way that slaves are questioned under torture.

2018—Question 4

> Cerberus haec ingens latratu regna trifauci
> personat adverso recubans immanis in antro.
> Cui vates horrere videns iam colla colubris
> melle soporatam et medicatis frugibus offam
> obicit. Ille fame rabida tria guttura pandens
> corripit obiectam, atque immania terga resolvit
> fusus humi totoque ingens extenditur antro. [*Aeneid* 6.417–23]

1. Name **one and only one** characteristic of Cerberus mentioned in lines 1–2 (Cerberus … antro). Write out the specific Latin word or words for that characteristic.

    - huge—*ingens*; three-throated barking—*latratu trifauci*; crouching—*recubans*; immense—*immanis*

2. Earlier in Book 6, which deity speaks through the Sibyl (vates, line 3)?

    - Apollo

3. Translate in context the word videns (line 3) **AND** identify its tense.

    - seeing; present

4. Write out **all** of line 4 (melle … offam) and mark the scansion.

    - melle soporatam et medicatis frugibus offam
    - ˘ ˘ | - - | — — ˘ ˘ | - - | - ˘ ˘ | - -

5. Name one and only one thing that Cerberus does in lines 5–7 (Ille … antro).

    - revealing his three throats; grabbed food having been tossed; turned his huge back; stretched himself out on the ground; having been spread through the whole cave

6. What mythical hero was sent to retrieve Cerberus from the Underworld?

    - Hercules

2018—Question 5

In omni Gallia eorum hominum qui aliquo sunt numero atque honore genera sunt duo. Nam plebes paene servorum habetur loco, quae nihil audet per se, nullo adhibetur consilio. Plerique, cum aut aere alieno aut magnitudine tributorum aut iniuria potentiorum premuntur, sese in servitutem dicant nobilibus: in hos eadem omnia sunt iura quae dominis in servos. [*Bellum Gallicum* 6.13]

1. Translate in context the words <u>aliquo numero atque honore</u> (line 1).

    - of some rank and worth

2. What Latin word is the antecedent of <u>quae</u> (line 2)?

    - plebes

3. Name **one and only one** of the circumstances that, according to lines 3–4 (<u>Plerique</u> … <u>nobilibus</u>), force the common people of Gaul to become slaves.

    - debt; large tribute; oppression of more powerful people

4. Translate in context the word <u>sese</u> (line 4) **AND** identify its case.

    - themselves; accusative

5. Identify the case of <u>dominis</u> (line 5).

    - dative

6. In Roman society, what was a slave called after manumission?

    - freedman

2017—Question 4

> "Heu pietas, heu prisca fides invictaque bello
> dextera! Non illi se quisquam impune tulisset
> obvius armato, seu cum pedes iret in hostem
> seu spumantis equi foderet calcaribus armos.
> Heu, miserande puer, si qua fata aspera rumpas,
> tu Marcellus eris. Manibus date lilia plenis
> purpureos spargam flores animamque nepotis
> his saltem accumulem donis, et fungar inani
> munere." [*Aeneid* 6. 878–86]

1. Who is the speaker of the lines above?

    - Anchises

2. In lines 1–2 (<u>Heu</u> … <u>dextera</u>), the speaker lists characteristics of Marcellus. Name **one and only one** of these characteristics. Write out the specific Latin word or words for that characteristic.

    - loyalty—*pietas*; ancient trust—*prisca fides*; unconquered right hand—*invicta dextera*

3. What are the tense and mood of the verb <u>tulisset</u> (line 2)?

    - pluperfect subjunctive

4. Write out and scan **all** of line 3 (<u>obvius</u> … <u>hostem</u>).

   - obvius armato, seu cum pedes iret in hostem

   ¯ ˘˘| ¯ ¯|¯ ¯| ¯ ¯ ˘ ˘|¯ ˘ ˘| ¯ ¯

5. Translate in context the words <u>miserande puer</u> (line 5) **AND** identify the case.

   - pitiable boy; vocative

6. In which Roman ritual would the actions described in lines 6–9 (<u>Manibus</u> … <u>munere</u>) be appropriate?

   - funeral

2017—Question 5

Caesar, quod memoria tenebat L. Cassium consulem occisum exercitumque eius ab Helvetiis pulsum et sub iugum missum, concedendum non putabat; neque homines inimico animo, data facultate per provinciam itineris faciendi, temperaturos ab iniuria et maleficio existimabat. Tamen, ut spatium intercedere posset dum milites quos imperaverat convenirent, legatis respondit diem se ad deliberandum sumpturum: si quid vellent, ad Id. April. reverterentur. [*Bellum Gallicum* 1.7]

1. Translate in context the phrase <u>memoria tenebat</u> (line 1).

   - he was holding in memory / he was remembering

2. Under what circumstances in war does the ritual indicated by the phrase <u>sub iugum missum</u> (line 2) occur?

   - the defeat of a people

3. Translate <u>data facultate</u> (line 3) **AND** identify the grammatical construction.

   - with help having been given; ablative absolute

4. According to lines 2–4 (<u>neque homines</u> … <u>existimabat</u>), why did Caesar not want to grant the Helvetii's request?

   - insult and ill-intent

5. According to lines 4–5 (<u>Tamen</u> … <u>convenirent</u>), why does Caesar want a delay?

   - to wait for his soldiers

6. Later in Book 1, where does Caesar send the Helvetii after he defeats them?

   - Spain

2016—Question 4

Primus ibi ante omnes magna comitante caterva
Laocoon ardens summa decurrit ab arce,

et procul "O miseri, quae tanta insania, cives?
Creditis avectos hostes? Aut ulla putatis
dona carere dolis Danaum? Sic notus Ulixes?
Aut hoc inclusi ligno occultantur Achivi,
aut haec in nostros fabricata est machina muros." [*Aeneid* 2.40–46]

1. Translate <u>magna comitante caterva</u> (line 1) in context **AND** name the grammatical construction.

     - with a large band accompanying; ablative absolute

2. According to line 2 (<u>Laocoon</u> … <u>arce</u>), what is Laocoon's state of mind?

     - burning

3. To what proposed action of the Trojans does <u>insania</u> (line 3) refer?

     - taking the horse into the city

4. Write out and scan **all** of line 4 (<u>Creditis</u> … <u>putatis</u>).

     - Creditis avectos hostes? Aut ulla putatis
     - ˘ ˘ | - - |- - - | - - | - ˘ ˘ ˘ | - -

5. Identify the case of <u>dolis</u> (line 5).

     - ablative

6. Name a stylistic device that occurs in line 6 (<u>Aut</u> … <u>Achivi</u>). **Write out** the specific Latin word or words that illustrate that figure.

     - metonymy—*ligno*; word picture—*hoc inclusi ligno*; synchesis—*hoc inclusi ligno Achivi*

2016—Question 5

Deum maxime Mercurium colunt. Huius sunt plurima simulacra, hunc omnium inventorem artium ferunt, hunc viarum atque itinerum ducem, hunc ad quaestus pecuniae mercaturasque habere vim maximam arbitrantur. Post hunc Apollinem et Martem et Iovem et Minervam. De his eandem fere quam reliquae gentes habent opinionem: Apollinem morbos depellere, Minervam operum atque artificiorum initia tradere, Iovem imperium caelestium tenere, Martem bella regere. Huic, cum proelio dimicare constituerunt, ea quae bello ceperint plerumque devovent. [*Bellum Gallicum* 6.17]

1. Identify **one and only one** of Mercury's roles described in lines 1–3 (<u>hunc omnium</u> … <u>arbitrantur</u>). **Write out** the specific Latin word or words for that role.

     - inventor of all arts—*omnium inventorem artium*; guide of roads and journeys—*viarum atque itinerum ducem*; patron of trade and commerce—*ad quaestus pecuniae mercaturasque vim maximam*

2. Translate <u>ferunt</u> (line 2) in context.

     - they say

3. According to lines 4–5 (<u>De his</u> … <u>opinionem</u>), how do the Gauls' beliefs about the gods compare with those of other peoples?

   - almost the same

4. According to Roman belief, Apollo is a god of many things other than healing. Name **one and only one** of these things.

   - medicine, art, poetry, sun, music, light, prophecy

5. Translate the words <u>cum constituerunt</u> (lines 6–7) **AND** identify the mood of <u>constituerunt</u>.

   - when they decided; indicative

6. Later in Book 6, Caesar describes the religious beliefs of another people. Name that people.

   - the Germans

2015—Question 4

"Tempus erat quo prima quies mortalibus aegris
incipit et dono divum gratissima serpit.
In somnis, ecce, ante oculos maestissimus Hector
visus adesse mihi largosque effundere fletus,
raptatus bigis ut quondam, aterque cruento
pulvere perque pedes traiectus lora tumentes." [*Aeneid* 2.268-73]

1. Name the speaker of these words.

   - Aeneas

2. Identify the case of <u>divum</u> (line 2).

   - genitive

3. Accurately write out and scan **all** of line 3 (<u>In somnis</u> … <u>Hector</u>).

   - In somnis, ecce, ante oculos maestissimus Hector

   - - | - - | — ˘ ˘ | - - | - ˘ ˘ | - -

4. Translate in context the word <u>fletus</u> (line 4) **AND** identify its case.

   - tears; accusative

5. Name **one and only one** aspect of Hector's physical appearance described in lines 5–6 (<u>ater-que</u> … <u>tumentes</u>).

   - dark from bloody dust; pierced through swollen feet

6. What decisive event prompted Hector's visit?

   - fall of Troy

7. According to what is described in Book 1, who dragged Hector's body around the walls of Troy three times?

   - Achilles

2015—Question 5

> Apud Helvetios longe nobilissimus fuit et ditissimus Orgetorix. Is, M. Messala et M. Pupio Pisone consulibus, regni cupiditate inductus coniurationem nobilitatis fecit et civitati persuasit ut de finibus suis cum omnibus copiis exirent: perfacile esse, cum virtute omnibus praestarent, totius Galliae imperio potiri. [*Bellum Gallicum* 1.2]

1. Translate in context the word <u>ditissimus</u> (line 1).

    - wealthiest

2. Based on your knowledge of Roman history, what was the usual length of time in office for a consul serving in Rome in the Roman Republic?

    - one year

3. Translate <u>ut de finibus suis exirent</u> (line 3) **AND** identify the type of subjunctive clause.

    - to leave from their borders; indirect command or purpose clause

4. Identify the case of <u>omnibus</u> in <u>cum virtute omnibus praestarent</u> (lines 3–4).

    - dative

5. According to lines 3–4 (<u>perfacile</u> … <u>potiri</u>), what was Orgetorix's goal?

    - to assume power over all of Gaul

6. Later in Book 1, which Gallic chieftain intercedes on behalf of the Helvetii in support of their migration?

    - Dumnorix; Divico; Verucloetius; Nammeius

2014—Question 4

> Instamus tamen immemores caecique furore
> et monstrum infelix sacrata sistimus arce.
> Tunc etiam fatis aperit Cassandra futuris
> ora dei iussu non umquam credita Teucris.
> Nos delubra deum miseri, quibus ultimus esset
> ille dies, festa velamus fronde per urbem. [*Aeneid* 2.244–49]

1. Translate <u>immemores caecique furore</u> (line 1) **AND** identify the use of the ablative in <u>furore</u>.

    - forgetting and blind with fury; ablative of cause or means

2. To what specifically does <u>monstrum infelix</u> (line 2) refer?

    - Trojan Horse

3. Accurately write out and **scan** all of line 2 (<u>et monstrum</u> … <u>arce</u>).

    - et monstrum infelix sacrata sistimus arce

    ‾ ‿ ‿ | ‾‾ ‾|‿ ‾|‿ ‿|‾ ‿ ‿|‾ ‿

4. To whom specifically does <u>quibus</u> (line 5) refer?

     - Trojans

5. What activity is described in lines 5–6 (<u>Nos</u> … <u>urbem</u>)?

     - celebration

6. In Book 1, Cupid is sent in disguise into the city of Carthage. What is his mission there?

     - to help Dido fall in love with Aeneas or to protect Aeneas or to make the Carthaginians welcoming to the Trojans

2014—Question 5

Moribus suis Orgetorigem ex vinclis causam dicere coegerunt. Damnatum poenam sequi oportebat ut igni cremaretur. Die constituta causae dictionis Orgetorix ad iudicium omnem suam familiam ad hominum milia decem undique coegit, et omnes clientes obaeratosque suos, quorum magnum numerum habebat, eodem conduxit: per eos, ne causam diceret, se eripuit. Cum civitas ob eam rem incitata armis ius suum exsequi conaretur, multitudinemque hominum ex agris magistratus cogerent, Orgetorix mortuus est; neque abest suspicio, ut Helvetii arbitrantur, quin ipse sibi mortem consciverit. [*Bellum Gallicum* 1.4]

1. According to line 1 (<u>Moribus</u> … <u>coegerunt</u>), why was Orgetorix forced to plead his case in chains?

     - it was customary

2. According to lines 1–2 (<u>Damnatum</u> … <u>cremaretur</u>), what was the specific punishment if Orgetorix lost the case?

     - burned to death

3. Name **one and only one** group mentioned in lines 2–4 (<u>Orgetorix</u> … <u>conduxit</u>) that helped Orgetorix to escape.

     - dependents, up to 10,000 men; clients; those that owe him money

4. Translate <u>ne causam diceret</u> (line 5) as literally as possible **AND** identify the type of ne-clause.

     - so that he didn't have to plead his case; purpose clause

5. According to lines 7–8 (<u>neque abest</u> … <u>consciverit</u>), what was suspected about Orgetorix's death? Write out the Latin that supports your answer.

     - that he committed suicide—*ipse sibi mortem consciverit*

6. Later in Book 1, what is **one and only one** strategy that Caesar uses to prevent the migration of the Helvetii?

     - stalls for time to organize his troops; fortifies Geneva; dismantles the bridge to Geneva; forbids them from entering Roman territory

2013—Question 4

> At vero Aeneas aspectu obmutuit amens,
> arrectaeque horrore comae et vox faucibus haesit.
> Ardet abire fuga dulcesque relinquere terras,
> attonitus tanto monitu imperioque deorum.
> Heu quid agat? Quo nunc reginam ambire furentem
> audeat adfatu? Quae prima exordia sumat? [*Aeneid* 4.279–84]

1. To what or whom is Aeneas reacting?

    - **the appearance of Mercury**

2. According to lines 1–2 (<u>At</u> … <u>haesit</u>), what is one physical effect of Aeneas' reaction? Write out the Latin to support your answer.

    - **grows silent—*obmutuit*; hair on end—*arrectae comae*; voice stuck in throat—*vox faucibus haesit***

3. Translate <u>fuga</u> (line 3) and identify the case.

    - **fleeing; ablative**

4. Accurately write out the Latin of line 4 (<u>attonitus</u> … <u>deorum</u>) and scan the line.

    - **attonitus tanto monitu imperioque deorum**

5. In lines 5–6 (<u>Heu</u> … <u>sumat</u>), Aeneas asks himself three questions. What is one of these questions?

    - **what should he do; how can he approach the crazed queen; how should he begin what he says**

6. Later in the *Aeneid*, what is one way by which Dido tries to prevent Aeneas from <u>dulcesque relinquere terras</u> (line 3)?

    - **invokes their marriage; expresses concern about him traveling in winter; cites the threats to her if he leaves; asks Anna to approach him**

2013—Question 5

> His rebus adducti et auctoritate Orgetorigis permoti constituerunt ea quae ad proficiscendum pertinerent comparare, iumentorum et carrorum quam maximum numerum coemere, sementes quam maximas facere ut in itinere copia frumenti suppeteret, cum proximis civitatibus pacem et amicitiam confirmare. Ad eas res conficiendas biennium sibi satis esse duxerunt: in tertium annum profectionem lege confirmant. Ad eas res conficiendas Orgetorix deligitur. Is sibi legationem ad civitates suscepit. [*Bellum Gallicum* 1.3]

1. In lines 1–2 (<u>constituerunt</u> … <u>comparare</u>), what do the Helvetii decide to do?

    - **to get ready the things they need to leave**

2. Identify the grammatical construction of <u>ut</u> ... <u>suppeteret</u> (line 3).

   - purpose clause

3. According to lines 4–5 (<u>Ad</u> ... <u>duxerunt</u>), how much time did the Helvetii estimate it would take them to get ready?

   - two years

4. Translate the phrase <u>Ad eas res conficiendas</u> (line 4) and identify the verb form of <u>conficiendas</u>.

   - for the purpose of completing these things; gerundive / future passive participle

5. To whom does <u>sibi</u> (line 6) refer?

   - Orgetorix

6. What is one reason Caesar gives later in the *Bellum Gallicum* for attacking the Helvetii?

   - The Helvetii couldn't be trusted; death of consul Lucius Cassius; capture of Roman army; entered Roman territory without permission; control of Gaul and/or Gallic tribes; self-defense

Chapter 3

GLOSSARY OF PROPER NAMES

- This glossary only includes names from the Latin syllabus; names that appear only in the English portion of the syllabus do not appear here.

- Use this glossary to study and keep track of the proper names that appear in each text.

- Such proper names are important because they can provide useful background information for analyzing a text and they can help you contextualize an otherwise isolated or unidentified passage; for example, in Caesar the names of the gods only appear in 6.17.

- Use this glossary also for grammatical information: you may already know who Caesar is but it is as important to remember that the Latin word *Caesar* is a 3rd declension noun whose genitive is *Caesaris* or that the Latin word *Aeneas* is a 1st declension masculine noun: *Aeneas, Aeneae*.

- Reference words appear as they appear in the text; for example, Caesar appears as Caesar rather than Gaius Julius Caesar because his full name is not used in the text; full names will be included in the definition.

- Different incarnations of the same place are combined; for example, Gaul and Troy appear as the place (*Gallia, -ae; Troia, -ae*), the people (*Galli, -orum; Troiani, -orum*), and the adjective (*Gallus, -a, -um; Troianus, -a, -um*). All three are combined in the glossary and the different Latin forms will be explained in the definition.

- The grammar of any non-obvious names will be explained; for example, Ariovistus is not explained because the -us ending is self-explanatory as a 2nd declension noun, while Catamantaloedis is explained because its nominative, genitive, and declension are not immediately apparent.

- The number in parentheses indicates how many times each proper name appears in the Latin selections of the syllabus.

- Both people and places are included together.

3.1 CAESAR PROPER NAME GLOSSARY

- Lists organized by type, for example, rivers, cities, and so on, are provided before the glossary with a map.

o   Use the maps as quizzes: can you identify in which episode each city appears? And then use the glossary to check yourself.

• Proper names with a cross (†) are not included on the map.

• Summary lists that organize by people, geographic feature, and frequency of occurrence appear before the glossary; use these to organize and focus your study, for example, Ambiorix appears 15 times in the Latin syllabus and so it is more important to know about him than, say, A. Gabinius, who appears only once.

• The names Gaius and Gnaeus are abbreviated C. and Cn., even when spelled out Gaius and Gnaeus. That convention is followed here.

TOPOGRAPHICAL FEATURES

RIVERS

Garumna (Garonne)
Matrona (Marne)
Mosa (Meuse)
†Padus (Po)
Rhenus (Rhine)
Rhodanus (Rhone)
Sequana (Seine)

MOUNTAINS

Iura (Jura)
Pyrenees

OTHER

(Lake) Lemannus
Oceanus

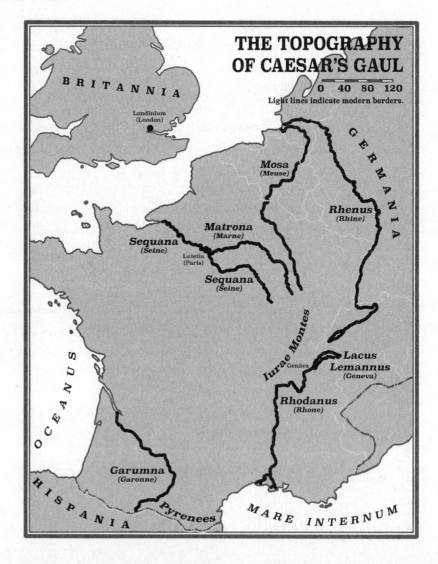

PEOPLES

Aduatuci	Ceutrones	Levaci
Aedui	Eburones	Morini
Allobroges	Esubii	Nervii
Aquitani	Geidumni	Pleumoxi
Atrebates	Germani	Raurici
Belgae	†Graeci	Remi
Bellovaci	Grudii	Sequani
Boii	Helvetii	Treveri
Carnutes	Latobrigi	Tulingi
†Celtae		

CITIES

Genava (Geneva)
†Noreia
Samarobriva (Amiens)

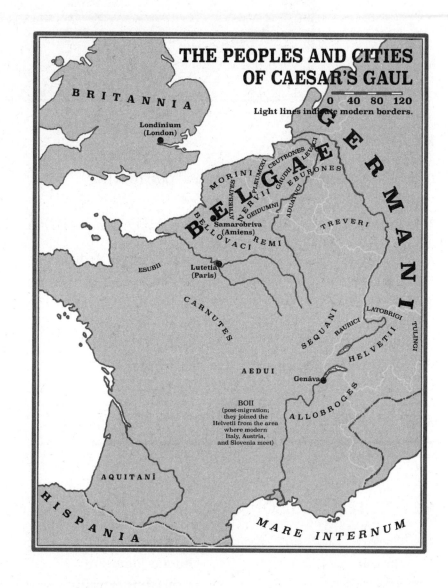

THE PEOPLES AND CITIES OF CAESAR'S GAUL

BY EPISODE

In order of appearance, reading down and then over.

1.1-7: INTRODUCTION TO GAUL AND THE MIGRATION OF THE HELVETII

the Belgae	Dumnorix, the Aeduan	the Allobroges
the Aquitani	the Raurici	Caesar
the Gauls	the Tulingi	Geneva (city)
the Helvetii	the Latobrigi	Lucius Cassius
Orgetorix	the Boii	
Casticus, the Sequanian	the Sequani	

4.24-35: THE BRITISH CAMPAIGN

the Britons	Caesar	Commius, the Atrebatian

5.24-37: THE SIEGE OF SABINUS AND COTTA'S CAMP

Caesar	Gaius Arpineius	Titus Balventius
the Carnutes	Quintus Junius	Quintus Lucanius
Tasgetius	Lucius Aurunculeius	Lucius Petrosidius
Ambiorix	Sabinus	Labienus
Catuvulcus	Cotta	

5.38–48: THE SIEGE OF CICERO'S CAMP

the Aduatuci	Titus Pullo	Marcus Crassus
the Nervii	Lucius Vorenus	Gaius Fabius
Cicero	Verticus, the Nervian	Labienus
the Germans	Caesar	

6.13–20: THE GAULS AND THE DRUIDS

Druids	Mercury	Jupiter
the Carnutes	Apollo	Minerva
Britain	Mars	Dis

ALPHABETICAL GLOSSARY

Starred words in definitions have their own entry.

the Aduatuci (5)

- a people that lived in modern Belgium, likely centered around the modern city of Namur, with the *Nervii to the west and the *Eburones to the east

- *Ambiorix, in the speech to the Roman ambassadors C. *Arpineius and Q. *Junius in which he sets up the deception that will lead to the Romans' demise, refers to the Aduatuci as those from whom *Caesar freed him from paying tribute and from whom *Caesar recovered *Ambiorix's son and nephew, whom they were holding hostage:

  o *sese pro Caesaris in se beneficiis plurimum ei confiteri debere, quod eius opera stipendio liberatus esset quod **Aduatucis** finitimis suis pendere consuesset, quodque ei et filius et fratris filius ab Caesare remissi essent, quos **Aduatuci** obsidum numero missos apud se in servitute et catenis tenuissent.* (5.27)

- *Ambiorix, after the defeat of the Romans, goes to the Aduatuci and enlists their help against the remaining Romans, weakened from their defeat:

  o *Hac victoria sublatus Ambiorix statim cum equitatu in **Aduatucos**, qui erant eius regno finitimi, proficiscitur; neque noctem neque diem intermittit peditatumque sese subsequi iubet. Re demonstrata **Aduatucis**que concitatis, postero die in Nervios pervenit.* (5.38)

the Aedui (1)

- a people that lived in modern central France, between the *Arar and the *Liger rivers

- In the Latin syllabus, they are used in their adjectival form to describe *Dumnorix (*item-que Dumnorigi **Aeduo**, 1.3*).

CHAPTER 3

the Allobroges (3)

- a people that lived in the northwestern corner of modern *Italy near *Italy's border with Switzerland and southeastern France

- Roughly bordered in the northeast by Lake Geneva and the ancient city of *Genava, the territory of the Allobroges stretched southwest to the *Rhone River, between the Alps and the southern end of the *Jura Mountains.

Ambiorix (15)

- leader of the *Eburones who, along with *Catuvulcus, attacked the camp of *Sabinus and *Cotta who were wintering nearby

- After the attack, Ambiorix received the embassy of C. *Arpineius and Q. *Iunius and explained to them that he had not ordered the attack, a lie, and advised them to leave before a large *German force could attack.

- As the Romans left, he and the *Eburones ambushed the Romans, easily defeating them.

Apollo (2)

- the god of the sun, poetry, music, and medicine, among others

- *Caesar refers to him along with four other Roman gods (*Mercury, *Mars, *Jupiter, *Minerva) as one of the five primary gods that the *Gauls worship.

- The *Gauls would have of course known these gods by local names rather than their Roman names, but *Caesar uses the Roman names for the familiarity of his readers.

- *Caesar specifically says that the *Gallic version of Apollo dispels disease (*morbos depellere*; 6.17).

the Aquitani / Aquitania (3) [Aquitani, -orum: the Aquitani; Aquitania, -ae: Aquitania, the territory of the Aquitani]

- a people that possessed the southwestern corner of modern-day France, bordered by the *Pyrenees to the south and the Garonne River (ancient *Garumna) to the north and east

- *Caesar mentions the Aquitani (in the Latin syllabus) only in 1.1, when he introduces the basic geography of Gaul:

  o *Gallia est omnis divisa in partes tres, quarum unam incolunt Belgae, aliam **Aquitani**, tertiam qui ipsorum lingua Celtae, nostra Galli appellantur. … Gallos ab **Aquitanis** Garumna flumen, a Belgis Matrona et Sequana dividit. … **Aquitania** a Garumna flumine ad Pyrenaeos montes et eam partem Oceani quae est ad Hispaniam pertinet; spectat inter occasum solis et septentriones.* (1.1)

Ariovistus (1)

- leader of the Suebi, a *Germanic people, whom *Caesar defeated in 58 BC

- The description of this conflict appears in 1.31–53, part of the English but not the Latin syllabus.

- In the Latin syllabus, Ariovistus is mentioned in passing as a source of great grief to the *Germans:

    o *magno esse Germanis dolori **Ariovisti** mortem.* (5.29)

C. Arpineius (2)

- a Roman *eques* sent to *Ambiorix as an ambassador along with Q. *Junius, whom *Ambiorix deceived by advising them to leave in the face of an imminent attack of a large *German force:

    o *Mittitur ad eos colloquendi causa **C. Arpineius**, eques Romanus, familiaris Q. Tituri, et Q. Iunius ex Hispania quidam, qui iam ante missu Caesaris ad Ambiorigem ventitare consuerat.* (5.27)

    o ***Arpineius** et Iunius quae audierunt ad legatos deferunt.* (5.28)

the Atrebates (3) [Atrebas, -atis: Atrebatian (adj); Atrebates, -um: the Atrebates]

- a people who lived in northeastern France

- *Commius appears twice described as an Atrebatian:

    o *una cum his legatis Commius **Atrebas** venit* (4.27)

    o *quos Commius **Atrebas**, de quo ante dictum est, secum transportaverat* (4.35)

- And, in book 5, *Caesar sends a message to C. *Fabius to bring his legion into their borders:

    o *Alterum ad C. Fabium legatum mittit, ut in **Atrebatum** finis legionem adducat, qua sibi iter faciendum sciebat.* (5.46)

T. Balventius (1)

- a respected soldier who was wounded in both thighs in the ambush set by *Ambiorix and the *Eburones:

    o *tum **T. Balventio**, qui superiore anno primum pilum duxerat, viro forti et magnae auctoritatis, utrumque femur tragula traicitur.* (5.35)

the Belgae (6)

- one of the three primary peoples, along with the *Gauls and the *Aquitani, identified by *Caesar in his introduction to *Gaul

- *Caesar identifies the Belgae as the bravest of the three because they are farthest from the Romans, whose civilization might soften them, and closest to the *Germans, with whom they are constantly warring.

- Their territory includes modern-day Belgium and extends into northeastern France, bordered on the east by the *Rhine (Rhenus) River and on the west by the *Sequana:

  o *Gallia est omnis divisa in partes tres, quarum unam incolunt **Belgae**, aliam Aquitani, tertiam qui ipsorum lingua Celtae, nostra Galli appellantur. ... Gallos ab Aquitanis Garumna flumen, a **Belgis** Matrona et Sequana dividit. Horum omnium fortissimi sunt **Belgae**, propterea quod a cultu atque humanitate provinciae longissime absunt, minimeque ad eos mercatores saepe commeant atque ea quae ad effeminandos animos pertinent important, proximique sunt Germanis qui trans Rhenum incolunt, quibuscum continenter bellum gerunt.* (1.1)

the Bellovaci (2)

- a *Belgian tribe that lived in modern northeastern France, bordered on the south by the river Seine (*Sequana) and the north by the coast

- M. *Crassus is quartered in the territory of the Bellovaci when *Caesar summons him and his legion:

  o *Caesar, acceptis litteris hora circiter undecima diei, statim nuntium in **Bellovacos** ad M. Crassum quaestorem mittit.* (5.46)

the Boii (1)

- a people that lived east of the *Rhine River and that joined the *Helvetii on their migration into *Gaul:

  o ***Boios**que, qui trans Rhenum incoluerant et in agrum Noricum transierant Noreiamque oppugnarant, receptos ad se socios sibi asciscunt.* (1.5)

Britannia (6)

- the territory of modern Great Britain

- *Caesar explores Britain as a potential future target and battles the Britons.

- As part of their negotiations, the Britons return *Commius the *Atrebatian whom they had seized when he went to them as an envoy:

  o *una cum his legatis Commius Atrebas venit, quem supra demonstraveram a Caesare in **Britanniam** praemissum* (4.27)

  o *his rebus pace confirmata, post diem quartum quam est in **Britanniam** ventum naves xviii. ... quae cum appropinquarent **Britanniae** et ex castris viderentur, tanta tempestas subito coorta est* (4.28)

o *quibus rebus cognitis, principes **Britanniae**, qui post proelium ad Caesarem convenerant, inter se collocuti, … quod eis superatis aut reditu interclusis neminem postea belli inferendi causa in **Britanniam** transiturum confidebant* (4.30)

Caesar (40)

- Roman magistrate with proconsular *imperium* who conquers Gaul and writes about this campaign in his *De bello Gallico*

- In that text, Caesar refers to himself in the 3rd person when he is a character in his own story and in the 1st person when he is functioning as an author.

- Caesar is also known for his later crossing of the Rubicon River (in northeastern *Italy) with his army, an act of war by Roman law and one that precipitated civil war against Caesar's rivals at Rome, led by Pompey the Great.

- Caesar prevails in the civil war and establishes himself as dictator at Rome but is killed by a conspiracy of Roman senators led by Brutus and Cassius, who hope that their assassination of Caesar will preserve the Republic. In the end, though, Caesar's death leaves a power vacuum that would be filled by further civil war, ultimately resulting in the final demise of the Republic and the eventual rise of the imperial monarchy of Augustus.

the Carnutes (4)

- a people living in modern central France, to the southwest of Paris, bordered by the river Seine (*Sequana) on their east

- *Caesar admires the Carnutian *Tasgetius and so installs him as leader of the tribe (*erat in **Carnutibus** summo loco natus Tasgetius*; 5.25).

- *Caesar also mentions in 6.13 that it is in the territory of the Carnutes that the Druids meet once a year:

  o *hi certo anni tempore in finibus **Carnutum**, quae regio totius Galliae media habetur, considunt in loco consecrato*

L. Cassius (1)

- consul in 107 BC whom the *Helvetii had defeated and killed and whom *Caesar remembers when negotiating with the *Helvetii

- The memory of Cassius' death causes *Caesar to refuse the request of the *Helvetii to pass through Roman territory:

  o *Caesar, quod memoria tenebat **L. Cassium** consulem occisum exercitumque eius ab Helvetiis pulsum et sub iugum missum, concedendum non putabat.* (1.7)

Casticus (1)

- a *Sequanian whom the *Helvetian *Orgetorix, in his mission to secure peace with neighboring tribes, convinced to seize the power over the *Sequani that his father *Catamantaloedis had held:

  - *in eo itinere persuadet **Castico** Catamantaloedis filio Sequano, cuius pater regnum in Sequanis multos annos obtinuerat* (1.3)

Catamantaloedis (1; Catamantaloedis, -is, m.)

- the father of the *Sequanian *Casticus and the former leader of the *Sequani:

  - *in eo itinere persuadet Castico **Catamantaloedis** filio Sequano, cuius pater regnum in Sequanis multos annos obtinuerat* (1.3)

Catuvulcus (2)

- Joint leader of the *Eburones with *Ambiorix:

  - *qui sub imperio Ambiorigis et **Catuvulci** erant* (5.24)

- along with *Ambiorix, attacked the camp of *Sabinus and *Cotta who were wintering nearby

- As the Romans left, the *Eburones ambushed the Romans, easily defeating them.

the Celtae (1)

- Caesar identifies Celtae in 1.1 as the word by which the *Gauls refer to themselves in their own language:

  - *Gallia est omnis divisa in partes tres, quarum unam incolunt Belgae, aliam Aquitani, tertiam qui ipsorum lingua **Celtae**, nostra Galli appellantur.* (1.1)

- The Celts as a people have a long history throughout Europe.

- Though their origins are disputed, the most accepted origin places them in central Europe, in modern Austria, from which they then expanded westward into France, Spain, and the British Isles, as well as eastward, potentially as far as modern central Turkey.

the Ceutrones (1)

- After *Ambiorix's defeat of *Sabinus' troops, he approached the *Nervii to assemble forces to attack *Cicero's winter camp.

- The *Nervii summoned peoples under their rule to join them against the Romans.

- The Ceutrones were one of these peoples:

  - *Itaque confestim dimissis nuntiis ad **Ceutrones**, Grudios, Levacos, Pleumoxios, Geidumnos, qui omnes sub eorum imperio sunt, quam maximas manus possunt cogunt et de improviso ad Ciceronis hiberna advolant.* (5.39)

Quintus Tullius Cicero (15)

- The younger brother of the famous Roman orator, Marcus Tullius Cicero, Quintus figures prominently in the Latin selections from book 5.

- He accompanied *Caesar on his reconnaissance mission to Britain and was in charge of the winter quarters besieged by *Ambiorix.

- Eventually Cicero was able to send word to Caesar, who rushed to aid him and, despite being outnumbered, defeated *Ambiorix.

Commius (2)

- an *Atrebatian whom Caesar installed as king upon conquering the *Atrebates (in 57; not part of the Latin syllabus) and whom *Caesar sent to *Britain to convince the Britons to receive *Caesar kindly

- Instead they seized Commius but returned him to *Caesar as part of negotiations when they could not prevent *Caesar from landing in *Britain:

  - *una cum his legatis* **Commius** *Atrebas venit, quem supra demonstraveram a Caesare in Britanniam praemissum* (4.27)

  - *tamen nactus equites circiter XXX, quos* **Commius** *Atrebas, de quo ante dictum est, secum transportaverat, legiones in acie pro castris constituit* (4.35)

L. Aurunculeius Cotta (9)

- one of the *legati*, along with Quintus Titurius *Sabinus, in charge of the Romans attacked by and eventually deceived by *Ambiorix and the *Eburones

- *Ambiorix told the embassy of C. *Arpineius and Q. *Iunius sent by Cotta that he did not want to attack but was pressured to do so and that the Romans should leave their camp because of the imminent attack of a large force of *Germans.

- Cotta's position was that the Romans should not abandon their camp without an order from *Caesar and that they could withstand the *German assault behind their fortifications.

- *Sabinus advised abandoning the camp and *Sabinus eventually prevailed.

- Upon leaving camp, the Romans were ambushed by the *Gauls, all but a few of them killed in the ambush.

Marcus Licinius Crassus (5)

- son of Marcus Crassus, who formed the political alliance with *Caesar and Pompey known as the First Triumvirate

- a quaestor, along with Gaius *Trebonius and Lucius Munatius *Plancus as legates, in charge of wintering three legions in the land of the *Belgae:

- o *Tres in Bellovacis collocavit: his **M. Crassum** quaestorem et L. Munatium Plancum et C. Trebonium legatos praefecit.* (5.24)

- When *Caesar hears that *Cicero's winter camp is under attack by the *Nervii, he summons Crassus' legion to help.

- Upon Crassus' approach, Caesar leaves him in charge of *Samarobriva (modern Amiens) to guard the army's valuables, while Caesar departs to help *Cicero:

  - o *Hora circiter tertia ab antecursoribus de **Crassi** adventu certior factus, eo die milia passuum XX procedit. **Crassum** Samarobrivae praeficit legionemque attribuit, quod ibi impedimenta exercitus, obsides civitatum, litteras publicas, frumentumque omne quod eo tolerandae hiemis causa devexerat relinquebat.* (5.47)

Dis (1; Dis, Ditis, m.)

- god of the Underworld; another name for Pluto

- *Caesar reports that the *Gauls claim Dis as their ancestor:

  - o *Galli se omnes ab **Dite** patre prognatos praedicant, idque ab Druidibus proditum dicunt.* (6.18)

Diviciacus (1)

- one of the *Aedui and brother of *Dumnorix, in which capacity alone Diviciacus is mentioned in the Latin syllabus:

  - o *itemque Dumnorigi Aeduo fratri **Diviciaci*** (1.3)

Dumnorix (1)

- one of the *Aedui and brother of *Diviciacus

- Dumnorix entered into an alliance with *Orgetorix, the *Helvetian, to consolidate power among the *Gauls as the *Helvetii moved into central *Gaul through *Roman territory; as part of the alliance, *Orgetorix gave Dumnorix his daughter in marriage:

  - o *In eo itinere persuadet Castico Catamantaloedis filio Sequano ... ; itemque **Dumnorigi** Aeduo fratri Diviciaci, qui eo tempore principatum in civitate obtinebat ac maxime plebi acceptus erat, ut idem conaretur persuadet, eique filiam suam in matrimonium dat.* (1.3)

the Eburones (5)

- a *Gallic people that lived in the area where modern Germany, Belgium, and the Netherlands meet

- *Ambiorix, the chief of the Eburones, led the attack on the winter camp of *Cotta and *Sabinus.

- After the attack, *Ambiorix received the embassy of C. *Arpineius and Q. *Iunius and explained to them that he had not ordered the attack, a lie, and advised them to leave before a large *German force could attack.

- As the Romans left, he and the Eburones ambushed the Romans, easily defeating them.

- The Eburones also attacked the winter camp of *Cicero:

  o *Eis circumventis, magna manu **Eburones**, Nervii, Aduatuci atque horum omnium socii et clientes legionem oppugnare incipiunt.* (5.39)

the Esubii (1)

- a tribe that lived in modern-day Normandy in northern France

- *Caesar sends a legion to winter among them under the leadership of L. *Roscius:

  o *ex quibus unam in Morinos ducendam C. Fabio legato dedit, alteram in Nervios Q. Ciceroni, tertiam in **Esubios** L. Roscio* (5.24)

C. Fabius (3)

- a *legatus* whom *Caesar charged with a legion to winter among the *Morini:

  o *ex quibus unam in Morinos ducendam **C. Fabio** legato dedit* (5.24)

- *Caesar then summoned Fabius' legion to assist against the *Atrebates.

A. Gabinius (1)

- Aulus Gabinius

- consul in 58 BC along with Lucius Calpurnius *Piso

- used by *Caesar to date the departure of the *Helvetii from their land into Roman territory, March 28, 58 BC:

  o *Omnibus rebus ad profectionem comparatis, diem dicunt, qua die ad ripam Rhodani omnes conveniant. Is dies erat a. d. V. Kal. April., L. Pisone **A. Gabinio** consulibus.* (1.6)

Gallia (34)

- Gaul, the name of the land roughly to the west of the *Rhine River, including modern France, Luxembourg, Belgium, and parts of Switzerland, *Italy, and Germany.

- The *Rhine River separated the Gauls from the *Germans.

the Garumna (3)

- the Garonne River that originates in the middle of the *Pyrenees, continues northwest through southern France, and ends at the Atlantic on the west coast of France

- *Caesar uses the Garonne to demarcate different parts of *Gaul:

  o *Gallos ab Aquitanis* **Garumna** *flumen, a Belgis Matrona et Sequana dividit.* (1.1)

  o *Eorum una pars, quam Gallos obtinere dictum est, initium capit a flumine Rhodano; continetur* **Garumna** *flumine, Oceano, finibus Belgarum; attingit etiam ab Sequanis et Helvetiis flumen Rhenum; vergit ad septentriones.* (1.1)

  o *Aquitania a* **Garumna** *flumine ad Pyrenaeos montes et eam partem Oceani quae est ad Hispaniam pertinet; spectat inter occasum solis et septentriones.* (1.1)

the Geidumni (1)

- After *Ambiorix's defeat of *Sabinus' troops, he approached the *Nervii to assemble forces to attack *Cicero's winter camp.

- The *Nervii summoned peoples under their rule to join them against the Romans.

- The Geidumni were one of these peoples:

  o *Itaque confestim dimissis nuntiis ad Ceutrones, Grudios, Levacos, Pleumoxios,* **Geidumnos**, *qui omnes sub eorum imperio sunt, quam maximas manus possunt cogunt et de improviso ad Ciceronis hiberna advolant.* (5.39)

Genava (3)

- modern Geneva in Switzerland

- An ancient city on Lake *Lemannus in the territory of the *Allobroges that bordered the territory of the *Helvetii:

  o *Extremum oppidum Allobrogum est proximumque Helvetiorum finibus* **Genava**. (1.6)

- The *Helvetii gather near Geneva to begin the migration west.

- *Caesar rushes to Geneva to meet the *Helvetii:

  o *Caesari cum id nuntiatum esset, eos per provinciam nostram iter facere conari, maturat ab urbe proficisci, et quam maximis potest itineribus in Galliam ulteriorem contendit, et ad* **Genavam** *pervenit.* (1.7)

the Germani (9)

- a war-loving people living on the east side of the *Rhine River

- *Caesar identifies those *Gauls that live closest to the Germani as the most warlike because their proximity to the Germani necessitates it:

  o *Horum omnium fortissimi sunt Belgae, propterea quod a cultu atque humanitate provinciae longissime absunt, minimeque ad eos mercatores saepe commeant atque ea quae ad effeminandos animos pertinent important, proximique sunt* **Germanis** *qui trans Rhenum incolunt, quibuscum continenter bellum gerunt.* (1.1)

- o *Qua de causa Helvetii quoque reliquos Gallos virtute praecedunt, quod fere cotidianis proeliis cum **Germanis** contendunt, cum aut suis finibus eos prohibent aut ipsi in eorum finibus bellum gerunt.* (1.1)

- When *Ambiorix tricks *Sabinus into abandoning his winter camp and ambushes the Romans, he claims that a large *German force has assembled and is marching to attack the camp:

  - o *Magnam manum **Germanorum** conductam Rhenum transisse: hanc adfore biduo.* (5.27)

- The *Nervii, when attempting to overcome *Cicero's winter camp, tell him a similar story about the *Germans massing to attack:

  - o *Facta potestate eadem quae Ambiorix cum Titurio egerat commemorant: omnem esse in armis Galliam; **Germanos** Rhenum transisse; Caesaris reliquorumque hiberna oppugnari.* (5.41)

the Graeci (2; both the adjective: Graecus, -a, -um)

- referring to the Greeks

- Both times, *Caesar describes the use of the Greek language to prevent the Gauls from understanding a message:

  - o *Hanc **Graecis** conscriptam litteris mittit, ne intercepta epistola nostra ab hostibus consilia cognoscantur.* (5.48)

  - o *Neque fas esse existimant ea litteris mandare, cum in reliquis fere rebus, publicis privatis- que rationibus, **Graecis** litteris utantur.* (6.14)

the Grudii (1)

- After *Ambiorix's defeat of *Sabinus' troops, he approached the *Nervii to assemble forces to attack *Cicero's winter camp.

- The *Nervii summoned peoples under their rule to join them against the Romans.

- The Grudii were one of these peoples:

  - o *Itaque confestim dimissis nuntiis ad Ceutrones, **Grudios**, Levacos, Pleumoxios, Gei- dumnos, qui omnes sub eorum imperio sunt, quam maximas manus possunt cogunt et de improviso ad Ciceronis hiberna advolant.* (5.39)

the Helvetii (15)

- a people living in modern-day Switzerland whose decision to move west into modern-day France causes the chain of events that lead *Caesar to *Gaul

Hispania (3)

- modern-day Spain and Portugal

- the origin of Q. *Iunius, the Spaniard sent to *Ambiorix as an ambassador along with C. *Arpinius:

  ○ *Mittitur ad eos colloquendi causa C. Arpineius, eques Romanus, familiaris Q. Tituri, et Q. Iunius ex* **Hispania** *quidam, qui iam ante missu Caesaris ad Ambiorigem ventitare consuerat.* (5.27)

  ○ *Arpineius et* **Iunius** *quae audierunt ad legatos deferunt.* (5.28)

Indutiomarus (1)

- a leader of the *Treveri who encourages *Ambiorix and *Catuvulcus to gather troops to attack the Romans:

  ○ *Diebus circiter quindecim quibus in hiberna ventum est initium repentini tumultus ac defectionis ortum est ab Ambiorige et Catuvulco; qui, cum ad fines regni sui Sabino Cottaeque praesto fuissent frumentumque in hiberna comportavissent,* **Indutiomari** *Treveri nuntiis impulsi suos concitaverunt subitoque oppressis lignatoribus magna manu ad castra oppugnatum venerunt.* (5.26)

Iove (2; Iupiter, Iovis, m.)

- the king of the gods and the god of thunder and lightning, among other things

- *Caesar refers to him along with four other Roman gods (*Mercury, *Apollo, *Mars, *Minerva) as one of the five primary gods that the *Gauls worship.

- The Gauls would have of course known these gods by local names rather than their Roman names, but *Caesar uses the Roman names for the familiarity of his readers.

- *Caesar specifically says that the *Gallic version of *Jupiter rules the skies (*imperium caelestium tenere*; 6.17).

Italia (1)

- the country of Italy

- In *Caesar's time, the Rubicon River to the east as well as the Arno River to the west marked the northern boundary of Italy, or Roman territory just below where modern Italy narrows from its northern, broader area.

- North of that border was *Gaul, Cisapline *Gaul being the Italian side of the Alps, Transalpine *Gaul being on the northern or non-Italian side of the Alps.

Q. Iunius (2)

- a Spaniard sent to *Ambiorix as an ambassador along with C. *Arpinius, whom *Ambiorix deceived by advising them to leave in the face of an imminent attack of a large *German force:

  o *Mittitur ad eos colloquendi causa C. Arpineius, eques Romanus, familiaris Q. Tituri, et **Q. Iunius** ex Hispania quidam, qui iam ante missu Caesaris ad Ambiorigem ventitare consuerat (5.27)*

  o *Arpineius et **Iunius** quae audierunt ad legatos deferunt. (5.28)*

the Iura (1)

- the Jura Mountains, running along the modern border of France and Switzerland

- *Caesar identifies the Jura Mountains as one of the natural features that contains the land of the *Helvetii.

- The Jura Mountains separate the *Helvetii from the *Sequani:

  o *altera ex parte monte **Iura** altissimo, qui est inter Sequanos et Helvetios (1.2)*

T. Labienus (5)

- Titus Atius Labienus, one of *Caesar's legates

- *Caesar assigns Labienus and a legion to the area of the *Remi, near the *Treveri:

  o *quartam in Remis cum **T. Labieno** in confinio Treverorum hiemare iussit (5.24)*

- *Ambiorix, when informing *Sabinus' envoys of the potential of a *German attack on the winter camp, suggests that the Romans can move to Labienus' camp, slightly farther from them than *Cicero's camp:

  o *Ipsorum esse consilium, velintne priusquam finitimi sentiant eductos ex hibernis milites aut ad Ciceronem aut ad **Labienum** deducere, quorum alter milia passuum circiter quinquaginta, alter paulo amplius ab eis absit. (5.27)*

- After the defeat of *Sabinus' men, the survivors are able to escape to Labienus' camp:

  o *Pauci ex proelio elapsi incertis itineribus per silvas ad **T. Labienum** legatum in hiberna perveniunt atque eum de rebus gestis certiorem faciunt. (5.37)*

- When *Cicero's camp is besieged, *Caesar sends word to Labienus to help.

- Labienus responds that it would be too risky to leave his camp exposed, given the proximity of the *Treveri; *Caesar agrees:

  o ***Labienus**, interitu Sabini et caede cohortium cognita, cum omnes ad eum Treverorum copiae venissent veritus ne, si ex hibernis fugae similem profectionem fecisset, hostium impetum sustinere non posset, praesertim quos recenti victoria efferri sciret, litteras Caesari remittit. (5.47)*

the Latobrigi (1)

- a small tribe about whom little is known linked to the *Helvetii

- They, along with the *Raurici and the *Tulingi, were among those tribes whom the *Helvetii convinced to move with them into western Gaul:

  o *Persuadent Rauricis et Tulingis et **Latobrigis** finitimis suis uti eodem usi consilio, oppidis suis vicisque exustis, una cum eis proficiscantur.* (1.5)

Lake Lemannus (1; Lemannus, -i, though often appearing, as it does here, with *lacus*)

- referring to Lake Geneva

- *Caesar identifies Lake Lemannus as one of the natural features that contains the land of the *Helvetii.

- Lake Lemannus, along with the *Rhone River, separates the *Helvetii from the Romans:

  o *tertia lacu **Lemanno** et flumine Rhodano, qui provinciam nostram ab Helvetiis dividit* (1.2)

the Levaci (1)

- After *Ambiorix's defeat of *Sabinus' troops, *Ambiorix approached the *Nervii to assemble forces to attack *Cicero's winter camp.

- The *Nervii summoned peoples under their rule to join them against the Romans.

- The Levaci were one of these peoples:

  o *Itaque confestim dimissis nuntiis ad Ceutrones, Grudios, **Levacos**, Pleumoxios, Geidumnos, qui omnes sub eorum imperio sunt, quam maximas manus possunt cogunt et de improviso ad Ciceronis hiberna advolant.* (5.39)

Q. Lucanius (1)

- a Roman soldier fighting in the siege of *Cicero's winter camp who was killed trying to save his son:

  o ***Q. Lucanius** eiusdem ordinis, fortissime pugnans, dum circumvento filio subvenit, interficitur.* (5.35)

Mars (2)

- the god of war

- *Caesar refers to him along with four other Roman gods (*Mercury, *Apollo, *Jupiter, *Minerva) as one of the five primary gods that the Gauls worship.

- The Gauls would have of course known these gods by local names rather than their Roman names, but *Caesar uses the Roman names for the familiarity of his readers.

- *Caesar specifically says that the *Gallic version of Mars oversees war (*bella regere*; 6.17).

the Matrona (1)

- the river Marne

- *Caesar identifies it as the river, along with the *Sequana, that divides the *Gauls from the *Belgae:

  o *Gallos ab Aquitanis Garumna flumen, a Belgis* **Matrona** *et Sequana dividit.* (1.1)

Mercury (1)

- the messenger god

- *Caesar refers to him along with four other Roman gods (*Apollo, *Mars, *Jupiter, *Minerva) as one of the five primary gods that the Gauls worship.

- The Gauls would have of course known these gods by local names rather than their Roman names, but *Caesar uses the Roman names for the familiarity of his readers.

- *Caesar specifically says that the *Gallic version of Mercury is the most worshipped of these gods and that he is considered the inventor of the arts, the presider over roads and journeys, and the judge and overseer of commerce:

  o *Deum maxime* **Mercurium** *colunt. Huius sunt plurima simulacra, hunc omnium inventorem artium ferunt, hunc viarum atque itinerum ducem, hunc ad quaestus pecuniae mercaturasque habere vim maximam arbitrantur.* (6.17)

M. Messalla (1)

- Marcus Valerius Messalla

- consul in 61 BC along with M. Pupius *Piso Calpernianus

- used by *Caesar to date the origin of *Orgetorix's conspiracy and plan to move the *Helvetii:

  o *Apud Helvetios longe nobilissimus fuit et ditissimus Orgetorix. Is,* **M. Messalla** *et M. Pupio Pisone consulibus, regni cupiditate inductus coniurationem nobilitatis fecit.* (1.2)

Minerva (2)

- the goddess of wisdom.

- *Caesar refers to her among four other Roman gods (*Mercury, *Apollo, *Mars, *Jupiter) as one of the five primary gods that the Gauls worship.

- The Gauls would have of course known these gods by local names rather than their Roman names, but *Caesar uses the Roman names for the familiarity of his readers.

- *Caesar specifically says that the *Gallic version of Minerva presides over inspiration (*operum atque artificiorum initia tradere*; 6.17).

the Morini (1)

- a people living on the northern coast of modern Belgium

- *Caesar sends a legion to winter among them under the leadership of C. *Fabius:

  o *ex quibus unam in **Morinos** ducendam C. Fabio legato dedit* (5.24)

Mosa (1)

- the Meuse River, which begins in eastern France and continues north through Belgium and the Netherlands before dumping into the North Sea

- *Caesar identifies the greatest part of the *Eburones as being located between the Meuse and the *Rhine rivers:

  o *Unam legionem, quam proxime trans Padum conscripserat, et cohortes V in Eburones, quorum pars maxima est inter **Mosam** ac Rhenum, qui sub imperio Ambiorigis et Catuvulci erant, misit.* (5.24)

Nammeius (1)

- an ambassador, along with *Verucloetius, at the head of the embassy sent by the *Helevetii to *Caesar to communicate that the *Helvetii intended no damage or violence and had no other route:

  o *Ubi de eius adventu Helvetii certiores facti sunt, legatos ad eum mittunt nobilissimos civitatis, cuius legationis **Nammeius** et Verucloetius principem locum obtinebant.* (1.7)

- *Caesar, remembering the death at the hands of the *Helvetii of Lucius *Cassius, refuses to admit them.

the Nervii (9)

- a *Gallic tribe that lived in modern-day Belgium

- *Caesar appointed Q. *Cicero legate in charge of a legion sent into the territory of the Nervii:

  o *Ex quibus unam in Morinos ducendam C. Fabio legato dedit, alteram in **Nervios** Q. Ciceroni, tertiam in Esubios L. Roscio.* (5.24)

- After the defeat of *Sabinus by *Ambiorix, *Ambiorix convinces the Nervii and their subject tribes to attack *Cicero's camp:

o   *Re demonstrata Aduatucisque concitatis, postero die in* **Nervios** *pervenit hortaturque ne sui in perpetuum liberandi atque ulciscendi Romanos pro eis quas acceperint iniuriis occasionem dimittant.* (5.38)

- The Nervii attempted to convince *Cicero to leave camp, ostensibly to ambush him as *Ambiorix did *Sabinus, but *Cicero proclaimed that he would leave only if they lay down their arms:

  o   *Tunc duces principesque* **Nerviorum** *qui aliquem sermonis aditum causamque amicitiae cum Cicerone habebant colloqui sese velle dicunt.* (5.41)

- The Nervii instead besieged *Cicero's camp until *Verticus, one of the Nervii loyal to *Cicero, bribed a slave to sneak out with a message for *Caesar, who eventually routed the Nervii.

Noreia (1)

- a town in *Noricum, a territory located in modern Austria
- The *Boii, who accompanied the *Helvetii on their migration, had entered the land of *Noricum and attacked there the town of Noreia:

  o   *Boiosque, qui trans Rhenum incoluerant et in agrum Noricum transierant* **Noreiam***que oppugnarant, receptos ad se socios sibi asciscunt.* (1.5)

Noricus (1; Noricus, -a, -um)

- referring to Noricum, a territory located in modern Austria
- The *Boii, who accompanied the *Helvetii on their migration, had entered the land of Noricum and attacked there the town of *Noreia:

  o   *Boiosque, qui trans Rhenum incoluerant et in agrum* **Noricum** *transierant Noreiamque oppugnarant, receptos ad se socios sibi asciscunt.* (1.5)

Oceanus (3)

- the Ocean, used by *Caesar in 1.1 as part of his description of *Gallic geography and in 4.29 during his description of his landing on the British coast

Orgetorix (6)

- the leader of the *Helvetii who planned and led the movement of the *Helvetii from their home in modern Switzerland into modern France
- He also conspired with the leaders of the *Aedui and the *Sequani, *Dumnorix and *Casticus respectively, to control all of *Gaul.

- The plot was discovered, he was brought before the *Helvetii, and died mysteriously, perhaps by suicide:

  o ***Orgetorix*** *mortuus est; neque abest suspicio, ut Helvetii arbitrantur, quin ipse sibi mortem consciverit.* (1.4)

Padus (1)

- the modern Po River in northern *Italy that flows from *Italy's northwestern Alps and ends in the Adriatic Sea on *Italy's east coast near Venice

- In 5.24 *Caesar describes the legion that he sends to the *Eburones as having originated north of the Po:

  o *Unam legionem, quam proxime trans **Padum** conscripserat, et cohortes V in Eburones ... qui sub imperio Ambiorigis et Catuvolci erant, misit.* (5.24)

L. Petrosidius (1)

- A standard-bearer in the army of *Sabinus and *Cotta who was killed during the return to the Roman camp after the ambush of *Ambiorix, he hurls the standard into the camp to save it from the enemy, sacrificing himself in the process. (The loss of the standard to the enemy was considered the greatest disgrace a Roman legion could suffer.)

- *Caesar describes his sacrifice with admiration:

  o *Ex quibus **L. Petrosidius** aquilifer, cum magna multitudine hostium premeretur, aquilam intra vallum proiecit; ipse pro castris fortissime pugnans occiditur.* (5.37)

L. Piso (1)

- Lucius Calpurnius Piso, the father-in-law of *Caesar

- consul in 58 BC along with Aulus *Gabinius

- used by *Caesar to date the departure of the *Helvetii from their land into Roman territory: March 28, 58 BC:

  o *Omnibus rebus ad profectionem comparatis, diem dicunt, qua die ad ripam Rhodani omnes conveniant. Is dies erat a. d. V. Kal. April., **L. Pisone** A. Gabinio consulibus.* (1.6)

L. Munatius Plancus (2)

- a legate along with Gaius *Trebonius, and M. *Crassus as quaestor, in charge of wintering three legions in the land of the *Belgae:

  o *Tres in Bellovacis collocavit: his M. Crassum quaestorem et **L. Munatium Plancum** et C. Trebonium legatos praefecit.* (5.24)

- L. Plancus was also sent by *Caesar to the land of the *Carnutes to investigate the death of *Tasgetius and punish those responsible:

  o *Ille veritus, quod ad plures pertinebat, ne civitas eorum impulsu deficeret, **L. Plancum** cum legione ex Belgio celeriter in Carnutes proficisci iubet ibique hiemare, quorumque opera cognoverat Tasgetium interfectum, hos comprehensos ad se mittere.* (5.25)

the Pleumoxi (1)

- After *Ambiorix's defeat of *Sabinus' troops, he approached the *Nervii to assemble forces to attack *Cicero's winter camp.

- The *Nervii summoned peoples under their rule to join them against the Romans.

- The Pleumoxi were one of these peoples:

  o *Itaque confestim dimissis nuntiis ad Ceutrones, Grudios, Levacos, **Pleumoxios**, Geidumnos, qui omnes sub eorum imperio sunt, quam maximas manus possunt cogunt et de improviso ad Ciceronis hiberna advolant.* (5.39)

Cn. Pompeius (1)

- interpreter of *Sabinus to *Ambiorix

- *Ambiorix had previously told *Sabinus that a *German force was amassing to attack the winter camp.

- There was disagreement among the Romans about whether or not they should abandon the winter camp while there was still time.

- *Sabinus led the faction that was for abandoning.

- *Ambiorix had set a trap for the Romans and Cn. Pompeius is sent to ask for a meeting with *Ambiorix:

  o *His rebus permotus Q. Titurius, cum procul Ambiorigem suos cohortantem conspexisset, interpretem suum **Cn. Pompeium** ad eum mittit rogatum ut sibi militibusque parcat.* (5.36)

T. Pullo (6: 5 as Pullo, 1 as T. Pullo)

- one of two legionaries, along with L. *Vorenus, who, in the attack by *Ambiorix on *Cicero's camp, were vying with each other for primacy in the legion

- Pullo, as he enters the battle, asks why *Vorenus is hanging back in the battle, so *Vorenus joins.

- But Pullo is gravely wounded and *Vorenus saves him. Both are praised equally for their valor and it can't be decided who is the braver:

o *Pullo*, *cum acerrime ad munitiones pugnaretur, "Quid dubitas," inquit, "Vorene?"… Transfigitur scutum* **Pulloni** *et verutum in balteo defigitur … Gladio comminus rem gerit Vorenus, atque uno interfecto reliquos paulum propellit … Huic rursus circumvento fert subsidium* **Pullo**, *atque ambo incolumes compluribus interfectis summa cum laude sese intra munitiones recipiunt. Sic fortuna in contentione et certamine utrumque versavit, ut alter alteri inimicus auxilio salutique esset neque diiudicari posset, uter utri virtute anteferendus videretur.* (5.44)

M. Pupius Piso (1)

- Marcus Pupius Piso Calpernianus

- consul in 61 BC along with M. *Messalla

- used by *Caesar to date the origin of *Orgetorix's conspiracy and plan to move the *Helvetii:

  o *Apud Helvetios longe nobilissimus fuit et ditissimus Orgetorix. Is, M. Messalla et* **M. Pupio Pisone** *consulibus, regni cupiditate inductus coniurationem nobilitatis fecit.* (1.2)

Pyrenees (1; here an adjective, Pyrenaeus, -a, -um)

- a mountain range on the border of Spain and France

- describes the southern border of *Aquitania:

  o *Aquitania a Garumna flumine ad* **Pyrenaeos** *montes et eam partem Oceani quae est ad Hispaniam pertinent.* (1.1)

the Raurici (1)

- a small tribe about whom little is known, linked to the *Helvetii

- They, along with the *Tulingi and the *Latobrigi, were among those tribes whom the *Helvetii convinced to move with them into western Gaul:

  o *Persuadent* **Rauricis** *et Tulingis et Latobrigis finitimis suis uti eodem usi consilio, oppidis suis vicisque exustis, una cum eis proficiscantur.* (1.5)

the Remi (1)

- a people living in southern modern Belgium

- *Caesar sends a legion to winter among them under the leadership of T. *Labienus:

  o *quartam in* **Remis** *cum T. Labieno in confinio Treverorum hiemare iussit* (5.24)

the Rhenus (9)

- The Rhine River begins in the southeastern Swiss Alps, forms the border between Switzerland and Liechtenstein, Austria, and Germany, continues as part of the border between

France and Germany, then into Germany and the Netherlands until it flows into the North Sea.

- *Caesar uses the Rhine primarily to describe the divisions of lands and tribes at the beginning of book 1.

the Rhodanus (5)

- The Rhone River begins in the central Swiss Alps, continues through Lake *Geneva, and, in southeastern France, empties into the Mediterranean after splitting into two branches.

- *Caesar uses the Rhone primarily to describe the divisions of lands and tribes at the beginning of book 1.

L. Roscius (2)

- a legate to whom *Caesar gave a legion to winter in the land of the *Esubii:

  o *ex quibus unam in Morinos ducendam C. Fabio legato dedit, alteram in Nervios Q. Ciceroni, tertiam in Esubios* **L. Roscio**. (5.24)

Q. Titurius Sabinus (14: 1 as Q. T. Sabinus; 2 as Q. Titurius; 5 as Titurius; 6 as Sabinus)

- one of the *legati*, along with L. Aurunculeius *Cotta, in charge of the Romans attacked by and eventually deceived by *Ambiorix and the *Eburones

- *Ambiorix told the embassy of C. *Arpineius and Q. *Iunius sent by *Cotta that he did not want to attack but was pressured to do so and that the Romans should leave their camp because of the imminent attack of a large force of *Germans.

- *Cotta's position was that the Romans should not abandon their camp without an order from *Caesar and that they could withstand the *German assault behind their fortifications.

- Sabinus advised abandoning the camp and Sabinus eventually prevailed.

- Upon leaving camp, the Romans were ambushed by the Gauls, all but a few of them killed in the ambush.

Samarobriva (2)

- the modern city of Amiens, located in northern France

- the location of a *Gallic council going into the winter:

  o *concilioque Gallorum* **Samarobrivae** *peracto, quod eo anno frumentum in Gallia propter siccitates angustius provenerat, coactus est aliter ac superioribus annis exercitum in hibernis collocare* (5.24)

- where *Crassus wintered his legion:

  o *Crassum* **Samarobrivae** *praeficit legionemque attribuit.* (5.47)

the Sequana River (1)

- the river Seine

- *Caesar identifies it as the river, along with the *Matrona, that divides the *Gauls from the *Belgae:

  o *Gallos ab Aquitanis Garumna flumen, a Belgis Matrona et **Sequana** dividit.* (1.1)

the Sequani (5)

- a *Gallic people that lived at the northeastern end of the *Jura Mountains in modern-day Switzerland near the *German border

Tasgetius (3)

- a leader of the *Carnutes whom *Caesar installed as leader for his continued loyalty

- He was killed after a couple of years and *Caesar sent L. Munatius *Plancus to investigate his death and punish those responsible:

  o *L. Plancum cum legione ex Belgio celeriter in Carnutes proficisci iubet ibique hiemare, quorumque opera cognoverat **Tasgetium** interfectum, hos comprehensos ad se mittere.* (5.25)

C. Trebonius (1)

- a legate along with L. Munatius *Plancus, and M. *Crassus as quaestor, in charge of wintering three legions in the land of the *Belgae:

  o *Tres in Bellovacis collocavit: his M. Crassum quaestorem et L. Munatium Plancum et **C. Trebonium** legatos praefecit.* (5.24)

the Treveri (4)

- a people that lived near what is now the Moselle River in modern northeastern France near the borders of Luxembourg, Germany, and Belgium

- Titus *Labienus winters a legion among the *Remi near the border of the Treveri:

  o *quartam in Remis cum T. Labieno in confinio **Treverorum** hiemare iussit* (5.24)

- During the siege by the *Nervii of *Cicero's winter camp, when *Caesar calls for reinforcement legions, *Labienus suggests that he should stay at his camp because of the aggressiveness of the *Treveri and his concern that they would take the camp if exposed:

  o *docet omnes equitatus peditatusque copias **Treverorum** tria milia passuum longe ab suis castris consedisse.* (5.47)

the Tulingi (1)

- a small tribe, about whom little is known, linked to the *Helvetii

- They, along with the *Raurici and the *Latobrigi, were among those tribes whom the *Helvetii convinced to move with them into western Gaul:

  - *Persuadent Rauricis et **Tulingis** et Latobrigis finitimis suis uti eodem usi consilio, oppidis suis vicisque exustis, una cum eis proficiscantur.* (1.5)

Verticus (1)

- during *Ambiorix's attack on *Cicero's winter camp, the *Nervian loyal to Rome who was able to bring a message to *Caesar to bring help

- As a Gaul, Verticus was able to circulate among the Gauls without difficulty:

  - *Erat unus intus Nervius, nomine **Vertico**, loco natus honesto, qui a prima obsidione ad Ciceronem perfugerat, suamque ei fidem praestiterat. Hic servo spe libertatis magnisque persuadet praemiis ut litteras ad Caesarem deferat.* (5.45)

Verucloetius (1)

- an ambassador, along with *Nammeius, at the head of the embassy sent by the *Helvetii to *Caesar to communicate that the *Helvetii intended no damage or violence and had no other route:

  - *Ubi de eius adventu Helvetii certiores facti sunt, legatos ad eum mittunt nobilissimos civitatis, cuius legationis Nammeius et **Verucloetius** principem locum obtinebant.* (1.7)

- *Caesar, remembering the death at the hands of the *Helvetii of Lucius *Cassius, refuses to admit them.

L. Vorenus (5: 4 as Vorenus; 1 as L. Vorenus)

- one of two legionaries, along with T. *Pullo, who, in the attack by *Ambiorix on *Cicero's camp, were vying with each other for primacy in the legion

- *Pullo, as he enters the battle, asks why Vorenus is hanging back in the battle so Vorenus joins.

- But *Pullo is gravely wounded and Vorenus saves him.

- Both are praised equally for their valor and it can't be decided who is the braver:

  - *Pullo, cum acerrime ad munitiones pugnaretur, "Quid dubitas," inquit, "**Vorene**?"... Transfigitur scutum Pulloni et verutum in balteo defigitur ... Gladio comminus rem gerit **Vorenus**, atque uno interfecto reliquos paulum propellit ... Huic rursus circumvento fert subsidium Pullo, atque ambo incolumes compluribus interfectis summa cum laude sese intra munitiones recipiunt. Sic fortuna in contentione et certamine utrumque versavit, ut alter alteri inimicus auxilio salutique esset neque diiudicari posset, uter utri virtute anteferendus videretur.* (5.44)

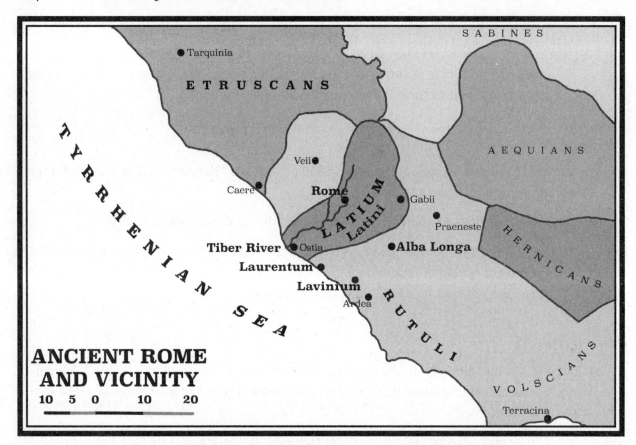

ANCIENT ROME
AND VICINITY

10 5 0   10   20

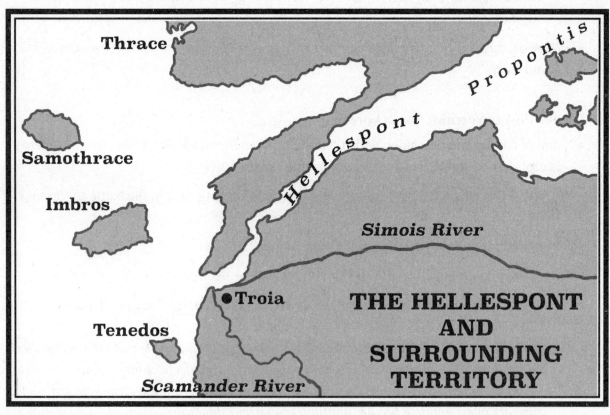

THE HELLESPONT
AND
SURROUNDING
TERRITORY

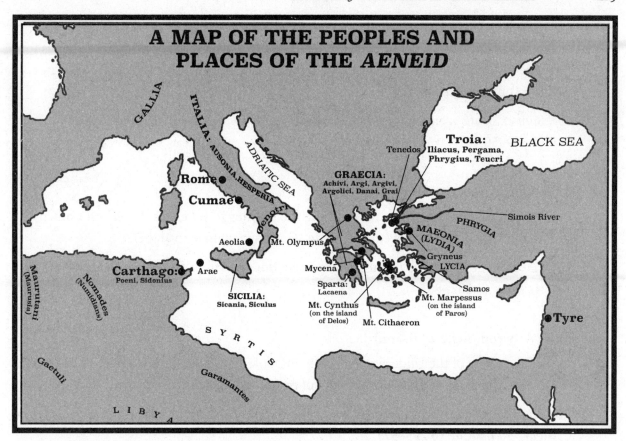

A MAP OF THE PEOPLES AND PLACES OF THE *AENEID*

3.2 *Aeneid* Proper Name Glossary

- Summary lists that organize by people, geographic feature, and frequency of occurrence appear before the glossary; use these to organize and focus your study; for example, Dido appears eleven times in the Latin syllabus and so it is more important to know about her than, say, Deiopea, who only appears once.

- Maps are included before the glossary for a visual reference.

  - The Ancient Rome and Vicinity map identifies the places and peoples of the region of Rome.

  - The Hellespont map is for general reference and to highlight the island of Tenedos.

  - The Peoples and Places of the *Aeneid* map includes all proper names except for the region of Rome places and peoples.

Abas (1; Abas, Abantis)

- a Trojan companion who accompanies *Aeneas from *Troy and who is caught in the storm sent by *Juno:

  - *Iam validam Ilionei navem, iam fortis Achatae, / et qua vectus **Abas**, et qua grandaevus Aletes, / vicit hiems.* (1.120–22)

Acestes (4; Acestes, -ae, m.)

- a Trojan king of Sicily who welcomed *Aeneas during his journey, held funeral games for the recently dead *Anchises, and offered to settle any Trojan with *Aeneas who did not wish to continue the journey:

  o *Sunt et Siculis regionibus urbes / armaque Troianoque a sanguine clarus **Acestes**.* (1.549–50)

Achates (3; Achates, -ae, m.)

- one of *Aeneas' closest companions during the journey to Italy, Achates is best known for accompanying *Aeneas as they explore *Carthage upon arrival there:

  o *Constitit hic arcumque manu celeresque sagittas / corripuit fidus quae tela gerebat **Achates**.* (1.187–88)

Acheron (1; Acheron, Acherontis, m.)

- one of the rivers of the Underworld; Vergil, in book 6, uses the name to refer to the river Styx, over which the unburied souls are not permitted to cross:

  o *Hinc via Tartarei quae fert **Acherontis** ad undas. / turbidus hic caeno vastaque voragine gurges / aestuat.* (6.295–97)

Achilles (2; Achilles, Achillis, m.)

- the great Greek fighter best known for his slaying and defiling of *Hector in the *Iliad*

- In the *Aeneid*, he appears once at 1.30 as one of those whom the Trojans fled and again at 2.275 when *Hector appears to *Aeneas in a dream.

- *Aeneas describes the contrast between the appearance of *Hector returning from battle wearing Achilles' armor and his appearance as a ghost bearing the wounds Achilles inflicted upon him:

  o *Ei mihi, qualis erat, quantum mutatus ab illo / Hectore qui redit exuvias indutus **Achilli**.* (2.274–75)

the Achivi (1; Achivi, -orum, m.)

- a term for the Greeks:

  o *Aut hoc inclusi ligno occultantur **Achivi**, / aut haec in nostros fabricata est machina muros.* (2.45–46)

Aeacides (1; Aeacides, -ae, m.)

- a patronymic for *Achilles, referring to his grandfather Aeacus:

- o *Mene Iliacis occumbere campis / non potuisse tuaque animam hanc effundere dextra, / saevus ubi **Aeacidae** telo iacet Hector.* (1.97–99)

Aeneades (2; Aeneadēs, -ae, m.)

- the followers of *Aeneas:

  - o *Quis genus **Aeneadum**, quis Troiae nesciat urbem, / virtutesque virosque aut tanti incendia belli?* (1.565–66)

Aeneas (23; Aeneas, -ae, m.)

- Trojan hero who escapes from the burning *Troy with the divine charge of traveling to Italy to establish a new *Troy

Aeolus (5)

- god of the winds whom *Juno bribes with a *nymph to send a storm to Aeneas and his fleet to blow them off their course for Italy

- *Neptune, when he discovers the storm and its origin, rebukes Aeolus:

  - o *Hic vasto rex **Aeolus** antro / luctantes ventos tempestatesque sonoras / imperio premit ac vinclis et carcere frenat.* (1.52–54)

Aeolia (1)

- the land where *Aeolus and the winds live:

  - o *Talia flammato secum dea corde volutans / nimborum in patriam, loca feta furentibus Austris, / **Aeoliam** venit.* (1.50–52)

Africus (1)

- the southwest wind and one of three winds identified by Vergil whom *Aeolus released to cause the storm in book 1:

  - o *Incubuere mari totumque a sedibus imis / una Eurusque Notusque ruunt creberque procellis / **Africus**, et vastos volvunt ad litora fluctus.* (1.84–86)

Aiax (1; Aiax, Aiacis, m.)

- Greek hero, son of *Oileus (not the more famous son of Telamon), who defiled *Cassandra in Minerva's temple and whom Minerva struck down with a thunderbolt

- *Juno uses Ajax's story to fuel her resentment over why she can't stop Aeneas:

  - o *Quippe vetor fatis. Pallasne exurere classem / Argivum atque ipsos potuit submergere ponto / unius ob noxam et furias **Aiacis** Oilei?* (1.39–41)

Albani (1; Albanus, -a, -um)

- referring to Alba Longa, the city that *Aeneas' son *Ascanius founded and that lasted 300 years before *Rome was founded:

  o *genus unde Latinum / **Albani**que patres atque altae moenia Romae* (1.6–7)

Alcides (1; Alcides, -ae, m.)

- a patronymic for Hercules from his grandfather Alceus:

  o *Nec vero **Alciden** me sum laetatus euntem / accepisse lacu.* (6.392–93)

Aletes (1; Aletes, -ae, m.)

- a Trojan companion who accompanies *Aeneas from *Troy and who is caught in the storm sent by *Juno:

  o *Iam validam Ilionei navem, iam fortis Achatae, / et qua vectus Abas, et qua grandaevus **Aletes**, / vicit hiems.* (1.120–22)

Amphrysia (1; Amphrysius, -a, -um)

- an obscure reference to *Apollo based on his temporary servitude to Admetus in Thessaly by the river Amphrysus:

  o *Quae contra breviter fata est **Amphrysia** vates.* (6.398)

Anchises (8; Anchises, Anchisae; acc: Anchisen, m.)

- father of *Aeneas and lover of *Venus

- When *Troy is burning, Anchises initially refuses to accompany *Aeneas, despite his entreaties.

- It is only an omen of tongues of fire appearing atop the head of Aeneas' son, *Ascanius, that convinces him that he should go:

  o *Non prius aspicies ubi fessum aetate parentem / liqueris **Anchisen**, superet coniunxne Creusa / Ascaniusque puer.* (2.596–98)

Antheus (2; Antheus, -i; acc: Anthea, m.)

- one of Aeneas' companions whose ship he tries to locate after surviving the storm that *Aeolus sends:

  o *Aeneas scopulum interea conscendit, et omnem / prospectum late pelago petit, **Anthea** si quem / iactatum vento videat Phrygiasque biremes / aut Capyn aut celsis in puppibus arma Caici.* (1.180–83)

- One of Aeneas' companions, along with *Sergestus and *Cloanthus, whom Aeneas sees entering Dido's temple:

  o *cum subito Aeneas concursu accedere magno / **Anthea** Sergestumque videt fortemque Cloanthum / Teucrorumque alios* (1.509–11)

Apollo (1; Apollo, Apollonis, m.)

- the god of the sun, medicine, music, poetry, and prophecy, the latter used most prominently throughout the *Aeneid*

- Apollo in book 4 is associated with two locations of his oracle, *Lycia and *Grynium:

  o *Sed nunc Italiam magnam Gryneus **Apollo**, / Italiam Lyciae iussere capessere sortes.* (4.345–46)

Aquilo (2; Aquilo, Aquilonis, m.)

- the north wind and bringer of cold:

  o *Talia iactanti stridens **Aquilone** procella / velum adversa ferit, fluctusque ad sidera tollit.* (1.102–3)

Arae (1; Arae, -arum)

- the name of a large and dangerous reef by which three of Aeneas' ships were dashed:

  o *(saxa vocant Itali mediis quae in fluctibus **Aras**, / dorsum inmane mari summo)* (1.109–10)

Argi / Argivi / Argolici (1 each; Argus, -a, -um; Argivus, -a, -um; Argolicus, -a, -um)

- a term for the Greeks, derived from Argos, one of ancient Greece's most famous cities:

  o *Id metuens veterisque memor Saturnia belli, / prima quod ad Troiam pro caris gesserat **Argis*** (1.23–24)

  o *Pallasne exurere classem / **Argivum** atque ipsos potuit submergere ponto / unius ob noxam et furias Aiacis Oilei?* (1.39–41)

  o *Et, si fata deum, si mens non laeva fuisset, / impulerat ferro **Argolicas** foedare latebras.* (2.54–55)

Ascanius (3)

- The son of *Aeneas, also known as *Iulus, he accompanies *Aeneas to *Italy and will establish *Alba Longa and the lineage that will eventually lead to *Romulus and Remus and the Romans.

- It is Ascanius who bears the divine omen that inspires *Anchises to leave the burning *Troy with *Aeneas and it is Ascanius on whom *Dido fixates when she is initially infatuated with *Aeneas.

- Julius *Caesar and Augustus use the linguistic affinity of *Iulus with the Julian family name to establish divine lineage for the Julians through Ascanius' grandmother *Venus:

  o *Si te nulla movet tantarum gloria rerum / nec super ipse tua moliris laude laborem, / **Ascanium** surgentem et spes heredis Iuli / respice, cui regnum Italiae Romanaque tellus / debetur.* (4.272–76)

Ausonia (1; here Ausonius, -a, -um)

- a name for ancient *Italy:

  o *Si te Karthaginis arces / Phoenissam Libycaeque aspectus detinet urbis, / quae tandem **Ausonia** Teucros considere terra / invidia est?* (4.347–50)

Auster (2; Auster, Austri)

- The south wind that brings wind and rain, Auster is used as a more general term for stormy winds than *Notus, also a word for the south wind:

  o *Talia flammato secum dea corde volutans / nimborum in patriam, loca feta furentibus **Austris**, / Aeoliam venit.* (1.49–51)

Bacchus (1)

- the Roman god of wine and disorder

- When *Dido learns of the rumor of *Aeneas' departure, she rages through the city like a Maenad, a crazed worshipper of Bacchus:

  o *Saevit inops animi totamque incensa per urbem / bacchatur, qualis commotis excita sacris / Thyias, ubi audito stimulant trieterica **Baccho** / orgia nocturnusque vocat clamore Cithaeron.* (4.300–303)

Caicus (1)

- a companion of *Aeneas feared lost at sea in the storm sent by *Juno:

  o *Aeneas scopulum interea conscendit, et omnem / prospectum late pelago petit, Anthea si quem / iactatum vento videat Phrygiasque biremes / aut Capyn aut celsis in puppibus arma **Caici**.* (1.180–83)

Capys (1; Capys, Capyos; acc: Capyn, m.)

- a companion of *Aeneas feared lost at sea in the storm sent by *Juno:

o *Aeneas scopulum interea conscendit, et omnem / prospectum late pelago petit, Anthea si quem / iactatum vento videat Phrygiasque biremes / aut **Capyn** aut celsis in puppibus arma Caici.* (1.180–83)

Carthage (4; Karthago, -inis, f.)

- an ancient city in North Africa on the coast of modern Tunisia at the point where Africa and Sicily are the closest

- Founded by *Dido after fleeing the Phoenician city of *Tyre and her brother *Pygmalion, Carthage would grow into *Rome's greatest rival for control of the Mediterranean Sea, over which they fought in the three Punic Wars of the 3rd and 2nd centuries BC.

- *Juno hopes to divert *Aeneas from reaching *Italy because she knows that his eventual descendants will conquer her prized city.

- The abandoning of *Dido by *Aeneas and her resulting curse of him is used to explain that later enmity between the two cultures:

  o *Urbs antiqua fuit (Tyrii tenuere coloni) / **Karthago**, Italiam contra Tiberinaque longe / ostia, dives opum studiisque asperrima belli, / quam Iuno fertur terris magis omnibus unam / posthabita coluisse Samo.* (1.12–16)

Cassandra (1)

- daughter of *Priam and Hecuba and cursed by *Apollo to know the future but not be able to convince others of her prescience

- After the death of *Laocoon and his sons, Cassandra is the final voice to express doubt about the Trojan Horse as the Trojans wheel it into *Troy:

  o *Tunc etiam fatis aperit **Cassandra** futuris / ora dei iussu non umquam credita Teucris.* (2.246–47)

Cerberus (1)

- the three-headed guard dog of the Underworld

- When *Aeneas and the *Sibyl first debark from *Charon's boat in the Underworld, Cerberus greets them violently.

- The *Sibyl soothes Cerberus by throwing him a treat:

  o ***Cerberus** haec ingens latratu regna trifauci / personat adverso recubans immanis in antro. / Cui vates horrere videns iam colla colubris / melle soporatam et medicatis frugibus offam / obicit.* (6.417–21)

CHAPTER 3

Ceres (2; 1 as noun Ceres, Cereris, f.; 1 as adjective Cerealis, -e)

- the goddess of grain and the harvest, used by Vergil not in her divine role but as a metonymy for grain:

  - *Tum **Cererem** corruptam undis **Cerealia**que arma / expediunt fessi rerum, frugesque receptas / et torrere parant flammis et frangere saxo.* (1.177–79)

Ceres, the goddess of grain and the harvest

Charon (2; Charon, Charontis, m.)

- the boatman of the Underworld, responsible for transporting the properly buried dead across the river Styx (referred to as *Acheron in the *Aeneid*):

  - *Portitor has horrendus aquas et flumina servat / terribili squalore **Charon**, cui plurima mento / canities inculta iacet, stant lumina flamma, / sordidus ex umeris nodo dependet amictus.* (6.298–301)

Cithaeron (1; Cithaeron, Cithaeronis, m.)

- a mountain in central Greece sacred to *Bacchus, the Roman god of wine and disorder

- When *Dido learns of the rumor of *Aeneas' departure, she rages through the city like a Maenad, a crazed worshipper of *Bacchus:

  - *Saevit inops animi totamque incensa per urbem / bacchatur, qualis commotis excita sacris / Thyias, ubi audito stimulant trieterica Baccho / orgia nocturnusque vocat clamore **Cithaeron**.* (4.300–303)

Cloanthus (1)

- one of Aeneas' companions, along with *Antheus and *Sergestus, whom Aeneas sees entering *Dido's temple:

  - *cum subito Aeneas concursu accedere magno / Anthea Sergestumque videt fortemque **Cloanthum** / Teucrorumque alios* (1.509–11)

Cocytus (2)

- one of the rivers of the Underworld, the river of lamentation:

  - *Anchisa generate, deum certissima proles, / **Cocyti** stagna alta vides Stygiamque paludem, / di cuius iurare timent et fallere numen.* (6.322–24)

Coeus (1)

- a Titan, the son of Mother Earth, the brother of the giant *Enceladus, and brother of Rumor or *Fama:

o   *Illam Terra parens ira inritata deorum / extremam, ut perhibent, **Coeo** Enceladoque sororem / progenuit pedibus celerem et pernicibus alis.* (4.178–80)

Creusa (2)

- Trojan wife of *Aeneas whom he lost during his flight from *Troy

- He went back to find her but only found her ghost who gave him her blessing to leave and find happiness in a new land:

    o   *Obstipui; subiit cari genitoris imago, / ut regem aequaevum crudeli vulnere vidi / vitam exhalantem, subiit deserta **Creusa** / et direpta domus et parvi casus Iuli.* (2.560–63)

Cyclops (1; used in its adjectival form: Cyclopius, -a, -um)

- a race of one-eyed monsters characterized by Homer in the *Odyssey* as lacking civilization

- In book 3 of the *Aeneid* (not in the syllabus), *Aeneas and his men arrive at the land of the Cyclopes and take on a Greek abandoned there by *Ulysses.

- In book 1, Aeneas refers to the Cyclopes as one of the dangers they have survived as he encourages his men to remain steadfast in the face of the storm sent by *Juno:

    o   *Vos et Scyllaeam rabiem penitusque sonantes / accestis scopulos, vos et **Cyclopia** saxa / experti: revocate animos maestumque timorem / mittite.* (1.200–203)

Cyllenius (1; Cyllenius, -a -um)

- referring to Cylene, the mother of Mercury, and used to mean Mercury, the messenger god

- Mercury delivers to *Aeneas in *Carthage the message from *Jupiter that he has tarried too long and must continue to pursue his destiny to reach *Italy:

    o   *Tali **Cyllenius** ore locutus / mortales visus medio sermone reliquit / et procul in tenuem ex oculis evanuit auram.* (4.276–78)

Cymothoe (1; Cymothoe, -es, f.)

- a sea *nymph who, along with *Triton, a sea god, rescues Aeneas' ships after *Neptune has calmed the storm that *Juno sent:

    o   ***Cymothoe** simul et Triton adnixus acuto / detrudunt naves scopulo.* (1.144–45)

Cynthus (1)

- a mountain on the island of Delos where *Apollo and Artemis were born:

    o   *Qualis in Eurotae ripis aut per iuga **Cynthi** / exercet Diana choros, quam mille secutae / hinc atque hinc glomerantur Oreades.* (1.498–500)

Danai (7; Danai, -orum)

- epithet for the Greeks from King Danaus (Danaos), a mythic king of *Argos:

  - *Quidquid id est, timeo **Danaos** et dona ferentes.* (2.49)

Dardani / Dardanides (6; Dardanus, -a, -um or Dardanius, -a, -um; Dardanides, -ae, m.)

- epithet for the Trojans from Dardanus, son of *Jupiter and Electra, who founded Dardania, near *Troy:

  - *O lux **Dardaniae**, spes o fidissima Teucrum, / quae tantae tenuere morae?* (2.281–82)

  - *O patria, o divum domus Ilium et incluta bello / moenia **Dardanidum**!* (2.241–42)

Deiopea (1)

- *nymph whom *Juno promises to *Aeolus in return for the storm he sends against Aeneas' fleet:

  - *Sunt mihi bis septem praestanti corpore Nymphae, / quarum quae forma pulcherrima **Deiopea**, / conubio iungam stabili propriamque dicabo.* (1.71–73)

Diana (1)

- goddess of the hunt to whom *Dido is compared when Aeneas sees her entering the temple in *Carthage:

  - *Qualis in Eurotae ripis aut per iuga Cynthi / exercet **Diana** choros, quam mille secutae / hinc atque hinc glomerantur Oreades.* (1.498–500)

Diana, the virginal goddess of the hunt

Dido (11; Dido, -onis, f.)

- queen of *Carthage who fled the Phoenician city of *Tyre after her brother *Pygmalion killed her husband *Sychaeus

- She founded *Carthage with money her husband revealed to her as a ghost after his death.

- She welcomed Aeneas and, from the influence of *Venus, fell in love with him.

- When he left, she committed suicide and said nothing to him when he tried to explain in the Underworld:

  - *regina ad templum, forma pulcherrima **Dido**, / incessit magna iuvenum stipante caterva* (1.496–97)

  - *Inter quas Phoenissa recens a vulnere **Dido** / errabat silva in magna.* (6.450–51)

Dis (2; Dis, Ditis, m.)

- an alternate name for Hades, god of the Underworld:

  - *Hunc ego **Diti** / sacrum iussa fero teque isto corpore solvo.* (4.702–3)

Elissa (1)

- an alternate name for *Dido:

  - *nec me meminisse pigebit **Elissae** / dum memor ipse mei, dum spiritus hos regit artus* (4.335–36)

Enceladus (1)

- a giant, the son of Mother Earth, brother to the Titan *Coeus, and brother to Rumor or *Fama:

  - *Illam Terra parens ira inritata deorum / extremam, ut perhibent, Coeo **Encelado**que sororem / progenuit pedibus celerem et pernicibus alis.* (4.178–80)

Erebus (1)

- another name for the Underworld:

  - *Troius Aeneas, pietate insignis et armis, / ad genitorem imas **Erebi** descendit ad umbras.* (6.403–4)

Erinys (1; Erinys, Erinyos, f.)

- the personification of Fury, whose plural refers to the mythological Furies; in the singular and at *Aeneid* 2.573 used as metonymy for "rage," "curse," or "destruction":

  - *[illa] Troiae et patriae communis **Erinys**, / abdiderat sese atque aris invisa sedebat* (2.573–74)

Eryx (1; Eryx, Erycis, m.)

- a half-brother of Aeneas by *Venus after whose name a town and mountain in Sicily is named:

  - *Seu vos Hesperiam magnam Saturniaque arva / sive **Erycis** fines regemque optatis Acesten.* (1.569–70)

Eurus (4)

- the east wind and one of three winds identified by Vergil whom *Aeolus released to cause the storm in book 1:

- o *Incubuere mari totumque a sedibus imis / una **Eurus**que Notusque ruunt creberque procellis / Africus, et vastos volvunt ad litora fluctus.* (1.84–86)

- Eurus is also the direct recipient of *Neptune's censure just before he calms the storm:

- o *Tenet ille immania saxa, / vestras, **Eure**, domos; illa se iactet in aula / Aeolus et clauso ventorum carcere regnet.* (1.139–41)

Eurotas (1; Eurotas, -ae, m.)

- a river in the Peloponnese of Greece on which *Sparta is located

- It is used in the simile that compares *Dido to *Diana dancing with her chorus:

- o *Qualis in **Eurotae** ripis aut per iuga Cynthi / exercet Diana choros.* (1.498–99)

Fama (4)

- rumor personified whose physical appearance Vergil describes in detail when she flies through *Carthage spreading word of the relationship of *Dido and Aeneas:

- o *Extemplo Libyae magnas it **Fama** per urbes, / **Fama**, malum qua non aliud velocius ullum: / mobilitate viget viresque adquirit eundo.* (4.173–75)

- Rumor is also responsible for hinting to *Dido that Aeneas was planning to leave *Carthage:

- o *Eadem impia **Fama** furenti / detulit armari classem cursumque parari.* (4.298–99)

Gaetulus (1)

- referring to the Gaetulians, an ancient people who lived in modern Morocco and to whom *Dido's suitor *Iarbus belonged:

- o *Quid moror? An mea Pygmalion dum moenia frater / destruat aut captam ducat **Gaetulus** Iarbas?* (4.325–26)

Gallus (1)

- referring to the Gauls, an ancient people who lived in modern France and throughout Western Europe

- In the Underworld, *Anchises identifies the Gauls as one of the peoples whose rebellion will be put down by the elder *Marcellus:

- o *Hic rem Romanam magno turbante tumultu / sistet eques, sternet Poenos **Gallum**que rebellem, / tertiaque arma patri suspendet capta Quirino.* (6.857–59)

Ganymede (1; Ganymedes, -is, m.)

The Trojan Ganymede and Jupiter's eagle

- a brother of *Priam whom *Jupiter coveted and brought to *Olympus where he became cupbearer to the gods

- He is used to explain *Juno's hatred of the Trojans.

- Ganymede was made cupbearer to the gods over *Juno's daughter Hebe:

  - *manet alta mente repostum / iudicium Paridis spretaeque iniuria formae / et genus invisum et rapti **Ganymedis** honores* (1.26–28)

Garamantidus (1)

- referring to the Garamantes, an ancient North African people that lived in modern *Libya and the location of the oracle of *Hammon, with whom *Jupiter was associated

- *Iarbas was the product of *Jupiter and a Garamantian *nymph whose identity is unknown:

  - *Hic Hammone satus rapta **Garamantide** nympha / templa Iovi centum latis immania regnis.* (4.198–99)

Gorgon (1; Gorgo, -onis, f.)

The head of Medusa

- snake-haired woman whose gaze turns people to stone

- Her head traditionally appears on Minerva's shield:

  - *Iam summas arces Tritonia, respice, Pallas / insedit nimbo effulgens et **Gorgone** saeva.* (2.615–16)

Grai (2; Graius, -a, -um; Grai, -orum)

- referring to the Greeks:

  - *Est locus, Hesperiam **Grai** cognomine dicunt.* (1.530)

Grynium (1; Grynium, -i)

- a city in modern western Turkey and the location of one of *Apollo's oracles:

  - *Sed nunc Italiam magnam **Gryneus** Apollo, / Italiam Lyciae iussere capessere sortes.* (4.345–46)

Hammon (1; Hammon, Hammonis, m.)

- referring to *Jupiter Hammon (or Ammon), an Egyptian incarnation of *Jupiter

- *Dido's suitor *Iarbas was the son of Hammon and a *nymph and he built, according to the *Aeneid*, 100 temples to his father:

  o *Hic **Hammone** satus rapta Garamantide nympha / templa Iovi centum latis immania regnis.* (4.198–99)

- It is to his father as well that he prays to address the insult of *Dido loving *Aeneas rather than him.

Hector (4; Hector, Hectoris, m.)

- prince and greatest fighter of *Troy who is killed by *Achilles after Hector kills *Achilles' best friend Patroclus (who was wearing *Achilles' armor)

- *Achilles not only kills Hector but also drags his body around the city three times and will not return it until *Priam begs him.

- In the *Aeneid*, Hector's death is not included but rather he appears to *Aeneas in a dream to inform him that *Troy has been taken and that he must flee:

  o *In somnis, ecce, ante oculos maestissimus **Hector** / visus adesse mihi largosque effundere fletus.* (2.270–71)

Hesperia (3)

- ancient name for *Italy used by the Greeks:

  o *Est locus, **Hesperiam** Grai cognomine dicunt.* (1.530)

Iarbas (2; Iarbas, -ae, m.)

- son of *Jupiter *Hammon and a *nymph and a local suitor of *Dido of the *Gaetulian tribe whom *Dido rejected in favor of *Aeneas:

  o *Protinus ad regem cursus detorquet **Iarban** / incenditque animum dictis atque aggerat iras.* (4.196)

- When *Aeneas leaves, *Dido accuses him of abandoning her to Iarbas:

  o *An mea Pygmalion dum moenia frater / destruat aut captam ducat Gaetulus **Iarbas**?* (4.325–26)

Iliacus (1; Iliacus, -a, -um)

- referring to *Troy; Trojan:

  o *Nec puer **Iliaca** quisquam de gente Latinos / in tantum spe tollet avos.* (6.875–76)

Ilioneus (3)

- a companion of *Aeneas whose ship was sunk in the storm sent by *Juno:

    o *Iam validam **Ilionei** navem.* (1.120)

- When he and the other Trojans arrive before *Dido in *Carthage, as the eldest, Ilioneus speaks first:

    o *Postquam introgressi et coram data copia fandi, / maximus **Ilioneus** placido sic pectore coepit.* (1.520–21)

Iris (2; Iris, Iridis; acc: Irim, f.)

- messenger goddess whom *Juno sends to release *Dido's soul from her body:

    o *Tum Iuno omnipotens longum miserata dolorem / difficilesque obitus **Irim** demisit Olympo … Ergo **Iris** croceis per caelum roscida pennis / mille trahens varios adverso sole colores / devolat et supra caput astitit.* (4.693–94, 700–702)

Italia (11)

- Italy, the land which *Aeneas is fated to reach to found his new *Troy:

    o *Arma virumque cano, Troiae qui primus ab oris / **Italiam** fato profugus Laviniaque venit / litora.* (1.1–3)

    o *gens inimica mihi Tyrrhenum navigat aequor / Ilium in **Italiam** portans victosque penates* (1.67–68)

Iulus (3)

- An alternate name for *Ascanius, the son of *Aeneas, he accompanies *Aeneas to *Italy and will establish *Alba Longa and the lineage that will eventually lead to *Romulus and Remus and the Romans.

- It is *Ascanius who bears the divine omen that inspires *Anchises to leave the burning *Troy with *Aeneas and it is *Ascanius on whom *Dido fixates when she is initially infatuated with *Aeneas.

- Julius Caesar and Augustus use the linguistic affinity of Iulus with the Julian family name to establish divine lineage for the Julians through *Ascanius' grandmother *Venus:

    o *Si te nulla movet tantarum gloria rerum / nec super ipse tua moliris laude laborem, / **Ascanium** surgentem et spes heredis Iuli / respice, cui regnum Italiae Romanaque tellus / debetur.* (4.272–76)

Iuno (8; Iuno, Iunonis, f.)

- Goddess of marriage and wife of *Jupiter, she tortures *Aeneas, as Vergil describes in *Aeneid* 1.26–28, for the following reasons:

  o the slight to her beauty in the Judgment of *Paris

  o the birth of the Trojan founder *Dardanus to *Jupiter and Electra, one of *Jupiter's many mistresses

  o the elevation of the Trojan youth *Ganymede to cupbearer to the gods over Juno's daughter Hebe

    ▪ *manet alta mente repostum / iudicium Paridis spretaeque iniuria formae / et genus invisum et rapti Ganymedis honores* (1.26–28)

Juno, queen of the gods and enemy of Aeneas

- She also hopes to divert *Aeneas from reaching *Italy because she knows that his eventual descendants will conquer her prized city of *Carthage in the Punic Wars of the 3rd and 2nd centuries BC, fought between *Rome and *Carthage for dominion over the Mediterranean.

- The abandoning of *Dido by *Aeneas and her resulting curse of him is used to explain that later enmity between the two cultures:

  o *Urbs antiqua fuit (Tyrii tenuere coloni) / Karthago, Italiam contra Tiberinaque longe / ostia, dives opum studiisque asperrima belli, / quam* **Iuno** *fertur terris magis omnibus unam / posthabita coluisse Samo.* (1.12–16)

Iupiter (9: 2 in the nominative, 7 in the non-nominative; Iūpiter, Iovis, m.; Iuppiter, Iovis, m.; Jupiter in English)

- king of the gods, husband of *Juno, and god of the sky and thunder

- He appears in the *Aeneid* as the presider over *Aeneas' destiny both (in the English syllabus) when *Venus complains to him that *Juno continues to harass *Aeneas and when he convinces *Juno to relent in that harassment.

- He is also, as Jupiter *Hammon, the father of *Iarbas to whom *Iarbas prays when *Dido chooses *Aeneas over him:

Jupiter, the king of the gods

  o ***Iuppiter** omnipotens, cui nunc Maurusia pictis / gens epulata toris Lenaeum libat honorem, / aspicis haec?* (4.206–8)

Lacaena (1)

- the term for a *Spartan woman, in the *Aeneid* Helen, whom *Aeneas sees hiding in the Temple of *Vesta during the fall of *Troy and whom *Aeneas wants to kill for her impact on *Troy

- *Venus appears to Aeneas, however, and saves Helen, claiming that it is not her fault that *Troy has fallen but rather the fault of the gods:

o *Non tibi Tyndaridis facies invisa **Lacaenae** / culpatusve Paris, divum inclementia, divum / has evertit opes sternitque a culmine Troiam.* (2.601–3)

Laocoon (4; Laocoon, Laocoontis, m.)

The death of Laocoon and his sons

- Trojan priest who rushes to the beach where the Trojan Horse has been left and claims correctly that it is a trick and should not be brought into the city

- Laocoon, along with his two sons, is killed by two sea serpents who come from the sea from the nearby island of *Tenedos where the Greek fleet is hiding:

  o *Primus ibi ante omnes magna comitante caterva / **Laocoon** ardens summa decurrit ab arce* (2.40–41)

  o *Illi [angues] agmine certo / **Laocoonta** petunt.* (2.212–13)

Latini (2; Latinus, -a, -um; Latini, -orum)

- the Latin people who live in the area of *Rome when *Aeneas arrives there

- *Aeneas, after the death of *Latinus, establishes Lavinium as the capital city.

- After the death of *Aeneas, *Ascanius establishes Alba Longa as the new capital:

  o *genus unde **Latinum** / Albanique patres atque altae moenia Romae.* (1.6–7)

Latinus (1)

- king of the *Latins, who live in the area around *Rome when *Aeneas arrives in *Italy

- He recognizes *Aeneas as the foreigner who it is prophesied will marry his daughter Lavinia.

- Betrothing Lavinia to *Aeneas, however, angers *Turnus, the king of the Rutulians to whom Lavinia was previously promised:

  o *exim bella viro memorat quae deinde gerenda, / Laurentesque docet populos urbemque **Latini*** (6.890–91)

Latium (4; Latium, -i)

- the area of *Italy where the *Latins lived and where *Latinus ruled:

  o *multa quoque et bello passus, dum conderet urbem / inferretque deos **Latio*** (1.5–6)

  o *Per varios casus, per tot discrimina rerum / tendimus in **Latium**, sedes ubi fata quietas / ostendunt; illic fas regna resurgere Troiae.* (1.204–6)

Latona (1)

- the Roman name for the Greek Leto, the mother of *Apollo and *Diana

- In the *Aeneid* she is referenced in the simile that compares *Dido to *Diana dancing with a chorus of *nymphs:

  - *illa [Diana] pharetram / fert umero gradiensque deas supereminet omnes / (**Latonae** tacitum pertemptant gaudia pectus).* (1.500–502)

Laurentine (1; Laurens, Laurentis, adj)

- referring to Laurentum, the capital city of the *Latins, ruled by *Latinus:

  - *exim bella viro memorat quae deinde gerenda, / **Laurentes**que docet populos urbemque Latini.* (6.890–91)

Lavinian (1; Lavinius, -a, -um)

- referring to Lavinium, the capital city of *Latium that *Aeneas founded:

  - *Arma virumque cano, Troiae qui primus ab oris / Italiam fato profugus **Lavinia**que venit / litora.* (1.1–3)

Libya (11; Libya, -ae; Libycus, -a, -um)

- referring to Libya or the Libyans, a people of North Africa

- *Dido laments that *Aeneas' departure will expose her to the odium of the locals, whom she specifies as Libyans and Numidians:

  - *te propter **Libycae** gentes Nomadumque tyranni / odere, infensi Tyrii;* (4.320–21)

- More generally, the term is used synonymously with (North) African.

Lycia (2)

- an area in modern southern Turkey and the location of one of *Apollo's oracles:

  - *Sed nunc Italiam magnam Gryneus Apollo, / Italiam **Lyciae** iussere capessere sortes.* (4.345–46)

Maeonian (1; Maeonius, -a, -um)

- *Phrygian or Lydian, so Trojan or, more generally, eastern

- Maeonia was an alternate name for Lydia, the ancient region of western modern Turkey:

  - *Et nunc ille Paris cum semiviro comitatu, / **Maeonia** mentum mitra crinemque madentem / subnexus, rapto potitur.* (4.215–17)

Manes (1; Manes, -ium)

- the souls of the dead, and so another word for the underworld:

  - *sed falsa ad caelum mittunt insomnia **Manes*** (6.896)

Marcellus (2)

- a Roman general of the Gallic War and the 2nd Punic War famous for acquiring the *spolia opima*, arms acquired from an opposing general in single combat, and whom *Anchises shows *Aeneas in the underworld as one of his glorious descendants

- The Romans recognized only three instances that merited the designation of *spolia opima* (however many other times the arms of an opposing general were acquired):

  - *Romulus over the general in the war with the Caeninenses

  - Cossus over the king of the Veientes, an Etruscan people

  - Marcellus over Viridomarus, a Gallic king:

    - *Aspice, ut insignis **spoliis Marcellus opimis** / ingreditur victorque viros supereminet omnes.* (6.855–56)

- The name Marcellus also, however, refers to Augustus' nephew who died prematurely in 23 BC, one of the prime candidates to succeed Augustus.

- It is reported that Marcellus' mother wept upon hearing 6.861 and the following lines when they were read to her:

  - *Quis, pater, ille, virum qui sic comitatur euntem? / Filius, anne aliquis magna de stirpe nepotum?* (6.863–64)

Marpessus (1; Marpesius, -a, -um)

- a mountain on the island of Paros from which white marble is quarried

- here used to represent *Dido's hardness in the face of *Aeneas' entreaties to her in the underworld:

  - *Illa solo fixos oculos aversa tenebat / nec magis incepto vultum sermone movetur / quam si dura silex aut stet **Marpesia** cautes.* (6.469–71)

Maurusian (1; Maurusius, -a, -um)

- referring to the Maurutanians, a people of northwest Africa, but here used to mean more generally African:

  - *Iuppiter omnipotens, cui nunc **Maurusia** pictis / gens epulata toris Lenaeum libat honorem, / aspicis haec?* (4.206–8)

Mavors (1; Mavors, Mavortis, m.)

- an old name for the war god Mars:

  - *Quantos ille virum magnam **Mavortis** ad urbem / campus aget gemitus!* (6.872–73)

Mnestheus (1)

- one of *Aeneas' companions, along with *Sergestus and *Serestus, whom he summons to prepare for their clandestine departure from *Carthage:

  - ***Mnesthea** Sergestumque vocat fortemque Serestum, / classem aptent taciti sociosque ad litora cogant, / arma parent et quae rebus sit causa novandis / dissimulent.* (4.288–91)

Musa (1)

- The nine Muses were the daughters of Jupiter and Mnemosyne, the goddess of memory, and presided over the arts: epic poetry, history, lyric poetry, love poetry, tragedy, sacred poetry, dance, comedy, astronomy.

- It is ancient epic convention to invoke the Muse at the beginning of the poetic endeavor.

- Although Calliope is the muse of epic poetry, Vergil invokes only a generalized Muse in the opening of the *Aeneid*:

  - ***Musa**, mihi causas memora, quo numine laeso / quidve dolens regina deum tot volvere casus / insignem pietate virum, tot adire labores / impulerit.* (1.8–11)

Calliope, the muse of epic poetry

Mycenae (1; Mycenae, -arum, f. pl)

- the ancient Greek city that Agamemnon ruled

- Vergil references Mycenae in book 2 when *Aeneas, fleeing the burning *Troy, sees *Helen and imagines killing her.

- He asks in essence why she should get to see her home when he and the Trojans are fleeing theirs:

  - *Scilicet haec Spartam incolumis patriasque **Mycenas** / aspiciet, partoque ibit regina triumpho?* (2.577–78)

Neptunus (3)

- The god of the seas, Neptune features most prominently when he realizes that *Aeolus has released the winds to cause the storm that *Aeneas encounters in book 1 and orders him to collect the winds to stop the storm:

o *Interea magno misceri murmure pontum / emissamque hiemem sensit* **Neptunus** *et imis / stagna refusa vadis, graviter commotus, et alto / prospiciens summa placidum caput extulit unda.* (1.124–27)

- He is mentioned too as the god of whom *Laocoon is priest and as the destroyer of *Troy:

o *Laocoon, ductus* **Neptuno** *sorte sacerdos, / sollemnes taurum ingentem mactabat ad aras.* (2.201–2)

o *Hic, ubi disiectas moles avulsaque saxis / saxa vides, mixtoque undantem pulvere fumum, /* **Neptunus** *muros magnoque emota tridenti / fundamenta quatit totamque a sedibus urbem / eruit.* (2.608–12)

Neptune, god of the sea

Nomades (1; Nomas, Nomadis, m.)

- referring to the Numidians, a people of North Africa

- *Dido laments that *Aeneas' departure will expose her to the odium of the locals, whom she specifies as *Libyans and Numidians:

o *te propter Libycae gentes* **Nomadum**que *tyranni / odere, infensi Tyrii* (4.320–21)

Notus (2)

- the south wind that brings wind and rain and one of three winds identified by Vergil whom *Aeolus released to cause the storm in book 1:

o *Incubuere mari totumque a sedibus imis / una Eurusque* **Notus**que *ruunt creberque procellis / Africus, et vastos volvunt ad litora fluctus.* (1.84–86)

Nymph (3; Nympha, -ae)

- minor female divinities, usually young and beautiful, associated with a specific place or geographic feature

- *Juno tells *Aeolus that she has fourteen nymphs, the most beautiful of whom is *Deiopea, whom she will give to him if he sends a storm to *Aeneas' fleet:

o *Sunt mihi bis septem praestanti corpore* **Nymphae**, / *quarum quae forma pulcherrima Deiopea, / conubio iungam stabili propriamque dicabo.* (1.71–73)

Oenotri (1; Oenotrus, Oenotra, Oenotrum)

- the Oenotrians, Arcadian Greeks who occupied the southeastern part of *Italy before the Romans

- in the *Aeneid*, used to refer to ancient Italians:

o **Oenotri** *coluere viri [locum / terram].* (1.532)

Oileus (1)

- father of *Ajax (rather than the Ajax who is the more famous son of Telamon)

- *Ajax defiled *Cassandra in Minerva's temple and for it Minerva struck him down with a thunderbolt.

- *Juno uses *Ajax's story to fuel her resentment over why she can't stop *Aeneas:

  o *Quippe vetor fatis. Pallasne exurere classem / Argivum atque ipsos potuit submergere ponto / unius ob noxam et furias Aiacis **Oilei**?* (1.39–41)

Olympus (2)

- Mt. Olympus, the home of the gods, used both times in the *Aeneid* as the place from which a god is sent to earth by another god.

- *Jupiter sends Mercury to *Carthage and *Aeneas, and *Juno sends *Iris to release *Dido's soul:

  o *Ipse deum tibi me claro demittit **Olympo** / regnator* (4.268–69)

  o *Tum Iuno omnipotens longum miserata dolorem / difficilesque obitus Irim demisit **Olympo**.* (4.694–95)

Orcus (1)

- another name for the Underworld:

  o *nondum illi flavum Proserpina vertice crinem / abstulerat Stygioque caput damnaverat **Orco**.* (4.698–99)

Oreades (1; Oreas, Oreadis, f.)

- a term for mountain *nymphs

- They appear in the simile that compares *Dido to *Diana dancing with her chorus:

  o *Qualis in Eurotae ripis aut per iuga Cynthi / exercet Diana choros quam mille secutae / hinc atque hinc glomerantur **Oreades**.* (1.498–500)

Orion (1; Orion, Orionis, m.)

- a mythological hunter whom, in the most common version, Artemis accidentally kills after *Apollo, jealous of Artemis' love for Orion, encourages her to shoot an arrow at a far away target, which in reality is Orion swimming

- Orion is memorialized in the sky as a constellation whose setting in the fall portends stormy weather and so is used here as a metonymy for a storm:

  o *Hic cursus fuit, / cum subito adsurgens fluctu nimbosus **Orion** / in vada caeca tulit.* (1.534–36)

Orontes (1; Orontes, -i; acc: Oronten, m.)

- a companion of *Aeneas whose ship is sunk in the storm sent by *Juno:

  - *Unam, quae Lycios fidumque vehebat* **Oronten**, / *ipsius ante oculos ingens a vertice pontus* / *in puppim ferit.* (1.113–15)

Pallas (2; Pallas, Palladis, f.)

- an epithet of Minerva:

  - *Iam summas arces Tritonia, respice,* **Pallas** / *insedit nimbo effulgens et Gorgone saeva.* (2.615–16)

- The name is derived either from the Greek word meaning young woman or from a myth whereby Minerva accidently killed her friend Pallas or killed in the Gigantomachy a giant named Pallas and the epithet originated in honor of that death.

Parcae (1; Parcae, -arum)

- the Fates

- There were three Fates, each of whom had a different job related to an individual's destiny: Clotho spun the thread of an individual's life, Lachesis measured the thread to determine when an individual would die, and Atropos cut the thread to mark an individual's death:

The three fates: Clotho, Atropos, and Lachesis

  - *hinc populum late regem belloque superbum* / *venturum excidio Libyae; sic volvere* **Parcas** (1.18–19)

- On the other hand, the abruptness of *Dido's death is underscored by the description of how she died before her fated time: *Juno had to send the messenger goddess *Iris to release her soul because the fates had not decreed this her time.

Paris (3; Paris, Paridis, m.)

- Trojan shepherd who was prophesied to bring about the fall of *Troy

- Because of the prophecy, he was sent from the city to tend sheep, where *Jupiter sent the three goddesses, *Venus, *Juno, Minerva, for him to determine the most beautiful:

  - *saevique dolores* / *exciderant animo; manet alta mente repostum* / *iudicium* **Paridis** (1.25–27)

- He chose *Venus and was rewarded with Helen, the most beautiful woman in the world and the husband of the Greek general Menelaus.

- Helen's carrying off by Paris prompted the Trojan War:

    o *Non tibi Tyndaridis facies invisa Lacaenae / culpatusve* **Paris**, *divum inclementia, divum / has evertit opes sternitque a culmine Troiam.* (2.601–3)

- Paris' fighting ability has always been questioned, from his role as an archer to his fleeing from Menelaus in battle (albeit helped by *Venus).

- Thus he becomes a symbol of effeminacy when *Iarbas prays to *Jupiter to vent his frustration over *Dido choosing *Aeneas:

    o *Et nunc* **ille Paris** *cum semiviro comitatu, / Maeonia mentum mitra crinemque madentem / subnexus, rapto potitur.* (4.215–17)

Pergama (3; Pergamum, -ī [usually pl])

- another name for *Troy:

    o *"Heu fuge, nate dea, teque his" ait "eripe flammis. / Hostis habet muros; ruit alto a culmine Troia. / Sat patriae Priamoque datum: si* **Pergama** *dextra / defendi possent, etiam hac defensa fuissent."* (2.289–92)

Phoenissus (2; Phoenissus, -a, -um)

- Phoenician, referring to the origin of *Dido and the *Carthagians in *Tyre, a Phoenician city:

    o *Inter quas* **Phoenissa** *recens a vulnere Dido / errabat silva in magna.* (6.450–51)

Phrygius (3; Phrygius, -a, -um)

- Phrygia was an area in western modern Turkey whose people were close allies of the Trojans in the Trojan War.

- It is thus used because of its proximity to *Troy to refer to the Trojans:

    o *Anthea si quem / iactatum vento videat* **Phrygias**que *biremes / aut Capyn aut celsis in puppibus arma Caici.* (1.180–83)

Pirithous (1; Pirithous, -i)

- friend of *Theseus, both of whom journeyed to the underworld to kidnap Persephone

- They were thwarted and their punishment was to be confined eternally to thrones in the underworld.

- The more common version of the story has Hercules rescue them when he comes to the underworld for *Cerberus. Vergil departs from that version (6.617–18, part of the English syllabus) by having neither of them rescued:

o *Nec vero Alciden me sum laetatus euntem / accepisse lacu, nec Thesea* **Pirithoum**que, ... / hi dominam Ditis thalamo deducere adorti.* (6.392–93, 397)

Poeni (2; Poeni, -orum)

- referring to the *Carthaginians by recalling their *Phoenician origins:

  o *Hic rem Romanam magno turbante tumultu / sistet eques, sternet* **Poenos** *Gallumque rebellem, / tertiaque arma patri suspendet capta Quirino.* (6.857–59)

Priam (4; Priamus, -i)

- king of *Troy and father of *Hector and *Paris, husband of Hecuba

- Priam in the Latin syllabus is used to represent *Troy:

  o *Et, si fata deum, si mens non laeva fuisset, / impulerat ferro Argolicas foedare latebras, / Troiaque nunc staret,* **Priami**que arx alta maneres.* (2.54–56)

- But he figures prominently in the English syllabus in the scene of his death at the hands of *Achilles' son Neoptolemus or Pyrrhus.

- Priam accuses Pyrrhus of being less of a man than his father because of Pyrrhus' merciless treatment of Priam's family during the fall of *Troy.

- Pyrrhus cruelly responds just before killing Priam that Priam can inform his father of his heartlessness when he meets him in the underworld.

Proserpina (2)

- wife of Hades and queen of the underworld

- Her most famous story is her kidnapping by Hades and the subsequent mourning over the absence of her mother *Ceres, goddess of the harvest.

- The story alluded to in the Latin syllabus is the failed attempt of *Theseus and *Pirithous to kidnap her:

  o *licet ingens ianitor antro / aeternum latrans exsangues terreat umbras, / casta licet patrui servet* **Proserpina** *limen* (6.400–402)

Pygmalion (1; Pygmalion, Pygmalionis, m.)

- the brother of *Dido who, without *Dido's knowledge, killed her husband *Sychaeus

- *Sychaeus eventually revealed himself to *Dido as a ghost in a dream and encouraged her to flee and found a new city, which became *Carthage.

- *Dido, when she learns that *Aeneas is leaving her, worries that she is being abandoned to her violent brother:

  o *Quid moror? An mea* **Pygmalion** *dum moenia frater / destruat aut captam ducat Gaetulus Iarbas?* (4.325–26)

CHAPTER 3

Quirinus (1)

- an early Roman deity associated with the deified *Romulus or the Sabine war god

- At 6.859 Vergil describes the future deeds of *Marcellus, one of which is his acquisition of the *spolia opima*, the highest honor that a general can earn.

- These *spolia* are traditionally dedicated at the Temple of *Jupiter Feretrius but Vergil follows an alternate tradition whereby they are dedicated to Quirinus, here associated with the deified *Romulus:

  o *Hic rem Romanam magno turbante tumultu / sistet eques, sternet Poenos Gallumque rebellem, / tertiaque arma patri suspendet capta* **Quirino**. (6.857–59)

Roma (6; Roma, -ae; Romanus, -a, -um; Romani, -orum)

- the city of Rome, which *Aeneas' descendants establish after he flees *Troy and, after many trials, arrives in *Italy:

  o *genus unde Latinum / Albanique patres atque altae moenia* **Romae** (1.6–7)

Romulus (1; Romulus, -a, -um, here the adjectival form of the proper name: "of Romulus")

- the founder and first king of *Rome, descended ultimately from *Aeneas through his mother Rhea Silvia:

  o *nec* **Romula** *quondam / ullo se tantum tellus iactabit alumno* (6.876–77)

Samos (1; Samos, Sami, f.)

- an island off of the central coast of modern-day Turkey in the northern Aegean Sea

- The island was sacred to *Juno but not, according to Vergil, as sacred as *Carthage was:

  o *quam Iuno fertur terris magis omnibus unam / posthabita coluisse* **Samo** (1.15–16)

Sarpedon (1; Sarpedon, Sarpedonis, m.)

- a *Lycian king who fought in the Trojan War on the side of the Trojans

- Jupiter wanted to save him from death in the war but ultimately did not.

- When *Aeneas is caught in the storm sent by *Aeolus, Sarpedon is one of the Trojan heroes by whose hand *Aeneas wishes he had been killed in the Trojan War rather than dying at sea:

  o *Mene Iliacis occumbere campis / non potuisse tuaque animam hanc effundere dextra, / saevus ubi Aeacidae telo iacet Hector, ubi ingens /* **Sarpedon**. (1.97–100)

Saturnius (2; Saturnius, -a, -um)

- referring to Saturn, an ancient Roman deity and the father of *Juno

- Here the term is used to refer to *Juno:

  - *Id metuens veterisque memor **Saturnia** belli, / prima quod ad Troiam pro caris gesserat Argis.* (1.23–24)

- And here to *Italy or Italian:

  - *Seu vos Hesperiam magnam **Saturnia**que arva / sive Erycis fines regemque optatis Acesten.* (1.569–70)

Scaean (1; Scaeus, -a, -um)

- referring to the Scaean gates, *Troy's most famous gates, whose survival was linked to the survival of the city; if the gates fell, the city would fall:

  - *Hic Iuno **Scaeas** saevissima portas / prima tenet sociumque furens a navibus agmen / ferro accincta vocat.* (2.612–14)

Scylla (1)

- a sea monster that lives in the channel between Sicily and *Italy along with Charybdis: Scylla is the dragon-like monster, while Charybdis is the deadly whirlpool, both of which destroy ships that pass.

- When *Aeneas is exhorting his men during the storm that *Aeolus sent, he evokes previous victories to inspire them, one of which is their survival of Scylla:

  - *Vos et **Scyllaeam** rabiem penitusque sonantes / accestis scopulos, Vos et Cyclopia saxa / experti.* (1.200–202)

Serestus (1)

- one of *Aeneas' companions, along with *Mnestheus and *Sergestus, whom he summons to prepare for their clandestine departure from *Carthage:

  - *Mnesthea Sergestumque vocat fortemque **Serestum**, / classem aptent taciti sociosque ad litora cogant, / arma parent et quae rebus sit causa novandis / dissimulent.* (4.288–91)

Sergestus (2)

- one of *Aeneas' companions, along with *Antheus and *Cloanthus, whom *Aeneas sees entering *Dido's temple:

  - *cum subito Aeneas concursu accedere magno / Anthea **Sergestum**que videt fortemque Cloanthum / Teucrorumque alios* (1.509–11)

- also, one of *Aeneas' companions, along with *Mnestheus and *Serestus, whom he summons to prepare for their clandestine departure from *Carthage:

  - *Mnesthea **Sergestum**que vocat fortemque Serestum, / classem aptent taciti sociosque ad litora cogant, / arma parent et quae rebus sit causa novandis / dissimulent.* (4.288–91)

CHAPTER 3

Sibylla (1; Sibylla, -ae)

- a prophetess associated with *Apollo whose temple is at Cumae on the Bay of Naples where *Aeneas lands when he arrives in *Italy

- *Aeneas asks the Sibyl to take him to the underworld to see his father, *Anchises, and to hear from him the glory of his descendants:

  o *His ibi tum natum Anchises unaque **Sibyllam** / prosequitur dictis portaque emittit eburna, / ille viam secat ad naves sociosque revisit.* (6.897–99)

Sicania (1)

- another name for the island of Sicily, where *Acestes, a Trojan, rules a kingdom

- *Aeneas and his men stop there on their journey and *Acestes welcomes them, holds funeral games for the dead *Anchises, and offers to anyone who no longer wants to travel a new home with him:

  o *at freta **Sicaniae** saltem sedesque paratas, / unde huc advecti, regemque petamus Acesten* (1.557–58)

Siculan (1; Siculus, -a, -um)

- Sicilian, referring to the inhabitants of the island of Sicily, where *Acestes, a Trojan, rules a kingdom

- *Aeneas and his men stop there on their journey and *Acestes welcomes them, holds funeral games for the dead *Anchises, and offers to anyone who no longer wants to travel a new home with him:

  o *Sunt et **Siculis** regionibus urbes / armaque Troianoque a sanguine clarus Acestes.* (1.549–50)

  o *Vix e conspectu **Siculae** telluris in altum / vela dabant laeti et spumas salis aere ruebant.* (1.34–35)

Sidonian (1; Sidonius, -a, -um)

- *Phoenician or *Carthaginian, referring to the origin of *Dido's people in *Tyre, a Phoenician city:

  o *Exstinxti te meque, soror, populumque patresque / **Sidonios** urbemque tuam.* (4.682–83)

Simois (1; Simois, Simoentis, m.)

- referring to the Simois River, a river near *Troy:

  o *ubi tot **Simois** correpta sub undis / scuta virum galeasque et fortia corpora volvit* (1.100–101)

Somnus (1)

- sleep personified

- *Aeneas and the *Sibyl encounter the gates of sleep as they leave the underworld:

  - *Sunt geminae **Somni** portae, quarum altera fertur / cornea, qua veris facilis datur exitus umbris, / altera candenti perfecta nitens elephanto, / sed falsa ad caelum mittunt insomnia Manes.* (6.893–96)

Sparta (1)

- the ancient Greek kingdom of Menelaus

- Vergil references Sparta in book 2 when *Aeneas, fleeing the burning *Troy, sees Helen and imagines killing her.

- He asks in essence why she should get to see her home when he and the Trojans are fleeing theirs:

  - *Scilicet haec **Spartam** incolumis patriasque Mycenas / aspiciet, partoque ibit regina triumpho?* (2.577–78)

Styx (4; Stygius, -a, -um: all 4 occurrences are the adjective)

- Stygian or referring to the river Styx

- the river in the underworld that a soul crosses in *Charon's boat to enter the underworld:

  - *Navita quos iam inde ut **Stygia** prospexit ab unda / per tacitum nemus ire pedemque advertere ripae, / sic prior adgreditur dictis atque increpat ultro* (6.385–87)

  - *Anchisa generate, deum certissima proles, / Cocyti stagna alta vides **Stygiam**que paludem.* (6.322–23)

Sychaeus (1)

- the Tyrian husband of *Dido, whom her brother *Pygmalion, without *Dido's knowledge, killed

- Sychaeus eventually revealed himself to *Dido as a ghost in a dream and encouraged her to flee and found a new city, which became *Carthage.

- Sychaeus is only named in the Latin syllabus in the underworld, when *Dido's ghost returns to his ghost after turning away from *Aeneas:

  - *Tandem corripuit sese atque inimica refugit / in nemus umbriferum, coniunx ubi pristinus illi / respondet curis aequatque **Sychaeus** amorem.* (6.472–74)

Syrtis (2; Syrtis, Syrtis, f.)

- an area of sandy shallows off the coast of modern *Libya in North Africa

- Used to mean sandbar or reef (and some editors in fact do not capitalize the S, rendering it, rather than the specific location, a more general term for "sandbar" or "reef"):

  o *tres Eurus ab alto / in brevia et **Syrtes** urget, miserabile visu, / inliditque vadis atque aggere cingit harenae* (1.110–12)

Tartarus (2; Tartareus, -a, -um: both times used as the adjective)

- a name for the underworld:

  o *Hinc via **Tartarei** quae fert Acherontis ad undas.* (6.295)

Teucer (10; Teucer, -cri; Teucrus, -a, -um)

- Son of the river Scamander and *nymph Idaea, Teucer came to the area of the Scamander River, near *Troy, and established a people.

- Thus, his name is used to refer to the Trojans:

  o *O lux Dardaniae, spes o fidissima **Teucrum**, / quae tantae tenuere morae?* (2.281–82)

Tellus (1)

- the earth personified, here a witness to the union of *Dido and *Aeneas:

  o *Prima et **Tellus** et pronuba Iuno / dant signum.* (4.166–67)

Tenedos (1; Tenedus, -i or Tenedos, -i)

- an island off of the northwestern coast of Turkey behind which the Greek fleet hid when they left behind the Trojan Horse

- It is also from Tenedos that the sea snakes that killed *Laocoon originated:

  o *Ecce autem gemini a **Tenedo** tranquilla per alta / (horresco referens) immensis orbibus angues / incumbunt pelago pariterque ad litora tendunt.* (2.203–5)

Terra (1)

- The goddess Earth, parent of both the Titans and, out of anger for the gods killing the Titans, the Giants, one of whom is Rumor:

  o *Illam **Terra** parens ira inritata deorum / extremam, ut perhibent, Coeo Enceladoque sororem / progenuit pedibus celerem et pernicibus alis, / monstrum horrendum, ingens.* (4.178–81)

Theseus (1)

- friend of *Pirithous, both of whom journeyed to the underworld to kidnap Persephone

- They were thwarted and their punishment was to be confined eternally to thrones in the underworld.

- The more common version of the story has Hercules rescue them when he comes to the underworld for *Cerberus.

- Vergil departs from that version (6.617–18, part of the English syllabus) by having neither of them rescued:

  - *Nec vero Alciden me sum laetatus euntem / accepisse lacu, nec **Thesea** Pirithoumque, … / hi dominam Ditis thalamo deducere adorti.* (6.392–93, 397)

Thyias (1; Thyias, Thyiadis, f.)

- a term for a Maenad, a worshipper of *Bacchus, the Roman god of wine and disorder

- When *Dido learns of the rumor of *Aeneas' departure, she rages through the city like a Maenad:

  - *Saevit inops animi totamque incensa per urbem / bacchatur, qualis commotis excita sacris / **Thyias**, ubi audito stimulant trieterica Baccho / orgia nocturnusque vocat clamore Cithaeron.* (4.300–303)

A *Thyias*, or Maenad,
a worshipper of Bacchus

Tiberinus (2; Tiberinus, -a, -um; Tiberinus, -i: once as the adjective; once as the noun)

- having to do with the Tiber, the river that runs through *Rome:

  - *Urbs antiqua fuit (Tyrii tenuere coloni) / Karthago, Italiam contra **Tiberina**que longe / ostia.* (1.12–14)

- or, the god of the river Tiber:

  - *Vel quae, **Tiberine**, videbis / funera, cum tumulum praeterlabere recentem!* (6.873–74)

Triton (3; Triton, Tritonis, m.)

- a sea god who, along with *Cymothoe, a sea *nymph, rescues *Aeneas' ships after *Neptune has calmed the storm that *Juno sent:

  - *Cymothoe simul et **Triton** adnixus acuto / detrudunt naves scopulo.* (1.144–45)

Troy (26; Troia, -ae)

- the city of Troy, located in the northwestern corner of modern Turkey, near the entrance to the Dardanelles

- The Trojan prince *Paris kidnapped the *Spartan queen Helen, which started the Trojan War.

- Troy eventually fell to the Greeks through the deception of the Trojan Horse.

- The Trojan *Aeneas fled Troy to found a new city in *Italy, whose descendents would become the Romans:

  o *Arma virumque cano, **Troiae** qui primus ab oris / Italiam fato profugus Laviniaque venit / litora.* (1.1–3)

Tydides (1; Tydides, -ae, m., voc. = Tydide)

- a patronymic for Diomedes from his father's name, Tydeus

- Diomedes was a fierce Greek fighter who fought *Aeneas and likely would have killed him had his mother *Venus not saved him:

  o *O terque quaterque beati, / quis ante ora patrum Troiae sub moenibus altis / contigit oppetere! O Danaum fortissime gentis / **Tydide!*** (1.94–97)

Tyndarides (2; Tyndaris, Tyndaridis, f.)

- a patronymic for Helen from her father's name Tyndareus:

  o *Non tibi **Tyndaridis** facies invisa Lacaenae / culpatusve Paris, divum inclementia, divum / has evertit opes sternitque a culmine Troiam.* (2.601–3)

Tyre (9; Tyrius, -i; Tyrius, -a, -um)

- a Phoenician city from which *Dido fled after her brother *Pygmalion killed her husband *Sychaeus

- *Dido would found *Carthage in modern Tunisia, which would grow into *Rome's greatest rival for control of the Mediterranean Sea, over which they fought in the three Punic Wars of the 3rd and 2nd centuries BC.

- *Juno hopes to divert *Aeneas from reaching *Italy because she knows that his eventual descendants will conquer her prized city and the abandoning of *Dido by *Aeneas and her resulting curse of him is used to explain that later enmity between the two cultures:

  o *Urbs antiqua fuit (**Tyrii** tenuere coloni) / Karthago, Italiam contra Tiberinaque longe / ostia, dives opum studiisque asperrima belli, / quam Iuno fertur terris magis omnibus unam / posthabita coluisse Samo.* (1.12–16)

Tyrrhenus (1)

- Tyrrhenian, referring to Etruria or the Etruscans

- The body of water off the southwestern coast of *Italy is called the Tyrrhenian Sea:

  - *gens inimica mihi **Tyrrhenum** navigat aequor / Ilium in Italiam portans victosque penates* (1.67–68)

Ulixes (1; Ulixes, Ulixis, m.)

- Ulysses, Greek *Odysseus*, hero of the *Odyssey*, known for his ten-year journey home to Ithaca from the Trojan War and on whose journey *Aeneas' journey from *Troy is based

- Ulysses also hatched the idea of the Trojan Horse, which is how he is referenced here by *Laocoon, as he doubts the veracity of the horse:

  - *O miseri, quae tanta insania, cives? / Creditis avectos hostes? Aut ulla putatis / dona carere dolis Danaum? Sic notus **Ulixes**? / Aut hoc inclusi ligno occultantur Achivi.* (2.42–45)

Venus (1; Venus, Veneris, f.)

- goddess of love and mother of *Aeneas by *Anchises

- She appears throughout the *Aeneid* but is only mentioned by name in the Latin syllabus when the storm that drives *Aeneas and *Dido to the same cave occurs:

  - *Interea magno misceri murmure caelum / incipit, insequitur commixta grandine nimbus, / et Tyrii comites passim et Troiana iuventus / Dardaniusque nepos **Veneris** diversa per agros / tecta metu petiere.* (4.160–64)

Vesta (2)

- Roman goddess of the hearth and home, Greek Hestia

- There was a temple to Vesta in the heart of *Troy and she was associated with the *penates*, which *Aeneas brings from *Troy to *Italy:

  - *"Sacra suosque tibi commendat Troia penates; / hos cape fatorum comites, his moenia quaere / magna pererrato statues quae denique ponto." / Sic ait et manibus vittas **Vestam**que potentem / aeternumque adytis effert penetralibus ignem.* (2.293–97)

- It is in this temple too that *Aeneas finds *Helen hiding as *Troy is falling:

  - *Iamque adeo super unus eram, cum limina **Vestae** / servantem et tacitam secreta in sede latentem / Tyndarida aspicio.* (2.567–69)

Zephyrus (1)

- the west wind, which portends mild air and spring, although here used as wind in a more general sense

- *Neptune calls Zephyrus and *Eurus to him just before he admonishes the winds for raising a storm without his approval:

  - *Eurum ad se **Zephyrum**que vocat, dehinc talia fatur.* (1.131)

CHAPTER 3

Chapter 4

SUMMARIES

- Below is summarized, in order, the entirety of the syllabus, both Latin and English.

- The English portions are *italicized*, the Latin unitalicized.

- Main points and proper names of the summary are **bolded**.

- For Caesar, ancient names for locations are used (with modern in parentheses) except for the most recognizable places, for example, Paris (Lutetia) vs. Avaricum (Bourges).

- These summaries should not be used as a replacement for the full texts but rather as a way to review quickly specific portions, especially those less familiar or more difficult.

- The summaries should recall for you the more detailed portion of the syllabus.

- When appropriate and notable, a brief Latin text is included for reference. (This occurs more for Vergil than for Caesar.)

> *The purpose of the English readings is to put the Latin passages in context with their significant themes, central characters, and key ideas. The English readings also help students relate the passages studied in Latin to the themes and essential questions proposed for the course. Understanding the broader context helps students to appreciate the meaning and significance of the passages read in Latin and to see what features are typical of the author's style and approach. For example, students have a richer understanding of the character of Aeneas when they discover how he acts at the end of the Aeneid. (Fall 2019 Course and Exam Description 128)*

CAESAR, *BELLUM GALLICUM*

Latin Syllabus:

- ✓ Book 1: Chapters 1–7
- ✓ Book 4: Chapters 24–35 and the first sentence of Chapter 36 (*Eodem die ... pace venerunt.*)
- ✓ Book 5: Chapters 24–48
- ✓ Book 6: Chapters 13–20

English Syllabus:

- ✓ (rest of) Book 1
- ✓ (rest of) Book 6
- ✓ Book 7

BELLUM GALLICUM SUMMARY

1.1–7 (Latin): Introduction to Gaul and the Migration of the Helvetii

Cast of Proper Names

the Belgae	Casticus, the Sequanian	the Sequani
the Aquitani	Dumnorix, the Aeduan	the Allobroges
the Gauls	the Raurici	Caesar
the Helvetii	the Tulingi	Geneva (city)
Orgetorix	the Latobrigi	Lucius Cassius
	the Boii	

MAP SUMMARY

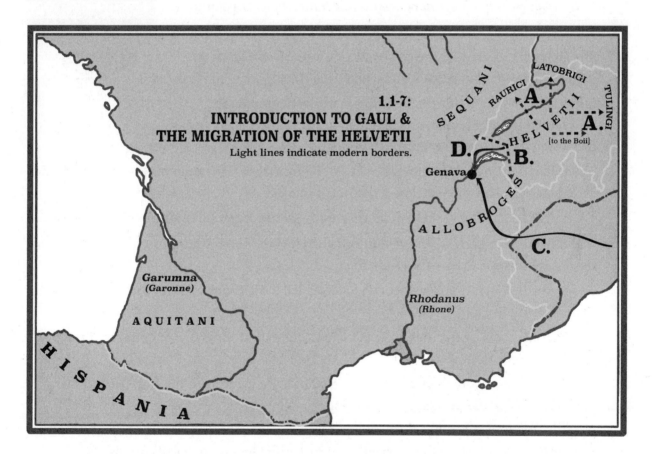

A. *The Helvetii, in preparation to migrate west, convince the Raurici, the Latobrigi, the Tulingi, and the Boii to join them.*

B. *The Helvetii debate which route west to take: through the mountains and the territory of the Sequani or through the territory of the Allobroges, who are allies of the Romans. They choose the route through the territory of the Allobroges because it is an easier route.*

C. *Caesar, hearing that the Helvetii plan to move through Roman territory, rushes to Geneva to intercept them.*

D. *The Helvetii send ambassadors to Caesar to reassure him that they only want safe passage and plan no harm or violence. Caesar, remembering that the Helvetii had killed a Roman consul, denies their request.*

TEXT SUMMARY

1   Introduction to Gaul and her people: **Belgae**, **Aquitani**, and **Gauls**.

  Gallia est omnis divisa in partes tres

1   The **Belgae are the toughest**: farthest from Rome, close to and at war with the Germans.

  Horum omnium fortissimi sunt Belgae

1   The **Helvetii** are also tough because of their proximity to the Germans.

1   Specifics about the geography of Gaul focusing on where each people lives in relationship to Gaul's rivers.

2   Introduction of **Orgetorix**: his desire to rule and his plan to persuade the **Helvetii** to leave their land.

  Apud Helvetios longe nobilissimus fuit et ditissimus Orgetorix

Modern Switzerland still refers to itself as the Confederatio Helvetica, as seen here on a Swiss coin.

2   The **Helvetii**'s current home was inadequate in accessibility and size.

3   The **Helvetii** prepare to move by purchasing animals, stockpiling grain, and negotiating peace with neighboring tribes.

3   **Orgetorix** allies himself with the **Sequanian Casticus** and the **Aeduan Dumnorix** by encouraging them to seize power and promising them **Helvetian military support**.

4   The **Helvetii** discover **Oregetorix's** plan and he is charged. He summons his supporters and escapes trial but dies nonetheless, a suspected suicide.

  Moribus suis Orgetorigem ex vinclis causam dicere coegerunt … Orgetorix mortuus est

5   The **Helvetii** continue their migration and burn their towns and surplus grain to ensure that they cannot return, even if they want to.

5   The **Helvetii** persuade four neighbors, the **Raurici**, the **Tulingi**, the **Latobrigi**, and the **Boii**, to do likewise and join them.

6   The **Helvetii** choose their route, either a dangerous path through the **Sequani** or through the Roman province.

6   The **Allobroges**, whom the **Romans** recently conquered, bordered the **Helvetii** and the Helvetii either would persuade the Allobroges to allow them safe passage or they would force the Allobroges to allow it.

7   **Caesar** hears of the plan of the **Helvetii** and rushes to **Geneva**, marshals troops, and destroys the bridge at **Geneva**.

7   The **Helvetii** send ambassadors to **Caesar** to say that they mean no harm and that this is their only route.

7   **Caesar** recalls how the **Helvetii** killed the consul **Lucius Cassius** and so he thinks that he should not agree.

1.8–54 (English)

8   *Caesar* buys time to organize his troops by telling the ambassadors that he will consider their request.

8   *Caesar* fortifies the defenses at **Geneva** by building a wall and a trench.

8   *Caesar* denies the request of the **Helvetii** to pass through the Roman province; they attempt to pass anyway but are thwarted by the newly built defenses.

9   The **Helvetii**, denied by the Romans, approach the **Sequani** to request passage through their territory.

9   The **Helvetii** approach **Dumnorix**, the **Aeduan**, to plead their case to the **Sequani**.

9   *Dumnorix*, because of his ambition to lead the **Aedui**, brokers with the **Sequani** passage for the **Helvetii** by exchanging hostages.

10   *Caesar* receives reports that the **Helvetii** will settle near a Roman border and he worries about the threat of their proximity to Roman lands.

10   *Caesar* leaves **Titus Labienus** in charge of **Geneva**, collecting **two legions from Italy** and **three from Aquileia** and returning to **Gaul**.

10   The **Ceutrones**, **Graioceli**, and **Caturiges** attempt to hinder **Caesar's** progress but he defeats them, and ends up among the **Segusiavi**, on the eastern side of the **Rhone River** in modern southern France.

11   The **Aedui** send ambassadors to **Caesar** for assistance against the **Helvetii**.

11   The **Ambarri** and the **Allobroges** also complain to **Caesar** and he resolves to take swift action against the **Helvetii**.

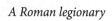

A Roman legionary

12   *Caesar* learns that the **Helvetii** are crossing the **river Seine** and defeats the group that hasn't yet crossed; some are killed and the rest flee to the woods.

12   *Caesar* describes how his defeat of the **Tigurini**, the people of one of the four cantons of **Helvetia**, avenges their defeat of the army of **Lucius Cassius**, whom they killed, and the death of **Lucius Piso**, killed in the same battle, who was the grandfather of Caesar's father-in-law.

13   *Caesar* builds a bridge over the **Seine**, complimenting himself for crossing the river in a day while the **Helvetii** took 20, to pursue the remaining Helvetii, who immediately sue for peace.

13   The **Helvetii** propose that **Caesar** settle them in a place of his choosing to avoid further conflict or, reminding Caesar of the Romans' previous defeat, resolve that they will continue to fight.

Pontem in flūmine faciunt

14   *Caesar* states that his resolve is increased because of that previous defeat and suggests that the

*arrogance of the **Helvetii**, thinking that they can defeat the Romans because they already have, will make their subsequent defeat all the more bitter.*

14   *Caesar suggests that, if the **Helvetii** provide hostages and placate the **Aedui**, the **Ambarri**, and the **Allobroges**, he will make peace.*

14   **Divico**, the **Helevtian ambassador**, refuses Caesar, saying that the **Helvetii take rather than give hostages**.

15   *Both the Romans and the **Helvetii** break camp, and **Caesar** sends his cavalry ahead to ascertain where the Helvetii are headed; they engage with and are defeated by the Helvetii, which encourages the Helvetii.*

16   *Caesar continues to ask the **Aedui** for grain for his men and they continue to stall; he summons their chiefs.*

16   *Caesar asks why they are not helping him after it was their summons that caused him to be there and fight the **Helvetii**.*

17   **Liscus**, one of the chiefs, admits that private citizens, more powerful than the chiefs, were encouraging the **Aedui** to refuse the Romans' request because it is better to be subject to other **Gauls** than to **Romans**.

18   *Caesar realizes that **Dumnorix**, **Diviciacus'** brother, is behind the resistance.*

18   *The origin of **Dumnorix's** power: he had assumed control of collecting taxes and had become rich from it; others didn't want to challenge him because of this power.*

18   **Dumnorix** was loyal to neighboring tribes because of alliances of marriage, especially the **Helvetii** because his wife was Helvetian; Dumnorix also resented the increase in the power of his brother **Diviciacus** and the decrease in his own power with the arrival of **Caesar** and **the Romans**.

18   **Dumnorix** was also in charge of the **Aeduan cavalry** attached to the Roman cavalry and had started the attack that had led to its defeat.

19   *Caesar determines that **Dumnorix** is behind the resistance to the Romans: he negotiated with the **Sequani** passage for **the Helvetii**.*

19   *Caesar addresses with **Diviciacus** the treachery of his brother and promises to hear the case himself.*

20   **Diviciacus** does not deny the treachery of his brother but asks **Caesar** for mercy, saying that it was through **Diviciacus' influence** that **Dumnorix** grew powerful.

20   **Diviciacus** is also concerned that harsh treatment of **Dumnorix** will be attributed to Diviciacus and will reflect poorly on him.

20   *Caesar sends for **Dumnorix**, reveals to him what he has heard, and forgives him because of his brother and his brother's loyalty, but he warns him against such behavior in the future and sends men to watch him.*

21   *Caesar hears that the enemy is stationed eight miles from camp and sends **Labienus** to a nearby hilltop, while he himself approaches along a lower route.*

22   Through a miscommunication with a scout that the **Helvetii** rather than **Labienus** possessed the hill, the battle does not occur. The Helvetii in the meantime move camp and **Caesar** follows.

23   Rather than pursue the **Helvetii**, **Caesar** turns toward **Bibracte**, **a primary Aeduan city**, to collect grain.

23   The **Helvetii**, partly because the Romans did not engage the previous battle, think that the Romans are retreating and pursue them.

24   **Caesar** establishes his men on a nearby hill and prepares to attack the **Helvetii**.

25   **Caesar's** men break the **Helvetian** formation with their spears and then attack with swords.

26   The **Helvetii**, pursued by the **Romans**, retreat to a hill, where the **Boii** and **Tulingi** reinforce them and surround the Romans.

26   This battle rages all day with the Romans eventually winning and taking **as hostage a son and daughter of Orgetorix**.

26   The **Helvetii** retreat to the land of the **Lingones**, whom **Caesar** contacts by letter to refuse entrance to the Helvetii or they will become enemies of the Romans too.

27   The **Helvetii** sue for peace and **Caesar** orders that they provide hostages, surrender their weapons, and turn over to him the deserters who had joined them.

27   The **Verbigeni** attempt to flee under cover of darkness.

28   **Caesar** orders those into whose territory the **Verbigeni** fled to return them to the Romans and they do.

28   The rest comply with **Caesar's** peace terms and he sends them back to their original lands, ordering the **Allobroges** to provide grain since there was none at home.

28   **Caesar** orders the **Helvetii** to rebuild their settlement to prevent the Germans from eyeing their fertile land.

28   The **Boii** settle with the **Aedui** who welcome them for their bravery.

29   **Caesar** discovers a census of the arms-bearing and non-arms-bearing people of the tribes that he had fought.

30   In the aftermath of the defeat of the **Helvetii**, chiefs from almost all of Gaul's tribes come to **Caesar** to thank him for preventing the Helvetii both from being able to choose a land that is fertile and convenient for them and from exacting tribute from the other tribes.

30   These chiefs ask **Caesar** if they can declare a day for all of the **Gallic leaders** to assemble; Caesar agrees.

31   The chiefs, led by **Diviciacus**, ask for a private meeting with **Caesar** to describe how the **Arverni** and **Sequani** sent for **German mercenaries** to help fight the **Aedui** and how the number of Germans had steadily increased.

31   The **Aedui** are defeated by this faction and have to hand over hostages but **Diviciacus** refuses, which explains his request for help from the **Romans**.

31   The **Germans**, however, turn on the **Sequani** and, led by their king **Ariovistus**, are demanding that the **Sequani** leave their land for the **Germans**.

31   **Diviciacus** is concerned that more and more **Germans** will cross the **Rhine** and occupy more and more of Gaul.

31   **Diviciacus** concludes by identifying **Caesar** as the only one who can prevent the further encroachment by the **Germans** on Gallic lands.

32   **Caesar** notices that the representatives of the **Sequani** seem concerned and asks why but receives no response. **Diviciacus** explains that, because the **Germans** live within the lands of the **Sequani**, they are in the most danger of reparations.

33   **Caesar** expresses his confidence that he can stem through diplomacy the advances of **Ariovistus** and the **Germans**.

33   **Caesar** considers the slight to the Romans that their subject people, the **Aedui**, are enslaved to the **Sequani** and the **Germans**.

33   **Caesar** also acknowledges the danger of a growing German presence in Gaul, fearing that eventually they will reach and cross into **the Province** (modern **Provence**, in southwestern France), a Roman territory.

34   **Caesar** sends envoys to **Ariovistus** to establish a meeting place midway between them.

34   **Ariovistus** replies that **Caesar** should come to him if he wants something from him.

35   **Caesar** then makes these demands of **Ariovistus**: that no more Germans cross into Gaul, that he return his **Aeduan hostages** and that the **Sequani** return their Aeduan hostages, and that he no longer attack the Aedui; Caesar pledges war if these demands are not met.

36   **Ariovistus** refuses to adhere to **Caesar's** demands and encourages him to declare war to see for himself the strength of **German soldiers**.

37   Ambassadors from the **Aedui** and the **Treveri** appear to describe further grievances against the **Germans**.

38   **Caesar** hears that **Ariovistus** is targeting **Besançon** (**ancient Vesontio**, in eastern France, north of Switzerland), the largest city of the **Sequani**, because it is a **storehouse of military supplies** and because of its situation on a hill that slopes directly to the river, a **naturally advantageous bastion**.

39   In **Besançon**, **Caesar** questions the inhabitants who describe the **size, strength, and bravery of the Germans**; such descriptions spook his soldiers so much that they begin to ask Caesar for permission to leave.

39   The panic among the troops continues, some drawing up wills, others attributing their concern to the perils of the narrow route necessary to reach **Ariovistus**.

40   **Caesar** addresses the troops directly about their concerns, first suggesting that **Ariovistus** is sensible enough to make peace with the **Romans**, then reinforcing his own leadership and their competence as soldiers, and finally pointing out that the **Helvetii**, whom the Romans defeated, experienced mostly success against the **Germans**.

40   *Caesar concludes by saying that he will leave then to test the men's mettle, and, if none follow him, he will fight only with **the 10th legion** (whom he admits **he has always favored and admired**).*

41   *Caesar's speech works: **the 10th legion** thanks him for his endorsement and the other legions express their confidence in his leadership.*

41   *Caesar sets out with all of his troops and is informed that he is 24 miles from **Ariovistus'** troops.*

42   *Ariovistus agrees to a meeting with **Caesar** but asks that no infantry be present for fear of treachery. Caesar agrees but mounts the **10th legion** on the Gauls' horses to have them with him.*

43   *Caesar and **Ariovistus** meet on a hill: Caesar reminds Ariovistus of his and the Romans' previous kindness toward him and reiterates his previous demands.*

44   *Ariovistus responds by defending his position and praising his actions: he came into **Gaul** on their invitation and they initiated hostilities, and his friendship with the **Romans** should yield benefits rather than disadvantages (if he were to yield his land).*

44   *Ariovistus' presence in **Gaul** predates the **Romans'** presence: why did they leave Roman lands?*

44   *The **Aedui**, whom **Caesar** professes to be helping, did not help the **Romans** against the **Allobroges**.*

44   *If **Caesar** were to be defeated, **Romans** themselves would be pleased, according to **Ariovistus'** contacts among the Romans.*

45   *Caesar evokes the defeat of the **Arverni** and the **Ruteni**, saying that the Romans neither occupied their land nor asked tribute of them (as **Ariovistus** did of the **Sequani** and **Aedui**).*

46   *Caesar concludes the meeting because he is informed that cavalry of **Ariovistus** is attacking the Roman cavalry. He tells his men not to return fire because he doesn't want it said that he broke his side of the bargain not to fight.*

46   *The **arrogance of Ariovistus** at the meeting inspires **Caesar's** men to want to fight.*

47   *Ariovistus asks for the meeting to be resumed but **Caesar** refuses to go himself and instead sends an ambassador who speaks the Gallic language; Ariovistus refuses to engage with the ambassador and takes him hostage.*

48   *Ariovistus advances his troops closer to **Caesar's** camp and in such a way to cut off his supply lines.*

48   *Caesar presents his troops to **Ariovistus** should he wish to fight but he does not engage.*

48   *Caesar describes the particular way of **German** fighting, that the cavalry is directly supported by the infantry, both in direct fighting and in tending to wounded cavalrymen.*

49   *Caesar positions his troops beyond **Ariovistus** to open up the supply lines and has a third of them fortify a camp while the other two-thirds defend.*

49   *Ariovistus presents his troops to scare off the **Romans** but the Romans hold their line and the camp is completed.*

49   *Caesar leaves a detachment at this newer camp and returns to the larger camp with the bulk of the troops.*

50   *Caesar again presents his troops for battle and Ariovistus doesn't engage but rather attacks the smaller camp. Ariovistus does not take the smaller camp and both sides take casualties.*

50   *Caesar asks his German prisoners why Ariovistus won't engage and they explain that it is German custom to use divination to predict the outcome of the battle and that it was predicted that the Germans wouldn't win until the new moon.*

51   *Caesar draws up his troops outside the German camp, forcing them to line up for battle, which they do by tribe.*

52   *The charge by both sides is so quick that the Romans can't use their spears.*

52   *The Romans are winning one side of the battle but the Germans the other until that side is reinforced and the Romans regain the upper hand.*

53   *Ariovistus and the Germans retreat to the Rhine and attempt to cross, whether by swimming or by boat, Ariovistus himself finding a small boat.*

53   *Two of Ariovistus' wives and a daughter are killed and one daughter is taken prisoner.*

53   *Caesar, in his pursuit of the Germans, finds the captured Roman who speaks Gallic being dragged by his guards.*

53   *He describes how chance kept him alive: three times the Germans drew lots to determine to kill him or spare him and three times he was spared.*

Rōmānī cum Germānīs pugnant

54   *The Suebi, hearing of Ariovistus' defeat, turn for home but are pursued by those tribes living near the Rhine who killed many of them.*

**4.24–35 and the first sentence of 36 (*Eodem die ... pace venerunt*). (Latin):
The British Campaign**

Cast of Proper Names

the Britons   Caesar   Commius, the Atrebatian

MAP SUMMARY

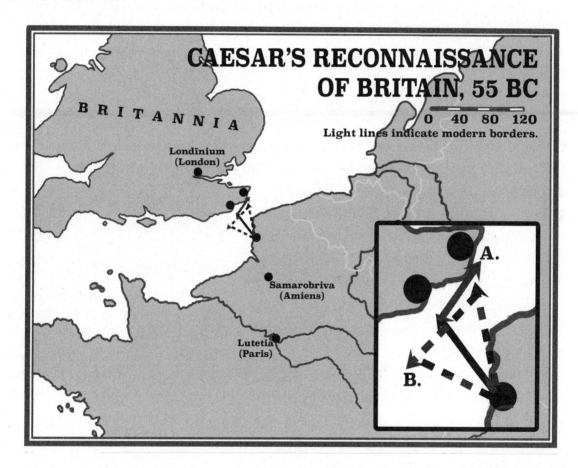

A. *[solid arrows] Caesar crosses to Britain but is met by a significant British force on the coast, so he shifts his landing to the northeast. Because of the unfamiliarity and the uncertainty of the terrain, Caesar has difficulty defeating the Britons. Additionally, the Britons fight with horse-drawn chariots, a technique archaic and unfamiliar to the Romans.*

B. *[dotted arrows] A force of cavalry sails a few days later to assist but is met by a fierce storm. The storm not only prevents the cavalry from landing and forces them to return to France but also damages Caesar's fleet. Caesar is forced to forage for food inland, which invites the British to attack, and to expend resources to repair his ships.*

TEXT SUMMARY

24   The **Britons** meet **Caesar's** fleet of troop transports at the coast and, because of the size of his ships, the weight of the soldiers' armor, and the unfamiliarity of the terrain, the **Britons** gain the upper hand in battle.

25   **Caesar** counters by having his warships, smaller and more maneuverable than the transports, forcibly run aground toward the exposed side of the **British** force; the British are intimidated by the **Roman** ships and artillery.

25   The standard-bearer of the **10th legion** leaps from the ship and leads a charge against the **British**.

26   Because of the lack of organization after the chaos of disembarking, the unfamiliarity of the terrain, and the British cavalry, the **Britons** again gain the upper hand.

26   **Caesar** sends troops to help and, once the **Romans** gain dry land, they are able to rout the **Britons**. They are unable to follow because the cavalry has not arrived in Britain.

27   The **Britons** send ambassadors to sue for peace; **Commius the Atrebatian**, whom the Britons had taken as hostage when he had reconnoitered Britain, was with them and was returned.

27   The **Britons** return home and chiefs from the island come to **Caesar** to pledge loyalty.

28   The ships carrying the cavalry approach Britain but are met with a fierce storm.

28   Some ships turn around and return to the coast while others are blown off course and eventually return.

29   This storm, because of the high tide at the full moon, destroys the **Roman ships** already landed. **Caesar** has no way to transport the troops back, no way of repairing the ships, and no supplies for wintering in **Britain**.

Roman legionaries on the march

30   The **Britons**, recognizing the uncertainty of the Roman situation, regroup and plot to renew hostilities, hoping that turning away one invader will prevent future invaders.

31   **Caesar** figures out the **British** plan because of the lack of hostages arriving and his understanding of his own situation.

31   **Caesar** salvages enough material from the destroyed ships to render the remaining ships seaworthy.

32   **Caesar** sends the 7th **legion** out of the camp to collect grain and the **Britons attack** them. The cloud of dust from the attack alerts the guards to the attack and Caesar sets out to assist.

32   The **Britons** know where the **Romans** will collect grain because there is only one place with available grain, so they lie in ambush and attack when the Romans have laid down their weapons to harvest the grain.

33   **Caesar** summarizes the chariot warfare of the **Britons**: the chariots and the horses themselves, because of their size, speed, and noise, disrupt the enemy, at which point the soldiers leave the chariots and fight on foot, with their chariot waiting just off the battlefield to provide protection if necessary.

34   **Caesar's** arrival calms the 7th **legion** and prevents the enemy from continuing the attack; he leads them back to camp and the **Britons** disperse.

34   **Bad weather** follows, which **keeps the Romans in camp** and allows the **Britons to assemble** from the neighboring country a sizable force.

35   **Caesar** uses the cavalrymen that **Commius** had brought with him to defeat the **Britons**.

36   The **Britons** send ambassadors to sue for peace.

CHAPTER 4

5.24–38 (Latin): The Siege of Sabinus' and Cotta's Camp

Cast of Proper Names

Caesar	Gaius Arpineius	Titus Balventius
the Carnutes	Quintus Junius	Quintus Lucanius
Tasgetius	Lucius Aurunculeius	Lucius Petrosidius
Ambiorix	Sabinus	Labienus
Catuvulcus	Cotta	

MAP SUMMARY—5.24–25: THE WINTERING OF CAESAR'S LEGIONS

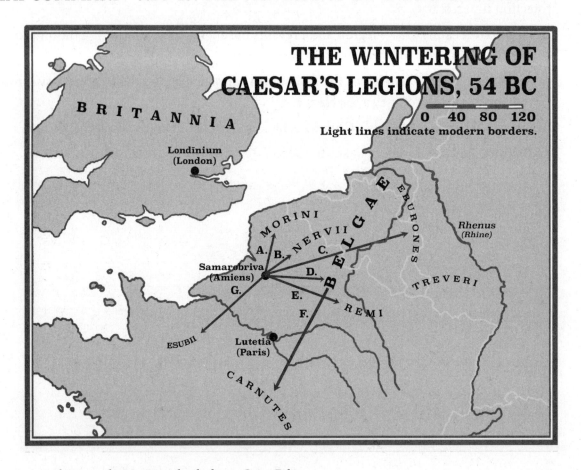

A. *one legion to the Morini under the legate Gaius Fabius*
B. *one legion to the Nervii under the legate Quintus Cicero*
C. *one legion and five cohorts to the Eburones under the legates Quintus Titurius Sabinus and Lucius Aurunculeius Cotta*
D. *three legions to the Belgae under the quaestor Marcus Crassus and the legates Lucius Munatius Plancus and Gaius Trebonius*
E. *one legion to the Remi under the legate Titus Labienus*
F. *one legion of the three with the Belgae to the Carnutes under Lucius Plancus to investigate the death of Tasgetius*
G. *one legion to the Esubii under the legate Lucius Roscius*

TEXT SUMMARY—5.24–25: THE WINTERING OF CAESAR'S LEGIONS

24   Because of a grain shortage, **Caesar** has to winter his legions in different places scattered throughout **Gaul**.

25   **Caesar** sends a legion to the **Carnutes** to investigate the death of **Tasgetius**, a **Caesar** loyalist whom Caesar installed as leader of the Carnutes. Caesar is concerned that there will be more revolt among the Carnutes.

MAP SUMMARY—5.26–37: THE SIEGE OF THE CAMP OF SABINUS AND COTTA

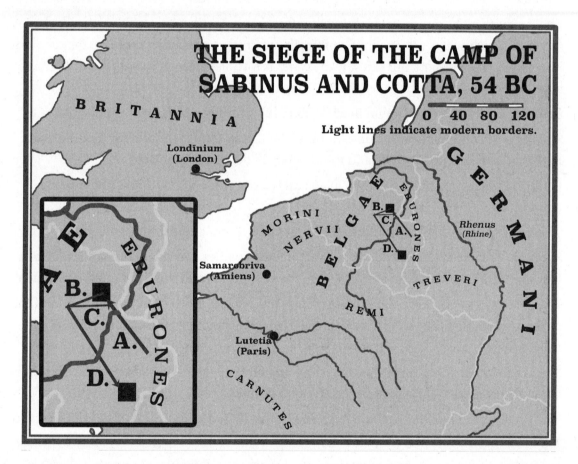

A.   *Ambiorix and Catuvulcus ambush a Roman foraging party and attack the camp of Sabinus and Cotta. When they meet with Sabinus and Cotta, they explain that the Germans are amassing a force to attack the camp and the Romans should flee.*

B.   *The Romans debate whether to flee or to stay; Sabinus advocates fleeing, while Cotta advocates staying. Eventually Sabinus' plan wins out and the Romans abandon the camp.*

C.   *Ambiorix and Catuvulcus ambush the Romans and, after much fighting, wipe out the Roman forces.*

D.   *The few that survive flee through the woods to the camp of Labienus.*

TEXT SUMMARY—5.26–37: THE SIEGE OF THE CAMP OF SABINUS AND COTTA

26   A foraging group of **Romans** are unexpectedly attacked by **Ambiorix** and **Catuvulcus**, who then attack the Roman camp. Spanish horsemen defeat the enemy who then ask to meet with the Romans.

27   **Gaius Arpineius** and **Quintus Junius** meet with **Ambiorix**, who first informs them of his indebtedness to **Caesar** and then claims that he was pressured by the tribes to attack.

27   **Ambiorix** continues to say that, because he cares so much about the **Romans**, they should leave quickly because of a large force of **Germans** that is assembling and preparing to attack.

27   **Ambiorix** concludes by pledging safe passage for the **Romans** through his territory.

28   The **Romans** meet to discuss **Ambiorix's** information. **Lucius Aurunculeius** leads the faction that advocates not heeding **Ambiorix's** warning and staying in camp: they shouldn't move without an order from **Caesar**, the camp is fortified enough to withstand an attack, and there is enough grain to sustain the troops.

29   **Sabinus** argues that they should heed **Ambiorix's** warning and leave.

30   The factions continue to argue until **Sabinus** proclaims loudly enough for the soldiers to hear that he is not afraid to die and that **Cotta** will be held responsible.

31   **Cotta** eventually relents to **Sabinus'** plan and the camp spends the night preparing to depart.

32   **The Gauls** realize that **the Romans** are about to leave and ambush them when they do.

33   **Sabinus**, because he failed to anticipate an ambush, panics and can no longer lead. **Cotta**, because he did anticipate an ambush, does the best he can and is able to maintain control.

33   The two legates encourage **the Romans** to form a defensive circle but the formation of that circle suggests that they are on the defensive, which encourages **the Gauls** and discourages the Romans.

34   **The Gauls** attack more from afar than close and retreat when the Romans attack, but pursue when the Romans return from the attack to their lines.

35   **The Romans**, despite the pressure from **the Gauls**, do not relent. **Titus Balventius** is pierced in both thighs, **Quintus Lucanius** is killed, and **Cotta** takes a sling-stone to the face.

36   **Sabinus** sends someone to **Ambiorix** to sue for peace and Ambiorix responds that Sabinus himself should come.

36   **Sabinus** suggests to the wounded **Cotta** that they both go but Cotta is wary of visiting **Ambiorix** while still at war.

37   **Sabinus** gathers high-ranking soldiers and approaches **Ambiorix**, who tells him to surrender his weapons.

37   During the discussion, **the Gauls** slowly surround **Sabinus** and
kill him.

37   **The Gauls**, encouraged by the death of **Sabinus**, charge and break
through the Roman lines, during which **Cotta is killed**. The **Romans**
retreat to the camp from which they had come.

37   **Lucius Petrosidius, a standard-bearer**, hurls the standard into camp,
rather than letting it be captured, and is killed. **Most Romans commit
suicide** in the face of certain death or capture. A handful are able to
reach Labienus' camp and explain what happened.

*From the tomb
of Pintaius, a
standard-bearer*

CHAPTER 4

5.38–48 (Latin): The Siege of Cicero's Camp

Cast of Proper Names

the Aeduatici   Titus Pullo   Marcus Crassus
the Nervii   Lucius Vorenus   Gaius Fabius
Cicero   Vertico, the Nervian   Labienus
the Germans   Caesar

MAP SUMMARY

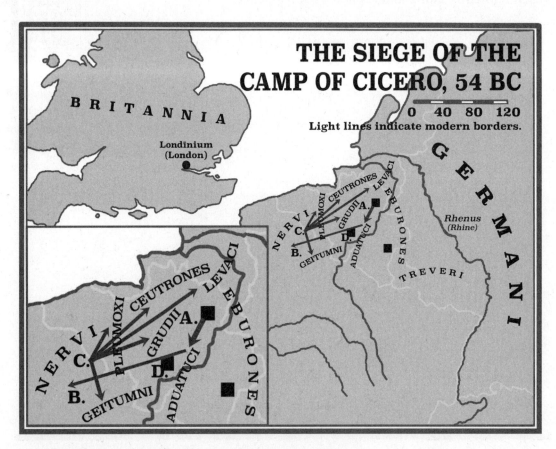

A. *Ambiorix goes to the Aduatici to persuade them to fight the Romans.*
B. *Ambiorix goes to the Nervii to persuade them to fight the Romans.*
C. *The Nervii go to their peoples, the Pleumoxi, the Ceutrones, the Levaci, the Grudii, and the Geitumni, to persuade them to join them.*
D. *The combined forces attack Cicero's camp.*

TEXT SUMMARY

38   **Ambiorix**, spurred by his victory, persuades the **Aeduatici** and the **Nervii** to join him against the **Romans**.

39   The **Nervii** gather their tribes and **attack Cicero's camp**. Cicero's men are surprised while gathering wood outside of the camp and then the Nervii attack the camp itself.

40 **Cicero** attempts to send letters to **Caesar** but cannot break through the enemy. The Romans spend each night fortifying the camp to meet the attack during the day. They are able to hold off the enemy and Cicero fights and leads despite his poor health.

41 The **chiefs of the Nervii** ask to speak with **Cicero** and they tell him that, because of the **Germans'** incursion into **Gaul**, all of Gaul is armed and attacking **Roman camps**.

41 The chiefs recall the **death of Sabinus** and explain that they **don't want Roman camps in their lands** and that the Romans can have **safe passage back to Italy**.

41 **Cicero** responds that Romans don't surrender to armed men and that he will support **the Nervii**, if they put down their arms, when they bring their concerns to **Caesar**.

42 The **Nervii build a rampart** around the Roman camp **in the style of a Roman fortification**, informed by observing the Romans and by Roman prisoners, that will allow them to assault the Roman camp more successfully.

43 The **Nervii launch flaming missiles** into the camp which ignite the thatched roofs of the huts, and they begin attempting to scale the walls.

43 **Caesar lauds the Romans** for their bravery, citing their dedication to the battle even when their possessions were burning behind them.

43 **The Romans inflict more damage on the Nervii** this day because the Nervii gathered as one beneath the rampart.

43 The **Nervii** manage to bring a tower to the wall but, because of the Romans' bravado, they do not enter the camp.

44 **Titus Pullo and Lucius Vorenus** are introduced, two soldiers exceedingly brave and equally matched, who were both **vying for promotion over the other**.

44 **Pullo chides Vorenus** for hanging back as he charges the **Nervii** at their thickest. **Vorenus follows** for fear of how he will be perceived.

44 The **Gauls surround the wounded Pullo and Vorenus rescues him** but is surrounded himself. **Pullo then rescues Vorenus** and they both return to camp **praised for their equal bravery**.

45 Because of the growing number of wounded **Romans**, the camp becomes more and more difficult to defend. **Cicero** continues to send letters to **Caesar** with no success until a **Nervian, Vertico, who had deserted**, sends a letter out with a **Gallic slave** who is able to pass through the enemy line.

46 **Caesar** orders **Marcus Crassus** to join him with his legion and **Gaius Fabius** to meet him with his legion on the way. He orders **Labienus** to proceed to the **Nervian frontier**.

47 **Crassus** is left at Amiens **to guard** the Roman equipment and winter food stores and **Fabius joins Caesar**.

47 **Labienus** explains to **Caesar** his concern that, if he leaves camp, it would be too exposed, especially because of the Gauls' increased confidence after their victory over **Sabinus**. **Caesar agrees** with his decision to stay, even though it means one fewer legion to help **Cicero**.

CHAPTER 4

48   **Caesar** decides to **attack quickly** and **sends a letter to Cicero**, via a **Gallic cavalryman, written in Greek** so that the **Gauls can't read it**.

48   **The Gaul** doesn't make it into camp but, **at Caesar's suggestion, throws it into camp** via a spear, where it sits unnoticed for two days.

48   Eventually, though, it is read and **Cicero and the Romans rejoice** at Caesar's presence and assistance.

6.1–12 (English)

1   *Caesar anticipates an uprising in Gaul and so mobilizes troops to compensate for the loss of the legion of Sabinus:* **Marcus Silanus, Gaius Antistius Reginus,** *and* **Titus Sextius** *are ordered to gather troops and* **Pompey** *is asked to order troops in* **Northern Italy** *to join Caesar. Pompey and the legates send their troops to form three legions new to* **Gaul**.

2   *The Treveri make an* **alliance** *with the* **Germans** *and* **Ambiorix joins their faction;** **Caesar** *realizes that, because of* **the Gauls**, *along with the Germans, mobilizing against him, he must prepare to fight.*

3   *Caesar surprises* **the Nervii** *by attacking before the winter is over.*

3   *Caesar then summons the* **Gallic chieftains**, *all of whom appear except for three, which Caesar interprets as a sign of impending rebellion. Of these three missing tribes, Caesar visits the* **Senones** *first.*

4   *Acco, the leader of the* **Senones'** *treachery, orders his people to retreat but they cannot retreat fast enough and so he sends ambassadors to sue for peace.*

4   *The Aedui approach* **Caesar** *on the* **Senones'** *behalf and Caesar accepts their apology, asking for hostages which he gives to the Aedui.*

4   *The* **Carnutes** *also send hostages and are similarly pardoned by* **Caesar**.

5   *Caesar now turns his attention to the* **Treveri and Ambiorix**.

5   *Caesar decides first to attack the* **Menapii, allies of Ambiorix**, *to prevent them from helping him or from hiding him in case of defeat.*

5   *The Menapii don't form up their battle line but rather hide in the forests and swamps.*

6   *Caesar burns enough of the property of the* **Menapii** *that they sue for peace.*

6   *Caesar pardons them but warns them that* **they cannot harbor Ambiorix** *in any way. He then sets off for the* **Treveri**.

7   *The Treveri have assembled troops and are* **waiting for German reinforcements** *to attack the* **winter quarters of Labienus**, *which are in their territory.*

7   *Labienus leaves behind guards at the camp and builds a smaller camp near the steep banks of a river. Neither he nor the* **Treveri** *would cross.*

7   *Labienus plants the information* that he will be leaving camp the next day in fear of the **Germans'** *arrival, assuming correctly that this information will be carried to the **Treveri** by **sympathetic Gauls** in his camp.*

7   *Labienus tells his generals, secretly, that they should make more noise than usual when leaving, suggesting a panic rather than an orderly departure.*

8   *The **Treveri**, because they thought **the Romans** were panicked and because they wanted the plunder of the Roman camp, **cross the river before the Germans arrive**. Labienus expects this and continues to retreat until all of the Treveri had crossed.*

8   *Labienus orders his men to turn and fight and the battle is quickly over. The surviving **Treveri** are chased and either captured or killed. **The Germans**, hearing that the Treveri were routed, turn around.*

9   *Caesar decides to **cross the Rhine** to punish the **Germans** for helping the **Treveri** and to prevent **Ambiorix** from taking refuge with the Germans.*

9   *Caesar builds a **bridge over the Rhine** and leaves troops on the side of the **Treveri** in case of any uprising.*

9   *The **Ubii** approach Caesar to repledge their loyalty and to assure him that they did not help the **Treveri**. Caesar investigates, corroborates their stance, and learns that the **Suebi** helped the Treveri, so Caesar sets off for the territory of the Suebi.*

10   *Caesar learns from the **Ubii** that the **Suebi are mobilizing**, so he orders the Ubii to retreat to their fort with their supplies, hoping that the Suebi would fight without full support.*

10   *Caesar orders the **Ubii** to patrol the territory of the **Suebi** to discover their intent. They report to Caesar that they have retreated into a forest in the farthest part of their territory and are waiting for the Romans at the edge of the forest.*

11   *Caesar pauses to describe **the mores of the Gauls and Germans**.*

11   *Every aspect of the life of the **Gauls**, from tribe down to household, is **divided into factions**, which prevents any one individual from accumulating too much power.*

12   *On **Caesar's arrival in Gaul, the Aedui** and **the Sequani** were the two dominant factions, with the Aedui the more powerful of the two.*

12   *Because of the primacy of the **Aedui**, the **Sequani** allied with **Ariovistus** and **the Germans**. This alliance defeated the Aedui enough that it took over many of the tribes of the Aedui, took Aeduan hostages, and made them swear that they would conspire against the Sequani.*

12   *In response to the **rise of the Sequani, Diviciacus went to Rome** to seek assistance but received none.*

12   *Caesar's arrival in Gaul, however, does help the **Aedui** by having their hostages returned and their tribes reinstated.*

12   *The prominence of the Sequani decreases and the Remi, whom Caesar trusts, **rise in prominence**.*

12   *Tribes that wouldn't ally with the **Aedui** because of previous conflicts, now ally themselves with **the Remi** and so with **Rome**.*

6.13–20 (Latin)

Cast of Proper Names:

Druids	Mercury	Jupiter
the Carnutes	Apollo	Minerva
Britain	Mars	Dis

13   **Caesar** introduces **the classes of the Gauls**: the common people have few to no rights and are subject to the wealthier nobles. The **two true classes are Knights and Druids**. The Druids cover religion and settle disputes where their ruling is sacrosanct. Anyone defying the ruling of a Druid is shunned by society and prevented from participating in ritual sacrifices.

13   **One Druid is in charge** and, upon his death, the next most powerful takes his place. If no clear successor exists, there is a vote.

13   On a set day each year, **the Druids meet in the territory of the Carnutes**, which is supposed to be the **center of Gaul**. Those with disputes present them here to the Druids and abide by their ruling.

13   **The Druids originated in Britain** and those preparing to be a Druid still go to Britain to learn.

14   **The Druids** do not fight in the army and do not pay taxes. Much of their training is spent memorizing texts, as they do not write them down. They do write down proceedings and for this they use Greek, so that others can't read them and to encourage students to utilize their memories.

14   **The Druids** believe in reincarnation, partly because the continuous survival of the soul reduces the fear of death among soldiers. The Druids also discuss aspects of philosophy: the stars and planets, natural phenomena, and the gods.

15   **The Knights** are constantly fighting and their prominence is tied to the number of people they can afford to attend them.

16   **The Gauls** participate in **human sacrifice** because they are superstitious: their belief is that the sacrificed life is exchanged for another life. Some sacrifices involve **the Wicker Man**: a large figure made of wicker in whose limbs are placed living men. The Wicker Man is then ignited. The Gauls prefer to sacrifice criminals but will sacrifice innocents if no criminals are available.

17   **The Gauls worship Mercury most commonly** but also worship **Apollo, Mars, Jupiter, and Minerva**. In war, they dedicate plunder, both cattle and equipment, to Mars.

18   **The Gauls**, according to **the Druids**, are descended from **Dis**, and so they organize the space of a day with night first rather than day.

18   **Sons are not allowed to be seen with their father in public** until they are old enough to fight in battle.

19   **Husband and wife contribute equally to a shared account**, whose initial amount and subsequent growth is tracked. At the death of either spouse, the other receives the total amount of the account.

19   **When a husband dies, his family assesses if his death is at all suspicious.** If it is deemed suspicious, the wife is tortured and, if found guilty, burned to death. The funeral pyre collects all of the man's possessions, even animals and, in the recent past, though no longer, slaves.

20   The most successful tribes manage rumor and news. It is required that, if any news is heard from a neighboring tribe, that news must be reported to the chieftains, who will determine if it is credible and worth publicizing. This approach minimizes impulsivity in the face of false information among the people.

6.21–44 (English)

21   *Caesar introduces the **mores** of the Germans.*

21   ***The Germans have no religious caste** like the Druids and they only worship the gods of things that are visible and tangible—for example, sun, fire, moon.*

21   *The **entire life of the Germans** is focused on **hunting and the military**.*

21   *The **Germans value chastity** and frown on sex before the age of 20 but do not separate men and women: they bathe together and dress in a way that leaves much of the body exposed.*

22   *The **Germans eat primarily milk, cheese, and meat** without much interest in farming.*

22   *The **Germans do not own their own land** but rather are given land by the chieftain, whose size and location vary year to year. This uncertainty prevents individuals from accumulating excessive land, prevents them from safeguarding themselves against the heat and cold, and gives the impression that each member of the tribe is equal.*

23   *The **greatest triumph for the Germans is to raze the land around them** so that it is unhabitable and no one wants to live next to them.*

23   *There is **no centralized government**. Leaders who have absolute power are elevated during wartime and chiefs decide disputes during peacetime.*

23   ***Armed raids** on neighboring peoples are **encouraged** because it maintains sharp military skills, especially for the younger men.*

23   *The **Germans welcome and protect guests**.*

24   *Caesar describes how the **Gauls used to surpass the Germans** in militancy and even sent a tribe over the **Rhine** to settle, **the Volcae Tectosages**, because Gaul was running out of land.*

24   *The **Volcae Tectosages** live similarly to **the Germans** while **the Gauls** on the Gallic side of the Rhine enjoy a more luxurious life because **they live near Roman provinces**.*

25   *Caesar describes the Hercynian forest; its size is such that a man would take nine days to traverse it. The Germans have to describe its size this way because they have no units of measurement.*

25   *The forest also **contains many species of animals that are unknown** outside of the forest.*

26   *Caesar begins his **description of these sometimes fantastical animals** [some editors believe that this section was not written by Caesar but rather inserted by later scribes].*

26   *First, the **ox that looks like a stag** with a single horn coming from its forehead that branches into tree-like antlers.*

27   *There are **elk, similar to but larger than goats, whose legs have no joints**. When they sleep, they lean against trees. Hunters ambush them by cutting the trees so that they look solid but, when the elks lean against them, the trees fall and the elks fall with them.*

28   ***The auroch** looks like a bull and is just smaller than an elephant. The Germans enjoy hunting the auroch because of its fierceness; the hunting of it hones their military skills. The Germans turn auroch horns into decorated drinking cups.*

29   ***Caesar decides not to pursue the Suebi into their forest**. Instead, he **dismantles the bridge** on the Ubian side and **builds a tower** on the other side to remind the Suebi that he can still attack.*

29   ***Caesar instead turns his attention to Ambiorix**. He marches through **the forest of the Ardennes** and sends cavalry ahead in case there is an opportunity for a quick strike.*

30   *Indeed **Lucius Minucius Basilus**, in charge of the cavalry, is able to reach the enemy more quickly than expected and to capture a number of them. Those that he captured **tell him where Ambiorix is believed to be** and he proceeds there.*

30   ***Basilus takes Ambiorix by surprise but Ambiorix is able to escape**, despite losing all of his equipment, because his house was in the woods, as is customary for the Gauls, and **the woods disguised his escape**.*

31   ***Ambiorix does not marshal his troops** but rather orders them to look out for themselves.*

31   *Catuvulcus is now **old and feeble** and cannot withstand the demands of war any longer. **He curses Ambiorix and poisons himself**.*

32   ***The Segni and the Condrusi ask Caesar for clemency**, claiming that not all **Germans in Gaul** are against him and that they **had never helped Ambiorix**. Caesar investigates their claims, asks for Eburonian hostages, and then does not attack them.*

32   *Caesar then splits his forces and heads with the military equipment for **Aduatuca, the fortress where Sabinus and Cotta had wintered**, because the fortress was largely still intact and his soldiers would not have to work to build a new one.*

33   *Caesar distributes his legions: **Titus Labienus** heads to the coast to an area bordering **the Menapii**; **Gaius Trebonius** attacks the land bordering **the Aduatuci**; and Caesar heads to the **Scheldt River** on the western end of **the Ardennes forest** in pursuit of **Ambiorix**.*

33   ***Caesar** says that he will **return in seven days** and asks the others to do likewise to be present for a measure of grain that would arrive.*

34   *The enemy being scattered poses problems not for the* **Roman army** *as a whole, who could easily defend against such small attacks, but rather for smaller bands of Romans outside of the protection of the garrison. Soldiers searching for plunder are easily vulnerable to* **ambushes by hidden Gauls.**

34   **Caesar** *either has to split his troops up and scatter them to root out the* **hiding Gauls,** *thereby making them vulnerable by their small numbers, or, if he attacks in formation, the* **terrain undermines his effectiveness** *by causing difficulties for the soldiers.*

34   **Caesar summons troops from neighboring Gallic tribes** *to assist, thereby putting Gauls at risk rather than Romans and increasing the numbers of soldiers. Many Gauls answer his summons.*

35   **Caesar** *was preparing to return after seven days when the* **Germans** *heard that the* **Eburones** *were being routed.* **The Sugambri cross the Rhine,** *capture a number of Eburones, and take their plunder. The Eburones, however, suggest that the Roman* **plunder held at Aduatuca** *is attainable and significantly better.* **The Sugambri set out for Aduatuca.**

36   **Cicero, in charge of Aduatuca,** *has kept the men in the garrison for the week. On the seventh day, however, because the men were complaining of inaction and because he* **heard that Caesar had traveled farther** *than expected,* **he lets the men out,** *confident that they are safe close to the garrison and with cavalry outside.*

37   *When the troops, and the servants attending them, have left the garrison,* **the German army appears.** *The nearby woods hide their attack and the garrison on guard barely holds them off. The camp is in chaos and* **the defeat of Sabinus and Cotta** *at that very garrison is on their mind.* **The Roman panic spurs the Germans** *on to attack the gates more fiercely.*

38   **Publius Sextius Baculus** *was a chief centurion under Caesar who was* **sick in camp,** *not having eaten in five days. Nonetheless, understanding the emergency, he* **leaves his tent and arms himself.** *Baculus and troops defend the gate and, though he is wounded and carried away,* **buy enough time for the Romans** *to organize themselves.*

39   *The cavalry outside the garrison hear the commotion and realize what is happening. The men with them, however, have no experience and panic.* **The Germans,** *seeing the standard, abandon the camp and turn to fight them.*

40   *There is* **debate among the Romans about how to proceed.** *Some suggest* **breaking for the safety of the garrison,** *even if it means losing some men. Others suggest* **maintaining the high ground** *and fighting together. The veterans, however, led by* **Gaius Trebonius,** *exhort the men to break for the garrison. Under their leadership, not only do they make it to the garrison but also* **not a single man is killed.**

40   *Some did indeed take position on the high ground but they were too disorganized to hold it, had to come down, and found themselves in danger. Some did make it to the camp because of the bravery of certain centurions who, having already acquired a reputation for valor, did not want to lose that reputation and defended those attempting to return to the garrison.*

41   *With the* **Romans organized,** *the* **Germans** *realize that they won't take the camp and* **retreat back across the Rhine** *with their plunder.*

41   *The soldiers, however, are still panicked enough that, when* **Caesar** *sends* **Gaius Volusenus** *ahead to herald his arrival, they don't believe that Caesar has returned.*

42   **Caesar's return ends the panic.** *His one criticism of the garrison is that no one should have left. Caesar acknowledges too the role of luck, that the* **Germans** *attacked when they did but that they didn't take the garrison when they could and that the Germans did the work of* **Ambiorix** *for him.*

43   **Caesar** *again turns his attention to* **the Eburones,** *burning villages and driving off cattle. He is confident that any remaining enemy will die of starvation.*

43   *Throughout this campaign,* **Caesar continues to seek Ambiorix** *who, however close Caesar might get, manages to elude him.*

44   **Caesar withdraws to Durocortorum,** *a town of* **the Remi,** *and calls a council.* **Acco,** *the mastermind behind the treachery of the* **Senones and the Carnutes,** *is sentenced to death and executed.*

44   **Caesar** *determines the winter quarters for the legions and* **returns to Italy.**

Book 7 (English)

1   **Caesar** *learns upon arriving* **in Italy** *that* **Publius Clodius was assassinated** *and that* **Italians** *who are eligible* **for the military are being recruited.** *He likewise recruits in* **northern Italy.**

1   **News from Italy reaches Gaul** *and* **the Gauls embellish** *the stories, using the perceived unrest as impetus to mobilize for war.*

1   *The Gauls meet and encourage each other to* **undertake war against Rome,** *fearing that* **the same fate that befell Acco could befall them.**

1   *The Gauls plan to* **prevent Caesar from meeting up** *with his armies in Gaul and the* **Carnutes volunteer to begin the hostilities.**

2   *The Carnutes state that hostages cannot be exchanged for fear of revealing the plan but that* **the Gauls should swear fealty** *to each other not to desert once the war has begun.*

3   **Cotuatus and Conconnetodumnus** *lead the* **Carnutes against Cenabum,** *where they* **kill all Roman citizens,** *and news of the victory* **travels quickly throughout Gaul.**

4   *The Arvernian Vercingetorix collects a number of* **young Gauls** *to his cause* **against the Romans** *but is expelled because the chieftains do not endorse his plan.*

4   *With the young Gauls he had originally collected plus a number of outcasts,* **Vercingetorix** *is able to oust the chieftains who expelled him and to* **become king.**

4   *All of the tribes on the coast of the Atlantic pledge* **loyalty to Vercingetorix** *who then demands both soldiers and weapons from them.*

4   **Vercingetorix leads** *his men with* **strict discipline:** *serious crimes brought death and less serious crimes brought expulsion and disfigurement, both intended as a deterrent.*

5   *Vercingetorix sends Lucterius* with troops to the land of **the Ruteni** and **he himself approaches the Bituriges**.

5   *The Bituriges send ambassadors to the Aedui* to help them resist and the Aedui approach the **Roman legates for advice**.

5   *The Aedui send troops* who stop at the river Loire and don't cross because they fear **treachery from the Bituriges**.

5   *They return home* and the **Bituriges ally themselves with the Arverni**.

6   *Caesar returns to Gaul* but is uncertain how to proceed to connect with his troops: should he risk his armies coming through hostile territory to him or should he travel with tribes whose loyalty is uncertain?

7   *Lucterius*, whom **Vercingetorix** had sent to **the Ruteni**, collects forces from them and other tribes and marches toward **Narbonne**, near enough to Roman territory to suggest an invasion. *Caesar* abandons his plans and **heads for Narbonne**, where he fortifies the territory against the enemy.

8   *Caesar's defenses work and Lucterius retreats*, so Caesar proceeds to the land of **the Helvii**. From there he proceeds to the land of **the Arverni**, which lies on the other side of the mountains. Because it is winter, drifts have to be cleared but, because of the hard work of his men, Caesar makes it through.

8   *Caesar takes the Arverni by surprise* because they assumed that none could traverse the mountains. He orders his troops to terrorize the countryside as much as possible.

8   *The Arverni approach Vercingetorix* and ask him to protect them from the Romans and so he moves his garrison closer to the Arverni.

9   *Caesar anticipates Vercingetorix's decision* and so **leaves Brutus in charge** of the troops, ordering him to continue to terrorize the countryside and saying that he will return in three days.

9   *Caesar* collects troops while he is gone. When **Vercingetorix** hears this, he **leaves the Arverni and attacks the Boii**, whom the **Aedui** protect under **Caesar's** orders.

10   *Vercingetorix's attack on the Boii* puts **Caesar** in a bad spot: if he remains in his winter quarters, he gives the impression that he won't protect his people; if he leaves his winter quarters, he risks his men in the face of grain shortages.

10   *Caesar decides to help the Boii* and **asks the Aedui to fortify his supplies**. He sends word to the Boii that he is coming and that they should stay strong.

11   *Caesar attacks Vellaunodonum*, a garrison of **the Senones**, on the way, for fear of them attacking his rear. The garrison relents easily and **Caesar leaves Gaius Trebonius** to oversee Caesar's demands of weapons, pack animals, and hostages.

11   *Next Caesar looks to attack Cenabum*, a garrison of **the Carnutes**, but he can't attack until the next day because of nightfall. Caesar is concerned about a bridge over **the nearby river Loire** and so stations guards there. Indeed, the people try to escape at night over the bridge, so Caesar burns the gates, takes the garrison, and captures most of its residents.

12   *Caesar is attacking Noviodunum*, a garrison of **the Bituriges**, when envoys approach asking for clemency. Caesar orders weapons, horses, and hostages from them. While these are being handed over, the **advance cavalry of Vercingetorix appears** and the Bituriges begin to take them back and arm themselves.

13   *A cavalry battle* ensues and **Caesar**, when **Vercingetorix** gains the upper hand, sends in German cavalry he had with him who put the Gauls to flight.

13   The **residents of Noviodunum** arrest those who incited the people to revolt and bring them to **Caesar**, surrendering in the process.

13   *Caesar then leaves for Avaricum* (modern Bourges), whose submission, because it is the **largest town among the Bituriges** and in the middle of fertile ground, should lead to the conquest of the whole tribe.

14   *Vercingetorix* realizes, because of the Roman victories, that he must **cut the Romans off from their supplies**. To do this he suggests that the **Gauls** wait until the Romans leave the protection of the camps to collect supplies and **ambush them** then.

14   Additionally, the **Gauls must sacrifice** their own structures within reach of the Roman camps to render the supplies therein inaccessible. He also suggests that **any Roman camps that are not protected must be burned** both to prevent the Romans from utilizing them and to prevent the Gauls who do not want to fight from hiding in them.

15   *The Gauls agree and set fire to 20 towns* in the territory of the **Bituriges**. The Bituriges, however, beg the Gauls **not to set fire to Avaricum** (Bourges) because of its size, beauty, and importance. **Vercingetorix agrees**.

16   *Vercingetorix* sets up his camp **16 miles from Avaricum** (Bourges) and, through a series of well-organized patrols, keeps tabs on the movements of the Romans. Any Roman mission farther afield is attacked by the Gauls, often with success.

17   *Caesar begins to construct the siege engines* necessary to take **Avaricum** (Bourges), which are limited by the terrain. Meanwhile the lack of grain becomes a problem: **the Aedui** were resistant to help and **the Boii** had little grain to give. The soldiers went three days without any grain at one point but did not complain and remained committed to the siege of Bourges, even when Caesar suggested that they depart to find grain.

18   *Caesar* hears from prisoners that **Vercingetorix is preparing an ambush** on a foraging party, so he moves his troops to Vercingetorix's camp under the cover of night. This approach is discovered, so Vercingetorix marshals his forces and both sides are ready for battle.

19   *The Gauls* draw themselves up on a hill surrounded by a marsh and **Caesar** realizes the difficulty of taking such a position. Despite the enthusiasm of his men to fight, **Caesar withdraws**, realizing the cost of such a victory.

20   *Vercingetorix is accused* of conspiring with the Romans because of the Romans' approach: the Gauls reason that Vercingetorix is plotting to have the Romans confer kingship on him if the Gauls won't.

20   **Vercingetorix addresses the Gauls' accusations**: *they were running out of grain and had to move camp; the cavalry he had with him would have been useless in marshy ground; the appearance of the Romans allowed them to see how paltry the Roman forces were.*

20   *Finally, Caesar describes* **Vercingetorix's address to the Gauls in direct speech**: *Vercingetorix doesn't need the Romans to confer power because the Romans are already almost defeated. And, if the Gauls still don't believe him, they can take his power back for themselves.*

20   **Vercingetorix then produces Roman servants** *whom he presents as soldiers and has told what to say: that, because of the lack of supplies, the Romans would break camp in three days and depart.*

21   **Vercingetorix's speech wins over the Gauls** *and renews their loyalty to him. They send* **10,000 men to Avaricum (Bourges) to help the Bituriges** *resist the Romans.*

22   **The Gauls are able to undermine the Romans' siege engines** *through cleverness: pulling their siege hooks into the town with rope and undermining the siege towers by utilizing mine shafts. They also counter more directly by attacking the soldiers building the siege engines or booby-trapping the tunnels the Romans dug.*

23   **Caesar describes how the Gauls build their walls,** *concluding that they are both attractively built and useful for defense.*

24   *The quality of the walls of* **Avaricum** *(Bourges), as well as cold weather and rain, make the* **Roman work slow** *but eventually they build a siege engine that nearly touches the wall of Avaricum (Bourges).*

24   **The Gauls, however, ambush the tower** *at night, setting fire to it and attacking the workers.*

24   *The chaos of the attack makes it difficult to know where to send reinforcements but* **Caesar** *has stationed two legions for just such a situation and eventually, by moving the engine away from the wall, they are able to regain some control.*

25   *But the fighting continues:* **the Gauls** *are constantly renewed by fresh troops, thinking that the entire siege depends on this one battle.*

25   **Caesar describes a Gaul** *standing in front of the gate and refreshing the fire burning a Roman tower. He is killed and another takes his place. This replacement is killed and another takes his place. This continues until the fire is extinguished and the fighting is over.*

26   **The Gauls,** *encouraged by* **Vercingetorix,** *plan an escape, leaving at night and using the marshes to hamper any Roman pursuit.*

26   *When* **the Gauls** *are ready to leave,* **the women beg them not to abandon them.** *The Gauls ignore their pleas, and so the* **women begin shouting to alert the Romans,** *which then dissuades the Gauls from leaving.*

27   **Caesar** *repositions his siege engines and, in a heavy rainstorm, notices that* **the Gallic sentries seem less carefully positioned.** *Caesar prepares an attack and offers a reward to the first soldiers to scale the wall.*

28   *The wall is taken easily and* **the Gauls are thrown into confusion.** *Expecting a battle within the walls, the Gauls form a wedge but the* **Romans** *instead begin to spread out on the wall.*

The Gauls, afraid of being surrounded, break formation and make for the farthest ends of the city, where some escape and some are killed.

28   **The Romans attack the city with no mercy,** *killing even the women and children. Those that do escape, some 800 of 40,000, are brought to Vercingetorix's camp at night by guards he had posted on the road.* **Vercingetorix tries to minimize the blow to morale** *that their arrival might inflict.*

29   **Vercingetorix calls a council** *to allay the fears of* **the Gauls: the Romans won by trickery** *rather than bravery and the* **Bituriges were foolish** *to try to defend the city.*

29   **Vercingetorix then fortifies the camp** *to withstand a potential attack by the Romans.*

30   **The Gauls are encouraged by Vercingetorix's speech** *because he maintained optimism and did not flee in the face of defeat. Additionally, his renown was increased because he was against defending* **Bourges** *to begin with; the* **Romans' victory** *proved him correct.*

31   **The Gauls** *set about fortifying the camp while* **Vercingetorix** *recruits other Gauls to their cause.*

31   **Vercingetorix** *arms those who escaped from* **Bourges** *and calls for any archers among the Gauls to be sent to the camp.*

31   **Teutomatus, chief of the Nitiobriges joins Vercingetorix.**

32   **Caesar** *restores his men with the grain stores in* **Bourges.**

32   **The Aedui approach Caesar with a problem:** *each year they elect a leader but there are two who are claiming that role and the people are split over who should rule.*

33   **Caesar** *does not want to leave the fight with* **Vercingetorix** *but realizes the importance of* **the Aedui** *to Rome and doesn't want the losing side to join Vercingetorix. Caesar goes to the Aedui and summons both men.*

33   **Caesar** *determines that* **Cotus'** *election was invalid and so appoints* **Convictolitavis** *as leader.*

34   **Caesar then encourages the Aedui to continue fighting,** *promising them rewards once all of Gaul is conquered.*

34   **Caesar divides his army,** *bringing four legions* **to the Arverni** *to meet* **Vercingetorix** *who, in response to Caesar's approach,* **burns the bridges over the river Elaver** *(Allier).*

35   *Both armies are positioned on* **opposite sides of the river Elaver** *(Allier). By hiding two legions and sending troops ahead as decoys,* **Caesar** *is able to rebuild one of the bridges and cross the river.*

35   *When* **Vercingetorix** *hears that* **Caesar** *has crossed, he* **retreats to Gergovia,** *the primary town of* **the Arverni,** *to prepare its defense.*

36   **Caesar arrives at Gergovia** *and, because of its situation atop a high mountain, realizes that it cannot be taken by force. Before setting up any siege engines, however, Caesar attends to a grain supply for his troops.*

36   **Vercingetorix** *stations his men atop the walls as a show of force.*

36 *Caesar* realizes that the taking of a hill opposite the city, defended by the Gauls but not strongly, would cut off their supply lines. He makes a night raid on the hill and takes it before reinforcements are sent from the city.

37 *Convictolitavis*, the Aeduan appointed by Caesar, is **approached by the Arverni** in an attempt to turn him to their cause: because of **the influence of the Aedui**, their turning against the Romans would turn other tribes and all but ensure victory for the Gauls.

37 *Convictolitavis* is convinced and a plan is hatched: **the Aeduan Litaviccus** would command the Aeduan troops headed for Caesar.

38 *Litaviccus concocts a false story* about the Romans, how they without a trial slaughtered two Aeduan cavalrymen. He brings forward men to tell a story he has prepared for them, which stirs up the Aeduan soldiers.

38 **The Aeduans then torture and kill the Roman citizens** with them and pledge their **loyalty to the Arverni** rather than to the Romans.

38 *Finally, messengers are distributed* **throughout Aeduan lands** to report the story and **incite the Aeduans against the Romans**.

39 **One of the Aeduans with Caesar** learns of the plan and informs him of it, begging him not to condemn the entirety of the Aeduans for the rashness of a small group of young men.

40 *Caesar* quickly leaves camp **to intercept the Aeduan forces**. He sends the two Aeduans who Litaviccus falsely reported were killed by the Romans to circulate among the Aeduans to convey **Litaviccus' deception**.

40 Once the **Aeduans understand Litaviccus' deception**, they surrender and **Litaviccus flees for Gergovia**.

41 *Caesar spares the Aeduan soldiers* but makes sure that the Aeduans hear of his clemency, despite his right to kill them for their betrayal.

41 *Caesar rests his army* but is intercepted by **Fabius**, whom he left **in charge of the camp at Gergovia**. Fabius describes how the **Gauls had attacked** and how, because the Roman detachment was depleted, the Gauls almost took the camp but didn't. The soldiers are now refortifying the camp.

41 *Caesar rushes back to the camp* to reinforce it with his men.

42 *The Aedui hear Litaviccus' story* of the Romans' deception and **react against the Romans**, plundering their property and killing or enslaving them.

42 *Marcus Aristius*, a military tribune, leaves camp with Roman merchants, all of whom were **attacked by the Aedui**.

43 *The Aedui* then hear that the Aeduan soldiers are under Roman control and **realize the deception of Litaviccus**. They send **ambassadors to Caesar** to beg for mercy but at the same time prepare for war, realizing that Caesar might not grant such mercy.

43 *Caesar understands the plans* of the Aedui and prepares to withdraw his troops to address them but does not want to appear to be leaving because of revolt.

CHAPTER 4

44   *Caesar notices a second hill* near the city that had been occupied by **the Arverni** but is **now abandoned**. *He questions the Arvernian deserters about it and they explain that the Arverni are worried about the access this hill gives to the city and so are fortifying the ridge to prevent the Romans from gaining access.*

45   *Caesar uses pack-horses and servants as decoys to make it appear as if cavalry are mobilizing and preparing to attack that hill.* **The Arverni**, *in response to this, mobilize their forces to defend the hill, thereby leaving the camps that guard the city empty.*

45   *Caesar moves his troops into position, concealing the standards and crests of their helmets so that* **the Arverni** *wouldn't notice.*

46   **Caesar's troops easily capture** *three of these unguarded camps, even such that* **Teutomatus, king of the Nitiobriges,** *has to flee shirtless and on a wounded horse because the attack disturbed his nap.*

47   **Caesar orders a retreat** *but only the 10th legion hears it. The leaders of the other legions attempt to restrain the men but the men taste victory and approach the gates of the city.*

47   *The women of the city begin to beg for mercy, knowing what happened at Bourges.*

47   **Lucius Fabius**, *a centurion in the 8th legion, is the first to climb the wall, wanting for himself plunder similar to that of Bourges.*

48   **The Gauls** *falsely defending the ridge on the other side of the city hear the commotion and return to find the same women who had just then been begging the Romans for mercy exhorting them to fight.*

48   **The Roman situation is dire**: *they are tired from the previous assault and are not as numerous as the Gauls.*

49   *Caesar calls in* **reinforcements from the legate Titus Sextius** *who is guarding the smaller camp.*

50   **The Gauls are gaining the upper hand**, *despite the appearance of the Aeduan troops, who the Romans fear are not on their side.*

50   **Lucius Fabius**, *who scaled the wall first,* **is killed** *along with his men.*

50   **Marcus Petronius** *with his soldiers is trying to break down the gate but is wounded. He* **sacrifices himself** *to allow his men to escape.*

51   **The Romans retreat** *and the 10th Legion, which was drawn up in support, prevents the Gauls from pursuing.*

51   *The Romans lose 700 men that day.*

52   **Caesar assembles the troops** *and, while lauding their bravery in the face of difficulty,* **scolds them** *for their lack of control and their overeagerness.*

53   *Caesar nonetheless blames the defeat on the uneven ground rather than the bravery of the Gauls.*

53   **Caesar engages with Vercingetorix in a brief cavalry skirmish** *twice, both of which he wins, and then removes his troops for the land of the Aedui.*

54   *Caesar encounters Viridomarus and Eporedorix*, the two Aeduans falsely reported by **Litaviccus** killed by the Romans. They insist on **going ahead to the Aedui** to prevent Litaviccus from turning the Aedui against the Romans. Caesar agrees, thinking, however, the revolt of the Aedui inevitable, but not wanting to slight their honor. Caesar reminds them of the kindness of the Romans and exhorts them to remind the Aedui of this.

55   When **Viridomarus and Eporedorix reach Noviodunum**, an important Aeduan city under Roman control, they hear that **Convictolitavis had met Litaviccus at Bibracte**, another important Aeduan city, and had **sent ambassadors to Vercingetorix** to form an alliance.

55   **Viridomarus and Eporedorix see this as an opportunity** and so turn against the Romans and **take Noviodunum**. They **send hostages to Bibracte**, burn Noviodunum to render it useless to the Romans, and begin gathering troops to try to cut off the Romans' grain supply. Finally they **march against Labienus**, stationed near the land of the **Menapii**.

56   *Caesar decides not to retreat* because he did not want to lose face and was concerned about **Labienus** and his troops. He finds a place to cross **the Loire** (Liger) more quickly than expected and, fortified by grain and cattle they found, heads for the land of **the Senones**.

57   *Labienus sets out for Paris* (Lutetia), then an island in the middle of the river Seine (Sequana).

57   The **nearby tribes marshal forces against Labienus**, positioning themselves near the marshes that drain into the Seine, and make it difficult to cross.

58   *Labienus* tries unsuccessfully to cross the marshes and so **approaches Metiosedum**, a city of **the Senones** also on an island in the Seine. From the Senones he takes ships, which he connects to form a bridge across the river to take Metiosedum.

58   **Labienus then marches toward Paris**, in response to which the enemy burns the city and the bridges that lead to it. The enemy establishes its troops on the banks of the Seine facing Labienus.

59   The **rumors of Caesar's retreat from Gergovia** and **the rebellion of the Aedui** increase the confidence of the Gauls that they can conquer the Romans. **The Bellovaci** begin to **marshal troops** in preparation to fight.

59   **Labienus realizes how difficult his situation** has become, cut off from supplies and reinforcements. He resolves to leave Paris but knows that it will require the courage of his men to do so.

60   **Labienus calls a council** where he orders first Roman Knights to take the ships from Metiosedum and sail four miles downriver at night.

60   He leaves the soldiers least reliable in battle to guard the camp while he sends the rest of the soldiers and some boats upstream, telling them to make as much noise as possible.

60   **Labienus quietly goes downstream** with three legions to meet the ships he had sent there.

61   Because of a storm they were able to take the enemy by surprise and they crossed the river.

61   The reports of **the Romans** crossing downstream and moving upstream cause **the Gauls** to think that the Romans are spreading out to ease their escape for fear of the Aeduan revolt.

61   In response, the enemy divides its forces to meet the different Roman groups.

62   *Despite a fierce battle, **the Romans defeat the Gauls** downstream and **Labienus is able to escape** and reconnect with his supplies and reinforcements.*

63   ***The Aeduans try to win over tribes** to their cause and **ask Vercingetorix to meet** to plan the war. **The Aeduans ask for joint command and Vercingetorix disagrees**, so an **assembly** of all of the Gauls is called **at Bibracte**.*

63   ***All of the Gauls appear except for the Remi and Lingones**, who remain loyal to Rome, and **the Treveri**, who were too far away and dealing with the Germans; the Treveri remained neutral, neither fighting nor lending troops to either side.*

63   *The council awards **Vercingetorix the leadership**, which the Aedui resent to the extent that they consider returning to the Romans. But they are too invested in the revolt to switch sides. **Viridomarus and Eporedorix** are now unwillingly taking orders from Vercingetorix.*

64   ***Vercingetorix demands hostages** from the other tribes and **assembles a cavalry at Bibracte**. His plan is to use the cavalry to prevent the Romans from resupplying, harassing them as they forage. He also suggests that the Gauls sacrifice their grain and their structures to prevent the Romans from utilizing them.*

64   ***Vercingetorix** sends troops to the lands of those still sympathetic to the Romans, **the Allobroges and the Helvii and the Volcae Arecomici**. Still, he secretly sends ambassadors to the Allobroges, hoping to turn them against the Romans.*

65   ***Caesar sends troops** to assist those tribes sympathetic to the Romans. **The Helvii are defeated** and must retreat to their walled city. **The Allobroges successfully defend** their land at the Rhone River.*

65   ***Caesar** acknowledges that the Gallic cavalry surpasses his own, so he **asks the Germans** he had previously conquered **to send cavalrymen** to counter the Gauls. The Germans' horses are not suitable and so Caesar gives them his Roman horses.*

66   ***Vercingetorix sets up camp** near the Romans and exhorts his army: the Romans are leaving but they will be back so we must defeat them here and now.*

67   ***Vercingetorix divides his cavalry** into threes, two on either side of the Romans and one blocking their approach. **Caesar responds by dividing his cavalry likewise**. The battle is equal until the **German cavalry** is able to take a hill and **kill and capture Aeduans**.*

67   *One of those captured is **Cotus** who had the leadership dispute with **Convictolitavis**.*

68   ***Vercingetorix retreats to Alesia**, a city of **the Mandubii**. **Caesar pursues** and kills about 3,000 of Vercingetorix's troops.*

68   ***The Gauls are shaken by the defeat** of their cavalry and Caesar begins to build siege engines around Alesia.*

69   ***Alesia** is situated atop a hill, with two rivers around it and a plain stretching before it. **The Gauls** occupy one fortified hill-slope.*

70   ***A cavalry battle** breaks out on the plain and **Caesar sends the Germans to reinforce** the Romans. **The Romans win** and pursue the Gauls to their walls where **the Gauls are killed**.*

The advance of the Germans causes the Gauls to think an attack on the city is imminent so they close the gates to prevent Gauls from leaving their guard posts outside.

71   **Vercingetorix** *sends out his cavalry at night to recruit reinforcements, telling them to remind the tribesmen how much Vercingetorix has done for them and the danger he faced at* **Alesia**.

71   **Vercingetorix** *also orders grain and cattle to be distributed and all guards to be pulled inside the city until reinforcements arrive.*

72   **Caesar** *takes this opportunity to continue to* **fortify his position against Alesia** *by building siege engines.*

73   **Caesar** *has to send troops out to forage for supplies which leaves him undermanned and vulnerable to attack. Because of this, he continues to augment his defenses.*

73   **Caesar** *describes the construction and type of fortifications that he builds.*

74   **Caesar** *orders his men to supply themselves with grain for 30 days.*

75   **The Gauls**, *rather than provide* **Vercingetorix** *with all men of fighting age, instead agree to provide a fixed number of men.*

76   **The Gauls assemble a force** *of 8,000 cavalry and 240,000 infantrymen under the leadership of* **Commius the Atrebatian**, *a previous friend of Caesar whom Caesar had rewarded for his assistance in Britain. Also in charge were* **Viridomarus and Eporedorix and Vercassivellaunus, an Arvernian**.

76   **The Gauls** *assume that such a large force, coming from the opposite direction, will intimidate* **the Romans** *to surrender or retreat.*

77   **At Alesia**, *however, the day for the expected arrival of the reinforcements has passed and the grain has run out, so a council is called, at which various options are proposed, both surrender and escape.*

77   **Caesar singles out the speech of Critognatus**, *an Arvernian noble, because of the cruelty of its suggestion.*

77   **Critognatus** *discounts those advocating slavery because of the shame of it and instead only addresses those advocating escape.*

77   **Critognatus** *identifies escape as lacking courage because it is easier to face the potential death that comes with escape than the suffering that would come with staying.*

77   **Critognatus** *cites the impact of their death on the morale of all of Gaul, especially with reinforcements coming.*

77   **Critognatus** *recalls* **the war against the Cimbri and the Teutones** *when a similar lack of supplies was faced. The Gauls in that war nourished themselves by killing and feeding on those that could not fight.*

77   **Critognatus** *further underscores how much more important it is to defeat the Romans than it was to defeat* **the Cimbri and the Teutones**, *who were attacking but not conquering. The Romans intend to subjugate the land and the people of Gaul.*

78   *The council agrees to stay but only to adopt* **the plan of Critognatus as a last resort**.

78   **The Mandubii abandon** their camp and beg for food in exchange for slavery from the Romans, but Caesar has ordered no one to be admitted.

79   **The Gallic reinforcements arrive, which cheers those inside Alesia,** and establish themselves on the plain outside of the city.

80   **Caesar orders his cavalry to attack.** The Gauls' archers and infantrymen stationed among their cavalry take Caesar's troops by surprise and wound many of them.

80   The battle is fought equally on both sides until **a German cavalry detachment breaks through** and routs the Gauls.

81   **The Gauls prepare a sneak attack** and assault the Roman position in the middle of the night. **Vercingetorix,** upon hearing the attack, leads his forces out of the city.

81   The Romans are struggling to defend, but continue to send reinforcements to points of weakness along the fortification.

82   **The Gauls have the advantage** when they are farther from the fortifications because of the weapons they throw. When they approach the fortifications, they are stopped by the Romans' preparations.

82   **The Gauls withdraw at dawn** without capturing any ground.

83   **The Gauls meet to decide next steps.** They focus on a nearby hill whose size prevented it from being fortified adequately by the Romans. One force approaches the camp on that hill while the rest of the forces return to the plain outside of Alesia and appear in front of the city.

84   **The width of the Gallic attack** forces the Romans to thin their ranks. The difficulty of fighting with fewer reinforcements and the noise of battle surrounding them shakes the Romans' nerves.

85   **Caesar positions himself** so that he can see the entirety of the battle and responds to Gallic advances accordingly. The underfortified hill fort is suffering the most.

86   **Caesar sends Labienus to assist** the hill fort, telling him only to withdraw if necessary.

87   **Labienus** realizes that the Gauls have the upper hand, even with further reinforcements, so he formulates a plan that he reports to Caesar.

88   **Caesar himself joins Labienus** and his presence increases the intensity of the battle on both sides. **The Romans gain the upper hand** by fighting with swords and with reinforcements from the cavalry.

88   The **battle is finally won by the Romans.** Some Gauls try to escape the city but are pursued and captured or killed by the Romans. Any that make it out return to their tribes.

89   **Vercingetorix assembles the Gauls and offers himself to them:** his death at their hands could soften the Romans toward them. Or they can surrender him to the Romans alive.

89   **Weapons and Vercingetorix are surrendered** to the Romans.

A dying Gaul

90   With **Alesia subdued, Caesar proceeds to the Aedui** who submit to him. **The Arverni** likewise submit and Caesar restores prisoners to both tribes.

90   **Caesar distributes his legions throughout Gaul** to winter and maintain peace.

AENEAS SUMMARY

(*Because many poetic translations use their own line numbering that does not correspond directly to the line numbers of the Latin, line numbers are only used for the Latin summaries.*)

Latin Readings:

- ✓ *Aeneid* 1.1–209; 1.418–40; 1.494–578
- ✓ *Aeneid* 2.40–56; 2.201–49; 2.268–97; 2.559–620
- ✓ *Aeneid* 4.160–218; 4.259–361; 4.659–705
- ✓ *Aeneid* 6.295–332; 6.384–425; 6.450–76; 6.847–99

Readings in English:

- ✓ *Aeneid* rest of 1, rest of 2, rest of 4, rest of 6; all of 8 and 12

1.1–208 (Latin)

1–7   Introduction of theme and broad summary of narrative.

> ***arma virumque cano***

8–11   Invocation of the Muse.

> ***Musa, mihi causas memora***

12–18   Introduction of Carthage and its importance to Juno.

> ***Urbs antiqua fuit***

19–22   Juno considers the Trojans' impact on Carthage.

> ***Progeniem Trōiānō ā sanguine***

23–32   Juno's anger over the Judgment of Paris and the Trojan War causes her to punish Aeneas.

33   ***Tantae mōlis erat Rōmānam condere gentem!***
> Of so great a burden was the founding of the Roman people!

34–49   Juno resolves to punish Aeneas despite the impediments of Fate and worries about who will worship her.

50–64	Juno travels to Aeolia to Aeolus, the god of the winds, to enlist his assistance.
65–75	Juno promises Aeolus her most lovely nymph if he will use his winds to impede Aeneas' progress.
76–86	Aeolus agrees and unleashes his winds on Aeneas' fleet.
87–101	The crew and Aeneas react to the sudden arrival of the storm. Aeneas wishes that he had died at Troy.
102–23	The storm begins to destroy Aeneas' fleet. Seven of Aeneas' ships are sunk.
124–31	Neptune realizes what has happened and summons the winds.
132–41	Neptune admonishes the winds and Aeolus for acting without his sanction.
	Quos ego –
142–56	Neptune calms the seas: the simile of the man who calms the crowd.
157–79	Aeneas and his men land on the shores of Carthage.
180–97	Aeneas and Achates explore and kill stags; they bring the stags and wine to the men.
198–207	Aeneas reminds his men of their strength by recalling past triumphs and reminding them of their destiny.
208–9	Aeneas finishes speaking, hiding his concern and appearing optimistic to his men.
	premit altum corde dolorem

1.210–417 (English)

- *Aeneas and his men prepare the stags that they caught, and they eat and drink wine.*

- *Aeneas and his men grieve for their lost men, hoping that they somehow survived.*

- *Jupiter is introduced looking toward Libya as Venus addresses him.*

- *Venus asks Jupiter why the Trojans suffer so and why he has broken his promise to her to keep them safe.*

- *Venus references the Trojan Antenor who escaped Troy and founded the Italian city of Padua.*

- *Jupiter comforts Venus by assuring her that Aeneas will reach Italy safely.*

- *Jupiter tells Venus Aeneas' future:*

  o *He will fight a war upon reaching Italy and rule for three years after the war is over.*

  o *After Aeneas' three years, Ascanius will rule for 30 years and will found Alba Longa.*

  o *Alba Longa will survive for 300 years until the twins Romulus and Remus are born.*

  o *Romulus will found Rome whose existence Jupiter puts no limits on.*

- *Jupiter assures Venus that even Juno, despite her enmity toward Aeneas, will come to appreciate the Romans.*

- *Jupiter also foretells the geographic extent of the Roman Empire and connects the Julian clan to Ascanius' alternate name, Iulus.*

- *Jupiter predicts the end of war and the imprisoning of Fury.*

- *Jupiter sends Mercury to Carthage so that Aeneas and his men will be welcome there.*

- *Aeneas and Achates explore the coast to try to determine where they are and who lives there.*

- *Venus, disguised as a huntress, approaches Aeneas and asks, in character, if he has seen any of her huntress sisters.*

- *Aeneas replies that he has not and asks who she is, since she neither looks nor sounds mortal.*

- *Aeneas asks her where they are.*

- *Venus responds that they are in Carthage, bordering Libya, a pugnacious land.*

- *Venus tells the story of Dido's arrival:*

  o *Dido was married to Sychaeus, a rich Phoenician, but he and her brother Pygmalion feuded and Pygmalion secretly killed Sychaeus.*

  o *Pygmalion kept the death of Sychaeus secret and Dido's hopes alive until Sychaeus appeared to Dido in a dream and explained his death.*

  o *Sychaeus also exhorted Dido to flee, showed her where a secret treasure was located to allow her to flee, and showed her where to flee, to Carthage.*

  o *Dido used the money to buy as much land as she could and to begin the construction of Carthage.*

- *Venus concludes by asking Aeneas who he is and where he is going.*

- *Aeneas identifies himself as a Trojan, driven from home by the war and driven to this coast by a storm.*

- *Aeneas explains that his destiny is Italy, aided by his mother Venus.*

- *Venus interrupts to explain that he does not seem cursed by the gods and that he should proceed to the city of Carthage.*

- *Venus assures him that his men are safe and have either landed or are arriving.*

- *Venus turns away and Aeneas recognizes her divinity.*

- *Aeneas rebukes his mother for disguising herself from him.*

- *Aeneas and Achates approach the city enfolded in a cloud provided by his mother to render them invisible.*

1.418–40 (Latin)

418–29   Aeneas and Achates ascend a hill and look down on Carthage in the process of being built. They are amazed at how extensive the city is: laws are enacted, magistrates and a senate are chosen, walls and a theater are being built.

430–36   The epic simile of the bees: the work of the Carthaginians bustling about below Aeneas and Achates is compared to the work of bees.

> ***Qualis apes aestate nova per florea rura / exercet sub sole labor***

437   ***O fortunati, quorum iam moenia surgunt!***
O fortunate ones, whose walls now grow!

438–40   Aeneas and Achates mingle within the city, still hidden by Venus' cloud.

1.441–93 (English)

- *Vergil describes the temple of Juno in Carthage, established in a spot where a horse's head was found in the ground when Dido arrived.*

- *Aeneas waits in the temple for Dido and, as he waits, admires the art depicting the Trojan War.*

- *Aeneas addresses Achates about the renown of the Trojan War, how its story has even reached Carthage, and how their reputation as Trojans will save them in Carthage.*

- *Descriptions of the scenes of the Trojan War:*
  - *Greeks in retreat*
  - *Achilles chasing in his chariot*
  - *Diomedes' ambush of Rhesus' camp and theft of his horses*
  - *Troilus being dragged by his own chariot after facing Achilles*
  - *Trojan women going to the temple of Athena*
  - *Achilles dragging Hector around the walls of Troy and Priam grieving over him*
  - *Aeneas himself fighting the Greeks*
  - *Memnon and Penthesilea fighting*

1.494–578 (Latin)

494–97   Dido approaches the temple.

498–502   The simile of Diana and her retinue: Diana is attended by a thousand nymphs and she leads, surpassing the other goddesses.

503–8   Dido enters the temple and ascends the throne from where she leads, settling disputes and overseeing the construction of the city.

509–19	Aeneas and Achates, still enclosed within the cloud, see their companions, both those with whom they landed and those thought lost at sea, and enter the temple; they are uncertain about what has happened and what they should do.
520–29	The eldest of the Trojans, Ilioneus, addresses Dido. He identifies them as Trojans, he asks for clemency, and he assures her that they have not arrived for conflict.
530–38	Ilioneus explains their quest for Italy and how they were blown off course by the storm.
539–43	Ilioneus wonders what kind of place would contest their landing and question their motives.
544–49	Ilioneus mentions Aeneas and suggests that Dido would do well to receive him kindly.
549–60	Ilioneus concludes by asking for materials to repair their ships: if Aeneas is alive and found, they can continue their quest for Italy; if he has perished, they can make for Sicily where the Trojan Acestes is.
561–78	Dido responds favorably, that she must protect her borders because she is founding a new city, that the Trojans are welcome in Carthage to rebuild their ships or even to stay permanently, and that she will send search parties out for Aeneas.

1.579–756 (end; English)

- *Aeneas and Achates are eager to reveal themselves.*

- *Achates addresses Aeneas in the cloud, reminding him that what Venus told them when they met her has come to pass.*

- *Suddenly, the cloud disappears and Aeneas is visible, made glorious before Dido and his companions by Venus.*

- *Aeneas thanks Dido for taking them in and offering them a new home. He has nothing with which to thank her but prays that the gods reward her.*

- *Aeneas praises Dido's parents and pledges that her kindness will be remembered forever.*

- *Dido confirms that Aeneas is in fact who he says he is.*

- *Dido evokes the connection between her father and Teucer; since that encounter, she has known about Troy.*

- *Dido identifies her own suffering as the reason why she is willing to help others also suffering.*

- *Dido announces sacrifices in the temples and sends to the Trojans on the coast supplies for a feast.*

- *Aeneas is grateful but is worried about his son Ascanius.*

- *Aeneas sends Achates to the ship to deliver the news and bring Ascanius to him, as well as gifts for Dido.*

- *Venus invents a scheme whereby Cupid would appear in the form of Ascanius to make Dido fall in love with Aeneas.*

- *Venus tells Cupid that she is concerned about Juno's hindrance of Aeneas' journey and, by making Dido fall in love with Aeneas, she can regain control of Aeneas' situation.*

- *Venus explains that she will spirit Ascanius away for a day while Cupid assumes his appearance and that, when Dido embraces Cupid-as-Ascanius at the feast, he should inflame her with love for Aeneas.*

- *Cupid assumes Ascanius' appearance and brings the gifts to the feast.*

The boy Cupid preparing his bow

- *During the feast, Dido cannot keep her eyes off Ascanius or the gifts he bears and, when he approaches her, she embraces him.*

- *In this embrace, Cupid begins replacing Sychaeus with Aeneas in Dido's heart.*

- *At the close of the feast, Dido blesses the gathering and calls on a bard to tell tales.*

- *Throughout the feast, Dido is inquiring about the Trojan War and finally calls on Aeneas to tell his story.*

AN OVERVIEW OF THE FALL OF TROY AND THE JOURNEY OF AENEAS

- *Book 2 begins the tale of Aeneas' wanderings from Troy to Italy: the Fall of Troy in book 2 and the wanderings themselves in books 3 and 5.*

- *By book 6, Aeneas has arrived in Italy.*

- *Most of the wanderings are excluded from the syllabus; only Troy, Carthage, and Cumae are included.*

- *Nonetheless, a familiarity with Aeneas' wanderings, especially because of their derivation from and comparison to the journey of Odysseus, is important for understanding the literary context of Aeneas' wanderings and the Aeneid itself.*

- *At the end of the book 2 summary is a keyed map that includes all stops of Aeneas' wanderings.*

- *Below is a map of the area around Troy for reference for book 2.*

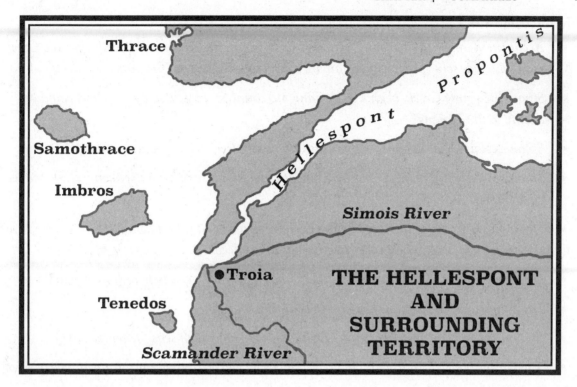

2.1–39 (English)

- *Aeneas describes how difficult it will be to tell his story but agrees to do so.*

- *Aeneas begins with the description of the Trojan Horse.*

- *The Greeks, after delivering the Trojan Horse, retreat to the island of Tenedos, near Troy but out of sight.*

- *The Trojans think that the Greeks have returned home and so, rejoicing, open their gates.*

- *The Trojans wander the now abandoned beach, marveling at their different memories of the war now that the Greeks have left.*

- *The horse prompts immediate debate: admit it to the city, throw it in the sea, burn it, or investigate its belly.*

2.40–56 (Latin)

40–44   The priest Laocoon runs down to the beach and admonishes the Trojans for even considering admitting the horse, reminding them how untrustworthy both the Greeks in general and specifically Odysseus are.

45–49   Laocoon speculates on the various ways the horse is a trick.

          Quidquid id est, timeo Danaos et dona ferentes.

50–56   Laocoon flings his spear into the side of the horse where it reveberates and Aeneas speculates that, had the gods not clouded their judgment and had they heeded Laocoon's warning, Troy would still stand.

CHAPTER 4

2.57–200 (English)

- At the moment when Laocoon flings his spear, Trojan shepherds bring forth a young Greek man who was sent specifically to convince the Trojans to admit the horse.

- Sinon, the young Greek, begins by claiming no country: unwanted by the Greeks and an enemy to the Trojans.

- Sinon explains that Palamedes, his kinsman, was falsely accused and killed by Odysseus.

- Sinon vowed vengeance for Palamedes' death and, because of his outspokenness, he too was condemned.

- Sinon, however, cuts himself off before explaining for what he was condemned to heighten the veracity of his story and the effectiveness of his deceit.

- He concedes that, if the Trojans are to kill him, they don't need to hear his story to do so.

- His plan works: the Trojans beg him to continue.

- Sinon explains that the Greeks were trying to leave but rough seas prevented them.

- The Greeks build the horse and the seas only grow worse, so they consult the oracle of Apollo.

- The oracle returns: as the Greeks sacrificed for favorable weather to come to Troy, so they must sacrifice for favorable weather to leave.

- Calchas, the Greek seer, refuses to name the one to be sacrificed for five days but finally relents and names Sinon.

- Sinon concludes by explaining how he escaped and, since he cannot return to the Greeks, begs the Trojans for mercy.

- Priam absolves him and welcomes him to Troy, concluding by asking him to explain the horse.

- Sinon prays to the gods, asking for mercy for breaking his oath of secrecy about the horse but asking the Trojans to be equally kind to him if his revelation leads to their salvation.

- Sinon explains that the theft of the Palladium by Diomedes and Odysseus from the temple of Athena turned her against the Greeks and turned their fortune in the war.

- The Greeks must leave and return, renewed by favorable omens at home.

- The Greeks are completing the return portion of the prophecy now and built the horse as a final gift to Athena.

- They built it so high so that it could not be brought into the city for, if the horse is destroyed, it will spell the doom of the Trojans, but, if it is brought into Troy, the Trojans will win.

- The Trojans are thoroughly convinced by Sinon's story.

2.201–49 (Latin)

201–11   Laocoon is sacrificing to Neptune when the Trojans spot two sea serpents coming toward the shore from Tenedos.

212–22   The serpents make for Laocoon and his sons, encircling the sons first and then Laocoon.

223–24   The simile of the bellowing bull.

> ***Qualis mugitus, fugit cum saucius aram /
> taurus et incertam excussit cervice securim.***

The death of Laocoon and his sons

225–27   The serpents kill Laocoon and slither off to the temple of Minerva.

228–33   The death of Laocoon convinces the Trojans that his spearing of the horse insulted Athena and that the horse should be admitted.

234–45   The Trojans break their walls and happily drag the horse inside. Even when it falters four times on the way in, causing the armor of the Greek soldiers to clatter, the Trojans ignore the sound and force it inside.

246–49   Cassandra, the Trojan princess cursed with knowing the future but having no one listen to her prophecies, warns against the horse but is ignored, as the Trojans garnish the altars of the gods with flowers.

2.250–67 (English)

- *As night falls, the Trojans are blissfully asleep and unaware of their coming doom.*

- *The Greeks return from Tenedos.*

- *Sinon, signaled by the lead ship, opens the door of the horse and releases the Greek soldiers, who kill the guards and open all of the gates of the city.*

2.268–97 (Latin)

268–79   Hector, wounded and bloodied from his death, appears in a dream to Aeneas.

279–86   Aeneas asks Hector why he appears now and why he retains his wounds.

287–92   Hector tells Aeneas that the city has fallen and that he must flee.

293–95   Hector entrusts to Aeneas the penates, the gods of Troy, to carry with him as he pursues his destiny.

296–97   Hector presents the fillets and eternal flame of Vesta.

CHAPTER 4

2.298–558 (English)

- The sounds of battle reach Aeneas and awaken him, confirming what Hector said.

- The simile of the south wind fanning flames and flattening fields, which the shepherd hears in increasing volume from afar.

- Aeneas sees the burning buildings and collapsing houses around him and rashly arms himself for battle.

- Panthus, the priest of Apollo, appears with his grandson fleeing the Greeks.

- Aeneas asks Panthus where he should fight, what position should be held.

- Panthus details Troy's destruction and the hopelessness of the situation.

- Aeneas pursues the battle anyway and a small group of Trojans fall in with him to fight.

- Aeneas addresses his new band: the gods have forsaken them, they pursue death by fighting for a conquered city, and they fight with little to no hope of success.

- Aeneas' words inspire his men and they make their way to the center of the city, witnessing the carnage and violence of war and the death of both Trojans and Greeks all around them.

- The Greek soldier Androgeos mistakes Aeneas' band for Greeks, chides them for being late, and realizes his mistake when they fail to respond immediately.

- The simile of the man stepping on an unseen snake.

- The Trojans, pressing their advantage, slay Androgeos and his men.

- Coroebus, one of the Trojans, suggests that they swap armor with the dead Greeks to blend in.

- The plan works, as Aeneas and his Trojans kill whichever Greeks they encounter.

- Next, the band sees Cassandra, bound, being dragged away.

- Coroebus attempts to rescue her but Aeneas and the Trojans are set upon from both sides: first the Trojans attack them because of their Greek armor and then, realizing the deception, the Greeks attack them.

- The simile of the hurricane and its devastating effects.

- All but three of Aeneas' group are killed and manage to escape to Priam's palace.

- The scene at Priam's palace is so grim that what they see before seemed barely a battle.

- Aeneas and his two companions attack with renewed energy to save Priam's palace.

- They use a secret entrance to go into the palace and then climb to the roof.

- On the roof, they dismantle a tower and send it crashing down on the Greeks.

- The character of Pyrrhus is introduced.

- The simile of the hungry snake emerging from winter.

- Pyrrhus and his band tear through the battlements to gain access to the palace.

- Pyrrhus and the Greeks move through the palace unstopped, killing any Trojans who resist them.

- The simile of a river flooding its banks.

- Pyrrhus, Menelaus, and Agamemnon stand on the threshold.

- Hecuba and the wounded Priam are exposed.

- Priam, in a feeble final attempt to defend his palace and his city, dons his armor and charges the Greeks.

- Hecuba and her daughters take shelter near a huge altar at the center of the palace as she addresses Priam.

- Hecuba exhorts Priam to join her at the altar, which will either save them or be the site of their death; she finally grabs Priam and brings him to the altar.

- Polites, a son of Priam and Hecuba, wounded and pursued by Pyrrhus, dies before them.

- Priam curses Pyrrhus for the insult of making him watch his own son's death.

- Priam rebukes Pyrrhus for lacking the honor that his father Achilles possessed when he and Priam met earlier in the war over Hector's body.

- Priam uselessly hurls his spear at Pyrrhus; it feebly strikes Pyrrhus' shield.

- Pyrrhus informs Priam that he can report his bad behavior to his father when he sees him in the underworld.

- Pyrrhus pulls Priam, unable to gain his footing in his son's spilled blood, to the altar and buries his sword in him.

2.559–620 (Latin)

559–63   Aeneas, seeing the death of Priam, imagines the deaths of his own family.

564–74   Aeneas, now alone, spies Helen hiding by the altar of Vesta.

575–87   Aeneas burns with resentment, which he verbalizes to himself:

  o Why should Helen get to see her home and family?

  o Did Priam die so she could return home?

  o It is not honorable to kill a woman.

  o I would be praised for killing such evil.

  o Her death would satisfy my need for revenge.

588–94   Venus, Aeneas' mother, appears just as he is about to attack Helen.

595–603   Venus asks why his anger is consuming him so much when his own family is in peril, saved only by her protection. Neither Paris nor Helen are at fault for Troy's fall but rather the gods.

604–18   Venus shows Aeneas the gods themselves destroying Troy: Neptune, Juno, Athena, Jupiter.

619–20   Venus promises to bring Aeneas to his father's house.

2.621–804 (end; English)

- *The simile of the ancient ash tree that slowly begins to falter and eventually falls before the persistent attempts of the axmen trying to chop it down.*

- *Aeneas reaches his father Anchises' house with the help of Venus and offers to carry him to safety.*

- *Anchises refuses, saying that he would rather take his own life and die in his city.*

- *Aeneas, along with his wife and son, implores Anchises to relent but he refuses.*

- *In desperation, Aeneas reaches for his arms and explains to Anchises the violence of Pyrrhus.*

- *Aeneas then wonders why Venus saved him only to see his father perish.*

- *He finally rearms himself, resigned to die at Troy if his father won't leave.*

- *As he is leaving the house, his wife grabs him and implores him first to defend their house and family.*

- *Just then, a small, harmless flame appears on the head of Ascanius.*

- *Aeneas and Creusa quickly extinguish the flame but Anchises prays to Jupiter to confirm that the flame is a sign from the gods with a second sign.*

- *Thunder booms and a shooting star illuminates the night sky.*

- *Anchises agrees to accompany Aeneas and his family as they escape, the flames of the burning city now coming closer.*

- *Aeneas tells his father that he will carry him on his shoulders, that Ascanius will walk next to him, and that Creusa will be behind them.*

- *Aeneas explains that they will meet at a cypress tree outside of the city.*

- *Aeneas entrusts the penates to his father because he doesn't want to handle them without purifying his bloodied hands.*

- *Aeneas and his group stay in the shadows and make it just to the gate without incident when they come upon Greek soldiers.*

Aeneas carries his father, Anchises, from the burning Troy, trailed by his son Ascanius.

- *Anchises encourages Aeneas to run but, as he runs, Creusa is no longer with them.*

- *Aeneas realizes that she is missing when they reach the meeting spot and curses himself and the gods for not realizing her absence.*

- *Aeneas hides his family and the men with them, dons his armor, and returns to the city, desperate to find his missing wife.*

- *Aeneas retraces his steps without finding her and then proceeds to his own house and Priam's palace, all the while witnessing the destruction of Troy.*

- *Aeneas even risks calling her name until her ghost appears before him.*

- *Creusa absolves him of any blame, citing the gods for her disappearance.*

- *She then explains to him his future:*
    - *He will endure a long journey.*
    - *Eventually he will come to Italy where the Tiber flows.*
    - *He will be happy, be king, and marry.*

- *She encourages him not to weep, reminding him that she will never be a Greek slave.*

- *As she finishes, Aeneas attempts to hug her unsuccessfully, hugging only the empty air.*

- *When Aeneas returns to his group, he finds that its number has grown and they depart.*

4.1–159 (English)

[At the end of book 3, Aeneas finishes his tale.]

- *Dido's love for Aeneas is intensified by the telling of his story.*

- *The next morning, Dido summons her sister Anna.*

- *Dido identifies Aeneas as divine because of his bravery before such trials.*

- *Dido admits that she has feelings for Aeneas but reiterates her commitment to her dead husband Sychaeus.*

- *Anna laments Dido's commitment to Sychaeus, suggesting that she is wasting her youth and that the dead hold no grudges: Sychaeus does not expect her to remain faithful.*

- *Anna acknowledges that no other men have been attractive but that she shouldn't ignore the one that is.*

- *Anna suggests that the mingling of Carthaginian and Trojan would create a mighty empire.*

- *Anna finally suggests that Dido should fabricate reasons for the Trojans to stay, like the weather is bad or the sea is too stormy.*

- *Anna's argument works and she and Dido sacrifice to the gods, especially Juno, the goddess of marriage, to bless her decision.*

- *Dido's feelings toward Aeneas drive her to wander the city.*

- *The simile of the wounded doe.*

- *Dido tours Aeneas through the growing city and has another feast where she implores him to tell his story again.*

- *Dido tries to recreate Aeneas' presence when he is absent by lying where he lay or by holding his son.*

- *The work on and construction of the city comes to a halt.*

- *Juno approaches Venus after seeing Dido so stricken and compliments her and Cupid on what they have accomplished.*

- *Juno proposes that they compromise by ruling the combined kingdom together.*

- *Venus cautiously agrees, realizing that Juno means to keep Aeneas from Italy.*

- *She asks Juno to confirm with Jupiter, her husband, that this plan in fact fulfills Aeneas' destiny.*

- *Juno agrees and outlines her plan: when the hunting party departs the next day, Juno will send a storm that will drive Dido and Aeneas to the same cave, where Juno will oversee their union.*

- *The hunting party departs, Aeneas' and Dido's companions forming into one group.*

- *Aeneas' splendor is compared to Apollo refreshing and restoring himself during winter on his home island of Delos.*

- *Ascanius ranges about, chasing deer and goats but yearning for more of a challenge, like a boar or lion.*

4.160–218 (Latin)

160–66   The storm arrives, everyone scatters, and Dido and Aeneas find themselves at the same cave.

166–72   Juno attends the union of Dido and Aeneas and, with it, Dido sacrifices her reputation for the sake of her love.

173–90   The origin and description of the allegorized Rumor.

        magnas it Fama per urbes

191–97   The rumor about Dido and Aeneas reaches Iarbas, a local ruler and previous suitor of Dido.

198–205   Iarbas, jealous, prays to his father Jupiter.

206–18   Iarbas resents not only that Dido, a newcomer, spurned him but also that she spurned him for the effeminate Aeneas.

        Et nunc ille Paris cum semiviro comitatu

4.219–58 (English)

- *Jupiter, in response to Iarbas' prayer, summons Mercury to bring a message to Aeneas:*

  - *Aeneas does not belong in Carthage nor is that why his mother saved him from the Greeks.*

  - *He should not cheat Ascanius of the kingdom that Aeneas will leave him.*

4.259–361 (Latin)

259–64   Mercury arrives in Carthage to find Aeneas in sumptuous finery and helping to build the city.

265–76   Mercury reminds Aeneas of his duty to himself, to the gods, and to his son.

277–82   Mercury vanishes and Aeneas immediately realizes that he has to and that he wants to leave Carthage.

283–86   Aeneas worries about how to handle his departure from Carthage and Dido.

287–95   Aeneas orders his men to prepare the ships while he determines how to approach Dido.

296–301   Dido hears a rumor of Aeneas' departure and rages through the city.

        At regina dolos (quis fallere possit amantem?) / praesensit

The messenger god Mercury, whom Jupiter sends to Aeneas

CHAPTER 4

301–3   The simile of the crazed Maenad.

> *qualis commotis excita sacris / Thyias ubi audito stimulant trieterica Baccho / orgia nocturnusque vocat clamore Cithaeron*

304–30   Dido addresses Aeneas.

    305–6   Did you think you could hide this?

    307   Do you not care about our love?

    308   Do you not care about my death?

    309–13   The weather is so bad that you wouldn't even flee Troy in it.

    314   Do you flee me?

> *Mene fugis?*

A Thyias, or Maenad, a worshipper of Bacchus

    314–19   If our love meant anything, if you have any pity, don't go.

    320–26   Our love has made everyone hate me and has ruined my reputation; either Iarbas will kill me or Pygmalion will destroy Carthage.

    327–30   A child by you would have made your departure easier.

331–61   Aeneas responds.

    333–36   I owe you and will always remember you.

    337–39   I did not intend to leave secretly and we never married.

    340–44   If it were up to me rather than Fate, Troy would still stand.

    345–47   Apollo orders me to go to Italy.

    347–50   You have your own kingdom; why can't I have mine?

    351–53   The ghost of my father encourages me to leave every night.

    354–55   Will I cheat my son of his kingdom?

    356–59   Mercury himself visited me to tell me to leave.

    360–61   This is painful enough; I don't want to leave.

4.362–658 (English)

- *Dido responds angrily.*

- *Dido ascribes Aeneas' birth to a rock or wild animal.*

- *Dido took Aeneas in and shared her kingdom only to be rewarded by the gods with his departure.*

- *Dido curses Aeneas by wishing on him death at sea while calling her name and she promises that her ghost will haunt him.*

- *Dido leaves Aeneas, who still has things to say and who still wishes to console Dido.*

- *Nonetheless, Aeneas returns to his fleet.*

- *Aeneas and the Trojans hurry to prepare their ships.*

- *The simile of the ants working.*

- *Dido sees the Trojans' preparations and weeps to her sister Anna.*

- *Dido asks Anna to beg Aeneas to delay his departure so that Dido can learn to live with the sorrow of his leaving.*

- *Anna brings Dido's request to Aeneas and he refuses.*

- *The simile of the strong oak resisting the winter winds.*

- *Dido prays for death and witnesses two evil omens: the libation she pours turns black and she hears Sychaeus' voice emanating from his altar.*

- *The simile of crazed Pentheus and Orestes.*

- *Dido formulates a plan for her death.*

- *She summons her sister to her.*

- *Dido explains that a priestess from Ethiopia has arrived and explained to her how to expiate her grief.*

- *Dido asks Anna to build a pyre on top of which she should put the weapons and clothes that Aeneas left behind and the bed that they shared.*

- *Anna can't fathom that Dido would kill herself and so does as she's asked.*

- *Dido decorates the pyre and arranges Aeneas' belongings.*

- *Dido incants prayers to dark deities.*

- *Dido can't sleep and finally speaks, wondering what she should do.*
  - *Should she approach her former suitors?*
  - *Would the Trojans take her aboard in return for her kindness toward them? Probably not.*
  - *Should Dido follow the Trojans with her own fleet?*

- *Dido resolves to die, blames her sister for convincing her to pursue Aeneas, and accepts responsibility for betraying Sychaeus.*

- *Mercury returns to Aeneas in his sleep to encourage him to leave, telling him that Dido is about to die and intends evil.*

CHAPTER 4

- *Aeneas wakes up, wakes his men up, and they quickly depart.*

- *Dido sees the fleet leave and calls to her people to pursue, realizing immediately her folly.*

- *Dido imagines if she had killed Aeneas or Ascanius or had burned the Trojans' camp.*

- *Dido prays to the Sun, Juno, Hecate, and the Furies, cursing Aeneas to prolonged battle in his new land and to die early.*

- *Dido also demands that her descendants never make peace with his descendants and constantly battle them. [This demand (fictionally) explains the historical enmity between Rome and Carthage, and the three Punic Wars.]*

- *Dido, preparing to kill herself, instructs Barce, the nurse of her dead husband Sychaeus, to fetch her sister Anna, and to both return to her.*

- *Dido climbs the pyre with Aeneas' sword unsheathed and delivers her final speech in which she resigns herself to her death and expresses on the one hand satisfaction with her accomplishments and on the other hand regret at the Trojans' arrival.*

4.659–705 (Latin)

659–62   Dido's final words, declaring her own death and the witness of the Trojans to it from the smoke.

666–71   Dido falls onto Aeneas' sword, Rumor swirls through the city, and all of Carthage mourns as if the entire city had been destroyed.

667–85   Anna discovers Dido's death and hurries to the pyre to address her, regretting that she couldn't die with Dido and declaring the destruction of the city by Dido's death.

668–92   Anna climbs the pyre to embrace her dying sister's body.

669–702   Juno sends Iris to Dido to complete the death ritual since Dido's premature death preempted any divine preparations.

700–705   Iris consecrates Dido and allows her to finally die.

6.1–294 (English)

[Aeneas in book 5 completes his journey and is now approaching Italy.]

- *Aeneas and his fleet land at Cumae and, while they forage for supplies, Aeneas seeks out the Cumaean Sibyl, priestess of Apollo.*

- *Her temple was established by Daedalus and depicts the story of Crete on its doors:*

  o *the murder of Androgeus*

Daedalus, Icarus, and the wings: the story that Daedalus couldn't sculpt on the temple doors

o   *the Athenian tribute*

o   *Pasiphae and the bull*

o   *the Minotaur and the Labyrinth*

o   *Ariadne helping Theseus*

- *The temple does not depict Icarus because Daedalus tried but his grief prevented him.*

- *Achates returns with Deïphobe, Apollo's priestess, who orders him to sacrifice in preparation.*

- *The priestess transforms and warns Aeneas that he cannot enter the temple until he has prayed.*

- *Aeneas prays to Apollo, who helped Paris kill Achilles, to stop Troy's fate from following Aeneas to Italy.*

- *Aeneas prays to the other gods whom Troy offended and to the priestess that they be able to settle in Italy.*

- *Aeneas pledges a temple to Phoebus and Trivia, a goddess of the underworld.*

- *The priestess struggles with Apollo's possession of her.*

- *Apollo through the priestess prophesies war, another Achilles with whom the Trojans must contend, and continued harassment by Juno.*

- *Apollo also encourages them to persist and to look for assistance from, of all places, a Greek city.*

- *Aeneas accepts the troubles that she has prophesied, saying that he has experienced trouble aplenty already.*

- *Aeneas asks instead to be admitted to the Underworld to see his dead father.*

- *The priestess informs Aeneas that admission to the Underworld is easy; it is returning that is difficult.*

- *Nonetheless, she gives Aeneas instructions on how to proceed:*

  o   *In a nearby wood, there is a golden branch which Persephone considers a gift.*

  o   *If Aeneas is meant to enter the underworld, the branch will break off in his hands; if not, he will not be able to break it.*

  o   *Aeneas also must bury the unburied body of his companion and lead black cattle to be sacrificed.*

- *Achates and Aeneas walk, trying to figure out whose body is unburied.*

- *As they walk, they come upon the body of Misenus who insulted Triton by claiming he could play the conch better; Triton drowned him.*

- *The Trojans build a pyre for Misenus with pine trees from the forest, where Aeneas prays that he will find the golden branch.*

- *After the prayer, two doves, the birds of Aeneas' mother Venus, appear and Aeneas prays that they lead him to the branch.*

- *The doves fly to the very gates of the Underworld and there Aeneas finds the tree with the golden branch.*

- *The simile of blooming mistletoe.*

- *Aeneas and the Trojans burn the body of Misenus.*

- *Aeneas and the Sibyl proceed to a cave near a forest and on a lake where nothing lived because of the foul stench, called Avernus.*

- *The priestess makes sacrifices and sends off everyone but Aeneas.*

- *She orders Aeneas to follow her and they enter the cave together.*

- *The simile of the path faintly lit by the light of the moon.*

- *First they encounter the Furies and other negative spirits.*

- *Next they find an elm tree whose branches encompass False Dreams.*

- *Then they encounter monsters, whose ghosts Aeneas would have attacked had the priestess not stopped him.*

6.295–332 (Latin)

295–304   Aeneas and the priestess reach the river Acheron and see Charon, the ferryman, who is described.

305–16   A crowd of people rushes Charon for passage; he takes some and leaves others.

The simile of falling leaves and migrating birds:

> **quam multa in silvis autumni frigore primo /**
> **lapsa cadunt folia, aut ad terram gurgite ab**
> **alto / quam multae glomerantur aves**

331–32   The priestess explains to the inquiring Aeneas why some are conveyed and some are left behind: those that have received a proper burial may cross while those that have not must wait.

6.333–83 (English)

- *Aeneas sees those that he recognizes and addresses his helmsman Palinurus.*

The gubernator, or helmsman, of a ship, as Palinurus was for one of Aeneas' ships

- *Palinurus explains that he was cast overboard with the rudder of the ship and was more concerned for the survival of the now rudderless ship than for his own.*

- *After four days lost and floating at sea, Palinurus finally reached Italy but was killed by bandits on the shore.*

- *His body remains unburied and he begs Aeneas to either bury it or, with the divine sanction of his mother, to bring Palinurus with him.*

- *The priestess rebukes Palinurus for thinking that divine rule can be skirted but promises him that the locals will bury him and name the area after him.*

6.384–425 (Latin)

384–97	Charon sees them approaching the river and challenges Aeneas as a mortal in the Underworld, begrudging previous heroes their journey.
398–407	The priestess assures Charon that Aeneas means no harm and is traveling to see his father, and shows him the golden branch as divine sanction for Aeneas' journey.
407–16	Charon accepts with awe the golden branch, dismisses the other spirits, and transports only Aeneas whose human weight causes the boat to take on water.
417–25	Cerberus rages on the other side but the Sibyl placates him with a treat and Aeneas enters the Underworld.

Charon (left) welcomes a soul, escorted by Mercury, to his boat.

Cerberus, the three-headed guard dog of the Underworld

6.426–49 (English)

- *Aeneas encounters the first souls in the Underworld: infants and those falsely executed.*

- *Minos is introduced as the judge that determines to what section the souls are assigned.*

- *Next are the suicides who regret their death and wish to be in the world above.*

- *Those that died of a broken heart are next, among whom is Dido.*

6.450–76 (Latin)

450–66   Aeneas recognizes Dido, with her wound still fresh, and, weeping, addresses her.

> ### Inter quas Phoenissa recens a vulnere Dido / errabat

- o   The simile of the new moon faint through the haze.

- o   Aeneas laments that the rumors of her death are true and hopes that he wasn't the cause of her death.

- o   Aeneas reiterates that he would have stayed but the gods forced him to leave.

- o   Aeneas begs Dido not to leave, claiming that this is their only chance to talk.

467–76   Dido keeps her eyes down and says nothing to Aeneas as she flees him and returns to her husband Sychaeus while Aeneas weeps and pities her.

6.477–846 (English)

- *Aeneas proceeds to where the war heroes are and mourns all of the Trojans he sees there.*

- *The Trojan shades try to talk with Aeneas but the Greek shades flee him.*

- *Aeneas recognizes the son of Priam, Deïphobus, horribly disfigured from his death and asks him who killed him and how he died.*

- *Deïphobus blames Helen, his wife after Paris' death, for his death and explains:*

  - o   *As Troy was being sacked, Helen hid his weapons and admitted Greek soldiers to their room.*

  - o   *The Greek soldiers, aided by Helen, kill Deïphobus.*

- *Deïphobus prays for vengeance on the Greeks and asks Aeneas why he is here.*

- *The Sibyl hurries Aeneas along on his journey and Deïphobus voluntarily withdraws, despite his desire to speak more.*

- *Aeneas sees a castle surrounded by Phlegethon, the river of fire.*

- *Tisiphone, one of the Furies, sits atop the gate and terrifies Aeneas.*

- *The Sibyl explains that only evil souls are admitted but that she will describe the punishments therein to Aeneas.*

  - o   *Rhadamanthus coerces a confession out of evil souls.*

  - o   *Tisiphone then pounces on the souls and sends them through the gate.*

  - o   *The Hydra therein is even more terrifying.*

  - o   *Tartarus is a pit two times as deep as Olympus' height.*

  - o   *In Tartarus lie the Titans and the Lapiths and other transgressors.*

- Aeneas completes his sacrifice by purifying himself with water and placing the golden branch.

- Thus they are admitted to Elysium.

- Aeneas sees Orpheus as well as Trojans.

- The Sibyl addresses Musaeus to learn where Aeneas' father Anchises is.

- When Aeneas sees Anchises, he is gazing over his descendants and their future deeds.

- Anchises weeps when he sees Aeneas.

- Aeneas attempts to hug Anchises three times but three times hugs only the air.

- Aeneas sees the river Lethe and the souls hovering nearby and asks Anchises what it is.

- The simile of the bees swarming on flowers.

- Anchises explain that they drink of the river Lethe and forget their previous life to be given another body and another life.

- Aeneas asks about the reincarnation of the souls and Anchises explains:

  o Humans begin with the divine spirit that is within all things.

  o The everyday failings of life gradually dull that spirit.

  o When humans die, those transgressions that dulled the spirit remain.

  o In the Underworld, those transgressions are cleansed and the souls enter Elysium.

  o In Elysium, time eventually returns the soul to its original divine, unstained state.

  o After 1,000 years, these souls will drink of Lethe, forget their previous lives, and assume new ones on earth.

- Anchises now says that he will show Aeneas his descendants and their glory:

  o Silvius, the son of Aeneas and Lavinia, who will rule Alba Longa

  o Procas, Capys, Numitor, Aeneas Sylvius

  o Romulus, honored by the gods, founder of Rome

  o Julius Caesar, whose ancestor is Aeneas' son Iulus

  o Augustus, expander of the Empire, institutor of a Golden Age

  o Numa, the Roman king who first provided laws

  o Tullus, organizer and inspirer of the army

  o Ancus, ever beholden to what the people want

  o Brutus, the first consul, who overthrew the kings

  o The Decii, the Drusi, Torquatus, and Camillus

  o Pompey and Caesar, in civic strife

  o Those who conquered Greece, in vengeance for the fall of Troy

6.847–99 (Latin)

847–53   Anchises concludes by stating the mission of the Roman people: "rule people with power, impose a habit of peace, spare those conquered and overcome those arrogant."

> ***tu regere imperio populos, Romane, memento / (hae tibi erunt artes), pacique imponere morem, / parcere subiectis et debellare superbos.***

854–59   Anchises describes how Marcellus, general in the Punic War, will save Rome.

860–66   Aeneas notices a young boy with Marcellus and asks Anchises who it is.

867–86   Anchises describes a descendant of Marcellus, also named Marcellus, who died in 23 BC at the age of 19. [He was Augustus' nephew and was in line to assume power after Augustus. The ancient commentator Servius describes how Octavia, Marcellus' mother, wept upon hearing this passage.]

886–92   Anchises explains to Aeneas his immediate future, how he will battle in Latium.

893–99   The two Gates of Sleep, one horn for the shades and one ivory that sends false dreams. Aeneas goes with the Sibyl through the gate of ivory and returns to his men.

8.all (English)

[In book 7, Aeneas meets the local king, Latinus, who betroths to him his daughter Lavinia, whom the local king Turnus had hoped to marry. Spurred on by Lavinia's mother, Amata, Turnus declares war on Aeneas and Latinus.]

- *Local rulers pledge allegiance to Turnus and his cause against Aeneas.*

- *Aeneas sees everyone mobilizing against him and is concerned.*

- *The simile of light reflecting off shimmering water in a bowl.*

- *Aeneas drifts to sleep on a riverbank and dreams of Tiberinus, the god of the river Tiber, who addresses him.*

  o *Tiberinus assures Aeneas that this is the land for his new Troy and that he should not be concerned about the coming war.*

  o *Tiberinus gives Aeneas a sign as reassurance: a white sow nursing thirty babies will mark the location of Aeneas' new city.*

  o *Tiberinus also advises Aeneas to ally himself with Evander and the Arcadians and promises to bring him upstream to Evander.*

- *Aeneas awakens and prays to the river nymphs and the river god.*

- *After Aeneas chooses two ships and crews, he spies the white sow and sacrifices her to Juno.*

- *Tiberinus calms the current so that Aeneas and his ships can sail upstream.*

- *When Aeneas reaches Evander's city, the residents are sacrificing to Hercules and prepare to confront Aeneas but Pallas, Evander's son, keeps his head and encourages them to continue the sacrifice while he meets the newcomers.*

- *Pallas asks who they are and why they have come and Aeneas responds, holding out an olive branch in peace.*

- *Aeneas states that they are Trojans and hope to make an alliance with Evander.*

- *Pallas welcomes Aeneas warmly and invites him inside.*

- *Aeneas tells Evander that he does not fear allying with Greeks because it was prophesied that he would and that they share common ancestry in Maia, the mother of Mercury and Atlas.*

- *Evander responds that he remembers when Priam and Anchises visited Arcadia and Anchises left him with gifts.*

- *Evander promises men and supplies to Aeneas and invites him to join their feast.*

- *At the feast Evander tells the story of Hercules and Cacus.*

  - *Cacus was a monster who sated himself on humans.*

  - *Hercules arrived, driving Geryon's cattle.*

  - *Cacus took four of the cattle, dragging them by their tails to disguise which direction they went.*

  - *As Hercules was leading the rest away, one of the kidnapped bellowed, revealing where they were.*

  - *Hercules rushes to the cave but Cacus blocks the door with a huge rock, which Hercules tries, but fails, three times to break.*

  - *Hercules spies a huge, peaked rock, which he removes and uses to break open Cacus' lair.*

  - *Hercules attacks and kills Cacus and frees the cattle.*

  - *This annual feast commemorates the death of Cacus at the hands of Hercules.*

- *The celebration continues with rituals that celebrate Hercules' deeds: the strangling of the serpents, his prowess in war, and the twelve labors.*

- *As Aeneas and Evander with Pallas return to the city, Aeneas asks Evander about the history of the place.*

  - *The land was inhabited originally by fauns and nymphs who had no infrastructure or agriculture.*

  - *Saturn, exiled from Olympus by Jupiter, arrived, organized them, and provided them laws, calling the area Latium.*

  - *Saturn ruled the Golden Age but eventually that was corrupted by an interest in war and possessions.*

  - *A succession of people followed and eventually Evander ended up here.*

CHAPTER 4

- Evander tours Aeneas around notable locations in the city, many of which still exist (albeit in different form) in contemporary Rome.

- Evander invites Aeneas into his house to rest.

- Venus approaches her husband Vulcan and, claiming that she didn't want to bother him during the Trojan War, now asks for armor for Aeneas.

- Vulcan hesitates so Venus seduces him into compliance.

- Vulcan maintains that he would have made armor during the war and will make it now.

- Vulcan proceeds to his workshop on an island off the coast of Sicily.

- He orders his Cyclopes workmen to stop what they're doing to begin forging Aeneas' armor.

The god Vulcan, husband of Venus, who makes Aeneas' armor

- Aeneas and Achates meet Evander and Pallas the next morning and they talk in the courtyard.

- Evander tells Aeneas the story of the Lydians, once ruled by Mezentius, a cruel and monstrous ruler against whom his people revolted.

- Mezentius escaped to Turnus and the Rutulians.

- Evander suggests that Aeneas assume leadership of the Lydians and their quest for vengeance against Mezentius; an oracle declared that they must be ruled by a foreigner.

- Evander also suggests that Pallas accompany Aeneas to learn from him.

- Venus at that moment sends a sign: thunder crashes and lightning flashes as Aeneas' new armor appears in the sky.

- Aeneas pledges death to Turnus' men, takes some Trojans from the ships with him, and sends the rest back to update Ascanius.

- Evander says goodbye to Pallas, praying for his safe return and fainting as he stops speaking.

- Aeneas and his troops leave Evander's city and approach a grove near the city of Caere where Tarchon, leader of the Lydians, is encamped.

The making of Achilles' armor from Homer's Iliad, upon which the making of Aeneas' armor is based

- Venus appears to Aeneas and presents to him his new armor.

- The description of the shield:

  o The future of Rome

  o The wars fought by the Romans

  o The she-wolf with Romulus and Remus

- o *The carrying off of the Sabine women and the eventual peace between those peoples*
- o *The death by drawing-and-quartering of the traitorous Alban Mettus*
- o *Porsenna attempting to restore the Tarquins to power*
- o *Cocles and the bridge*
- o *Cloelia swimming the river*
- o *Manlius and the goose*
- o *The Salii and the Luperci*
- o *Tartarus, Dis, and the consequences of transgression*
- o *Catiline and Cato*
- o *Around this was the sea and the Battle of Actium*
  - ▪ *Augustus, divinely sanctioned*
  - ▪ *Agrippa and his fleet*
  - ▪ *Antony and his shameful Egyptian wife*
  - ▪ *The battle between Egyptian and Roman gods*
  - ▪ *Apollo and his bow*
  - ▪ *The desperation of Cleopatra*
- o *Augustus' triumphant return to Rome*
  - ▪ *Sacrifices and feasts*
  - ▪ *Augustus before the doors of the Temple of Apollo*

12.all (English)

[Books 9–11: The two sides battle and Pallas is killed.]

- *Turnus' army has just endured a significant defeat and his people are despondent.*
- *The simile of the Carthaginian lion, fervent for battle because of his wound.*
- *Turnus approaches Latinus and asks for single combat with Aeneas.*
- *Latinus wavers, regretting that Turnus and Lavinia can't be married but admitting that the oracles stated that she couldn't marry a local.*
- *Turnus reiterates his interest in fighting Aeneas and states his lack of fear of death.*
- *Amata, Latinus' wife and Lavinia's mother, begs Turnus not to face Aeneas alone.*
- *Turnus rebuffs Amata and calls for a messenger to suggest to Aeneas the duel.*
- *Turnus considers his weapons and addresses his spear directly.*

- The simile of the bull preparing to fight.

- Aeneas agrees to the duel, comforts Ascanius who is concerned for him, and sends a messenger to Latinus confirming the duel and the ensuing peace.

- The Trojans prepare for Aeneas' battle by preparing sacrifices and laying down their weapons.

- Juno addresses Juturna, Turnus' sister, a nymph, and explains that Turnus is fated to die but perhaps there is a chance that she can still help him.

- Juturna weeps but Juno encourages her to act: break the treaty and force war.

- Turnus with Latinus and Aeneas with Ascanius approach each other.

- They along with a priest prepare a sacrifice.

- Aeneas prays that, if Turnus wins, Ascanius and the Trojans will leave the land and not continue fighting and that, if Aeneas wins, the Trojans will not subjugate the Italians but rather will build their new city and name it Lavinium after Aeneas' new wife Lavinia.

- Latinus prays, affirming Aeneas' prayers.

- The Rutulians, however, are not confident in the duel; Turnus' downcast attitude does not help.

- Juturna, disguised as one of the Rutulians, goes among the Rutulians and goads them into wanting to fight.

- Juturna also sends a sign: an eagle taking a swan being attacked by other birds until it drops the swan and flees.

- Tolumnius, the Rutulian seer, interprets the omen as a sign to fight and hurls his spear at the Trojans.

- The spear strikes one of nine brothers; the other eight charge and the war is on.

- Aeneas begs his men not to fight and reassures them that the fight is his alone.

- As he says this, an arrow wounds Aeneas in the leg.

- When Turnus sees Aeneas wounded, he is inspired and hops in his chariot, mowing down Trojans as he ranges the field.

- The Rutulians kill many Trojans, both in close combat and by running them over.

- Ascanius, Achates, and Mnestheus bring Aeneas into camp to tend to his wound.

- Aeneas advocates digging into the leg so that the point of the arrow can be removed.

- Iapyx the healer appears but even he cannot extract the arrow.

- Venus acquires from Mt. Ida an herb that she gives to Iapyx; once it is applied, the pain stops and the bleeding stops and the arrow is removed easily.

- *Iapyx recognizes that Aeneas was healed through divine intervention and uses this to inspire Aeneas and the troops.*

- *Before Aeneas leaves for battle, he tells Ascanius to take inspiration in battle from him and his Trojan forebears.*

- *Aeneas and his troops make an intimidating approach to battle; even Juturna flees.*

- *The simile of the wind signaling the coming storm.*

- *Aeneas and the Trojans rout the Rutulians but Aeneas doesn't chase; he's looking for Turnus.*

- *Juturna, worried for Turnus, takes the form of his chariot driver.*

- *The simile of the swallow in the mansion.*

- *Juturna moves Turnus in his chariot about the battlefield but never stops him long enough to fight.*

- *Aeneas rages on the battlefield, waiting for his opportunity to fight Turnus.*

- *Venus plants in Aeneas' head the idea of charging the walls.*

- *Aeneas orders his men to take the city and burn it down.*

- *The residents of the city are divided: some want to surrender while others want to fight.*

- *The simile of the shepherd smoking the bee hive.*

- *Amata sees the Trojans attacking the city and fears that Turnus is dead.*

- *She hangs herself; Lavinia, Latinus, and the rest of the city mourn.*

- *Turnus wonders about the commotion from the town but Juturna, still as his charioteer, suggests that they continue fighting outside.*

- *Turnus wonders why she is prolonging the fight with other men losing their lives.*

- *Turnus then receives an update that Amata is dead and Aeneas is storming the city.*

- *He informs Juturna that he will face Aeneas, come what may, but will rage before that.*

- *The simile of the stone rolling down the mountain.*

- *Turnus reaches the walls of the city and tells the Rutulians to fall back, that he will accept whatever fate awaits.*

- *The battle pauses as Aeneas and Turnus draw up against each other and engage.*

- *The simile of the bulls butting heads.*

- *Jupiter weighs the destinies of each man.*

- *Turnus attacks but his sword shatters against Aeneas' divine armor.*

- *Turnus flees but the Trojans keep him penned in as Aeneas pursues.*

- *The simile of the hunting dog cornering the stag.*

- *Turnus calls for a new sword but Aeneas prevents it.*

- *Aeneas chases but, because of his wound, cannot catch Turnus.*

- *A spear Aeneas had thrown was lodged in the roots of a sacred olive tree that the Trojans had cut down.*

- *He tries to pull it out but the prayers of Turnus to the gods of the tree work and they hold fast the spear.*

- *In the meantime, Juturna delivers Turnus a sword.*

- *Venus, incensed at Juturna's temerity, releases the spear.*

- *Turnus and Aeneas face each other, both now armed.*

- *Jupiter addresses Juno as they view the battle.*

- *Jupiter questions why Juno persists in trying to thwart Aeneas' destiny and encourages her to give up her enmity toward him.*

- *Juno agrees to let fate run its course but requests of Jupiter that the Trojan name be lost as the city was lost, that the Latins remain the Latins, and that they retain their language and their customs.*

- *Jupiter agrees: the Trojans will be absorbed into the Latins and their descendants, the Romans, will worship Juno fervently.*

- *Jupiter sends a demon to Juturna to convince her to quit the battle.*

- *The simile of the flying arrow.*

- *The demon takes the form of an owl and flies in front of Turnus during the battle.*

- *Both Turnus and Juturna recognize the owl as an omen portending his death.*

- *Juturna says goodbye to her brother and leaves.*

- *Aeneas challenges Turnus and questions why he is afraid.*

- *Turnus responds that he is only afraid of Jupiter and heaves a huge rock toward Aeneas, which does not reach Aeneas.*

- *The simile of our body unable to function in dreams.*

- *Turnus falters, unable to get his bearings, and Aeneas' spear strikes him in the thigh.*

- *Turnus submits to Aeneas and asks him to return his body to his parents.*

- *Aeneas is about to grant Turnus mercy when he sees Pallas' belt on Turnus.*

- *Aeneas kills Turnus, proclaiming vengeance for Pallas' death.*

- *Turnus' soul leaves his now dead body.*

THE WANDERINGS OF AENEAS

- bold names are included in the syllabus

THE JOURNEY OF AENEAS

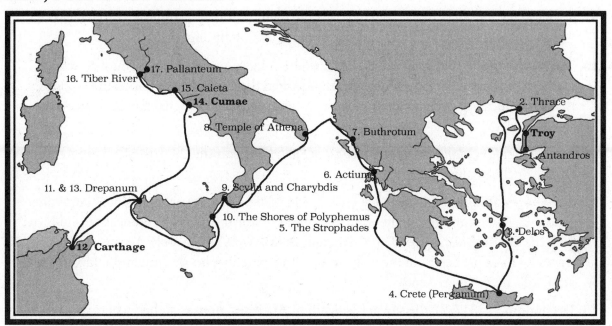

1. **Antandros** (3.5–6), where Aeneas assembled his fleet to begin his journey to Italy.

2. **Thrace** (3.13–68), where Aeneas first landed upon fleeing Troy and where he founded his first city, named after his descendants; Aeneas soon fled after encountering the Trojan Polydorus in the form of a bush that, when Aeneas broke off a branch, bled and told him his story, that the king to whom Priam had entrusted him and the Trojan gold had killed him, kept the gold, and allied himself with the Greeks.

3. **Delos** (3.69–120), where Aeneas is welcomed by King Anius, a friend of his father, and where Aeneas prays to Apollo to grant the Trojans a new home; Apollo tells Aeneas to seek out his mother and Anchises interprets the prophecy as advising them to sail to Crete.

4. *[121–27: sailing on the Aegean through the Cyclades islands to Crete]* **Crete** (Pergamum) (3.128–91), where Aeneas and his men begin to settle until a plague arrives and besets them and their crops with disease; the penates, the household gods that Aeneas brought with him from Troy, speak to him in a dream and tell him to travel to Italy, that that is where he is destined to settle.

5. *[192–210: sailing through a storm to the Strophades]* **The Strophades** (3.210–69), where Aeneas encounters the Harpies, bird-monsters with the faces of women, whose cattle Aeneas and his men kill; for this, Celaeno, the head Harpy, curses Aeneas by saying that he will reach Italy but will not settle until his hunger is such that he and his men eat the very plates on which their food is served.

6. **Actium** (3.270–89), where Aeneas hosts games for the Trojans.

7. **Buthrotum** (3.291–520), where Aeneas is reunited with Andromache, the wife of Hector, who is living with Helenus, a Trojan, who prophesies for Aeneas the route he should take and the signs that he will see when he arrives.

8. **The Temple of Athena** (3.529–47), where Aeneas and the Trojans pay tribute to Athena and Juno, as Helenus had ordered, and continue on their journey.

9. **Scylla and Charybdis** (3.548–69) Scylla is the many-headed sea monster and Charybdis the violent whirlpool that appear in the strait between Italy and Sicily.

10. **The Shores of the Cyclopes** (3.570–681), where Aeneas and his men encounter Achaemenides, a comrade of Odysseus, left behind when the Greek hero escaped the Cyclops; Achaemenides begs Aeneas to take him away and, despite that Achaemenides is Greek, Aeneas agrees.

11. *[682–706: sailing along the southern coast of Sicily]* **Drepanum** (3.707–15), where Aeneas' father, Anchises, dies.

12. **The Shores of Libya and Carthage** (1.157–58 and ff.; 4.1–583.), where Aeneas lands after Juno asks Aeolus, the god of the winds, to send the storm, and where Aeneas falls in love with the Carthaginian queen Dido, who falls in love with him as well; Aeneas eventually leaves Dido, at the behest of the gods, to continue pursuing his destiny, and Dido, in her grief, kills herself over Aeneas.

13. **Drepanum** (5.28–777), the site of the death of Anchises, Aeneas' father, where Aeneas returns after leaving Carthage and hosts funeral games in his father's honor.

14. **Cumae** (6.1–899) where Aeneas encounters the Sibyl who leads him to the Underworld; there, Aeneas sees the shades of Palinurus, his helmsman; Dido; and Deiphobus, a son of Priam and husband of Helen after Paris' death, whose weapons Helen removed so that the Greeks could kill him. Aeneas also sees the souls punished in Tartarus as well as those joyous in the Elysian Fields, among whom is his father, who shows Aeneas his illustrious descendants.

15. **Caieta** (6.900–901; 7.1–7), where Aeneas' nurse Caieta died and where he erected a burial mound in her honor.

16. **Tiber River** (7.29–36 and following), where Aeneas finally lands near Rome.

17. **Pallanteum** (8.97–101 and following), the future site of Rome, where King Evander lives.

Chapter 5

CLEAN TEXTS

INTRODUCTION

- When reviewing for the test, do not mark up this text; it should remain free of notes, vocabulary, diagrams, and so on.

- You want to study as much as possible from a clean text so that you are ready for the clean texts of the AP® Exam.

- Feel free to begin your studying with an annotated text (perhaps you marked up the text in your textbook as you were reading in class) but transition yourself from that annotated text to this clean text as soon as you can.

- The more practice you have with a clean text, the better prepared you will be for your AP® Exam.

THE LATIN READING LIST

Caesar, *Bellum Gallicum*

- ✓ Book 1: Chapters 1–7
- ✓ Book 4: Chapters 24–35 and the first sentence of Chapter 36 (*Eodem die ... pace venerunt.*)
- ✓ Book 5: Chapters 24–48
- ✓ Book 6: Chapters 13–20

Vergil, *Aeneid*

- ✓ Book 1: Lines 1–209, 418–40, 494–578
- ✓ Book 2: Lines 40–56, 201–49, 268–97, 559–620
- ✓ Book 4: Lines 160–218, 259–361, 659–705
- ✓ Book 6: Lines 295–332, 384–425, 450–76, 847–99

CAESAR, *BELLUM GALLICUM*

- The text below is based on the 1900 Oxford Classical Text of Rene L. A. Du Pontet via the online version available at oxfordscholarlyeditions.com (subscription required):

  o Scan the code at right to go directly to the website.

- Macrons are not used in the text because they are not used on the AP® Exam.

- Spellings have been updated to reflect modern American textbook conventions:

  o long -*is* has been changed to -*es*

  o "j" has been changed to consonantal "i"

  o consonantal "u" has been changed to "v"

- **Assimilation** is the process by which a root and its prefix are smoothed for the sake of pronunciation or euphony: the first letter of the root absorbs or assimilates the last letter of the prefix.

  o "Correspondence" is a combination of "con-" and "respond"; the "r" in "respond" absorbs the "n" in "con-" to form the assimilated "correspondence."

  o The same process happens in Latin:

    ▪ sub + mergo = submergo or summergo

    ▪ in + motus = inmotus or immotus

  o The text reflects the convention used in Lewis and Short's *Latin Dictionary*; for example, *submergo* is not assimilated while *immotus* is.

  o It is important to be aware of assimilation for the recognition of words, although the AP® Exam will often notate alternate forms of words when reproducing a text.

- The following editions were also consulted in the preparation of this text.

  o Dickinson College Commentaries

    ▪ Scan the code at right to go directly to the website.

    ▪ Or use the direct link here: http://dcc.dickinson.edu/caesar/caesar -introduction

  o The Packard Humanities Institute's Classical Latin Texts

    ▪ Scan the code at right to go directly to the website.

    ▪ Or use the direct link here: http://latin.packhum.org/loc/448/1/0#0

  o Caesar. *Selections from his* Commentarii de bello gallico. By Hans-Friedrich Mueller. Mundelein, IL: Bolchazy-Carducci, 2012.

- Alternate readings are included in footnotes throughout the text.

BOOK 1, CHAPTERS 1–7

(1.1) Gallia est omnis divisa in partes tres, quarum unam incolunt Belgae, aliam Aquitani, tertiam qui ipsorum lingua Celtae, nostra Galli appellantur. Hi omnes lingua, institutis, legibus inter se differunt. Gallos ab Aquitanis Garumna flumen, a Belgis Matrona et Sequana dividit. Horum omnium fortissimi sunt Belgae, propterea quod a cultu atque humanitate provinciae longissime absunt, minimeque ad eos mercatores saepe commeant atque ea quae ad effeminandos animos pertinent important, proximique sunt Germanis qui trans Rhenum incolunt, quibuscum continenter bellum gerunt. Qua de causa Helvetii quoque reliquos Gallos virtute praecedunt, quod fere cotidianis proeliis cum Germanis contendunt, cum aut suis finibus eos prohibent aut ipsi in eorum finibus bellum gerunt. Eorum una pars, quam Gallos obtinere dictum est, initium capit a flumine Rhodano; continetur Garumna flumine, Oceano, finibus Belgarum; attingit etiam ab Sequanis et Helvetiis flumen Rhenum; vergit ad septentriones. Belgae ab extremis Galliae finibus oriuntur; pertinent ad inferiorem partem fluminis Rheni; spectant in septentrionem et orientem solem. Aquitania a Garumna flumine ad Pyrenaeos montes et eam partem Oceani quae est ad Hispaniam pertinet; spectat inter occasum solis et septentriones.

(1.2) Apud Helvetios longe nobilissimus fuit et ditissimus Orgetorix. Is, M. Messala et M.[1] Pupio Pisone consulibus, regni cupiditate inductus coniurationem nobilitatis fecit et civitati persuasit ut de finibus suis cum omnibus copiis exirent: perfacile esse, cum virtute omnibus praestarent, totius Galliae imperio potiri. Id hoc facilius eis persuasit, quod undique loci natura Helvetii continentur: una ex parte flumine Rheno latissimo atque altissimo, qui agrum Helvetium a Germanis dividit; altera ex parte monte Iura altissimo, qui est inter Sequanos et Helvetios; tertia lacu Lemanno et flumine Rhodano, qui provinciam nostram ab Helvetiis dividit. His rebus fiebat ut et minus late vagarentur et minus facile finitimis bellum inferre possent: qua ex parte homines bellandi cupidi magno dolore adficiebantur. Pro multitudine autem hominum et pro gloria belli atque fortitudinis angustos se fines habere arbitrabantur, qui in longitudinem milia passuum CCXL, in latitudinem CLXXX patebant.

(1.3) His rebus adducti et auctoritate Orgetorigis permoti constituerunt ea quae ad proficiscendum pertinerent comparare, iumentorum et carrorum quam maximum numerum coemere, sementes quam maximas facere ut in itinere copia frumenti suppeteret, cum proximis civitatibus pacem et amicitiam confirmare. Ad eas res conficiendas biennium sibi satis esse duxerunt: in tertium annum profectionem lege confirmant. Ad eas res conficiendas Orgetorix deligitur. Is sibi legationem ad civitates suscepit. In eo itinere persuadet Castico, Catamantaloedis filio Sequano, cuius pater regnum in Sequanis multos annos obtinuerat et a senatu populi Romani amicus

---

1. First names in Latin are often abbreviated in texts. Here, the M. stands for Marco in both instances, in the ablative because of the ablative absolute. Some textbooks expand the abbreviation, but it is left abbreviated here because the AP® Exam will abbreviate it: on the 2015 Exam, question 5 included this passage with the M. left abbreviated.

appellatus erat, ut regnum in civitate sua occuparet quod pater ante habuerat; itemque Dumnorigi Aeduo fratri Diviciaci, qui eo tempore principatum in civitate obtinebat ac maxime plebi acceptus erat, ut idem conaretur persuadet, eique filiam suam in matrimonium dat. Perfacile factu esse illis probat conata perficere, propterea quod ipse suae civitatis imperium obtenturus esset: non esse dubium quin totius Galliae plurimum Helvetii possent; se suis copiis suoque exercitu illis regna conciliaturum confirmat. Hac oratione adducti inter se fidem et ius iurandum dant et regno occupato per tres potentissimos ac firmissimos populos totius Galliae sese potiri posse sperant.

(1.4) Ea res est Helvetiis per indicium enuntiata. Moribus suis Orgetorigem ex vinclis causam dicere coegerunt. Damnatum poenam sequi oportebat ut igni cremaretur. Die constituta causae dictionis Orgetorix ad iudicium omnem suam familiam, ad hominum milia decem, undique coegit, et omnes clientes obaeratosque suos, quorum magnum numerum habebat, eodem conduxit: per eos ne causam diceret se eripuit. Cum civitas ob eam rem incitata armis ius suum exsequi conaretur, multitudinemque hominum ex agris magistratus cogerent, Orgetorix mortuus est; neque abest suspicio, ut Helvetii arbitrantur, quin ipse sibi mortem consciverit.

(1.5) Post eius mortem nihilo minus Helvetii id quod constituerant facere conantur, ut e finibus suis exeant. Ubi iam se ad eam rem paratos esse arbitrati sunt, oppida sua omnia, numero ad duodecim, vicos ad quadringentos, reliqua privata aedificia incendunt; frumentum omne, praeterquam quod secum portaturi erant, comburunt, ut domum reditionis spe sublata paratiores ad omnia pericula subeunda essent; trium mensum molita cibaria sibi quemque domo efferre iubent. Persuadent Rauricis et Tulingis et Latobrigis finitimis suis, uti eodem usi consilio, oppidis suis vicisque exustis, una cum eis proficiscantur, Boiosque, qui trans Rhenum incoluerant et in agrum Noricum transierant Noreiamque oppugnarant, receptos ad se socios sibi asciscunt.

(1.6) Erant omnino itinera duo, quibus itineribus domo exire possent: unum per Sequanos, angustum et difficile, inter montem Iuram et flumen Rhodanum, vix qua singuli carri ducerentur; mons autem altissimus impendebat, ut facile perpauci prohibere possent: alterum per provinciam nostram, multo facilius atque expeditius, propterea quod inter fines Helvetiorum et Allobrogum, qui nuper pacati erant, Rhodanus fluit, isque nonnullis locis vado transitur. Extremum oppidum Allobrogum est proximumque Helvetiorum finibus Genava. Ex eo oppido pons ad Helvetios pertinet. Allobrogibus sese vel persuasuros, quod nondum bono animo in populum Romanum viderentur, existimabant vel vi coacturos ut per suos fines eos ire paterentur. Omnibus rebus ad profectionem comparatis, diem dicunt, qua die ad ripam Rhodani omnes conveniant. Is dies erat a. d. V. Kal. Apr., L. Pisone A. Gabinio consulibus.

(1.7) Caesari cum id nuntiatum esset, eos per provinciam nostram iter facere conari, maturat ab urbe proficisci et quam maximis potest itineribus in Galliam ulteriorem contendit et ad Genavam pervenit. Provinciae toti quam maximum potest militum numerum imperat (erat omnino in Gallia ulteriore legio una), pontem, qui erat ad Genavam, iubet rescindi. Ubi de eius adventu Helvetii certiores facti sunt, legatos ad eum mittunt nobilissimos civitatis, cuius legationis Nammeius et Verucloetius principem locum obtinebant, qui dicerent sibi esse in animo sine ullo maleficio iter per provinciam facere, propterea quod aliud iter haberent nullum: rogare ut eius voluntate id sibi facere liceat. Caesar, quod memoria tenebat L. Cassium consulem occisum exercitumque eius ab Helvetiis pulsum et sub iugum missum, concedendum non putabat; neque homines inimico animo, data facultate per provinciam itineris faciendi, temperaturos ab iniuria et maleficio existimabat. Tamen, ut spatium intercedere posset dum milites quos imperaverat convenirent, legatis respondit diem se ad deliberandum sumpturum: si quid vellent, ad Id. Apr., reverterentur.

BOOK 4, CHAPTERS 24–36, 1ST SENTENCE (*eodem die … pace venerunt*)

(4.24) At barbari, consilio Romanorum cognito praemisso equitatu et essedariis, quo plerumque genere in proeliis uti consuerunt, reliquis copiis subsecuti nostros navibus egredi prohibebant. Erat ob has causas summa difficultas, quod naves propter magnitudinem nisi in alto constitui non poterant, militibus autem, ignotis locis, impeditis manibus, magno et gravi onere armorum oppressis, simul et de navibus desiliendum et in fluctibus consistendum et cum hostibus erat pugnandum, cum illi aut ex arido aut paulum in aquam progressi, omnibus membris expeditis, notissimis locis, audacter tela coicerent et equos insuefactos incitarent. Quibus rebus nostri perterriti atque huius omnino generis pugnae imperiti, non eadem alacritate ac studio quo in pedestribus uti proeliis consuerant utebantur.

(4.25) Quod ubi Caesar animadvertit, naves longas, quarum et species erat barbaris inusitatior et motus ad usum expeditior, paulum removeri ab onerariis navibus et remis incitari et ad latus apertum hostium constitui atque inde fundis, sagittis, tormentis hostes propelli ac submoveri iussit; quae res magno usui nostris fuit. Nam et navium figura et remorum motu et inusitato genere tormentorum permoti barbari constiterunt ac paulum modo pedem rettulerunt. Atque nostris militibus cunctantibus, maxime propter altitudinem maris, qui decimae legionis aquilam ferebat, obtestatus[2] deos, ut ea res legioni feliciter eveniret, "Desilite," inquit, "commilitiones,[3] nisi vultis aquilam hostibus prodere: ego certe meum rei publicae atque imperatori officium praestitero." Hoc cum voce magna dixisset, se ex navi proiecit atque in hostes aquilam ferre coepit. Tum nostri cohortati inter se, ne tantum dedecus admitteretur,

---

2. Some texts read *contestatus* here.
3. Some texts read *milites* here.

universi ex navi desiluerunt. Hos item ex proximis primi[4] navibus cum conspexissent, subsecuti hostibus appropinquarunt.

(4.26) Pugnatum est ab utrisque acriter. Nostri tamen, quod neque ordines servare neque firmiter insistere neque signa subsequi poterant atque alius alia ex navi quibuscumque signis occurrerat se adgregabat, magnopere perturbabantur; hostes vero, notis omnibus vadis, ubi ex litore aliquos singulares ex navi egredientes conspexerant, incitatis equis impeditos adoriebantur, plures paucos circumsistebant, alii ab latere aperto in universos tela coiciebant. Quod cum animadvertisset Caesar, scaphas longarum navium, item speculatoria navigia militibus compleri iussit et, quos laborantes conspexerat, his subsidia submittebat. Nostri, simul in arido constiterunt, suis omnibus consecutis, in hostes impetum fecerunt atque eos in fugam dederunt; neque longius prosequi potuerunt, quod equites cursum tenere atque insulam capere non potuerant. Hoc unum ad pristinam fortunam Caesari defuit.

(4.27) Hostes proelio superati, simul atque se ex fuga receperunt, statim ad Caesarem legatos de pace miserunt; obsides daturos quaeque imperasset sese facturos[5] polliciti sunt. Una cum his legatis Commius Atrebas venit, quem supra demonstraveram a Caesare in Britanniam praemissum. Hunc illi e navi egressum, cum ad eos oratoris modo Caesaris mandata deferret, comprehenderant atque in vincula coiecerant: tum proelio facto remiserunt et[6] in petenda pace eius rei culpam in multitudinem contulerunt[7] et propter imprudentiam ut ignosceretur petiverunt. Caesar questus quod, cum ultro in continentem legatis missis pacem ab se petissent, bellum sine causa intulissent, ignoscere imprudentiae dixit obsidesque imperavit; quorum illi partem statim dederunt, partem ex longinquioribus locis arcerssitam paucis diebus sese daturos dixerunt. Interea suos remigrare in agros iusserunt, principesque undique convenire et se civitatesque suas Caesari commendare coeperunt.

(4.28) His rebus pace confirmata, post diem quartum quam est in Britanniam ventum naves XVIII, de quibus supra demonstratum est, quae equites sustulerant, ex superiore portu leni vento solverunt. Quae cum appropinquarent Britanniae et ex castris viderentur, tanta tempestas subito coorta est ut nulla earum cursum tenere posset, sed aliae eodem unde erant profectae referrentur, aliae ad inferiorem partem insulae, quae est propius solis occasum, magno suo[8] cum periculo deicerentur; quae tamen, ancoris iactis, cum fluctibus complerentur, necessario adversa nocte in altum provectae continentem petierunt.

---

4. There are multiple readings here: *proximis primis* or *proximis*, with *primis/-is* deleted.
5. Some texts reverse these words: *facturos sese.*
6. Some texts eliminate this *et* and read a period after *remiserunt*: "*remiserunt. In petenda*"
7. Some texts read *coiecerunt.*
8. Some texts read *sui* here.

(4.29) Eadem nocte accidit ut esset luna plena, qui dies maritimos aestus maximos in Oceano efficere consuevit, nostrisque id erat incognitum. Ita uno tempore et longas naves, quibus Caesar[9] exercitum transportandum curaverat, quasque in aridum subduxerat, aestus compleverat et onerarias, quae ad ancoras erant deligatae, tempestas adflictabat, neque ulla nostris facultas aut administrandi aut auxiliandi dabatur. Compluribus navibus fractis, reliquae cum essent funibus, ancoris, reliquisque armamentis amissis ad navigandum inutiles, magna, id quod necesse erat accidere, totius exercitus perturbatio facta est. Neque enim naves erant aliae quibus reportari possent, et omnia deerant quae ad reficiendas naves erant usui et, quod omnibus constabat hiemare in Gallia oportere, frumentum in his[10] locis in hiemem provisum non erat.

(4.30) Quibus rebus cognitis, principes Britanniae, qui post proelium ad Caesarem convenerant, inter se collocuti, cum equites et naves et frumentum Romanis deesse intellegerent et paucitatem militum ex castrorum exiguitate cognoscerent, quae hoc erant etiam angustiora quod sine impedimentis Caesar legiones transportaverat, optimum factu esse duxerunt, rebellione facta, frumento commeatuque nostros prohibere et rem in hiemem producere, quod eis superatis aut reditu interclusis neminem postea belli inferendi causa in Britanniam transiturum confidebant. Itaque, rursus coniuratione facta, paulatim ex castris discedere et[11] suos clam ex agris deducere coeperunt.

(4.31) At Caesar, etsi nondum eorum consilia cognoverat, tamen et ex eventu navium suarum et ex eo quod obsides dare intermiserant fore id quod accidit suspicabatur. Itaque ad omnes casus subsidia comparabat. Nam et frumentum ex agris cotidie in castra conferebat et, quae gravissime adflictae erant naves, earum materia atque aere ad reliquas reficiendas utebatur et quae ad eas res erant usui ex continenti comportari[12] iubebat. Itaque, cum summo studio a militibus administraretur, XII navibus amissis, reliquis ut navigari commode posset effecit.

(4.32) Dum ea geruntur, legione ex consuetudine una frumentatum missa, quae appellabatur septima, neque ulla ad id tempus belli suspicione interposita, cum pars hominum in agris remaneret, pars etiam in castra ventitaret, ei qui pro portis castrorum in statione erant Caesari nuntiaverunt pulverem maiorem quam consuetudo ferret in ea parte videri quam in partem legio iter fecisset. Caesar id quod erat suspicatus, aliquid novi a barbaris initum consilii, cohortes quae in stationibus erant secum in eam partem proficisci, ex reliquis duas in stationem cohortes succedere, reliquas armari et confestim sese subsequi iussit. Cum paulo longius a castris processisset, suos ab hostibus premi atque aegre sustinere et conferta legione ex omnibus partibus tela coici animadvertit. Nam quod omni ex reliquis partibus demesso frumento pars una erat reliqua, suspicati hostes huc nostros esse venturos noctu in silvis delituerant; tum dispersos,

---

9. Some texts read *Caesar* after *quasque*: "*quibus exercitum transportandum curaverat, quasque Caesar in aridum subduxerat.*"
10. Some texts read *his in locis* here.
11. Some texts read *ac* here.
12. Some texts read *comparari* here.

depositis armis in metendo occupatos subito adorti, paucis interfectis reliquos incertis ordinibus perturbaverant, simul equitatu atque essedis circumdederant.

(4.33) Genus hoc est ex essedis pugnae. Primo per omnes partes perequitant et tela coiciunt atque ipso terrore equorum et strepitu rotarum ordines plerumque perturbant et, cum se inter equitum turmas insinuaverunt, ex essedis desiliunt et pedibus proeliantur. Aurigae interim paulatim ex proelio excedunt atque ita currus collocant ut, si illi a multitudine hostium premantur, expeditum ad suos receptum habeant. Ita mobilitatem equitum, stabilitatem peditum in proeliis praestant, ac tantum usu cotidiano et exercitatione efficiunt uti in declivi ac praecipiti loco incitatos equos sustinere et brevi moderari ac flectere et per temonem percurrere et in iugo insistere et se inde in currus citissime recipere consuerint.

(4.34) Quibus rebus perturbatis nostris novitate pugnae tempore opportunissimo Caesar auxilium tulit: namque eius adventu hostes constiterunt, nostri se ex timore receperunt. Quo facto, ad lacessendum[13] et ad committendum proelium alienum esse tempus arbitratus suo se loco continuit et, brevi tempore intermisso, in castra legiones reduxit. Dum haec geruntur, nostris omnibus occupatis, qui erant in agris reliqui discesserunt. Secutae sunt continuos complures dies tempestates quae et nostros in castris continerent et hostem a pugna prohiberent. Interim barbari nuntios in omnes partes dimiserunt paucitatemque nostrorum militum suis praedicaverunt et quanta praedae faciendae atque in perpetuum sui liberandi facultas daretur, si Romanos castris expulissent, demonstraverunt. His rebus celeriter magna multitudine peditatus equitatusque coacta ad castra venerunt.

(4.35) Caesar etsi idem quod superioribus diebus acciderat fore videbat, ut, si essent hostes pulsi, celeritate periculum effugerent, tamen nactus equites circiter XXX, quos Commius Atrebas, de quo ante dictum est, secum transportaverat, legiones in acie pro castris constituit. Commisso proelio, diutius nostrorum militum impetum hostes ferre non potuerunt ac terga verterunt. Quos tanto spatio secuti quantum cursu et viribus efficere potuerunt, complures ex eis occiderunt, deinde omnibus longe lateque aedificiis incensis se in castra receperunt.

(4.36) Eodem die legati ab hostibus missi ad Caesarem de pace venerunt.

BOOK 5: CHAPTERS 24–48

(5.24) Subductis navibus, concilioque Gallorum Samarobrivae peracto, quod eo anno frumentum in Gallia propter siccitates angustius provenerat, coactus est aliter ac superioribus annis exercitum in hibernis collocare legionesque in plures civitates distribuere.

---

13. Some texts include *hostem* with *lacessendum*: "*lacessendum hostem*."

Ex quibus unam in Morinos ducendam C.[14] Fabio legato dedit, alteram in Nervios Q. Ciceroni, tertiam in Esubios L. Roscio; quartam in Remis cum T. Labieno in confinio Treverorum hiemare iussit. Tres in Bellovacis[15] collocavit: his[16] M. Crassum quaestorem et L. Munatium Plancum et C. Trebonium legatos praefecit. Unam legionem, quam proxime trans Padum conscripserat, et cohortes V in Eburones, quorum pars maxima est inter Mosam ac Rhenum, qui sub imperio Ambiorigis et Catuvolci erant, misit. His militibus Q. Titurium Sabinum et L. Aurunculeium Cottam legatos praeesse iussit. Ad hunc modum distributis legionibus, facillime inopiae frumentariae sese mederi posse existimavit. Atque harum tamen omnium legionum hiberna praeter eam quam L. Roscio in pacatissimam et quietissimam partem ducendam dederat, milibus passuum centum continebantur. Ipse interea, quoad legiones collocatas munitaque hiberna cognovisset, in Gallia morari constituit.

(5.25) Erat in Carnutibus summo loco natus Tasgetius, cuius maiores in sua civitate regnum obtinuerant. Huic Caesar pro eius virtute atque in se benevolentia, quod in omnibus bellis singulari eius opera fuerat usus, maiorum locum restituerat. Tertium iam hunc annum regnantem inimici multis palam ex civitate[17] auctoribus interfecerunt. Defertur ea res ad Caesarem. Ille veritus, quod ad plures pertinebat, ne civitas eorum impulsu deficeret, L. Plancum cum legione ex Belgio celeriter in Carnutes proficisci iubet ibique hiemare quorumque opera cognoverat Tasgetium interfectum, hos comprehensos ad se mittere. Interim ab omnibus legatis quaestoribusque, quibus legiones tradiderat, certior factus est in hiberna perventum locumque hibernis esse munitum.

(5.26) Diebus circiter quindecim, quibus in hiberna ventum est, initium repentini tumultus ac defectionis ortum est ab Ambiorige et Catuvulco; qui, cum ad fines regni sui Sabino Cottaeque praesto fuissent frumentumque in hiberna comportavissent, Indutiomari Treveri nuntiis impulsi suos concitaverunt subitoque oppressis lignatoribus magna manu ad castra oppugnatum venerunt. Cum celeriter nostri arma cepissent vallumque ascendissent atque una ex parte Hispanis equitibus emissis equestri proelio superiores fuissent, desperata re hostes suos ab oppugnatione reduxerunt. Tum suo more conclamaverunt, uti aliqui ex nostris ad colloquium prodiret: habere sese, quae de re communi dicere vellent, quibus rebus controversias minui posse sperarent.

(5.27) Mittitur ad eos colloquendi causa C. Arpineius, eques Romanus, familiaris Q. Tituri, et Q. Iunius ex Hispania quidam, qui iam ante missu Caesaris ad Ambiorigem ventitare consuerat; apud quos Ambiorix ad hunc modum locutus est: sese pro

---

14. The name Gaius is typically abbreviated C. (Caius is an alternate spelling but the abbreviation is still C, even if the G- spelling is used when written in full.)
15. Some texts read *Belgis* here.
16. Some texts read *eis* here.
17. Some texts read *et eis* here: "*ex civitate et eis auctoribus.*" But *ex civitate auctoribus* is the largely accepted reading.

Caesaris in se beneficiis plurimum ei confiteri debere, quod eius opera stipendio liberatus esset quod Aduatucis, finitimis suis, pendere consuesset, quodque ei et filius et fratris filius ab Caesare remissi essent, quos Aduatuci obsidum numero missos apud se in servitute et catenis tenuissent; neque id, quod fecerit de oppugnatione castrorum, aut iudicio aut voluntate sua fecisse, sed coactu civitatis, suaque esse eiusmodi imperia ut non minus haberet iuris in se multitudo quam ipse in multitudinem. Civitati porro hanc fuisse belli causam, quod repentinae Gallorum coniurationi resistere non potuerit. Id se facile ex humilitate sua probare posse, quod non adeo sit imperitus rerum ut suis copiis populum Romanum superari posse confidat. Sed esse Galliae commune consilium: omnibus hibernis Caesaris oppugnandis hunc esse dictum diem, ne qua legio alterae legioni subsidio venire posset. Non facile Gallos Gallis negare potuisse, praesertim cum de recuperanda[18] communi libertate consilium initum videretur. Quibus quoniam pro pietate satisfecerit, habere nunc se rationem offici pro beneficiis Caesaris: monere, orare Titurium pro hospitio ut suae ac militum saluti consulat. Magnam manum Germanorum conductam Rhenum transisse: hanc adfore biduo. Ipsorum esse consilium, velintne priusquam finitimi sentiant eductos ex hibernis milites aut ad Ciceronem aut ad Labienum deducere, quorum alter milia passuum circiter quinquaginta, alter paulo amplius ab eis absit. Illud se polliceri et iure iurando confirmare, tutum iter per fines daturum. Quod cum faciat, et civitati sese consulere, quod hibernis levetur, et Caesari pro eius meritis gratiam referre. Hac oratione habita discedit Ambiorix.

(5.28) Arpineius et Iunius, quae audierunt, ad legatos deferunt. Illi repentina re perturbati, etsi ab hoste ea dicebantur, tamen non neglegenda existimabant, maximeque hac re permovebantur, quod civitatem ignobilem atque humilem Eburonum sua sponte populo Romano bellum facere ausam vix erat credendum. Itaque ad consilium rem deferunt magnaque inter eos exsistit controversia. L. Aurunculeius compluresque tribuni militum et primorum ordinum centuriones nihil temere agendum neque ex hibernis iniussu Caesaris discedendum existimabant; quantasvis magnas etiam copias Germanorum sustineri posse munitis hibernis docebant: rem esse testimonio, quod primum hostium impetum multis ultro vulneribus illatis fortissime sustinuerint; re frumentaria non premi; interea et ex proximis hibernis et a Caesare conventura subsidia; postremo quid esset[19] levius aut turpius quam auctore hoste de summis rebus capere consilium?

(5.29) Contra ea Titurius sero facturos clamitabat, cum maiores manus hostium adiunctis Germanis convenissent aut cum aliquid calamitatis in proximis hibernis esset acceptum. Brevem consulendi esse occasionem. Caesarem arbitrari profectum in Italiam; neque aliter Carnutes interficiendi Tasgeti consilium fuisse capturos neque Eburones, si ille adesset, tanta contemptione nostri ad castra venturos esse. Non hostem

---

18. Some texts read *reciperanda* here.
19. Some texts read *esse* here.

auctorem sed rem spectare: subesse Rhenum; magno esse Germanis dolori Ariovisti mortem et superiores nostras victorias; ardere Galliam tot contumeliis acceptis sub populi Romani imperium redactam, superiore gloria rei militaris exstincta. Postremo quis hoc sibi persuaderet, sine certa re Ambiorigem ad eiusmodi consilium descendisse? Suam sententiam in utramque partem esse tutam: si nihil esset durius, nullo cum periculo ad proximam legionem perventuros: si Gallia omnis cum Germanis consentiret, unam esse in celeritate positam salutem. Cottae quidem atque eorum qui dissentirent consilium quem haberet[20] exitum, in quo[21] si praesens periculum non, at certe longinqua obsidione fames esset timenda?

(5.30) Hac in utramque partem disputatione habita, cum a Cotta primisque ordinibus acriter resisteretur, "Vincite," inquit, "si ita vultis," Sabinus, et id clariore voce, ut magna pars militum exaudiret: "Neque is sum," inquit, "qui gravissime ex vobis mortis periculo terrear: hi sapient; si gravius quid acciderit, abs te rationem reposcent qui, si per te liceat, perendino die cum proximis hibernis coniuncti communem cum reliquis belli casum sustineant, non reiecti et relegati longe ab ceteris aut ferro aut fame intereant."

(5.31) Consurgitur ex consilio; comprehendunt utrumque et orant, ne sua dissensione et pertinacia rem in summum periculum deducant: facilem esse rem, seu maneant, seu proficiscantur, si modo unum omnes sentiant ac probent; contra in dissensione nullam se salutem perspicere. Res disputatione ad mediam noctem perducitur. Tandem dat Cotta permotus manus: superat sententia Sabini. Pronuntiatur prima luce ituros. Consumitur vigiliis reliqua pars noctis, cum sua quisque miles circumspiceret, quid secum portare posset, quid ex instrumento hibernorum relinquere cogeretur. Omnia excogitantur, quare nec sine periculo maneatur et languore militum et vigiliis periculum augeatur. Prima luce sic ex castris proficiscuntur ut quibus esset persuasum non ab hoste sed ab homine amicissimo Ambiorige consilium datum, longissimo agmine maximisque impedimentis.

(5.32) At hostes, posteaquam ex nocturno fremitu vigiliisque de profectione eorum senserunt, collocatis insidiis bipertito in silvis opportuno atque occulto loco a milibus passuum circiter duobus Romanorum adventum exspectabant et, cum se maior pars agminis in magnam convallem demisisset, ex utraque parte eius vallis subito se ostenderunt, novissimosque premere et primos prohibere ascensu atque iniquissimo nostris loco proelium committere coeperunt.

(5.33) Tum demum Titurius, qui nihil ante providisset, trepidare et concursare cohortesque disponere, haec tamen ipsa timide atque ut eum omnia deficere viderentur; quod plerumque eis accidere consuevit qui in ipso negotio consilium capere coguntur.

---

20. Some texts read *habere* here.
21. Some texts punctuate this as a new sentence: "*quem haberet exitum? In quo*"

At Cotta, qui cogitasset haec posse in itinere accidere atque ob eam causam profectionis auctor non fuisset, nulla in re communi saluti deerat et in appellandis cohortandisque militibus imperatoris et in pugna militis officia praestabat. Cum propter longitudinem agminis minus facile omnia per se obire et quid quoque loco faciendum esset providere possent, iusserunt pronuntiare ut impedimenta relinquerent atque in orbem consisterent. Quod consilium etsi in eiusmodi casu reprehendendum non est, tamen incommode accidit: nam et nostris militibus spem minuit et hostes ad pugnam alacriores effecit, quod non sine summo timore et desperatione id factum videbatur. Praeterea accidit, quod fieri necesse erat, ut vulgo milites ab signis discederent, quae quisque eorum carissima haberet ab impedimentis petere atque arripere properaret, clamore et fletu omnia complerentur.

(**5.34**) At barbaris consilium non defuit. Nam duces eorum tota acie pronuntiare iusserunt, ne quis ab loco discederet, illorum esse praedam atque illis reservari quaecumque Romani reliquissent: proinde omnia in victoria posita existimarent. Erant et virtute et studio[22] pugnandi pares. Nostri, tametsi ab duce et a fortuna deserebantur, tamen omnem spem salutis in virtute ponebant, et quotiens quaeque cohors procurrerat, ab ea parte magnus numerus hostium cadebat. Qua re animadversa, Ambiorix pronuntiari iubet ut procul tela coiciant neu propius accedant et quam in partem Romani impetum fecerint cedant (levitate armorum et cotidiana exercitatione nihil his noceri posse), rursus se ad signa recipientes insequantur.

(**5.35**) Quo praecepto ab eis diligentissime observato, cum quaepiam cohors ex orbe excesserat atque impetum fecerat, hostes velocissime refugiebant. Interim eam partem nudari necesse erat et ab latere aperto tela recipi. Rursus cum in eum locum unde erant egressi reverti coeperant, et ab eis qui cesserant et ab eis qui proximi steterant circumveniebantur. Sin autem locum tenere vellent, nec virtuti locus relinquebatur neque ab tanta multitudine coiecta tela conferti vitare poterant. Tamen tot incommodis conflictati, multis vulneribus acceptis resistebant et magna parte diei consumpta, cum a prima luce ad horam octavam pugnaretur, nihil quod ipsis esset indignum committebant. Tum T. Balventio, qui superiore anno primum pilum duxerat, viro forti et magnae auctoritatis, utrumque femur tragula traicitur; Q. Lucanius eiusdem ordinis, fortissime pugnans, dum circumvento filio subvenit, interficitur; L. Cotta legatus omnes cohortes ordinesque adhortans in adversum os funda vulneratur.

(**5.36**) His rebus permotus Q. Titurius, cum procul Ambiorigem suos cohortantem conspexisset, interpretem suum Cn.[23] Pompeium ad eum mittit rogatum ut sibi militibusque parcat. Ille appellatus respondit: si velit secum colloqui, licere; sperare a multitudine impetrari posse, quod ad militum salutem pertineat; ipsi vero nihil nocitum iri, inque eam rem se suam fidem interponere. Ille cum Cotta saucio communicat, si

---

22. Some texts read *numero* here but *studio* seems the stronger reading.

23. The name Gnaeus is typically abbreviated Cn. (Cnaeus is an alternate spelling but the abbreviation is still Cn., even if the Gn-spelling is used when written in full.)

videatur, pugna ut excedant et cum Ambiorige una colloquantur: sperare ab eo de sua ac militum salute impetrari posse. Cotta se ad armatum hostem iturum negat atque in eo perseverat.

(5.37) Sabinus quos in praesentia tribunos militum circum se habebat et primorum ordinum centuriones se sequi iubet et, cum propius Ambiorigem accessisset, iussus arma abicere imperatum facit suisque ut idem faciant imperat. Interim, dum de condicionibus inter se agunt longiorque consulto ab Ambiorige instituitur sermo, paulatim circumventus interficitur. Tum vero suo more victoriam conclamant atque ululatum tollunt impetuque in nostros facto ordines perturbant. Ibi L. Cotta pugnans interficitur cum maxima parte militum. Reliqui se in castra recipiunt unde erant egressi. Ex quibus L. Petrosidius aquilifer, cum magna multitudine hostium premeretur, aquilam intra vallum proiecit; ipse pro castris fortissime pugnans occiditur. Illi aegre ad noctem oppugnationem sustinent: noctu ad unum omnes desperata salute se ipsi interficiunt. Pauci ex proelio elapsi incertis itineribus per silvas ad T. Labienum legatum in hiberna perveniunt atque eum de rebus gestis certiorem faciunt.

(5.38) Hac victoria sublatus Ambiorix statim cum equitatu in Aduatucos, qui erant eius regno finitimi, proficiscitur; neque noctem neque diem intermittit peditatumque sese[24] subsequi iubet. Re demonstrata Aduatucisque concitatis, postero die in Nervios pervenit hortaturque ne sui in perpetuum liberandi atque ulciscendi Romanos pro eis quas acceperint iniuriis occasionem dimittant; interfectos esse legatos duo magnamque partem exercitus interisse demonstrat; nihil esse negoti subito oppressam legionem quae cum Cicerone hiemet interfici; se ad eam rem profitetur adiutorem. Facile hac oratione Nerviis persuadet.

(5.39) Itaque confestim dimissis nuntiis ad Ceutrones, Grudios, Levacos, Pleumoxios, Geidumnos, qui omnes sub eorum imperio sunt, quam maximas manus possunt cogunt et de improviso ad Ciceronis hiberna advolant, nondum ad eum fama de Tituri morte perlata. Huic quoque accidit, quod fuit necesse, ut nonnulli milites qui lignationis munitionisque causa in silvas discessissent repentino equitum adventu interciperentur. His[25] circumventis, magna manu Eburones, Nervii, Aduatuci atque horum omnium socii et clientes legionem oppugnare incipiunt. Nostri celeriter ad arma concurrunt, vallum conscendunt. Aegre is dies sustentatur, quod omnem spem hostes in celeritate ponebant atque hanc adepti victoriam in perpetuum se fore victores confidebant.

(5.40) Mittuntur ad Caesarem confestim ab Cicerone litterae, magnis propositis praemiis, si pertulissent: obsessis omnibus viis missi intercipiuntur. Noctu ex materia, quam munitionis causa comportaverant, turres admodum CXX[26] excitantur incredibili celeritate; quae deesse operi videbantur perficiuntur. Hostes postero die multo maioribus

---

24. Some texts read *se* instead of *sese* here and some texts eliminate the pronoun: "*peditatumque subsequi iubet.*"

25. Some texts read *eis* here.

26. Some texts spell the number out in various forms, either *centum viginti* or *centum XX*.

coactis copiis castra oppugnant, fossam complent. Eadem ratione, qua pridie, ab nostris resistitur. Hoc idem reliquis deinceps fit diebus. Nulla pars nocturni temporis ad laborem intermittitur; non aegris, non vulneratis facultas quietis datur. Quaecumque ad proximi diei oppugnationem opus sunt noctu comparantur: multae praeustae sudes, magnus muralium pilorum numerus instituitur; turres contabulantur, pinnae loricaeque ex cratibus attexuntur. Ipse Cicero, cum tenuissima valetudine esset, ne nocturnum quidem sibi tempus ad quietem relinquebat, ut ultro militum concursu ac vocibus sibi parcere cogeretur.

(5.41) Tunc duces principesque Nerviorum qui aliquem sermonis aditum causamque amicitiae cum Cicerone habebant colloqui sese velle dicunt. Facta potestate eadem quae Ambiorix cum Titurio egerat commemorant: omnem esse in armis Galliam; Germanos Rhenum transisse; Caesaris reliquorumque hiberna oppugnari. Addunt etiam de Sabini morte; Ambiorigem ostentant fidei faciendae causa. Errare eos dicunt, si quicquam ab eis praesidi sperent qui suis rebus diffidant; sese tamen hoc esse in Ciceronem populumque Romanum animo ut nihil nisi hiberna recusent[27] atque hanc inveterascere consuetudinem nolint: licere illis incolumibus per se ex hibernis discedere et quascumque in partes velint sine metu proficisci. Cicero ad haec unum modo respondit: non esse consuetudinem populi Romani accipere ab hoste armato condicionem: si ab armis discedere velint, se adiutore utantur legatosque ad Caesarem mittant; sperare pro eius iustitia quae petierint impetraturos.

(5.42) Ab hac spe repulsi Nervii vallo pedum IX et fossa pedum XV hiberna cingunt. Haec et superiorum annorum consuetudine ab nobis cognoverant et quos clam[28] de exercitu habebant captivos ab eis docebantur; sed nulla ferramentorum copia quae esset ad hunc usum idonea, gladiis caespites circumcidere, manibus sagulisque terram exhaurire videbantur.[29] Qua quidem ex re hominum multitudo cognosci potuit: nam minus horis tribus milium pedum XV in circuitu[30] munitionem perfecerunt reliquisque diebus turres ad altitudinem valli, falces testudinesque, quas idem captivi docuerant, parare ac facere coeperunt.

(5.43) Septimo oppugnationis die maximo coorto vento ferventes fusili ex argilla glandes fundis et fervefacta iacula in casas, quae more Gallico stramentis erant tectae, iacere coeperunt. Hae celeriter ignem comprehenderunt et venti magnitudine in omnem locum castrorum distulerunt. Hostes maximo clamore, sicuti parta iam atque explorata victoria, turres testudinesque agere et scalis vallum ascendere coeperunt. At tanta militum virtus atque ea praesentia animi fuit ut, cum ubique[31] flamma torrerentur maximaque telorum multitudine premerentur suaque omnia impedimenta atque

---

27. Some texts read *recusant* here.
28. Some texts read *quosdam* for *quos clam* here: "*et quosdam de exercitu habebant.*"
29. Some texts read *cogebantur* here.
30. Some texts eliminate the *pedum XV* here.
31. Some texts read *undique* here.

omnes fortunas conflagrare intellegerent, non modo demigrandi causa de vallo decederet nemo sed paene ne respiceret quidem quisquam, ac tum omnes acerrime fortissimeque pugnarent. Hic dies nostris longe gravissimus fuit, sed tamen hunc habuit eventum ut eo die maximus numerus hostium vulneraretur atque interficeretur, ut se sub ipso vallo constipaverant recessumque primis ultimi non dabant. Paulum quidem intermissa flamma et quodam loco turri adacta et contingente vallum, tertiae cohortis centuriones ex eo, quo stabant, loco recesserunt suosque omnes removerunt, nutu vocibusque hostes, si introire vellent, vocare coeperunt: quorum progredi ausus est nemo. Tum ex omni parte lapidibus coiectis deturbati, turrisque succensa est.

(5.44) Erant in ea legione fortissimi viri, centuriones, qui primis ordinibus appropinquarent, T. Pullo et L. Vorenus. Hi perpetuas inter se controversias habebant, quinam anteferretur, omnibusque annis de locis summis simultatibus contendebant. Ex his Pullo, cum acerrime ad munitiones pugnaretur, "Quid dubitas," inquit, "Vorene? Aut quem locum tuae pro laude[32] virtutis spectas?[33] Hic dies de nostris controversiis iudicabit." Haec cum dixisset, procedit extra munitiones, quaeque pars hostium confertissima est visa irrumpit. Ne Vorenus quidem sese[34] vallo continent, sed omnium veritus existimationem subsequitur. Tum[35] mediocri spatio relicto Pullo pilum in hostes immittit, atque unum ex multitudine procurrentem traicit; quo percusso et exanimato, hunc scutis protegunt, in hostem tela universi coiciunt neque dant regrediendi facultatem. Transfigitur scutum Pulloni et verutum in balteo defigitur. Avertit hic casus vaginam et gladium educere conanti dextram moratur manum, impeditumque hostes circumsistunt. Succurrit inimicus illi Vorenus et laboranti subvenit. Ad hunc se confestim a Pullone omnis multitudo convertit; illum veruto arbitrantur occisum. Gladio comminus rem gerit Vorenus, atque uno interfecto reliquos paulum propellit: dum cupidius instat, in locum deiectus inferiorem concidit. Huic rursus circumvento fert subsidium Pullo, atque ambo incolumes compluribus interfectis summa cum laude sese intra munitiones recipiunt. Sic fortuna in contentione et certamine utrumque versavit, ut alter alteri inimicus auxilio salutique esset neque diiudicari posset, uter utri virtute anteferendus videretur.

(5.45) Quanto erat in dies gravior atque asperior oppugnatio, et maxime quod magna parte militum confecta vulneribus res ad paucitatem defensorum pervenerat, tanto crebriores litterae nuntiique ad Caesarem mittebantur; quorum pars deprehensa in conspectu nostrorum militum cum cruciatu necabatur. Erat unus intus Nervius, nomine Vertico, loco natus honesto, qui a prima obsidione ad Ciceronem perfugerat, suamque ei fidem praestiterat. Hic servo spe libertatis magnisque persuadet praemiis ut litteras ad Caesarem deferat. Has ille in iaculo inligatas effert, et Gallus inter Gallos

---

32. Some texts read *probandae* for *pro laude*.
33. Some texts read *exspectas* here.
34. Some texts include *tum* here: "*quidem tum sese.*"
35. Some texts eliminate this *tum* and move it to the previous sentence (see n.32 above).

sine ulla suspicione versatus ad Caesarem pervenit. Ab eo de periculis Ciceronis legionisque cognoscitur.

(5.46) Caesar, acceptis litteris hora circiter XI[36] diei, statim nuntium in Bellovacos ad M. Crassum quaestorem mittit, cuius hiberna aberant ab eo milia passuum XXV; iubet media nocte legionem proficisci celeriterque ad se venire. Exit cum nuntio Crassus. Alterum ad C. Fabium legatum mittit, ut in Atrebatium fines legionem adducat, qua sibi iter faciendum sciebat. Scribit Labieno, si rei publicae commodo facere posset, cum legione ad fines Nerviorum veniat. Reliquam partem exercitus, quod paulo aberat longius, non putat exspectandam; equites circiter quadringentos ex proximis hibernis colligit.

(5.47) Hora circiter tertia ab antecursoribus de Crassi adventu certior factus, eo die milia passuum XX procedit. Crassum Samarobrivae praeficit legionemque[37] attribuit, quod ibi impedimenta exercitus, obsides civitatum, litteras publicas, frumentumque omne quod eo tolerandae hiemis causa devexerat relinquebat. Fabius, ut imperatum erat, non ita multum moratus in itinere cum legione occurrit. Labienus, interitu Sabini et caede cohortium cognita, cum omnes ad eum Treverorum copiae venissent veritus ne, si ex hibernis fugae similem profectionem fecisset, hostium impetum sustinere non posset, praesertim quos recenti victoria efferri sciret, litteras Caesari remittit: quanto cum periculo legionem ex hibernis educturus esset; rem gestam in Eburonibus perscribit; docet omnes equitatus peditatusque copias Treverorum tria milia passuum longe ab suis castris consedisse.

(5.48) Caesar, consilio eius probato, etsi opinione trium legionum deiectus ad duas redierat, tamen unum communis salutis auxilium in celeritate ponebat. Venit magnis itineribus in Nerviorum fines. Ibi ex captivis cognoscit quae apud Ciceronem gerantur quantoque in periculo res sit. Tum cuidam ex equitibus Gallis magnis praemiis persuadet uti ad Ciceronem epistolam deferat. Hanc Graecis conscriptam litteris mittit, ne intercepta epistola nostra ab hostibus consilia cognoscantur. Si adire non possit, monet ut tragulam cum epistola ad amentum deligata intra munitionem castrorum abiciat. In litteris scribit se cum legionibus profectum celeriter adfore; hortatur ut pristinam virtutem retineat. Gallus periculum veritus, ut erat praeceptum, tragulam mittit. Haec casu ad turrim adhaesit neque ab nostris biduo animadversa tertio die a quodam milite conspicitur, dempta ad Ciceronem defertur. Ille perlectam in conventu militum recitat maximaque omnes laetitia adficit. Tum fumi incendiorum procul videbantur, quae res omnem dubitationem adventus legionum expulit.

---

36. Some texts read *undecima* here.
37. Some texts read an *ei* here: "*legionemque ei attribuit.*"

BOOK 6: CHAPTERS 13–20

(**6.13**) In omni Gallia eorum hominum qui aliquo sunt numero atque honore genera sunt duo. Nam plebes paene servorum habetur loco, quae nihil audet per se, nullo adhibetur consilio. Plerique, cum aut aere alieno aut magnitudine tributorum aut iniuria potentiorum premuntur, sese in servitutem dicant nobilibus: in[38] hos eadem omnia sunt iura quae dominis in servos. Sed de his duobus generibus alterum est Druidum, alterum equitum. Illi rebus divinis intersunt, sacrificia publica ac privata procurant, religiones interpretantur: ad hos magnus adulescentium numerus disciplinae causa concurrit, magnoque hi sunt apud eos honore. Nam fere de omnibus controversiis publicis privatisque constituunt et, si quod est admissum facinus, si caedes facta, si de hereditate, de finibus controversia est, idem decernunt, praemia poenasque constituunt; si qui aut privatus aut populus eorum decreto non stetit, sacrificiis interdicunt. Haec poena apud eos est gravissima. Quibus ita est interdictum, hi numero impiorum ac sceleratorum habentur, his omnes decedunt, aditum sermonemque defugiunt, ne quid ex contagione incommodi accipiant, neque his petentibus ius redditur, neque honos ullus communicatur. His autem omnibus Druidibus praeest unus, qui summam inter eos habet auctoritatem. Hoc mortuo, aut, si qui ex reliquis excellit dignitate, succedit, aut, si sunt plures pares, suffragio druidum, nonnumquam etiam armis de principatu contendunt. Hi certo anni tempore in finibus Carnutum, quae regio totius Galliae media habetur, considunt in loco consecrato. Huc omnes undique qui controversias habent conveniunt eorumque decretis iudiciisque parent. Disciplina in Britannia reperta atque inde in Galliam translata esse existimatur, et nunc, qui diligentius eam rem cognoscere volunt, plerumque illo discendi causa proficiscuntur.

(**6.14**) Druides a bello abesse consuerunt, neque tributa una cum reliquis pendunt; militiae vacationem omniumque rerum habent immunitatem. Tantis excitati praemiis et sua sponte multi in disciplinam conveniunt et a parentibus propinquisque mittuntur. Magnum ibi numerum versuum ediscere dicuntur. Itaque annos nonnulli XX in disciplina permanent. Neque fas esse existimant ea litteris mandare, cum in reliquis fere rebus, publicis privatisque rationibus, Graecis litteris utantur. Id mihi duabus de causis instituisse videntur, quod neque in vulgum disciplinam efferri velint neque eos, qui discunt, litteris confisos minus memoriae studere; quod fere plerisque accidit ut praesidio litterarum diligentiam in perdiscendo ac memoriam remittant. In primis hoc volunt persuadere, non interire animas sed ab aliis post mortem transire ad alios, atque hoc maxime ad virtutem excitari putant, metu mortis neglecto. Multa praeterea de sideribus atque eorum motu, de mundi ac terrarum magnitudine, de rerum natura, de deorum immortalium vi ac potestate disputant et iuventuti tradunt.

(**6.15**) Alterum genus est equitum. Hi, cum est usus atque aliquod bellum incidit (quod fere ante Caesaris adventum quot annis accidere solebat, uti aut ipsi iniurias inferrent

---

38. Some texts include *quibus* before the *in*: "*quibus in hos....*"

aut inlatas propulsarent), omnes in bello versantur; atque eorum ut quisque est genere copiisque amplissimus, ita plurimos circum se ambactos clientesque habet. Hanc unam gratiam potentiamque noverunt.

(6.16) Natio est omnis[39] Gallorum admodum dedita religionibus, atque ob eam causam qui sunt adfecti gravioribus morbis quique in proeliis periculisque versantur aut pro victimis homines immolant aut se immolaturos vovent, administrisque ad ea sacrificia Druidibus utuntur, quod, pro vita hominis nisi hominis vita reddatur, non posse deorum immortalium numen placari arbitrantur, publiceque eiusdem generis habent instituta sacrificia. Alii immani magnitudine simulacra habent, quorum contexta viminibus membra vivis hominibus complent; quibus succensis circumventi flamma exanimantur homines. Supplicia eorum qui in furto aut in latrocinio aut aliqua noxia sint comprehensi gratiora dis immortalibus esse arbitrantur, sed, cum eius generis copia deficit, etiam ad innocentium supplicia descendunt.

(6.17) Deum maxime Mercurium colunt. Huius sunt plurima simulacra: hunc omnium inventorem artium ferunt, hunc viarum atque itinerum ducem, hunc ad quaestus pecuniae mercaturasque habere vim maximam arbitrantur. Post hunc Apollinem et Martem et Iovem et Minervam. De his eandem fere, quam reliquae gentes, habent opinionem: Apollinem morbos depellere, Minervam operum atque artificiorum initia tradere, Iovem imperium caelestium tenere, Martem bella regere. Huic, cum proelio dimicare constituerunt, ea quae bello ceperint plerumque devovent: cum superaverunt,[40] animalia capta immolant, reliquasque res in unum locum conferunt. Multis in civitatibus harum rerum exstructos tumulos locis consecratis conspicari licet, neque saepe accidit ut neglecta quispiam religione aut capta apud se occultare aut posita tollere auderet, gravissimumque ei rei supplicium cum cruciatu constitutum est.

(6.18) Galli se omnes ab Dite patre prognatos praedicant, idque ab Druidibus proditum dicunt. Ob eam causam spatia omnis temporis non numero dierum sed noctium finiunt; dies natales et mensum et annorum initia sic observant ut noctem dies subsequatur. In reliquis vitae institutis hoc fere ab reliquis differunt quod suos liberos, nisi cum adoleverunt ut munus militiae sustinere possint, palam ad se adire non patiuntur filiumque puerili aetate in publico in conspectu patris adsistere turpe ducunt.

(6.19) Viri, quantas pecunias ab uxoribus dotis nomine acceperunt, tantas ex suis bonis aestimatione facta cum dotibus communicant. Huius omnis pecuniae coniunctim ratio habetur fructusque servantur: uter eorum vita superarit, ad eum pars utriusque cum fructibus superiorum temporum pervenit. Viri in uxores, sicuti in liberos, vitae necisque habent potestatem; et cum pater familiae illustriore loco natus decessit, eius propinqui conveniunt et, de morte si res in suspicionem venit, de uxoribus in

---

39. Some texts read *omnium* here.
40. Some texts read *quae superaverint* for *cum superaverunt*.

servilem modum quaestionem habent et, si compertum est, igni atque omnibus tormentis excruciatas interficiunt. Funera sunt pro cultu Gallorum magnifica et sumptuosa; omniaque quae vivis cordi fuisse arbitrantur in ignem inferunt, etiam animalia; ac paulo supra hanc memoriam servi et clientes quos ab eis dilectos esse constabat iustis funeribus confectis una cremabantur.

(6.20) Quae civitates commodius suam rem publicam administrare existimantur habent legibus sanctum, si quis quid de re publica a finitimis rumore aut fama acceperit, uti ad magistratum deferat neve cum quo alio communicet: quod saepe homines temerarios atque imperitos falsis rumoribus terreri et ad facinus impelli et de summis rebus consilium capere cognitum est. Magistratus quae visa sunt occultant, quaeque esse ex usu iudicaverunt multitudini produnt. De re publica nisi per concilium loqui non conceditur.

VERGIL, *AENEID*

- The text below is based on the 1969 Oxford Classical Text of R. A. B. Mynors via the online version available at oxfordscholarlyeditions.com (subscription required):
  - Scan the code at right to go directly to the website.
- **Macrons** are not used in the text because they are not used on the AP® Exam.
- **Spellings** have been updated to reflect modern American textbook conventions:
  - long *-is* has been changed to *-es*
  - "j" has been changed to consonantal "i"
  - consonantal "u" has been changed to "v"
- **Assimilation** is the process by which a root and its prefix are smoothed for the sake of pronunciation or euphony: the first letter of the root absorbs or assimilates the last letter of the prefix.
  - "Correspondence" is a combination of "con-" and "respond"; the "r" in "respond" absorbs the "n" in "con-" to form the assimilated "correspondence."
  - The same process happens in Latin:
    - sub + mergo = submergo or summergo
    - in + motus = inmotus or immotus
  - The text uses the convention reflected in Lewis and Short's *Latin Dictionary*; for example, *submergo* is not assimilated while *immotus* is.
  - It is important to be aware of assimilation for the recognition of words, although the AP® Exam will often notate alternate forms of words when reproducing a text.
- The following editions were also consulted in the preparation of this text.

CHAPTER 5

- o Dickinson College Commentaries
  - ▪ Scan the code at right to go directly to the website.
  - ▪ Or use the direct link here: http://dcc.dickinson.edu/vergil-aeneid /preface

- o The Packard Humanities Institute's Classical Latin Texts
  - ▪ Scan the code at right to go directly to the website.
  - ▪ Or use the direct link here: http://latin.packhum.org/loc/690/3/0#0
- • Alternate readings are included in footnotes throughout the text.

BOOK 1.1–209

Arma virumque cano, Troiae qui primus ab oris
Italiam fato profugus Laviniaque venit
litora, multum ille et terris iactatus et alto
vi superum, saevae memorem Iunonis ob iram,
multa quoque et bello passus, dum conderet urbem   5
inferretque deos Latio; genus unde Latinum
Albanique patres atque altae moenia Romae.
Musa, mihi causas memora, quo numine laeso
quidve dolens regina deum tot volvere casus
insignem pietate virum, tot adire labores   10
impulerit. Tantaene animis caelestibus irae?
Urbs antiqua fuit (Tyrii tenuere coloni)
Karthago,[41] Italiam contra Tiberinaque longe
ostia, dives opum studiisque asperrima belli,
quam Iuno fertur terris magis omnibus unam   15
posthabita coluisse Samo. Hic illius arma,
hic currus fuit; hoc regnum dea gentibus esse,
si qua fata sinant, iam tum tenditque fovetque.
Progeniem sed enim Troiano a sanguine duci
audierat Tyrias olim quae verteret arces;   20
hinc populum late regem belloque superbum
venturum excidio Libyae; sic volvere Parcas.
Id metuens veterisque memor Saturnia belli,
prima quod ad Troiam pro caris gesserat Argis –
necdum etiam causae irarum saevique dolores   25
exciderant animo; manet alta mente repostum
iudicium Paridis spretaeque iniuria formae
et genus invisum et rapti Ganymedis honores –
his accensa super iactatos aequore toto
Troas, reliquias Danaum atque immitis Achilli,   30

---

41. The Latin word for Carthage can be alternately spelled with K or C. Most texts seem to use the K so that will be used here and throughout.

arcebat longe Latio, multosque per annos
errabant acti fatis maria omnia circum.
Tantae molis erat Romanam condere gentem.

      Vix e conspectu Siculae telluris in altum
vela dabant laeti et spumas salis aere ruebant,   35
cum Iuno aeternum servans sub pectore vulnus
haec secum: "Mene incepto desistere victam
nec posse Italia Teucrorum avertere regem –
quippe vetor fatis! Pallasne exurere classem
Argivum atque ipsos potuit submergere ponto   40
unius ob noxam et furias Aiacis Oilei?
Ipsa, Iovis rapidum iaculata e nubibus ignem,
disiecitque rates evertitque aequora ventis,
illum exspirantem transfixo pectore flammas
turbine corripuit scopuloque infixit acuto;   45
ast ego, quae divum incedo regina Iovisque
et soror et coniunx, una cum gente tot annos
bella gero. Et quisquam numen Iunonis adorat
praeterea aut supplex aris imponet honorem?"

      Talia flammato secum dea corde volutans   50
nimborum in patriam, loca feta furentibus Austris,
Aeoliam venit. Hic vasto rex Aeolus antro
luctantes ventos tempestatesque sonoras
imperio premit ac vinclis et carcere frenat.
Illi indignantes magno cum murmure montis   55
circum claustra fremunt; celsa sedet Aeolus arce
sceptra tenens mollitque animos et temperat iras.
Ni faciat, maria ac terras caelumque profundum
quippe ferant rapidi secum verrantque per auras;
sed pater omnipotens speluncis abdidit atris   60
hoc metuens molemque et montes insuper altos
imposuit, regemque dedit qui foedere certo
et premere et laxas sciret dare iussus habenas.

      Ad quem tum Iuno supplex his vocibus usa est:
"Aeole (namque tibi divum pater atque hominum rex   65
et mulcere dedit fluctus et tollere vento),
gens inimica mihi Tyrrhenum navigat aequor,
Ilium in Italiam portans victosque penates:
incute vim ventis submersasque obrue puppes,
aut age diversos et disice[42] corpora ponto.   70
Sunt mihi bis septem praestanti corpore Nymphae,
quarum quae forma pulcherrima Deïopea,
conubio iungam stabili propriamque dicabo,

---

42. Some texts spell this verb *dissice*; with the single *s*, the preceding *i* is naturally long; the double *s* makes the *i* long by position.

omnes ut tecum meritis pro talibus annos
exigat et pulchra faciat te prole parentem."   75
     Aeolus haec contra: "Tuus, o regina, quid optes
explorare labor; mihi iussa capessere fas est.
Tu mihi quodcumque hoc regni, tu sceptra Iovemque
concilias, tu das epulis accumbere divum
nimborumque facis tempestatumque potentem."   80
     Haec ubi dicta, cavum conversa cuspide montem
impulit in latus; ac venti, velut agmine facto,
qua data porta, ruunt et terras turbine perflant.
Incubuere mari totumque a sedibus imis
una Eurusque Notusque ruunt creberque procellis   85
Africus, et vastos volvunt ad litora fluctus.
Insequitur clamorque virum stridorque rudentum;
eripiunt subito nubes caelumque diemque
Teucrorum ex oculis; ponto nox incubat atra;
intonuere poli et crebris micat ignibus aether   90
praesentemque viris intentant omnia mortem.
Extemplo Aeneae solvuntur frigore membra;
ingemit et duplices tendens ad sidera palmas
talia voce refert: "O terque quaterque beati,
quis ante ora patrum Troiae sub moenibus altis   95
contigit oppetere! O Danaum fortissime gentis
Tydide! Mene Iliacis occumbere campis
non potuisse tuaque animam hanc effundere dextra,
saevus ubi Aeacidae telo iacet Hector, ubi ingens
Sarpedon, ubi tot Simois correpta sub undis   100
scuta virum galeasque et fortia corpora volvit!"
     Talia iactanti stridens Aquilone procella
velum adversa ferit, fluctusque ad sidera tollit.
Franguntur remi, tum prora avertit et undis
dat latus, insequitur cumulo praeruptus aquae mons.   105
Hi summo in fluctu pendent; his unda dehiscens
terram inter fluctus aperit, furit aestus harenis.
Tres Notus abreptas in saxa latentia torquet
(saxa vocant Itali mediis quae in fluctibus Aras,
dorsum immane mari summo), tres Eurus ab alto   110
in brevia et Syrtes urget, miserabile visu,
inliditque vadis atque aggere cingit harenae.
Unam, quae Lycios fidumque vehebat Oronten,
ipsius ante oculos ingens a vertice pontus
in puppim ferit: excutitur pronusque magister   115
volvitur in caput, ast illam ter fluctus ibidem
torque, agens circum, et rapidus vorat aequore vertex.

Apparent rari nantes in gurgite vasto,
arma virum tabulaeque et Troia[43] gaza per undas.
Iam validam Ilionei navem, iam fortis Achatae,   120
et qua vectus Abas, et qua grandaevus Aletes,
vicit hiems; laxis laterum compagibus omnes
accipiunt inimicum imbrem rimisque fatiscunt.
        Interea magno misceri murmure pontum
emissamque hiemem sensit Neptunus et imis   125
stagna refusa vadis, graviter commotus, et, alto
prospiciens, summa placidum caput extulit unda.
Disiectam Aeneae toto videt aequore classem,
fluctibus oppressos Troas caelique ruina;
nec latuere doli fratrem Iunonis et irae.   130
Eurum ad se Zephyrumque vocat, dehinc talia fatur:
"Tantane vos generis tenuit fiducia vestri?
Iam caelum terramque meo sine numine, venti,
miscere et tantas audetis tollere moles?
Quos ego—sed motos praestat componere fluctus.   135
Post mihi non simili poena commissa luetis.
Maturate fugam regique haec dicite vestro:
non illi imperium pelagi saevumque tridentem,
sed mihi sorte datum. Tenet ille immania saxa,
vestras, Eure, domos; illa se iactet in aula   140
Aeolus et clauso ventorum carcere regnet."
        Sic ait, et dicto citius tumida aequora placat
collectasque fugat nubes solemque reducit.
Cymothoe simul et Triton adnixus acuto
detrudunt naves scopulo; levat ipse tridenti   145
et vastas aperit Syrtes et temperat aequor
atque rotis summas levibus perlabitur undas.
Ac veluti magno in populo cum saepe coorta est
seditio saevitque animis ignobile vulgus
iamque faces et saxa volant, furor arma ministrat;   150
tum, pietate gravem ac meritis si forte virum quem
conspexere, silent arrectisque auribus astant;
ille regit dictis animos et pectora mulcet:
sic cunctus pelagi cecidit fragor, aequora postquam
prospiciens genitor caeloque invectus aperto   155
flectit equos curruque volans dat lora secundo.
        Defessi Aeneadae quae proxima litora cursu
contendunt petere, et Libyae vertuntur ad oras.
Est in secessu longo locus: insula portum

---

43. The Latin noun *Troia, -ae* can be read as disyllabic or trisyllabic, based on whether the *i* is read as a consonant or a vowel. Here it is trisyllabic, as it often is in the *Aeneid*.

efficit obiectu laterum, quibus omnis ab alto   160
frangitur inque sinus scindit sese unda reductos.
Hinc atque hinc vastae rupes geminique minantur
in caelum scopuli, quorum sub vertice late
aequora tuta silent; tum silvis scaena coruscis
desuper, horrentique atrum nemus imminet umbra.   165
Fronte sub adversa scopulis pendentibus antrum;
intus aquae dulces vivoque sedilia saxo,
Nympharum domus. Hic fessas non vincula naves
ulla tenent, unco non alligat ancora morsu.
Huc septem Aeneas collectis navibus omni   170
ex numero subit ac, magno telluris amore
egressi, optata potiuntur Troes harena
et sale tabentes artus in litore ponunt.
Ac primum silici scintillam excudit Achates
suscepitque ignem foliis atque arida circum   175
nutrimenta dedit rapuitque in fomite flammam.
Tum Cererem corruptam undis Cerealiaque arma
expediunt fessi rerum, frugesque receptas
et torrere parant flammis et frangere saxo.
       Aeneas scopulum interea conscendit, et omnem   180
prospectum late pelago petit, Anthea si quem
iactatum vento videat Phrygiasque biremes
aut Capyn aut celsis in puppibus arma Caici.
Navem in conspectu nullam, tres litore cervos
prospicit errantes; hos tota armenta sequuntur   185
a tergo et longum per valles pascitur agmen.
Constitit hic arcumque manu celeresque sagittas
corripuit, fidus quae tela gerebat Achates,
ductoresque ipsos primum capita alta ferentes
cornibus arboreis sternit, tum vulgus et omnem   190
miscet agens telis nemora inter frondea turbam;
nec prius absistit quam septem ingentia victor
corpora fundat humi et numerum cum navibus aequet;
hinc portum petit et socios partitur in omnes.
Vina bonus quae deinde cadis onerarat Acestes   195
litore Trinacrio dederatque abeuntibus heros
dividit, et dictis maerentia pectora mulcet:
"O socii (neque enim ignari sumus ante malorum),
o passi graviora, dabit deus his quoque finem.
Vos et Scyllaeam rabiem penitusque sonantes   200

accestis scopulos, vos et Cyclopia saxa
experti: revocate animos maestumque timorem
mittite; forsan et haec olim meminisse iuvabit.
Per varios casus, per tot discrimina rerum
tendimus in Latium, sedes ubi fata quietas   205
ostendunt; illic fas regna resurgere Troiae.
Durate, et vosmet rebus servate secundis."
Talia voce refert curisque ingentibus aeger
spem vultu simulat, premit altum corde dolorem.   209

BOOK 1.418–40

Corripuere viam interea, qua semita monstrat,   418
iamque ascendebant collem, qui plurimus urbi
imminet adversasque aspectat desuper arces.   420
Miratur molem Aeneas, magalia quondam,
miratur portas strepitumque et strata viarum.
Instant ardentes Tyrii: pars ducere muros
molirique arcem et manibus subvolvere saxa,
pars optare locum tecto et concludere sulco;   425
iura magistratusque legunt sanctumque senatum.
Hic portus alii effodiunt; hic alta theatris
fundamenta locant alii, immanesque columnas
rupibus excidunt, scaenis decora apta futuris:
qualis apes aestate nova per florea rura   430
exercet sub sole labor, cum gentis adultos
educunt fetus, aut cum liquentia mella
stipant et dulci distendunt nectare cellas,
aut onera accipiunt venientum, aut agmine facto
ignavum fucos pecus a praesepibus arcent;   435
fervet opus redolentque thymo fragrantia mella.
"O fortunati, quorum iam moenia surgunt!"
Aeneas ait et fastigia suspicit urbis.
Infert se saeptus nebula (mirabile dictu)
per medios, miscetque viris neque cernitur ulli.   440

BOOK 1.494–578

Haec dum Dardanio Aeneae miranda videntur,
dum stupet obtutuque haeret defixus in uno,   495
regina ad templum, forma pulcherrima Dido,
incessit magna iuvenum stipante caterva.
Qualis in Eurotae ripis aut per iuga Cynthi
exercet Diana choros, quam mille secutae

hinc atque hinc glomerantur Oreades; illa pharetram   500
fert umero gradiensque deas supereminet omnes
(Latonae tacitum pertemptant gaudia pectus):
talis erat Dido, talem se laeta ferebat
per medios instans operi regnisque futuris.
Tum foribus divae, media testudine templi,   505
saepta armis solioque alte subnixa resedit.
Iura dabat legesque viris, operumque laborem
partibus aequabat iustis aut sorte trahebat:
cum subito Aeneas concursu accedere magno
Anthea Sergestumque videt fortemque Cloanthum   510
Teucrorumque alios, ater quos aequore turbo
dispulerat penitusque alias avexerat oras.
Obstipuit simul ipse, simul percussus Achates
laetitiaque metuque; avidi coniungere dextras
ardebant, sed res animos incognita turbat.   515
Dissimulant et nube cava speculantur amicti
quae fortuna viris, classem quo litore linquant,
quid veniant; cunctis nam lecti navibus ibant
orantes veniam et templum clamore petebant.
　　　Postquam introgressi et coram data copia fandi,   520
maximus Ilioneus placido sic pectore coepit:
"O regina, novam cui condere Iuppiter urbem
iustitiaque dedit gentes frenare superbas,
Troes te miseri, ventis maria omnia vecti,
oramus: prohibe infandos a navibus ignes,   525
parce pio generi et propius res aspice nostras.
Non nos aut ferro Libycos populare penates
venimus, aut raptas ad litora vertere praedas;
non ea vis animo nec tanta superbia victis.
Est locus, Hesperiam Grai cognomine dicunt,   530
terra antiqua, potens armis atque ubere glaebae;
Oenotri coluere viri; nunc fama minores
Italiam dixisse ducis de nomine gentem.
Hic cursus fuit,
cum subito adsurgens fluctu nimbosus Orion   535
in vada caeca tulit penitusque procacibus Austris
perque undas superante salo perque invia saxa
dispulit; huc pauci vestris adnavimus oris.
Quod genus hoc hominum? Quaeve hunc tam barbara morem
permittit patria? Hospitio prohibemur harenae;   540

bella cient primaque vetant consistere terra.
Si genus humanum et mortalia temnitis arma,
at sperate deos memores fandi atque nefandi.
Rex erat Aeneas nobis, quo iustior alter
nec pietate fuit, nec bello maior et armis.   545
Quem si fata virum servant, si vescitur aura
aetheria neque adhuc crudelibus occubat umbris,
non metus, officio nec te certasse priorem
paeniteat. Sunt et Siculis regionibus urbes
armaque Troianoque a sanguine clarus Acestes.   550
Quassatam ventis liceat subducere classem
et silvis aptare trabes et stringere remos,
si datur Italiam sociis et rege recepto
tendere, ut Italiam laeti Latiumque petamus;
sin absumpta salus, et te, pater optime Teucrum,   555
pontus habet Libyae nec spes iam restat Iuli,
at freta Sicaniae saltem sedesque paratas,
unde huc advecti, regemque petamus Acesten."
Talibus Ilioneus; cuncti simul ore fremebant
Dardanidae.   560
     Tum breviter Dido vultum demissa profatur:
"Solvite corde metum, Teucri, secludite curas.
Res dura et regni novitas me talia cogunt
moliri et late fines custode tueri.
Quis genus Aeneadum, quis Troiae nesciat urbem,   565
virtutesque virosque aut tanti incendia belli?
Non obtunsa adeo gestamus pectora Poeni,
nec tam aversus equos Tyria Sol iungit ab urbe.
Seu vos Hesperiam magnam Saturniaque arva
sive Erycis fines regemque optatis Acesten,   570
auxilio tutos dimittam opibusque iuvabo.
Vultis et his mecum pariter considere regnis?
Urbem quam statuo, vestra est; subducite naves;
Tros Tyriusque mihi nullo discrimine agetur.
Atque utinam rex ipse Noto compulsus eodem   575
adforet Aeneas! Equidem per litora certos
dimittam et Libyae lustrare extrema iubebo,
si quibus eiectus silvis aut urbibus errat."   578

CHAPTER 5

[Double quotes are used for direct quotations within the book 2 selections. Although, because book 2 is Aeneas' narration of his journey to Dido and her audience, these direct quotations are quotes-within-a-quote, which would conventionally be punctuated with single quotes, this excess of quotation marks, double and single, seems unnecessary because the AP® Latin selection does not include the entirety of book 2.]

BOOK 2.40–56

Primus ibi ante omnes magna comitante caterva	40
Laocoon ardens summa decurrit ab arce,	
et procul, "O miseri, quae tanta insania, cives?	
Creditis avectos hostes? Aut ulla putatis	
dona carere dolis Danaum? Sic notus Ulixes?	
Aut hoc inclusi ligno occultantur Achivi,	45
aut haec in nostros fabricata est machina muros,	
inspectura domos venturaque desuper urbi,	
aut aliquis latet error; equo ne credite, Teucri.	
Quidquid id est, timeo Danaos et dona ferentes."	
Sic fatus validis ingentem viribus hastam	50
in latus inque feri curvam compagibus alvum	
contorsit. Stetit illa tremens, uteroque recusso	
insonuere cavae gemitumque dedere cavernae.	
Et, si fata deum, si mens non laeva fuisset,	
impulerat ferro Argolicas foedare latebras,	55
Troiaque nunc staret, Priamique arx alta maneres.	

BOOK 2.201–49

Laocoon, ductus Neptuno sorte sacerdos,	201
sollemnes taurum ingentem mactabat ad aras.	
Ecce autem gemini a Tenedo tranquilla per alta	
(horresco referens) immensis orbibus angues	
incumbunt pelago pariterque ad litora tendunt;	205
pectora quorum inter fluctus arrecta iubaeque	
sanguineae superant undas, pars cetera pontum	
pone legit sinuatque immensa volumine terga.	
Fit sonitus spumante salo; iamque arva tenebant	
ardentesque oculos suffecti sanguine et igni	210
sibila lambebant linguis vibrantibus ora.	
Diffugimus visu exsangues. Illi agmine certo	
Laocoonta petunt; et primum parva duorum	
corpora natorum serpens amplexus uterque	
implicat et miseros morsu depascitur artus;	215
post ipsum auxilio subeuntem ac tela ferentem	

corripiunt spirisque ligant ingentibus; et iam
bis medium amplexi, bis collo squamea circum
terga dati, superant capite et cervicibus altis.
Ille simul manibus tendit divellere nodos   220
perfusus sanie vittas atroque veneno,
clamores simul horrendos ad sidera tollit:
quales mugitus, fugit cum saucius aram
taurus et incertam excussit cervice securim.
At gemini lapsu delubra ad summa dracones   225
effugiunt saevaeque petunt Tritonidis arcem,
sub pedibusque deae clipeique sub orbe teguntur.
Tum vero tremefacta novus per pectora cunctis
insinuat pavor, et scelus expendisse merentem
Laocoonta ferunt, sacrum qui cuspide robur   230
laeserit et tergo sceleratam intorserit hastam.
Ducendum ad sedes simulacrum orandaque divae
numina conclamant.
Dividimus muros et moenia pandimus urbis.
Accingunt omnes operi pedibusque rotarum   235
subiciunt lapsus, et stuppea vincula collo
intendunt; scandit fatalis machina muros
feta armis. Pueri circum innuptaeque puellae
sacra canunt funemque manu contingere gaudent;
illa subit mediaeque minans inlabitur urbi.   240
O patria, o divum domus Ilium et incluta bello
moenia Dardanidum! Quater ipso in limine portae
substitit atque utero sonitum quater arma dedere;
instamus tamen immemores caecique furore
et monstrum infelix sacrata sistimus arce.   245
Tunc etiam fatis aperit Cassandra futuris
ora, dei iussu non umquam credita Teucris.
Nos delubra deum miseri, quibus ultimus esset
ille dies, festa velamus fronde per urbem.   249

BOOK 2.268-97

Tempus erat quo prima quies mortalibus aegris   268
incipit et dono divum gratissima serpit.
In somnis, ecce, ante oculos maestissimus Hector   270
visus adesse mihi largosque effundere fletus,
raptatus bigis ut quondam, aterque cruento
pulvere perque pedes traiectus lora tumentes.
Ei mihi, qualis erat, quantum mutatus ab illo
Hectore qui redit exuvias indutus Achilli   275

CHAPTER 5

vel Danaum Phrygios iaculatus puppibus ignes!
Squalentem barbam et concretos sanguine crines
vulneraque illa gerens, quae circum plurima muros
accepit patrios. Ultro flens ipse videbar
compellare virum et maestas expromere voces: 280
"O lux Dardaniae, spes o fidissima Teucrum,
quae tantae tenuere morae? Quibus Hector ab oris
exspectate venis? Ut te post multa tuorum
funera, post varios hominumque urbisque labores
defessi aspicimus! Quae causa indigna serenos   285
foedavit vultus? Aut cur haec vulnera cerno?"
Ille nihil, nec me quaerentem vana moratur,
sed graviter gemitus imo de pectore ducens,
"Heu fuge, nate dea, teque his," ait, "eripe flammis.
Hostis habet muros; ruit alto a culmine Troia.   290
Sat patriae Priamoque datum: si Pergama dextra
defendi possent, etiam hac defensa fuissent.
Sacra suosque tibi commendat Troia penates;
hos cape fatorum comites, his moenia quaere
magna pererrato statues quae denique ponto."   295
Sic ait et manibus vittas Vestamque potentem
aeternumque adytis effert penetralibus ignem.   297

BOOK 2.559–620

At me tum primum saevus circumstetit horror.
Obstipui; subiit cari genitoris imago,   560
ut regem aequaevum crudeli vulnere vidi
vitam exhalantem; subiit deserta Creusa
et direpta domus et parvi casus Iuli.
Respicio et quae sit me circum copia lustro.
Deseruere omnes defessi, et corpora saltu   565
ad terram misere aut ignibus aegra dedere.
        Iamque adeo super unus eram, cum limina Vestae
servantem et tacitam secreta in sede latentem
Tyndarida aspicio; dant claram[44] incendia lucem
erranti passimque oculos per cuncta ferenti.   570
Illa sibi infestos eversa ob Pergama Teucros
et Danaum poenam et deserti coniugis iras
praemetuens, Troiae et patriae communis Erinys,
abdiderat sese atque aris invisa sedebat.
Exarsere ignes animo; subit ira cadentem   575

---

44. Some texts read *clara* here.

ulcisci patriam et sceleratas sumere poenas.
"Scilicet haec Spartam incolumis patriasque Mycenas
aspiciet, partoque ibit regina triumpho?
Coniugiumque domumque patres natosque videbit
Iliadum turba et Phrygiis comitata ministris?   580
Occiderit ferro Priamus? Troia arserit igni?
Dardanium totiens sudarit sanguine litus?
Non ita. Namque etsi nullum memorabile nomen
feminea in poena est, habet haec[45] victoria laudem;
exstinxisse nefas tamen et sumpsisse merentes   585
laudabor poenas, animumque explesse iuvabit
ultricis flammae et cineres satiasse meorum."
Talia iactabam et furiata mente ferebar,
cum mihi se, non ante oculis tam clara, videndam
obtulit et pura per noctem in luce refulsit   590
alma parens, confessa deam qualisque videri
caelicolis et quanta solet, dextraque prehensum
continuit roseoque haec insuper addidit ore:
          "Nate, quis indomitas tantus dolor excitat iras?
Quid furis? Aut quonam nostri tibi cura recessit?   595
Non prius aspicies ubi fessum aetate parentem
liqueris Anchisen, superet coniunxne Creusa
Ascaniusque puer? Quos omnes undique Graiae
circum errant acies et, ni mea cura resistat,
iam flammae tulerint inimicus et hauserit ensis.   600
Non tibi Tyndaridis facies invisa Lacaenae
culpatusve Paris, divum inclementia, divum
has evertit opes sternitque a culmine Troiam.
Aspice (namque omnem, quae nunc obducta tuenti
mortales hebetat visus tibi et umida circum   605
caligat, nubem eripiam; tu ne qua parentis
iussa time neu praeceptis parere recusa):
hic, ubi disiectas moles avulsaque saxis
saxa vides, mixtoque undantem pulvere fumum,
Neptunus muros magnoque emota tridenti   610
fundamenta quatit totamque a sedibus urbem
eruit. Hic Iuno Scaeas saevissima portas
prima tenet sociumque furens a navibus agmen,
ferro accincta, vocat.
Iam summas arces Tritonia, respice, Pallas   615
insedit nimbo effulgens et Gorgone saeva.
Ipse pater Danais animos viresque secundas

---

45. Some texts read *nec habet* here rather than *habet haec.*

sufficit, ipse deos in Dardana suscitat arma.
Eripe, nate, fugam finemque impone labori;
nusquam abero et tutum patrio te limine sistam."   620

BOOK 4.160–218

Interea magno misceri murmure caelum   160
incipit, insequitur commixta grandine nimbus,
et Tyrii comites passim et Troiana iuventus
Dardaniusque nepos Veneris diversa per agros
tecta metu petiere; ruunt de montibus amnes.
Speluncam Dido dux et Troianus eandem   165
deveniunt. Prima et Tellus et pronuba Iuno
dant signum; fulsere ignes et conscius aether
conubiis summoque ululararunt vertice Nymphae.
Ille dies primus leti primusque malorum
causa fuit; neque enim specie famave movetur   170
nec iam furtivum Dido meditatur amorem:
coniugium vocat, hoc praetexit nomine culpam.
    Extemplo Libyae magnas it Fama per urbes,
Fama, malum qua non aliud velocius ullum:
mobilitate viget viresque adquirit eundo,   175
parva metu primo, mox sese attollit in auras
ingrediturque solo et caput inter nubila condit.
Illam Terra parens ira inritata deorum
extremam, ut perhibent, Coeo Enceladoque sororem
progenuit pedibus celerem et pernicibus alis,   180
monstrum horrendum, ingens, cui quot sunt corpore plumae,
tot vigiles oculi subter (mirabile dictu),
tot linguae, totidem ora sonant, tot subrigit aures.
Nocte volat caeli medio terraeque, per umbram
stridens, nec dulci declinat lumina somno;   185
luce sedet custos aut summi culmine tecti
turribus aut altis, et magnas territat urbes,
tam ficti pravique tenax quam nuntia veri.
Haec tum multiplici populos sermone replebat
gaudens, et pariter facta atque infecta canebat: 190
venisse Aenean Troiano sanguine cretum,
cui se pulchra viro dignetur iungere Dido;
nunc hiemem inter se luxu, quam longa, fovere
regnorum immemores turpique cupidine captos.
Haec passim dea foeda virum diffundit in ora.   195
Protinus ad regem cursus detorquet Iarban
incenditque animum dictis atque aggerat iras.

Hic Hammone satus rapta Garamantide nympha,
templa Iovi centum latis immania regnis,
centum aras posuit vigilemque sacraverat ignem,   200
excubias divum aeternas, pecudumque cruore
pingue solum et variis florentia limina sertis.
Isque amens animi et rumore accensus amaro
dicitur ante aras media inter numina divum
multa Iovem manibus supplex orasse supinis: 205
"Iuppiter omnipotens, cui nunc Maurusia pictis
gens epulata toris Lenaeum libat honorem,
aspicis haec? An te, genitor, cum fulmina torques
nequiquam horremus, caecique in nubibus ignes
terrificant animos et inania murmura miscent?   210
Femina, quae, nostris errans in finibus, urbem
exiguam pretio posuit, cui litus arandum
cuique loci leges dedimus, conubia nostra
reppulit ac dominum Aenean in regna recepit.
Et nunc ille Paris cum semiviro comitatu,   215
Maeonia mentum mitra crinemque madentem
subnexus, rapto potitur: nos munera templis
quippe tuis ferimus famamque fovemus inanem."   218

BOOK 4.259–361

Ut primum alatis tetigit magalia plantis,
Aenean fundantem arces ac tecta novantem   260
conspicit. Atque illi stellatus iaspide fulva
ensis erat Tyrioque ardebat murice laena
demissa ex umeris, dives quae munera Dido
fecerat, et tenui telas discreverat auro.
Continuo invadit: "Tu nunc Karthaginis altae   265
fundamenta locas pulchramque uxorius urbem
exstruis? Heu, regni rerumque oblite tuarum!
Ipse deum tibi me claro demittit Olympo
regnator, caelum et terras qui numine torquet,
ipse haec ferre iubet celeres mandata per auras: 270
quid struis? Aut qua spe Libycis teris otia terris?
Si te nulla movet tantarum gloria rerum
[nec super ipse tua moliris laude laborem,][46]
Ascanium surgentem et spes heredis Iuli
respice, cui regnum Italiae Romanaque tellus   275
debetur." Tali Cyllenius ore locutus,

---

46. This line is considered spurious because it is not included in the most important Vergil manuscripts, but it is more often than not included, usually bracketed to indicate its uncertainty, in textbooks, so it is included here.

mortales visus medio sermone reliquit
et procul in tenuem ex oculis evanuit auram.
      At vero Aeneas aspectu obmutuit amens,
arrectaeque horrore comae et vox faucibus haesit.   280
Ardet abire fuga dulcesque relinquere terras,
attonitus tanto monitu imperioque deorum.
Heu quid agat? Quo nunc reginam ambire furentem
audeat adfatu? Quae prima exordia sumat?
Atque animum nunc huc celerem nunc dividit illuc   285
in partesque rapit varias perque omnia versat.
Haec alternanti potior sententia visa est:
Mnesthea Sergestumque vocat fortemque Serestum,
classem aptent taciti sociosque ad litora cogant,
arma parent et quae rebus sit causa novandis   290
dissimulent; sese interea, quando optima Dido
nesciat et tantos rumpi non speret amores,
temptaturum aditus et quae mollissima fandi
tempora, quis rebus dexter modus. Ocius omnes
imperio laeti parent et iussa facessunt.   295
      At regina dolos (quis fallere possit amantem?)
praesensit, motusque excepit prima futuros,
omnia tuta timens. Eadem impia Fama furenti
detulit armari classem cursumque parari.
Saevit inops animi totamque incensa per urbem   300
bacchatur, qualis commotis excita sacris
Thyias, ubi audito stimulant trieterica Baccho
orgia nocturnusque vocat clamore Cithaeron.
      Tandem his Aenean compellat vocibus ultro:
"Dissimulare etiam sperasti, perfide, tantum   305
posse nefas tacitusque mea decedere terra?
Nec te noster amor nec te data dextera quondam
nec moritura tenet crudeli funere Dido?
Quin etiam hiberno moliri sidere classem
et mediis properas Aquilonibus ire per altum,   310
crudelis? Quid, si non arva aliena domosque
ignotas peteres, et Troia antiqua maneret,
Troia per undosum peteretur classibus aequor?
Mene fugis? Per ego has lacrimas dextramque tuam te
(quando aliud mihi iam miserae nihil ipsa reliqui),   315
per conubia nostra, per inceptos hymenaeos,
si bene quid de te merui, fuit aut tibi quicquam
dulce meum, miserere domus labentis et istam,
oro, si quis adhuc precibus locus, exue mentem.
Te propter Libycae gentes Nomadumque tyranni   320

odere, infensi Tyrii; te propter eundem
exstinctus pudor et, qua sola sidera adibam,
fama prior. Cui me moribundam deseris, hospes
(hoc solum nomen quoniam de coniuge restat)?
Quid moror? An mea Pygmalion dum moenia frater 325
destruat aut captam ducat Gaetulus Iarbas?
Saltem si qua mihi de te suscepta fuisset
ante fugam suboles, si quis mihi parvulus aula
luderet Aeneas, qui te tamen ore referret,
non equidem omnino capta ac deserta viderer." 330
      Dixerat. Ille Iovis monitis immota tenebat
lumina et obnixus curam sub corde premebat.
Tandem pauca refert: "Ego te, quae plurima fando
enumerare vales, numquam, regina, negabo
promeritam, nec me meminisse pigebit Elissae 335
dum memor ipse mei, dum spiritus hos regit artus.
Pro re pauca loquar. Neque ego hanc abscondere furto
speravi (ne finge) fugam, nec coniugis umquam
praetendi taedas aut haec in foedera veni.
Me si fata meis paterentur ducere vitam 340
auspiciis et sponte mea componere curas,
urbem Troianam primum dulcesque meorum
reliquias colerem, Priami tecta alta manerent,
et recidiva manu posuissem Pergama victis.
Sed nunc Italiam magnam Gryneus Apollo, 345
Italiam Lyciae iussere capessere sortes;
hic amor, haec patria est. Si te Karthaginis arces
Phoenissam Libycaeque aspectus detinet urbis,
quae tandem Ausonia Teucros considere terra
invidia est? Et nos fas extera quaerere regna. 350
Me patris Anchisae, quotiens umentibus umbris
nox operit terras, quotiens astra ignea surgunt,
admonet in somnis et turbida terret imago;
me puer Ascanius capitisque iniuria cari,
quem regno Hesperiae fraudo et fatalibus arvis. 355
Nunc etiam interpres divum Iove, missus ab ipso
(testor utrumque caput), celeres mandata per auras
detulit: ipse deum manifesto in lumine vidi
intrantem muros vocemque his auribus hausi.
Desine meque tuis incendere teque querelis; 360
Italiam non sponte sequor."

CHAPTER 5

BOOK 4.659–705

Dixit, et os impressa toro, "Moriemur inultae,
sed moriamur," ait. "Sic, sic iuvat ire sub umbras.   660
Hauriat hunc oculis ignem crudelis ab alto
Dardanus, et nostrae secum ferat omina mortis."
Dixerat, atque illam media inter talia ferro
conlapsam aspiciunt comites, ensemque cruore
spumantem sparsasque manus. It clamor ad alta   665
atria: concussam bacchatur Fama per urbem.
Lamentis gemituque et femineo ululatu
tecta fremunt, resonat magnis plangoribus aether,
non aliter quam si immissis ruat hostibus omnis
Karthago aut antiqua Tyros, flammaeque furentes   670
culmina perque hominum volvantur perque deorum.
Audiit, exanimis trepidoque exterrita cursu
unguibus ora soror foedans et pectora pugnis
per medios ruit, ac morientem nomine clamat:
"Hoc illud, germana, fuit? Me fraude petebas?   675
Hoc rogus iste mihi, hoc ignes araeque parabant?
Quid primum deserta querar? Comitemne sororem
sprevisti moriens? Eadem me ad fata vocasses,
idem ambas ferro dolor atque eadem hora tulisset.
His etiam struxi manibus patriosque vocavi   680
voce deos, sic te ut posita, crudelis, abessem?
Exstinxti te meque, soror, populumque patresque
Sidonios urbemque tuam. Date, vulnera lymphis
abluam et, extremus si quis super halitus errat,
ore legam." Sic fata gradus evaserat altos,   685
semianimemque sinu germanam amplexa fovebat
cum gemitu atque atros siccabat veste cruores.
Illa, graves oculos conata attollere, rursus
deficit; infixum stridit sub pectore vulnus.
Ter sese attollens cubitoque adnixa levavit,   690
ter revoluta toro est oculisque errantibus alto
quaesivit caelo lucem ingemuitque reperta.

Tum Iuno omnipotens, longum miserata dolorem
difficilesque obitus, Irim demisit Olympo
quae luctantem animam nexosque resolveret artus.   695
Nam quia nec fato merita nec morte peribat,
sed misera ante diem subitoque accensa furore,
nondum illi flavum Proserpina vertice crinem

abstulerat Stygioque caput damnaverat Orco.
Ergo Iris croceis per caelum roscida pennis,   700
mille trahens varios adverso sole colores,
devolat et supra caput astitit. "Hunc ego Diti
sacrum iussa fero teque isto corpore solvo."
Sic ait et dextra crinem secat, omnis et una
dilapsus calor atque in ventos vita recessit.   705

BOOK 6.295–332

Hinc via Tartarei quae fert Acherontis ad undas.   295
Turbidus hic caeno vastaque voragine gurges
aestuat atque omnem Cocyto eructat harenam.
Portitor has horrendus aquas et flumina servat
terribili squalore Charon, cui plurima mento
canities inculta iacet, stant lumina flamma,   300
sordidus ex umeris nodo dependet amictus.
Ipse ratem conto subigit velisque ministrat
et ferruginea subvectat corpora cumba,
iam senior, sed cruda deo viridisque senectus.
Huc omnis turba ad ripas effusa ruebat,   305
matres atque viri defunctaque corpora vita
magnanimum heroum, pueri innuptaeque puellae,
impositique rogis iuvenes ante ora parentum:
quam multa in silvis autumni frigore primo
lapsa cadunt folia, aut ad terram gurgite ab alto   310
quam multae glomerantur aves, ubi frigidus annus
trans pontum fugat et terris immittit apricis.
Stabant orantes primi transmittere cursum
tendebantque manus ripae ulterioris amore.
Navita sed tristis nunc hos nunc accipit illos,   315
ast alios longe summotos arcet harena.
Aeneas miratus enim motusque tumultu,
"Dic," ait, "o virgo, quid vult concursus ad amnem?
Quidve petunt animae? Vel quo discrimine ripas
hae linquunt, illae remis vada livida verrunt?"   320
Olli sic breviter fata est longaeva sacerdos:
"Anchisa generate, deum certissima proles,
Cocyti stagna alta vides Stygiamque paludem,
di cuius iurare timent et fallere numen.
Haec omnis, quam cernis, inops inhumataque turba est;   325
portitor ille Charon; hi, quos vehit unda, sepulti.
Nec ripas datur horrendas et rauca fluenta

CHAPTER 5

transportare prius quam sedibus ossa quierunt.
Centum errant annos volitantque haec litora circum;
tum demum admissi stagna exoptata revisunt."   330
Constitit Anchisa satus et vestigia pressit
multa putans sortemque animo miseratus iniquam.

BOOK 6.384–425

Ergo iter inceptum peragunt fluvioque propinquant.
Navita quos iam inde ut Stygia prospexit ab unda   385
per tacitum nemus ire pedemque advertere ripae,
sic prior adgreditur dictis atque increpat ultro:
"Quisquis es, armatus qui nostra ad flumina tendis,
fare age, quid venias, iam istinc et comprime gressum.
Umbrarum hic locus est, somni noctisque soporae: 390
corpora viva nefas Stygia vectare carina.
Nec vero Alciden me sum laetatus euntem
accepisse lacu, nec Thesea Pirithoumque,
dis quamquam geniti atque invicti viribus essent.
Tartareum ille manu custodem in vincla petivit   395
ipsius a solio regis traxitque trementem;
hi dominam Ditis thalamo deducere adorti."
Quae contra breviter fata est Amphrysia vates:
"Nullae hic insidiae tales (absiste moveri),
nec vim tela ferunt; licet ingens ianitor antro   400
aeternum latrans exsangues terreat umbras,
casta licet patrui servet Proserpina limen.
Troius Aeneas, pietate insignis et armis,
ad genitorem imas Erebi descendit ad umbras.
Si te nulla movet tantae pietatis imago,   405
at ramum hunc" (aperit ramum qui veste latebat)
"agnoscas." Tumida ex ira tum corda residunt;
nec plura his. Ille admirans venerabile donum
fatalis virgae longo post tempore visum
caeruleam advertit puppim ripaeque propinquat.   410
Inde alias animas, quae per iuga longa sedebant,
deturbat laxatque foros; simul accipit alveo
ingentem Aenean. Gemuit sub pondere cumba
sutilis et multam accepit rimosa paludem.
Tandem trans fluvium incolumes vatemque virumque   415
informi limo glaucaque exponit in ulva.
        Cerberus haec ingens latratu regna trifauci
personat adverso recubans immanis in antro.
Cui vates horrere videns iam colla colubris

melle soporatam et medicatis frugibus offam   420
obicit. Ille fame rabida tria guttura pandens
corripit obiectam, atque immania terga resolvit
fusus humi totoque ingens extenditur antro.
Occupat Aeneas aditum custode sepulto
evaditque celer ripam inremeabilis undae.   425

BOOK 6.450–76

Inter quas Phoenissa recens a vulnere Dido   450
errabat silva in magna; quam Troius heros
ut primum iuxta stetit agnovitque per umbras
obscuram, qualem primo qui surgere mense
aut videt aut vidisse putat per nubila lunam,
demisit lacrimas dulcique adfatus amore est: 455
"Infelix Dido, verus mihi nuntius ergo
venerat exstinctam ferroque extrema secutam?
Funeris heu tibi causa fui? Per sidera iuro,
per superos et si qua fides tellure sub ima est,
invitus, regina, tuo de litore cessi.   460
Sed me iussa deum, quae nunc has ire per umbras,
per loca senta situ cogunt noctemque profundam,
imperiis egere suis; nec credere quivi
hunc tantum tibi me discessu ferre dolorem.
Siste gradum teque aspectu ne subtrahe nostro.   465
Quem fugis? Extremum fato quod te adloquor hoc est."
Talibus Aeneas ardentem et torva tuentem
lenibat dictis animum lacrimasque ciebat.
Illa solo fixos oculos aversa tenebat
nec magis incepto vultum sermone movetur   470
quam si dura silex aut stet Marpesia cautes.
Tandem corripuit sese atque inimica refugit
in nemus umbriferum, coniunx ubi pristinus illi
respondet curis aequatque Sychaeus amorem.
Nec minus Aeneas casu percussus[47] iniquo   475
prosequitur lacrimis longe et miseratur euntem.

BOOK 6.847–99

"Excudent alii spirantia mollius aera   847
(credo equidem), vivos ducent de marmore vultus,
orabunt causas melius, caelique meatus
describent radio et surgentia sidera dicent: 850

---

47. Some texts read *concussus* here.

CHAPTER 5

tu regere imperio populos, Romane, memento
(hae tibi erunt artes), pacique[48] imponere morem,
parcere subiectis et debellare superbos."
        Sic pater Anchises, atque haec mirantibus addit:
"Aspice, ut insignis spoliis Marcellus opimis   855
ingreditur victorque viros supereminet omnes.
Hic rem Romanam, magno turbante tumultu,
sistet eques, sternet Poenos Gallumque rebellem,
tertiaque arma patri suspendet capta Quirino."
Atque hic Aeneas (una namque ire videbat   860
egregium forma iuvenem et fulgentibus armis,
sed frons laeta parum et deiecto lumina vultu):
"Quis, pater, ille, virum qui sic comitatur euntem?
Filius, anne aliquis magna de stirpe nepotum?
Qui strepitus circa comitum! Quantum instar in ipso!   865
Sed nox atra caput tristi circumvolat umbra."
Tum pater Anchises lacrimis ingressus obortis:
"O gnate, ingentem luctum ne quaere tuorum;
ostendent terris hunc tantum fata nec ultra
esse sinent. Nimium vobis Romana propago   870
visa potens, superi, propria haec si dona fuissent.
Quantos ille virum magnam Mavortis ad urbem
campus aget gemitus! Vel quae, Tiberine, videbis
funera, cum tumulum praeterlabere recentem!
Nec puer Iliaca quisquam de gente Latinos   875
in tantum spe tollet avos, nec Romula quondam
ullo se tantum tellus iactabit alumno.
Heu pietas, heu prisca fides invictaque bello
dextera! Non illi se quisquam impune tulisset
obvius armato, seu cum pedes iret in hostem   880
seu spumantis equi foderet calcaribus armos.
Heu, miserande puer, si qua fata aspera rumpas,
tu Marcellus eris. Manibus date lilia plenis
purpureos spargam flores animamque nepotis
his saltem accumulem donis et fungar inani   885
munere." Sic tota passim regione vagantur
aëris in campis latis atque omnia lustrant.
Quae postquam Anchises natum per singula duxit
incenditque animum famae venientis amore,
exim bella viro memorat quae deinde gerenda,   890
Laurentesque docet populos urbemque Latini,
et quo quemque modo fugiatque feratque laborem.

---

48. Some texts read *pacisque* here.

    Sunt geminae Somni portae, quarum altera fertur
cornea, qua veris facilis datur exitus umbris,
altera candenti perfecta nitens elephanto,   895
sed falsa ad caelum mittunt insomnia Manes.
His ibi tum natum Anchises unaque Sibyllam
prosequitur dictis portaque emittit eburna.
Ille viam secat ad naves sociosque revisit.   899

CHAPTER 5

Chapter 6

VOCABULARY

INTRODUCTION

- One of the most difficult aspects of the AP® Exam is mastering the sheer number of vocabulary words that the syllabus includes.

- To that end, vocabulary frequency lists for Caesar and Vergil are included.

- Separate lists for each author are included for both organizational reasons and in case you know one author better or you were not able to complete the syllabus in class.

- You should use the lists as a checklist.

- Begin with the most frequent words and make sure you know them.

- Move down the lists as far as you can, mastering the words as you go.

- The lists do not include definitions.

- It is assumed that you will know the definition, will be aided by looking up the definition, or definitions will be too limited in scope for the variety of meanings of words to be included.

- Principal parts will be included except for regular 1st conjugation verbs; these verbs will be listed as *-ō, -āre* with their 3rd and 4th principal parts being *-āvī, -ātus*.

- Verbs with unattested (missing) principal parts will be indicated by a dash (-), except for the three standard principal parts of deponents.

- Parts of speech will be identified for forms that could otherwise be confusing—for example, two-termination 3rd declension adjectives.

- Macrons are included, if it is helpful to know naturally long syllables that might exist.

- Some difficulty in compiling frequency lists occurs with overlapping or derivative forms; for example, is *immōtus* included as a form of the verb *immōveō, -ēre* or as its own adjectival form?

- There is no right answer to these choices; I have in most cases let the dictionary be my guide; that is, if a word is included separately there (as *immōtus* is), then it is included separately here and vice versa.

- The primary exceptions to this approach are words which are more common to Latin students in their derivative form than their original form; for example, *serpens, -ntis* is a substantive participle of *serpō, -ere*, but students are more likely to know the noun *serpens, -ntis* than the verb *serpō, -ere. Potens, -ntis* as a form of *possum* works similarly.

- Negative forms will be treated similarly; that is, less common negated versions of more common positive words: *impius, -a, -um* is the negative of the much more common *pius, -a, -um*; these words are listed separately.

- And finally a note on vocabulary in general.

  o Memorizing definitions out of context can be dangerous.

  o You want to avoid knowing a definition alone without a specific context.

  o Avoid using online dictionaries or glossaries to look up words unless those sites are specific to the text that you are reading (and, even then, make sure it is its own glossary and does not link to an external, more general, glossary).

  o Use the glossary or vocabulary lists in your textbook whenever possible; these definitions are tailored to the context of the texts and so will be more helpful, rather than an online dictionary which will give a broader definition.

  o The goal with vocabulary is to have a sense of the range of meanings of a word that you can apply flexibly to different contexts.

  o Ideally, know words in each of the contexts in which they appear in the texts.

List of abbreviations used:

abbrev	abbreviated	impers	impersonal
abl	ablative	indef	indefinitie
acc	accusative	inter	interrogative
adj	adjective	m	masculine
adv	adverb	n	neuter
comp	comparative	pers	personal
conj	conjunction	pl	plural
demon	demonstrative adjective / pronoun	prep	preposition
		pron	pronoun
dep	deponent	refl	reflexive
encl	enclitic	rel	relative
f	feminine	semidep	semideponent

LIST OF EASILY CONFUSED VOCABULARY WORDS

- These words either have nominatives that are easily confused with other cases or are words that are easily confused with similar words.

- In some examples, only one of the easily confused words appears in the syllabus (e.g., only *audeo, -ere* appears), but it is included to highlight the potential confusion.

  ✓ **audeo, -ere**, to dare, vs. **audio, -ire**, to hear

  o Nam plebes paene servorum habetur loco, quae nihil **audet** per se, nullo adhibetur consilio. (*audeo, -ere*: *Bellum Gallicum* 6.13)

  o Multis in civitatibus harum rerum exstructos tumulos locis consecratis conspicari licet, neque saepe accidit ut neglecta quispiam religione aut capta apud se occultare aut posita tollere **auderet**, gravissimumque ei rei supplicium cum cruciatu constitutum est. (*audeo, -ere*: *Bellum Gallicum* 6.17)

  o Iam caelum terramque meo sine numine, venti, / miscere et tantas **audetis** tollere moles? (*audeo, -ere*: *Aeneid* 1.133–34)

  o Quo nunc reginam ambire furentem / **audeat** adfatu? (*audeo, -ere*: *Aeneid* 4.283–84)

  ✓ **custos**, custodis: the nominative singular looks like an accusative plural

  o luce sedet **custos** aut summi culmine tecti / turribus aut altis (*Aeneid* 4.186–87)

  ✓ **imago**, imaginis: the nominative singular looks like a dative or ablative singular (or a 1ˢᵗ person present indicative verb)

  o subiit cari genitoris **imago** (*Aeneid* 2.560)

  o Me patris Anchisae, quotiens umentibus umbris / nox operit terras, quotiens astra ignea surgunt, / admonet in somnis et turbida terret **imago**; (*Aeneid* 4.351–53)

  o "Si te nulla movet tantae pietatis **imago**, / at ramum hunc" (aperit ramum qui veste latebat) / "agnoscas." (*Aeneid* 6.405–7)

  ✓ **metuo, -ere**, to fear, vs. **meto, -ere**, to reap or to harvest

  o depositis armis in **metendo** occupatos subito adorti (*meto, -ere*: *Bellum Gallicum* 4.32)

  o id **metuens** veterisque memor Saturnia belli (*metuo, -ere*: *Aeneid* 1.23)

  ✓ **omina**, nominative and accusative plural of omen, ominis vs. **omnia**, nominative and accusative plural of omnis, -e, 3ʳᵈ declension adjective

  o Hauriat hunc oculis ignem crudelis ab alto / Dardanus, et nostrae secum ferat **omina** mortis. (*omen, ominis*: *Aeneid* 4.661–62)

  o Sic tota passim regione vagantur / aëris in campis latis atque **omnia** lustrant. (*omnis, -e*: *Aeneid* 6.886–87)

✓ **pareo, -ere**, to obey, vs. **paro, -are**, to prepare

- o Huc omnes undique qui controversias habent conveniunt eorumque decretis iudiciis- que **parent**. (pareo, -ere: *Bellum Gallicum* 6.13)

- o Tum Cererem corruptam undis Cerealiaque arma / expediunt fessi rerum, frugesque receptas / et torrere **parant** flammis et frangere saxo. (paro, -are: *Aeneid* 1.177–79)

- o tu ne qua parentis / iussa time neu praeceptis **parere** recusa (pareo, ere: *Aeneid* 2.606–7)

- o Mnesthea Sergestumque vocat fortemque Serestum, / classem aptent taciti sociosque ad litora cogant, / arma **parent** (*Aeneid* 4.288–90)

  - ▪ *Parent* here is the subjunctive of *paro, -are*, though it looks exactly like the indicative of *pareo, -ere*.

- o Ocius omnes / imperio laeti **parent** et iussa facessunt. (pareo, -ere: *Aeneid* 4.294–95)

✓ **sacerdos**, sacerdotis: the nominative singular looks like an accusative plural

- o Laocoon, ductus Neptuno sorte **sacerdos**, / sollemnes taurum ingentem mactabat ad aras. (*Aeneid* 2.201–2)

- o Olli sic breviter fata est longaeva **sacerdos**: (*Aeneid* 6.321)

✓ **tero, -ere**, to wipe or to waste, vs. **terra, -ae**, land

- o Aut qua spe Libycis **teris** otia **terris**? (*Aeneid* 4.271)

DEALING WITH PROPER NAMES

- Often, students forget that proper names are nouns like any other nouns: they are declined in all cases.

- This confusion most commonly occurs when two proper nouns are next to each other in different cases.

  - o Gallos ab **Aquitanis Garumna** flumen, a **Belgis Matrona** et Sequana dividit. (Caesar 1.1)

    - ▪ *Aquitanis* and *Belgis* are the ablative objects of *ab*; *Garumna* and *Matrona* are the nominative names of rivers.

  - o Ex quibus unam in Morinos ducendam G. Fabio legato dedit, alteram in **Nervios Q. Ciceroni**, tertiam in **Esubios L. Roscio** (*Bellum Gallicum* 5.24)

    - ▪ *Nervios* and *Eusebios* are the names of peoples and the accusative objects of *in*; *Q. Ciceroni* and *L. Roscio* are datives.

  - o **Crassum Samarobrivae** praeficit legionemque attribuit (*Bellum Gallicum* 5.47)

    - ▪ *Crassum* is the accusative direct object; *Samarobrivae* is the locative.

Bellum Gallicum **Frequency List**

225 times

quī, quae, quod (rel pron or adj; inter adj)

175 times

in (prep + abl or acc)

155 times

et (conj)

145 times

is, ea, id (demon)

144 times

sum, esse, fuī, futūrus

111 times

ad (prep + acc)

-que (encl conj added to end of word)

92 times

hic, haec, hoc (demon)

87 times

-, suī, sibi, sē, sē (refl pron)

81 times

a/ab (prep + abl)

79 times

cum (conj or prep + abl)

72 times

e/ex (prep + abl)

omnis, -e (adj)

64 times

rēs, reī

62 times

atque (conj)

56 times

ut / utī (conj)

55 times

suus, -a, -um

43 times

pars, -tis (f)

42 times

faciō, -ere, fēcī, factus

hostis, -is (m)

41 times

dē (prep + abl)

40 times

Caesar, -aris (m)

possum, posse, potuī, -

37 times

nōn (adv)

36 times

noster, -tra, -trum

33 times

diēs, diēī

32 times

aut (conj)

legiō, -ōnis (f)

31 times

locus, -ī (loca, -ōrum in pl)

magnus, -a, -um
sī (conj)

28 times

habeō, -ēre, habuī, habitus
reliquus, -a, -um
ūnus, -a, -um; adv ūnā = together

27 times

neque (conj)

26 times

hīberna, -ōrum (n pl)

24 times

ac (conj)

23 times

castra, -ōrum (n pl)
nāvis, -is (f)

22 times

ille, illa, illud (demon)

21 times

causa, -ae
consilium, -ī
maximus, -a, -um
mittō, -ere, mīsī, missus

20 times

cīvitas, -ātis (f)

19 times

dō, dare, dedī, datus

18 times

iubeō, -ēre, iussī, iussus
per (prep + acc)

17 times

dīcō, -ere, dīxī, dictus
fīnis, -is (m)
Gallia, -ae
ipse, ipsa, ipsum
iter, itineris (n)
prō (prep + abl)

16 times

Helvētius, -a, -um / Helvētiī, -ōrum
lēgātus, -ī

15 times

Ambiorīx, -īgis (m)
Gallus, -a, -um / Gallī, -ōrum
homo, -inis (m)
inter (adv and prep + acc)
multitūdo, -inis (f)
prīmus, -a, -um
proelium, -ī
Rōmānus, -a, -um
videō, -ēre, vīdī, vīsus

14 times

Cicero, -ōnis (m)
cognoscō, -ere, cognōvī, cognitus
īdem, eadem, idem (pron or adj)
imperium, -ī
interficiō, -ere, -fēcī, -fectus
nē (conj)
numerus, -ī
perīculum, -ī
tamen (adv)
volō, velle, voluī

13 times

accidō, -ere, accīdī, -
eques, -itis (m)
ita (adv)
sed (conj)

12 times

alter, altera, alterum

annus, -ī

cōgō, -ere, coēgī, coactus

copia, -ae

littera, -ae

Lūcius, -ī (abbrev: L.)

multus, -a, -um

paulātim / paulō / paulum (adv)

persuādeō, -ēre, -suāsī, -suāsus

proximus, -a, -um

quis, quid (inter pron)

tum (adv)

veniō, -īre, vēnī, ventus

11 times

cōgō, -ere, coēgī, coactus

constituō, -ere, -stituī, -stitūtus

proficiscor, -ī, -fectus

pūblicus, -a, -um

tempus, -oris (n)

vallum, -ī

virtūs, virtūtis (f)

10 times

accipiō, -ere, accēpī, acceptus

alius, -a, -ud

arbitror, -ārī, -ātus (dep)

arma, -ōrum (n pl)

capiō, -ere, cēpī, captus

contineō, -ēre, -tinuī, -tentus

conveniō, -īre, -vēnī, -ventus

Cotta, -ae (m)

facilis, -e (adj)

frūmentum, -ī

genus, -eris (n)

manus, -ūs

nihil / nihilo

nullus, -a, -um

ordo, -inis (m)

recipiō, -ere, -cēpī, -ceptus

salūs, -ūtis (f)

summus, -a, -um

tantus, -a, -um

9 times

aliquis, -quid / aliqui, aliquae, aliquod (once, qua after ne)

coepī, -isse (defec vb)

cohors, -rtis (f)

coniciō, -ere, coiēcī, coiectus

discēdō, -ere, -cessī, -cessus

exercitus, -ūs

existimō, -āre

flūmen, -inis (n)

Germānus, -a, -um / Germānī -ōrum

gravis, -e

longus, -a, -um

mille, milia

mors, mortis (f)

nam / namque

nox, noctis (f)

populus, -ī

pugnō, -āre

Rhēnus, -ī

sine (prep + abl)

superus, -a, -um

tēlum, -ī

ūtor, ūtī, ūsus (dep)

8 times

ager, -grī

certus, -a, -um

consuescō, -ere, -suevī, -suētus (often syncopated in the perfect, so the stem consu- plus endings, e.g., consuerunt)

dēferō, dēferre, -tulī, -lātus

duō, -ae, -ō (pl adj)

etiam (adv)

gerō, -ere, gessī, gestus

Nerviī, -ōrum (m pl)

perveniō, -īre, -vēnī, -ventus

regnum, -ī

sustineō, -ēre, -tinuī, -tentus

tertius, -a, -um

Titūrius, -ī

usus, -ūs

uterque, utraque, utrumque (adj)

victōria, -ae

7 times

adventus, -ūs

apud (prep + acc)

at (conj)

celer, -eris, -ere (adv: celeriter)

circiter (adv)

contrōversia, -ae

dūcō, -ere, dūxī, ductus

ferē (adv)

ferō, ferre, tulī, lātus

fortis, -e (adj)

imperō, -āre

inferō, inferre, intulī, illātus

minor, minus (comp adj)

mūnītiō, -ōnis (f)

passus, -ūs

pertineō, -ēre, -uī, -

petō, -ere, -īvī, -ītus

plērusque, -raque, -rumque (adj)

premō, -ere, pressī, pressus

prōvincia, -ae

pugna, -ae

relinquō, -ere, -līquī, -lictus

Sabīnus, -ī

subsequor, -sequī, -secūtus

tōtus, -a, -um (*five of which are the irregular genitive* tōtius)

trēs, tria (adj)

turris, -is (m) (acc: turrim)

6 times

absum, abesse, āfuī, -

animus, -ī

barbarus, -a, -um

Belgae, -ārum (f pl)

Britannia, -ae

circumveniō, -īre, -vēnī, -ventus

commūnis, -e (adj)

compleō, -ēre, -ēvī, -ētus

cōnor, -ārī, -ātus (dep)

dēsum, deesse, -fuī, -futūrus

Druidēs, -um (m pl)

dum (conj)

fīnitimus, -a, -um

flūmen, -inis (n)

impedīmentum, -ī

instituō, -ere, -stituī, -stitūtus

iūs, iūris (n)

māior, māius (comp adj)

nisi (conj)

nuntius, -ī

obtineō, -ēre, -tinuī, -tentus

oppugnātiō, -ōnis (f)

oppugnō, -āre

Orgetorix, -igis (m)

pax, pācis (f)

perturbō, -āre

pōnō, -ere, posuī, positus

prohibeō, -ēre, -uī, -itus

Pullō, -ōnis (m)

quantus, -a, -um

quidem (adv)

Quintus, -ī (abbrev: Q.)

Sēquanus, -a, -um / Sēquanī, -ōrum / Sēquana, -ae (m)

spērō, -āre

spes, speī (f)

superō, -āre

teneō, -ēre, -uī, tentus

transeō, -īre, -iī, -itus

5 times

Aduatucī, -ōrum (m pl)

altus, -a, -um

animadvertō, -ere, advertī, adversus

ante (adv or prep + acc)

appellō, -āre

autem (adv)

cāsus, -ūs

celeritās, -ātis (f)

collocō, -āre

colloquor, -ī, collocūtus

complūrēs, -a (pl adj)

comprehendō, -ere, -prehendī, -prehensus

confirmō, -āre

conspiciō, -ere, -spexī, -spectus

constō, -āre, -stitī, -stātus

consuētūdo, -inis (f)

Crassus, -ī

dēmonstrō, -āre

deus, -ī

discīplīna, -ae

Eburōnēs, -um (m pl)

efficiō, -ere, effēcī, effectus

ēgredior, egredī, egressus

equitātus, -ūs

etsi (conj)

facultas, -ātis (f)

fīlius, -ī

iam / iamque (adv)

ibi (adv)

incitō, -āre

interim (adv)

intermittō, -ere, -mīsī, -missus

Labiēnus, -ī

licet, licēre, licuit, licitum (impers)

longē (adv)

magnitūdo, -inis (f)

ob (prep + acc)

obsideō, -ēre, -sēdī, -sessus

pater, -tris (m)

permoveō, -ēre, -mōvī, -mōtus

post (adv and prep + acc)

praemium, -ī

praestō, -āre, -stitī, -stātus

prīvātus, -a, -um

profectiō, -ōnis (f)

propter (prep + acc)

quam *with superlative*

ratiō, -ōnis (f)

resistō, -ere, -stitī, -

Rhodanus, -ī

sub (prep + acc or abl)

subitō (adv)

subsidium, -ī

tollō, -ere, sustulī, sublātus

ubi (adv)

ullus, -a, -um

ventus, -ī

vīta, -ae

Vorēnus, -ī

4 times

ācer, acris, acre

aeger, aegra, aegrum

agō, -ere, ēgī, actus

angustus, -a, -um

aquila, -ae

auctor, -ōris (m/f)

audeō, -ēre, ausus (semidep)

Carnūtes, -um (m pl)

centuriō, -ōnis (m)

cliens, -ntis (m/f)

committō, -ere, commīsī, commissus

commūnicō, -āre

comparō, -āre

confestim (adv)

conficiō, -ere, -fēcī, -fectus

confīdō, -ere, -fisus sum (semidep)

consulō, -ere, -suluī, -sultus

contendō, -ere, -tendī, -tentus

cōtīdiānus, -a, -um

dēsiliō, -īre, -siluī, -sultus

dīvidō, -ere, dīvīsī, dīvīsus

doceō, -ēre, docuī, doctus

dux, ducis (m/f)

efferō, -ferre, extulī, ēlatus

eō, īre, īvi, itus

equus, -ī
exeō, -īre, -iī, -itus
expediō, -īre, -īvī, -ītus
fīdēs, -eī
fortūna, -ae
Gaius, -ī
hiemō, -āre
hōra, -ae
ignis, -is (m)
impediō,- īre, -pedīvī, -pedītus
inimīcus, -a, -um
initium, -ī
iniūria, -ae
inquit (defec)
Marcus, -ī (abbrev: M.)
memoria, -ae
modō (adv)
modus, -ī
mons, montis (m)
mos, mōris (m)
necesse (indecl adj)
noctū (adv)
occīdo, -ere, -cīdī, -cīsus
occupō, -āre
oppidum, -ī
ōrātiō, -ōnis (f)
paucī, -ae, -a (pl adj)
perpetuus, -a, -um
pēs, pedis (m)
plūrimus, -a, -um
plūs, plūris (comp adj)
princeps, -cipis (m)
probō, -āre
prōnuntiō, -āre
proptereā (adv)
quīcumque, quaecumque, quodcumque
remittō, -ere, -mīsī, -missus
repentīnus, -a, -um
rursus (adv)
sacrificium, -ī
sequor, -ī, secutus
servus, -ī

signum, -ī
silva, -ae
simul (adv)
spatium, -ī
spectō, -āre
statim (adv)
suspīciō, -ōnis (f)
Titus, -ī (abbrev: T.)
Trēvir, Trēverī
undique (adv)
vereor, -ērī, veritus (dep)
versō, -āre
vir, virī
vīs, vis (f)
vox, vōcis (f)

3 times

addūcō, -ere, addūxī, adductus
administrō, -āre
adsum, adesse, adfuī, adfutūrus
aestus, -ūs
afficiō, ere, affēcī, affectus
agmen, agminis (n)
Allōbrogēs, -um
ancora, -ae
aperiō, -īre, aperuī, apertus
approprinquō, -āre
āridus, -a, -um
armō, -āre
Atrebas, -atis (m)
auctōritas, -ātis (f)
auxilium, -ī
brevis, -e (adj)
captīvus, -a, -um
cohortō, -āre
commodus, -a, -um
comportō, -āre
concēdō, -ere, -cessī, -cessus
conferciō, -īre, -, confertus
conferō, -ferre, -tulī, -lātus
coniūratiō, -ōnis (f)

consul, -ulis (m)

cursus, -ūs

dēcernō, -ere, -crēvī, -crētus

dēdūcō, -ere, -dūxī, -ductus

dēficiō, -ere, -fēcī, -fectus

dēiciō, -ere, -iēcī, -iectus

differō, -ferre, distulī, dīlātus

dimittō, -ere, dimīsī, dimissus

domus, -ūs / -ī

ēdūcō, -ere, ēduxī, ēductus

eiusmodī (adv)

epistola, -ae

essedum, -ī

ēveniō, -īre, -vēnī, -ventus

excēdō, -ere, excessī, excessus

excitō, -āre

Fabius, -ī

fiō, -erī, factus

flamma, -ae

fuga, -ae

funda, -ae

Garumna, -ae (m)

Genāva, -ae

gladius, -ī

hiems, -emis (f)

honor / honos, -ōris (m)

immolō, -āre

immortālis, -e (adj)

imperītus, -a, -um

impetrō, -āre

incolō, -ere, -coluī, -

incommodus, -a, -um

inde (adv)

inferior, -ius (comp adj)

intercipiō, -ere, -cēpī, -ceptus

intereā (adv)

intereō, -īre, -iī, -itus

intrā (adv and prep + acc)

item (adv)

iūdicium, -ī

latus, lateris (n)

lex, lēgis (f)

līberō, -āre

lux, lūcis (m)

magistrātus, -ūs

medius, -a, -um

moror, -ārī, -ātus

mōtus, -ūs

mūniō, -īre, -īvi, -ītus

nascor, nascī, nātus

neglegō, -ere, -lexī, -lectus

nēmō, -inis (pron)

nōbilis, -e (adj)

nocturnus, -a, -um

nōndum (adv)

Ōceanus, -ī

officium, -ī

omnīno (adv)

opera, -ae

opprimō, -ere, -pressī, -pressus

opus, -eris (n)

orior, -īrī, ortus

parō, -āre

paucitas, -ātis (f)

pecūnia, -ae

peditātus, -ūs

perficiō, -ere, -fēcī, -factus

pīlum, -ī

poena, -ae

potestas, -ātis (f)

praesens, -ntis (adj)

prōcēdō, -ere, -cessī, -cessus

procul (adv)

prōficiō, -ere, -fēcī, -fectus

prōprius, -a, -um

prōvideō, -ēre, -vīdī, -vīsus

putō, -āre

quaestor, -ōris (m)

quies, -ētis (f or adj)

quisque, quaeque, quodque (indef pron)

referō, -ferre, -tulī, -lātus

religiō, -ōnis (f)

rēmus, -ī

rēspondeō, -ēre, -dī, -sus

saepe (adv)
sentiō, -īre, sēnsī, sēnsus
septentriōnes, -um (m pl)
sermo, -ōnis (m)
sīc (adv)
sōl, sōlis (m)
statiō, -ōnis (f)
stō, stāre, stetī, status
supplicium, -ī
sūprā (adv and prep + acc)
suspicor, -ārī, -ātus
Tasgetius, -ī
tempestās, -ātis (f)
tormentum, -ī
trādō, -ere, trādidī, trāditus
trāgula, -ae
trans (prep + acc)
transportō, -āre
ultrō (adv)
unde (adv)
ūniversus, -a, -um
uxor, uxōris (f)
verō (adv)
vigilla, -ae
vulnerō, -āre
vulnus, -eris (n)

2 times

abiciō, -ere, abiēcī, abiectus
accēdō, -ere, accessī, accessus
aciēs, -ēī
adeō, -īre, -iī, -itus
aditus, -ūs
adiūtor, -ōris (m)
admittō, -ere, admīsī, admissus
admodum (adv)
adorior, -īrī, adortus
advertō, -ere, advertī, adversus
aedificium, -ī
aes, aeris (n)
aestus, -ūs

aliēnus, -a, -um
aliter (adv)
alius, -a, -ud
altitūdo, -inis (f)
amīcitia, -ae
āmittō, -ere, āmīsī, āmissus
amplus, -a, -um
animal, -ālis (n)
anteferō, -ferre, -tulī, -lātus
Apollo, -onis
Aprīlis, -is (m)
Aquītānī, -ōrum
Arpineius, -ī
ascendō, -ere, ascendī, ascensus
Aurunculēius, -ī
beneficium, -ī
biduus, -a, -um
bonus, -a, -um
caedes, -is (f)
carrus, -ī
Catuvulcus, -ī
cēdō, -ere, cessī, cessus
circum (adv or prep + acc)
circumsistō, -ere, -stetī, -
clam (adv)
clāmor, -ōris (m)
commeō, -āre
Commius, -ī
concilium, -ī
concitō, -āre
conclāmō, -āre
concurrō, -ere, -currī, -cursus
condiciō, -ōnis (f)
condūcō, -ere, -duxī, -ductus
conscrībō, -ere, -scripsī, -scriptus
consecrō, -āre
consīdō, -ere, consēdī, consessus
consistō, -ere, -stitī, -stitus
conspectus, -ūs
consūmō, -ere, -sumpsī, -sumptus
contrā (adv or prep + acc)
coorior, -īrī, coortus

cremō, -āre

crucciō, -āre

cultus, -ūs

cupidus, -a, -um

currus, -ūs

dēcēdō, -ere, -cessī, -cessus

dēligō, -āre

dēscendō, -ere, -scendī, -scensus

dēspērō, -āre

dīligens, -ntis (adj)

discō, -ere, didicī, discitūrus

disputātiō, -ōnis (f)

dissensiō, -ōnis (f)

distribuō, -ere, -tribuī, -tribūtus

dolor, -ōris (m)

dōs, dōtis (f)

egō, meī, mihi, mē, mē

exanimō, -āre

exercitātiō, -ōnis (f)

expellō, -ere, -pulī, -pulsus

exspectō, -āre

extrēmus, -a, -um

facinus, -oris (n)

fāma, -ae

fames, -is (f)

familiae, -ae

firmus, -a, -um

fluctus, -ūs

fossa, -ae

frater, -tris (m)

fructus, -ūs

frūmentārius, -a, -um

fūnus, -eris (n)

glōria, -ae

Graecus, -a, -um / Graecī, -ōrum

grātia, -ae

Hispānia, -ae

hortor, -ārī, -ātus

hūc (adv)

iaciō, -ere, iēcī, iactus

iaculum, -ī

ignoscō, -ere, -nōvī, -nōtus

impellō, -ere, -pulī, -pulsus

imperātor, -ōris (m)

imprūdentia, -ae

incendō, -ere, -cendī, -census

incertus, -a, -um

incolumis, -e (adj)

ineō, -īre, -īvī, -itus

insistō, -ere, -stitī, -

insula, -ae

intellegō, -ere, -lexī, -lectus

interdīcō, -ere, -dixī, -dictus

interpōnō, -ere, -posuī, -positus

inūsitātus, -a, -um

iūdicō, -āre

iugum, -ī

Iūnius, -ī

Iūppiter, Iovis (m)

iūrō, -āre

labōrō, -āre

lātē (adv)

laus, laudis (f)

lēgātiō, -ōnis (f)

līber, liberī

lībertas, -ātis (f)

lingua, -ae

longinquus, -a, -um

longitūdo, -inis (f)

loquor, -ī, locūtus

maleficium, -ī

mandō, -āre

maneō, -ēre, mansī, mansus

Mars, Martis (m)

māteria, -ae

membrum, -ī

mensis, -is (m)

metus, -ūs

mīlitia, -ae

Minerva, -ae

minuō, ere, -uī, -ūtus

moneō, -ēre, -uī, -itus

morbus, -ī

mortuus, -a, -um

nātūra, -ae

nāvigō, -āre

nec (conj)

negō, -āre

negōtium, -ī

noceō, -ēre, -uī, -itus

nōmen, -inis (n)

nōnnullus, -a, -um

nōtus, -a, -um

novus, -a, -um

nunc (adv)

nuntiō, -āre

observō, -āre

obsidiō, -ōnis (f)

occāsiō, -ōnis (f)

occidō, -ere, -cidī, -cāsus

occultō, -āre

occurrō, -ere, -currī, -cursus

opīniō, -ōnis (f)

oportet, -ēre, -uit

opportūnus, -a, -um

orbis, -is (m)

ōrō, -āre

ostendō, -ere, ostendī, ostentus

pācātus, -a, -um

paene (adv)

palam (adv)

pār, paris (adj)

parcō, -ere, pepercī, parsurus

pateō, -ēre, -uī, -

pellō, -ere, pepulī, pulsus

pendō, -ere, pependī, pensus

perfacilē (adv)

perferō, -ferre, -tulī, -lātus

Pīso, -ōnis (m)

Plancus, -ī

plebs, -bis (f)

polliceor, -ērī, -itus

pons, -ntis (m)

portō, -āre

posteā (adv)

posterus, -a, -um

postrēmo (adv)

potens, -ntis (adj)

potior, -īrī, -itus

praeda, -ae

praedicō, -āre

praeficiō, -ere, -fēcī, -fectus

praemittō, -ere, -mīsī, -missus

praesertim (adv)

praesidium, -ī

praesum, -esse, -fuī, -

praetereā (adv)

principātus, -ūs

pristinus, -a, -um

prōcurrō, -ere, -currī / -cucurrī, -cursus

prōdeō, -īre, -ii, -itus

prōgredior, -ī, -gressus

prōiciō, -ere, -iēcī, -iectus

prōpellō, -ere, -pulī, -pulsus

propinquus, -a, -um

quadringentī, -ae, -a (pl adj)

quam *with comparative*

quartus, -a, -um

quīdam, quaedam, quoddam

quīn (conj)

quīque, quaeque, quodque

recēdō, -ere, -cessī, -cessus

reddō, -ere, -didī, -ditus

redūco, -ere, -xī, -ctus

reficiō, -ere, -fēcī, -fectus

removeō, -ēre, -mōvī, -mōtus

revertō, -ere, -vertī, -versus

rogō, -āre

Roscius, -ī

rūmor, -ōris (m)

Samarobrīva, -ae

sciō, -īre, -īvī, -ītus

scrībō, -ere, scripsī, scriptus

scūtum, -ī

sententia, -ae

septimus, -a, -um

servitūs, -ūtis (f)

servō, -āre

seu (conj)

sīcutī (adv)

simulācrum, -ī

singulāris, -e (adj)

socius, -ī

sponte (abl n)

studium, -ī

subdūcō, -ere, -xī, -ctus

subveniō, -īre, -vēnī, -ventus

succēdō, -ere, -cessī, -cessus

succendō, -ere, -cendī, -census

sumptuōsus, -a, -um

terra, -ae

terreō, -ēre, -uī, -itus

testūdo, -inis (f)

timor, -ōris (m)

tot (indecl adj)

traiciō, -icere, -iēcī, -iectus

tribūnus, -ī

tribūtum, -ī

tū, tuī, tibi, tē, tē

turpis, -e (adj)

tūtus, -a, -um

ulterior, ultierius (comp adj)

uter, utra, utrum (adj)

vadum, -ī

vel (conj)

ventitō, -āre

verūtum, -ī

via, -ae

vīcus, -ī

vinculum, -ī

vīvus, -a, -um

vix (adv)

voluntās, -ātis (f)

vulgus, -ī (n)

1 time

accersō, -ere, -īvī, -ītus

addō, -ere, addidī, additus

adeō (adv)

adflictō, -āre

adfligō, -ere, adflixī, adflictus

adgrego, -āre

adhaereō, -ēre, adhaesī, adhaesus

adhibeō, -ēre, -uī, -ītus

adhortor, -ārī, -ātus

adigō, -ere, adēgī, adactus

adipiscor, -ī, adeptus

adiungō, -ere, adiunxī, adiunctus

administer, -trī

adolescō, -ere, adolēvī, adultus

adripiō, -ere, adripuī, adreptus

adsistō, -ere, adstitī, -

adulescens, -ntis (m/f)

advolō, -āre

Aeduus, -a, -um

aestimātiō, -ōnis (f)

aetas, aetātis (f)

alacer, -cris, -cre (adj)

alacritās, -ātis (f)

ambactus, -ī

ambō, -ae, -o (pl adj)

amentum, -ī

amīcus, -a, -um

amīcus, -ī

anima, -ae

antecursor, -ōris (m)

aqua, -ae

aquilifer, -fēri

Aquītānia, -ae

ardeō, -ēre, arsī, arsus

argilla, -ae

Ariovistus, -ī

armamenta, -ōrum (n pl)

ars, artis (f)

artificium, -ī

ascensus, -ūs

adsciscō, -ere, adsciscīvī, adsciscītus

asper, -era, -erum

attexō, -ere, attexuī, attextus

attingō, -ere, attigī, attactus

attribuō, -ere, attribuī, attribūtus

audax, -ācis (adj)

audiō, -īre, audīvī, audītus

augeō, -ēre, auxī, auctus

auriga, -ae (m)

auxilior, -ārī

āvertō, -ere, āvertī, āversus

balteus, -ī

Balventius, -ī

Belgium, -ī

bellō, -āre

Bellovacī, -ōrum

benevolentia, -ae

biennium, -ī

bipertiō, -īre, -, bipertītus

Boii, -ōrum (m pl)

cadō, -ere, cecedī, cāsus

caelestis, -e (adj)

caespes, -itis (m)

calamitas, -ātis (f)

cārus, -a, -um

casa, -ae

Cassius, -ī

Casticus, -ī

Catamantaloedis, -is (m)

catēna, -ae

Celtae, -ārum

centum (indecl)

certāmen, -inis (n)

cēterus, -a, -um

Ceutronēs, -um (m pl)

cibārius, -a, -um

cingō, -ere, cinxī, cinctus

circuitus, -ūs

circumcīdō, -ere, -cīdī, -cīsus

circumdō, -are, -dedī, -datus

circumspiciō, -ere, -spexī, -spectus

citus, -a, -um

clāmitō, -are

clārus, -a, -um

coactus, -ūs

coemō, -ere, -ēmī, -emptus

cōgitō, -āre

colligō, -ere, collēgī, collectus

colloquium, -ī

colō, -ere, coluī, cultus

combūrō, -ere, combussī, combustus

commemorō, -āre

commendō, -āre

commīliō, -ōnis (m)

comminus (adv)

comperiō, -īre, -perī, -pertus

conciliō, -āre

concursō, -āre

concursus, -ūs

confīnium, -ī

confiteor, -ērī, confessus (semidep)

conflagrō, -āre

conflictō, -āre

coniunctim (adv)

coniungō, -ere, -iunxī, -iunctus

conscendō, -ere, -scendī, -scensus

consciscō, -ere, -scīvī, -scītus

consentiō, -īre, -sensī, -sensus

consequor, -ī, consecūtus

conspicor, -ārī, conspicātus

constīpō, -āre

consurgō, -ere, -surrexī, -surrectus

contabulō, -āre

contāgiō, -ōnis (f)

contemptiō, -ōnis (f)

contentiō, -ōnis (f)

contexō, -ere, -texuī, -textus

continenter (adv)

contingō, -ere, -tigī, -tactus

continuus, -a, -um

contumēlia, -ae

convallis, -is (f)

convertō, -ere, -vertī, -versus

cor, -dis (n)

cratis, -is (f)

crēber, -bra, -brum

crēdō, -ere, credidī, creditus

culpa, -ae

cunctor, -ārī

CHAPTER 6

cupiditās, -ātis (f)

cūrō, -āre

damnō, -āre

dēbeō, -ēre, dēbuī, dēbitus

dēcēdō, -ere, -cessī, -cessus

decem (indecl noun)

decimus, -a, -um

dēclīvis, -e (adj)

decus, -oris (n)

dēdō, -ere, -didī, -ditus

dēfectiō, -ōnis (f)

dēfensor, -ōris (m)

dēfīgō, -ere, -fīxī, -fixus

dēfugiō, -ere, -fūgī, -

deinceps (adj and adv)

deinde (adv)

dēlīberō, -āre

dēligō, -ere, -lēgī, -lectus

dēlitescō, -ere, -lituī, -

dēmetō, -ere, -messuī, -messus

dēmigrō, -āre

dēmittō, -ere, -mīsī, -missus

dēmō, -ere, dempsī, demptus

dēmum (adv)

dēpellō, -ere, -pulī, -pulsus

dēpōnō, -ere, -posuī, -positus

dēprehendō, -ere, -prehendī, -prehensus

dēsero, -ere, -seruī, -sertus

dēspērātiō, -onis (f)

dēturbō, -āre

dēvehō, -ere, -vexī, -vectus

dēvoveō, -ēre, -vōvī, -vōtus

dexter, -tera, -terum

dicō, -āre

dictiō, -ōnis (f)

difficilis, -e (adj)

difficultās, -ātis (f)

diffīdō, -ere, -fīsus (semidep)

dignitās, -ātis (f)

dīiūdicō, -āre

dīligentia, -ae

dīligō, -ere, -lexī, -lectus

dīmicō, -āre

Dīs, Dītis (m)

dispergō, -ere, -sparsī, -sparsus

dispōnō, -ere, -posuī, -positus

disputō, -āre

dissentiō, -īre, -sesnī, -sensus

diū (adv)

dīves, -itis (adj)

Dīviciācus, -ī

dīvīnus, -a, -um

dominus, -ī

dubitātiō, -ōnis (f)

dubitō, -āre

dubius, -a, -um

Dumnorix, -igis (m)

duodecim (indecl)

dūrus, -a, -um

ēdiscō, -ere, -didicī, -

effēminō, -āre

effugiō, -ere, effūgī, -

ēlābor, -ī, elapsus

ēmittō, -ere, ēmīsī, ēmissus

enim (adv)

ēnuntiō, -āre

equester, -tris, -tre (adj)

ēripiō, -ere, ēripuī, ēreptus

errō, -āre

essedārius, -a, -um

Esubiī, -ōrum (m pl)

exaudiō, -īre, -īvī, -ītus

excellō, -ere, -celluī, -celsus

excōgitō, -āre

excruciō, -āre

exhauriō, -īre, -hausī, -haustus

exiguitās, -ātis (f)

existimātiō, -ōnis (f)

exitus, -ūs

explōrō, -āre

exsequor, -ī, -secūtus

exsistō,- ere, -stitī, -stitus

exstinguō, -ere, exstinxī, exstinctus

exstruō, -ere, -struxī, -structus

extrā (prep + acc)

exūrō, -ere, exussī, exustus

falsus, -a, -um

falx, falcis (f)

familiāris, -e (adj)

fas (indecl)

fēliciter (adv)

femur, -oris (n)

ferrāmentum, -ī

ferrum, -ī

fervefaciō, -ere, -fēcī, -factus

ferveō, -ēre, -ferbuī, -

figūra, -ae

fīlia, -ae

fīniō, -īre, -īvī, -ītus

flectō, -ere, flexī, flectus

flētus, -ūs

fluō, -ere, fluxī, fluxus

fortitūdō, -inis (f)

frangō, -ere, frēgī, fractus

fremitus, -ūs

frūmentor, -ārī, -ātus

fūmus, -ī

fūnis, -is (m)

furtum, -ī

fūsilis, -e (adj)

Gabīnius, -ī

Gallicus, -a, -um

Geidumnī, -ōrum (m pl)

gens, gentis (f)

glans, -ndis (f)

Gneus, -ī

grātus, -a, -um

Grudiī, -ōrum (m pl)

hērēditās, -ātis (f)

Hispānus, -a, -um / Hispānī, ōrum

honestus, -a, -um

hospitium, -ī

hūmānitās, -ātis (f)

humilis, -e (adj)

humilitās, -ātis (f)

idōneus, -a, -um

ignōbilis, -e (adj)

ignōtus, -a, -um

immānis, -e (adj)

immittō, -ere, -mīsī, -missus

immūnitās, -ātis (f)

impendeō, -ēre, -, -

impius, -a, -um

importō, -āre

imprōvīsus, -a, -um

incendium, -ī

incidō, -ere, -cidī, -cāsus

incipiō, -ere, -cēpī, -ceptus

incognitus, -a, -um

incrēdibilis, -e (adj)

indicium, -ī

indignus, -a, -um

indūcō, -ere, -dūxī, -ductus

Indutiomarus, -ī

inīquus, -a, -um

iniussus, -ūs

inligō, -āre

inlustris, -e (adj)

innocens, -entis (adj)

inopia, -ae

insequor, -ī, insecūtus

insidiae, -ārum

insinuō, -āre

instō, -āre

instrūmentum, -ī

insuēfactus, -a, -um

intercēdō, -ere, -cessī, -cessus

interclūdō, -ere, -clūsī, -clūsus

interitus, -ūs

interpres, interpretis (m/f)

interpretor, -ārī, -ātus

intersum, -esse, -fuī, -futūrus

introeō, -īre, -īvi, -itus

intus (adv)

inūtilis, -e (adj)

inventor, -ōris (m)

inveterasco, -ere, -rāvī, -

irrumpō, -ere, -rūpī, -ruptus

Ītalia, -ae

iūmentum, -ī

Iura, -ae (m)

iustitia, -ae

iuventūs, iuventūtis (f)

Kalendae, -ārum (pl n; abbrev: Kal.)

labor, labōris (m)

lacessō, -īre, -īvi, -ītus

lacus, -ūs

laetitia, -ae

languor, -ōris (m)

lapis, -idis (m)

lātitūdō, -inis (f)

Latobrigī, -ōrum (m pl)

latrōcinium, -ī

lātus, -a, -um

Lemannus, -ī

lēnis, -e (adj)

Levācī, -ōrum

levis, -e (adj)

levitās, -ātis (f)

levō, -āre

lignātiō, -ōnis (f)

lignātor, -ōris (m)

lītus, -oris (n)

lōrica, -ae

Lūcānius, -ī

lūna, -ae

magnoperē (adv)

mare, -is (n)

maritimus, -a, -um

mātrimōnium, -ī

mātrōna, -ae

mātūrō, -āre

medeor, -ērī, -

mediōcris, -e (adj)

mercātor, -ōris (m)

mercor, -ārī, -ātus

Mercurius, -ī

mereō, -ēre, -uī, -itus

Mesala, -ae (m)

metō, -ēre, messuī, messus

meus, -a, -um

mīlitāris, -e (adj)

minimē (adv)

mōbilitās, -ātis (f)

moderor, -ārī, -ātus

mōlior, -īrī, -ītus

Morinī, -ōrum (m pl)

Mosa, -ae

Munātius, -ī

mundus, -ī

mūnus, -eris (n)

mūrālis, -e (adj)

Nammēius, -ī

nanciscor, -ī, nactus

nātālis, -e (adj)

nātiō, -ōnis (f)

nāvigium, -ī

necessārius, -a, -um

necō, -āre

Nervius, -a, -um

neu (conj)

nex, necis (f)

nōbilitās, -ātis (f)

nōlō, nolle, noluī, -

Norēia, -ae

Nōricum, -ī

nōs (pron)

noscō, -ere, nōvī, nōtus

novitās, -ātis (f)

noxius, -a, -um

nūdō, -āre

nūmen, -inis (n)

nōnnumquam (adv)

nūper (adv)

nūtus, -ūs

obaerātus, -a, -um

obeō, -īre, -iī, -itus

obses, -idis (m/f)

obtestor, -ārī, obtestātus

occulō, -ere, -culuī, -cultus

octāvus, -a, -um

onerārius, -a, -um

onus, -eris (n)

optimus, -a, -um

ōs, ōris (n)

Padus, -ī

parens, -ntis (m/f)

pāreō, -ēre, paruī, pāritus

pariō, -ere, peperī, paritus / partus

patior, patī, passus

pedes, -itis (m)

pedester, -tris, -tre (adj)

penna, -ae

peragō, -ere, -ēgī, -actus

percurrō, -ere, -cucurrī, -cursus

percutiō, -ere, -cussī, -cussus

perdiscō, -ere, -didicī, -

perdūcō, -ere, -dūxī, -ductus

perendinus, -a, -um

perequitō, -āre

perfugiō, -ere, -fūgī, -

perlegō, -ere, -lēgī, -lectus

permaneō, -ēre, -mansī, -mansus

perpaucus, -a, -um

perscrībō, -ere, -scrīpsī, -scriptus

persevērō, -āre

perspiciō, -ere, -spexī, -spectus

perterreō, -ēre, -uī, -itus

pertinācia, -ae

perturbātiō, -ōnis (f)

pēs, pedis (m)

Petrosidius, -ī

pietās, -ātis (f)

plācō, -āre

plēnus, -a, -um

Pleumoxiī, -ōrum (m pl)

Pompēius, -ī

porrō (adv)

porta, -ae

portus, -ūs

postequam (adv)

potentia, -ae

praecēdō, -ere, -cessī, -cessus

praeceps, -cipitis

praeceptum, -ī

praecipiō, -ere, -cēpī, -ceptus

praestō (adv)

praeter (prep + acc)

praeterquam (adv)

praeūrō, -ere, -ussī, -ustus

prīdiē (adv)

prior / prius, priōris

priusquam (adv)

prōcūrō, -āre

prōdō, -ere, -didī, -ditus

prōdūcō, -ere, -dūxī, -ductus

proelior, -ārī, -ātus

profiteor, -ērī, -fessus

prōgnātus, -a, -um

proindē (adv)

properō, -āre

prōpōnō, -ere, -posuī, -positus

prōpulsō, -āre

prōsequor, -ī, -secūtus

prōsum, prōdesse, -fuī, -

prōtegō, -ere, -texī, -tectus

prōvehō, -ere, -vexī, -vectus

prōveniō, -īre, -vēnī, -ventus

puerīlis, -e (adj)

pulvis, -eris (m)

Pūpius, -ī

Pȳrēnaeus, -a, -um

quaestiō, -ōnis (f)

quaestus, -ūs

quam = postquam

quantusvīs, -avīs, -umvīs

quārē (adv)

questus, -ūs

quīdam, quaedam, quoddam

quīnam, quaenam, quodnam

quindecim (indecl)

quinquāgintā (indecl)

quispiam, quaepiam, quodpiam

quisquam, quaequam, quid- / quicquam

quoad (adv)

quoniam (adv)

quot (adj plur indecl)

quotiens (adv)

Rauracī, -ōrum (m pl)

rebelliō, -ōnis (f)

recens, -ntis (adj)

recitō, -āre

recuperō, -āre

recusō, -āre

redeō, -īre, -iī, -itus

redigō, -ere, -dēgī, -dactus

reditiō, -ōnis (f)

reditus, -ūs

refugiō, -ere, -fūgī, -

regiō, regiōnis (f)

regnō, -āre

regō, -ere, rexī, rectus

regredior, -ī, -gressus

rēiciō, -ere, -iēcī, -iectus

relegō, -āre

remaneō, -ēre, -mansī, -

remigrō, -āre

repellō, -ere, reppulī, repulsus

reperiō, -īre, repperī, repertum

reportō, -āre

reposcō, -ere, -, -

reprehendō, -ere, -prehendī, -prehensus

rēscindō, -ere, -scidī, -scissus

reservō, -āre

respiciō, -ere, -pexī, -spectus

retineō, -ēre, -tinuī, -tentus

rīpa, -ae

rota, -ae

sagitta, -ae

sagulum, -ī

sanctus, -a, -um

sapiō, -ere, -īvī, -

satis (adv and indecl adj and noun)

satisfaciō, -ere, -fēcī, -factus

saucius, -a, -um

scālae, -ārum (f pl)

scapha, -ae

scelerātus, -a, -um

sēmentis, -is (f)

senātus, -ūs

serō (adv)

servīlis, -e (adj)

siccitās, -ātis (f)

sīdus, -eris (n)

similis, -e (adj)

simultās, -ātis (f)

sīn (conj)

singulī, -ae, -a

soleō, -ēre, - , -

solvō, -ere, -ī, solūtus

speciēs, -eī

speculātōrius, -a, -um

stabilitās, -ātis (f)

stīpendium, -ī

strāmentum, -ī

strepitus, -ūs

studeō, -ēre, -uī, -

subeō, -īre, -iī, -itus

submittō, -ere, -mīsī, -missus

subsum, -esse, -fuī, -

succurrō, -ere, -cursī, -cursus

sudis, -is (f)

suffrāgium, -ī

summoveō, -ēre, -mōvī, -mōtus

suppetō, -ere, -petīvī, -petītus

suscipiō, -ere, -cēpī, -ceptus

sustento, -āre

tametsī (conj)

tandem (adv)

tegō, -ere, -xī, -ctus (also, tectum, -ī)

temerārius, -a, -um

temerē (adv)

temō, -ōnis (m)

temperō, -āre

tenuis, -e (adj)

tergum, -ī

terror, -ōris (m)

testimōnium, -ī

timeō, -ēre, -uī, -

timidē (adv)

tolerō, -āre

torreō, -ēre, -uī, tostus

transferō, -ferre, -tulī, -lātus

transfīgō, -ere, -fīxī, -fīxus

Trebōnius, -ī

trepidō, -āre

Tulingī, -ōrum (m pl)

tumultus, -ūs

tumulus, -ī

tunc (adv)

turma, -ae

tuus, -a, -um

ulciscor, -ulciscī, -ultus

ultimus, -a, -um

ululō, -āre

urbs, urbis (f)

uter, utra, utrum (adj)

vacātiō, -ōnis (f)

vāgīna, -ae

vagor, -ārī, -ātus

valetūdō, -inis (f)

vēlox, vēlōcis (adj)

vergō, -ere, -, -

versus, -ūs

Verticō, -ōnis (m)

vertō, -ere, vertī, versus

Verucloetius, -ī

victima, -ae

victor, -ōris (m)

vīmen, -inis (n)

vincō, -ere, vīcī, victus

vītō, -āre

vocō, -āre

vōs (pers pron)

voveō, -ēre, vōvī, vōtum

Vergil Frequency List

174 times

et (conj)

111 times

quī, quae, quod (rel pron or adj; inter adj)

85 times

hic, haec, hoc (demon)

55 times

in (prep + acc or abl)

52 times

sum, esse, fuī, futūrus

45 times

per (prep + acc)

44 times

tū, tuī, tibi, tē, tē (pers pron)

40 times

ille, illa, illud (demon)

36 times

egō, meī, mihi, mē, mē (pers pron)

31 times

atque (conj)

aut (conj)

nec (conj)

29 times

ad (prep + acc)

dō, dare, dedī, datus

27 times

altus, -a, -um
omnis, -e (adj)
urbs, urbis (f)

26 times

sī (conj)
videō, -ēre, vīdī, vīsus

25 times

a/ab (prep + abl)

24 times

vir, virī

23 times

Aenēas, -ae (m)
cum (conj or prep + abl)
ferō, ferre, tulī, lātus
prīmus, -a, -um

22 times

ipse, ipsa, ipsum
nōn (adv)

20 times

-, suī, sibi, sē, sē (refl pron)
terra, -ae

19 times

animus, -ī
deus, -ī
dīcō, -ere, dīxī, dictus
iam / iamque (adv)
magnus, -a, -um
quis, quid (inter pron)

18 times

arma, -ōrum (n pl)
sīc (adv)
tantus, -a, -um

17 times

tum (adv)

16 times

fātum, -ī

15 times

ignis, -is (m)
lītus, -oris (n)
nunc (adv)
sed (conj)
tālis, -e (adj)

14 times

eō, īre, īvi, itus
petō, -ere, -īvī, -ītus
regnum, -ī
rex, rēgis (m)
Trōia, -ae
unda, -ae

13 times

caelum, -ī
ingens, -ntis (adj)
ō (interj)
ōs, ōris (n)
pater, -tris (m)
sub (prep + acc or abl)
veniō, -īre, vēnī, ventus

12 times

ac (conj)
dīvus, -a, -um
manus, -ūs
medius, -a, -um
oculus, -ī
pectus, -oris (n)
rēs, reī
umbra, -ae

11 times

aequor, -oris (n)

arx, -cis (f)

bellum, -ī

circum (adv or prep + acc)

corpus, -oris (n)

Dīdō, -ōnis (f)

fluctus, -ūs

gens, gentis (f)

īra, -ae

Ītalia, -ae

nāvis, -is (f)

saxum, -ī

teneō, -ēre, -uī, tentus

tuus, -a, -um

ut / utī (conj)

ventus, -ī

10 times

ante (adv or prep + acc)

caput, -itis (n)

de (prep + abl)

errō, -āre

iubeō, -ēre, iussī, iussus

noster, -tra, -trum

rēgīna, -ae

Teucer, -crī / Teucrus, -a, -um

ubī (conj)

ūnus, -a, -um; adv ūnā = together

9 times

alius, -a, -ud

amor, -ōris (m)

aspiciō, -ere, aspexī, aspectus

dexter, -tera, -terum

dūcō, -ere, dūxī, ductus

fāma, -ae

for, fārī, fātus

Iūno, Iūnōnis (f)

Iūppiter, Iovis (m)

meus, -a, -um

multus, -a, -um

pontus, -ī

summus, -a, -um

8 times

agō, -ere, ēgī, actus

Anchīses, -ae

ardeō, -ēre, arsī, arsus

āter, ātra, ātrum

classis, -is (f)

corripiō, -ere, corripuī, correptus

domus, -ūs / -ī

ē / ex (prep + abl)

flamma, -ae

inter (adv and prep + acc)

labor, labōris (m)

locus, -ī (loca, -ōrum in pl)

moveō, -ēre, mōvī, mōtus

mūrus, -ī

rīpa, -ae

ruō, -ere, -uī, -utus

saevus, -a, -um

tendō, -ere, tetendī, tentus

tot (indecl adj)

tōtus, -a, -um

Tyrius, -a, -um

vocō, -āre

vox, vōcis (f)

7 times

accipiō, -ere, accēpī, acceptus

advertō, -ere, advertī, adversus

ait

āra, -ae

at

aura, -ae

causa, -ae

cūra, -ae

Danaus, -a, -um

dea, -ae

dulcis, -e (adj)

etiam (adv)

faciō, -ere, fēcī, factus

ferrum, -ī

furo, -ere, furuī, -

genus, -eris (n)

heu (interj)

hinc (adv)

iactō, -āre

misceō, -ēre, -uī, mixtus

miser, -era, -erum

moenia, -ium (n pl)

nascor, nascī, nātus

nox, noctis (f)

nūmen, -inis (n)

ōrō, -āre

pātria, -ae

quālis, -e (adj)

sīdus, -eris (n)

simul (adv)

tegō, -ere, -xī, -ctus (also, tectum, -ī)

vulnus, -eris (n)

6 times

celer, -eris, -ere (adv = celeriter)

coniunx, coniugis (m/f)

crūdēlis, -e (adj)

cursus, -ūs

dēsero, -ere, -seruī, -sertus

dolor, -ōris (m)

dōnum, -ī

dum (conj)

harēna, -ae

īdem, eadem, idem

immānis, -e (adj)

imperium, -ī

incipiō, -ere, -cēpī, -ceptus

longus, -a, -um

mereō, -ēre, -uī, -itus

nam / namque (adv)

nūbēs, -is (f)

nullus, -a, -um

parens, -ntis (m/f)

pēs, pedis (m)

pietās, -ātis (f)

pōnō, -ere, posuī, positus

populus, -ī

porta, -ae

possum, posse, potuī, -

prior / prius, priōris (comp adj)

puer, -ī

rapiō, -ere, rapuī, raptus

sanguis, -inis (m)

scopulus, -ī

sēdes, -is (f)

servō, -āre

socius, -ī

spes, speī

stō, stāre, stetī, status

subeō, -īre, -iī, -itus

tellūs, -ūris (f)

Trōiānus, -a, -um

vastus, -a, -um

vērus, -a, -um

vīs, vis (f)

volvō, -ere, -ī, -ūtus

vos (pers pron)

vultus, -ūs

5 times

Aeolus, -ī

agmen, -inis (n)

anima, -ae

annus, -ī

antrum, -ī

aperiō, -īre, aperuī, apertus

capiō, -ere, cēpī, captus

clāmor, -ōris (m)

cor, -dis (n)

crēdō, -ere, credidī, creditus

cunctus, -a, -um

Dardanius, -a, -um

dēmittō, -ere, -mīsī, -missus

extrēmus, -a, -um

fīnis, -is (m)

fortis, -e (adj)

fuga, -ae

fugiō, -ere, fūgī, fugitus

gemitus, -ūs

gerō, -ere, gessī, gestus

hūc (adv)

impōnō, -ere, -posuī, -positus

imus, -a, -um

intereā (adv)

is, ea, id (demon pron / adj)

lācrima, -ae

laetus, -a, -um

lateō, -ēre, -uī, -

latus, lateris (n)

Libya, -ae

līmen, -inis (n)

lūmen, -inis (n)

lux, lūcis (m)

mare, -is (n)

memor, -oris (adj)

mens, -ntis (f)

metus, -ūs

mīror, -ārī

mōles, -is (f)

mons, montis (m)

morior, morī

nē (conj)

neque (conj)

nōmen, -inis (n)

nōs (pron)

ōra, -ae

pars, -tis (f)

poena, -ae

post (adv and prep + acc)

premō, -ere, pressī, pressus

prōspiciō, -ere, -spexī, -spectus

pulcher, -chra, -chrum

puppis, -is (f)

quaerō, -ere, quaesīvi, -sītus

referō, -ferre, -tulī, -lātus

Rōmānus, -a, -um

sacer, -cra, -crum

sedeō, -ēre

silva, -ae

sōlus, -a, -um

somnus, -ī

soror, -ōris (f)

sors, -tis (f)

surgō, -ere, surrexī, surrectus

taceō, -ēre, -uī, -itus

tandem (adv)

tēlum, -ī

templum, -ī

tergum, -ī

tollō, -ere, sustulī, sublātus

ullus, -a, -um

varius, -a, -um

vester, -tra, -trum

vincō, -ere, vīci, victus

4 times

Acestēs, -ae (m)

Achātes, -ae (m)

adeō, -īre, -iī, -itus

aeternus, -a, -um

antīquus, -a, -um

artus, -ūs

arvum, -ī

āvertō, -ere, āvertī, āversus

cadō, -ere, cecedī, cāsus

cāsus, -ūs

cernō, -ere, crēvī, crētus

certus, -a, -um

clārus, -a, -um

comes, comitis (m/f)

comitō, -āre

condō, -ere, condidī, conditus

cōnūbium, -i

crīnis, -is (m)

culmen, -inis (n) (columen, -inis)

custōs, -ōdis (m/f)

diēs, diēī

dīsiciō, -ere, dīsiēcī, dīsiectus

enim (adv)

equus, -ī

ēripiō, -ere, ēripuī, ēreptus

Eurus, -ī

forma, -ae

foveō, -ēre, fōvī, fōtus

fūnus, -eris (n)

geminus, -a, -um

genitor, -ōris (m)

Hector, -oris (m)

homō, -inis (m)

horrendus, -a, -um

hostis, -is (m)

incendō, -ere, -cendī, -census

inimīcus, -a, -um

iuvō, -āre

Karthāgo, Karthāginis (f)

Lāocoon, Lāocoontis (m)

lātē (adv)

legō, -ere, lēgī, lectus

Libycus, -a, -um

linquō, -ere

longē (adv)

maneō, -ēre, mansī, mansus

miseror, -ārī, -ātus

mōlior, -īrī, -ītus

mortālis, -e (adj)

murmur, -uris (n)

nemus, -oris (n)

nimbus, -ī

nympha, -ae

optō, -āre

opus, -eris (n)

parō, -āre

passim (adv)

pātrius, -a, -um

pelagus, -ī (n)

plūrimus, -a, -um

potens, -ntis (adj)

Priamus, -ī

quantus, -a, -um

quisquam, quaequam, quicquam

quondam

sequor, -ī, secutus

sistō, -ere, stitī, status

sōl, sōlis (m)

spērō, -āre

spūmō, -āre, -āvī, -ātus

sternō, -ere, strāvī, strātus

Stygius, -a, -um

subitō (adv)

super (adv and prep + acc)

superō, -āre

tam (adv)

ter (adv)

timeō, -ēre, -uī, -

torqueō, ēre, torsī, tortus

trēs, tria (adj)

turba, -ae

tūtus, -a, -um

vadum, -ī

vehō, -ere, vexī, vectus

vertex, -icis (m)

via, -ae

vinculum, -ī

vīta, -ae

3 times

accendō, -ere, accendī, accensus

accipiō, -ere, accēpī, acceptus

aeger, aegra, aegrum

aequō, -āre

aether, -eris (m)

aliquis, aliquid (indef pron)

alter, -era, -erum

amplector, -ī, amplexus

aqua, -ae

arceō, -ēre, arcuī, arctus

armō, -āre

arrectus, -a, -um

Ascanius, -ī

aspectus, -ūs

ast (conj)

attollō, -ere, -, -

audiō, -īre, audīvī, audītus

bis (adv)

breviter (adv)

caecus, -a, -um

campus, -ī

canō, -ere, cecinī, cantus

cārus, -a, -um

cavus, -a, -um

centum (indecl adj)

cōgō, -ere, coēgī, coactus

collum, -ī

colō, -ere, coluī, cultus

consistō, -ere, -stitī, -stitus

contrā (adv or prep + acc)

cruor, cruōris (m)

dēfessus, -a, -um

dēsuper (adv)

discrīmen, -inis (n)

dissimulō, -āre

dīvidō, -ere, dīvīsī, dīvīsus

dolus, -ī

effundō, -ere, effūdī, effūsus

ensis, -is (m)

equidem (adv)

ergo (adv)

ēvertō, -ere, ēvertī, ēversus

exstinguō, -ere, exstinxī, exstinctus

fas (indecl)

fātālis, -e (adj)

fessus, -a, -um

foedō, -āre

frangō, -ere, frēgī, fractus

fremō, -ere, -uī, -itus

fundāmentum, -ī

furor, -ōris (m)

gravis, -e (adj)

gurges, -itis (m)

habeō, -ēre, habuī, habitus

hauriō, -īre, hausī, haustus

hēros, -ōis (m)

Hesperia, -ae

hiems, -emis (f)

honor / honos, -ōris (m)

horreō, -ēre, -uī, -

Īlioneus, -ei (m)

imāgō, -inis (f)

impellō, -ere, -pulī, -pulsus

inānis, -e (adj)

ingredior, -dī, ingressus

insequor, -ī, insecūtus

insignis, -e (adj)

instō, -āre

invideō, -ēre, -vīdī, -vīsus

iste, ista, istum (adj)

Iulius, -ī

iungō, -ere, iunxī, iunctus

iuvenis, -is (m/f)

Latīnus, -a, -um (also, Latīnus, -ī)

licet, licēre, licuit, licitum (impers)

maestus, -a, -um

malus, -a, -um

mel, -mellis (n)

meminī, -isse (defec vb)

mittō, ere, mīsī, missus

mors, mortis (f)

mulceō, -ēre, mulsī, mulsus

mūnus, -eris (n)

nefās (indecl n)

nepos, -ōtis (m/f)

Neptūnus, -i

Notus, -ī

novus, -a, -um

ob (prep + acc)

ōbiciō, -ere, -iēcī, -iectus

omnipotens, -ntis (adj)

ops, opis (f)

Paris, -idis (m)

pariter (adv)

parvus, -a, -um

paucī, -ae, -a (pl adj)

penātēs, -ium (m pl)

penitus, -a, -um

Pergama, -ōrum (pl)

Phrygius, -a, -um

portus, -ūs

postquam (conj)

potior, -īrī, -itus

prō (prep + abl)

putō, -āre

quater (adv)

quippe (adv and conj)

rapidus, -a, -um

recipiō, -ere, -cēpī, -ceptus

regō, -ere, rexī, rectus

relinquō, -ere, -līquī, -lictus

rēmus, -ī

respiciō, -ere, -spexī, -spectus

saltem (adv)

secundus, -a, -um

septem (indecl adj)

sermō, -ōnis (m)

seu (conj)

sinō, -ere, sīvi, situs

solvō, -ere, -ī, solūtus

stagnum, -ī

strīdō, -ere, strīdī, -

superbus, -a, -um

superus, -a, -um

supplex, -icis (adj)

tamen (adv)

tempus, -oris (n)

torus, -ī

trahō, -ere, traxī, tractus

tridens, -ntis (adj)

Trōs, Trōis (m)

tueor, tuērī, tuitus

tumultus, -ūs

turbō, -inis (m)

ultrō (adv)

umerus, -ī

vātēs, -is (m/f)

vel (conj)

vēlum, -ī

vertō, -ere, vertī, versus

volō, -āre

2 times

abdō, -ere, -didī, -dītus

abeō, -īre, abiī, abītus

absistō, -ere, -stitī, -

absum, abesse, āfuī, āfutūrus

accingō, -ere, accinxī, accinctus

Achillēs, Achillis (m)

acūtus, -a, -um

addō, -ere, addidī, additus

adfātus, -ūs

adhūc (adv)

aditus, -ūs

adnītor, -ī, -nīsus / -nixus

adsum, -esse, adfuī, adfutūrus

Aeneadēs, -ae

aes, aeris (n)

agger, -eris (m)

agnoscō, -ere, agnōvī, agnōtus

aliquis, -quid / aliquī, aliquae, aliquod

alveus, -ī

alvus, -ī

amens, -ntis (adj)

amnis, -is (m)

an (conj)

Antheus, -os (Gr acc: Anthea)

aptō, -āre

Aquilō, -ōnis (m)

asper, -era, -erum

audeō, -ēre, ausus (semidep)

aula, -ae

auris, -is (f)

auster, -trī

auxilium, -ī

āvehō, -ere, avexī, avectus

bacchor, -ārī, -ātus (dep)

capessō, -ere, capessīvī, capessītus

carcer, -eris (m)

caterva, -ae

celsus, -a, -um

cervix, -icis (f)

Charon, -ontis (m)

cieō, -ere, cīvī, citus

Cōcȳtus, -ī

colligō, -ere, collēgī, collectus

compāges, -is (f)

compellō, -āre

compōnō, -ere, composuī, compositus

concursus, -ūs

coniugium, -ī

consīdō, -ere, consēdī, consessus

conspectus, -ūs

conspiciō, -ere, -spexī, -spectus

contingō, -ere, -tigī, -tactus

copia, -ae

crēber, -bra, -brum

Creūsa, -ae

currus, -ūs

cuspis, -idis (f)

cymba, -ae (cumba, -ae)

Dardanus, -a, -um

dēfendō, -ere, -fendī, -fensus

dēferō, dēferre, -tulī, -lātus

deinde (adv)

dēlūbrum, -ī

dimittō, -ere, dimīsī, dimissus

Dīs, Dītis (m)

dispellō, -ere, dispulī, dispulsus

dīversus, -a, -um

dīves, -itis (adj)

dūrus, -a, -um

dux, ducis (m/f)

ecce

efferō, -ferre, extulī, ēlatus

ēmittō, -ere, ēmīsī, ēmissus

ēvādō, -ere, ēvāsī, ēvāsus

excidō, ere, excidī, -

excitō,-āre

excūdō, -ere, excūdī, excūsus

exerceō, ēre, exercuī, exercitus

exsanguis, -e (adj)

extemplō (adv)

fallō, -ere, fefellī, falsus

fēmineus, -a, -um

feriō, -īre, -, -

fētus, -a, -um

fidēs, -eī

fīdus, -a, -um

fingō, -ere, finxī, fictus

flūmen, -inis (n)

fluvius, -ī

foedus, -eris (n)

folium, -ī

frater, -tris (m)

frēnō, -āre

frīgus, -oris (n)

frons, -dis (f)

frūgēs, -um (f)

fugō, -āre

fulgeō,-ēre, fulsī, -

fundō, -ere, fūdī, fūsus

furiō, -āre

gaudeō, -ēre, gāvīsus (semidep)

germānus, -a, -um

glomerō, -āre

gradior, -ī, gressus

gradus, -ūs

Grāius, -a, -um

graviter (adv)

haereō, -ēre, haesī, haesus

hasta, -ae

horror, -ōris (m)

humus, -ī

iaceō, -ēre, iacuī, iacitus

iaculor, -ārī, -ātus

Iarbas, -ae (m)

ibī (adv)

Īliacus, -a, -um

Īlium, -ī

immemor, -oris (adj)

immensus, -a, -um

immineō, -ēre

immittō, -ere, -mīsī, -missus

incēdō, -ere, -cessī, -cessus

incendium, -ī

incolumis, -e (adj)

incubō, -āre

inde (adv)

infēlix, -icis (adj)

inferō, inferre, intulī, illātus

infīgō, -ere, infīxī, infixus

ingemō, -ere, ingemuī , -

inīquus, -a, -um

iniūria, -ae

innupta, -ae

inops, -opis (adj)

insuper (adv)

invictus, -a, -um

Īris, Īris (f; or Īridis)

iugum, -ī

iūrō, -āre

iūs, iūris (n)

iustus, -a, -um

lābor, labī, lapsus

laedō, -ere, laesī, laesus

lapsus, -ūs

Latium, -iī

lātrō, -āre

lātus, -a, -um

laus, laudis (f)

laxō, -āre

levō, -āre

lex, lēgis (f)

lingua, -ae

locō, -āre

loquor, -ī, locūtus

lōrum, -ī

luctor, -ārī, -ātus

māchina, -ae

māgālia, -ium (n pl)

magis (adv)

mandō, -āre

Marcellus, -ī

metuō, -ēre, -uī, -ūtus

mille, milia

ministrō, -āre

minor, -ārī

minor, minus (comp adj)

mīrābilis, -e (adj)

modus,-ī

mollis,- e (adj)

moneō, -ēre, -uī, -itus

monstrum, -ī

moror, -ārī, -ātus

morsus, -ūs

mos, mōris (m)

nāvita, -ae (m)

nectō, -āre

nesciō, -īre

nī (adv)

nihil

nōdus, -ī

novō, -āre

nūbilus, -a, -um

numerus, -ī

nuntius, -a, -um

obstipescō, -ere, -puī, -

ōlim (adv)

Olympus, -ī

optimus, -a, -um

orbis, -is (m)

ostendō, -ere, ostendī, ostentus

Pallas, -adis (f)

palus, -ūdis (f)

pandō, -ere, pandī, passus

parcō, -ere, pepercī, parsurus

patior, patī, passus

pecus, -udis (f)

pendō, -ere, pependī, pensus

Phoenissa, -ae

placidus, -a, -um

Poenī, -ōrum (m pl)

portitor, -ōris (m)

praestō, -āre, -stitī, -stātus

priusquam (*1 is* prius *and* quam *by tmesis*)

procella, -ae

procul (adv)

profundus, -a, -um

prohibeō, -ēre, -uī, -itus

prōles, -is (f)

propinquō, -āre

prōprius, -a, -um

propter (prep + acc)

prōsequor, -ī, -secūtus

Prōserpina, -ae

puella, -ae

pulvis, -eris (m)

quandō (adv and conj)

quiescō, -ere, -ēvi, -ētus

quisquis, quidquid (indef pron)

quotiens (adv)

rāmus, -ī

ratis, -is (f)

recēdō, -ere, -cessī, -cessus

recens, -ntis (adj)

redūco, -ere, -xī, -ctus

regiō, regiōnis (f)

reliquiae, -ārum

resolvō, -ere, -solvī, -solūtus

rēstō, -are, -stitī, -

revīsō, -ere, -, -

rogus, -ī

rota, -ae

rumpō, -ere

rūpes, -is (f)

sacerdōs, -ōtis (m/f)

sacrō, -āre

saepiō, -īre, -psī, -ptus

saeviō, -īre, -iī, -itus

sāl, salis (n)

salum, -ī

Saturnius, -a, -um

scaena, -ae

secō, -are, -uī, -tus

sepeliō, -īre, sepelīvi, sepultus

Sergestus, -ī

serō, -ere, sēvī, satus

Siculus, -a, -um

sileō, -ere, -uī

silex, -icis (m)

sinus, -ūs

solium, -ī

sonitus, -ūs

sonō, -āre, -uī, -ītus

spargō, -ere, sparsī, sparsus

spelunca, -ae

spernō, -ere, sprēvī, sprētus

sponte (adv or abl noun)

statuō, -ere, -uī, -ūtus

stīpō, -āre

strepitus, -ūs

struō, -ere, struxī, structus

subdūcō, -ere, -xī, -ctus

sūbiciō, -ere, -iēcī, -iectus

submergō, -ere, -sī, -sus

sufficiō, -ere, -fēcī, -fectus

sūmō, -ere, sumpsī, sumptus

superēmineō, -ēre, -uī, -

suscipiō, -ere, -cēpī, -ceptus

suus, -a, -um

syrtis, -is (f)

Tartareus, -a, -um

taurus, -ī

temperō, -āre

tempestās, -ātis (f)

tenuis, -e (adj)

terreō, -ere, -uī, -itus

Tiberīnus, -a, -um

trans (prep + acc)

tremō, -ere, -uī, -

tristis, -e (adj)

Trōas, -adis (adj)

Trōius, -a, -um

tumidus, -a, -um

turbidus, -a, -um

turbō, -āre

Tyndaris, -idis (f)

umquam

unde (adv)

uterque, utraque, utrumque (adj)

uterus, -ī

validus, -a, -um

velut / veluti (adv)

verrō, -ere, verrī, versus

Vesta, -ae

vestis, -is (f)

vetō, -āre

victor, -ōris (m)

vigil, -ilis (adj)

vitta, -ae

vīvus, -a, -um

volō, velle, voluī, -

1 time

Abas, Abantis (m)

abferō, abferre, abstulī, ablātus

abluō, -ere, abluī, ablūtus

abripiō, abripere, abripuī, abreptus

abscondō, abscondere, abscondidī,
    absconditus

absūmō, absumere, absumpsī,
    absumptum

accēdō, -ere, accessī, accessus

accumbō, -ere, accubuī, accubitus

accumulō, -āre

Acherōn, Acherontis (m)

Achīvus, -a, -um

aciēs, -ēi (f)

adgredior, -ī, adgressus

adloquor, -ī, adlocūtus

admīror, -ārī, -ātus

admittō, -ere, admīsī, admissus

admoneō, -ēre, admonuī, admonitus

adnō, -āre

adorior, -īrī, adortus

adorō, -āre

adpāreō, -ēre, adparuī, adparitus

adquirō, -ere, adquisīvī, adquisītus

adsistō, -ere, adstitī, -

adspectō, -āre

adstō, -āre, astitī, -

adsurgō, -ere, adsurrexī, adsurrectus

adultus, -a, -um

advehō, -ere, advexī, advectus

adytum, -ī

Aeacidēs, -ae (m)

Aeolia, -ae

aequaevus, -a, -um

āēr, āeris (m)

aestās, -ātis (f)

aestuō, -āre

aestus, -ūs

aetās, aetātis (f)

aetherius, -a, -um

Africus, -a, -um

ager, -grī

aggerō, -āre

Āiax, Āiācis (m)

āla, -ae

ālātus, -a, -um

Albānus, -a, -um

Alcīdes, -ae (m)

Alētēs, -ī

aliēnus, -a, -um

aliter (adv)

alligō, -āre

almus, -a, -um

alternō, -āre

alumnus, -ī

amans, amantis (m/f)

amārus, -a, -um

ambiō, -īre, -īvī, -ītus

ambō, -ae, -ō (pl adj)

amiciō, -īre, amixī, amictus

amictus, -ūs

Amphrȳsus / -os, -ī

ancora, -ae

anguis, -is (m/f)

anne (conj: an + ne)

apis, -is (f)

Apollō, -onis

aprīcus, -a, -um

Arae, -ārum

arboreus, -a, -um

arcus, -ūs

Argī, -ōrum

Argīvus, -a, -um

Argolicus, -a, -um

āridus, -a, -um

armentum, -ī

armus, -ī

arō, -āre

ars, artis (f)

ascendō, -ere, ascendī, ascensus

astrum, -ī

atrium, -ī

attonitus, -a, -um

aurum, -ī

Ausonius, -a, -um

auspicium, -ī

autem (adv)

autumnus, -a, -um

āvellō, -ere, avulsī, avulsus

avidus, -a, -um

avis, -is (f)

avus, -ī

Bacchus, -ī

barba, -ae

barbarus, -a, -um

beātus, -a, -um

bene (adv)

bīgae, -ārum

birēmis, -e (adj)

bonus, -a, -um

brevis, -e (adj)

caelestis, -e (adj)

caelicola, -ae

caenum, -ī

caeruleus, -a, -um

Caīcus, -i

calcar, -āris (n)

cālīgō, -āre

calor, -ōris (m)

candens, -ntis

cānities, -is (f)

Capys, Capyos / -is

careō, -ēre

carīna, -ae

Cassandra, -ae

castus, -a, -um

cautēs, -is (f)

caverna, -ae

cēdō, -ere, cessī, cessus

cella, -ae

Cerberus, -ī

Cereālis, -e (adj)

Cerēs, -eris (f)

certō, -āre

cervus, -ī

cēterus, -a, -um

chorus, -ī

cingō, -ere, cinxī, cinctus

cinis, -eris (m)

circā (adv)

circumstō, -āre, circumstetī, -

circumvolō, -āre

Cithaeron, -ōnis (m)

citus, -a, -um

cīvis, -is (m/f)

clāmō, -āre

claudō, -ere, clausī, clausus

claustra, -ōrum

clipeus, -ī

Cloanthus, -ī

coepī, -isse (defec vb)

Coeus, -ī

cognōmen, -inis (n)

collis, -is (m)

colōnus, -ī

color, -ōris (m)

coluber, -brī

columna, -ae

coma, -ae

comitātus, -ūs

commendō, -āre

commisceō, -ēre, commixuī, commixtus

committō, -ere, commīsī, commissus

commotus, -ūs

commoveō, -ēre, commōvī, commōtus

commūnis, -e (adj)

compellō, -ere, compulī, compulsus

comprimō, -ere, compressī, compressus

conciliō, -āre

conclāmō, -āre

concludō, -ere, conclūsī, conclūsus

concrētus, -ūs

concutiō, -ere, concussī, concussus

confiteor, -ērī, confessus (semidep)

coniungō, -ere, -iunxī, -iunctus

conlābor, -ī, conlapsus

cōnor, -ārī, conātus

conscendō, -ere, -scendī, -scensus

conscius, -a, -um

contendō, -ere, -tendī, -tentus

contineō, -ēre, -tinuī, -tentus

continuō (adv)

contorqueō, -ēre, -torsī, -tortus

contus, -ī

convertō, -ere, -vertī, -versus

coorior, -īrī, coortus

cōram (adv)

corneus, -a, -um

cornū, -ūs

coruscus, -a, -um

croceus, -a, -um

crūdus, -a, -um

cruentus, -a, -um

cubitum, -ī

culpa, -ae

culpō, -are

cumulus, -ī

cupīdō, -inis (f)

cur (adv)

curva, -ae

Cȳclōpēus, -a, -um

Cyllēnius, -a, -um

Cȳmothoē, -es (f)

Cynthus, -ī

damnō, -āre

Dardanidēs, -ae (m)

Dardanis, -idis (adj)

dēbellō, -āre

dēbeō, -ēre, dēbuī, dēbitus

dēcēdō, -ere, -cessī, -cessus

dēclīnō, -āre

dēcurrō, -ere, -cucurrī, -

decus, -oris (n)

dēdūcō, -ere, -dūxī, -ductus

dēficiō, -ere, -fēcī, -fectus

dēfīgō, -ere, -fīxī, -fixus

dēfungor, -ī, -functus

dehinc (adv)

dēhiscō, -ere, dēhīvī, -

dēiciō, -ere, -iēcī, -iectus

Dēiopēa, -ae (f)

dēmum (adv)

dēniquē (adv)

dēpascor, dēpascī, -pastus

dēpendeō, -ēre, -, -

dēscendō, -ere, -scendī, -scensus

dēscrībō, -ere, -scripsī, -scriptus

dēsinō, -ere, -siī, -situs

dēsistō, -ere, -stitī, -stitus

dēstruō, -ere, -struxī, -structus

dētineō, -ēre, -tinuī, -tentus

dētorqueō, -ēre, -torsī, -tortus

dētrūdō, -ere, -trūsī, -trūsus

dēturbō, -āre

dēveniō, -īre, dēvēnī, dēventus

dēvolō, -āre

Dīana, -ae

dico, -āre

difficilis, -e (adj)

diffugiō, -ere, diffūgī, -

diffundō, -ere, diffūdī, diffūsus

dignor, -ārī, -ātus

dīlābor, -ī, dīlāpsus

dīripiō, -ere, dīripuī, dīreptus

discernō, -ere, discrēvī, discrētus

discessus, -ūs

distendō, -ere, distendī, distentus

dīvellō, -ere, dīvellī, dīvulsus

doceō, -ēre, docuī, doctus

doleō, -ēre, doluī, dolitus

domina, -ae

dominus, -ī

dorsum, -ī

dracō, -ōnis (m)

ductor, ductōris (m)

duō, -ae, -ō (pl adj)

dūplex, -icis

dūrō, -āre

eburnus, -a, -um

ēdūcō, -ere, ēdūxī, ēductus

efficiō, -ere, effēcī, effectus

effodiō, -ere, effōdī, effosus

effugiō, -ere, effūgī, -

effulgeō, -ēre, effulsī, -

egeō, -ēre, eguī, -

ēgredior, -ī, egressus

ēgregius, -a, -um

ēiciō, -ere, ēiēcī, ēiectus

elephantus, -ī

Elissa, -ae

ēmoveō, -ēre, -mōvī, -mōtus

Enceladus, -ī

ēnumerō, -āre

epulae, -ārum (f)

epulor, -ārī, -ātus

eques, -itis (m)

Ērebus, -ī

Erīnÿs, -ÿos (f)

error, -ōris (m)

ēructō, -āre

ēruō, -ere, ēruī, ērutus

Eryx, Erycis (m)

etsī (conj)

Eurōtās, -ae (m)

ēvānescō, -ere, ēvānuī, ēvānitūrus

exanimus, -a, -um

exardescō, -ere, exarsī, exarsus

excēdō, -ere, excessī, excessus

excidium, -ī

excipiō, -ere, excēpī, exceptus

excubiae, -ārum

excutiō, -ere, excussī, excussus

exhālō, -āre

exigō, -ere, -egī, -actus

exiguus, -a, -um

exim (adv; equivalent to exindē)

exitus, -ūs

exoptō, -āre

exordium, -ī

expediō, -īre, -īvī, -ītus

expendō, -ere, expendī, expensus

expertus, -a, -um

expleō, -ēre, explēvī, explētus

explōrō, -āre

expōnō, -ere, exposuī, expositus

exprōmō, -ere, exprompsī, expromptus

exspectō, -āre

exspīrō, -āre

exstinguō, -ere, -stinxī, -stinctus

exstruō, -ere, exstruxī, exstructus

extendō, -ere, extendī, extentus

exterreō, -ēre, exterruī, exterritus

exterus, -a, -um

exuō, -ere, exuī, exūtus

exūrō, -ere, exussī, exustus

exuviae, -ārum

fabricō, -āre

facessō, -ere, facessī, facessītus

faciēs, -eī

facilis, -e (adj)

falsus, -a, um

famēs, -is (f)

fastigium, -ī

fatiscō, -ere, -, -

faucēs, -ium

fax, facis (f)

fēmina, -ae

ferrūgineus, -a, -um

ferus, -a, -um

fervescō, -ere, -, -

festus, -a, -um

fētus, -ūs

fīducia, -ae

fidus, -a, -um

figō, -ere, fixī, fixus

fīlius, -ī

fīō, -erī, factus

flammō, -āre

flāvus, -a, -um

flectō, -ere, flexī, flectus

fleō, -ēre, flēvī, flētus

flētus,-ūs

flōreō, -ēre, flōruī, -

flōreus, -a, -um

flōs, -ōris (m)

fluō, -ere, fluxī, fluxus

fodiō, -ere, fōdī, fossus

foedus, -a , -um

fōmes, -itis (m)

foris, -is (f)

forsan (adv)

fortē (adv)

fortūna, -ae

fortūnō, -āre

forus, -ī

fragor, -ōris (m)

frāgrō, -āre

fraudō, -āre

fraus, -dis (f)

fretum, -ī

frīgidus, -a, -um

frondeus, -a, -um

frons, -ntis (f)

fūcus, -ī

fulmen, -inis (n)

fulvus, -a, -um

fūmus, -ī

fundō, -āre

fungor, -ī, functus

fūnis, -is (m)

furtīvus, -a, -um

furtum, -ī

Gaetūlus, -ī (Gaetūlus, -a, -um)

galea, -ae

Gallus, -ī (Gallus, -a, -um)

Ganymēdes, -is (m)

Garamantis, -idis (m)

gaudium,-ī

gaza, -ae

gemō, -ere, gemuī, gemitus

generō, -āre

gestō, -āre

gignō, -ere, genuī, genitus

glaeba, -ae

glaucus, -a, -um

glōria, -ae

gnātus, -a, -um (*equivalent to*
    nātus, -a, -um fr. nascor, -ī)

Gorgō, -onis (f)

grandaevus, -a, -um

grandō, -inis (m)

grātus, -a, -um

Grȳnēus, -a, -um

guttur, -uris (n)

habēna, -ae

hālitus, -ūs

Hammōn, -ōnis (m)

hebetō, -āre

hēres, -ēdis (m/f)

hībernus, -a, -um

hōra, -ae

horresco, -ere, -uī, -

hospes, -itis (m)

hospitium, -ī

hūmānus, -a, -um

hymenaeus, -i

iānitor, -ōris (m)

iaspis, -idis (f)

ibīdem (adv)

īdem, eadem, idem

ignārus, -a, -um

ignāvus, -a, -um

igneus, -a, -um

ignōbilis, -e (adj)

ignōtus, -a, um

Īlias, -adis (m)

illīc (adv)

illūc (adv)

imber, -bris (m)

immītis, -e (adj)

immōtus, -a, -um

impius, -a, -um

implicō, -āre

imprimō, -ere, -pressī, -pressus

impūne (adv)

incertus, -a, -um

inclēmens, -ntis (adj)

inclūdō, -ere, -clūsī, -clūsus

inclutus, -a, -um

incognitus, -a, -um

increpō, -āre

incultus, -a, -um

incumbō, -ere, -cubuī, -cubitus

incutiō, -ere, -cussī, -cussus

indignor, -ārī, -ātus

indignus, -a, -um

indomitus, -a, -um

induō, -ere, -duī, -dūtus

infandus, -a, -um

infectus, -a, -um

infensus, -a, -um

infestus, -a, -um

informis, -e (adj)

inhumātus, -a, -um

inlabor, -ī, inlapsus

inlīdō, -ere, illīsī, illīsus

inremeābilis, -e (adj)

insānia, -ae

insideō, -ēre, -sēdī, -sessus

insidiae, -ārum

insinuō, -āre

insomnia, -ae

insonō, -āre

inspiciō, -ere, -spexī, -spectus

instar (indecl)

insula, -ae

intendō, -ere, -tendī, -tentus

intentō, -āre

interpres, interpretis (m/f)

intonō, -āre

intorqueō, -ēre, -torsī, -tortus

intrō, -āre

intrōgredior, -ī, -gressus

intus (adv)

inultus, -a, -um

invādō, -ere, -vāsī, -vāsus

invehō, -ere, -vexī, -vectus

invidia, -ae

invītus, -a, -um

invius, -a, -um

irrītō, -āre

istinc (adv)

ita (adv)

Ītalus, -a, -um

iter, itineris (n)

iuba, -ae

iūdicium, -ī

iustitia, -ae

iuventus, iuventūtis (f)

iuxtā (adv)

Lacaena, -ae (f)

lacus, -ūs

laena, -ae

laetitia, -ae

laetor, laetārī, laetātus

laevus, -a, -um

lambō, -ere, lambī, lambitus

lāmentum, -ī

largus, -a, -um

latēbra, -ae

Lātōna, -ae

laudō, -āre

Laurens, Laurentis (adj)

Lāvīnius, -a, -um

laxus, -a, -um

Lēnaeus, -a, -um

lēniō, -īre, lenīvi, lenītus

lētum, -ī

levis, -e (adj)

lībō, -āre

lignum, -ī

ligō, -āre

līlium, -ī

līmus, -a, -um

līvidus, -a, -um

longaevus, -a, -um

luctus, -ūs

lūdō, -ere, lūsī, lūsus

lūna, -ae

luō, -ere, luī, luitūrus

lustrō, -āre

luxus, -ūs

Lycia, -ae

Lycius, -a, -um

lympha, -ae

mactō, -āre

madeō, -ēre, maduī, -

Maeonia, -ae

maereō, -ēre, maeruī, -

magister, -tri

magistrātus, -ūs

magnanimus, -a, -um

māior, māius (comp adj)

Mānes, -ium (m)

manifestus, -a, -um

marmor, -oris (m)

Marpēsius, -a, -um

māter, -tris (f)

mātūrō, -āre

Maurūsia, -ae

Māvors, -rtis (m)

maximus, -a, -um

meātus, -ūs

medicō, -āre

meditor, -ārī, -ātus

melior, melius (comp adj)

membrum, -ī

memorābilis, -e (adj)

memorō, -āre

mensis, -is (m)

mentum, -ī

micō, -āre

minister, -tra, -trum

miserābilis, -e (adj)

misereō, -ēre, -uī, -itus

mītra, -ae

Mnestheus, -eī

mōbilitās, -ātis (f)

molliō, -īre, -īvī, -ītus

monstrō, -āre

mora, -ae

moribundus, -a, -um

mox (adv)

mūgītus, -ūs

multiplex, -icis (adj)

mūrex, -icis (m)

Mūsa, -ae

mūtō, -āre

Mycēnae, -ārum

nāvigō, -āre

nebula, -ae

necdum (conj)

nefandus, -a, -um

negō, -āre

nēquīquam

neu (conj)

nimbōsus, -a, -um

nimium (adv)

nītor, -ī, nīsus / nixus

no, nāre

nocturnus, -a, -um

Nomās, -adis (m/f)

nōndum (adv)

noscō, -ere, nōvi, nōtum

novitās, -ātis (f)

noxa, -ae

numquam (adv)

nusquam (adv)

nūtrimentum, -ī

obdūcō, -ere, -xī, -ctus

obeō, -īre, -ii, -itus

obferō, -ferre, -tulī, -lātus

oblīviscor, -ī, oblītus

obmūtescō, -ere, obmutuī, -

obnītor, -ī, obnīxus

oborior, -īrī, -ortus

obruō, -ere, -uī, -utus

obscūrus, -a, -um

obtundō, -ere, -tudī, -tūsus

obtūtus, -ūs

obvius, -a, -um

occīdō, -ere, -cīdī, -cīsus

occubō, -āre

occultō, -āre

occumbō, -ere, -cubuī, -cubitus

occupō, -āre

ōcior, ōcius (comp adj)

ōdī, ōdisse (defec vb)

Oenōtrus, -a, -um

offa, -ae

officium, -ī

Oīleus, -ī

ollus, -a, -um (old form of ille, illa, illud)

ōmen, -inis (n)

omnīno (adv)

onerō, -āre

onus, -eris (n)

operiō, -īre, -uī, opertus

opīmus, -a, -um

oppetō, -ere, -īvī, -ītus

opprimō, -ere, -pressī, -pressus

Orcus, -ī

orēas, -adis (f)

orgia, -ōrum (n pl)

Ōrīōn, -ōnis (m)

Orontes, -is (m)

os, ossis (n)

ostium, -ī

ōtium, -ī

paenitet (impers)

palma, -ae

Parca, -ae

pāreō, -ēre, -uī, -itus

pariō, -ere, peperī, paritus / partus

parō, -āre

partiō, -īre, -īvī, -ītus

parum (adv)

parvulus, -a, -um

pascō, -ere

pateō, -ēre, -uī, -

patruus, -ī

pavor, -ōris (m)

pax, pācis (f)

penētrālis, -e (adj)

penna, -ae

peragō, -ere, -ēgī, -actus

percellō, -ere, -culī, -culsus

percutiō, -ere, -cussī, -cussus

pereō, -īre, -ii, -itus

pererrō, -āre

perficiō, -ere, -fēcī, -factus

perfidus, -a, -um

perflō, -āre

perfundō, -ere, -fūdī, -fūsus

perhibeō, -ēre, -ui, -itus

perlābor, -ī, -lapsus

permittō, -ere, -mīsī, -missus

pernix, -īcis (adj)

personō, -āre, -ui, -itus

pertemptō, -āre

pharētra, -ae

pigeō, -ēre, -uī, -itus

pingō, -ere, -xī, pictum

pinguis, -e (adj)

Pīrithous, -ī

pius, -a, -um

plācō, -āre

plangor, -ōris (m)

planta, -ae

plēnus, -a, -um

plūma, -ae

plūs, plūris (comp adj)

polus, -ī

pondus, ponderis (n)

populor, -ārī, -ātus

portō, -āre

posthabeō, -ēre, -uī, -itus

praeceptum, -ī

praeda, -ae

praemetuō, -ere, -, -

praerumpō, -ere, praerūpī, praeruptus

praesaepe, -is (n)

praesens, -ntis (adj)

praesentiō, -īre, praesensī, sensus

praetendō, -ere, -ī, praetentus

praetereā (adv)

praeterlābor, -ī, lapsus

praetexō, -ere, -uī, praetextus

prāvus, -a, -um

prehendō, -ere, -ī, prehensus

pretium, -ī

prex, precis (f)

priscus, -a, -um

pristinus, -a, -um

procax, -ācis (adj)

profor, -ārī, -ātus

profugus, -a, -um

prōgenies, -ēī

prōgignō, -ere, prōgenuī, prōgenitus

prōmereō, -ēre, -uī, -itus

prōnubus, -a, -um

prōnus, -a, -um

prōpāgō, -āre

properō, -āre

propior, propius (comp adj)

prōra, -ae

prōtinus (adv)

proximus, -a, -um

pudor, -ōris (m)

pugna, -ae

purpureus, -a, -um

pūrus, -a, -um

Pygmalion, -ōnis (m)

quam with comparative

quamquam (conj)

quassō, -āre

quatiō, -ere, -, quassus

queō, quīre, quīvī, quitus

querēla, -ae

queror, -ī, questus

quia (conj)

quīcumque, quaecumque, quodcumque

quies, -ētis (f)

quīn (conj)

quīque, quaeque, quodque

Quirīnus, -ī

quōnam (adv)

quoniam (adv)

quot (indecl pl adj)

rabidus, -a, -um

rabiēs, -iēī (f)

radius, -iī

raptō, -āre

rārus, -a, -um

raucus, -a, -um

rebellis, -is (adj)

recidīvus, -a, -um

recumbō, -ere, -cubuī, -

recusō, -āre

recutiō, -ere, -, -cussus

redeō, -īre, -iī, -itus

redoleō, -ēre, -uī, -

refugiō, -ere, -fūgī, -

refulgeō, -ēre, -fulsi, -

refundō, -ere, -fūdī, -fusus

regnātor, -ōris (m)

regnō, -āre

repellō, -ere, reppulī, repulsus

reperiō, -īre, repperī, repertum

repleō, -ēre, -ēvi, -ētus

repōnō, -ere, -posuī, -postus

resideō, -ēre, -sēdī, -

resīdō, -ere, -sēdī, -

resistō, -ere, -stitī, -

resonō, -āre

rēspondeō, -ēre, -dī, -sus

resurgō, -ere, -surrexī, -surrectus

revocō, -āre

revolvō, -ere, -volvī, -volūtus

rīma, -ae

rīmōsus, -a, -um

rōbur, -oris (n)

Rōma, -ae

Romulus, -ī

roscidus, -a, -um

roseus, -a, -um

rudens, -ntis (m)

ruīna, -ae

rūmor, -ōris (m)

rursus (adv)

rūs, rūris (n)

saepe (adv)

sagitta, -ae

saltus, -ūs

salūs, ūtis (f)

Samus, -ī

sanctus, -a, -um

sanguineus, -a, -um

saniēs, -eī

Sarpēdōn, -onis (m)

sat (adv)

satiō, -āre

saucius, -a, -um

Scaeus, -a, -um

scandō, -ere, scandī, -

scelerō, -āre

scelus, -eris (n)

sceptrum, -ī

scīlicet (adv)

scindō, -ere, scidi, scissus

scintilla, -ae

sciō, -īre, -īvī, -ītus

scūtum, -ī

Scyllaeus, -a, -um

sēcernō, -ere, secrēvī, -crētus

secessus, -ūs

sēclūdō, -ere, -sī, -sus

secūris, -is (f) (acc: secūrim)

sedīle, -is (n)

sēditiō, -ōnis (f)

sēmianimis, -e (adj)

sēmita, -ae

sēmivir, -ī

senātus, -ūs

senectūs, -ūtis (f)

senior, -ōris (comp adj)

sententia, -ae

sentiō, -īre, sensī, sensus

sentus, -a, -um

serēnus, -a, -um

Serestus, -ī

serō, -ere, -uī, -tus

serpens, -ntis (f)

serpō, -ere, -sī, -tus

sībilia, -ōrum (n pl)

Sibylla, -ae

Sicānus, -a, -um

siccō, -āre

Sīdonius, -a, -um

signum, -ī

similis, -e (adj)

Simoīs, -entis (m)

simulācrum, -ī

simulō, -āre

sīn (conj; si + nē)

sine (prep + abl)

singulī, -ae, -a

sinuō, -āre

sīve (conj)

soleō, -ēre, - , -

sollemnis, -e (adj)

sonōrus, -a, -um

sopōrō, -āre

sopōrus, -a, -um

sordidus, -a, -um

Sparta, -ae

speciēs, -eī

speculor, -ārī, -ātus

spīra, -ae

spīritus, -ūs

spīrō, -āre

spolium, -ī

squāleō, -ēre, -uī, -ītus

squālor, -ōris (m)

squāmeus, -a, -um

stabilis, -e (adj)

stello, -āre, -, -ātus

stimulō, -āre

stirps, -pis (f)

strīdor, -ōris (m)

stringō, -ere, strinxī, strictus

studeō, -ēre, studuī, -

stupeō, -ēre, -uī, -

stuppeus, -a, -um

subigō, -ere, -ēgī, -actus

subnectō, -ere, -nexuī, -nexus

subnixus, -a, -um

subolēs, -is (f)

subrigō, -ere, surrexī, surrectus

substō, -āre

subter (adv or prep + acc)

subtrahō, -ere, traxī, -tractus

subvectō, -āre

subvolvō, -ere, -, -

sūdō, -āre

sulcus, -ī

summoveō, -ēre, -mōvī, -mōtus

sumpsō, -ere, sumpsī, sumptus

superbia, -ae

supīnus, -a, -um

sūprā (adv and prep + acc)

suscitō, -āre

suspendō, -ere, -dī, suspensus

suspiciō, -ere, -spexī, -spectus

sūtilis, -e (adj)

Sӯchaeus, -ī

tābeō, -ēre, -, -

tabula, -ae

taeda, -ae

tangō, -ere, tetigī, tactus

tēla, -ae

temnō, -ere, -, -

temptō, -āre

tenax, -ācis (adj)

Tenedos, -ī (f)

terō, -ere, trīvī, trītus

terribilis, -e (adj)

terrificō, -āre

territō, -āre

tertius, -a, -um

testor, -ārī, -ātus

testūdo, -inis (f)

thalamus, -ī

theātrum, -ī

Thēseus, -a, -um

Thӯias, -adis (f)

thymum, -ī

timor, -ōris (m)

torreō, -ēre, -uī, tostus

torvus, -a, -um

totidem (adv)

totiens (adv)

trabs, trabis (f)

trāiciō, -ere, -iēcī, -iectus

tranquillus, -a, -um

transfīgō, -ere, -fīxī, -fīxus

transmittō, -ere, -mīsī, -missus

transportō, -āre

tremefaciō, -ere, -fēcī, -factus

trepidus, -a, -um

trietēricus, -a, -um

trifaux, -cis (adj)

Trīnācrius, -a, -um

Trītōn, -ōnis (m)

Trītōnis, -idis (adj)

Trītōnius, -a, -um

triumphus, -ī

tumeō, -ēre, -, -

tunc (adv)

turpis, -e (adj)

turris, -is (f)

Tӯdīdes, -ae (m)

tyrannus, -ī

Tyrrhēnus, -a, -um

Tӯrus, -ī (f)

ūber, -eris (adj)

ulciscor, ulciscī, ultus

Ulixēs, Ulixis (m)

ulterior, ultierius (comp adj)

ultimus, -a, -um

ultrā (adv and prep)

ultrix, ultrīcis (adj)

ululātus, -ūs

ululō, -āre

ulva, -ae

umbrifer, -era, -erum

ūmeo, -ēre

ūmidus, -a, -um

uncus, -a, -um

undique (adv)

undō, -āre

undōsus, -a, -um

unguis, -is (m)

urgeō, -ēre, ursī, ursus

utinam (adv)

utor, utī, usus

uxōrius, -a, -um

vagor, -ārī, -ātus

valeō, -ēre, -ui, -

vallum, -ī

vānus, -a, -um

vectō, -āre

vēlō, -āre

vēlox, vēlōcis (adj)

venēnum, -ī

venerābilis, -e (adj)

venia, -ae

Venus, -eris (f)

versō, -āre

vertex, -icis (m)

vescor, -ī, -

vestigium, -ī

vetus, -eris (adj)

vibrō, -āre

victōria, -ae

vigeō, -ēre, -, -

vīnum, -ī

virga, -ae

virgō, -inis (f)

viridis, -e (adj)

virtūs, virtūtis (f)

vīvō, -ere, vixi, victus

vix (adv)

volitō, -āre

volūmen, -inis (n)

volūtō, -āre

vorāgō, -inis (f)

vorō, -āre

vulgus, -ī (n)

Zephyrus, -ī

Chapter 7

GRAMMAR REVIEW

- The Grammar Review presents grammatical constructions with explanations and Latin and English examples.

- It includes information that some students might find unnecessary or overly basic, but I would rather include too much than include too little.

- Use the Grammar Review as a checklist: go down the constructions and check off the ones with which you're comfortable so that you can focus on the ones you need to review.

7.1   TERMS TO KNOW

- This is the list of terminology included on p.129 of the College Board's 2019 Course Description. The general terms will be defined below the list, while the grammar-specific terms will be defined and explained in their specific section.

- The Grammar Review will also include constructions not included on this list.

  o Constructions from this list will be starred (*).

  o Constructions not from this list will be *italicized*.

modifies	indirect command	dative of reference
complements	conditionals	dative with special verb
is dependent on	mood	accusative of duration of time
antecedent	imperative	accusative of respect
gerundive	hortatory or jussive subjunctive	ablative absolute
gerund	passive periphrastic	ablative of separation
supine	deponent	ablative of comparison
fearing clause	partitive genitive	ablative of specification
result clause	genitive with impersonal verb	ablative of cause
purpose clause	genitive with adjective	ablative of description
relative clause	genitive with verb of remembering (forgetting)	ablative of degree of difference
relative clause of characteristic	objective genitive	ablative with special verbs

relative clause of purpose	dative of possession	ablative of time when
cum clauses	dative of purpose	ablative of time within which
indirect statement	dative with compound verb	vocative
indirect question	dative of agent	

- modifies—when one word is linked grammatically with another
  - an adjective modifies a noun
  - an adverb modifies a verb, adjective, or other adverb
- complements—when one word completes the meaning of another word by expanding it
  - The loyalty of Diviciacus made Caesar **happy**.
    - "Happy" is the object complement.
  - Aeneas was able **to reach** Italy.
    - "To reach" is the complementary infinitive of "was able."
- is dependent on—when one word requires another word to make it fit in the sentence or make sense in the sentence
  - The number **of Germans** frightened the Romans.
    - "Of Germans" is dependent on "number."

7.2   NOUNS

- It is assumed that you either do not need to review forms or that you can easily review them elsewhere.
- Included here will be all five cases with both common case uses and case uses popular with Caesar and Vergil.

7.2.1   CASE USES

7.2.1.1 Nominative

- *Irregular or Confusing Nominatives*
  - Certain nominative forms of the 3rd declension have endings that are more commonly associated with other cases and declensions.
  - Make sure to know these forms, as their endings can be misleading.

- o custos, custodis
  - ▪ Luce sedet **custos**. (*Aeneid* 4.186)
  - ▪ **The guard** sits under the light.
- o imago, imaginis
  - ▪ Obstipui; subiit cari genitoris **imago**. (*Aeneid* 2.560)
  - ▪ I stood amazed; **the image** of my dear father appeared.
- o sacerdos, sacerdotis
  - ▪ Laocoon, ductus Neptuno sorte **sacerdos**, / sollemnes taurum ingentem mactabat ad aras. (*Aeneid* 2.201–2)
  - ▪ Laocoon, chosen by lot **as priest** to Neptune, was slaughtering a huge bull at solemn altars.
- o tempestas, tempestatis
  - ▪ Tanta **tempestas** subito coorta est. (*Aeneid* 4.28)
  - ▪ So great **a storm** suddenly rose up.

- • *Subject*
  - o The doer of the action of an active verb:
    - ▪ Sic **fortuna** in contentione et certamine utrumque **versavit**. (*Bellum Gallicum* 5.44)
    - ▪ Thus **fortune turned** each within their disagreement and conflict.
    - ▪ **Aeneas** scopulum interea **conscendit**. (*Aeneid* 1.180)
    - ▪ **Aeneas** meanwhile **ascended** the cliff.

  - o The receiver of the action of a passive verb:
    - ▪ Ad eas res conficiendas **Orgetorix deligitur**. (*Bellum Gallicum* 1.3)
    - ▪ **Orgetorix is chosen** to take care of these matters.
    - ▪ cui **regnum** Italiae **Romanaque tellus** / **debetur** (*Aeneid* 4.275–76)
    - ▪ to whom **the kingdom** of Italy **and the Roman land is owed**.

  - o When a form of *sum, esse* begins the sentence, often the sense is "There" + [*sum, esse*] + [nominative noun]:
    - ▪ **Erant** omnino **itinera duo**. (*Bellum Gallicum* 1.6)
    - ▪ **There were** all together **two routes**.
    - ▪ **Sunt** mihi **bis septem** praestanti corpore **Nymphae**. (*Aeneid* 1.71)
    - ▪ **There are fourteen Nymphs** for me of significant attractiveness.

- *Predicate noun or adjective*—the noun or adjective linked to the subject by *sum, esse*:

  o **qui erant** eius regno **finitimi** (*Bellum Gallicum* 5.38)

  o **who were neighbors of / next to** his kingdom

  o ut … **paratiores** ad omnia pericula subeunda **essent** (*Bellum Gallicum* 1.5)

  o so that **they would be more prepared** to face all of the dangers

  o umbrarum **hic locus est** (*Aeneid* 6.390)

  o **this is the place** of shades

7.2.1.2 Genitive

- The genitive functions like an adjective and so will most often be associated with a noun.

  o the **tall** man

  o the man **of great height**

    ▪ Both convey the same idea and both are associated with "man."

    ▪ The first is an adjective ("tall") and the second is a genitive ("of great height").

- When faced with a genitive, look for a noun with which it is translated.

- *with Adjective—used after certain adjectives, some of which use "of" in English, some of which do not

  o quibus rebus nostri perterriti atque **huius** omnino **generis** pugnae *imperiti* (*Bellum Gallicum* 4.24)

  o because of these things, our men were scared and *inexperienced* **in this type** of fighting altogether

  o *dives* **opum** studiisque asperrima belli (*Aeneid* 1.14)

  o *rich* **in resources** and very coarse in its enthusiasm for war

    ▪ *Opum* can also be read as a genitive of respect, especially since *studiis* is an ablative of respect.

- *Description*—used to specify the quality of someone (or thing)

  o Tum T. Balventio, … viro forti et **magnae auctoritatis**, utrumque femur tragula traicitur. (*Bellum Gallicum* 5.35)

  o Then each leg of Titus Balventius, a brave man and a man **of great authority**, is pierced by a spear.

- *Objective
    - Expresses the "direct object" of the implied action of a noun that comes from a verb (contrasted with the subjective genitive which expresses the "subject" of the implied action of a noun that comes from a verb):
        - **The Judgment of Paris** is a subjective genitive (because Paris is doing the judging) but, if you didn't know the story, the question becomes whether Paris is doing the judging or being judged: if he is being judged, it is an objective genitive because he is the direct object of the implied act of judging in the noun judgment.
    - **regnī** *cupiditāte* inductus (*Bellum Gallicum* 1.2)
    - motivated *by his desire* **for power**
        - "Power" is the direct object of the implied act of desiring and so is the objective genitive.
    - dives opum *studiisque* asperrima **belli** (*Aeneid* 1.14)
    - rich in resources and very coarse *in its enthusiasm* **for war**
        - "War" is the direct object of the implied act of being enthusiastic and so is the objective genitive.

- *Partitive—represents the whole in a part-of-a-whole expression.
    - ***Horum omnium*** *fortissimi* sunt Belgae. (*Bellum Gallicum* 1.1)
    - *The bravest **of all of these*** [peoples] are the Belgae.
        - The whole is "all of these peoples," the partitive genitive.
        - The part is the "the bravest."
    - Tu mihi *quodcumque hoc* **regni** … concilias. (*Aeneid* 1.78)
    - You grant to me *whatever* **power** I have.

- *Possession*—shows the possessor of the noun to which it is attached:
    - cum legione *ad fines* **Nerviorum** veniat (*Bellum Gallicum* 5.46)
    - [if] he could come with his legion *to the borders* **of the Nervii**
    - Et primum *parva* **duorum** / *corpora* **natorum** serpens amplexus uterque / implicat. (*Aeneid* 2.213–15)
    - And first each serpent, embracing *the small bodies* **of [Laocoon's] two sons**, folded over them.

- *with Special Verbs—certain verbs take their objects in the genitive:

  o This category combines all special verbs that take the genitive, including the Genitive with Impersonal Verb and the Genitive with Verb of Remembering (Forgetting) in the AP® List of Terminology to Know.

  o *memini, -isse*

    - Nec me *meminisse* pigebit **Elissae**. (*Aeneid* 4.335)

    - Nor will it grieve me *to remember* **Dido**.

  o *misereor, -eri*

    - *Miserere* **domus labentis**. (*Aeneid* 4.318)

    - *Pity* **this collapsing house**.

  o *obliviscor, -i*

    - Heu, **regni rerumque** *oblite* **tuarum**! (*Aeneid* 4.267)

    - Alas, *forget* **this kingdom and your current situation**!

  o *potior, potiri*

    - This verb usually takes its object in the ablative but can on occasion take it in the genitive, as it does here:

      - Et regno occupato per tres potentissimos ac firmissimos populos **totius Galliae** sese *potiri* posse sperant. (*Bellum Gallicum* 1.3)

      - They hope that, after the kingdom is occupied, they can *control* **all of Gaul** through the three most powerful and resolute people.

- *Subjective*

  o Expresses the "subject" of the implied action of a noun that comes from a verb (contrasted with the objective genitive which expresses the "object" of the implied action of a noun that comes from a verb):

    - **The Judgment of Paris** is a subjective genitive (because Paris is doing the judging) but, if you didn't know the story, the question becomes whether Paris is doing the judging or being judged: if he is being judged, it is an objective genitive because he is the direct object of the implied act of judging in the noun judgment. Because he is doing the judging, it is a subjective genitive.

  o Ipso *terrore* **equorum** et *strepitu* **rotarum** ordines plerumque perturbant. (*Bellum Gallicum* 4.33)

- Over and over they disturbed the ranks (of soldiers) *with the terror* **of the horses** and *the noise* **of the wheels.**

  - "The horses" is the subject of the implied act of experiencing terror and "the wheels" of making noise and so they are subjective genitives.

7.2.1.3 Dative

- *with Adjective*—the dative is used after certain adjectives; English idiom will determine whether or not the dative is translated with "to" or "for" or with a different preposition.

  - *Iniquissimo* **nostris** *loco proelium committere coeperunt.* (*Bellum Gallicum* 5.32)

  - They began to undertake the battle in a place *most hated* **to our men.**

  - *Gens* inimica **mihi** *Tyrrhenum navigat aequor.* (*Aeneid* 1.67)

  - A tribe *unfriendly* **to me** sails the Tyrrhenian sea.

- *of Agent

  - The dative is sometimes used to show agency—that is, the doer of a passive action.

  - This most commonly occurs with the future passive participle but can occur with other passive verbs (though rarely), usually perfect passive participles and more a feature of poetry than prose.

  - **Militibus** *autem … de navibus* desiliendum *et in fluctibus* consistendum *et cum hostibus erat* pugnandum. (*Bellum Gallicum* 4.24)

  - **The soldiers** *had to jump down* from the ships and *stand firm* in the waves and *fight* with the enemy.

    - In this example, the passive periphrastic is used impersonally: literally, "it is for the soldiers to jump down … to stand firm … to fight" or "there is a necessity for the soldiers to jump down … to stand firm … to fight."

    - The dative of agent seems to have its origins in the dative of possession; these more literal translations illustrate that connection.

  - *Miscetque* [Aeneas] *viris neque* cernitur **ulli**. (*Aeneid* 1.440)

  - And Aeneas mixes with men and *is not seen* **by anyone.**

- *Of Direction*—the dative is sometimes used with verbs of motion to show direction, similar in meaning to the preposition *ad* plus the accusative.

  - *Huc pauci* **vestris** *adnavimus* **oris**. (*Aeneid* 1.538)

  - A few of us swam **to your shores.**

- o Ei mihi, qualis erat, quantum mutatus ab illo / Hectore qui redit exuvias indutus Achilli / vel Danaum Phrygios iaculatus **puppibus** ignes. (*Aeneid* 2.274–76)

- o Woe is me, what sort was he, how much he had changed from that Hector who returned covered in the spoils of Achilles or having flung Trojan fire **to the ships** of the Greeks.

- • *Double Dative*

  - o A combination of the Dative of Purpose and the Dative of Reference.

  - o Most often occurs with a form of *sum, esse.*

  - o The Dative of Purpose is translated like a predicate of "to be" and the Dative of Reference like a traditional dative with "to" or "for":

    - ▪ **magno** esse **Germanis** *dolori* Ariovisti mortem et superiores nostras victorias (*Bellum Gallicum* 5.29)

    - ▪ that the death of Ariovistus and our overwhelming victories were *a great tragedy* **for the Germans**

  - o In non-*sum-esse* uses, the datives are translated more conventionally:

    - ▪ ne qua legio **alterae legioni** *subsidio* venire posset (*Bellum Gallicum* 5.27)

    - ▪ lest any legion is able to come *for the assistance* **of another legion**

- • *Indirect Object*

  - o The dative is used to show the recipient of the direct object.

  - o English can express this in two ways:

    - ▪ Caesar gives **his men** an order.

    - ▪ Caesar gives an order **to his men**.

  - o Certain verbs take an indirect object; examples from the syllabus are listed here:

    - ▪ verbs of giving

      - • *do, dare*

      - • *pendo, -ere*

      - • *refero, -ferre* (with *gratiam*, to give thanks)

    - ▪ verbs of showing

      - • *remitto, -ere*

    - ▪ verbs of telling

      - • *commendo, -are*

- *confiteor, -eri*
- *dico, -ere*
- *enuntio, -are*
- *nuntio, -are*
- *praedico, -are*
- *scribo, -ere*

o **ei**que filiam suam in matrimonium dat (*Bellum Gallicum* 1.3)

o and he gives **him** his daughter in marriage / and he gives his daughter in marriage **to him**

o Maturate fugam **regi**que haec dicite **vestro**. (*Aeneid* 1.137)

o Hurry your flight and tell **your leader** these things. / Hurry your flight and tell these things **to your leader**.

- *of Possession

  o The dative is used to show possession.

  o The verb "to be" is commonly used with the dative of possession.

    ▪ Tantaene **animis caelestibus** irae? (*Aeneid* 1.11)

    ▪ Do the **heavenly spirits** have so much anger?

    ▪ Sunt **mihi** bis septem praestanti corpore Nymphae. (*Aeneid* 1.71)

    ▪ **I** have fourteen Nymphs of exceptional beauty.

      • Note how the dative of possession, in English, becomes the subject of the verb "to have."

      • There is a more literal but more awkward translation:

        ◊ Is there so much anger **for heavenly spirits**?

        ◊ There are **for me** fourteen Nymphs of exceptional beauty.

  o Most often with pronouns, the dative of possession can be equivalent in meaning to a possessive adjective:

    ▪ Rex erat Aeneas **nobis**. (*Aeneid* 1.544)

    ▪ **Our** king was Aeneas. (Aeneas was king **to us**.)

- *of Purpose

  o Tunc etiam **fatis** aperit Cassandra **futuris** / ora (*Aeneid* 2.246–47)

  o Then also Cassandra opened her mouth **for [the purpose of saying]** future fates.

- o Audierat … hinc populum late regem belloque superbum / venturum **excidio** Libyae. (*Aeneid* 1.20–21)

- o She had heard that this people and proud king would come from afar **for the destruction** of Libya.

- *Of Reference—the dative is used to specify to whom or what the meaning of the sentence refers.

  - o Tum **T. Balventio … viro forti** et magnae auctoritatis utrumque femur tragula traicitur. (*Bellum Gallicum* 5.35)

  - o Then, **in reference to Titus Balventius, a brave man** and one of great authority, each thigh is pierced by a spear.

  - o Talia **iactanti** stridens Aquilone procella / velum adversa ferit. (*Aeneid* 102–3)

  - o **For the man uttering** such words, the approaching storm, roaring with the North Wind, beats his sail.

- *with Special Verbs

  - o compound verbs

    - ▪ Some compound verbs take what looks like their direct object in the dative.

    - ▪ This noun is in reality an indirect object with sometimes an accusative direct object included and sometimes not.

    - ▪ Sometimes the dative will be translated as the object of the preposition that forms the compound.

    - ▪ The compound verbs that take the dative found in the syllabus:

accumbo, -ere	*intendo, -ere*
circumvenio, -ire	*intento, -are*
desum, -esse	*occumbo, -ere*
immineo, -ere	*praeficio, -ere*
impono, -ere	*praesto, -are*
incumbo, -ere	*praesum, -esse*
infingo, -ere	*subvenio, -ire*
inlabor, -i	*succurro, -ere*
inlido, -ere	*suscipio, -ere*
insto, -are	

- translated as a direct object:
    - cum virtute **omnibus** *praestarent* (*Bellum Gallicum* 1.2)
    - since they *surpassed* **everyone** in virtue
- translated as the object of the prefix-preposition:
    - **scopulo**que [Pallas] *infixit* **acuto** (*Aeneid* 1.45)
    - and Athena *tossed* him **onto a sharp crag**

o impersonal verbs
- licet, licere
    - *licere* **illis incolumibus** per se ex hibernis discedere (*Bellum Gallicum* 5.41)
    - (they said that,) according to them, *it is permitted* **to those inhabitants** to leave from their winter quarters

o intransitive verbs
- The intransitive verbs that take the dative found in the syllabus (some of these verbs are transitive in meaning but the use of the dative stems from their history as intransitive verbs):

accido, -ere	*parco, -ere*
credo, -ere	*pareo, -ere*
ignosco, -ere	*persuadeo, -ere*
impero, -are	*praesto sum, esse**
medeor, -eri	

*not strictly speaking a verb but an expression that functions similarly

- eorumque **decretis iudiciisque** *parent.* (*Bellum Gallicum* 6.13)
- and they *obeyed* their **decrees and orders**.
- facile hac oratione **Nerviis** *persuadet.* (*Bellum Gallicum* 5.38)
- he easily *persuaded* **the Nervii** with this speech.
- **equo** ne *credite*, Teucri (*Aeneid* 2.48)
- don't **believe the horse**, Trojans

7.2.1.4 Accusative

- *Duration of Time—expresses how long the action of the verb takes
    o cuius pater regnum in Sequanis **multos annos** obtinuerat (*Bellum Gallicum* 1.3)
    o whose father had ruled among the Sequani **for many years**

- *Extent of Space*—expresses how far the action of the verb happens

  o qui in longitudinem **milia passuum CCXL**, in latitudinem **CLXXX** patebant (*Bellum Gallicum* 1.2)

  o which extend in length **for 240 miles**, in width **for 180**

- *Place to which*—usually with the prepositions *ad* or *in* except with cities, towns, small islands, *domus*, and *rus*:

  o **In Galliam ulteriorem** contendit, et **ad Genavam** pervenit. (*Bellum Gallicum* 1.7)

  o He quickly traveled **to farther Gaul** and came **to Geneva**.

  o tendens **ad sidera** palmas (*Aeneid* 1.93)

  o stretching his hands **to the stars**

  o Per varios casus, per tot discrimina rerum / tendimus **in Latium**. (*Aeneid* 1.204–5)

  o Through various misfortunes, through so many dangers, we stretched **to Latium**.

- *Respect—the accusative is sometimes used, primarily in poetry, to show respect or specification (identical to the ablative of respect in meaning)

  o Nec magis incepto **vultum** sermone movetur / quam si dura silex aut stet Marpesia cautes (*Aeneid* 6.470–71)

  o Nor is [Dido] moved **in / with respect to her face** more by that speech having been begun than if hard stone or Marpesian cliffs stand.

  o Dixit, et **os** impressa toro, "Moriemur inultae, / sed moriamur," ait. (*Aeneid* 4.659–60)

  o She spoke and, having been pressed **with respect to her mouth** on the bed, said, "Unavenged, I will die, but let me die."

    - *os impressa* can also be read as a middle participle with a direct object

7.2.1.5 Ablative—most commonly provides adverbial information: when, how, where, with what, and so on, and so will most often be associated with a verb, adjective, or (rarely) an adverb.

- *Absolute—expresses the circumstances or situation of the main clause: time, cause, concession, condition (in rough order of frequency)

  o The ablative absolute is the construction that is both most common to and most difficult in the AP® syllabus.

  o There are over 60 ablatives absolute in the Caesar syllabus alone.

  o It is usually composed of a participle and a noun.

    - The most common participle is the perfect passive participle.

- The present active participle is used but not nearly as frequently.

- Rare is either of the future participles.

o It can also be composed of two nouns or a noun and an adjective.

- In both of these situations, there is an understood participle of *sum, esse*, which is why no participle is expressed.

o There is no grammatical distinction among time, cause, concession, condition; context and what makes sense is the only way to know what the ablative absolute is expressing and how to translate it.

o It is often translated as a clause that begins with the appropriate subordinate conjunction: when, after, since, because, although, if.

o It can be translated with "with" plus a participle: this is the most literal but also the most vague translation.

o For the AP® Exam, either the clause translation or the "with" translation is acceptable but **the voice of the participle must be maintained**; for example, the perfect passive participle must be translated as a passive and the present active as an active.

o Additionally, **the tense relationship between the participle and the main verb should be maintained**; for example, a perfect passive participle with a past main verb will be translated as a pluperfect.

- time

  - Deinde **omnibus** longe lateque **aedificiis incensis** se in castra receperunt. (*Bellum Gallicum* 4.35)

  - Then, **after all of the buildings** far and wide **had been burned**, they took themselves back into camp.

  - Then, **with all of the buildings** far and wide **having been burned,** they took themselves back into camp.

    ◊ *Incensis* is translated "had been burned" because it is a perfect passive participle with a perfect main verb (*receperunt*); "had" maintains the tense relationship.

  - Ac venti velut **agmine facto**, / qua data porta, ruunt. (*Aeneid* 1.82–83)

  - And the winds, just as **when a battle line was drawn up**, when the gate has been presented, rush out.

    ◊ The *velut* makes it difficult to translate this ablative absolute with the "with" translation.

◊ *Facto* is translated "was drawn up" because it is a perfect passive participle with a present main verb (*ruunt*); "was" maintains the tense relationship.

- Fit sonitus **spumante salo**. (*Aeneid* 2.209)

- A sound happens as the sea foams.

  ◊ A good example of a more ambiguous ablative absolute: "as" could be "while" or the more literal "with": "a sound happened with the sea foaming."

▪ cause

- Primus ibi ante omnes **magna comitante caterva** / Laocoon ardens summa decurrit ab arce. (*Aeneid* 2.40–41)

- There, in front of everyone, **because a great crowd is gathering**, first fuming Laocoon runs down from the top of the citadel.

- There, in front of everyone, **with a great crowd gathering**, first fuming Laocoon runs down from the top of the citadel.

  ◊ This has been translated as cause but could easily be read as time: "while a great crowd gathers."

  ◊ Neither is incorrect but rather is dependent on the interpretation of the reader.

▪ concession

- Quae tamen, **ancoris iactis**, cum fluctibus complerentur, necessario adversa nocte in altum provectae, continentem petierunt. (*Bellum Gallicum* 4.28)

- Which (ships), **although their anchors had been cast**, when they were covered with waves, having been conveyed unavoidably into the deep water in the unforgiving night, sought the continent.

▪ condition

- Neque homines inimico animo, **data facultate** per provinciam itineris faciendi, temperaturos ab iniuria et maleficio existimabat. (*Bellum Gallicum* 1.7)

- Nor was he thinking that men of an unfriendly spirit, **if the ease** of making a journey through the province **were granted**, would avoid violence and ill will.

o The ablative absolute can also occur with two ablative nouns.

○ With two ablative nouns, the participle is that of *sum, esse* understood.

  ▪ **Marco Messala et Marco Pupio Pisone consulibus** (*Bellum Gallicum* 1.2)

  ▪ **when Marcus Mesala and Marcus Pupius Piso were consuls**

    • The "were" is the understood *sum, esse.*

    • The two names are the subjects and *consulibus* the predicate.

○ The ablative absolute can also occur with an ablative noun and an ablative adjective, also with *sum, esse* understood.

  ▪ Paucis interfectis reliquos **incertis ordinibus** perturbaverant. (*Bellum Gallicum* 4.32)

  ▪ Because few had been killed, they had disturbed the rest **because their formation *was* chaotic**.

    • The "was" is the understood *sum, esse.*

    • *Incertis* is the adjective and *ordinibus* the noun.

• *Accompaniment*—specifies with whom the action of the verb is being done

○ uses the preposition *cum* with an ablative object

  ▪ **cum legione** ad fines Nerviorum veniat (*Bellum Gallicum* 5.46)

  ▪ [if] he could come **with his legion** to the borders of the Nervii

  ▪ Et nunc ille Paris **cum semiviro comitatu**, / Maeonia mentum mitra crinemque madentem / subnexus, rapto potitur. (*Aeneid* 4.215–17)

  ▪ And now that Paris, **along with his band of half-men**, wrapping his head and his glistening hair in an Asian turban, acquires my plunder.

○ In Caesar, sometimes when used with a military phrase, the preposition *cum* will be omitted.

  ▪ At barbari … **reliquis copiis** subsecuti nostros navibus egredi prohibebant. (*Bellum Gallicum* 4.24)

  ▪ But the enemy, following **with the rest of their troops**, prevented our men from leaving on their ships.

  ▪ Subitoque oppressis lignatoribus **magna manu** ad castra oppugnatum venerunt. (*Bellum Gallicum* 5.26)

  ▪ And suddenly, after those getting wood had been attacked, they came to the camp **with a sizable force** to attack it.

- *Agent*

  - the doer of the action of a passive verb

  - requires three elements:

    - a passive verb

    - the preposition *a/ab*

    - a person or sometimes an animal

  - be careful of other uses of *a/ab* that are not the ablative of agent:

    - Caesar questus quod, cum ultro in continentem legatis missis pacem **ab se** *petissent,* (*Bellum Gallicum* 4.27)

    - Caesar, complaining because, although *they had sought* peace **from him** after envoys had been sent voluntarily to the continent

      - *Ab se* might look like an ablative of agent but the verb *petissent* is not passive.

  - *Mittuntur* ad Caesarem confestim **ab Cicerone** litterae, magnis propositis praemiis, si pertulissent. (*Bellum Gallicum* 5.40)

  - Immediately letters *are sent* to Caesar **by Cicero**, with great rewards offered, if they would deliver them.

  - Nunc etiam interpres divum **Iove** *missus* **ab ipso** / (testor utrumque caput) celeres mandata per auras / detulit. (*Aeneid* 4.356–58)

  - Even now the messenger of the gods, *having been sent* **by Jupiter himself** (I swear on my and your head), brought orders through the swift air.

- *Cause

  - does not use a preposition

  - translated "because of"

  - ille veritus, quod ad plures pertinebat, ne civitas eorum **impulsu** deficeret (*Bellum Gallicum* 5.25)

  - that man, fearing, because it concerned more people, that the state would revolt **because of** their **attack**

  - saevus ubi Aeacidae **telo** iacet Hector (*Aeneid* 1.99)

  - where fierce Hector lies dead **because of the weapon** of Achilles

- *Comparison
  - indicates the person or thing compared to
    - He is shorter **than his sister**.
  - does not use a preposition
  - translated with "than"
  - requires a comparative word

  - Nam *minus* **horis tribus** milium pedum XV in circuitu munitionem perfecerunt. (*Bellum Gallicum* 5.42)
  - For in *less* **than three hours** they constructed a rampart of 15 thousand feet in circumference.
  - Extemplo Libyae magnas it Fama per urbes, / Fama, malum **qua** non aliud *velocius* ullum. (*Aeneid* 4.173–74)
  - Immediately Rumor went through the great cities of Africa, / Rumor, **than which** no other evil moves *more quickly*.

  - Latin also uses *quam* with a comparative word to mean "than."
  - This is not the ablative of comparison but expresses the same idea and is translated the same way as the ablative of comparison.
  - In the ablative of comparison, the English "than" is contained in the ablative; *quam* is translated as "than" in this non-ablative-of-comparison construction.
    - Postremo quid esset *levius aut turpius*, **quam** auctore hoste de summis rebus capere consilium? (*Bellum Gallicum* 5.28)
    - Finally, what could be *more trivial or shameful* **than**, with the enemy as instigator, to take his advice concerning the most important matters?
    - Nec *magis* incepto vultum sermone movetur / **quam** si dura silex aut stet Marpesia cautes. (*Aeneid* 6.470–71)
    - Nor is [Dido] moved in her face *more* by that speech having been begun **than** if hard stone or Marpesian cliffs stand.
  - The ablative of comparison will more often be used with nouns rather than clauses and *quam* more often with clauses rather than nouns alone.

- *Degree of Difference
  - specifies the amount by which two things differ
  - does not use a preposition

- - most often translated with "by" or as an adverb
    - She beat him **by three seconds**.
    - He enjoys Latin **[by] so much**.

  - alterum per provinciam nostram, **multo** *facilius atque expeditius* (*Bellum Gallicum* 1.6)
  - the other [journey], through our province, **much** *easier and more efficient* [*easier and more efficient* **by a lot**]

- *Description (Quality)
  - does not use a preposition
  - often used with a form of *sum, esse*
  - often translated with "of" when used with *sum, esse*
    - The woman is **of impressive strength**.

  - often accompanied by an adjective or genitive

  - Ipse Cicero, cum **tenuissima valetudine** esset, ne nocturnum quidem sibi tempus ad quietem relinquebat. (*Bellum Gallicum* 5.40)
  - Cicero himself, although he was **of very dubious health**, left for himself not even time at night for recovery.
  - Sunt mihi bis septem **praestanti corpore** Nymphae. (*Aeneid* 1.71)
  - I have fourteen Nymphs **of significant attractiveness**.

- *Manner*
  - indicates the emotion with which the action of the verb is done
  - sometimes uses the preposition *cum*, sometimes uses no preposition
  - translated "with"

  - Atque ambo incolumes compluribus interfectis **summa cum laude** sese intra munitiones recipiunt. (*Bellum Gallicum* 5.44)
  - And both men, **with the highest praise,** brought themselves back to the fortifications unharmed after many had been killed.
  - Illi indignantes **magno cum murmure** montis / circum claustra fremunt. (*Aeneid* 1.55–56)

- o   Those [winds] chafing **with the great rumbling** of a mountain / roar around the locks [of the door].

- o   The difference between means and manner when a preposition is not used is a nuanced one and often both difficult and immaterial to distinguish.

  - ▪   Hostes **maximo clamore** … turres testudinesque agere et scalis vallum ascendere coeperunt. (*Bellum Gallicum* 5.43)

  - ▪   The enemy **with a ton of noise** began to advance the towers and their formation and to scale the rampart with ladders.

    - •   The meaning of *maximo clamore* is relatively clear.

    - •   Is it means, though, or manner?

    - •   Means would suggest an element of motivation: it is the shouting that assists them.

    - •   Manner would suggest something more circumstantial: the shouting is happening as the action happens.

- •   *Means*

  - o   expresses how or by what means the action of a verb is completed

  - o   does not use a preposition

  - o   usually translated with "with" with an active verb and "by" with a passive verb

  - o   quod undique loci **natura** Helvetii *continentur* (*Bellum Gallicum* 1.2)

  - o   because on all sides the Helvetii *are contained* **by the nature** of the place

  - o   Facile **hac oratione** Nerviis *persuadet*. (*Bellum Gallicum* 5.38)

  - o   He easily *persuaded* the Nervii **with this speech**.

  - o   Extemplo Aeneae *solvuntur* **frigore** membra. (*Aeneid* 1.92)

  - o   Immediately Aeneas' limbs *are weakened* **by fear**.

  - o   Et igni / sibila *lambebant* **linguis vibrantibus** ora. (*Aeneid* 2.210–11)

  - o   And [the snakes] *were licking* their hissing mouths **with flickering tongues**.

- •   *Place Where*

  - o   expresses where the action of the verb is happening

  - o   most often used in Latin with the prepositions *in* and *sub*

    - ▪   sometimes used without a preposition, especially with cities, towns, small islands, *domus*, and *rus* o   translated into English with "in," "on," "at," and so forth, depending on context

o   Isque non **nullis locis** vado transitur. (*Bellum Gallicum* 1.6)

o   And it is crossed **in no places** by a shallow.

o   Ipse interea … **in Gallia** morari constituit. (*Bellum Gallicum* 5.24)

o   Meanwhile he himself … decided to delay **in Gaul**.

o   Et cohortes V in Eburones … qui **sub imperio** Ambiorigis et Catuvulci erant, misit. (*Bellum Gallicum* 5.24)

o   And he sent 5 cohorts to the Eburones … who were **under the control** of Ambiorix and Catuvulcus.

- *Place from Which*—expresses the place from which the action of the verb is happening; often used with the prepositions *a/ab, e/ex,* or *de*, except with cities, towns, small islands, *domus,* or *rus*, which use no preposition:

o   Gallōs **ab Aquitanis** Garumna flumen dividit. (*Bellum Gallicum* 1.1)

o   The river Garumna divides the Gauls **from the Aquitani**.

o   Trium mensum molita cibaria sibi quemque **domo** efferre iubent (*Bellum Gallicum* 1.5)

o   They ordered them to bring flour for three months for themselves **from home**.

  ▪   no preposition with *domo*

- *Separation—expresses the separation or removal of one noun from another; the ablative of place from which is a subset of the ablative of separation

o   sometimes used with the preposition *a/ab, de,* or *e/ex* but can also be used without a preposition

o   translated "from" or similar

o   cum aut **suis finibus** eos prohibent (*Bellum Gallicum* 1.1)

o   when they keep them **from our borders**

o   qui agrum Helvetium **a Germanis** dividit. (*Bellum Gallicum* 1.2)

o   which divides Helvetian land **from the Germans**

o   Ipsa Iovis rapidum iaculata **e nubibus** ignem. (*Aeneid* 1.42)

o   She herself threw the rapid fire of Jupiter **from the clouds**.

- *Special Verbs (VPUFF)—five deponent verbs, plus their compounds, take their direct objects in the ablative: *vescor, potior, utor, fungor, fruor* (hence VPUFF).

CHAPTER 7

- o Perfacile esse … totius Galliae **imperio** *potiri*. (*Bellum Gallicum* 1.2)

- o It would be easy … *to enjoy* **power** over all of Gaul.

- • *Specification—also called the ablative of respect, it specifies a verb or adjective or expresses in what respect the action is done (when used with a verb) or what quality exists (when used with an adjective):

  - o cum **virtute** omnibus *praestarent* (*Bellum Gallicum* 1.2)

  - o since they *surpassed* everyone **in virtue**

- • *Time When—expresses when the action of the verb happens

  - o no preposition

  - o must be a time word, for example, "day," "summer," and so on

  - o translated with "in," "at," "on," and so forth, depending on the English idiom

  - o **Eodem die** legati ab hostibus missi ad Caesarem de pace venerunt. (*Bellum Gallicum* 4.36)

  - o **On the same day** the legates sent by the enemy came to Caesar about peace.

  - o Qualis apes **aestate nova** per florea rura / exercet sub sole. (*Aeneid* 1.430–31)

  - o Just as a bee **in the new summer** works throughout the blooming countryside under the sun.

- • *Time Within Which—expresses the time within which the action of the verb happens

  - o covers a range of time rather than a single moment (which is the ablative of time when):

    - ▪ **Within five days**, Caesar will have conquered Gaul = time within which

    - ▪ **On the fifth day**, Caesar will have conquered Gaul = time when

  - o hanc adfore **biduo** (*Bellum Gallicum* 5.27)

  - o that this band of men would be present **within two days**

7.2.1.6 *Vocative

- • used for direct address—that is, when someone is speaking directly to someone else:

  - o **Caesar**, *order* the men to charge.

    - ▪ "Caesar" is the vocative because he is being spoken to.

- The vocative is often associated with the imperative ("order" in the above example), but an imperative does not need a vocative and a vocative does not need an imperative.

  o **Caesar**, the troops are prepared to charge.

    ▪ "Caesar" is vocative but in a declarative rather than an imperative sentence.

  o *Order* the troops to charge.

    ▪ an imperative sentence without a vocative

- In Latin, the vocative uses the same form as the nominative (except for two instances, explained below):

  o "Desilite," inquit, "**milites**, nisi vultis aquilam hostibus prodere." (*Bellum Gallicum* 4.25)

  o He said, "Hop down, **soldiers**, unless you want to surrender the standard to the enemy."

  o Hoc illud, **germana**, fuit? (*Aeneid* 4.675)

  o This was it, **sister**?

  o This overlap in forms can create some ambiguity:

    ▪ Cui me moribundam deseris, hospes (*Aeneid* 4.323)

    ▪ Cui me moribundam deseris **hospes**? (*Aeneid* 4.323)

      • Some editors include a comma between *deseris* and *hospes*.

      • The presence or absence of the comma renders *hospes* as vocative or nominative (which have the same forms).

      • Vocative: "To whom do you abandon me, dying, friend?"

      • Nominative: "To whom do you, as a friend, abandon me, dying?"

- two exceptions when the vocative has a different ending from the nominative:

  o 2nd declension -*us*, which becomes -*e*:

    ▪ Dissimulare etiam sperasti, **perfide**, tantum / posse nefas tacitusque mea decedere terra? (*Aeneid* 4.305–6)

    ▪ Did you hope to deceive me, **jerk**? Did you hope that so great an injustice was possible and that you could leave my land quietly?

      • The nominative of *perfide* is *perfidus*.

      • As an -*us* adjective (and the same for a noun), its vocative becomes *perfide*.

- o 2nd declension *-ius*, which becomes *-i*
    - ▪ This vocative seems not to appear in the Latin syllabus but could appear in the multiple choice section.

- Sometimes, but not always, the word "O" will be included to signal a vocative:
    - o "Dic," ait, "**o virgo**, quid vult concursus ad amnem?" (*Aeneid* 6.318)
    - o "Tell me," he said, "**maiden**, what does this gathering at the river mean?"

- The vocative is often set apart by commas.
    - o Especially if you have a single word surrounded by commas, there is a good chance that it will be vocative.
        - ▪ Tenet ille immania saxa, / vestras, **Eure**, domos. (*Aeneid* 1.139–40)
        - ▪ That man holds immense stones, **Eurus**, your homes.

7.2.1.7 Locative

- the case of place where
- The meaning of the locative overlaps with the ablative of place where.
- The use of the locative is restricted to cities, towns, and small islands, as well as the nouns *domus* and *rus*.
    - o Small islands have one primary town and that town has the same name as the island; large (not small) islands have multiple towns and none are the same name as the island.
    - o The locative of *domus* and *rus* does not appear in the Latin syllabus but might appear in the multiple choice section.
- The locative uses the same ending as the genitive for 1st and 2nd declension singular nouns.
    - o *Roma, -ae* = *Romae* in the locative
- The locative uses the same ending as the ablative for all other nouns (1st and 2nd declension plural and all 3rd declension nouns).
    - o *Athenae, -arum* = *Athenis* in the locative

- concilioque Gallorum **Samarobrivae** peracto (*Bellum Gallicum* 5.24)
- and after a council of Gauls had been held **at Samarobriva (Amiens)**.

7.3   ADJECTIVES AND ADVERBS

- In English, adjectives agree with their noun by proximity; that is, the adjective will be next to the noun with which it agrees.

    o   the **tall** sailor

- In Latin, adjectives agree with their noun in gender, number, and case.

    o   **alta** puella

    o   **altus nauta**

        ▪   Sometimes the same gender, number, and case will mean the same ending, as in the first example.

        ▪   But if a noun has an irregular gender or is a different declension from the adjective, the endings will be different, as in the second example: *nauta* is a masculine noun, so the adjective has to have a masculine ending to agree, even if that ending is different from the noun's ending.

- Adverbs describe a verb, adjective, or other adverb.

- Adverbs derived from *-us, -a, -um* adjectives will tend to use an *-e* ending.

- Adverbs derived from 3rd declension adjectives will tend to use a *-ter* ending.

    o   Caesar, however, often uses the neuter accusative adjective ending for the adverbial form of 3rd declension adjectives, especially *facilis, -e*.

        ▪   His rebus fiebat ut et *minus* **late** vagarentur et *minus* **facile** finitimis bellum inferre possent. (*Bellum Gallicum* 1.2)

        ▪   Because of these factors, it happened that they wandered *less* **widely** and the were able to battle with their neighbors *less* **easily**.

            •   *Late* is from *latus, -a, -um*; the *-e* ending is expected for this adverb.

            •   *Facile* is from *facilis, -e*; Caesar here uses the neuter accusative adjective ending instead of the *-ter* ending.

            •   *Minus* in both instances is an adverb modifying another adverb.

7.3.1   COMPARATIVE ADJECTIVES AND ADVERBS

- All comparative adjectives are 2-form 3rd declension adjectives with *-ior, -ius* as their nominatives.

- Comparative adjectives are translated with "more" or *-er*: "more extreme"; "taller."

- Comparative adverbs are translated with "more": "more quickly."

- o The most common comparative adjectives that Caesar uses are:
  - *certior, certius*
  - *maior, maius*
  - *superior, superius*
- o Examples of other adjectives are included below; Vergil uses fewer comparative adjectives than Caesar.

- o quanto erat in dies **gravior atque asperior** oppugnatio (*Bellum Gallicum* 5.45)
- o the **more serious and dangerous** the attack was every day
- o Nam et nostris militibus spem minuit et hostes ad pugnam **alacriores** effecit. (*Bellum Gallicum* 5.33)
- o For this reduced the hope of our soldiers and made the enemy **more keen** for battle.
- o "Vincite," inquit, "si ita vultis," Sabinus, et id **clariore** voce, ut magna pars militum exaudiret. (*Bellum Gallicum* 5.30)
- o "Win, if you want," Sabinus said, and he said this in a **louder** voice so that a great number of soldiers heard him.
- o Rex erat Aeneas nobis, quo **iustior** alter / nec pietate fuit, nec bello **maior** et armis. (*Aeneid* 1.544–45)
- o Aeneas was our king, than whom no other was **more just** nor **greater** in respect to war and arms.

- The comparative adverb uses the neuter accusative form, *-ius*.
- Only context can distinguish between a comparative adverb and a neuter comparative adjective.
  - o Neque **longius** prosequi potuerunt. (*Bellum Gallicum* 4.26)
  - o Nor could they pursue **farther**.
  - o cum *paulo* **longius** a castris processisset (*Bellum Gallicum* 4.32)
  - o when they had proceeded *a little* **farther** from camp
  - o alterum [iter] per provinciam nostram, multo **facilius** atque **expeditius**, (*Bellum Gallicum* 1.6)
  - o (there was) another (route) through our province, (a route) much **easier** and more **efficient**
    - *Longius* in the first two examples is a comparative adverb explaining how far they went.

- *Facilius* and *expeditius* in the third example are neuter comparative adjectives agreeing with *iter*.

7.3.2   SUPERLATIVE ADJECTIVES AND ADVERBS

- All superlative adjectives are *-us, -a, -um* adjectives with *-issimus, -a, -um.*

- Superlative adjectives are translated with "most" or *-est*: "most extreme"; "tallest."

- All superlative adverbs are formed with the *-e* ending.

- Superlative adverbs are translated with "most": "most quickly."

- Caesar uses superlative forms more frequently than Vergil.

  o Apud Helvetios longe **nobilissimus** fuit et **ditissimus** Orgetorix. (*Bellum Gallicum* 1.2)

  o Among the Helvetii, Orgetorix was by far **the most noble** and the **wealthiest**.

  o Una ex parte flumine Rheno **latissimo** atque **altissimo**, qui agrum Helvetium a Germanis dividit; altera ex parte monte Iura **altissimo**, qui est inter Sequanos et Helvetios. (*Bellum Gallicum* 1.2)

  o On one side was the river Rhine at its **widest** and **deepest**, which divided the Helvetian land from the Germans; on the other side were the **very tall** Iura Mountains, which are between the Helvetii and the Sequani.

  o Quo praecepto ab eis **diligentissime** observato, cum quaepiam cohors ex orbe excesserat atque impetum fecerat, hostes **velocissime** refugiebant. (*Bellum Gallicum* 5.35)

  o After this order had been followed **most carefully** by them, once the cohort had departed from the circle and had attacked, the enemy was retreating **most quickly**.

- Be careful of the rare superlative *-e* ending that is not an adverb:

  o O Danaum **fortissime** gentis / Tydide! (*Aeneid* 1.96–97)

  o O Diomedes, **bravest** of the tribe of the Greeks!

    ▪ In this example, the *-e* ending is a vocative ending rather than an adverbial ending.

7.3.3   SUBSTANTIVE ADJECTIVES

- adjectives without a stated noun to agree with or an adjective used in place of a noun

- The translation of the substantive depends on the gender of the adjective and is general in meaning: "men," "women," "things," "people," and so forth.

- The most common substantives are the demonstratives, which are first adjectives meaning "this" or "that" but are often used substantively as pronouns:

  o *is, ea, id*: this man / he; this woman / she; this thing / it

- o *hic, haec, hoc*: this man / he; this woman / she; this thing / it

- o *ille, illa, illud*: that man / he; that woman / she; that thing / it

- Possessive adjectives function similarly to the demonstratives:

- o *mei*: my people, my friends, my companions

- o *tuae*: your (female) people, your (female) friends, your (female) companions

- Caesar uses substantives considerably less than Vergil.

- cum virtute **omnibus** praestarent (*Bellum Gallicum* 1.2)

- since they exceed **everyone (all people)** in virtue

- O socii (neque enim ignari sumus ante malorum), / o passi **graviora**, dabit deus **his** quoque finem. (*Aeneid* 1.198–99)

- O companions, o those suffering **pretty serious things (difficulties, troubles, etc.)**, god will eventually give an end **to these things (difficulties, troubles, etc.)**

- Et duplices tendens ad sidera palmas / **talia** voce refert. (*Aeneid* 1.93–94)

- And stretching his two palms to the stars he spoke **such things** with his voice.

- o Vergil commonly uses *talia* in the *Aeneid* as a substantive referring to the words spoken in direct speech.

- Atque animum nunc huc celerem nunc dividit illuc / in partesque rapit varias perque **omnia** versat. (*Aeneid* 4.285–86)

- And now he divided his swift mind this way and that and he went through various options and he turned over **all possibilities / all things**.

- Any adjective referring to a people is commonly used as a substantive:

- o Romanus, -a, -um = Roman; Romanus, -i / -a, -ae = a Roman

- o Troianus, -a, -um = Trojan; Troianus, -i / -a, -ae = a Trojan

- As adjectives, participles can be used substantively as well.

- Substantive participles are more difficult because not only must the noun that the participle modifies be included in the translation but there is also the possibility of a direct object or other modifier with the participle.

- o *talia* **iactanti** (*Aeneid* 1.102)

- o as **for the one tossing out** *such words*

  - ▪ The "for" in the translation comes from the dative ending.

  - ▪ The "the one" is the understood noun that the substantive participle modifies.

- The "tossing out" is the participle itself.

- The "such words" is *talia*, the direct object of the active participle *iactanti*.

  o Vina bonus quae deinde cadis onerarat Acestes / litore Trinacrio dederatque **abeuntibus** heros / dividit, et **dictis** maerentia pectora mulcet. (*Aeneid* 1.195–97)

  o [Aeneas] as hero divided the wine that good Acestes had stored in jugs and had given **to them as they departed** from the Sicilian shore, and he soothed their grieving hearts **with these words**.

- Some nouns are in actuality substantive participles used so commonly that they become nouns.

  o *Parens, parentis* is the present participle of *pario, -ire*, to give birth, so *parens* is literally "one giving birth" or a "parent"

  o *Dictum, -i* in the *Aeneid* example above is the perfect passive participle of *dico, -ere*, so a *dictum* is literally "something having been spoken" or a "word."

7.3.4   IRREGULAR ADJECTIVES

- There are nine adjectives whose genitive and dative singular follow the -ius, -i pattern (perhaps familiar from the genitive and dative singulars of *hic, ille, qui*, etc.):

  o *Forms with an asterisk do not appear in the Latin syllabus in their irregular genitive or dative singular forms.*

  o alius, -a, -ud

  o alter, alterius

  o *neuter, -tra, -trum

  o *nullus, -a, -um

  o *solus, -a, -um

  o totus, -a, -um

  o ullus, -a, -um

  o unus, -a, -um

  o uter, -tra, -trum

- the genitive in *-ius*

  o Magna … **totius exercitus** perturbatio facta est. (*Bellum Gallicum* 4.29)

  o A great disturbance **of the whole army** happened.

- There are four other occurrences of *totius* in the Latin Caesar syllabus, all of which agree with *Galliae*.

  o Pallasne exurere classem / Argivum atque ipsos potuit submergere ponto / **unius** ob noxam et furias **Aiacis Oilei**? (*Aeneid* 1.39–41)

  o Could Athena burn the Argive fleet and submerge those very ships in the ocean on account of the anger and passion **of one Ajax, son of Oileus**?

  o Uter eorum vita superarit, ad eum pars **utriusque** cum fructibus superiorum temporum pervenit. (*Bellum Gallicum* 6.19)

  o Whichever of them outlives the other, to this one comes the share **of the first** along with any gains up to that point.

- the dative in *-i*: more difficult to recognize because the *-i* ending is a common ending

  o **Provinciae toti** quam maximum potest militum numerum imperat. (*Bellum Gallicum* 1.7)

  o He ordered as great a number of soldiers as was possible from **the whole province**.

  o Sic fortuna in contentione et certamine utrumque versavit, ut alter **alteri** inimicus auxilio salutique esset neque diiudicari posset, uter **utri** virtute anteferendus videretur. (*Bellum Gallicum* 5.44)

  o Thus fortune toyed with each in struggle and in battle, such that one was unfriendly **to the other** in assistance and safety and couldn't be judged better; each seemed preferred **to the other** in virtue.

  o Miscetque viris neque cernitur **ulli**. (*Aeneid* 1.440)

  o And he mixes with men and isn't seen **by anyone**.

7.4   PRONOUNS

- A word that replaces a noun.
- The noun that a pronoun replaces is called the antecedent.

7.4.1   PERSONAL

- Personal pronouns represent people: the 1st, 2nd, and 3rd persons that are used with verbs:

  o 1st person: the person speaking — I / me, we / us

  o 2nd person: the person spoken to — you, you (all)

  o 3rd person: the person spoken about — he / him, she / her, it, they / them

- In English, subject personal pronouns are necessary:

  o **She** runs.

    ▪ English can't say simply "runs"; the subject is necessary.

- In Latin, subject personal pronouns are optional:

  o **Ea** currit = She runs

  o Currit = She runs

- 1st and 2nd person has dedicated pronoun forms:

  o ego = I / me

  o nos = we / us

  o tu = you (sing)

  o vos = you (pl)

- 3rd person pronouns do not have their own forms but use demonstratives instead:

  o is, ea, id; hic, haec, hoc; ille, illa, illud

- The pronouns also have possessive adjective forms:

  o meus, -a, -um = my

  o noster, -tra, -trum = our

  o tuus, -a, -um = your (sing)

  o vester, -tra, -trum = your (pl)

- 1st and 2nd pronouns and possessive adjectives will appear more frequently in direct speech—that is, when people are talking to each other directly.

> **Me**ne fugis? Per **ego** has lacrimas dextramque *tuam* **te**
> (quando aliud **mihi** iam miserae nihil ipsa reliqui),   315
> per conubia nostra, per inceptos hymenaeos,
> si bene quid de **te** merui, fuit aut **tibi** quicquam
> dulce *meum*, miserere domus labentis et istam,
> oro, si quis adhuc precibus locus, exue mentem.
> **Te** propter Libycae gentes Nomadumque tyranni   320
> odere, infensi Tyrii; **te** propter eundem
> exstinctus pudor et, qua sola sidera adibam,
> fama prior. (*Aeneid* 4.314–23)

Do you flee **me**? By these tears and by **your** right hand, **I** beg **you** (since I myself have left no other thing to now miserable **me**), by our bond, by our celebrated wedding, if I well deserved anything from **you**, or **you** have anything sweet **of mine**, pity a collapsing house and, if there is still a place for entreaties, turn that mind of yours. On account of **you**, Libyan tribes and the tyrants of the Nomads hate me; on account of **you** as well, my honor and my previous reputation have been destroyed, by which alone I was approaching the stars.

7.4.2   REFLEXIVE

- Reflexive pronouns reflect on the subject of the sentence; that is, they are used when the subject and the non-subject are the same person.

- Reflexive pronouns use the -self ending in English.

  o **Caesar** tells **himself** to remain calm.

  o **Anna** scolds **herself** for leaving Dido alone.

- Reflexive pronouns do not have nominative forms.

- In Latin, the 1st and 2nd person reflexive pronoun uses the same forms as the personal pronoun; only context distinguishes between them.

  o Caesar **me** videt = Caesar sees **me**

    ▪ Personal because the subject and the pronoun are not the same person.

  o **Ego me** video = **I** see **myself**

    ▪ Reflexive because the subject and the pronoun are the same person.

  o quando aliud **mihi** iam miserae nihil ipsa **reliqui** (*Aeneid* 4.315)

  o since **I** myself **left** nothing at all **for my** now miserable **self**

- The reflexive pronouns do not have nominative forms.

  o -, mei, mihi, me, me = myself

  o -, nostri, nobis, nos, nobis = ourselves

  o -, tui, tibi, te, te = yourself (sing)

  o -, vestri, vobis, vos, vobis = yourselves (pl)

- Because there is no true 3rd person personal pronoun, the 3rd person reflexive has its own form: *-, sui, sibi, se, se*

  o Q. Titurius … interpretem *suum* Cn. Pompeium ad *eum* mittit rogatum ut **sibi** militi-busque parcat (*Bellum Gallicum* 5.36)

  o Quintus Titurius sent *his* interpreter, Gnaius Pompeius to *him* to ask to spare **himself** and his soldiers

    ▪ *Suum* is the reflexive possessive adjective, confirming that the interpreter is in fact the interpreter of Quintus Titurius, the subject of the sentence, instead of some-one else's interpreter.

- *Eum* is the demonstrative used as a 3rd person (non-reflexive) pronoun, confirming that the "him" is a different person.

  - *Sibi* is the reflexive pronoun, confirming that Quintus Titurius is asking that Quintus Titurius be spared, instead of that someone else be spared.

- *Ipse* Cicero, cum tenuissima valetudine esset, ne nocturnum quidem **sibi** tempus ad quietem relinquebat, ut ultro militum concursu ac vocibus **sibi** parcere cogeretur. (*Bellum Gallicum* 5.40)

- Cicero *himself*, although he was of very poor health, forfeited **his** time, even at night, for rest with the result that he was forced by a group of soldiers and their entreaties to spare **himself**.

  - The *ipse* "himself" and the *sibi* "himself" illustrate an ambiguity that exists in English, because these different words use the same -self ending.

  - *Ipse* is the intensive, which English translates with -self but which does not reflect on the subject; *sibi* is the reflexive.

- Eurum ad **se** Zephyrumque vocat. (*Aeneid* 1.131)

- He calls the Eurus and the Zephyrus **to himself**.

- The reflexive *se* is used in indirect statement when the subject of the main verb is the same as the subject of the indirect statement.

- Although Latin uses the reflexive for this subject of the indirect statement, English will use a personal pronoun (he, she, it).

  - Tunc *duces principesque* Nerviorum qui aliquem sermonis aditum causamque amicitiae cum Cicerone habebant colloqui **sese** *velle dicunt*. (*Bellum Gallicum* 5.41)

  - Then *the leaders and chiefs* of the Nervii, who had with Cicero some form of rapport and some reason for friendship, *said* that **they** *wanted* to talk to him.

    - *Sese* is an alternate form of *se*.

    - The use of the reflexive *sese* indicates that the subject of *velle*, the infinitive in indirect statement dependent on *dicunt*, is the same as the subject of *dicunt*: *duces principesque*.

    - Note that in English the personal pronoun "they" is used to translate the Latin reflexive *sese*.

- The Latin reflexive does not distinguish among gender or number in its form; -, *sui, sibi, se, se* is used for all three genders and singular and plural.

- The gender of the translation of the Latin reflexive is dependent on its antecedent:

  - If it refers to a male, it will be translated "himself."

o   If it refers to a female, it will be translated "herself."

o   If it refers to a neuter object, it will be translated "itself."

- The number of the translation of the Latin reflexive is also dependent on its antecedent:

o   If it refers to a singular, it will be translated "himself," "herself," "itself."

o   If it refers to a plural, it will be translated "themselves."

7.4.3   DEMONSTRATIVES

- Demonstratives is an umbrella term for a series of adjectives with their genitive in *-ius* and their dative in *-i*.

- The most common meaning is "this" or "that" but other words are counted as demonstratives as well.

7.4.3.1 *Hic* and *Ille*

- *Hic* and *ille* are declined like irregular adjectives, with *-ius* in the genitive and *-i* in the dative.

- Some of the forms of *hic, haec, hoc* end in *-c* (as the nominatives do).

o   The *-c* is a vestige of the archaic emphatic ending *-ce*.

o   The *-c* as an ending does not provide any grammatical information.

o   Rather, the ending appears before the *-c*; for example, *haec* is *hae* + *-c*.

- The first use of *hic* and *ille* is as adjectives.

o   Una cum **his legatis** Commius Atrebas venit. (*Bellum Gallicum* 4.27)

o   Commius the Atrebatian came together with **these legates**.

o   licere **illis incolumibus** per se ex hibernis discedere (*Bellum Gallicum* 5.41)

o   that it is permitted **to those inhabitants** to depart from their winter quarters

o   ad quem tum Iuno supplex **his vocibus** usa est (*Aeneid* 1.64)

o   with whom Juno then as suppliant used **these words**

o   squalentem barbam et concretos sanguine crines / **vulnera**que **illa** gerens (*Aeneid* 2.277–78)

o   (he), bearing **those wounds** and his rigid beard and his hair, caked with blood

- *Hic* and *ille* are used also as pronouns, either with a clear antecedent or substantively (without an expressed noun to modify) as a 3rd person personal pronoun.

o **Hic** servo spe libertatis magnisque persuadet praemiis ut *litteras* ad Caesarem deferat. **Has** ille in iaculo *inligatas* effert. (*Bellum Gallicum* 5.45)

o **He / This man** persuades his servant out of a hope for liberty and great rewards to bring a letter to Caesar. He carries **this letter** *lashed* to a spear.

   ▪ The *hic* refers to a person in the previous sentence.

   ▪ *Litteras* is the antecedent of the pronoun *has*, with *inligatas* a participle agreeing with *has*.

o Defertur ea res ad *Caesarem*. **Ille** … L. Plancum cum legione ex Belgio celeriter in Carnutes proficisci iubet. (Caear 5.25)

o This situation is related to *Caesar*. **He / That man** orders Lucius Plancus to depart with his legion from Belgium quickly for the Carnutes.

o Sacra suosque tibi commendat Troia *penates*; / **hos** cape fatorum comites, **his** moenia quaere / magna. (*Aeneid* 2.293–95)

o Let Troy commend her sacred rites and household gods to you; take **them** as companions of fate, seek great walls **for them**.

   ▪ Both *hos* and *his* have *penates* as their antecedent.

o Maturate fugam *regi*que haec dicite vestro: / non **illi** imperium pelagi saevumque tridentem, / sed mihi sorte datum. Tenet **ille** immania saxa, / vestras, Eure, domos; **illa** se iactet **in aula** / Aeolus et clauso ventorum carcere regnet. (*Aeneid* 1.137–41)

o Hurry your flight and tell these words *to your king*: power over the sea and the harsh trident are not **for him** but given to me by lot. **He / That man** holds immense rocks, your homes, Eurus; let Aeolus throw himself **in that space** and rule with the prison of winds closed.

• The substantive use is most often (but not always) a plural nominative or accusative.

o Aeolus **haec** contra. (*Aeneid* 1.76)

o Aeolus (spoke) **these things / words** in response.

o Navita sed tristis nunc **hos** nunc accipit **illos**. (*Aeneid* 6.315)

o The sad sailor now accepts **these men**, now accepts **those men**.

o **Hi** perpetuas inter se controversias habebant. (*Bellum Gallicum* 5.44)

o **They / these people** had eternal disagreement among them.

o **Illi** aegre ad noctem oppugnationem sustinent. (*Bellum Gallicum* 5.37)

o **They / those soldiers** wearily sustain the battle into the night.

o levitate armorum et cotidiana exercitatione nihil **his** noceri posse (*Bellum Gallicum* 5.34)

o because of the lightness of weapons and their daily exercise, nothing could harm **them / these people**

- *Hīc* and *illīc* with a long *-ī-* is used adverbially to mean "here" and "there." (The nominative masculine singular *hic* has a short *-i-*.)

- *Illīc* only appears once in the Latin syllabus.

  o **Hic** vasto rex Aeolus antro / luctantes ventos tempestatesque sonoras / imperio premit. (*Aeneid* 1.52–54)

  o **Here** king Aeolus holds back in his cave with his power the raging winds and the roaring storms.

  o **Hic** portus alii effodiunt; **hic** alta theatris / fundamenta locant alii. (*Aeneid* 1.427–28)

  o **Here** some dig out harbors; **here** others establish deep foundations for theaters.

  o **Illic** fas regna resurgere Troiae. (*Aeneid* 1.206)

  o **There** it is right for the kingdom of Troy to rise again.

- *Hinc* is an adverbial form derived from *hic, haec, hoc* that means "from here" or "from this place."

  o *Hinc* does not appear in the Caesar syllabus.

  o **Hinc atque hinc** vastae rupes geminique minantur / in caelum scopuli. (*Aeneid* 1.162–63)

  o **On this side and this side / all over** vast cliffs and twin crags stretch into the sky.

- *Illinc*, the corresponding form of *ille, illa, illud*, does not appear in the Latin syllabus.

- *Hūc* and *illūc* are adverbial forms derived from *hic* and *ille* that mean "to here / there" or "to this / that place."

  o **Huc** omnes undique qui controversias habent convenient. (*Bellum Gallicum* 6.13)

  o **To this place** all those from everywhere who disagreed will come together.

  o **Huc** septem Aeneas collectis navibus omni / ex numero subit. (*Aeneid* 1.170–71)

  o **To this place** Aeneas comes with seven of his whole number of ships collected.

  o Atque animum nunc **huc** celerem nunc dividit **illuc**. (*Aeneid* 4.285)

  o And he shifts his mind swiftly now **in this direction**, now **in that direction**.

- *Illūc* only appears once in the Latin syllabus.

7.4.3.2 *Is, Ea, Id*

- similar in meaning and usage to *hic* and *ille*

- a less forceful demonstrative and so traditionally recognized as the 3rd person personal pronoun

- Caesar uses *is, ea, id* much more than Vergil; as best I can tell, Vergil uses *is, ea, id* four times in the Latin syllabus.

- Adjectival Use

  o Ex **eo oppido** pons ad Helvetios pertinet. (*Bellum Gallicum* 1.6)

  o From **this town** a bridge stretched to the Helvetii.

  o Non **ea vis** animo. (*Aeneid* 1.529)

  o **This power** is not in our mind.

- Pronominal Use

  o Nostri … in hostes impetum fecerunt atque **eos** in fugam dederunt. (*Bellum Gallicum* 4.26)

  o Our men … made an attack against the enemy and put **them** to flight.

  o **Is**que … dicitur … Iovem manibus supplex orasse supinis. (*Aeneid* 4.203–5)

  o And **he** … is said … to have prayed to Jove as suppliant with upturned hands.

- Possessive Use

  o Cum aut *suis* finibus eos prohibent aut ipsi in **eorum** finibus bellum gerunt. (*Bellum Gallicum* 1.1)

  o Since they [the Belgae] either keep them [the Germans] from *their own* [the Belgian] borders or they themselves [the Belgae] wage war on **their** [the Germans'] borders.

    ▪ The use of *eorum* here rather than *suis*, the reflexive possessive adjective, indicates that the borders are not the borders of the "they" that is the subject.

    ▪ *Suis*, in the first half of the excerpt, indicates that the borders belong to the "they" that is the subject.

7.4.3.3 *Idem, Eadem, Idem*

- a compound of *is, ea, id* and the suffix *-dem*

- The *-dem* is fixed; it doesn't change. The ending comes before the *-dem*.

- Any form of *is, ea, id* that ends in *-m* ends with an *-n* in *idem, eadem, idem*

CHAPTER 7

- o *Eam* becomes *eandem*.

- translation: "same"

- *Idem* is primarily an adjective but can be used substantively as well.

- Persuadent Rauricis et Tulingis et Latobrigis finitimis suis, uti **eodem** usi **consilio**. (*Bellum Gallicum* 1.5)

- They persuade the Raurici and the Tulingi and the Latobrigi, their neighbors, to use the **same approach**.

- **Eadem nocte** accidit ut esset luna plena. (*Bellum Gallicum* 4.29)

- **On the same night** it happened that the moon was full.

- Q. Lucanius **eiusdem ordinis**, fortissime pugnans … interficitur. (*Bellum Gallicum* 5.35)

- Q. Lucanius **of the same rank**, fighting most bravely … is killed.

- **Speluncam** Dido dux et Troianus **eandem** / deveniunt. (*Aeneid* 4.165–66)

- Dido, the leader, and the Trojan approached **the same cave**.

- **Eadem** me ad **fata** vocasses, / **idem** ambas ferro **dolor** atque **eadem hora** tulisset. (*Aeneid* 4.678–79)

- You could have called me to **the same fates**, **the same grief** could have borne both of us with the sword and **at the same time**.

7.4.3.4 *Ipse, Ipsa, Ipsum*

- translation: "myself," "yourself," "himself," "itself"; "ourselves," "yourselves," "themselves"

- *Ipse* is translated with the same English form as the Latin reflexive pronoun (-, *sui, sibi, se, se*) but they have different functions; the ambiguity is an English, rather than a Latin, one.

- o The president sees **herself** in the mirror.

- o The president **herself** is attending the meeting.

  - The first sentence contains a reflexive pronoun because it reflects on the subject; that is, the pronoun is the same person as the subject.

  - The second sentence contains an intensive because it intensifies or emphasizes the noun it modifies: not the president's secretary, but the president *herself*.

- o Noctu ad unum omnes desperata salute *se* **ipsi** interficiunt. (*Bellum Gallicum* 5.37)

- o At night to a man **they themselves** kill *themselves*, with their safety cast aside.

- It is not uncommon among students to translate the intensive as the reflexive or vice versa because of their overlapping translations in English.

- It is imperative, however, to distinguish between them in the Latin and translate them accordingly in English.

- **Ipse Cicero** … ne nocturnum quidem sibi tempus ad quietem relinquebat. (*Bellum Gallicum* 5.40)

- **Cicero himself**, although he was of very dubious health, left for himself not even time at night for recovery.

- **Ductores**que **ipsos** primum … sternit. (*Aeneid* 188–90)

- And [Achates] first took down **the leaders themselves**.

- *Ipse* can be used substantively, in which case a pronoun in English must be supplied for the -self form to modify.

    o cum aut suis finibus eos prohibent aut **ipsi** in eorum finibus bellum gerunt (*Bellum Gallicum* 1.1)

    o when they keep them from their borders or ***they* themselves** wage war at their borders

    o **Ipse** interea … in Gallia morari constituit. (*Bellum Gallicum* 5.24)

    o ***He* himself**, meanwhile, … decided to stay in Gaul.

        ▪ *Ipsi* and *ipse* are nominative but require English pronouns to complete their translation.

- Also translated "very": "You are the **very** person I wanted to see."

    o Quater **ipso in limine** portae / substitit. (*Aeneid* 2.242–43)

    o Four times he stopped **on the very threshold** of the door.

- *Ipse* is most commonly used with the 3rd person but can be 1st or 2nd person.

    o quando aliud mihi iam miserae nihil **ipsa** reliqui (*Aeneid* 4.315)

    o when **I myself** left nothing else to now miserable me

    o **Ipse** deum manifesto in lumine vidi / intrantem muros. (*Aeneid* 4.358–59)

    o **I myself** saw the god in the clear light entering the city.

        ▪ The 1st person ending on the verbs determines the translation of *ipsa* and *ipse*.

7.4.3.5 *Iste, Ista, Istud*

- similar in meaning and usage to *ille*

- often carries the implication of "of yours" in its meaning

CHAPTER 7

- sometimes used with a negative connotation

- Caesar does not use *iste, ista, istud* in the Latin syllabus; Vergil uses it three times.

- Adjectival Use

  o Miserere domus labentis et **istam**, / oro, si quis adhuc precibus locus, exue **mentem**. (*Aeneid* 4.318–19)

  o Pity this collapsing house and, please, if there is any room for pleading, change **that mind of yours**.

  o Hoc illud, germana, fuit? Me fraude petebas? / Hoc **rogus iste** mihi, hoc ignes araeque parabant? / Quid primum deserta querar? (*Aeneid* 4.675–77)

  o This was it, sister? Were you deceiving me? Did **this pyre of yours**, fires and altars prepare this for me?

  o Teque **isto corpore** solvo. (*Aeneid* 4.703)

  o And I release you from **that body of yours**.

7.4.4   RELATIVE AND INTERROGATIVE PRONOUNS

- The relative and the interrogative pronouns are unique in English because their form rather than word order indicates meaning: they must occur at the beginning of their clause, whatever their grammatical function.

- This phenomenon proves difficult because it violates every instinct of the English speaker: "whom" is rarely used in all but the most formal English, however correct it might be, because the English speaker is not accustomed to having a non-subject as the first noun in a clause.

- Consider the following examples of the relative and interrogative pronouns:

  o The boy loves Latin. **He** studies hard. / The boy, **who** loves Latin, studies hard.

  o **Who** went to the movies? **He** went to the movies.

    ▪ The pronouns are the subjects of their clauses / sentences, and occur at the beginning.

    ▪ All of the pronouns occur in the standard grammatical position for the English subject, at the beginning.

  o The girl loves Latin. Her teacher admires **her**. / The girl, **whom** her teacher admires, loves Latin.

  o **Whom** did you see? We saw **them**.

- The personal pronouns "her" and "them" are the direct objects of their clauses / sentences and occur after the verb.

- While the personal pronouns appear in the standard grammatical position for English direct objects after the verb, the relative and interrogative pronouns remain at the beginning of the clause / sentence.

- Its form, "whom" with its "m" ending, indicates that it is the direct object, rather than its position in the word order of the clause / sentence.

- The neuter relative and interrogative pronoun is even more difficult because in both English and Latin its nominative and accusative (subjective and objective) forms are identical.

  o I read the book **which** is good.

  o The book **which** I read was good.

  o **What** did that? **It** did that.

  o **What** did you see? We saw **it**.

  o Tum suo more conclamaverunt … habere sese **quae** de re communi dicere **vellent**. (*Bellum Gallicum* 5.26)

  o Then, according to their custom, they shouted that they had things **which** they wanted to say about their shared situation.

- A good rule is the following:

  o A nominative Latin relative or interrogative pronoun will be followed in English by the main verb (rather than a helping verb).

    - I read the book **which** *is* good.

    - **Who** *saw* it? **What** *did* it?

- An accusative (or non-nominative) Latin relative or interrogative pronoun will most often be followed in the English version by a noun (sometimes with a helping verb in between).

  o The book **which** I̲ *read* was good. [I = subject; read = verb]

  o **Whom** *did* y̲o̲u̲ *see*? **What** d̲i̲d̲ *you* s̲e̲e̲? [did = helping verb; you = subject; see = main verb]

  o Atque harum tamen omnium legionum hiberna praeter eam **quam** L. Roscio in pacatissimam et quietissimam partem ducendam *dederat*, milibus passuum centum continebantur. (*Bellum Gallicum* 5.24)

  o And the winter quarters of all of these legions were contained within a hundred miles except for the legion **which** h̲e̲ *had given* to Lucius Roscius to be led into the most peaceful and tranquil part.

- o **Quem** *fugis*? (*Aeneid* 6.466)

- o **Whom** *do* <u>you</u> *flee*?

- The relative pronoun does not have to be 3rd person.

  - o "Neque is sum," inquit, "**qui** gravissime ex vobis mortis periculo *terrear*." (*Bellum Gallicum* 5.30)

  - o He said, "*I* am not one **who** *am* most gravely *scared* by the danger of death from you."

    - ▪ The *qui terrear* is the relative pronoun plus the verb with "I" as its antecedent, which produces the "who am" translation.

7.4.4.1 Substantive Relative Pronouns

- Relative pronouns can sometimes be used in Latin without a stated antecedent.

- The translation of these relative pronouns requires an English antecedent.

- That English antecedent will be based on the gender of the relative pronoun.

  - o Arpineius et Iunius **quae audierunt** ad legatos deferunt. (*Bellum Gallicum* 5.28)

  - o Arpineius and Iunius reported **what / those things that they heard** to the envoys.

    - ▪ "Those things" is the supplied antecedent, unstated in the Latin.

    - ▪ The neuter *quae* determines "things."

7.4.4.2 Interrogative Adjectives

- Compare the following questions:

  - o Who attacked the Gauls? Which general attacked the Gauls?

- The first sentence begins with the interrogative pronoun; in Latin, it would be *quis*.

- The second sentence, however, illustrates the interrogative adjective.

- As its name implies, the interrogative adjective is a word that introduces a question by agreeing with a noun: "who" operates by itself and asks a general question; "which" agrees with "person" and asks a more specific question.

- The interrogative adjective has forms identical to the relative pronoun.

- **Quod** *genus* hoc hominum? **Quae**ve hunc tam barbara morem / permittit *patria*? (*Aeneid* 1.539–40)

- **What** *type* of men is this? Or **what** *land* so barbarous permits this custom?

- O lux Dardaniae, spes o fidissima Teucrum, **quae** tantae tenuere *morae*? **Quibus** Hector ab *oris* / exspectate venis? … **Quae** *causa* indigna serenos / foedavit *vultus*? (*Aeneid* 2.281–86)

- O light of Troy, o most faithful hope of the Trojans, **what** *delays* so great kept you? From **which** *shores*, Hector having been expected, do you come? … **Which** unworthy *cause* has fouled your peaceful face?

- Aut **qua** *spe* Libycis teris otia terris? (*Aeneid* 4.271)

- Or because of **which** *hope* do you waste time in Libyan lands?

7.5   VERBS

7.5.1   VERBS—OVERVIEW

- verb terminology
    - principal parts—the standardized forms of a verb from which other forms are made
        - Latin has four principal parts:
            - 1st person present indicative; present infinitive; 1st person perfect indicative; perfect passive participle
            - duco, ducere, duxi, ductus
    - mood—the function of a verb
- indicative—states a fact
- imperative—issues a command
- infinitive—the variable form: completes the meaning of a verb and a building block form to create other forms
- subjunctive—expresses doubt or uncertainty
- *Some teachers and textbooks consider the four moods above the only four moods; for convenience's sake, I include participle, gerund, and supine among the moods.*
- participle—a verbal adjective
- gerund—a verbal noun
- supine—a verbal noun
    - tense—when the action of a verb happens
        - six indicative tenses: present, imperfect, future, perfect, pluperfect, future perfect
        - one imperative tense: present (there is a rare future imperative but it does not occur in the Latin syllabus)
        - three infinitive tenses: present, perfect, future
        - four subjunctive tenses: present, imperfect, perfect, pluperfect
        - three participle tenses: present, perfect, future

- one gerund and supine tense: present
  - voice—expresses the relationship of the subject to the verb
    - active: the subject is doing the action of the verb
    - passive: the subject is receiving the action of the verb
    - middle: the subject is doing the action of the verb to itself
      - the middle voice is a Greek form that Latin does not have
      - occasionally Latin passive forms will carry a middle sense; that is, they look passive in Latin but they reflect a middle meaning
        - ◊ tum breviter Dīdō vultum **dēmissa** profātur: (*Aeneid* 1.561)
        - ◊ then Dido, **having put herself down** with respect to her face, spoke briefly:
          - ▷ *Vultum* is an accusative of respect, a construction that often accompanies the Latin middle voice.
  - person—who is doing the action of the verb
    - 1st person: the person speaking—I, we
    - 2nd person: the person spoken to—you, you (all)
    - 3rd person: the person spoken about—he, she, it, they
  - number—singular or plural
  - deponent—a verb that has only passive forms but is translated actively
    - A deponent can have three active forms:
      - present active participle
      - future active participle
      - future active infinitive
    - potior, potiri, potitus
      - potiens, potientis
      - potitus, -a, -um
      - potiturus, -a, -um

7.5.2   INFINITIVES

- at its core, a verbal noun that, unlike the gerund (another verbal noun), expresses distinctions in tense
- exists in three tenses: present, perfect, and future

- traditionally translated "to"

- translated as an indicative verb when used in indirect statement

- The farther down the list of infinitives, the more likely they will be used in indirect statement rather than being translated with "to"; that is, present active and passive are used roughly equally with both translations, while, starting with perfect active, indirect statement use becomes more common.

7.5.2.1 Infinitive Forms

- Present Active

  o formation: present stem + *-re*; also, for most verbs, the 2nd principal part

    ▪ hiemo, -are → hiema- → hiem**are**

  o translation: "to verb"

  o The *-ere* ending can also be used as a syncopated form for the *-erunt* ending of the perfect active indicative.

  o This form will look like a present active infinitive but in reality is a 3rd person indicative.

  o The clues to distinguish them are:

    ▪ The infinitive generally requires a verb on which to depend; the indicative functions on its own.

    ▪ The infinitive comes from the 2nd principal part, while the syncopated perfect indicative comes from the 3rd.

    ▪ A 3rd conjugation infinitive will have a short *-ere*, while the syncopated perfect indicative will have a long *-ēre*.

- Present Passive

  o formation: present stem + *-ri* for 1st, 2nd, and 4th conjugations; + *-i* for 3rd and 3rd *-io*

    ▪ hiemo, -are → hiema- → hiem**ari**

    ▪ capio, -ere → cape- → cap**i**

  o translation: "to be verbed"

  o Interim eam partem **nudari** necesse erat et ab latere aperto tela **recipi**. (*Bellum Gallicum* 5.35)

  o Meanwhile it was necessary for that part **to be exposed** and for weapons **to be received** from that open side.

CHAPTER 7

- Irregular verbs and their compounds often have irregular present active and passive infinitives (though their other infinitives are regular)

  o *fero, ferre*

    ▪ the active infinitive appears six times total, including the two below

      • In hostes aquilam **ferre** coepit. (*Bellum Gallicum* 4.25)

      • He began **to carry** the standard toward the enemy.

      • Ipse haec **ferre** iubet celeres mandata per auras. (*Aeneid* 4.270)

      • He himself ordered him **to bring** these orders through the swift breezes.

    ▪ The passive infinitive appears twice, including the example below:

      • praesertim quos recenti victoria **efferri** sciret (*Bellum Gallicum* 5.47)

      • especially those whom he knew **were boosted** by the recent victory

  o *fio, fieri*

    ▪ The infinitive appears once in the Latin syllabus.

      • Praeterea accidit, quod **fieri** necesse erat, ut vulgo milites ab signis discederent. (*Bellum Gallicum* 5.33)

      • It happens especially, because it was necessary **that it happen**, that soldiers everywhere departed from the standards.

  o *volo, velle*

    ▪ The active infinitive appears once in the Latin syllabus.

      • Tunc duces principesque Nerviorum … colloqui sese **velle** dicunt. (*Bellum Gallicum* 5.41)

      • Then the leaders and rulers of the Nervii say that **they want** to speak (with Cicero).

- Perfect Active

  o formation: perfect stem + *-isse*

    ▪ hiemo, -are, hiemavi → hiemav- → hiemav**isse**

  o translation: "to have verbed"

  o quam Iuno fertur terris magis omnibus unam posthabita **coluisse** Samo (*Aeneid* 1.15–16)

  o which alone Juno is said **to have loved** more than all lands, with Samos put aside

  o omnem esse in armis Galliam; Germanos Rhenum **transisse** (*Bellum Gallicum* 5.41)

  o that all of Gaul was in arms; that the Germans **had crossed** the Rhine

- Perfect Passive

    o formation: perfect passive participle + *esse* as separate word

        ▪ hiemo, -are, hiemavi, hiematus → hiematus → hiematus **esse**

    o translation: "to have been verbed"

    o disciplina in Britannia **reperta** atque inde in Galliam **translata esse** existimatur (*Bellum Gallicum* 6.13)

    o this approach is thought **to have been invented** in Britain and then **to have been transferred** to Gaul

- Future Active

    o formation: perfect passive participle + -ur- + -esse as separate word

        ▪ hiemo, -are, hiemavi, hiematus → hiematus → hiema**tur**us **esse**

    o Every future active infinitive appears in the syllabus with the *esse* understood except for one.

    o translation: "to be about to verb"

    o neque Eburones, si ille adesset, tanta contemptione nostri ad castra **venturos esse** (*Bellum Gallicum* 5.29)

    o nor that the Eburones, if Caesar were present, **would have come** to camp out of such contempt for us

- Future Passive

    o The future passive infinitive is rare enough that its very existence is questioned.

    o There are two primary ways to form it.

    o Of the five future passive infinitives that appear in the Latin syllabus, four follow formation #2; one follows formation #1.

    o Formation #1: supine (which looks like the perfect passive participle) + *iri* as separate word

        ▪ hiemo, -are, hiemavi, hiematus → hiematum → hiematum **iri**

            • Ille appellatus respondit ... ipsi vero nihil **nocitum iri**. (*Bellum Gallicum* 5.36)

            • He, having been called, responded that indeed no **injury would be done** to him.

    o Formation: #2: future passive participle + esse as a separate word

        ▪ hiemo, -are, hiemavi, hiematus → hiemandus → hiemandus **esse**

- **Ducendum (esse)** ad sedes simulacrum **oranda**que **(esse)** divae / numina conclamant. (*Aeneid* 2.232–33)

- They proclaim that the statue [here the Trojan horse to replace the stolen Palladium] **must be brought** to the temple and the power of the goddess **must be prayed to.**

7.5.2.2 Infinitive Uses

- *Complementary Infinitive*

  o used with a verb to complete its meaning

  o does not have a subject; that is, there is no noun between the introductory verb and the infinitive

    ▪ Caesar *wants* **to conquer** Gaul.

  o The complementary infinitive, depending on syntax, can easily overlap with the objective infinitive.

  o Post eius mortem nihilo minus Helvetii id quod constituerant **facere** *conantur*. (*Bellum Gallicum* 1.5)

  o After his death, the Helvetii *tried* no less **to do** that which they had decided.

  o Quis **fallere** *possit* amantem? (*Aeneid* 4.295)

  o Who *could* **deceive** a lover?

- *Indirect Statement / Indirect Discourse—reports direct speech

  o Latin requirements:

    ▪ head verb—verb of thinking, feeling, saying, and so on

    ▪ Subject accusative—the English will have a subject but the Latin will not necessarily express that subject, especially if it's the same as the subject of the head verb.

    ▪ infinitive

  o translation: that …

    ▪ Jupiter *says* that <u>Aeneas</u> **will reach** Italy.

      • "Says" is the head verb that introduces the indirect statement.

      • "That" is not expressed in the Latin.

      • "Aeneas" is the subject accusative.

      • "Will reach" is the Latin infinitive.

    ▪ <u>Illum</u> veruto *arbitrantur* **occisum**. (*Bellum Gallicum* 5.44)

- *They think* that <u>he</u> **was killed** with a spear.
  - *Arbitrantur* is the head verb.
  - no word for "that" in the Latin
  - *Illum* is the subject accusative.
  - *Occisum (esse)* is the infinitive.
- <u>Progeniem</u> sed enim Troiano a sanguine **duci** / *audierat. (Aeneid* 1.19–20)
- But she *had heard* that <u>a race</u> **was springing** from Trojan blood.
  - *Audierat* is the head verb.
  - no word for "that" in the Latin
  - *Progeniem* is the subject accusative.
  - *Duci* is the infinitive.

- The Tense of the Infinitive in Indirect Statement
  o The indicative utilizes absolute tense; that is, each tense represents a specific time.
  o Each tense of the infinitive (present, perfect, future) represents a relative tense—that is, a tense that changes based on the tense of the main verb.
  o The infinitive represents a time relationship rather than an absolute tense:
    - present infinitive = same time
    - perfect infinitive = before
    - future infinitive = after
  o This relationship can also be considered in mathematical terms
    - present = equal
    - perfect = minus 1
    - future = plus 1
  o If the main verb is present tense, the infinitive will be translated by whatever tense it is.

- Present Tense Main Verb
  o Neque fas **esse** *existimant* ea litteris mandare. (*Bellum Gallicum* 6.14)
  o And *they think* that **it is** not right to entrust these things to writing.
    - *Existimant* is the present tense main (head) verb.
    - no word for "that" in the Latin

- no subject accusative

- *(Fas) esse* is the infinitive.

- A present tense main verb (*existimant*) with a present tense infinitive (*esse*) means both verbs will be translated in the present.

○ Interea magno **misceri** murmure <u>pontum</u> / **emissam**que <u>hiemem</u> *sensit* Neptunus et imis <u>stagna</u> **refusa** vadis, graviter commotus. (*Aeneid* 1.124–26)

○ Meanwhile, Neptune *senses* that <u>the sea</u> **is turned** over by a great murmur and <u>a storm</u> **has been raised up** and that <u>the still water</u> **has been churned up** by its deepest water.

- *Sensit* is the present tense main (head) verb that governs the three infinitives.

- no word for "that" in the Latin

- *Pontum, hiemem,* and *stagna* are the subjects accusative.

- *Misceri, emissam (esse), refusa (esse)* are the infinitives.

- *Sensit* is a present tense main verb with one present tense infinitive, translated in the present, and two perfect tense infinitives, translated in the perfect.

○ *Docet* <u>omnes</u> equitatus peditatusque <u>copias</u> Treverorum tria milia passuum longe ab suis castris **consedisse**. (*Bellum Gallicum* 5.47)

○ *He tells* (him) that all of the cavalry and infantry of the Treveri **established** their camp three miles away from his own camp.

- *Docet* is the present tense main (head) verb that governs *consedisse*.

- no word for "that" in the Latin

- *Omnes copias* is the subject accusative.

- *Consedisse* is the infinitive.

- *Docet* is a present tense main verb with a perfect infinitive, translated in the perfect, because it is time before the present.

○ Aut <u>se</u> **immolaturos** *vovent*. (*Bellum Gallicum* 6.16)

○ Or *they pray* that <u>they</u> **will burn**.

- *Vovent* is the present tense main (head) verb.

- no word for "that" in the Latin

- *Se* is the subject accusative which, as the reflexive, means that the subject of *immolaturos* is the same "they" as the subject of *vovent*.

- *Immolaturos (esse)* is the future active infinitive.

- A present main verb with a future infinitive means that the infinitive will be translated in the future tense.

- o Mnesthea Sergestumque *vocat* fortemque Serestum ..., / <u>sese</u> interea ... / **temptaturum** aditus. (*Aeneid* 4.288–93)

- o He *calls* Mnestheus and Sergestus and brave Serestus, that meanwhile <u>he</u> will **try** an approach.

  - ▪ *Vocat* is the present tense main (head) verb.

  - ▪ no word for "that" in the Latin

  - ▪ *Sese* is the subject accusative which, as the reflexive (an alternate form of *se*), means that the subject of *temptaturum* is the same "he" as the subject of *vocat*.

  - ▪ *Temptaturum (esse)* is the future active infinitive.

  - ▪ A present main verb with a future infinitive means that the infinitive will be translated in the future tense.

- o Non *putat* **exspectandam**. (*Bellum Gallicum* 5.46)

- o He does not think that it (the remaining part) **should be expected**.

  - ▪ *Putat* is the present tense main (head) verb.

  - ▪ no word for "that" in the Latin

  - ▪ no subject accusative

  - ▪ *Exspectandam (esse)* is the future passive infinitive.

  - ▪ A present main verb with a future infinitive means that the infinitive will be translated in the future tense.

- o **Ducendum** ad sedes <u>simulacrum</u> **oranda**que divae / <u>numina</u> *conclamant*. (*Aeneid* 2.232–33)

- o *They proclaim* that the <u>statue</u> [here the Trojan horse to replace the stolen Palladium] **must be brought** to the temple and <u>the power</u> of the goddess **must be prayed to**.

  - ▪ *Conclamant* is the present tense main (head) verb that governs the two infinitives.

  - ▪ no word for "that" in the Latin

  - ▪ *Simulacrum* and *numina* are the subjects accusative.

  - ▪ *Ducendum (esse)* and *oranda (esse)* are the future passive infinitives.

  - ▪ *Conclamant* is a present tense main verb with two future passive infinitives, translated with "must" because they are passive periphrastics.

- • Perfect Tense Main Verb

  - o quod saepe <u>homines temerarios atque imperitos</u> falsis rumoribus **terreri** et ad facinus **impelli** et de summis rebus consilium **capere** *cognitum est* (*Bellum Gallicum* 6.20)

- o because it *was* often *thought* that <u>rash and reckless men</u> **were scared** by false rumors and **were driven** to transgression and **took** steps about the most important matters

  - *Cognitum est* is the perfect tense main (head) verb.

  - no word for "that" in the Latin

  - *Homines* (modified by two adjectives) is the subject accusative.

  - *Terreri* and *impelli* are present passive infinitives and *capere* is a present active infinitive.

  - A perfect main verb with a present infinitive means that the infinitive will be translated in the perfect tense because the present infinitive is the same time infinitive.

- o *Certior factus est* in hiberna **perventum** <u>locum</u>que hibernis **esse munitum**. (*Bellum Gallicum* 5.25)

- o *He was made more certain* that **they had arrived** in the winter quarters and that <u>the place</u> for the winter quarters **had been fortified**.

  - *Certior factus est* is the perfect tense main (head) verb.

  - no word for "that" in the Latin

  - no subject accusative for the first infinitive and *locum* the subject accusative for *esse munitum*

  - *Perventum (esse)* and *esse munitum* are perfect passive infinitives.

  - A perfect main verb with a perfect infinitive means that the infinitive will be translated in the pluperfect tense because the perfect infinitive is the before infinitive and before the perfect is the pluperfect.

- o Obsides **daturos** quaeque imperasset <u>sese</u> **facturos** polliciti sunt. (*Bellum Gallicum* 4.27)

- o *They promised* that <u>they</u> **would provide** hostages and that **they would do** what he had ordered.

  - *Polliciti sunt* is the perfect tense main (head) verb (it is a deponent).

  - no word for "that" in the Latin

  - *Sese* is the subject accusative which, as the reflexive (an alternate form of *se*), means that the subject of *daturos (esse)* and *facturos (esse)* is the same "they" as the subject of *polliciti sunt*.

  - *Daturos (esse)* and *facturos (esse)* are future active infinitives.

  - A perfect main verb with a future infinitive means that the infinitive will be translated "would" because the future infinitive is the after infinitive.

- *Infinitive of Exclamation*

  - o Often connotes a sense of resentment or indignation.

  - o Translated like an indicative.

  - o Only two appear in the Latin syllabus, both in Vergil.

    - ▪ Mene incepto **desistere** victam / nec **posse** Italia Teucrorum avertere regem! (*Aeneid* 1.37–38)

    - ▪ Will I, conquered, **stop** my plan and not **be able** to turn the king of the Trojans from Italy?

    - ▪ Mene Iliacis occumbere campis / non **potuisse** tuaque animam hanc **effundere** dextra. (*Aeneid* 1.97–98)

    - ▪ If only I **could** have died on Trojan plains and **poured out** this soul by your right hand.

- *Objective Infinitive*

  - o an infinitive used as the direct object of the verb

  - o will often have an accusative noun as its subject

    - ▪ This accusative noun simultaneously functions as the object of the introductory verb and the subject of the infinitive.

  - o L. Plancum cum legione ex Belgio celeriter in Carnutes **proficisci** *iubet* ibique **hiemare**. (*Bellum Gallicum* 5.25)

  - o He *orders* Lucius Plancus **to depart** with his legion quickly from Belgium for the Carnutes and **to winter** there.

  - o Quidve dolens regina deum tot **volvere** casus / insignem pietate virum, tot **adire** labores / *impulerit*. (*Aeneid* 1.9–11)

  - o Or why the grieving queen of the gods *forces* a man distinguished in loyalty **to suffer** so many misfortunes, **to undergo** so many trials.

- *Subjective Infinitive*

  - o an infinitive used as the subject of a verb

  - o Often in English an impersonal construction will be used with the subjective infinitive.

    - ▪ **To run** is fun = non-impersonal construction.

    - ▪ It is fun **to run** = impersonal construction.

  - o Et omnia deerant quae ad reficiendas naves erant usui et, quod omnibus constabat **hiemare** in Gallia *oportere*. (*Bellum Gallicum* 4.29)

o   And everything which was for repairing ships was lacking and, because it was clear to everyone that *it was appropriate* **to winter** in Gaul.

- The non-impersonal translation, "to winter in Gaul was appropriate," better illustrates the infinitive as subject.

7.5.3   THE SUBJUNCTIVE

7.5.3.1 Overview

- As a general definition, the subjunctive indicates doubt or uncertainty (in contrast to the indicative, which indicates certainty or fact).

- English expresses the subjunctive with "may," "might," "could," "should," "would."

- Not every Latin subjunctive will be translated into English with an English subjunctive.

  o   *cum* clause:

  - Hoc **cum** voce magna **dixisset**, se ex navi proiecit atque in hostes aquilam ferre coepit. (*Bellum Gallicum* 4.25)

  - **After** he **had said** this in a great voice, he threw himself from the ship and began to bear the standard toward the enemy.

  o   result clause:

  - **Tanta** tempestas subito coorta est **ut** nulla earum cursum tenere **posset**. (*Bellum Gallicum* 4.28)

  - **So great** a storm arose suddenly **that** none of them **could** hold their course.

- The Latin subjunctive has dependent and independent uses.

  o   independent uses:

  - deliberative

  - optative

  - volitive (jussive and hortatory)

  o   dependent uses:

  - conditional

  - *cum* clause

  - with *dum*

  - fearing clause

  - indirect command

- indirect question
- noun clause of result
- with *priusquam*
- purpose clause
- with *quin*
- with *quoad*
- relative clause expressing cause
- relative clause of characteristic
- relative clause of purpose
- relative clause of result
- result clause
- subordinate clause in indirect statement

7.5.3.2 Formation

- There is no set translation for the subjunctive, so translations are not included in this section.

- Use-specific translations will be included with each use of the subjunctive below.

Present Tense

- General rule: same formation as the present indicative active and passive but with a different characteristic vowel

- the characteristic vowels for the subjunctive:

  o 1st conjugation: -**e**- (-a- for indicative)

  o 2nd conjugation: -**ea**- (-e- for indicative)

  o 3rd conjugation: -**a**- (-i- for indicative)

  o 3rd io conjugation: -**ia**- (-ī- for indicative)

  o 4th conjugation: -**ia**- (-ī- for indicative)

- The -*e*- form now has three different possibilities that can only be distinguished by knowing the conjugation of the verb:

  o amet = present subjunctive, 1st conjugation

  o docet = present indicative, 2nd conjugation

  o ponet = future indicative, 3rd conjugation

- There is nothing in these forms to tell them apart; only context and vocabulary information can distinguish them.

Imperfect Tense

- General rule: present active infinitive plus the active and passive personal endings

- All conjugations, including irregular verbs, are formed the same way.

  o premo, premere → premere → premerem, premeres, premeret, and so on

  o possum, posse → posse → possem, posses, posset, and so on

- For deponent verbs, the passive imperative, which looks like a present active infinitive, is used, plus passive endings (because they are deponents).

  o arbitror, arbitrari → arbitrari → arbitrare → arbitrarer, arbitrareris, arbitraretur, and so on

Perfect Tense

- General rule for the active: perfect stem (3rd principal part minus the -i) plus -eri- plus the active personal endings

  o There are no changes to the -eri-; even the 3rd person plural stays -erint (rather than the more customary change to a -u-, -erunt).

- All conjugations, including irregular verbs, are formed the same way.

  o mitto, mittere, misi, missus→ misi → mis- → miseri- → miserim, miseris, miserit, and so on

  o volo, velle, volui, - → volui → volu- → volueri- → voluerim, volueris, voluerit, and so on

- General rule for the passive: perfect passive participle (4th principal part) + the present subjunctive of *sum, esse* as a separate word

- All conjugations, including irregular verbs, are formed the same way.

  o accipio, accipere, accepi, acceptus → acceptus → acceptus sim, acceptus sis, acceptus sit, and so on

  o fio, fieri, factus → factus → factus sim, factus sis, factus sit, and so on

Pluperfect Tense

- General rule for the active: perfect stem (3rd principal part minus the -i) plus -isse plus the active personal endings

- All conjugations, including irregular verbs, are formed the same way.

  o dico, dicere, dixi, dictus → dixi → dix- → dixisse- → dixissem, dixisses, dixisset, and so on

- o   fero, ferre, tuli, latus → tuli → tul- → tulisse- → tulissem, tulisses, tulisset, and so on
- General rule for the passive: perfect passive participle (4th principal part) + the imperfect subjunctive of *sum, esse* as a separate word
- All conjugations, plus irregular verbs, are formed the same way.
  - o   video, videre, vidi, visus → visus → visus essem, visus esses, visus esset, and so on
  - o   fio, fieri, factus → factus → factus essem, factus esses, factus esset, and so on

7.5.3.3 Uses

*Conditionals

- both dependent (protasis) and independent (apodosis) clauses
- Latin requirements: *si*
- translation: "If … (then) …"

- Conditionals are composed of two parts:
  - o   the apodosis, which is the main clause of the conditional
  - o   the protasis, which is the dependent, or "if," clause of the conditional
    - ▪ If Caesar attacks *[protasis]*, the Romans will be victorious *[apodosis]*.
- Conditionals are broadly divided into **indicative or simple** conditions and **subjunctive or contrary-to-fact** conditionals.
- Simple conditions express an actual or realistic situation:
  - o   If Caesar attacks, the Romans will be victorious.
- Contrary-to-fact conditionals express a hypothetic situation:
  - o   If Caesar were to attack *[which he might not]*, the Romans would be victorious.
- The Latin syllabus contains mostly contrary-to-fact (subjunctive) conditionals.
- The majority of simple conditionals occur in the Vergil syllabus rather than Caesar.

- Latin conditionals can occur in all tenses of the indicative and the subjunctive.
- Verbs in conditionals will, in general, be translated the way they look; that is, present tense verbs will be translated in the present, perfect in the perfect, and so on
- The primary exception is pluperfect subjunctive verbs.
  - o   A pair of pluperfect subjunctives in a conditional will be translated "had … would have"
  - o   If Caesar had attacked, he would have been victorious.

- Simple Present (present indicative)

  o Hoc mortuo, aut, **si** qui ex reliquis **excellit** dignitate **succedit**, aut, **si sunt** plures pares, suffragio druidum (succedunt). (*Bellum Gallicum* 6.13)

  o Once this man dies, either, **if** anyone of the rest **is exemplary** in dignity, **he takes over**, or, **if there are** many people that are equal, **they take over** by a vote of the Druids.

  o De morte **si** res in suspicionem **venit**, de uxoribus in servilem modum quaestionem **habent** et, **si compertum est**, igni atque omnibus tormentis excruciatas **interficiunt**. (*Bellum Gallicum* 6.19)

  o **If** the circumstances of his death **become** suspicious, they **question** the wives the way they question slaves and, **if it is proved**, they **kill** them, after they have been tortured, by burning or other tortures.

  o Tum, pietate gravem ac meritis **si** forte [**est**] virum quem / conspexere, **silent** arrectisque auribus **astant**. (*Aeneid* 1.151–52)

  o Then, **if** by chance **there is** a man, serious in dignity and merits, whom they see, they **are silent** and **they stand** with their ears primed.

- Present Contrary-to-Fact (imperfect subjunctive)

  o **Si** quid **vellent**, ad Id. April, **reverterentur**. (*Bellum Gallicum* 1.7)

  o **If** they **wanted** something, **they could return** on the Ides of April.

  o **Si** non arva aliena domosque / ignotas **peteres**, et Troia antiqua **maneret**, / Troia per undosum **peteretur** classibus aequor? (*Aeneid* 4.311–13)

  o **If you were not to seek** foreign lands and unknown homes and **if** ancient Troy **remained**, **would** Troy **be sought** by your fleet over the wavy sea?

- Future-Less-Vivid / Future Contrary-to-Fact (present subjunctive)

  o **Si** ab armis discedere **velint**, se adiutore **utantur** legatosque ad Caesarem **mittant**. (*Bellum Gallicum* 5.41)

  o **If they (should) want** to stop fighting, they **would use** him as an advocate and **send** ambassadors to Caesar.

  o **Ni faciat**, maria ac terras caelumque profundum / quippe **ferant** rapidi secum **verrant**que per auras. (*Aeneid* 1.58–59)

  o **If** he **(shouldn't) doesn't** [control the winds], **they would** quickly and certainly **take over** the seas and the lands and the wide sky for themselves and **sweep** them through the air.

Cum Clause—expresses circumstance: time, cause, concession

- dependent clause

- Latin requirements: *cum*

- translation: "when," "after," "since," "because," "although"

- Be careful of the confusion between *cum* the conjunction (used in a *cum* clause) and *cum* the preposition, meaning "with."

- *Cum* the preposition will be followed by an ablative noun or adjective (or perhaps a genitive that comes before the ablative noun).

- *Cum* the conjunction will, in general, not be followed by an ablative noun, but it can be:

  o **cum** virtute omnibus **praestarent** (*Bellum Gallicum* 1.2)

  o since they excelled everyone in virtue

    ▪ *Cum* the conjunction is followed by an ablative noun, which might suggest that *cum* here is a preposition; *virtute*, however, is an ablative of respect, which does not take a preposition, and so *cum* is a conjunction, further suggested by the subjunctive *praestarent*.

- If *cum* is followed by a nominative, it is most likely *cum* the conjunction.

- The majority of the subjunctive *cum* clauses in the syllabus come from Caesar; Vergil much more often uses *cum* with the indicative.

- Examples are included below of the different meanings of *cum* but time and cause will often overlap; that is, "when" or "after" can sometimes imply cause.

- Time

  o Caesari **cum** id **nuntiatum esset**, eos per provinciam nostram iter facere conari, maturat ab urbe proficisci. (*Bellum Gallicum* 1.7)

  o **When** this **had been reported** to Caesar, that they were trying to journey through our province, he hurries to depart from the city.

  o Hoc **cum** voce magna **dixisset**, se ex navi proiecit atque in hostes aquilam ferre coepit. (*Bellum Gallicum* 4.25)

  o **After** he **had said** this in a great voice, he threw himself from the ship and began to bear the standard toward the enemy.

- Cause

  o Hos item ex proximis primis navibus **cum conspexissent**, subsecuti hostibus appropinquarunt. (*Bellum Gallicum* 4.25)

  o **Because these from the closest ships had seen** these men [jumping from the ship into battle], having followed, they approached the enemy.

    ▪ *Cum* here can also be interpreted as time, "when" or "after."

- o Principes Britanniae ... **cum** equites et naves et frumentum Romanis deesse **intellegerent** et paucitatem militum ex castrorum exiguitate **cognoscerent**, ... optimum factu esse duxerunt. (*Bellum Gallicum* 4.30)

- o The leaders of Britain, **because they thought** that the horsemen and ships and grain were absent to the Romans and **they knew** the lack of soldiers from the camp because of its size ... held that the best thing to do was.

- Concession

  - o **Cum** a prima luce ad horam octavam **pugnaretur**, nihil quod ipsis esset indignum committebant. (*Bellum Gallicum* 5.35)

  - o **Although** [the army] **fought** from dawn to the eighth hour, they did nothing that was unworthy of them themselves.

  - o Ipse Cicero, **cum** tenuissima valetudine **esset**, ne nocturnum quidem sibi tempus ad quietem relinquebat. (*Bellum Gallicum* 5.40)

  - o Cicero himself, **although** he **was** of very dubious health, left for himself not even time at night for recovery.

Deliberative—an independent use of the subjunctive that expresses doubt or indignation

- Quis genus Aeneadum, quis Troiae **nesciat** urbem, / virtutesque virosque aut tanti incendia belli. (*Aeneid* 1.565–66)

- Who **wouldn't know** the tribe of the Trojans, who **wouldn't know** the city of Troy, and the virtues and men and the fires of so great a war.

with dum—translated "until" when used with the present or imperfect subjunctive to express expectancy or potentiality

- Tamen, ut spatium intercedere posset **dum** milites quos imperaverat **convenirent**, legatis respondit. (*Bellum Gallicum* 1.7)

- Nevertheless, so that a moment might intervene **until** the soldiers whom he had ordered could come together, he responded to the envoys.

- Multa quoque et bello passus, **dum conderet** urbem / **inferret**que deos Latio. (*Aeneid* 1.5–6)

- Also suffering many things in war, **until he can found** the city and **establish** the gods in Latium.

*Fearing Clause

- a dependent noun clause that expresses what the subject fears

- Latin requirements:

o   verb of fearing as the main verb

-   *Veritus*, the perfect participle of *vereor, vereri* introduces both fearing clauses in the Latin syllabus.

o   *ne* or *ut* as the introductory clause word

-   The use of *ne* or *ut* is reversed from other clauses.

-   *Ne* indicates the positive (where it indicates the negative in other clauses).

-   *Ne … non* or *ut* indicates the negative (where *ut* indicates the positive in other clauses).

-   This reversal occurs because the verb of fearing is considered a negative, so the negative verb of fearing plus the negative *ne* equals a positive, and the negative verb of fearing plus the positive (or, really, null) *ut* equals a negative.

- translation:

  o   "that"

  o   Caesar *is afraid* **that** the Germans are coming. → Caesar *timet* **ne** Germani veniant.

  o   Caesar *is afraid* **that** Roman soldiers are **not** coming. → Caesar *timet* **ut** Romani milites veniant.

- ille **veritus**, quod ad plures pertinebat, **ne** civitas eorum impulsu **deficeret** (*Bellum Gallicum* 5.25)

- that man, **fearing**, because this pertained to many people, **that** the state **might revolt** because of their encouragement

- Labienus … **veritus ne**, si ex hibernis fugae similem profectionem fecisset, hostium impetum sustinere non **posset** … litteras Caesari remittit. (*Bellum Gallicum* 5.47)

- Labienus, **fearing that**, if he departed from his winter quarters similar to fleeing, **he could not sustain** an enemy attack, sends letters to Caesar.

[for the Hortatory, see Volitive below]

*Indirect Command—the reporting of a command

[For a comparison of indirect command, indirect question, and indirect statement, see the chart below indirect question.]

- a dependent clause

- Latin requirements:

  o   verb of ordering

  o   *ut* (positive) or *ne* (negative)

- translation:
  - ○ "to" as an infinitive or "that" with an indicative (or, strictly speaking, a subjunctive in English)
  - ○ Caesar *orders* his troops **to** attack / **that** his troops attack → Caesar *imperat* **ut** milites petant.
  - ○ Caesar *orders* his troops **not to** attack / **that** his troops **not** attack → Caesar *imperat* **ne** milites petant.

- In the Latin syllabus, as best I can tell, indirect commands are only used by Caesar.

- These are the verbs of ordering used by Caesar:
  - ○ *cohortor, -ari*
  - ○ *communico, -are*
  - ○ *contestor, -ari*
  - ○ *hortor, -ari*
  - ○ *impero, -are*
  - ○ *moneo, -ere*
  - ○ *oro, -are*
  - ○ **persuadeo, -ere** (most frequently used)
  - ○ *pronuntio, -are*
  - ○ *rogo, -are*

- The verb of ordering *iubeo, -ere* takes a subject accusative and the infinitive rather than *ut* plus the subjunctive.

- Both Vergil and Caesar use *iubeo* with an infinitive in the Latin syllabus.

- From a strictly grammatical standpoint, this use of *iubeo* constitutes an indirect statement but expresses what an indirect command expresses.
  - ○ Trium mensum molita cibaria sibi quemque domo **efferre** iubent. (*Bellum Gallicum* 1.5)
  - ○ *They order* **that** each **bring** from home enough flour for themselves for three months.
  - ○ Ipse haec **ferre** iubet celeres mandata per auras. (*Aeneid* 4.270)
  - ○ He himself *orders* **that** he **bear** these orders through the sky.

- Civitati *persuasit* **ut** de finibus suis cum omnibus copiis **exirent**. (*Bellum Gallicum* 1.2)

- He *persuaded* the state **to depart** from its borders with all of their supplies.

- *Orant* **ne** sua dissensione et pertinacia rem in summum periculum **deducant**. (*Bellum Gallicum* 5.31)

- *They beg* them **not to move** the situation into the gravest danger by their disagreement and rashness.

*Indirect Question—the reporting of a question

- a dependent clause

- Latin requirements:

  o   verb of asking

  o   interrogative word to introduce the indirect question

- a direct question: Where are Caesar's troops? → Ubi Caesaris milites sunt?

- an indirect question: Caesar *wonders* <u>where</u> his troops **are** → Caesar *miratur* <u>ubi</u> milites **sint**.

- Ibi ex captivis *cognoscit* <u>quae</u> apud Ciceronem **gerantur** <u>quantoque</u> in periculo res **sit**. (*Bellum Gallicum* 5.48)

- There *he learned* from the captives <u>what</u> **happened** at Cicero's fort and <u>how</u> dangerous the situation **was**.

- Nube cava *speculantur* amicti / <u>quae</u> fortuna viris, classem <u>quo litore</u> **linquant**, / <u>quid</u> **veniant**. (*Aeneid* 1.516–18)

- Covered in a thick cloud, *they wonder* <u>what</u> fortune their men have, <u>on what shore</u> **they leave** their fleet, <u>why</u> **they come** here.

- The three Latin indirect constructions can easily be confused. The chart below lays out the basic information for all three:

	introductory verb type	introductory Latin word	mood of Latin verb	translation
indirect statement / discourse	head verb / verb of saying or speaking	[none]	infinitive	that …
indirect question	verb of asking	[interrogative word]	subjunctive	[interrogative word]
indirect command	verb of ordering	*ut / ne*	subjunctive	that … / to …

[for the Jussive, see Volitive below]

Noun Clause of Result

- a dependent clause

CHAPTER 7

- Latin requirements:

  o verb of happening or effecting (i.e., bringing something about or making happen)

  o *ut*

- translation:

  o "that"

  o *It happened* **that** Caesar arrived in time.

  o Caesar *brought it about / effected / made happen* **that** his troops were victorious.

- In the Latin syllabus, as best I can tell, noun clauses of result are only used by Caesar.

- These are the verbs of happening used by Caesar:

  o **accido, -ere** (most frequently used)

  o *efficio, -ere*

  o *evenio, -ire*

  o *fio, fieri*

  o *oportet, -ere*

- Eadem nocte **accidit ut** esset luna plena. (*Bellum Gallicum* 4.29)

- On the same night **it happened that** there was a full moon.

- XII navibus amissis, reliquis **ut** navigari commode posset **effecit**. (*Bellum Gallicum* 4.31)

- Once 12 ships were lost, *he effected / made it happen* **that** the others could be sailed easily.

Optative—expresses a wish

- an independent use

- Latin requirements:

  o *utinam*

- translation:

  o "would that"

  o **Would that** Caesar had arrived sooner!

- Both uses of the optative occur in the *Aeneid*, one with *utinam* and one without.

- Atque **utinam** rex ipse Noto compulsus eodem / **adforet** Aeneas. (*Aeneid* 1.575–76)

- And **would that** the king himself, Aeneas, moved by that same wind, **were present**.

- Eadem me ad fata **vocasses**, / idem ambas ferro dolor atque eadem hora **tulisset**. (*Aeneid* 4.678–79)

- **Would that you had called** me to the same fate, **would that** the same grief and the same time **had taken** both of us with the sword.

with priusquam

- a dependent clause

- Latin requirements:

  o *priusquam*

- translation:

  o before" or "until"

- *Priusquam* with the subjunctive is often separated into two words which often have words between them.

- *Priusquam* with the subjunctive occurs twice in the syllabus, once in Caesar and once in Vergil.

- Ipsorum esse consilium, velintne **priusquam** finitimi **sentiant** eductos ex hibernis milites aut ad Ciceronem aut ad Labienum deducere. (*Bellum Gallicum* 5.27)

- It was their decision whether they wanted to lead away their soldiers, drawn from winter quarters, either to Cicero or to Labienus, **before** those nearby **figured it out**.

- Nec **prius** absistit **quam** septem ingentia victor / corpora **fundat** humi et numerum cum navibus **aequet**. (*Aeneid* 1.192–93)

- Nor does the victor cease **until** he **spreads** seven huge bodies on the ground and **makes** the number **equal** to his ships.

*Purpose Clause

- a dependent clause expressing purpose or answering the question "for what purpose"

- Latin requirements:

  o *ut* (positive) or *ne* (negative)

- translation:

  o "to" as an infinitive or "that" with an indicative (positive); "not to," "so that … not," or "lest" (negative)

    ▪ The infinitive can be used when the subject of the main verb and the subject of the purpose clause are the same.

      - Caesar rushes to aid his soldiers → Caesar ruit ut milites iuvet.

- ▪ "That" must be used when the subject of the main verb and the subject of the purpose clause are different.

    - Caesar sends troops so that Cicero might live → Caesar milites mittit ut Cicero vivat.

- The majority of purpose clauses in the syllabus appears in Caesar; as best I can tell there are only two in the Vergil syllabus.

- Helvetii id quod constituerant facere conantur, **ut** e finibus suis **exeant**. (*Bellum Gallicum* 1.5)

- The Helvetii try to do what they had decided **so that** they **could leave** from their borders.

- Hanc Graecis conscriptam litteris mittit, **ne** intercepta epistola nostra ab hostibus consilia **cognoscantur**. (*Bellum Gallicum* 5.48)

- He sends it written in Greek letters, **so that** our plans **might not be known** if the letter was intercepted by the enemy / **lest** our plans be known.

- Quassatam ventis liceat subducere classem / et silvis aptare trabes et stringere remos … **ut** Italiam laeti Latiumque **petamus**. (*Aeneid* 1.553–54)

- Let it be permitted that our fleet, battered by storms, land and that we form beams from trees and shape oars **so that** we happily **might seek** Italy and Latium.

- His etiam struxi manibus patriosque vocavi / voce deos, sic te **ut** posita, crudelis, **abessem**. (*Aeneid* 4.680–81)

- I built it with these hands and summoned the gods of our homeland with this voice, **so that**, with you thus having been taken away, I, cruel, **might be absent**.

with quamquam

- a dependent clause introduced by *quamquam*

- Latin requirements:

    ○ *quamquam*

- translation:

    ○ "although"

- Nec vero Alciden me sum laetatus euntem / accepisse lacu, nec Thesea Pirithoumque, / dis **quamquam** geniti atque invicti viribus **essent**. (*Aeneid* 6.392–94)

- Indeed I was not happy to have accepted Hercules arriving on the lake, nor Theseus and Pirithoos, **although they were** born to gods and unconquerable in strength.

with quin *after a Verb of Doubting*

- a dependent clause after a negative verb of doubting to express that which is doubted

- Latin requirements:

  o *quin*

- translation:

  o "that"

- *Quin* after a verb of doubting occurs twice in the Latin syllabus, both in Caesar.

- It does appear once in Vergil with the indicative as an interrogative (4.309).

- *non esse dubium* **quin** *totius Galliae plurimum Helvetii* **possent** (*Bellum Gallicum* 1.3)

- *that there is no doubt* **that** *the Helvetii* **could** *obtain all of Gaul*

- *Neque abest suspicio ...* **quin** *ipse sibi mortem* **consciverit.** (*Bellum Gallicum* 1.4)

- *Nor was the suspicion absent* **that he** *himself* **killed** *himself.*

with quoad

- a dependent clause

- Latin requirements:

  o quoad

- translation:

  o "until"

- Ipse interea, **quoad** legiones collocatas munitaque hiberna **cognovisset**, in Gallia morari constituit. (*Bellum Gallicum* 5.24)

- He himself, meanwhile, **until** he **knew** that the legions were assembled and the winter quarters were fortified, decided to stay in Gaul.

The next four subjunctives involve relative pronouns and clauses. There exists a good amount of ambiguity among these constructions; different editors identify relative clauses with the subjunctive as different relative clauses. That's not to say, of course, that there are no wrong answers; of course, a relative clause with the subjunctive can be misidentified. But there can be more than one right answer when interpreting one of these relative clauses.

Relative Clause expressing Cause

- a dependent clause with the relative pronoun to express cause

- Latin requirements:

  o a relative pronoun

- translation:

  o "because"

- tum demum Titurius, **qui** nihil ante **providisset** (*Bellum Gallicum* 5.33)

- then finally Titurius, **because he had anticipated** nothing before

  o Some interpret this as a relative clause of characteristic.

- At Cotta, **qui cogitasset** haec posse in itinere accidere atque ob eam causam profectionis auctor **non fuisset**. (*Bellum Gallicum* 5.33)

- But Cotta, **because he had known** that these things could happen on the journey and **because he had not been** the originator of the journey because of this reason.

- Labienus … praesertim **quos** recenti victoria efferri **sciret**, litteras Caesari remittit. (*Bellum Gallicum* 5.47)

- Labienus … especially **because he knew** that **they** were motivated by the recent victory, sends letters to Caesar.

*Relative Clause of Characteristic

- a dependent clause with the relative pronoun to identify a general category

- Latin requirements:

  o a relative pronoun

- translation:

  o however the relative pronoun is translated otherwise, sometimes with a statement of generality: "the type of man who …"

    ▪ regular relative clause: Caesar praises the soldier *who is brave*.

    ▪ relative clause of characteristic: Caesar praises the soldier *who is the type of man who is brave*.

  o can be translated no differently from an indicative relative clause; that is, the distinction is one of nuance in English

- All relative clauses of characteristic in the syllabus appear in Caesar.

- Constituerunt **ea quae** ad proficiscendum **pertinerent** comparare. (*Bellum Gallicum* 1.3)

- They decided to prepare **those things (of the type) that are relevant** to departure.

  o The Latin subjunctive verb is translated with an indicative English verb:

    ▪ pertinerent = are relevant

- o   The relative pronoun can include something that generalizes it: rather than "that" alone, "of the type that" or "the sort of thing(s) that."

- Erant in ea legione fortissimi viri, centuriones, **qui** primis ordinibus **appropinquarent**. (*Bellum Gallicum* 5.44)

- There were in that legion very brave men, centurions, **of the type who approach** the highest ranks.

*Relative Clause of Purpose

- a dependent clause with the relative pronoun to express purpose

  - o   The relative pronoun is an expression of *ut* (or *ne*) plus a personal pronoun.

  - o   This combination creates a closer link between the purpose clause and the main clause, somewhat similar to how a semicolon works in English.

- Latin requirements:

  - o   a relative pronoun

- translation:

  - o   no different from a regular purpose clause

  - o   "to" as an infinitive or "that" with an indicative (positive); "not to," "so that … not," or "lest" (negative)

    - ▪ The infinitive can be used when the subject of the main verb and the subject of the purpose clause are the same.

      - Caesar rushes to aid his soldiers → Caesar ruit qui milites iuvet.

    - ▪ "That" must be used when the subject of the main verb and the subject of the purpose clause are different.

      - Caesar sends troops so that Cicero might live → Caesar milites mittit qui Cicero vivat.

- Diem dicunt, **qua** die ad ripam Rhodani omnes **conveniant**. (*Bellum Gallicum* 1.6)

- They specify the day **on which they** all **should meet** on the shore of the Rhone / **to meet** on the shore of the Rhone.

- Progeniem sed enim Troiano a sanguine duci / audierat Tyrias olim **quae verteret** arces. (*Aeneid* 1.19–20)

- She had heard that a race was being brought forth from Trojan blood **who would overturn** Carthaginian citadels one day / **to overturn** Carthaginian citadels one day.

Relative Clause of Result

- a dependent clause with the relative pronoun to express result

- o   The relative pronoun is an expression of *ut* (or *ut ... non*) plus a personal pronoun.

- o   This combination creates a closer link between the result clause and the main clause, somewhat similar to how a semicolon works in English.

- Latin requirements:

  - o   a relative pronoun

- translation:

  - o   no different from a regular result clause

  - o   "that" or "with the result that"

- As best I can tell there is only one relative clause of result in the syllabus

- Secutae sunt continuos complures dies tempestates **quae** et nostros in castris **continerent** et hostem a pugna **prohiberent**. (*Bellum Gallicum* 4.34)

- Many storms followed day after day **with the result that they kept** our men in camp and **kept** the enemy from the fight.

*Result Clause

- a dependent clause expressing result

- Latin requirements:

  - o   *ut* (positive) or *ut ... non* (negative)

  - o   often preceded in the main clause by a signal word meaning "so"

  - o   These are the "so" words used in the syllabus:

    - *adeo*

    - *eiusmodi*

    - *ita*

    - ***tantus, -a, -um*** (most frequently used)

- translation:

  - o   "that" or "with the result that"

    - "That" is used when there is a "so" word in the main clause.

      - Caesar was **so** angry **that** he left → Caesar erat **tam** iratus **ut** proficisceretur.

    - "With the result that" is used when there is no "so" word in the main clause.

      - Caesar attacked swiftly **with the result that** he defeated the Gauls → Caesar celeriter petivit **ut** Gallos oppugnaret.

- The majority of result clauses in the syllabus appears in Caesar; as best I can tell there is only one in the Vergil syllabus.

- **Tanta** tempestas subito coorta est **ut** nulla earum cursum tenere **posset**. (*Bellum Gallicum* 4.28)

- **So great** a storm suddenly arose **that** no ship **could** maintain its course.

- Caesar etsi idem quod superioribus diebus acciderat fore videbat, **ut**, si essent hostes pulsi, celeritate periculum **effugerent**. (*Bellum Gallicum* 4.35)

- Caesar understood that the same thing that had happened on previous days would happen again, **with the result that**, if the enemy were to be pushed back, **they would flee** the danger quickly.

Subordinate Clause in Indirect Statement

- Latin requirements:
  - indirect statement
  - a subordinate clause
- translation:
  - no different from the subordinate clause's translation outside of indirect statement

- All subordinate clauses in indirect statement in the syllabus appear in Caesar.

- (Cicero *respondit*) *sperare* pro eius iustitia **quae petierint** impetraturos (esse). (*Bellum Gallicum* 5.41)

- Cicero *responded that he hoped* in light of Caesar's justice that they would collect **those things which they sought**.

*Volitive

- an independent subjunctive expressing a wish or desire
- Traditionally, the 1st person volitive is called the hortatory and the 3rd person the jussive.
- translation:
  - "let" or "may"
  - May Caesar triumph today → Hodie Caesar oppugnet.
  - Let us proceed to Gaul → Ad Galliam procedamus.

- The volitive appears in the syllabus only in the *Aeneid*.

- Quassatam ventis **liceat** subducere classem / et silvis aptare trabes et stringere remos. (*Aeneid* 1.551–52)

- **Let it be permitted** that our fleet, battered by storms, land and that we form beams from trees and shape oars so that we happily might seek Italy and Latium.

7.5.4   PARTICIPLES

- The participle is a verbal adjective; that is, it is a verb that functions like an adjective.

- Like an adjective, the participle must agree with a noun.

- Latin uses participles more frequently than English does.

- There are then multiple ways to translate a Latin participle into English:

  o   as a straight participle

  o   as a relative clause with the Latin participle as the English verb of that clause

  o   as an adverbial subordinate clause with the Latin participle as the English verb of that clause

- There are four participles in Latin.

7.5.4.1 Formation

Present Active Participle

- a 1-stem 3rd declension adjective with *-ns, -ntis* as its nominative and genitive

  o   tendo, -ere → **tendens, tendentis**

- translated with the -ing form in English

  o   The **fighting** soldier is killed.

- The present active participle / -ing form can also be used as part of a main verb in English (but cannot in Latin).

  o   The **fighting** soldier was *fleeing* the battle.

    ▪   "Fleeing" is a present active participle but it is used with the helping verb "was" as the main verb of the sentence.

    ▪   "Fighting" remains a present active participle used as an adjective because it agrees with "soldier."

    ▪   When translating on the AP® Exam, make sure not to translate Latin present active participles as main verbs.

- hostes vero, notis omnibus vadis, ubi ex litore aliquos singulares ex navi **egredientes** conspexerant, (*Bellum Gallicum* 4.26)

- indeed the enemy, because all of the shallows were known to them, when they spied from the shore some of our men **departing** from the ship one-by-one

- **tendens** ad sidera palmas (*Aeneid* 1.93)

- **stretching** his hands to the stars

Perfect Passive Participle

- For most verbs, the perfect passive participle is the 4th principal part of the verb.

  - *interficio, interficere, interfeci, **interfectus***

  o Verbs with *-urus* in the 4th principal part don't have passive forms; any 4th principal part in *-urus* is already the future active participle rather than the perfect passive participle.

  - *sum, esse, fui, **futurus***

  o Deponent verbs only have three principal parts (the 3rd principal part has only active forms so doesn't exist for passive-only deponents); I still, however, use the term "4th principal part" for consistency's sake.

- Translated with the past participle in English, which is most commonly the -ed form, but it can take other forms as well:

  o **(Having been) Dispersed** through the field, the soldiers *prepared* to fight.

  o First **(having been) seen** from afar, the enemy ships *approached*.

  o **(Having been) Told** the situation, Caesar *ordered* his men to retreat.

  o The English past participle form can be used as an adjective (strictly participial) or as a main verb.

  o In the above examples, "dispersed," "seen," and "told" are the participles, while "prepared," "approached," and "ordered" are main verbs.

  o The "having been" that is often used to translate the perfect passive participle is used to ensure that the Latin participle is translated as an English participle rather than as a main verb: "having been dispersed" can't be the main verb of a sentence.

- Nam quod omni ex reliquis partibus **demesso** frumento pars una erat reliqua, **suspicati** hostes huc nostros esse venturos noctu in silvis delituerant; tum **dispersos, depositis** armis in metendo **occupatos** subito **adorti**, paucis **interfectis** reliquos incertis ordinibus perturbaverant, simul equitatu atque essedis circumdederant. (*Bellum Gallicum* 4.32)

- For, because there was only one part left after all of the grain **had been cut** from the other parts, the enemy, **having guessed** that our men would go there, had hidden in the woods at night; then, they, **having attacked** suddenly our men who **were spread out** and **busy** with harvesting, **with** their weapons **put aside**, forced the rest into a chaotic formation,

after a few **had been killed**, at the same time scattering others with their horsemen and light chariots.

- Tum pater Anchises lacrimis **ingressus obortis**. (*Aeneid* 6.867)

- Then father Anchises (spoke), **having entered** as tears **rose up**.

  o Latin prefers participles more than English and so English will translate the Latin participle in often nonparticipial ways—for example, relative clauses, subordinate clauses, and so on

  o The examples above are intended to illustrate that range of translations.

Future Active Participle

- For most verbs, the future active participle is the 4ᵗʰ principal part of the verb plus the infix *-ur-*:

  ▪ *interficio, interficere, interfeci, interfectus → **interfecturus***

  o Verbs with *-urus* in the 4ᵗʰ principal part don't have passive forms; any 4ᵗʰ principal part in *-urus* is already the future active participle.

  ▪ *sum, esse, fui, **futurus***

  o Deponent verbs only have three principal parts (the 3ʳᵈ principal part has only active forms so doesn't exist for passive-only deponents); I still, however, use the term "4ᵗʰ principal part" for consistency's sake.

- Translated "about to verb":

  o **About to fall**, the soldier braced himself.

  o Caesar saw the ships, **about to sink**. / Caesar saw the ships **that were about to sink**.

- The future active participle can also be used, with *esse*, as the future active infinitive, almost always in indirect statement.

- The *esse* of that future active infinitive is often omitted.

- Immanesque columnas / rupibus excidunt, scaenis decora apta **futuris**. (*Aeneid* 1.428–29)

- They cut huge columns from rocks, decorations appropriate for **future** stages / stages **about to exist**.

- Aut haec in nostros fabricata est machina muros, / **inspectura** domos **ventura**que desuper urbi. (*Aeneid* 2.46–47)

- Or this machine was made against our walls, **about to inspect / for the purpose of inspecting** our homes and **about to come / for the purpose of coming** right up to our city.

   o   The future active participle here expresses purpose, as is not uncommon in poetic and later Latin.

- Nec **moritura** tenet crudeli funere Dido? (*Aeneid* 4.307–8)

- Nor does Dido **about to die** in her cruel funeral hold you?

Future Passive Participle [see Gerund and Gerundive below]

7.5.5   *GERUND AND GERUNDIVE—OVERVIEW

- The gerund and gerundive share their stem and some endings.

- The gerund and gerundive also share some uses but have uses unique to them as well.

- There are, however, fundamental differences between the two.

   o   The gerund is a verbal noun, has only four forms (because it is a neuter singular noun), and cannot agree with anything.

   o   The gerundive is a verbal adjective, has 30 endings (to cover all three genders, singular and plural), and must agree with something.

   o   The gerundive can also be viewed as and is sometimes called the future passive participle.

- The use of the term "gerundive" can be confusing.

   o   another name for the future passive participle when used to replace the gerund to express purpose with *ad*, *causā*, or *gratiā*

   o   Many students only hear the "gerund" part of the word and think that the gerund and gerundive are the same form.

   o   While they do share some of the same uses and the same basic form, the "ive" is the important part because it indicates that the gerundive is gerund-like, but not a gerund.

7.5.5.1 Gerund and Gerundive—Forms

- Both the gerund and the gerundive are formed using the present stem + the infix -*nd*-.

- The gerund uses only 2nd declension neuter endings from the genitive to the ablative:

   o   -*ī*: genitive

   o   -*ō*: dative and ablative

   o   -*um*: accusative after *ad*

- For the nominative subject and accusative direct object, the present infinitive is used; there is no *-um* gerund form in the nominative.

- The gerundive is an *-us, -a, -um* adjective.

duco, -ere	*gerund*	*gerundive*
nom	ducere	ducendus, -a, -um
gen	ducendī	ducendī, -ae, -ī
dat	ducendō	ducendō, -ae, -ō
acc	ducendum	ducendum, -am, -um
abl	ducendō	ducendō, -ā, -ō

7.5.5.2 Gerund and Gerundive—Uses

Case Uses

- In English, as in Latin, both the infinitive and the -ing form are used as gerunds, depending on the grammatical function.

  o English

  o subject, predicate nominative, direct object = infinitive or -ing

    ▪ **To winter** in Gaul is not fun. / **Wintering** in Gaul is not fun.

    ▪ Caesar's least favorite is **to winter** in Gaul. / Caesar's least favorite is **wintering** in Gaul.

    ▪ Caesar doesn't love **to winter** in Gaul. / Caesar doesn't love **wintering** in Gaul.

  o possessive, object of a preposition, and so on = -ing only

    ▪ His love **of fighting** brought him to Gaul. / ~~His love **of to fight** brought him to Gaul.~~

    ▪ He reaches Gaul **by marching**. / ~~He reaches Gaul **by to march**.~~

  o Latin

  o subject and direct object = infinitive

  o genitive, dative, accusative with preposition, ablative = *-nd-*

    ▪ for accusative with preposition, see *ad* and purpose below

- Qua ex parte homines **bellandi** cupidi magno dolore adficiebantur. (*Bellum Gallicum* 1.2)

- From which part men, desirous **of fighting**, were being approached with great grief.

  o *Bellandi* is a gerund in the genitive dependent on *cupidi*.

○   The two -*i* endings on *cupidi* and *bellandi* might cause confusion, that *cupidi* agrees with *homines* while *bellandi* is a genitive dependent on *cupidi*; as a gerund, a verbal noun, *bellandi* can't agree with anything.

- Mobilitate viget viresque adquirit **eundo**. (*Aeneid* 4.175)

- [Rumor] grows strong in its movement an acquires strength **by going**.

○   *Eundo* is a gerund in the ablative expressing means or how strength is acquired.

Passive Periphrastic

- The gerundive can also be used in the passive periphrastic: the participle plus a form of *sum, esse* indicates obligation or necessity and is translated with "must" or "have / has to."

- The gerundive used with a form of *sum, esse* in the passive periphrastic expresses necessity or obligation.

- **Ducendum** ad sedes simulacrum **oranda**que divae / numina conclamant. (*Aeneid* 2.232–33)

- They shout that the form (*simulacrum*; the horse) **must be led** (*ducendum [esse]*) to the temple and the power (*numina*) of the goddess **must be worshipped** (*oranda [esse]*).

○   *Ducendum* and *oranda* are gerundives used as a passive periphrastic with an understood *esse* in an indirect statement governed by *conclamant*.

- Incenditque animum famae venientis amore, / exim bella viro memorat quae deinde **gerenda**. (*Aeneid* 6.889–90)

- [After] [Anchises] fires [Aeneas'] soul with a love of his / their coming fame, he reminds him of the wars that **must be fought** in the future.

○   *Gerenda* is a future passive participle modifying *bella*.

- in quo si praesens periculum non, at certe longinqua obsidione fames **esset timenda** (*Bellum Gallicum* 5.29)

- in which, even if the present danger **must not be feared**, then certainly starvation, distant because of the siege, **must be feared**

Purpose with *ad, causā,* or *gratiā*

- *Ad* takes the gerund and gerundive in the accusative.

- *Causā* and *gratiā* take the gerund and gerundive in the genitive.

○   *Causā* and *gratiā* are ablatives of their respective nouns.

- Constituerunt ea quae **ad proficiscendum** pertinerent comparare. (*Bellum Gallicum* 1.3)

- They decided to prepare those things which are necessary **for departing**.

  o *Proficiscendum* is a gerund expressing purpose; as a (verbal) noun, it stands alone as the accusative object of *ad*.

- Atque ea quae **ad effeminandos animos** pertinent important. (*Bellum Gallicum* 1.1)

- And they import [the least] those things which exist **to make soft their spirits**.

  o *Effeminandos* is a gerundive that agrees with *animos* expressing purpose with *ad*.

  o As a gerundive, it is the same gender, number, and case as *animos*; it agrees with *animos*.

  o The gerundive is used instead of the gerund when there is a direct object.

  o Rather than using a gerund with a direct object, Latin uses a gerundive that agrees with what would be the direct object.

    ▪ not ~~ad effeminandum animos~~: gerund plus direct object

    ▪ rather *ad effeminandos animos*: gerundive agreeing with what would be the direct object

- Mittitur ad eos **colloquendi causa** G. Arpineius (*Bellum Gallicum* 5.27)

- Gaius Arpineuius is sent to them **for the purpose of conversing**.

  o *Colloquendi* is a gerund in the genitive dependent on *causā* expressing purpose.

- Frumentumque omne quod eo **tolerandae hiemis causa** devexerat relinquebat. (*Bellum Gallicum* 5.47)

- And he was leaving behind all of the grain that he had brought there **for the sake of surviving the winter**.

  o *Tolerandae* is a gerundive in the genitive agreeing with *hiemis*, both of which are dependent on *causa*.

- *Gratiā* with the gerund or gerundive, as far as I can tell, is not used in the Latin syllabus.

7.5.6   *THE SUPINE

- The supine is a verbal noun.

7.5.6.1 The Supine—Forms

- The supine uses the stem of the 4th principal part.

- The supine occurs only in the accusative and ablative singular.

- The supine uses fourth declension endings: *-um, -ū*.

7.5.6.2 The Supine—Uses

Ablative of Respect or Specification

- The supine in the ablative expresses respect or specification.

- It is often used with an adjective.

- It is often translated "[adjective] to [verb]."

- Tres Eurus ab alto / in brevia et Syrtes urget, *miserabile* **visu**. (*Aeneid* 1.110–11)

- Three times the Eurus and the Syrtis raised them from the deep onto the shoals, *miserable* **to behold**.

- *mirabile* **dictu** (*Aeneid* 1.439; 4.182)

- *wondrous* **to say**

  o *Visu* and *dictu* are supines in the ablative expressing respect or specification with *miserabile* and *mirabile*: in what area or with what respect is something "miserable" or "wondrous."

- *Perfacile* **factu** esse illis probat. (*Bellum Gallicum* 1.3)

- He agrees with them that it is *very easy* **to do**.

Purpose with Verbs of Motion

- The supine in the accusative after a verb of motion expresses purpose.

- Interpretem suum Cn. Pompeium ad eum *mittit* **rogatum** ut sibi militibusque parcat. (*Bellum Gallicum* 5.36)

- *He sends* his interpreter, Gnaius Pompeius, to him **to ask** him to spare himself and his soldiers.

  o *Rogatum* is the accusative supine after the verb of motion *mittit* expressing purpose: why he was sent.

Chapter 8

LITERARY STYLE

- The most recent AP® Latin Course and Exam Description (effective fall 2019) provides a non-exhaustive list of terms that "attempts to avoid both highly specialized and very basic terms, and focuses instead on those that are most important for precise translation, comprehension, and literary analysis in the AP® course." (129)

- These are the terms listed under the "Literary Style" heading. Make sure that you know the meanings of these terms and can recognize them in Latin texts.

✓ alliteration	✓ metonymy
✓ anaphora	✓ onomatopoeia
✓ apostrophe	✓ personification
✓ asyndeton	✓ polysyndeton
✓ chiasmus	✓ rhetorical question
✓ enjambment	✓ simile
✓ hyperbaton	✓ synchesis
✓ hyperbole	✓ synecdoche
✓ litotes	✓ tmesis
✓ metaphor	✓ transferred epithet

- This glossary includes not only the rhetorical figures listed above (which in the list below will be starred) but also those rhetorical figures commonly covered in upper-level Latin classes and included explicitly on previous AP® syllabi and tests.

- Latin examples are included from the Latin syllabus of Vergil and Caesar whenever possible, although Vergil, as a poet, tends to use these figures more commonly than Caesar.

- English examples are included to help you better hear the effect of a given rhetorical figure.

- Too often, such figures are learned in a way that focuses too much on the definition of the term and not enough on the rhetorical impact of the figure; English examples will help you hear that rhetorical impact in a more familiar linguistic context.

Resources online for rhetorical figures can provide further and more varied examples:

- American Rhetoric (http://www.americanrhetoric.com) is perhaps the most comprehensive site, including definitions as well as examples, plus a comprehensive library of full speeches from both politics/history and movies. As a non-Latin site it does not necessarily include every figure here.

- BYU's Silva Rhetoricae (http://rhetoric.byu.edu/) is a comprehensive site that includes definitions and examples. The list of figures is in a menu at the right of the page and includes many more than are included here but is a great resource for those looking for more in depth information.

- Literary Terms (http://literaryterms.net) includes an exhaustive list of terms, although a majority of the terms included is literary (e.g., protagonist) rather than rhetorical. The site includes a good variety of examples, from both literary and pop culture sources, for each term.

- A Running, Cited List of Rhetorical Figures (http://rhetoricalfigs.wordpress.com; full disclosure: this is the author's website) includes examples of rhetorical figures from pop culture and is updated as new examples are identified. Use the categories menu on the right of the site to focus on examples of specific figures.

allegory. A form of comparative representation that uses an extended narrative to stand for an abstract idea, a series of relationships, or another narrative, often without specifying explicitly the connection between the two.

Latin example. The relationship between Aeneas and Dido has been read as an allegory for the relationship between the Roman general Marc Antony and the Egyptian queen Cleopatra: both Aeneas and Marc Antony were ensnared by powerful Eastern queens who corrupted their Roman values (the anachronism of Aeneas having Roman values notwithstanding) and both were in danger of losing themselves to their emotions. Aeneas, of course, resisted this temptation (with some help from Mercury and Jupiter) while Marc Antony could not.

Vergil's description of *Fama* in *Aeneid* 4 is a different kind of allegory, a visual allegory, in which the physical description of something represents its character or personality. *Fama*, rumor, is described as originally small but grown to huge proportions, as rumors themselves begin small and snowball out of control as they are spread. She is nourished by speed and grows stronger in her spreading.

English example. George Orwell's *Animal Farm,* in which the Russian Revolution and the ensuing political wrangling is allegorized via an animal fable in which the animals overthrow their human overseer and then struggle among themselves to establish power.

*alliteration. The repetition of the same letter or sounds.

> *Latin example.*   Interea m̲agno m̲isceri m̲ur̲m̲ure pontum (*Aeneid* 1.124)

> C̲oncilio c̲onvoc̲ato c̲onsolatus c̲ohortatusque. (*Bellum Gallicum* 7.29)

> *English example.* "A b̲ridal b̲ower b̲ecomes a b̲urial b̲ier of b̲itter b̲ereavement." (*A Funny Thing Happened on the Way to the Forum*)

> *Discussion.* Alliteration can also be used in shorter phrases with fewer alliterative words for a more immediate effect. Malcolm X's perhaps most famous speech is entitled, after the most memorable phrase from the speech, "The B̲allot or the B̲ullet."

*anaphora. The unnecessary repetition of words for emphasis.

> *Latin example.*   V̲os̲ e̲t̲ Scyllaeam rabiem penitusque sonantes   200
> accestis scopulos, v̲os̲ e̲t̲ Cyclopia saxa
> experti: (*Aeneid* 1.200–202)

> Huius sunt plurima simulacra: h̲unc̲ omnium inventorem artium ferunt, h̲unc̲ viarum atque itinerum ducem, h̲unc̲ ad quaestus pecuniae mercaturasque habere vim maximam arbitrantur. (*Bellum Gallicum* 6.17)

> *English example.* "To raise a happy, healthy, and hopeful child, it t̲akes̲ a family; it t̲akes̲ teachers; it t̲akes̲ clergy; it t̲akes̲ business people; it t̲akes̲ community leaders; it t̲akes̲ those who protect our health and safety. It t̲akes̲ all of us." (Hillary Clinton, 1996 Democratic National Convention)

aposiopesis. The abrupt breaking off in midsentence for rhetorical effect.

> *Latin example.*   Iam caelum terramque meo sine numine, venti,
> miscere, et tantas audetis tollere moles?
> Q̲uos̲ e̲go̲— (*Aeneid* 1.135)

> *English example.* "And to attain the ultimate prize of global reach, business would exude multiculturalism—t̲he̲ U̲nited̲ C̲olors̲ o̲f̲ …" (Franklin Foer, *How Soccer Changed the World: An Unlikely Theory of Globalization*, p.38)

> *Discussion.* Benetton was a company most popular in the 1980s and known for the multicultural approach to its marketing which, at the time, was relatively innovative and which was marked by its slogan "The United Colors of Benetton." Thus the aposiopesis in the English example both anticipates completing the sentence with "Benetton" but also suggests that the goal of all companies was to emulate Benetton's multiculturalism.

*apostrophe. The direct address of someone or something not present.

Latin example.   "O terque quaterque beati,
quis ante ora patrum Troiae sub moenibus altis   95
contigit oppetere! O Danaum fortissime gentis
Tydide! (*Aeneid* 1.94–97)

English example. "It grieves me to say today we mourn the loss of Craig Sager [sports reporter & NBA sideline reporter], a colleague and friend of so many in this business, a reporter and man who was larger than life in so may ways. He was always there. Look: this is Craig on the field with Hank Aaron for his 715th homerun. And this is Craig as we last saw him at the ESPYs. Craig, the world was literally and figuratively more joyful with you in it. To your family, and to your family at Turner [Broadcasting], to everybody you touched in this business and out, our deepest condolences. Rest in peace." (Tony Reali on Craig Sager, *Around the Horn*, December 15, 2016)

Discussion. The first part of the quote highlights the rhetorical shift that the apostrophe creates; beginning in 3rd person and shifting to 2nd makes the shift more dramatic.

*asyndeton. The conspicuous lack of a conjunction.

Latin example.   eiectum litore, egentem
excepi et regni demens in parte locavi. (*Aeneid* 4.373–74)

Gallos ab Aquitanis Garumna flumen, a Belgis Matrona et Sequana dividit. (*Bellum Gallicum* 1.1)

English example. "But, in a larger sense, we cannot dedicate, we cannot consecrate, we cannot hallow this ground." (President Abraham Lincoln, Gettysburg Address)

*chiasmus. The arranging of words, phrases, or clauses in an A B B A format.

Latin example.   apparet domus intus et atria longa patescunt (*Aeneid* 2.483)

Caesar … tamen unum communis salutis auxilium in celeritate ponebat (*Bellum Gallicum* 5.48)

English example. "We don't stop playing because we grow old; we grow old because we stop playing" (George Bernard Shaw)

"And so, my fellow Americans, ask not what your country can do for you; ask what you can do for your country." (John F. Kennedy, Inaugural Address, January 20, 1961)

ecphrasis. The verbal or literary description of an image or visual, usually nature or a work of art.

Latin example.

Namque videbat, uti bellantes Pergama circum
hac fugerent Graii, premeret Troiana iuventus,
hac Phryges, instaret curru cristatus Achilles.
Nec procul hinc Rhesi niveis tentoria velis
adgnoscit lacrimans, primo quae prodita somno   470
Tydides multa vastabat caede cruentus,
ardentisque avertit equos in castra, prius quam
pabula gustassent Troiae Xanthumque bibissent.
(*Aeneid* 1.466–73)

English Example.

"Landscape with the Fall of Icarus"
by poet William Carlos Williams

"Ode on a Grecian Urn"
by poet John Keats

ellipsis. The omission of an easily understood syntactical element. (The bracketed words in the examples are not included in the original text; their omission is the ellipsis.)

Latin example.   Ille ubi <u>matrem</u>
adgnovit, tali fugientem [eam] <u>est</u> voce <u>secutus</u>: …
Talibus [eam] <u>incusat</u>, gressumque ad moenia tendit: (*Aeneid* 1.405–
6, 410)

Gallia est omnis dīvīsa in partēs trēs, quārum ūnam <u>incolunt</u> <u>Belgae</u>,
aliam <u>Aquītānī</u> [incolunt], tertiam quī ipsōrum linguā <u>Celtae</u> [incolunt],
nostrā Gallī appellantur. (*Bellum Gallicum* 1.1)

English example. And he to England shall [<u>go</u>] along with you. (Shakespeare, *Hamlet* 3.3.4)

*enjambment. When a sentence or clause no longer aligns with the poetic structure. Or, when a sentence or clause begins at the end of a poetic line or ends at the beginning of a poetic line. (End-stopping or end-stopped lines are the opposite of enjambment; i.e., when a clause aligns with the poetic structure.)

Latin example.   "O regina, novam cui condere Iuppiter urbem
iustitiaque dedit gentes frenare superbas,
Troes te miseri, ventis maria omnia vecti,
<u>oramus</u>: prohibe infandos a navibus ignis (*Aeneid* 1.522–25)

English example. I think that I shall never see
<u>A poem</u> as lovely as a tree. (Joyce Kilmer, "Trees")

Discussion. Enjambment, unlike many of the figures here, is unique to poetry because it depends on the poetic structure for its existence. Enjambment renders poetry more conversational (we don't pause at regular intervals when we speak) and is the reason why, when we read poetry, we don't pause at the end of lines, but rather at the end of syntactical units. In the English example above, the meaning becomes very different if the reader pauses at the end of the first line. In the Latin example, it is unclear what the verb is preparing until the first word of the fourth line, thereby creating suspense.

hendiadys. Two nouns joined by a conjunction that would otherwise be a noun-adjective pair or a noun-genitive pair.

> *Latin example.*   Hic vasto rex Aeolus antro
> luctantes ventos tempestatesque sonoras
> imperio premit ac <u>vinclis et carcere</u> frenat. (*Aeneid* 1.52–54)
>
> Hac oratione adducti inter se <u>fidem et ius iurandum</u> dant (*Bellum Gallicum* 1.3)

English example. Law and Order (= the order of law; TV show); Love and Transformation (= the transformation of love / that love brings, or a love of transformation; Ovid book title).

Discussion. A hendiadys lends equal emphasis to two concepts rather than, in the non-hendiadys version, one concept having a more prominent syntactical place. The effect can be simply one of emphasis or can introduce an element of ambiguity. The second English example above more likely means "the transformation that love brings," but, because the book is an Ovid book, the opposite reading becomes a more plausible reading than it might have otherwise been because of Ovid's interest in metamorphosis—that is, "the love of transformation."

*hyperbaton. A deliberate confusion of normal word order.

> *Latin example.*   <u>speluncam Dido dux et Troianus eandem</u> devenient.
> (*Aeneid* 4.124–25)
>
> Debere se suspicari <u>simulata Caesarem amicitia</u>,
> (*Bellum Gallicum* 1.44)

English example. "A prophecy that misread, could have been." (Yoda from the movie *Star Wars, Episode III: Revenge of the Sith*; even for Yoda, a particularly confused sentence)

*hyperbole. A deliberate and extreme exaggeration for emphasis or rhetorical effect.

Latin example.   Talia iactanti stridens Aquilone procella
velum adversa ferit, <u>fluctusque ad sidera tollit</u>. (*Aeneid* 1.102–3)

et demonstrant sibi <u>praeter agri solum</u> nihil esse reliqui. (*Bellum Gallicum* 1.11)

English example. "My guest tonight: an actor who has starred in over <u>500 million</u> films. His latest is *Snakes on a Plane.*" (Jon Stewart, introducing an interview with Samuel Jackson on *The Daily Show*)

hysteron proteron. The reversal of the natural order of events.

Latin example.   <u>Moriamur</u>, et in media arma <u>ruamus</u> (*Aeneid* 2.353)

atque inde fundis, sagittis, tormentis hostes <u>propelli ac submoveri</u> iussit (*Bellum Gallicum* 4.25)

English example. to put on one's shoes and socks

*litotes. An understatement achieved by emphasizing something's opposite.

Latin example.   Quisquis es, <u>haud</u>, credo, <u>invisus</u> caelestibus auras
vitalis carpis, Tyriam qui adveneris urbem. (*Aeneid* 1.387–88)

<u>Minime</u>que ad eos mercatores <u>saepe</u> commeant: (*Bellum Gallicum* 1.1)

English example. "So I think those are <u>not implausible</u> businesses." (from a November 20, 2017, *New York Times* article on for-profit schools); "Bill, what's your level of certainty?" "I am <u>not uncertain</u>." (*Billions*, season 4, episode 3)

*metaphor. A direct comparison between a narrative element and an element independent of the narrative for emphasis or clarification. The metaphor, unlike the simile, includes no introductory words (in English, "like" or "as"; in Latin, *ut, velut, veluti,* or *qualis*), which creates a more direct comparison.

Latin example.   volat ille per aera magnum
<u>remigio alarum</u> (*Aeneid* 1.300–301)

At Cytherea novas artes, nova pectore versat
consilia, ut faciem mutatus et ora Cupido
pro dulci Ascanio veniat, donisque furentem
<u>incendat</u> reginam, atque ossibus implicet <u>ignem</u>;
(*Aeneid* 1.657–60)

> non reiecti et relegati longe ab ceteris <u>aut ferro aut fame</u> intereant. (*Bellum Gallicum* 5.30)

English example. "Why, this country is a shining city on a hill." (Mario Cuomo, 1984 Democratic National Convention); "What emotions, John? I'm an emotionless, igneous news-rock." (Stephen Colbert, *The Colbert Report*, December 18, 2014)

*metonymy. Identifying something by way of association or suggestion

Latin example.   Vix e conspectu Siculae telluris in altum
vela dabant laeti, et spumas <u>salis</u> aere ruebant, (*Aeneid* 1.34–35)

English example. "City Hall" or "the White House" for the government: "You can't fight City Hall" or "The White House issued a statement today"; the Italian "*calcio*," meaning "kick" for soccer.

Discussion. Some overlap exists between metonymy and synecdoche. For example, referring to someone as a "suit" could be construed as a synecdoche because the suit is a part of its wearer, or as a metonymy because the suit suggests the profession of its wearer. Some have suggested not distinguishing between the two.

*onomatopoeia. When the sound of a word represents the meaning of the word.

Latin example.   Illi indignantes <u>magno</u> cum <u>murmure montis</u>
circum claustra fremunt; (*Aeneid* 1.55–56)

English example.   The <u>moan</u> of doves in immemorial elms
And <u>murmuring</u> of innumerable bees (Alfred Lord Tennyson, "The Princess")

Also, common words like "bang," "crash," "moo," and so on

*personification. Imbuing an inanimate object with human qualities.

Latin example.   Hic <u>fessas</u> non vincula <u>naves</u>
ulla tenent, unco non alligat ancora morsu. (*Aeneid* 1.168–69)

> Reversus ille eventus belli non ignorans unum, quod cohortes ex statione et praesidio essent emissae, questus ne minimo quidem casu locum relinqui debuisse, multum <u>fortunam</u> in repentino hostium adventu <u>potuisse iudicavit</u>, multo etiam amplius, quod paene ab ipso vallo portisque castrorum barbaros avertisset. (*Bellum Gallicum* 6.42)

English example. "Once again, the heart of America is heavy. The spirit of America weeps for a tragedy that denies the very meaning of our land." (Lyndon Baines Johnson on the death of Martin Luther King Jr., April 5, 1968)

pleonasm. The use of excessive or syntactically unnecessary words; repetition of the same idea with different words.

Latin example.   ingemit, et duplices tendens ad sidera palmas
talia voce refert: "O terque quaterque beati,
quis ante ora patrum Troiae sub moenibus altis
contigit oppetere! (*Aeneid* 1.93–96)

Ubi de eius adventu Helvetii certiores facti sunt, legatos ad eum mittunt nobilissimos civitatis, cuius legationis Nammeius et Veru-cloetius principem locum obtinebant, qui dicerent sibi esse in animo sine ullo maleficio iter per provinciam facere, propterea quod aliud iter haberent nullum: rogare ut eius voluntate id sibi facere liceat. (*Bellum Gallicum* 1.7)

English example. "No one anywhere in the world can doubt the enduring resolve and boundless capacity of the American people." (President Bill Clinton, State of the Union address, January 19, 1999)

polyptoton. The use of two or more forms of the same word or root.

Latin example.   Hectoris hic magni fuerat comes, Hectora circum
et lituo pugnas insignis obibat et hasta. (*Aeneid* 6.166–67)

stipendium capere iure belli, quod victores victis imponere consuerint. (*Bellum Gallicum* 1.44)

English example. There is no end of it, the voiceless wailing, / No end to the withering of withered flowers, / To the movement of pain that is painless and motionless, / To the drift of the sea and the drifting wreckage, / The bone's prayer to Death its God. Only the hardly, barely prayable / Prayer of the one Annunciation … (T. S. Eliot, "The Dry Salvages")

*polysyndeton. The use of more conjunctions than necessary.

Latin example.   Incubuere mari, totumque a sedibus imis
una Eurusque Notusque ruunt creberque procellis
Africus, et vastos volvunt ad litora fluctus. (*Aeneid* 1.84–86)

Persuadent Rauricis et Tulingis et Latobrigis finitimis suis, uti eodem usi consilio oppidis suis vicisque exustis una cum eis proficiscantur, Boiosque, qui trans Rhenum incoluerant et in agrum Noricum transierant Noreiamque oppugnarant, receptos ad se socios sibi adsciscunt. (*Bellum Gallicum* 1.5)

English example. "It's more than a game. And regardless of what level it is played upon, it still demands those attributes of courage <u>and</u> stamina <u>and</u> coordinated efficiency <u>and</u> goes even beyond that." (Vince Lombardi, former Green Bay Packers coach)

Discussion. Polysyndeton often conveys a sense of enthusiasm or energy, sometimes with an element of youthfulness or naïvete. The extra conjunctions give the impression that the speaker is thinking too quickly to be able to foresee when the series will end.

praeteritio. Saying something by saying that it will not be said.

> *Latin example.*   Quid Thesea magnum
> quid memorem Alciden? (*Aeneid* 6.122–23)
>
> "Nihil," inquit, "de eorum sententia dicturus sum, qui turpissimam servitutem deditionis nomine appellant, neque hos habendos civium loco neque ad concilium adhibendos censeo." (*Bellum Gallicum* 7.77)

English example. "I'm not going to tell you what they spent on that wedding, but $40,000 is a lot of money." (Elliot Gould as Monica's father from the TV show *Friends*); "There's a tradition in tournament play to not talk about the next step until you've climbed the one in front of you. I'm sure going to the State finals is beyond your wildest dreams, so let's just keep it right there." (Coach Norman Dale, played by Gene Hackman, in the movie *Hoosiers*)

prolepsis. The introduction of a syntactical unit before it is appropriate—that is, a word, phrase, or clause that cannot mean anything until some additional element is read after it, or the suggestion of an event that has not yet happened. (The Vergil example illustrates the latter, the Caesar the former.)

> *Latin example.*   incute vim ventis <u>submersasque</u> <u>obrue puppes</u>,
> aut age diversos et disice corpora ponto. (*Aeneid* 1.69–70)
>
> aut rem frumentariam, ut satis commode supportari posset, timere dicebant. (*Bellum Gallicum* 1.39)

English example. "<u>Whatever I give her</u>, she's going to be bringing in experts from all over the country to interpret the meaning behind <u>it</u>." (Jerry Seinfeld from *Seinfeld*, "The Deal," May 2, 1991)

prosopopoeia. When the words or actions of someone absent are introduced by the narrator.

> Latin example.   tu quoque magnam
> partem opere in tanto, sineret dolor, Icare, haberes. (*Aeneid* 6.30–31)

English example. "My momma always said, 'Life was like a box of chocolates. You never know what you're gonna get.'" (Forrest Gump from the movie *Forrest Gump*)

Discussion. Prosopopoeia can, and often will, overlap with allusion. Note that the English example, because it does not involve anyone famous, is a prosopopoeia without an allusion.

*rhetorical question. A question that expects no answer and is asked for rhetorical effect only.

> *Latin example.*   ipse deum tibi me claro demittit Olympo
> regnator, caelum et terras qui numine torquet,
> ipse haec ferre iubet celeres mandata per auras:
> quid struis? aut qua spe Libycis teris otia terris? (*Aeneid* 4.268–71)
>
> Quod si veteris contumeliae oblivisci vellet, num etiam recentium iniuriarum, quod eo invito iter per provinciam per vim temptassent, quod Aeduos, quod Ambarros, quod Allobrogas vexassent, memoriam deponere posse? (*Bellum Gallicum* 1.14)

English example. If you prick us, do we not bleed? / If you tickle us, do we not laugh? / If you poison us, do we not die? / And if you wrong us, shall we not revenge? (Shakespeare, *Merchant of Venice* 3.1)

Discussion. The rhetorical question asks a question that only has one answer. By introducing that answer in the form of a question, the rhetorical question forces the audience itself to in effect make the point of the speaker.

*simile. An indirect comparison between a narrative element and an element independent of the narrative for emphasis or clarification. Latin similes will be often introduced by *ut, velut, veluti,* or *qualis,* while English similes will be introduced by "like" or "as." These introductory words create distance between the comparison and the element compared, while a metaphor, without these introductory words, creates a more direct comparison between the two.

> *Latin example.*   ac venti, velut agmine facto,
> qua data porta, ruunt et terras turbine perflant. (*Aeneid* 1.82–83)
>
> Qualis apes aestate nova per florea rura
> exercet sub sole labor, cum gentis adultos
> educunt fetus, aut cum liquentia mella
> stipant et dulci distendunt nectare cellas,
> aut onera accipiunt venientum, aut agmine facto
> ignavum fucos pecus a praesepibus arcent:
> fervet opus, redolentque thymo fragrantia mella.
> (*Aeneid* 1.430–36)

English example. "Let us go then, you and I, / While the evening is spread out against the sky, / Like a patient etherized upon a table" (T. S. Eliot, "The Love Song of J. Alfred Prufrock"); "He sat as still as a mouse, in the futile hope that whoever it was might go away after a single attempt. But no, the knocking was repeated. The worst thing of all would be to delay. His heart was thumping <u>like a drum</u>, but his face, from long habit, was probably expressionless." (George Orwell, *1984*)

*synchesis (interlocked word order). The arrangement of words, phrases, or clauses in an A B A B pattern.

Latin example.   cui pharetra ex auro, crines nodantur in aurum,
<u>aurea</u> <u>purpuream</u> subnectit <u>fibula</u> <u>vestem</u>. (*Aeneid* 4.138–39)

hos item ex <u>proximis</u> <u>primi</u> <u>navibus</u> <u>cum conspexissent</u> (*Bellum Gallicum* 4.25)

English example. "We have seen a <u>steady</u> <u>erosion</u> of American power, and an <u>unsteady</u> <u>exercise</u> of American influence." (George W. Bush, 2000 Republican Convention Acceptance Speech); "[The] Y2k computer bug will be remembered as the <u>last head-ache</u> <u>of the 20th century</u>, not the <u>first crisis</u> <u>of the 21st</u>." (Bill Clinton, State of the Union address, January 19, 1999)

*synecdoche. The use of a whole to represent the part or a part to represent the whole.

Latin example.   hic vero ingentem pugnam, ceu cetera nusquam
bella forent, nulli tota morerentur in urbe,
sic Martem indomitum Danaosque ad <u>tecta</u> ruentis
cernimus obsessumque acta testudine limen. (*Aeneid* 2.438–41)

Gallis magno ad pugnam erat impedimento quod pluribus eorum scutis uno ictu pilorum transfixis et conligatis, cum <u>ferrum</u> se inflexisset, neque evellere neque sinistra impedita satis commode pugnare poterant, 4 multi ut diu iactato bracchio praeoptarent scutum manu emittere et nudo corpore pugnare. (*Bellum Gallicum* 1.25)

English example. "Nice wheels"; "Nice threads"; "Hand me the phone" (the whole phone standing for the receiver which is really what will be handed); "To watch the tube" (i.e., the cathode ray tube that generates the picture of a TV); and so on

Discussion. See the discussion on "metonymy" above.

*tmesis. The cutting or splitting of a word for the insertion of another word.

Latin example.   at Venus obscuro gradientes aere saepsit,
et multo nebulae <u>circum</u> dea <u>fudit</u> amictu, (*Aeneid* 1.411–12)

His rebus pace confirmata, <u>post</u> diem quartum <u>quam</u> est in Britanniam ventum naves XVIII, de quibus supra demonstratum est, quae equites sustulerant, ex superiore portu leni vento solverunt. (*Bellum Gallicum* 4.28)

Ita proelium restitutum est, atque omnes hostes terga verterunt nec <u>prius</u> fugere destiterunt <u>quam</u> ad flumen Rhenum milia passuum ex eo loco circiter L pervenerunt. (*Bellum Gallicum* 1.53)

English example. "This is not Romeo, he's <u>some other where</u>." (Shakespeare, *Romeo and Juliet* 1.1); "Oh so lovely sitting <u>abso-blooming-lutely</u> still" (from *My Fair Lady*)

Discussion. The 4.28 example is not strictly speaking a tmesis but a worthwhile example of ambiguity. It is on the one hand a splitting of postquam *into two parts as a tmesis would, but, conventionally, the grammar of the tmesis would remain unchanged, as if the split word were not split. In this example, however, the* post *of* postquam *becomes the preposition that takes* diem quartum *as its object and the* quam *is left floating.*

*transferred epithet. An adjective that agrees with a noun that it does not describe, or an adjective that describes a noun with which it does not agree.

Latin example.   Arma virumque cano, Troiae qui primus ab oris
Italiam, fato profugus, Laviniaque venit
litora, multum ille et terris iactatus et alto
vi superum saevae <u>memorem</u> Iunonis ob <u>iram</u>;
(*Aeneid* 1.1–4)

magnum reginae sed enim miseratus amorem
Daedalus ipse dolos tecti ambagesque resolvit,
<u>caeca</u> regens filo <u>vestigia</u>. (*Aeneid* 6.28–30)

Legiones, ubi primum planitiem attigerunt, <u>infestis</u> contra hostes <u>signis</u> constiterunt. (*Bellum Gallicum* 7.51)

English example. Celebrity chef Jamie Oliver is known as the Naked Chef, also the title of his first and most prominent TV show. He, however, is hardly naked; rather, his food is naked, or unadorned.

tricolon crescens. A group of three or more elements (usually nouns or clauses), the last of which is more complex than the previous.

> *Latin example.*   nec te noster amor nec te data dextera quondam
> nec moritura tenet crudeli funere Dido? (*Aeneid* 4.307–8)

> *English example.* "But if we keep our religion at home, keep our religion in the closet, keep our religion between ourselves and our God" (Malcolm X, The Ballot or the Bullet Speech); "Single moms struggling to feed the kids and pay the rent. Immigrants starting a hard life in a new world. Children without fathers in neighborhoods where gangs seem like friendship, where drugs promise peace, and where sex sadly seems the closest thing to belonging." (George W. Bush, 2000 Republican National Convention; one tricolon crescens within another)

zeugma. The use of a word (usually a verb) in a both a literal and figurative sense. Or the use of a word (usually a verb) in two senses, only one of which reflects common usage.

> *Latin example.*   "Aeole, namque tibi divum pater atque hominum rex
> et mulcere dedit fluctus et tollere vento,
> gens inimica mihi Tyrrhenum navigat aequor,
> Ilium in Italiam portans victosque penates: (*Aeneid* 1.65–68)
>
> sed nulla ferramentorum copia quae esset ad hunc usum idonea,
> gladiis caespites circumcidere, manibus sagulisque terram exhaurire
> cogebantur. (*Bellum Gallicum* 5.42)

> *English example.* "Dangers, Frustrations and Snow Keep Piling Up in New England" (February 15, 2015, headline from the *New York Times*); "I will work to reduce nuclear weapons and nuclear tension in the world." (from President George W. Bush's 2000 Republican Convention nomination acceptance speech); "I need to work out these feelings, and my deltoids." (Jack from the TV show *Will and Grace*)

Chapter 9

SCANSION

- The following summary is intended to provide a reference for the information necessary to scan successfully the dactylic hexameter of Vergil's *Aeneid*.

- A general overview of scansion and its process is included at the outset as a quick review.

- More detailed information on specific topics is included later in the chapter.

- All examples are from the *Aeneid* unless otherwise specified.

- The scansion of elegiac couplets can appear in the multiple choice section.

- The general information for scansion applies to both dactylic hexameter and elegiac couplets.

- A review of elegiac couplet–specific information is included at the end of the chapter.

9.1 TERMINOLOGY

Words that are starred in a definition are also defined in the list.

- **dactyl**. A poetic *foot composed of one long *syllable followed by two short *syllables.

- **dactylic hexameter**. The *meter of epic poetry, composed of six feet of *dactyls or *spondees (see also *substitution).

- **dieresis**. A double dot, resembling only in appearance the more common umlaut (ü), that indicates that a vowel combination that would normally function as a *diphthong is in fact functioning as two separate *syllables.

- **diphthong**. Two or more vowels that are pronounced as one sound and so create only one *syllable.

- **elision**. When two words, most commonly when the first ends in a vowel and the second begins with a vowel, are blended together in pronunciation. (The specific rules for elision are explained in greater detail below.) Each elision results in one fewer *syllable in a line.

- **foot**. The building block of a *meter. A metric line will be composed of a fixed number of feet; for example, *dactylic hexameter has six feet.

- **hiatus**. When an *elision should occur, but does not occur. Hiatus often occurs with single letter vowel words (*o!*) or at a clause break, but there is no rule or set pattern for anticipating hiatus.

- **macron**. The mark used to label a long *syllable: a straight line over the vowel (ā).

- **meter**. A specific rhythmic pattern for poetic lines.

- **quantity**. The length of a *syllable, either long or short, measured by how long it takes to speak the syllable: compare English "the" (short) and "catch" (long).

- **spondee**. A poetic *foot composed of two long *syllables.

- **substitution**. The phenomenon by which the second long *syllable of a *spondee can replace the two short *syllables of a *dactyl. Thus, the first four *feet in a line of *dactylic hexameter can be either four *dactyls or, by substitution, four *spondees, or any combination thereof.

- **syllable**. A group of letters that form a sound; each syllable must have a vowel.

- **synizesis**. When two otherwise separate vowel sounds are blended into one vowel sound. Compare the English word "oil" which can be distinctly two syllables or, especially with a regional accent, can be blended into one syllable.

9.2   DACTYLIC HEXAMETER

- A line of dactylic hexameter consists of six feet of dactyls (long-short-short) or spondees (long-long).

- The last two feet of a line of dactylic hexameter will almost always be dactyl-spondee or the syllable pattern long-short-short-long-long.

  o Only eight lines in the first six books of the *Aeneid* have the fifth foot as a spondee rather than a dactyl, none of which appear in the Latin syllabus.

9.3   THE PROCESS FOR SCANNING A LINE OF DACTYLIC HEXAMETER

Hi summo in fluctu pendent; his unda dehiscens (1.106)

1. Identify elisions.

   a. summo in = summin

   b. It is essential to scan for elisions first because it will change the number of syllables in the line.

      i.   Each elision creates one fewer syllable in the line.

         1. Without the elision, the line has 14 syllables.

         2. With the elision, the total number is reduced to 13 syllables.

2. Mark the final five syllables / two feet with dactyl-spondee: long-short-short-long-long.

   unda dehiscens = | ūndă dě | hīscēns

3. Mark the known long syllables in the line:

   Hī sūmmīn flūctu pēndēnt; his | ūnda de | hīscēns

   a. the first syllable

   b. vowels followed by double consonants

      i. If a word ends in a vowel and is followed by a word that begins with two consonants, check for a stop-liquid combination (explained below), which could render the vowel short.

   c. diphthongs

4. If you can, mark any definitive feet at either end of a line.

   Hī sūm | mīn flūc | tu pēndēnt; his | ūnda de | hīscēns

   a. You cannot mark feet that are not anchored: *pendent* is two long syllables, which in theory make a spondee, but, because there are no definitive, or anchored, feet around it, you can't know whether it is a spondee or whether each of its long syllables belong to another foot.

   b. *Hī sūmm-* is a spondee because it occurs at the beginning of the line and so is anchored.

   c. *Mīn flūc* is now anchored because *hī sūm* is anchored; it is a spondee.

5. Mark the necessarily long syllables: those syllables that metrical context forces to be long.

   Hī sūm | mīn flūc | tū pēn | dēnt; hīs | ūnda de | hīscēns

   a. Because there cannot be a single short syllable in dactylic hexameter, any single syllable between two long syllables must be long.

      i. The "i" in *his* is long because it is preceded and followed by a long syllable.

   j. The first syllable of any foot will always be long because both dactyls and spondees begin with a long syllable.

      i. The "u" in *tu* is long because it is the first syllable of a new foot; both dactyls and spondees begin with a long syllable and so, as with the first syllable of a line, any first syllable of a foot will be long.

6. Any unmarked (i.e., not-long) syllables will at this point most likely be short.

   a. See below for naturally long syllables that can violate this rule.

9.4 OVERVIEWS

9.4.1 ELISION

- When one word ends with a vowel and the following word begins with a vowel, the last syllable of the first word will drop out.

  o suscepitque ignem foliis, atque arida circum (1.175)

  o suscepitqu(e) ignem foliis, atqu(e) arida circum

  o suscepitquignem foliis, atquarida circum

- There are four instances when elision occurs, listed in order of most to least common:

first word ends in …	second word begins with …
vowel	vowel
-m	vowel
vowel	h-
-m	h-

- Elision is essential to scansion because it affects the total number of syllables in a line and so the metrical pattern of the line.

- *Aeneid* 1.175 would be 16 syllables without the elisions but 14 syllables with the elisions.

9.4.2 LONG BY POSITION

- A vowel followed by two or more consonants is long by position.

  - vela **dabant** laeti et spumas salis aere ruebant (1.35)

    - The second "a" in *dabant* is long because of the -*nt* following it.

  o These two or more consonants can stretch across word breaks; that is, the final syllable of a word that ends in a single consonant and is followed by a word that begins with a single (or double) consonant will be long.

    - turbine corripuit scopuloque infixit acuto (1.45)

      - The second "i" in *corripuit* is long because of the -*t s*- double consonant following it.

  o Similarly, the final syllable of a word that ends in a vowel and is followed by a word that begins with two consonants can be long but doesn't have to be.

  o The example below is a lengthened short syllable; for syllables that stay short even before the following word beginning with a double consonant, see the stop-liquid combination rule below.

    - *notitiam* **primosque gradus** *vicinia fecit* (Ovid, *Metamorphoses* 4.59): the "e" in *primosque* is naturally short but made long by the "gr" in *gradus*. [As far as I could find, there was no example in the entirety of the Vergil Latin syllabus of a naturally short syllable lengthened by the following word beginning with two consonants, but non-syllabus lines could appear in the multiple choice section.]

9.4.3   LONG BY NATURE: DIPHTHONGS

- Latin has six diphthongs:

    o   ae

    o   au

    o   ei

    o   eu

    o   oe

    o   ui

- Diphthongs do not exist when straddling the stem and ending of a form.

    o   Saltem si qua mihi de te suscepta **fuisset** (4.327)

        ▪   The "ui" in *fuisset* is not a diphthong because the "u" is part of the stem and the "i" is part of the ending; *fuisset* is a three syllable word without the diphthong, rather than a two-syllable word.

- The letter "u" in "qu" and "gu" does not form a diphthong when followed by another vowel. It is considered part of the preceding "q" or "g" instead (much the same way that in English the "q" cannot function without a corresponding "u").

    o   The "i" in the Latin verb *quiesco* is short because the "u" is part of the "q" rather than part of a "ui" diphthong.

9.4.4   LONG BY NATURE: COMMON NATURALLY LONG SYLLABLES

- all declensions, except 3rd, ablative singular

    o   -ā, -ō, -ū, -ē

- all declensions nominative plural except neuter forms

    o   -ae, -ī, -ēs, -ūs, -ēs

- all declensions accusative plural except neuter forms

    o   -ās, -ōs, -ēs, -ūs, -ēs

- 1st, 2nd, and 5th declensions, dative and ablative plural

    o   -īs, -ēbus

- 1st, 2nd, and 5th declensions, genitive plural

    o   -ārum, -ōrum, -ērum

- all conjugations, 1st person singular present active

- all conjugations, 1st person singular perfect active

- 1st, 2nd, 4th conjugations, present active infinitive characteristic vowel

9.4.5   AMBIGUITY: STOP-LIQUID COMBINATION

- When a vowel is followed by the combination of a stop and a liquid consonant, that vowel can be either long or short, depending on the poet's metrical needs.

- the stop-consonants: b, c, d, g, k, p, t

- the liquid-consonants: l, r

9.4.6   AMBIGUITY: *SYLLABA ANCEPS*

- The last syllable of a line is considered long, whether it is naturally long or short, because of the natural lengthening that will occur on that last syllable.

- The proper symbol for a *syllaba anceps* is a short symbol over a macron, indicating its potentially dual nature.

- The AP® Exam allows the *syllaba anceps* to be scanned long in all instances.

9.5   MORE DETAILS

9.5.1   ELISION

- When the second word in an elision is *es* or *est* (forms of *sum, esse*), the "e" of *es* or *est* drops out instead of the terminal vowel of the first word. This anomaly only affects the pronunciation of the line; it does not affect the scansion of the line.

    o   ut primum lux alma data est, exire locosque (1.306)

    o   ut primum lux alma data (e)st, exire locosque

    o   ut primum lux alma datast, exire locosque

- When the first word ends in -m and the following word begins with a vowel, elision occurs:

    o   lītora, multum ille et terrīs iactātus et alto (1.3)

    o   lītora, mult(um) ill(e) et terrīs iactātus et alto

    o   lītora, multillet terrīs iactātus et alto

- It is not technically the -*m* that elides but rather the vowel that precedes the -*m*; in the example above, the -*um* elides.

    o   The -*[vowel]m* elides because, in the earliest Latin, the terminal -*m* was originally not a letter but rather a variant in pronunciation.

o It was only as Latin evolved that that variant in pronunciation came to be represented by the letter -*m*.

o But, for scansion purposes, that -m remains essentially invisible and so -*[vowel]m* elides.

• When the first word ends in a vowel and the following word begins with an *h*-, elision occurs:

o Perge modo atqu<u>e hi</u>nc te reginae ad limina perfer. (1.389)

o Perge modo atqu(<u>e h)</u>inc te reginae ad limina perfer.

o Perge modo <u>atquinc</u> te reginae ad limina perfer.

• Note that it is not technically the h- that elides but rather the vowel that follows the h-; in the example above, the *hi*- elides.

o The h[vowel]- elides because, in ancient Greek, the letter "h" was not a letter but rather a punctuation mark that indicated whether to breathe or not when pronouncing an initial vowel. (Consider the English letter "i": "i" without breathing is the pronoun "I"; "i" with breathing is the greeting "Hi.")

o Latin, of course, does not use this punctuation mark and does use the letter "h" but, because dactylic hexameter has its origins in Homer and ancient Greek, Latin adopts this Graecism for scansion purposes.

• Least common, when the first word ends in an -*m* and the following word begins with an *h*-, elision occurs:

o non potuisse, tuaqu<u>e anim**am ha**</u>nc effundere dextra, (1.98)

o non potuisse, tuaqu(<u>e) </u>anim(<u>am h)</u>anc effundere dextra,

o non potuisse, <u>tuaquanimanc</u> effundere dextra,

• On occasion an elision will not occur when it should occur. This is called *hiatus*.

o Tun<u>e ille </u>Aeneas, quem Dardani<u>o </u>Anchisae (1.617)

o Tun(<u>e) </u>ill(<u>e) </u>Aeneas, quem Dardani<u>o </u>Anchisae

o <u>TunillAeneas</u>, quem Dardani<u>o </u>Anchisae

• In the example above, the scansion cannot work if Dardanio Anchisae elides.

• (And, even without the elision, the last two feet are spondees, which is a rare metrical occurrence in Vergil.)

9.5.2   LONG BY POSITION

• The letter "i" can function as a vowel or consonant.

o Vocalic "i" will most often be followed immediately by a consonant.

▪ Tenet **ille immania** saxa (1.139)

• The "i" in both *immania* and *ille* are vowels.

- Consonantal "i" will most often be followed immediately by a vowel.

  - Anthea si quem / **iactatum** vento videat (1.181–82)

    - The "i" in *iactatum* is a consonant.

    - It is followed by "a" and is pronounced "y."

- Consonantal "i" will most often occur at the beginning of words or after the prefix in a compound word.

  - me puer Ascanius capitisque **iniuria** cari (4.354)

    - The second "i" in *iniuria* is a consonant (the first is a vowel); the word is a compound of *in* and *ius, iuris.*

- Distinguishing between consonantal and vocalic "i" is important because it will:

  - affect the number of syllables in a line; that is, if you misinterpret a consonant as a vowel, you will add an extra syllable when scanning;

    - canities **inculta iacet**, stant lumina flamma (6.300)

      ◊ The "i" in *inculta* is a vowel, while the "i" in *iacet* is a consonant; the line has 15 syllables.

      ◊ Misinterpreting "i" can result in a two-syllable discrepancy in this particular line.

  - affect double consonants on preceding syllables; that is, if you misinterpret a consonant as a vowel, you might leave a vowel short when a double consonant would have lengthened it;

    - Inde alias animas, quae per **iuga** longa sedebant (6.411)

      ◊ The "i" in *iuga* is a consonant which, in combination with the "r" in *per* lengthens the "e" in *per.*

      ◊ If that "i" is interpreted as a vowel, the "e" in *per* mistakenly remains short.

  - create (or not) elisions, which also affect the number of syllables in a line; that is, if you misinterpret a consonant as a vowel, you might identify an elision where there isn't one.

    - quotiens astra **ignea** surgunt (4.352)

      ◊ The "i" in *ignea* is a vowel and so will elide with *astra: astr-ignea* = 4 (rather than 5) syllables.

    - Nunc etiam interpres divum **Iove** missus ab ipso (4.356)

      ◊ The "I" in *Iove* is a consonant and so will not elide with *divum: divum Iove* = 4 (rather than 3) syllables.

- Certain consonants function contrary to expectation.

  o The letter "h" is not considered a consonant for the purpose of long by position.

    ▪ A syllable that ends a word with a single consonant followed by a word that begins with "h" is not long by position. ("h" will also affect elisions; see above.)

      • **Funeris heu** tibi causa fui? Per sidera iuro (6.458)

        ◊ The "i" in *funeris* is short; if the "h" is read as a consonant, the combination of "s" and "h" would lengthen the "i."

  o The letter "m," although it does not count as a consonant for the purpose of elision (see above), does count as a consonant when it ends a word that is followed by a word that begins with a consonant.

    ▪ Ac **primum** silici **scintillam** excudit Achates (1.174)

      • The "u" in *primum* is long because of the double consonant *-m s-*.

      • The "am" in *scintillam* elides with *excudit* because the "m" doesn't count as a consonant.

  o The letters "x" and "z" are considered double consonants and will render vowels preceding them long.

    ▪ Tres Notus abreptas in **saxa** latentia torquet (1.108)

      • The first "a" in *saxa* is long because the "x" counts as a double consonant.

    ▪ arma virum tabulaeque et Troia **gaza** per undas (1.119)

      • The first "a" in *gaza* is long because the "z" counts as a double consonant.

  o The letter "k" is considered a double consonant and will render vowels preceding it long.

  o The letters "ph" and "th" are considered single consonants and will not render vowels preceding them long.

    ▪ hinc atque hinc glomerantur Oreades; illa **pharetram** (1.500)

      • The "a" in *illa* remains short even though it is followed by the two consonants "ph."

    ▪ orgia nocturnusque vocat clamore **Cithaeron**. (4.303)

      • The "i" in *Cithaeron* is short even though it is followed by the two consonants "th."

9.6   OVERVIEW OF ELEGIAC COUPLET

- The meter of elegiac couplet can appear in the multiple choice section.

- The majority of principles, terms, and approaches that you would use to scan dactylic hexameter can be applied to scanning elegiac couplet as well.

- An elegiac couplet consists of two lines (couplet), the first of which is a traditional line of dactylic hexameter and the second of which is a line of dactylic pentameter.

- The dactylic pentameter consists of five feet with one of the feet split in half, resulting in two repetitions of two and a half feet of dactylic hexameter.

    o   The first two feet will scan like dactylic hexameter—that is, either dactyls or spondees.

    o   The second two full feet will generally be dactyls only.

    o   The half feet will always be long.

        ▪   Arma gravi numero violentaque bella parabam
            edere, materia conveniente modis. (Ovid, *Amores* 1.1–2)

        - Line 1 scans like dactylic hexameter:

        - Arma gravi numero violentaque bella parabam
            - ˇ ˇ| - ˇ ˇ| - ˇˇ| - ˇ ˇ | - ˇ ˇ| - -

        - Line 2 is the pentameter (the half feet are bolded)

        - edere, materia conveniente mo**dis**
            - ˇ ˇ| - ˇ ˇ|-| - ˇ ˇ|- ˇ ˇ| -

IMAGE CREDITS

All images, maps, and photographs, unless otherwise stated, are scanned and edited by the author from public domain sources owned by the author.

CHARACTER GLOSSARIES

The topography of Caesar's Gaul, map; and the peoples and cities of Caesar's Gaul, map. Scanned from D'Ooge, Benjamin L. *Elements of Latin*. Boston: Ginn, 1921, p.49.

A map of the people and places of the *Aeneid*. Scanned from Comstock, David Y. *Virgil's "Aeneid" Books I–VI, VII, IX and Selections from the Other Books*. Boston: Allyn and Bacon, 1897, p.52.

The Hellespont and surrounding territory, map. Scanned from Botsford, George Willis. *A History of the Ancient World*. New York: Macmillan, 1917, p.236.

Ancient Rome and vicinity, map. Scanned from Botsford, George Willis. *A History of the Ancient World*. New York: Macmillan, 1917, p.352.

Ceres, the goddess of grain and the harvest. Scanned from Seyffert, Oskar. *A Dictionary of Classical Antiquities, Mythology, Religion, Literature and Art*. London: Swan Sonnenschein, 1899, p.178.

Diana, the virginal goddess of the hunt. Scanned from Seyffert, Oskar. *A Dictionary of Classical Antiquities, Mythology, Religion, Literature and Art*. London: Swan Sonnenschein, 1899, p.72.

The Trojan Ganymede and Jupiter's eagle. Scanned from Peck, Harry Thurston, ed. *Harper's Dictionary of Classical Literature and Antiquities*. New York: Harper, 1897, p.713.

The head of Medusa. Scanned from Seyffert, Oskar. *A Dictionary of Classical Antiquities, Mythology, Religion, Literature and Art*. London: Swan Sonnenschein, 1899, p.259.

Juno, queen of the gods and enemy of Aeneas. Scanned from Comstock, David Y. *Virgil's "Aeneid" Books I–VI, VII, IX and Selections from the Other Books*. Boston: Allyn and Bacon, 1897, p.55.

Jupiter, the king of the gods. Scanned from Peck, Harry Thurston, ed. *Harper's Dictionary of Classical Literature and Antiquities*. New York: Harper, 1897, p.388.

The death of Laocoon and his sons. Scanned from Peck, Harry Thurston, ed. *Harper's Dictionary of Classical Literature and Antiquities*. New York: Harper, 1897, p.920.

Calliope, the muse of epic poetry. Scanned from Comstock, David Y. *Virgil's "Aeneid" Books I–VI, VII, IX and Selections from the Other Books*. Boston: Allyn and Bacon, 1897, title page.

Neptune, god of the sea. Scanned from Seyffert, Oskar. *A Dictionary of Classical Antiquities, Mythology, Religion, Literature and Art*. London: Swan Sonnenschein, 1899, p.507.

The three fates: Clotho, Atropos, and Lachesis. Scanned from Seyffert, Oskar. *A Dictionary of Classical Antiquities, Mythology, Religion, Literature and Art*. London: Swan Sonnenschein, 1899, p.397.

A Thyias, or Maenad, a worshipper of Bacchus. Scanned from Seyffert, Oskar. *Classical Antiquities, Mythology, Religion, Literature and Art*. London: Swan Sonnenschein, 1899, p.193.

SUMMARIES

1.1–7: Introduction to Gaul and the migration of the Helvetii, map. Scanned from D'Ooge, Benjamin L. *Elements of Latin*. Boston: Ginn, 1921, p.49.

Modern Swiss coin. Photo credit: Phoebe Field; edited by Ed DeHoratius.

A Roman legionary. Scanned from Botsford, George Willis. *A History of the Ancient World*. New York: Macmillan, 1917, p.500.

Pontem in flumine faciunt. Scanned from Pearson, Henry Carr. *Essentials of Latin for Beginners*. New York: American Book, 1905, p.178.

Romani cum Germanis pugnant. Scanned from Pearson, Henry Carr. *Essentials of Latin for Beginners*. New York: American Book, 1905, p.97.

Caesar's reconnaissance of Britain, 55 BC, map. Scanned from D'Ooge, Benjamin L. *Elements of Latin*. Boston: Ginn, 1921, p.49.

Roman legionaries on the march. Scanned from Seyffert, Oskar. *A Dictionary of Classical Antiquities, Mythology, Religion, Literature and Art*. London: Swan Sonnenschein, 1899, p.348.

The wintering of Caesar's legions, 54 BC, map. Scanned from D'Ooge, Benjamin L. *Elements of Latin*. Boston: Ginn, 1921, p.49.

The siege of the camp of Sabinus and Cotta, 54 BC, map. Scanned from D'Ooge, Benjamin L. *Elements of Latin*. Boston: Ginn, 1921, p.49.

From the tomb of Pintaius, a standard-bearer. Scanned from Seyffert, Oskar. *A Dictionary of Classical Antiquities, Mythology, Religion, Literature and Art*. London: Swan Sonnenschein, 1899, p.586.

The siege of the camp of Cicero, 54 BC, map. Scanned from D'Ooge, Benjamin L. *Elements of Latin*. Boston: Ginn, 1921, p.49.

A dying Gaul. Scanned from Seyffert, Oskar. *A Dictionary of Classical Antiquities, Mythology, Religion, Literature and Art*. London: Swan Sonnenschein, 1899, p.568.

The boy Cupid preparing his bow. Scanned from Seyffert, Oskar. *A Dictionary of Classical Antiquities, Mythology, Religion, Literature and Art*. London: Swan Sonnenschein, 1899, p.226.

The Hellespont and surrounding territory, map. Scanned from Botsford, George Willis. *A History of the Ancient World*. New York: Macmillan, 1917, p.236.

The death of Laocoon and his sons. Scanned from Peck, Harry Thurston, ed. *Harper's Dictionary of Classical Literature and Antiquities*. New York: Harper, 1897, p.920.

Aeneas carries his father, Anchises, from the burning Troy, trailed by his son Ascanius. Scanned from Peck, Harry Thurston, ed. *Harper's Dictionary of Classical Literature and Antiquities*. New York: Harper, 1897, p.31.

The messenger god Mercury, whom Jupiter sends to Aeneas. Scanned from Comstock, David Y. *Virgil's "Aeneid" Books I–VI, VII, IX and Selections from the Other Books*. Boston: Allyn and Bacon, 1897, p.130.

A Thyias, or Maenad, a worshipper of Bacchus. Scanned from Seyffert, Oskar. *A Dictionary of Classical Antiquities, Mythology, Religion, Literature and Art*. London: Swan Sonnenschein, 1899, p.193.

Daedalus, Icarus, and the wings; the story that Daedalus couldn't sculpt on the temple doors. Scanned from Seyffert, Oskar. *A Dictionary of Classical Antiquities, Mythology, Religion, Literature and Art*. London: Swan Sonnenschein, 1899, p.171.

The gubernator, or helmsman, of a ship, as Palinurus was for one of Aeneas' ships. Scanned from Peck, Harry Thurston, ed. *Harper's Dictionary of Classical Literature and Antiquities*. New York: Harper, 1897, p.754.

Charon (left) welcomes a soul, escorted by Mercury, to his boat. Scanned from Peck, Harry Thurston, ed. *Harper's Dictionary of Classical Literature and Antiquities*. New York: Harper, 1897, p.325.

Cerberus, the three-headed guard dog of the Underworld. Scanned from Peck, Harry Thurston, ed. *Harper's Dictionary of Classical Literature and Antiquities*. New York: Harper, 1897, p.319.

The god Vulcan, husband of Venus, who makes Aeneas' armor. Scanned from Peck, Harry Thurston, ed. *Harper's Dictionary of Classical Literature and Antiquities*. New York: Harper, 1897, p.788.

The making of Achilles' armor from Homer's *Iliad*, upon which the making of Aeneas' armor is based. Scanned from Seyffert, Oskar. *A Dictionary of Classical Antiquities, Mythology, Religion, Literature and Art*. London: Swan Sonnenschein, 1899, p.644.

The wanderings of Aeneas, map. Scanned from Comstock, David Y. *Virgil's "Aeneid" Books I–VI, VII, IX and Selections from the Other Books*. Boston: Allyn and Bacon, 1897, p.52.